International Cuisine

THE
INTERNATIONAL
CULINARY
SCHOOLS ℠
at The Art Institutes

Michael F. Nenes, CEC, CCE

Photography by Joe Robbins

WILEY

JOHN WILEY & SONS, INC.

Published by John Wiley & Sons, Inc., Hoboken, New Jersey.

Published simultaneously in Canada.

For general information on our other products and services, or technical support, please contact our Customer Care Department within the United States at 800-762-2974, outside the United States at 317-572-3993 or fax 317-572-4002.

Wiley also publishes its books in a variety of electronic formats. Some content that appears in print may not be available in electronic books.

For more information about Wiley products, visit our Web site at http://www.wiley.com.

Library of Congress Cataloging-in-Publication Data:

Nenes, Michael F.
    International cuisine / Michael F. Nenes; photography by Joe Robbins.
        p. cm.
    Includes index.
    ISBN 978-0-470-05240-2 (cloth)
    ISBN 978-0-470-41076-9 (custom)
    1. Cookery, International.   I. Title.
    TX725.A1N46 2009
    641.59–dc22

                                                            2008009580

Printed in the United States of America
10   9   8

Contents

Foreword

Despite my training in classical French cooking techniques, I have long valued the cuisines of countries from all over the world and found great inspiration in them. As a young apprentice, I was fortunate to have trained in France's most famous kitchens including those of Paul Bocuse, Roger Vergé, and Paul Haeberlin, and then spent a number of years on cruise ships that exposed me to the excitement of world cuisines. Later, after a two-year stint in Brazil, I settled in San Francisco, a city with a food community that has always deeply appreciated a wide variety of international cuisines. At Fleur de Lys and more recently at our Burger Bar restaurants, I have created dishes which are sometimes directly—sometimes subtly—enhanced with flavors and cooking techniques found outside my original French classical training, and I have seen how these international influences have drawn enthusiasm from my diners.

I am delighted that The International Culinary Schools at The Art Institutes have put together this comprehensive book of world cuisines that is certain to become a treasured resource for anyone who cooks, both professionally and at home. It has everything needed to truly understand and master a wide array of international cuisines, especially Asian cuisines, which are now such an important part of the American dining landscape. The detailed and vivid descriptions of the history of the food culture for each cuisine are not only fascinating, but also give the reader an understanding of how each cuisine evolved. The comprehensive ingredient lists are a tremendous resource for anyone wishing to recreate the recipes. It is also extremely interesting to read about the cooking utensils from each cuisine along with the detailed descriptions of the cooking techniques. Finally, the book contains a treasure of authentic recipes that not only look delicious, but truly and accurately reflect the featured cuisine.

I know that *International Cuisine* is certain to have a prominent place in my culinary library and I hope yours as well.

Hubert Keller
Chef-Owner
Fleur de Lys, San Francisco and Las Vegas
Burger Bar, Las Vegas, San Francisco, and St. Louis
SLeeK Steakhouse, St. Louis

Acknowledgments

The International Culinary Schools at The Art Institutes wish to thank the following contributors for their efforts on behalf of *International Cuisine*:

Author Michael F. Nenes, MBA, CEC, CCE. This first edition of **International Cuisine** is the result of intensive cooperative and collaborative effort by many individuals. Thanks to Lois Nenes, M.Ed., for her tremendous amount of research, writing, editing, and support. Every effort was made to find information that could be supported by at least two documented sources. Lois was a supportive colleague and we both enjoyed the tremendous amount of exploring and learning needed to complete this project.

Photographer Joe Robbins of Joe Robbins Photography, Houston, Texas. Joe taught at The Art Institute of Houston for over 15 years, helping to shape the careers of students in the visual arts. His collaboration and outstanding photography contribute to the effectiveness of this book.

Certified Master Chef Klaus Friedenreich, Chef Hugh Chang, and Chef Scott Fernandez worked with culinary students at The Art Institute of Houston, testing recipes to prepare and plate the food photographed for the book. This was a tremendous task made possible by hard work, organization, and culinary passion.

Thank you to the following Art Institutes' instructors, staff, and students for their efforts on behalf of *International Cuisine*: Staff members Jose Ferreira and Waldemar "Wally" Marbach; Instructors Soren Fakstrop; Joseph Bonaparte, CCE, CCC, MHM; Mark Matin, MBA; Michael Edrington, CCC, MHM; Nathan Hashmonay; Shannon Hayashi, CEC, M.Ed; Anita Bouffard, MBA, CWA, CWS; Jeff Kennedy, CHE; Scott Maxwell, M.Ed; Stephan Kleinman, CEC, CCE, AAC; Matthew J. Bennett, M.Ed, CEC, CCE, CWPC, CFBE; Ricardo Castro; Simon Vaz, MBA, Ed.S. CHE; Eyad Joseph, CEC, CCE, CCA; Mark Mattern, MBA, CEC; Hugh Chang; and Scott Fernandez; and students Claudia Turcios; Bryce Smith; Ian Caughey; Camilla Guerrero; Amber Bush; and Elizabeth Sanchez.

Introduction

The idea for **International Cuisine** seemed natural and obvious in light of the importance of increased globalization. At the same time, The International Culinary School at The Art Institutes went through an extensive review process that emphasizes an international focus. The most compelling concept, explored with industry professionals, current students, our faculty, and prospective students, centered on teaching students about a wide variety of countries and regions, cultures, and ingredients and the crucial role they play in a variety of cuisines. Industry professionals acknowledge that while fundamental skills are still most critical, it is important for culinary students to have exposure to a wide range of cultural, sociological, and geographical information because the marketplace is demanding it. Due to changing demographics and evolving tastes of consumers, restaurateurs are under increasing pressure to offer more diverse and/or creative menus. Culinary students who have had a broader exposure to a variety of international cuisines will be more versatile and creative culinarians. We believe students who develop a good palate, expand their range of taste, and develop the techniques gain a better understanding of the culinary arts.

The intent of **International Cuisine** is to serve as a window for students to explore the different cultures and cuisines of the world. Culinary programs have always taught some type of international cuisine course, but while there are numerous good books centered on a particular country (such as Italy) or region (such as Latin America), there has been no one book that adequately brings together the world's regions. **International Cuisine** does just that, teaching the wide range of regions around the world and how history, geography, and religion—not to mention the ingredients—influence the different cuisines.

International Cuisine is unique. Many of a cuisine's culinary traits result from conditions that naturally exist in the region or country—factors such as geography, climate, agriculture, as well as historical, cultural and religious influences from settlers, invaders, and neighboring countries. Each chapter is divided into the geography of the area (including a map of the country or countries being discussed), the history, the people and their contributions, and the foods particular to the region. Some chapters are countries discussed individually, others include two or more countries, and several discuss an entire continent. The effort was to choose countries that are culinary representatives of the world. Following this introduction of each country or countries, each chapter contains a glossary of ingredients and dishes as well as a selection of menus and recipes characteristic of the cuisine and its heritage.

Each menu and recipe in *International Cuisine* was selected and tested for its representation of the cuisine, to insure a variety of culinary techniques, a variety of ingredients, and availability of ingredients. However, many of the recipes have been influenced by local customs, ingredient availability, and the inspiration of international chefs, so they have been reformulated to conform to current practices. Methods of preparation are clearly broken down into straightforward steps, and follow a logical progression for completion of the recipe.

Here are some important tips for using *International Cuisine*:

- It is important to understand that to yield a superior dish, you must start with high-quality ingredients. Good results cannot be obtained with substandard ingredients.

- Some ingredients are highly specific to a region and may be difficult to obtain elsewhere. The goal was to keep the unusual ingredients to a minimum so that the recipes can be prepared in areas that do not have large ethnic communities. These recipes are followed by Chef Tips, which indicate suitable substitutions.

- All herbs called for in recipes should be fresh unless specified as dried.

- All butter called for in recipes should be unsalted unless specified otherwise.

- It is recommended that the olive oil produced by each country be used for that country's recipes. For countries that do not produce olive oil but the ingredient is used in its recipes, use a good quality olive oil.

- It is recommended that both white and black pepper be ground fresh to the level of coarseness called for in the recipes. Ground pepper loses strength over time, making it difficult to judge the quantity needed.

- When citrus juice is called for in the recipes, it should be squeezed from fresh fruit rather than reconstituted from concentrate.

- Many of the cooking times indicated in the recipes are approximations. The altitude, type of cookware used, and amount of heat applied are all variables that affect cooking time. Professional cooks use these times as a guide but determine doneness by appropriate means.

One of the wonderful outcomes of our exploration turned out to be the discovery that most of these cuisines are based on sustainable food choices. Sustainable production enables the resources from which it was made to continue to be available for future generations. We support the positive shift in America and world-wide toward local, small-scale sustainable farming.

An *Instructor's Manual* (978-0-470-25406-6) is also available to qualified adopters of this book. It contains chapter objectives, the skills and techniques required to prepare the recipes, suggestions for mise en place demonstrations, additional information on each menu, expanded and detailed chef's tips, and a chapter test. For an electronic version of this *Instructor's Manual*, please visit www.wiley.com/college and click on Culinary Arts.

The Land

Long and narrow, Mexico forms what looks like a curved horn between the United States to the north and Guatemala and Belize to the south. To the west is the Pacific Ocean. The Gulf of Mexico and the Caribbean Sea lie to the east. Two huge mountain ranges, the Sierra Madre Occidental to the west, and the Sierra Madre Oriental to the east, run the length of the country, forming a giant V. Between these mountain ranges lie a series of plateaus. The plateau in the north is largely desert land, while the long central plateau father south is more fertile. Near the tip of the horn, the Yucatan Peninsula juts into the Atlantic Ocean. A long, narrow peninsula called Baja dangles from California's southern border. The southern coasts are home to tropical rain forests and jungles.

With most of its eastern and western borders being on the coast, some Mexican cuisine is based on seafood. There are good grazing areas in the north, with some fertile agricultural land to the south; however, between arid conditions and challenging terrain, only 12 percent of the country gets enough rain for crops.

History

Mexico is a country of great contrasts. Within its borders, there are scorching deserts, snow-capped volcanoes, and lush tropical rain forests. Mexico is also one of the twenty richest nations in the world but, as in nearby Central American countries, there are big differences between standards of living of the rich and the poor. Long before the first European explorers arrived in 1519, Mexico was the home of some of the world's greatest civilizations.

A thousand years ago, Mexico was inhabited by groups of Mayan Indians, who had developed a very advanced civilization. They built large cities out of stone, developed systems of writing and arithmetic, and created beautiful works of art. Mayan settlements were situated close to *cenotes*, natural water holes that allowed for survival in an inhospitable tropical climate. The basis of the culture was farming, which included the cultivation of corn, beans, squash, and chile peppers. Chiles, both fresh and dried, are used more for flavor than heat and popular varieties include jalapeño, poblano, serrano, guajillo, chipotle, pasilla, habanero, ancho, mulatto, and cascabel. Squash, including pumpkins, and zucchini are used as vegetables; their blossoms are stuffed or incorporated in soups and sauces; and squash seeds are dried, ground, and used in sauces. Tomatoes were cultivated and became an essential ingredient along with tomatillos, small green tomatoes encased in papery husks.

It was the conquest of Mexico by Spain in 1521 that had the most influence on Mexican cuisine. Not only did the conquistadors introduce new types of livestock to the area, such as pigs, cows, and sheep, but they also introduced dairy products such as cheese and the fat from the cattle. The Spanish, themselves heavily influenced by the Arabic Moors of western Africa, introduced the most distinctive features of their cuisine to Mexico. Perhaps most characteristic is the combination in one dish of various finely chopped ingredients. Highly seasoned and spiced meat casseroles, hot pots of meats and vegetables, fruit syrups, and pasta and rice pilaf are Arab in origin. The Spanish brought many herbs as well as an abundance of Far Eastern spices like cinnamon and cloves. Wheat, an essential staple of the Spanish diet, was introduced to the region. Citrus fruits, peaches, melons, figs, and cherries as well as garlic, carrots, turnips, and eggplants became regular items in the diet.

Sugarcane was cultivated and became an important trade item, and with this widely available sweet Mexicans developed many deserts and sweets. Many Spanish-style "convent" desserts were developed by the nuns and priests who came to cook for the viceroys (royal officials that governed the provinces). For many years convents all over Mexico have supported themselves by making marzipan-like candies, with almonds and *pepitas* (pumpkin seeds). This period also saw the assimilation of many other cultures, cuisines, and ingredients, including French, Portuguese, Caribbean (particularly in the Veracruz area in the southeast), West African, and South American.

Today, almost 80 percent of contemporary Mexicans are descendants of both native and Spanish cultures and are called *mestizo*. There are more than fifty native groups, including the Nahua, Zapotec, Mixtec, Maya, Purepecha, Trahumara, Huastec, Mayo, Yaqui, and Otomi Indians, who account for fewer than 10 percent of the population. The remaining 10 percent comprises others of European descent. The Roman Catholic Church plays an important part in the everyday life of most Mexicans and religious festivals and celebrations take place in towns and cities across the country throughout the year.

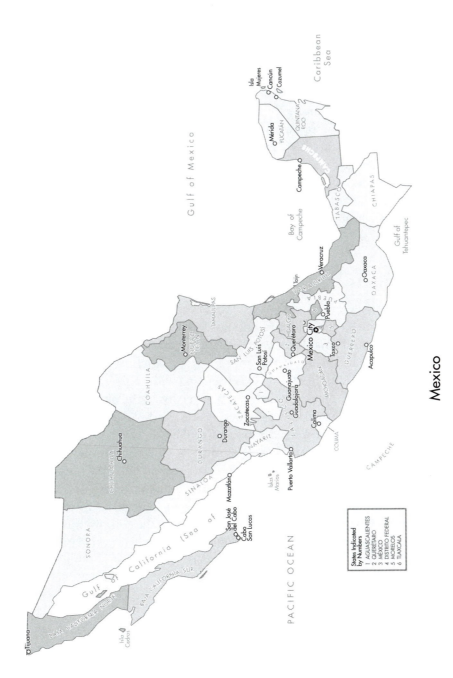

Mexico

Caribbean
Sea

Gulf of Mexico

Isla
Mujeres
Cancún
Cozumel

Mérida
YUCATÁN

QUINTANA
ROO

Bay
of
Campeche

Campeche

TABASCO

CHIAPAS

Gulf
of
Tehuantepec

Veracruz

Oaxaca

OAXACA

Tajín

VERACRUZ

Puebla

Mexico City

Querétaro

Taxco

Acapulco

GUERRERO

HIDALGO

MICHOACÁN

Monterrey

San Luis
Potosí

SAN LUIS POTOSÍ

Guanajuato

Guadalajara

Colima

COLIMA

COAHUILA

ZACATECAS

Zacatecas

DURANGO

Durango

NAYARIT

Puerto Vallarta

Islas
Marías

CAMPECHE

Mazatlán

Chihuahua

CHIHUAHUA

SINALOA

San José
del Cabo
Cabo
San Lucas

SONORA

Gulf of California (Sea of

BAJA CALIFORNIA SUR

Tijuana

BAJA CALIFORNIA NORTE

Isla
Cedros

PACIFIC OCEAN

TAMAULIPAS

States Indicated
by Numbers
1 AGUASCALIENTES
2 QUERÉTARO
3 MÉXICO
4 DISTRITO FEDERAL
5 MORELOS
6 TLAXCALA

3

The Food

Although it is very diverse among the various Mexican regions, Mexican food is rich in color and flavor. Areas along the ocean are famous for their abundant *mariscos* (seafood dishes). Inland and highland mountain areas are famous for stews, intricate sauces, and corn-based recipes. Desert areas have cultivated delicacies of different sorts. In some desert regions, for example, there are numerous dishes containing varieties of cactus plants. While Mexico is made up of thirty-one states and one federal district, the country can be divided into six regions: northern Mexico, central Mexico, southern Mexico and the Gulf of Mexico, the Yucatan Peninsula, the Pacific Coast, and the Baja Peninsula.

NORTHERN MEXICO

The north is mostly desert—a vast, high, windswept plateau flanked by the Occidental and Oriental chains of the Sierra Madre Mountains. The states of Chihuahua, Coajuila, Durango, Nuevo Leon, Sonora, Tamaulipas, and Zacatecas are part of this region. The cooking of northern Mexico gets its strongest influence from the ranching culture, predominately cattle, goats, pigs, and sheep. Ranch-style food is prepared with indigenous ingredients and cooked over an open fire. Cabrito is roast kid goat, a specialty of the city of Monterrey and its state of Nuevo Leon. Flour tortillas were created when the Spanish brought wheat to the New World; however, they are considered a bread staple in the northern states only. In the valleys of the eastern states farmers raise peaches, melons, nuts, and more than thirty varieties of apples. Queso Chihuahua or Chihuahua cheese is a soft white cow's milk cheese available in braids, balls or rounds. The cheese is named after its place of origin and is also called *queso menonita* after the Mennonite communities that first produced it. In the 1920s the Mexican government wanted to settle the barren northern areas of the country with industrious farmers. At the invitation of the then-president, 20,000 Mennonites left Canada and settled in the state of Chihuahua where the community still flourishes.

CENTRAL MEXICO

The Distrito Federal, or Mexico City as it is called in English, is the Mexican capital in every sense of the word. With over 20 million people, it is not only many times larger than any other city in Mexico, but is also the second most populous city in the world, just behind Tokyo. There has been a capital here since before the arrival of the Spanish, although then it was the Aztec capital of Tenoctitlan. Unfortunately, almost all this old city was destroyed by the Spanish in their zeal to convert the Indians to Christianity. One impressive remain, however, still survives. El Templo Mayor is what's left of the Great Temple of the Aztecs. The ruin sits off the northeast corner of the Zocalo, the city's massive main square. In Mexico City, there is a full range of national cuisine. Because it is the capital, cooking from every region is available here.

The state of Michoacán derives its name from the Náhuatl terms *michin* (fish), *hua* (those who have), and *can* (place), which roughly translates into "place of the fisherman." Today there are national fishing tournaments and annual international sport fishing competitions focusing upon catching sailfish, marlin, and mahi-mahi. This state, along with the states of Morelas, Puebla, Queretaro, and Tlaxcala, are known as "the Central Breadbasket," and are one of Mexico's most important agricultural regions. Sugarcane fields, rice fields, coffee plantations, and macadamia trees are cultivated. Michoaca is the largest producer of avocados in the country. The area also produces large quantities of corn, beans, chickpeas, and potatoes. Fruit crops such as mangoes, strawberries, papaya, bananas, lemons, and limes are grown as well.

The food in this region is based heavily on corn. The early Indian tribes served it as a kind of porridge, called *atoll*. Corn kernels were also softened in water and lime and then ground into a fine meal known as *masa*. The *masa* is then shaped into flat, round cakes called tortillas, which are cooked on a *comal*, or griddle. Specialties include *corundas*, a triangular puffy tamale made with white corn and unfilled. *Huitacoche*, a small, dark fungus that grows on a cornstalk, is considered a particular delicacy. One of the other important crops is agave (also known as maguey), used to produce syrup, vinegar, and *pulque*, an alcoholic beverage. *Pulque* was the historical predecessor of mescal and tequila, which wielded a heavy sociological influence during both pre-Hispanic and Colonial periods of Mexican history. There are more than 400 species of agave native to North America and Mexico. It was one of the most sacred and important plants in ancient Mexico and had a privileged place in mythology, religious rituals, and the economy. *Pulque* is still made and drunk in limited quantities in parts of Mexico today. However, because it cannot easily be stored or preserved, it is not well known outside the country. Mezcal (or mescal) is the name given to a double-distilled spirit that comes from the maguey plant. Tequila is made exclusively from the agave azul that grows in semiarid soils and takes from eight to twelve years to mature.

The state of Puebla has been considered the gastronomic capital of Mexico. Its location between the coastal city of Veracruz and Mexico City gives it ample access to fresh seafood. The state produces fresh fruits and vegetables year-round, and raises some of the best beef and pork in the world. It cultivates cinnamon and nuts, as well as different types of hot peppers. *Mole* (the word means stew, or "concoctions") is a dish regarded with national pride and a culinary touchstone of Mexican cooking. It is a rich dark sauce with chocolate, chiles, spices, herbs, groundnuts, seeds, and a variety of other ingredients. Every Mexican household has its version of a *mole*, most of which are named for the color given by the variety of chiles used. Without a doubt the most famous type of *mole* is *mole poblano* (made from any fresh or dried chiles from the poblano pepper family). Other commonly prepared *moles* include *mole verde* (uses green chiles), *mole rojo* (uses red chiles) and *mole pipian* (uses pumpkin seeds).

The cities in this region all have their own enchiladas, from the Enchiladas Potosinas of San Luis Potosí (cheese and onion, with red chile ground into the masa tortillas) to the Enchiladas Mineras (miners' enchiladas) of Guanajuato (cheese or chicken filling topped with potatoes and carrots in a *guajillo* salsa). The *zacahuil*, a three-foot-long tamale that may weigh as much as 150 pounds, is perhaps the most famous food of the region. Stuffed with pork and a variety of ingredients including potatoes, hard-boiled eggs, and vegetables, the *zacahuil* requires nearly all the leaves of a banana tree to wrap it.

SOUTHERN MEXICO AND THE GULF OF MEXICO

This region lies between two major bodies of water—the Gulf and Mexico and the Pacific Ocean—and includes the states of Veracruz, Chiapas, and Tabasco. Veracruz is located on the eastern shore of Mexico known as the Gulf Lowlands as it stretches along the Gulf Coast. Veracruz is the busiest port in Mexico and home to one of the most fertile fishing banks in the world. This is where the European conquest started and where the Spanish first settled, so there are significant Mediterranean influences. *Red Snapper Veracruz* is considered representative of the area. Traditionally, the whole fish is covered in a sauce of tomatoes, onions, capers, Spanish olives, olive oil, and pickled jalapeños. Veracruz is one of the few places in Mexico where people cook with olive oil, and ingredients like green olives and capers and raisins have been incorporated into the cuisine. In the city of Pampantla, vanilla pods are harvested from an orchid-type plant called *tlixochitl*.

During the first years after the Spanish arrived, diseases brought by the Europeans and unknown to the indigenous people decimated the population. Sugarcane production made heavy demands on labor, and African slaves were brought to work in the plantations. These slaves were some of the many thousands to bring their culinary influence with them. The peanut, an important ingredient in West African cooking, was added to meat, fish, and vegetable dishes and ground with spices as part of a paste-like condiment. Plantains, yucca, and sweet potatoes, all important elements of West African cooking, also became part of this region's cuisine.

More than half of Mexico's coffee beans are grown in Chiapas, and this state is one of the largest producers of cacao, used to make chocolate. The ancient Maya were the first to cultivate the cacao tree, native to the Central American rainforest. They found that by first fermenting the pulpy seeds, then drying, roasting, and crushing them, they could make a potent and delicious drink that they called *xocoatl* or *chocoatl*. When the Aztecs conquered the Maya in Central America, they demanded cacao seeds as tribute, and in their empire the seeds became a kind of currency. The Aztecs, like the Maya before them, used the chocoatl in religious ceremonies and considered the seeds a gift from the gods.

Here the tamales are made of fresh corn and pork wrapped in the large leaf of the *hoja santa* herb. When heated, the leaves produce a sweet, musky anise steam that flavors the tamale.

THE YUCATAN PENINSULA

This region comprises the states of Campeche, Yucatan, and Quintana Rol. The Yucatan was once an isolated region of Mexico due to the mountainous terrain surrounding it. The Mayan civilization originated in the Yucatan near 2500 B.C. The Toltec culture arrived in A.D. 987, followed by the Spanish in the 1500s. Game meats such as venison and wild turkey, and vegetables like squash, cucumbers, chiles, and tomatoes are from the Mayans. Black beans, rather than pinto beans or kidney beans, are used in this area. Cooking methods like the *pib*, a hand-dug pit lined with stones and coals in which meats wrapped in banana leaves are cooked, are typical of Mayan cooking. The Spanish introduced pork, beef, and chicken. The Mayans had never fried foods before, but with the pig came lard, and with lard came frying. This produced one of the most significant changes in Mexican cooking.

Seville oranges came from Spain and are a key ingredient in this region's cuisine along with herbs and spices such as garlic, oregano, cinnamon, and cumin. Northern Europeans have a legacy in this region as well, especially the Dutch. Holland was an active trading partner in the nineteenth century and Edam cheese continues to be a regional staple. Ground spice pastes used for marinades are called *recado*. The red version (*rojo*) contains annatto, Mexican oregano, cumin, clove, cinnamon, black pepper, allspice, garlic, and salt. The annatto seeds dye the mixture red, which gives the meat or vegetables cooked with it a distinctive red hue. There are hundreds of variations and each *recado* is for a different dish.

THE PACIFIC COAST

Many of the traditions considered characteristically "Mexican" were created in Guadalajara in the state of Jalisco. It is the country's second-largest city and has large mountain ranges, volcanoes, valleys, and plateaus. Guadalajara is the origin for traditions such as mariachi music, the Mexican hat dance, broad-brimmed sombrero hats, the Mexican rodeo, and tequila. The most important crops in this region include peanuts, sugarcane, and agave (for the production of tequila). In the mountainous regions ranch cooking dominates. *Pozole*, Mexico's pork and hominy stew, originated here, as did *birria*, mutton or goat prepared in an adobo sauce and served in a rich tomato and meat broth.

The state of Oaxaca is one of the most mountainous states in Mexico. Most of the people today are farmers and the most common crops are mangoes and coffee. A festival every December celebrates the radish, which was introduced to Mexico by the Spanish in the late 1500s. Specially grown radishes, some reaching over seven pounds, are carved into works of art. Sometimes called the "land of seven moles," Oaxaca is best known for its seven major varieties of mole. From the most elaborate to the simplest, the seven types are *mole negro* (black mole, the one that uses cocoa), *mole amarillo* (yellow), *mole coloradito* (little red), *mole almendrado* (with almonds), *mole chichilo* (a local name without translation), *mole verde* (green), and *mole colorado* (red). In the way of wine tasting, *mole* tasting is also practiced in several regions of Mexico.

Chocolate con leche, or more commonly *chocolate con agua* (hot chocolate prepared with milk or with water) is one of the most famous products of Oaxaca. The drink is prepared with fresh paste or tablets of cocoa, which in some stores are custom made with a mix of fresh cocoa, sugar, and cinnamon. The paste or tablets are dissolved in either water or milk. The hot liquid is mixed with a special wooden shaker (*molinillo*), which has loose rings that help produce foam. In many places it is served inside a large bowl accompanied with traditional bread made with egg and anise (*pan de huevo*).

The states of Colima, Nayarit, and Sinoloa border the Pacific Ocean. Sinaloa is one of Mexico's largest agricultural states, and also has one of the largest fishing fleets. The coast provides deep-sea fish such as marlin, swordfish, tuna, and sea bass as well as shallow-water fish and shellfish. All three states are important for their coconut, coffee, and banana plantations and orchards of avocado, limes, mango, mamey, and tamarind. Nayarit is famous for its chile sauce, called *Salsa Huichol*. This sauce is made from a variety of chiles, spices, vinegar, and salt and is used like American Tabasco.

THE BAJA CALIFORNIA PENINSULA

This territory is divided into two states, Baja California and Baja California Sur. In Baja California, Tijuana is one of the most visited border cities in the world. The fertile valleys of Guadalupe, San Antonio, Santo Tomas, and San Vicente make up part of Mexico's famous wine-producing region. The state also hosts many food festivals throughout the year, including the Paella and Wine Fair, the Seafood and Fish Festival, the Tequila Festival, and the Caesar Salad Festival (the caesar salad was created in this state). The food in this region tends to be influenced by the north with the use of flour tortillas, burritos, tacos, red meat, and *machaca* (the Mexican equivalent of beef jerky). Baja California Sur only became a state in 1974, when tourist resorts such as Cabo San Lucas and San José del Cabo were developed. In the coastal waters off Baja California and Baja California Sur the seafood harvested includes sole, tuna, sardines, mackerel, clams, shrimp, and lobster.

Glossary

Achiote Small, hard red seeds of the annatto tree, known as achiote, which are used to give color and flavor. Achiote seeds are widely available in Caribbean and Latin groceries. The seeds should have a healthy, earthy-red color; avoid seeds that have a dull brown color. The seeds alone have a slightly musky flavor, but they are most often combined with other herbs and seasoning to make achiote paste, which is popular in the Yucatan for marinades and sauces. In Mexico, the whole seeds are ground and used. Achiote should always be cooked in fat to remove any chalkiness.

Avocado The avocado tree, a member of the laurel family, is native of the tropical Americas. The pear-shaped fruit is sometimes known as the alligator pear. The word "avocado" is derived from the Nahuatl word *ahuacatl*, meaning "testicle." The medicinal properties of the avocado have been lauded since the Spanish conquest.

Avocado Leaves Fresh or dried; used for their flavor in Mexican cooking, particularly in the states of Morelos, Puebla, and Oaxaca. Avocado leaves should be stored dried in an airtight container away from light.

Banana Leaves Available year-round, fresh or frozen, in most Latin American markets. Banana leaves are popular in the southern and Gulf coast Mexican states for wrapping fish, tamales, pork, and chicken. Items wrapped with banana leaves stay moist during the cooking process, plus they pick up a fruity flavor.

Beans Two beans are typically associated with Mexican cooking: black beans and larger mottled pink pintos. Small black beans, eaten extensively in Latin regions of the world including Mexico, are small and quite hard, requiring a longer cooking time than other dried beans such as the pinto. Beans and rice are normally served at every meal and are a complete protein.

Cactus Paddles (Nopales) The prickly pear cactus is the most common type of cactus eaten in Mexico. *Nopal* means cactus in Spanish and *nopales* is the term for "cactus stem." *Nopalitos* refers to the pads once they are cut up and prepared for eating. Nopales are usually sold already cleaned (needles removed); look for bright green and firm pads. They are typically eaten grilled or boiled.

Chayote The chayote, or vegetable pear, is a native of Mexico, and its name is derived from the Nahuatl word *chayutli*. Chayote was one of the principal foods of the Aztec and Mayan people. This pear-shaped squash has the mild taste of zucchini. The flesh is quite crisp, something like a water chestnut. Chayotes come in both smooth and prickly varieties (covered in spines).

Cheeses

Fresh Cheeses

Queso Blanco A creamy white cheese made from skimmed cow's milk. It is described as being a cross between salty cottage cheese and mozzarella. It is traditionally coagulated with lemon juice, giving it a fresh, distinctive lemon flavor, although today it is often commercially made with rennet.

Queso Fresco A pale cream-colored, moist, crumbly, soft cheese made in round cakes of different sizes. It has a slight acidity but with a creamy flavor. It is sometimes called *queso* *de metate* because the curds are pressed out on the *metate* (grinding stone) until compact enough to be packed into the small wooden hoops that give them shape. It is usually made with a combination of cow's milk and goat's milk.

Panela The most popular fresh cheese in Mexico, also called *queso de canasta* because it carries the imprint of the basket in which it is molded. It is a white, spongy, salty, semi-soft cheese mild in flavor. It absorbs other flavors easily.

Requesón A loose, ricotta-like cheese used to fill *enchiladas* and to make cheese spreads. It is typically sold in the markets wrapped in fresh corn husks. *Requesón* has a very mild and semisweet flavor. Its color is white and its texture is soft, moist, and grainy.

Soft Cheeses

Oaxaca Also referred to as Asadero or Queso Oaxaca cheese. It is a semi-soft, white, string-type cheese. It is stretched, kneaded, then formed into a ball shape, which is plunged in brine for several minutes. The flavor ranges from mild to sweet and buttery.

Semi-Soft Cheeses

Asadero The literal translation of this cheese's name is "broiler" or "roaster"; the cheese itself is made by the same method as the braided Oaxaca cheese. The cheese melts easily when heated and strings appropriately.

Chihuahua Also called *queso menonita*, after the Mennonite communities of northern Mexico that first produced it. This is a mild, spongy, pale-yellow cheese. Unlike most Mexican cheeses, it is pale yellow rather than white, and can vary in taste from mild to a nearly cheddar-like sharpness.

Queso Jalapeño A smooth, soft white cow's milk cheese with bits of jalapeño chile in it.

Queso Quesadilla This cheese is smooth, soft, mild, and white. It melts easily to make dishes rich and creamy.

Semi-Firm Cheeses

Queso Criollo This pale yellow cheese is a specialty of the region around Taxco, Guerrero, and is similar to Munster.

Edam Although not considered a Mexican cheese, edam has become an intrinsic part of Yucatan regional cooking.

Manchego This cheese has a black, gray, or buff-colored rind with a crosshatch pattern. The interior ranges from stark white to yellowish, depending on age. It has a number of holes and a mild, slightly briny, nutty flavor.

Firm Cheeses

Añejo An aged cheese, white and crumbly, often very dry and salty, rather resembling a dry feta. This cheese is not as strongly flavored as cotija, but can be easily shredded or grated.

Cotija This is a sharp, crumbly goat cheese. This cheese is strongly flavored, firm and perfect for grating. It was originally made with goat's milk but today cow's milk is preferred.

Chicharrón Crispy fried pig skin used in salads, fillings, and as a snack.

Chiles, Canned Many Mexican recipes call for chiles serranos or jalapeños *en escabeche*, which means that they are canned in a souse, or pickled. Traditionally this includes vinegar, oil, herbs, garlic, onion, and slices of carrot. Canned *chiles chipotles en vinagre* or *adobo* are also widely used.

Chiles The most prominent feature of Mexican cooking is the emphasis it places on chiles, with more than seventy varieties.

Dried Chiles

Each chile has its own characteristics, flavor, and quality; you should not interchange chiles within a recipe unless it is indicated in the recipe.

Ancho Chile A ripened and dried *chile poblano*, one of the most commonly used throughout Mexico. Chile Ancho has a deep, reddish-brown color—brick red when soaked in water—and a wrinkled, fairly shiny skin. It is triangular in shape, and measures about 3 inches at its widest point and 5 inches in length. The ancho has a pleasant, sweet flavor, similar to a bell pepper. It may be stuffed; however, it is mostly soaked and ground for cooked sauces. It rates between 1,000 and 2,000 Scoville units on the heat index.

Árbol Chile The name means "tree chile." It is long and skinny, $2\frac{1}{2}$ by $\frac{1}{2}$ inches on average, and has a brilliant red, thin, smooth, shiny skin. This chile has a vicious bite, and should be treated with caution. It has a tannic, smoky, and grassy flavor, and a searing, acidic heat on the tip of the tongue. It rates between 15,000 and 30,000 Scoville units on the heat index.

Cascabel Chile Small and round, it is so named because it sounds like a rattle when it is shaken (cascabel means "jingle bells" in Spanish). It has a smooth, brownish-red skin, and usually measures 1 inch in diameter. Cascabel adds a deep smoky, nutty flavor to dishes. It is typically toasted and ground for sauce. The cascabel rates between 1,500 and 2,500 Scoville units on the heat index.

Chipotle Chile This is chile jalapeño, ripened, dried, and then smoked. Its light brown, wrinkled skin smells distinctly of smoke and its name means "smoked chile." It measures

Where's the Chile's Heat?

Chiles get their "heat"—or "pungency"—from a group of chemical compounds called capsaicinoids, the best known of which is capsaicin. According to the Chile Pepper Institute, a research and education center housed at New Mexico State University, capsaicin is produced in the whitish pith (also called membranes or ribs), not by the seeds.

HEAT SCALE

The pungency of chile peppers is measured in multiples of 100 units. It ranges from the sweet bell peppers at zero Scoville units to the habanero at 300,000-plus Scoville units! One part of chile "heat" per 1,000,000 drops of water is rated at only 1.5 Scoville Units. The substance that makes a chile so hot is called capsaicin. Pure capsaicin rates between 15,000,000 and 16,000,000 Scoville units! Today a more scientific and accurate method called liquid chromatography is used to determine capsaicin levels.

GENERAL NOTES

- Smaller peppers are usually hotter than larger peppers.
- Peppers often become hotter as they ripen, and hotter still when they're dried. Dried peppers tend to have a richer, more concentrated flavor.
- The majority of the chile's heat is concentrated in the seeds and ribs. To tone down the heat of a pepper, remove some or all of the seeds and the white ribs.
- When working with peppers, wear rubber gloves or coat your hands with vegetable oil. Wash your hands carefully afterward.
- Chiles don't freeze well.

TIPS FOR WORKING WITH FRESH CHILES

- It is advisable to wear gloves when handling fresh or dried chiles.
- Never bring your hands near your eyes during or after working with fresh chiles.
- Keep some vinegar or bleach on hand to neutralize the capsaicin, if it comes in contact with your skin.
- Be very careful of the hotter chiles like the habanero. It has been known to create first-degree burns.
- Gently wash your hands and arms after working with the chiles. The chile oils will need soap to break them up. Scrub fingertips, especially under the nails, and then soak them for a few minutes in strongly salted water, if necessary.

approximately 2 to 4 inches in length and about an inch wide. As much as one-fifth of the Mexican jalapeño crop is processed into chipotles. It rates between 5,000 and 8,000 Scoville units on the heat index.

Guajillo Chile A long, slender, pointed chile whose brownish-red skin is smooth, shiny, and tough, the *guajillo* averages $4\frac{1}{2}$ inches in length and $1\frac{1}{4}$ inches in width. Sweet and mild, this chile is a base for rich chile con carne and classic Tex-Mex cuisine. The *guajillo* is used in table and cooked sauces. The skin is extra tough, so it needs longer time for cooking. It rates between 2,000 and 4,500 Scoville units on the heat index.

Mora Chile This is a smoked and dried large red jalapeño pepper. Blackish red in color, it has a wrinkled, tough skin, with a round tip. A typical size is 2 inches long and $\frac{3}{4}$ inch wide. Like the *chipotle*, it has a smoky flavor and is very *picante* (hot and spicy). It rates between 5,000 and 8,000 Scoville units on the heat index.

Morita Chile A small, mulberry-red chile, triangular in shape and about 1 inch long and $\frac{1}{2}$ inch wide, with a slightly smoky flavor. This smoked and dried small red jalapeño pepper is very hot and spicy. It rates between 5,500 and 8,500 Scoville units on the heat index.

Mulato Chile This very popular chile looks like the ancho, only slightly larger with tougher and smoother skin and a brownish black hue. It's fairly mild and has an earthy flavor; when soaked in water it has a sweetish, almost chocolaty flavor. This chile is normally used soaked and ground in cooked sauces, the classic example being *mole poblano*. It rates between 900 and 1,500 Scoville units on the heat index.

Pasilla Chile This is a long, slender chile with a rounded tip. The skin is wrinkled with a blackish tone. It is a standard ingredient in mole sauces. The average size is 6 inches long and $\frac{3}{4}$ to 1 inch wide. The seeds and veins clustered at the top by the stem are very hot; however, the flesh is generally mild and has a slight "tobaccoish" flavor. It is toasted and ground for table sauces and soaked and ground for cooked sauces. It rates between 1,000 and 1,500 Scoville units on the heat index.

Chile de la Tierra, Colorado Chile This is the *chile verde*, or Anaheim, ripened and dried. When dried it has a tough, dark, reddish brown matte skin. It is very mild and does not have much flavor. It rates between 700 and 1,000 Scoville units on the heat index.

Fresh Chiles

Güero Chile A pale yellow chile that varies in size, averaging 4 to 5 inches long and 1 inch wide. It is pointed at the end, with a smooth, small-ridged, undulated surface. This chile can be very hot and has a delicious and distinctive flavor. It rates between 2,000 and 6,500 Scoville units on the heat index.

Habanero Chile This chile is shaped like a small lantern, about 1 inch across as its widest part and a bit over 2 inches long. This extremely hot chile has a distinctive fruity flavor. It is a light green color and as it ripens it turns to one of various colors including red, orange, salmon, white, and chocolate, depending on the variety. It rates 200,000 to 300,000 Scoville units.

Jalapeños Chile The most well known of Mexico's chiles. It is a mid- to dark-green chile with a smooth surface and more often rounded at the tip than pointed. It averages $2\frac{1}{2}$ inches long and $\frac{3}{4}$ inch at its widest part. It has a unique rich fresh flavor and is hot. *Jalapeños*, like *serranos*, are used in various ways: fresh in a relish, cut and cooked, boiled and blended. It rates between 2,500 and 8,000 Scoville units on the heat index.

Poblano Chile The poblano can vary in shape, color, size, and flavor, depending on where it was grown, the time of year, and so forth. Typically, they are mild, large, heart-shaped peppers with very thick walls, 5 inches long and about 3 inches wide at the top, tapering to the apex. They are great for stuffing. They can be fairly mild to hot. With minor exceptions they are always charred and peeled. It rates between 1,200 and 2,500 Scoville units on the heat index.

Serrano Chile A small, smooth, mid-green chile, mostly rounded but sometimes pointed at the end. It averages $1\frac{1}{2}$ inch long and about $\frac{1}{2}$ inch wide. The flesh has a strong, fresh flavor, and the seeds and veins are very hot and spicy. It has thin walls, so it doesn't need to be charred, steamed, and peeled before using. It rates between 8,000 and 22,000 Scoville units on the heat index.

Chile Verde, Anaheim Chile A light green chile with a rounded tip, averaging 1 inch wide and 6 inches long. Anaheim chiles range from mild to hot. They have a tough skin that is typically charred and peeled before being used. When mature and red, an Anaheim is called a *chile colorado*. It rates between 1,000 and 2,000 Scoville units on the heat index.

Chorizos Brought to Mexico by Spanish explorers, this pork sausage is made all over Mexico, and each region has its own balance of spices, chiles, and herbs. Many cooks believe that lean pork is *the* important factor when making chorizos. The pork for Mexican *chorizos* is chopped (not ground), seasoned, and stuffed into casings made from pigs' small intestine.

Cilantro The fresh green leaves and tender stems of coriander, or Chinese parsley. The dried seed is occasionally used, but the two are not interchangeable. There is no substitute for its crisp and pungent flavor. Thick stems should be discarded and only thin stems and leaves used.

Cinnamon The light brown cinnamon bark originally from Ceylon is used extensively in Mexican cooking. Mexican cinnamon has a softer and more delicate flavor, and flavors both savories and sweets.

Corn Husks The dried outer sheath that surrounds each ear of corn. They are the traditional wrappers for tamales, but they can be used to wrap other foods for steaming or grilling. In addition to protecting foods as they cook, they also impart a mild corn essence. Cornhusks are used fresh as well as dried.

Cumin The flavor of cumin plays a major role in Mexican cuisine. Cumin is the dried seed of the herb *Cuminum cyminum*, a member of the parsley family. The cumin plant grows to about 1 to 2 feet tall and is harvested by hand. Cumin is a key component in both chile powder and curry powder. Always develop the flavor by cooking it first in fat.

Epazote A weed that grows all over North America. It is a strong-tasting herb; the flavor is dominant and should be used alone, not in combination with other herbs. It is quite pungent and some say it smells like gasoline or kerosene. It is most commonly used in black bean recipes to ward off some of the "negative" side affects of eating beans.

Huitlacoche An exotic fungus that grows naturally on ears of corn. The kernels are swollen and deformed, black and juicy inside and covered with a crisp, slivery-gray skin. The texture and inky flavor is unique. The earthy and somewhat smoky fungus is used to flavor quesadillas, tamales, soups, and other specialty dishes.

Jicama Like potatoes, jicama grows underground as a tuber. It is a round brown-skinned vegetable that yields crisp white flesh that looks like an apple or raw potato. Raw jicama is sweet and juicy. Always remove the fibrous brown skin. Cooked lightly it becomes milder but retains its crispness, like a water chestnut. Jicama is primarily a texture food since its flavor is rather bland.

Lime Mexican cooks use the yellow-skinned key lime, because it tastes sweeter than other limes. If key limes are unavailable, use half lemon juice and half lime juice. Mexican cuisine uses limes for marinating fish and chicken, in salsas, soups, and best of all balancing margaritas.

Masa, Masa Harina Masa means "dough" in Spanish, but in Mexico it is generally understood as "corn dough." It is made by boiling corn kernels in powdered lime (calcium oxide), washing them, and then grinding; water is mixed in to make dough. Smoother, soft masa is required for tortillas, and coarser, stiff masa is used for tamales. Masa harina is factory-made powdered masa. It can be used to make anything that calls for masa. Ordinary yellow cornmeal for making cornbread is not a substitute.

Oregano Mexican oregano has a more assertive flavor than the Mediterranean oregano. Thirteen varieties of oregano grow throughout Mexico. However, Mexican cooks normally use dried oregano.

Pepitas or Pumpkin Seeds These seeds have been used in Mexican cuisine since pre-Columbian times. Toasted in their hulls or hulled but unroasted and unsalted, they are used in moles, sauces, salads, and snack foods.

Plantains Plantains are popular in Latin American, Asian, and African cuisines, and are prepared and eaten in a number of ways. Unlike their common sweet banana cousin, plantains have to be cooked. They are starchy, only slightly sweet, and are no more appealing to eat raw than a potato. They can be pink, green, red, blackish-brown, and yellow with black spots. In Mexican cooking they must be very ripe, almost juicy, and sweet.

Sesame Seeds Widely used as a topping for breads and pastries or as a thickener for sauces.

Seville or Sour Oranges Small, brilliantly orange, thin-skinned oranges. There is no real substitute for the sharp, fragrant juice.

Tamarind Seeds and Paste Widely grown in Mexico since the sixteenth century, this is a 3- to 8-inch-long, brown, irregularly curved pod, which produces a juicy brown to reddish brown acidulous pulp. When fully ripe, the shells are brittle and easily broken. The pulp dehydrates to a sticky paste enclosed by a few coarse stands of fiber. The pods may contain from one to twelve large, flat, glossy brown seeds embedded in the brown, edible pulp. The pulp has a pleasing sweet-sour flavor and is high in both acid and sugar.

Tomatillos (Tomates Verdes, Mexican Green Tomatoes) The *tomatillo* is of Mexican origin; however, it now grows everywhere in the Western Hemisphere. It is a pale green fruit enclosed in a green, papery husk that ripens to yellow. It is not an ordinary unripe tomato. In central Mexico it is called *tomate verde*, and in the northeast *fresadilla*; elsewhere it is *tomatillo, tomate de cascara*, or *tomate de bolsa*. Generally used when they are green rather than yellow, *tomatillos*, vary in acidity and have a very tart flavor. When working with *tomatillos* always remove the husks and wash the fruit.

Tomatoes Tomatoes are indigenous to Mexico and South America, and are grown year round. The Italian plum tomato, called *jitomato guaje* ("gourd" tomato) or *guajillo*, like the chile, is also grown extensively. However, the skin of the plum tomato is much tougher than an ordinary tomato.

Tortillas Indispensable in Mexican cuisine, made with either corn or wheat flour. Available both fresh and frozen.

KITCHEN TOOLS

Cazuela An earthenware casserole used to make moles. Its great advantage is that it heats evenly, eliminating that nemesis of all cooks, the dreaded "hot spot."

Coffee/Spice Grinder A necessity for many Mexican dishes that call for ground *achiote*, pumpkin or sesame seeds, or spices.

Comal A round plate, usually made of unglazed earthenware, cast iron, or tin, about $\frac{1}{2}$ inch thick. It is a Mexican griddle used for cooking tortillas, toasting chiles, garlic, and the like.

Molcajete y Tejolote This mortar and pestle combination, made of basalt, is used for grinding. The tejolote is a heavy, oval shaped rock used to grind spices, onions, peppers, and tomatoes into thick purees in a molcajete.

Molinillo Found in every Mexican kitchen, this wooden implement will, when twirled between the palms of both hands, give hot chocolate a spectacular collar of froth.

Tortilla Press An absolute must if you plan to make your own tortillas, the wooden variety of tortilla presses have largely been replaced by the cast-iron variety. There is also an aluminum model that is decidedly less popular.

COOKING METHODS

Charring, Peeling, and Cleaning Fresh Chiles and Bell Peppers In Mexican peasant cooking this is done by charring peppers right on the charcoal or wood fire, which also serves to enhance the flavor. They can also be put directly over a gas flame, grill, or on a tray under the broiler. Char the pepper, turning it frequently, until the skin is blackened. The entire chile will not be completely black, but it should be charred about 60 percent. They will char evenly and in all the little irregular surfaces if they are first lightly coated with oil. After charring, place the pepper immediately into a plastic bag to "sweat" for about 15 minutes. Remove from the bag and when cool enough to work with, remove the blackened skin. You can use your hands, continually dipping them in water to remove the blackened bits, or use a paper towel. Use a knife to remove any skin that sticks. Do not peel roasted peppers under running water because this will wash away juices and flavor.

Guisar (Braising or Stewing) This is the most common way of cooking meat and poultry (with the possible exception of northern Mexico, where much of it is grilled). The meat, poultry, and in some cases vegetables are prepared separately from the sauce in the making of *mole*, *pipian*, and other complex dishes. A heavy-bottomed Dutch oven is a good substitute for a *cazuela* when doing this long, slow type of cooking.

Moler (Grinding) This is traditionally done in a *molcajete* but today a blender is more frequently used. The *molcajete* allows more control over the final texture of a *salsa;* however, if the sauce is a smooth one, a blender does quite well. The process of grinding chiles, herbs, spices, and tomatoes in a *molcajete* is labor-intensive, and an alternative is to grind dry ingredients in a spice or coffee mill before combining them with other ingredients. Whether using a *molcajete*, blender, or food processor, garlic and salt should be ground together before adding the remaining ingredients.

Poner a Sudar (Sweating) This refers to the method used for removing the skins from fresh chiles, especially poblanos, which are usually cooked without skins, either for stuffing or for making *rajas*, strips of chiles that are used in a great number of dishes.

Sofreir (Soft-Frying/Sautéing) Not much deep-frying is done in Mexican cooking, with the exception of some street snacks. A far more common technique is "soft-frying" or sautéing, which is done to soften ingredients and intensify their flavor. Dried chiles, for example, are sometimes soft-fried in combination with dry-roasting. Tortillas usually need to be soft-fried before being covered with sauce, as with *enchiladas.*

Tostar/Asar Toasting or dry-roasting. This is commonly done on the *comal*, but any well-seasoned griddle or dry skillet will work. It is a quick process, done over high heat and involving no liquid or oil. Toasting ingredients adds a distinctive flavor to the dish in which they are cooked.

Menus and Recipes from Mexico

Sopa de Lima con Pollo y Elote
Chicken, Corn, and Lime Soup   SERVES 4–6

AMOUNT	MEASURE	INGREDIENT
I tablespoon	$\frac{1}{2}$ ounce, 14 ml	Vegetable oil
I cup	4 ounces, 112 g	White onion, $\frac{1}{4}$ inch (.6 cm) dice
2		Garlic cloves, minced
3 cups	18 ounces, 504 ml	Chicken stock
I$\frac{1}{2}$ cups	9 ounces, 252 g	Roma tomatoes, peeled, seeded, $\frac{1}{4}$ inch (.6 cm) dice
I$\frac{1}{2}$ cups	8 ounces, 224 g	Corn kernels
2		Jalapeño chiles, seeded, minced
I teaspoon		Cumin, ground
I cup	6 ounces, 168 g	Chicken thigh meat, fat trimmed, thinly sliced
3 tablespoons	8 g	Cilantro, chopped
I$\frac{1}{2}$ tablespoons	$\frac{3}{4}$ ounce, 21 ml	Fresh lime juice
To taste		Salt and pepper

PROCEDURE

1 Heat oil over medium heat, add onion and garlic, cook 8–10 minutes or until very soft.

2 Add chicken stock, tomatoes, corn, chiles, and cumin, bring to boil, reduce to simmer, and cook 5–8 minutes to blend flavors.

3 Add chicken and simmer about 3 minutes to cook meat.

4 Stir in cilantro and lime juice.

5 Correct seasoning.

Arroz Blanco con Verduras
White Rice with Vegetables   SERVES 4

Chef Tip For all Mexican rice dishes, the grains are soaked, drained, and sautéed before steaming, then cooked with onion and garlic, as one would make a pilaf. This method produces fluffy, separate grains and a nutty, full flavor.

AMOUNT	MEASURE	INGREDIENT
1 cup	7 ounces, 198 g	Long-grain, unconverted white rice
2 tablespoons	1 ounce, 28 g	Corn oil
$\frac{1}{4}$ cup	1 ounce, 28 g	White onion, $\frac{1}{4}$ inch (.6 cm) dice
$\frac{1}{2}$ cup	1 ounce, 28 g	Green onions and tops, finely chopped
2		Garlic cloves, minced
1 cup	$2\frac{1}{2}$ ounces, 70 g	White mushrooms, $\frac{1}{4}$ inch (.6 cm) slices
1		Serrano chile, seeds and veins removed, minced
$1\frac{1}{2}$ cups	12 ounces, 353 ml	Chicken stock
$\frac{1}{2}$ cup	2 ounces, 56 g	Corn kernels
1 cup	4 ounces, 113 g	Queso fresco, grated
2 tablespoons	$\frac{1}{4}$ ounce, 7 g	Cilantro, chopped
To taste		Salt and pepper

PROCEDURE

1 Cover the rice with hot water and let stand for 20 minutes. Drain and rinse well under cold water. Let drain for 10 minutes.

2 Heat the oil until it smokes and add the rice; stir until all the grains are well coated.

3 Cook until the rice just begins to take on a color.

4 Add the onions, garlic, mushrooms, and chile; cook over high heat for 10 minutes, until white onion and garlic are translucent, stirring constantly.

5 Add chicken stock and corn; cook uncovered over medium heat—do not stir again—until the liquid has been absorbed and small air holes appear in the rice.

6 Remove from heat and let stand, covered, for 10 to 15 minutes.

7 Add the cheese and cilantro, and stir into the rice with a fork.

Mole Verde con Hierbas
Pork Herbed Green Mole   SERVES 4

Green mole is most commonly found in the states of Puebla, Tlaxcala, and Oaxaca, where it is one of *los siete moles*—the seven famous moles, each with a distinctive color, flavor, and aroma. Unlike the other moles, which nearly always contain nuts and seeds, this recipe gets its characteristic flavor and bright green color from fresh herbs. If you prefer chicken, it may be substituted for pork in this recipe

AMOUNT	MEASURE	INGREDIENT
$1\frac{1}{2}$ pounds	24 ounces, 672 g	Pork stew meat, $1\frac{1}{2}$ inch (3.8 cm) cube
$\frac{1}{2}$ teaspoon	1 g	Black peppercorns, bruised
1 cup	4 ounces, 112 g	White onion, cut $1\frac{1}{2}$ inch (3.8 cm) cube
10		Garlic cloves, peeled and split lengthwise
8		Cloves, whole, or $\frac{1}{4}$ teaspoon ground
1 teaspoon	2 g	Cumin seeds
2		Jalapeño chiles, seeds removed
1 pound	16 ounces, 448 g	Tomatillos, husks removed
2		Thyme sprigs, fresh
2		Marjoram sprigs, fresh
1 cup	8 ounces, 224 g	Masa, either fresh or reconstituted by mixing 6 tablespoons masa harina to a smooth paste with 1 cup water
$\frac{1}{2}$ cup	1 ounce, 28 g	Italian parsley, chopped
$\frac{1}{2}$ cup	1 ounce, 28 g	Cilantro leaves, chopped
$\frac{1}{4}$ cup	$\frac{1}{2}$ ounce, 14 g	Epazote, fresh or $\frac{1}{8}$ cup dried, crumbled
$\frac{1}{4}$ cup	$\frac{1}{2}$ ounce, 14 g	Hoja santa leaves, fresh, or 3 dried leaves (Also called hierba santa or root beer plant, it has a distinctive anise flavor that's hard to duplicate.)
2 cups	14 ounces, 392 g	White beans, cooked
To taste		Salt and pepper

PROCEDURE

1   Combine pork stew meat, peppercorns, $\frac{1}{2}$ cup white onions, and 5 garlic cloves, cover by 1 inch with cold water. Bring to a boil, cover, and reduce to simmer. Cook until just tender, 30–45 minutes. Remove meat and strain stock, reserve.

2   Grind the cloves and cumin seeds with a spice grinder or a mortar and pestle.

3   In a blender combine ground spices, jalapeño, tomatillos, thyme, marjoram, remaining garlic cloves and onions and $\frac{1}{2}$ cup stock from the cooked pork. Blend until smooth.

4   Combine reserved pork stock and tomatillo mixture; simmer, uncovered, 3 minutes.

5   Whisk masa into pork and tomatillo liquid; whisking constantly, return to simmer.

6   Cook, uncovered, over low heat 10 minutes, whisking occasionally. If lumps form, pass through a medium-mesh sieve and return to heat. Mixture should thicken to the consistency of whipping cream; if necessary, reduce to correct consistency or thin with more stock.

7   Combine parsley, cilantro, *epazote*, and *hoja santa* in a blender or food processor. If necessary, add a few tablespoons of liquid; process to a smooth puree.

8   Add beans, cooked pork, and pureed herbs to the *masa*-thickened sauce and let return to a simmer. Correct seasoning and serve.

Mole Verde con Hierbas – Pork Herbed Green Mole,
Arroz Blanco con Verduras – White Rice with Vegetables

Corn Tortillas   YIELD: 1 POUND

AMOUNT	MEASURE	INGREDIENT
2 cups	10 ounces, 280 grams	Prepared masa harina
1⅓ cups	21 ounces, 588 ml	Warm water, approximately
1 teaspoon		Salt

PROCEDURE

1 Dissolve the salt in the warm water. To the masa harina, add the water all at once (this keeps lumps from forming) and mix quickly, just until the ingredients are combined.

2 Let rest 5 minutes. Masa will dry out quickly, so keep covered with plastic wrap or a damp cloth.

3 Pinch off golf-ball-sized pieces and roll into balls.

4 Flatten the balls and roll out to $\frac{1}{8}$ inch (.3 cm) thick or use a tortilla press. If using a tortilla press, line both sides with plastic.

5 Gently place the tortilla on a hot skillet or griddle. It should make a soft sizzling sound. Cook for 30–40 seconds or until the tortilla starts to bubble on top. Turn tortilla over and cook an additional 20–30 seconds.

6 Remove the tortilla from pan and keep warm.

7 To reheat, bake covered in a 350°F (176°C) oven for 10–12 minutes.

Flan de Naranja Orange Flan

SERVES 4

AMOUNT	MEASURE	INGREDIENT
$\frac{1}{2}$ cup	$3\frac{1}{2}$ ounces, 98 g	Sugar, granulated
1 tablespoon	$\frac{1}{2}$ ounce, 15 ml	Water
$\frac{1}{4}$ teaspoon		Lemon juice
Pinch		Cayenne pepper
$\frac{1}{2}$ cup	2 ounces, 56 g	Blanched almonds
$\frac{1}{4}$ cup	$1\frac{3}{4}$ ounces, 50 g	Sugar
		Finely grated zest of 1 orange
4		Eggs
$\frac{1}{4}$ cup	2 ounces, 60 ml	Heavy cream
$\frac{3}{4}$ cup	6 ounces, 180 ml	Orange juice

PROCEDURE

1   Preheat oven to 350°F (176°C).

2   Make caramel by melting $\frac{1}{2}$ cup sugar ($3\frac{1}{2}$ ounces, 98 g), water, lemon juice (lemon juice keeps the mixture from hardening or crystallizing), and cayenne over low heat and cook for 8 to 10 minutes, without stirring. Gently tilt the pan off the heat to distribute color evenly as sugar caramelizes. When sugar reaches a uniform golden brown (light amber) color, immediately remove from heat.

3   Pour caramel into 4 individual custard cups; tip the molds side to side until there is an even coating of caramel over the bottom and halfway up the sides. Set aside.

4   Grind the almonds in a food processor.

5   Add the remaining sugar, orange zest, and the eggs, process until smooth.

6   Add cream and orange juice, process to mix.

7   Let the froth subside before pouring into custard cup.

8   Bake in a water bath, covered, until the flan is set. Test by inserting the blade of a knife into the center of the custard. If the blade comes out clean, cooking is done.

9   Set aside to cool before unmolding.

Sopa de Ajo Garlic Soup

SERVES 4

AMOUNT	MEASURE	INGREDIENT
¼ cup	2 ounces, 56 ml	Vegetable oil
1 cup	4 ounces, 112 g	Leeks, white and light green parts, cleaned, thinly sliced
⅓ cup	2 ounces, 56 g	Garlic cloves, peeled, thinly sliced
1		Chile morita or arbol, seeded and soaked in hot water until soft
1 cup	6 ounces, 168 g	Roma tomatoes, roasted and peeled, rough chopped
3 cups	24 ounces, 672 ml	Chicken stock
3		Eggs, lightly beaten with 1 tablespoon oil
2 tablespoons	6 g	Parsley, chopped
To taste		Salt
4		2-inch round croutons
2 tablespoons	1 ounce, 56 g	Panela or queso fresco cheese, crumbled

PROCEDURE

1. Heat oil over medium high heat; add leeks and garlic and sauté until soft but not brown.
2. Puree the chile and tomatoes and add to the leek mixture.
3. Cook over medium high heat until mixture is thick.
4. Add chicken stock and bring to boil; return to simmer and cook 10–12 minutes.
5. Add beaten eggs, stirring constantly in a circular motion. Add parsley and simmer until eggs are set.
6. Correct seasoning.
7. Serve with a crouton in each bowl and sprinkle with cheese.

Nopales en Chipotle Adobado

Nopales in Chipotle Sauce   SERVES 4

The mild flavor of nopales makes them ideal for combining with strong-flavored ingredients.

Chef Tip **Nopal means cactus in Spanish and nopales is the term for "cactus stem." The term nopalitos refers to the pads once they are cut and prepared for eating. Nopales can be eaten grilled or boiled. Overcooking may give them a slightly slimy texture.**

AMOUNT	MEASURE	INGREDIENT
2 cups	12 ounces, 336 g	Nopales paddles, cleaned and $\frac{1}{2}$ inch (1.27 cm) dice
$1\frac{1}{2}$ pounds	672 g	Tomatillos, husked and roasted on a dry griddle or comal until soft
2		Garlic cloves, peeled and chopped
2		Chipotles in adobo sauce
1 tablespoon	$\frac{1}{2}$ ounce, 14 ml	Vegetable oil
1 cup	4 ounces, 112 g	White onion, sliced very thin
To taste		Salt
2 cups		Arroz blanco

PROCEDURE

1   To prepare the nopales remove the thorns and the "eyes" with a vegetable peeler or small paring knife. Wash the pads well with cool water and peel or trim off any blemished or discolored areas.

2   Combine nopales with enough salted water to cover. Bring to a boil and cook 10 minutes. Drain and set aside.

3   Combine tomatillos, garlic, and chipotles in a blender and blend until smooth.

4   Heat oil and sauté onions over low heat until transparent.

5   Add puree and nopales, stir and cook over low heat 10–15 minutes. Season to taste.

6   Serve hot with rice and warm tortillas

Pavo con Salsa de Achiote a la Yucataneca Yucatán-Style Steamed Turkey in Achiote Sauce SERVES 4

AMOUNT	MEASURE	INGREDIENT
$\frac{1}{2}$ cup	4 ounces, 112 g	Achiote paste (recipe follows)
3 cups	18 ounces, 504 ml	Seville or sour orange juice
$\frac{1}{4}$ cup	2 ounces, 46 ml	Honey
1 tablespoon	$\frac{1}{4}$ ounce, 6 grams	Cumin seeds, toasted and ground
1 teaspoon	1 g	Oregano, dried
1	47 ounces, 1.33 kg	Turkey breast, bone in, skin on
$\frac{1}{4}$ cup	2 ounces, 46 g	Butter, softened, or lard
3		Banana leaves or enough fresh corn husks to line the roasting pan and cover the turkey
2 tablespoons	1 ounce, 28 ml	Vegetable oil
$1\frac{1}{2}$ cups	12 ounces, 336 ml	Beer
1 cup	8 ounces, 113 g	Pickled red onion, thinly sliced (recipe follows)
1	8 ounces, 224 g	Avocado, sliced
8		Corn tortillas, 8 inches (20 cm), warmed
		Pico de Gallo (see p. 34)
		Salsa de Jitomate Cocida (see p. 32)

PROCEDURE

1 Combine achiote paste, juice, honey, cumin, and oregano.

2 Lift the turkey skin and rub softened butter over meat.

3 Spread the achiote mixture evenly over turkey; let marinate at room temperature for 45 minutes or under refrigeration 3–4 hours.

4 Line a pan with half the banana leaves or corn husks. Place the turkey on a rack on top of the banana leaves and cover with excess marinade.

5 Add beer to pan, cover turkey with remaining banana leaves or cornhusks.

6 Wrap pan with foil or use an airtight lid.

7   Steam until turkey reaches an internal temperature of 165°F (74°C). Steaming may be done in a preheated 350°F (176°C) oven. Check liquid level and add more beer or water if necessary. (Some Mexican cooks place a coin at the bottom of the steamer; when the coin begins to rattle, they add more water.)

8   When cooked, remove from pan and let cool. Shred as for tacos, combining meat with any sauce left in steamer. Turkey can also be placed on a platter, whole or in pieces, with any remaining sauce poured over it.

9   Serve turkey with pickled onion, avocado, tortillas, salsa (Pico de Gallo) and Salsa de Jitomate Cocida (p. 32; cooked tomato sauce).

Achiote Paste   MAKES ¼ CUP

AMOUNT	MEASURE	INGREDIENT
4 tablespoons		Achiote seeds
15		Peppercorns
1 tablespoon		Oregano
1 tablespoon		Cumin seeds
2		Whole cloves
1 tablespoon		Coriander seeds
6		Garlic cloves
4 tablespoons		White wine vinegar

PROCEDURE

1   Grind all but the garlic and vinegar in a coffee grinder. Crush the garlic in a mortar; gradually add the vinegar. Add the ground spices to the crushed garlic and mix well.

Pickled Red Onions   SERVES

AMOUNT	MEASURE	INGREDIENT
I pound	16 ounces, 448 g	Red onions, $\frac{1}{4}$ inch slices
I tablespoon	18 g	Kosher salt
I tablespoon	2 g	Oregano
I teaspoon	I g	Cumin seeds
I $\frac{1}{4}$ cup	10 ounces, 280 ml	Vinegar
5–6 tablespoons	I $\frac{3}{4}$ ounces, 49 g	Granulated sugar
I teaspoon	2 g	Black pepper

PROCEDURE

1   Separate the onion rings, toss with the salt until coated, and let stand 30 minutes.

2   Rinse the onions under cold water, drain very well, and pat dry with paper towels.

3   Combine well the oregano, cumin seeds, vinegar, sugar, and black pepper; pour over the rings in the bowl; toss to coat well. Chill for at least 2 hours before serving.

Frijoles Refritos Well-Fried Beans   SERVES 4

AMOUNT	MEASURE	INGREDIENT
3 tablespoons	I $\frac{1}{2}$ ounce, 42 g	Pork lard or vegetable oil
$\frac{1}{4}$ cup	I ounce, 28 g	White onion, $\frac{1}{4}$ inch (.6 cm) dice
2 cups	9 ounces, 252 g	Black, pink, or pinot beans, cooked, with cooking liquid
To taste		Salt and pepper

PROCEDURE

1   In a heavy pan, heat the lard or oil over medium-high heat.

2   Sauté the onions until brown, 3–4 minutes.

3   Increase heat to high and add half the beans and all the cooking liquid; mash well.

4   Gradually add the remaining beans and mash to a coarse puree.

5   Cook additional 10–12 minutes or until the beans begin to dry out and sizzle at the edges.

Arroz Blanco White Rice   SERVES 4

AMOUNT	MEASURE	INGREDIENT
		Hot water to cover
1 cup	$6\frac{1}{2}$ ounces, 184 g	Long-grain rice
$\frac{1}{4}$ cup	2 ounces, 56 ml	Vegetable oil
$\frac{1}{4}$ cup	1 ounce, 28 g	Carrots, $\frac{1}{4}$ inch (.6 cm) dice
$\frac{1}{4}$ cup	1 ounce, 28 g	Onions, thinly sliced
1		Garlic clove, minced
2 cups	16 ounces, 470 ml	Chicken stock
2 tablespoons	$\frac{1}{2}$ ounce, 14 g	Green peas, cooked

PROCEDURE

1 Soak rice in hot water for 20 minutes.

2 Drain and rinse well in cold water, let drain 10 minutes.

3 Heat oil to smoke point, add rice and stir to cover well with oil.

4 Cook, stirring, until rice is just turning color.

5 Add carrots, onions, and garlic; cook until onions are translucent, stirring constantly. Allow about 10 minutes over high heat to color rice and cook vegetables.

6 Add chicken stock and cook uncovered over medium heat—do not stir—until the liquid has been absorbed and small air holes appear.

7 Cover rice with a tight lid or aluminum foil, to prevent steam from escaping. Let set for 25 minutes.

8 Remove cover; stir in peas.

Salsa de Jitomate Cocida
Cooked Tomato Sauce   YIELD: 1 ½ CUPS

AMOUNT	MEASURE	INGREDIENT
1		Poblano chile, charred, peeled, seeded, and ¼ inch (.6 cm) dice (see step 1)
8 ounces	224 g	Tomatoes, charred, seeded, and chopped (see step 1)
1 tablespoon	½ ounce, 14 ml	Vegetable oil
½ cup	3 ounces, 84 g	Red onion, ¼ inch (.6 cm) dice
2		Garlic cloves, minced
1 teaspoon	3 g	Oregano, fresh, or ½ teaspoon dried
1 teaspoon	3 g	Basil, fresh, or ½ teaspoon dried
½ cup	4 ounces, 112 g	Tomato sauce
1 teaspoon	5 g	Fresh lime juice
To taste		Salt and pepper

PROCEDURE

1 Char poblano and tomatoes, turning frequently, until lightly charred on all sides, 3 to 5 minutes for chiles, 6 to 8 minutes for tomatoes (flesh should be soft).

2 Heat oil over medium heat and sauté onion and garlic until translucent, about 5 minutes.

3 Puree charred tomato and poblano.

4 Combine all ingredients except lime juice and salt and pepper, and cook over medium heat until slightly thickened and flavors are blended, about 5 minutes.

5 Add lime juice and correct seasoning.

Churros   SERVES 4

Churros are fried strips of dough typically served hot and sprinkled with powdered sugar or cinnamon and sugar, or dipped in chocolate. While the churro is actually an import from Spain, the dessert became very popular in Mexico. It is customary to serve churros with Mexican hot chocolate (see p. 34) or Cafe de Olla.

AMOUNT	MEASURE	INGREDIENT
1½ cups	6 ounces, 168 g	All-purpose flour
1 teaspoon	2 g	Baking powder
1¼ cups	10 ounces, 280 ml	Water
¼ teaspoon	1 g	Salt
1½ tablespoons	21 g	Brown sugar
1		Egg yolk
		Oil for deep frying
1		Lime, cut into wedges
		Powdered sugar for dusting

PROCEDURE

1   Sift the flour and baking powder together; set aside.

2   Bring water to a boil, add salt and brown sugar, stirring constantly, until both have dissolved.

3   Remove from heat, add the flour and baking powder mixture, and beat continuously until smooth.

4   Beat in the egg yolk until the mixture is smooth and glossy. Set the batter aside to cool. Have ready a churro maker or a piping bag fitted with a large star nozzle, which will give the churros their traditional shape.

5   Heat to the oil to 375°F (190°C) or until a cube of dried bread floats and turns golden after 1 minute.

6   Spoon the batter into a churros maker or a piping bag. Pipe five or six 4-inch lengths of the mixture into the hot oil, using a knife to slice off each length as it emerges from the nozzle.

7   Fry for 3–4 minutes or until golden brown.

8   Drain the churros on paper towels while cooking successive batches. Arrange on a plate with lime wedges, dust with powdered sugar, and serve warm.

Mexican Hot Chocolate   SERVES 4

Mexican chocolate is a grainy chocolate disk flavored with sugar, cinnamon, almonds, and vanilla. It is used to prepare hot chocolate and mole sauces. For I ounce Mexican chocolate, substitute I ounce semisweet chocolate, $\frac{1}{2}$ teaspoon ground cinnamon, and I drop almond extract.

AMOUNT	MEASURE	INGREDIENT
I quart	32 ounces, 896 ml	Milk
I pound	16 ounces, 448 g	Mexican chocolate or dark bitter chocolate
2		Vanilla beans, split lengthwise

PROCEDURE

1   Warm milk and chocolate.

2   Scrape seeds from the vanilla bean and add the seeds and beans to milk.

3   Stir with a *molinillo* or whisk until the chocolate is melted and the mixture begins to boil. Remove the vanilla beans. Remove from the heat and froth the chocolate with the *molinillo* or the whisk. Serve immediately in ample mugs.

Pico de Gallo   SERVES 4

AMOUNT	MEASURE	INGREDIENT
I tablespoon	$\frac{1}{2}$ ounce, 0.015 l	Olive oil
I cup	4 ounces, 113 g	Yellow onion, $\frac{1}{4}$ inch (.6 cm) dice
I		Serrano pepper, minced
I		Garlic clove, minced
I $\frac{1}{2}$ tablespoons		Cilantro, minced
I cup	6 ounces, 170 g	Tomatoes, peeled, seeded, $\frac{1}{4}$ inch (.6 cm) dice
I tablespoon	$\frac{1}{2}$ ounce, 0.015 l	Fresh lime juice
To taste		Salt and black pepper

PROCEDURE

1   Heat oil over medium heat. Add onions, serrano pepper, garlic, and cilantro. Toss and remove from heat. Let cool.

2   Combine onion mixture with tomatoes and lime juice and correct seasoning.

3   Serve warm or at room temperature.

Guacamole Avocado Dip

The word *guacamole* comes from the Nahuatl words for avocado (*ahuacatl*) and "mixture" or "concoction" (*molli*). It should be made in the *molcajete*, never in a blender or food processor. Guacamole can contain a seemingly infinite variety of ingredients; however, it is best when kept simple: avocados, chiles, onions, cilantro, and seasoning. Even tomatoes may cause problems if they are too watery.

Guacamole is usually eaten in Mexico at the beginning of a meal with a pile of hot, freshly made tortillas, crisp pork skins (*chicharron*), or little pieces of crispy pork (*carnitas*).

YIELD: 2 CUPS

AMOUNT	MEASURE	INGREDIENT
$\frac{1}{2}$ cup	2 ounces, 56 g	White onion, $\frac{1}{8}$ inch (.3 cm) dice
2		Jalapeño chiles, stemmed, seeded, and $\frac{1}{8}$ inch (.3 cm.) dice
$\frac{1}{4}$ cup	1 ounce, 28 g	Cilantro, chopped fine
2 tablespoons	1 ounce, 28 ml	Fresh lime juice
To taste		Salt
3		Hass avocados, ripe
Optional		
$\frac{3}{4}$ cup	5 ounces, 140 g	Tomatoes, $\frac{1}{4}$ inch (.6 cm) dice
Garnish		
$\frac{1}{4}$ cup	1 ounce, 28 g	White onion, $\frac{1}{8}$ inch (.3 cm) dice
1 tablespoon	2 g	Cilantro, chopped fine
As needed		Tortilla chips

PROCEDURE

1 In a *molcajete* or with a regular mortar and pestle, grind together the onion, chiles, cilantro, lime juice, and salt until smooth.

2 Cut the avocadoes in half. Remove the pits, scoop out the flesh, and mash roughly into the chile mixture in the *molcajete*. Mix well to incorporate flavors.

3 Stir in tomatoes, if desired.

4 Adjust the salt.

5 Sprinkle with garnish and serve immediately with warm tortilla chips.

Sopa de Fideos Aguada
Noodles in Tomato Broth   SERVES 4

AMOUNT	MEASURE	INGREDIENT
2 tablespoons	1 ounce, 28 g	Chicken fat or vegetable oil
	3 ounces, 84 g	Mexican fideos, angelhair pasta, or vermicelli
$1\frac{1}{2}$ cups	9 ounces, 252 g	Roma tomatoes, roasted and peeled
1		Garlic clove, chopped
$\frac{1}{4}$ cup	1 ounce, 28 g	White onion, roughly chopped
$5\frac{1}{4}$ cups	42 ounces, 1.24 liter	Chicken stock, heated
1 tablespoon	3 g	Italian parsley, roughly chopped
To taste		Salt

PROCEDURE

1   Heat fat or oil until it begins to smoke; add the whole bundles of noodles without breaking them up.

2   Sauté, stirring constantly to prevent scorching, until they are just golden brown.

3   Drain off excess fat; reserve 2 tablespoon in pan.

4   In a blender, combine tomatoes, garlic, and onions; blend until smooth.

5   Add mixture to the browned noodles; stir to coat noodles.

6   Add hot chicken stock and parsley; bring to a boil.

7   Reduce heat and simmer until pasta is cooked (soft).

8   Adjust seasoning.

Sopa de Fideos Aguada – Noodles in Tomato Broth

Chiles en Nogada
Chiles in Walnut Sauce   SERVES 4

This is one of the famous dishes of Mexico: large, dark green chiles poblanos stuffed with a pork meat picadillo and covered with a walnut sauce. It is decorated with red pomegranate seeds and large-leafed Italian parsley. The recipe is said to have been concocted by the grateful people of Puebla, for a banquet in honor of Don Agustin de Iturbide's saint's day, August 28, in 1821. He and his followers had led the final revolt against Spanish domination; as self-proclaimed emperor he had just signed the Treaty of Cordoba. All the dishes at the banquet were made with ingredients the colors of the Mexican flag: in this dish green chiles, white sauce, and red pomegranate seeds.

AMOUNT	MEASURE	INGREDIENT
4		Chiles poblano, large and smooth
1 tablespoon	$\frac{1}{2}$ ounce, 14 ml	Vegetable oil
1$\frac{1}{2}$ cups	12 ounces, 336 g	Pork, chopped fine
$\frac{1}{2}$ cup	2 ounces, 56 g	White onion, $\frac{1}{4}$-inch (.6 cm) dice
1		Garlic clove, minced
1 cup	6 ounces, 170 g	Tomato, peeled, seeded, $\frac{1}{4}$-inch (.6) dice
1		Apple, sweet or tart, $\frac{1}{4}$-inch (.6 cm) dice
$\frac{1}{2}$ cup	2 ounces, 56 g	Peaches, $\frac{1}{4}$-inch (.6 cm) dice
$\frac{1}{4}$ cup	1 ounce, 28 g	Plantain, $\frac{1}{4}$-inch (.6 cm) dice
$\frac{1}{4}$ cup	1 ounce, 28 g	Raisins
$\frac{1}{4}$ cup	1 ounce, 28 g	Almond slivers
2 teaspoons	$\frac{1}{2}$ ounce, 14 g	Pine nuts
1 tablespoon	$\frac{1}{3}$ ounce, 10 g	Lemon zest
$\frac{1}{4}$ cup	2 ounces, 56 ml	Chicken stock
$\frac{1}{2}$ teaspoon	1 g	Coriander seeds
To taste		Salt and black pepper
3		Eggs, separated
As needed		Flour
As needed		Oil
2 cups	16 ounces, 448 ml	Walnut sauce (recipe follows)
Garnish		Seeds of two pomegranates

Chiles en Nogada – Chiles in Walnut Sauce

PROCEDURE

1   Roast (char) the chiles, steam, and peel off outer skin without removing the stem.

2   Make a lengthwise slit in each chile and remove the veins. Optional: Soak in a salt water and vinegar solution for up to 2 hours to reduce the heat of the pepper.

3   Heat oil and brown the pork. Remove and drain meat; leave fat in pan.

4   Cook onion and garlic until translucent. Add tomatoes and cook 2 minutes.

5   Combine pork, apples, peaches, plantain, raisins, almonds, pine nuts, lemon zest, and chicken stock with onion mixture. Add coriander and season with salt and pepper.

6   Cook over slow heat until almost dry. Allow to cool.

7   Stuff chiles with pork mixture. Reshape and secure openings with a toothpicks; chill for 30 minutes.

8   Beat egg whites until stiff peaks form. Lightly beat the egg yolk and mix into whites.

9   Heat oil to 350°F (175°C) in a deep fryer or pan fry using enough oil so it comes up half the thickness of the chiles.

10   Dip the stuffed chiles in flour and then in the egg batter, and fry until golden brown on each side. Drain on paper towels and remove toothpicks.

11   Just before serving, coat with warm walnut sauce and garnish with pomegranate seeds.

Walnut Sauce

AMOUNT	MEASURE	INGREDIENT
I cup	4 ounces, 112 g	Walnut halves
I cup	8 ounces, 240 ml	Milk
I ounce	28 grams	Sliced bread, torn in pieces
I cup	8 ounces, 224 g	Queso fresco or whole-milk ricotta cheese
I cup	8 ounces, 240 g	Heavy cream
$\frac{1}{2}$ teaspoon	2 g	Sugar

PROCEDURE

1   Soak walnuts in half the milk for 1 hour. Strain and reserve the milk. Rub walnuts in a clean towel to remove the skin.

2   Soak the bread in remaining milk for at least 30 minutes.

3   Combine all ingredients in a blender and process until smooth.

Frijoles de Olla "Pot" Beans SERVES 4

This is traditionally served in a small earthenware bowl.

AMOUNT	MEASURE	INGREDIENT
2 cups	15 ounces, 420 g	Dried beans, black, pink, or pinto
$\frac{1}{2}$ cup	2 ounces, 56 g	White onion, $\frac{1}{4}$ inch (.6) dice
2 tablespoon	1 ounce, 28 g	Pork lard or vegetable oil
1 tablespoon	15 g	Salt
To taste		Salt and pepper

PROCEDURE

1 Rinse beans in cold water and check for and remove small stones.

2 Cover beans with hot water, add onion and lard, and bring to boil.

3 Reduce to simmer; cover and cook until they are just soft and the skins are breaking open, $1\frac{1}{2}$–2 hours.

4 Add salt and continue to cook until the beans are soft and the liquid is somewhat thick.

5 Correct seasoning.

Arroz con Leche Mexican Rice Pudding
SERVES 4

AMOUNT	MEASURE	INGREDIENT
2 cups	16 ounces, 480 ml	Milk
1		Cinnamon stick
1 cup	$6\frac{1}{2}$ ounces, 184 g	Long-grain rice
$\frac{1}{2}$ cup	$3\frac{1}{2}$ ounces, 98 g	Granulated sugar
$\frac{1}{2}$ cup	4 ounces, 112 ml	Sweetened condensed milk
$1\frac{1}{2}$ teaspoons	8 ml	Vanilla extract

PROCEDURE

1 Combine milk and cinnamon; bring to boil.

2 Add rice, reduce to a simmer, cover, and cook 15 minutes.

3 Combine sugar, condensed milk, and vanilla; stir to dissolve. Stir into rice and simmer 5 minutes. Remove from heat and serve warm.

Mole Negro Oaxaqueño
Oaxacan Black Mole   SERVES 4–6

The most famous of *Oaxaca*'s many moles, traditionally served with pork, chicken, or particularly turkey, this is the choice for festive occasions. In Mexico, the ingredients for large batches of mole are usually taken to a *molino*-mill to eliminate the laborious process of grinding with the *metate* (stone mortar and pestle).

AMOUNT	MEASURE	INGREDIENT
	5 ounces, 140 g	Mulato chiles
	4 ounces, 112 g	Ancho chiles
	2 ounces, 56 g	Pasilla chiles
	4 ounces, 114 g	Chile negro
2 cups	16 ounces, 448 ml	Chicken stock
1		Dried avocado leaves
$\frac{1}{4}$ cup	1 ounces, 56 g	Sesame seeds
1	2 ounces, 56 g	Corn tortilla, finely chopped
	2 ounces, 56 g	Bolillo or French roll, crumbled
$\frac{1}{4}$ cup	2 ounces, 56 ml	Lard or vegetable oil
$\frac{1}{2}$ cup	2 ounces, 56 g	Almonds, sliced
$\frac{1}{2}$ cup	2 ounces, 56 g	Peanuts, shelled and skinned
$\frac{1}{4}$ cup	2 ounces, 56 g	Raisins
$\frac{1}{4}$ cup	2 ounces, 56 g	Prunes, pitted and chopped
$\frac{1}{2}$ cup	3 ounces, 84 g	Plantain, peeled and chopped
1 teaspoon	2 g	Black pepper
2		Allspice, whole
$\frac{1}{8}$ teaspoon		Marjoram
$\frac{1}{8}$ teaspoon		Thyme
$\frac{1}{8}$ teaspoon		Oregano
1		Cinnamon stick, 2 inches

(Continued)

AMOUNT	MEASURE	INGREDIENT
Pinch		Anise
$\frac{1}{2}$ teaspoon	3 g	Cumin, ground
$\frac{1}{4}$ cup	1 ounce, 28 g	Garlic clove, minced
1 cup	4 ounces, 112 g	White onion, chopped
$\frac{1}{2}$ cup	2 ounces, 56 g	Tomatillos, husked
$\frac{1}{2}$ cup	2 ounces, 56 g	Tomato
$\frac{1}{2}$ cup	4 ounces, 112 ml	Vegetable oil
	2 ounce, 56 g	Mexican chocolate
To taste		Sugar and salt

PROCEDURE

1 Roast chiles and remove the veins and seeds; soak in chicken stock for 20 minutes. Puree chiles in a blender or food processor with stock. Reserve.

2 Dry-toast the avocado leaves, sesame seeds, tortillas, and *bolillo* until browned, set aside.

3 Heat the lard and fry the almonds, peanuts, raisins, prunes, plantain, herbs, spices, garlic, and onions until the onion begin to soften. Add more oil if needed.

4 Roast the *tomatillos* and tomatoes on the *comal* or on a sheet pan under the broiler.

5 Blend all ingredients in a food processor, blender, or mortar except chile puree, vegetable oil, and chocolate; puree until smooth, adding enough water or stock to allow the blades to move. May be done in batches.

6 Heat the vegetable oil over medium heat.

7 Add blended ingredients and cook over low heat for 35 minutes.

8 Add chile puree and continue to cook 30 minutes or until thickened.

9 Add chocolate; stir until melted.

10 Adjust seasoning with sugar and salt.

Pozole Blanco White Pozole SERVES 4–6

Pozole, a Mexican soup, is made with a special type of corn that has been slaked (soaked) in a solution of lime. The traditional corn used is *maiz blanco* or *cacahuazintle* [kaw-kaw-WAH-SEEN-til]. This is a very large-kerneled white corn grown in Mexico.

AMOUNT	MEASURE	INGREDIENT
		Water to cover
2 cups	13 ounces, 364 g	Hominy
1 pound	16 ounces, 448 g	Pork stew meat, $\frac{1}{2}$ inch (1.2 cm) cubes
1 pound	16 ounces, 448 g	Pork neck bones
1		Pork trotters (optional), cut in 4 pieces
1 cup	4 ounces, 112 g	White onion, $\frac{1}{2}$ inch (1.2 cm) dice
$\frac{1}{4}$ cup	1 ounce, 28 g	Garlic cloves, minced
To taste		Salt and pepper
Garnish		
2		Limes, quartered
2 cups	4 ounces, 112 g	Lettuce or cabbage, shredded
$\frac{1}{2}$ cup	2 ounces, 56 g	Radishes, washed, sliced thin
1 tablespoon		Dried oregano
1 tablespoon		Crumbled chiles piquin or other small, dried hot red chiles
1 cup	4 ounces, 112 g	White onion, $\frac{1}{4}$ inch (.6) dice
8		Corn tortillas, 4 inch, fried crisp

PROCEDURE

1 Add water to hominy to cover by $\frac{1}{2}$ inch (1.2 cm).

2 Bring to boil and cook until corn kernels start to blossom or "flower" (they will open out at one end).

3 Add all pork items, first quantity of onion, and garlic; cook until pork is tender, adjusting water as needed.

4 Correct seasoning.

5 Arrange lime wedges, shredded lettuce or cabbage, radishes, oregano, chiles, and onions in bowls.

6 Ladle soup over garnish.

7 Serve with fried tortillas.

Arroz à la Mexicana
Mexican Rice   SERVES 4–6

AMOUNT	MEASURE	INGREDIENT
		Hot water to cover
1 cup	$6\frac{1}{2}$ ounces, 184 g	Long-grain rice
$\frac{1}{4}$ cup	2 ounces, 56 ml	Vegetable oil
1 cup	6 ounces, 168 g	Tomato, $\frac{1}{4}$ inch (.6 cm) dice
$\frac{1}{4}$ cup	1 ounce, 28 g	Onions, thinly sliced
1		Garlic clove, minced
$\frac{1}{4}$ cup	1 ounce, 28 g	Carrots, $\frac{1}{4}$ inch (.6 cm) dice
2 cups	16 ounces 470 ml	Chicken stock
2 tablespoons	$\frac{1}{2}$ ounce, 14 g	Green peas, cooked

PROCEDURE

1 Add hot water to cover rice and soak for 20 minutes.

2 Drain and rinse well in cold water; let drain 10 minutes.

3 Heat oil until smoke point; add rice and stir to cover well with oil.

4 Cook, stirring, until rice is light golden, stirring and turning so the rice cooks evenly. This process should take about 8 minutes and should be done over high heat or the rice will become mushy in its final cooking stage.

5 Blend the tomato, onion, and garlic until smooth; add to the fried rice.

6 Cook until the mixture is dry.

7 Add carrots and chicken stock; cook uncovered over medium heat—do not stir—until the liquid has been absorbed and small air holes appear.

8 Cover rice with a tight lid or aluminum foil to prevent steam from escaping. Let set for 25 minutes.

9 Remove cover; stir in peas.

Pescado à la Veracruzana
Fish Veracruz Style   SERVES 4

Pescado à la Veracruzana is one of the most famous dishes of Veracruz, which lies on the Caribbean coast of eastern Mexico. This dish shows a strong influence of Spanish cuisine.

Chef Tip Be careful with how much salt you add to this dish. The olives and capers will add their own salt to the sauce.

Red snapper is the fish most commonly associated with this dish, but any firm white fish fillet may be used.

AMOUNT	MEASURE	INGREDIENT
4	4–6 ounces, 113–1170 g	Fish fillets, boneless white firm flesh
1 tablespoon	$\frac{1}{2}$ ounce, 14 ml	Fresh lime juice
1 teaspoon	8 g	Salt
2 tablespoons	1 ounce, 28 ml	Vegetable oil
1 cup	4 ounces, 112 g	White onion, sliced thin
2		Garlic cloves, minced
3 cups	18 ounces, 508 ml	Tomatoes, peeled, seeded, $\frac{1}{4}$ inch (.6 cm) dice
1 cup	8 ounces, 224 ml	Fish stock or water
$\frac{1}{3}$ cup	2 ounces, 56 g	Green olives, pitted, sliced thin
2 tablespoon	6 g	Parsley, minced
1 teaspoon	1 g	Oregano, dried
1		Bay leaf
1 tablespoon	$\frac{1}{2}$ ounce, 14 g	Capers, rinsed, drained
2		Jalapeños, seeds and veins removed, sliced thin
1		Cinnamon stick
2		Whole cloves
To taste		Salt and pepper
		Rice, for serving

PROCEDURE

1. Marinate the fish in the lime juice and salt, 30 minutes to 1 hour.

2. Heat oil over medium heat; add onion and cook until translucent.

3. Add garlic and cook 1 minute.

4. Add remaining ingredients, bring to simmer, and cook 15 minutes until almost sauce consistency.

5. Add fish to tomato sauce, cover with sauce; cover and simmer until fish is cooked.

6. Serve with rice.

Pescado à la Veracruzana – Fish Veracruz-style

Jicama Salad

SERVES 4

AMOUNT	MEASURE	INGREDIENT
$\frac{1}{2}$ cup	2 ounces, 56 g	Red bell pepper, julienned
$\frac{1}{2}$ cup	2 ounces, 56 g	Green bell pepper, julienned
$\frac{1}{2}$ cup	2 ounces, 56 g	Yellow bell pepper, julienned
$\frac{1}{2}$ cup	2 ounces, 56 g	Carrot, julienned
2 cups	8 ounces, 224 g	Jicama, peeled, julienned
$\frac{1}{2}$ cup	3 ounces, 84 g	Cucumber, peeled, seeded, julienned
I tablespoon	3 g	Fresh cilantro, minced
I teaspoon		Fresh parsley, minced
I teaspoon		Fresh chives, minced
2		Shallot, minced
I		Garlic clove, minced
2 tablespoons	I ounce, 28 ml	Vinegar or sherry wine vinegar
$\frac{1}{4}$ cup	2 ounce, 56 ml	Olive oil
To taste		Salt and pepper

PROCEDURE

1   Combine the first six ingredients.

2   Combine the remaining ingredients and whisk mixture until well incorporated.

3   Toss vegetables with dressing; refrigerate until ready to serve.

South America

The Land

South America, the fourth largest continent, contains the world's highest waterfall, Angel Falls; the largest river (by volume), the Amazon River; the longest mountain range, the Andes; the driest desert, Atacama; the largest rain forest, the Amazon rain forest; the highest capital city, La Paz, Bolivia; and the world's southernmost city, Ushuaia, Argentina.

In the high reaches of the Andes Mountains, along the border between Bolivia and Peru, lies one of the highest regions inhabited by people anywhere in the world. Here in the altiplano farmers raise sheep, llamas, and alpacas, as they have for thousands of years. But unlike most farmlands, the altiplano is surrounded by jagged mountains, volcanic peaks that drop steeply down to deserts in some places, to rain forests in others, and on the western side, to the deep trench of the Pacific Ocean. South America is home to some of the planet's largest volcanoes, and in the far south along the coast of Chile, large ice sheets are commonplace.

The Amazon River Basin is roughly the size of the forty-eight contiguous United States and covers some 40 percent of the South American continent. Reflecting environmental conditions as well as past human influence, the Amazon is made up of ecosystems and vegetation types that include rain forests, seasonal forests, deciduous forests, flooded forests, and savannas.

The Eastern Highlands of South America belong to the older geologic period (almost of the same time as that of North America's Appalachian Mountains). The northern section of the Eastern Highlands is known as Guiana Highlands, which consists of a vast plateau marked by deep gorges and tropical rain forests, and is home to Angel Falls. The southern section is known as the Brazilian Highlands and includes several mountain ranges.

Venezuela's rugged Llanos are one of the world's richest tropical grasslands. This large, very fertile plain is located in central and southern Venezuela and eastern and central Colombia. It is drained by the Orinoco River and its many tributaries. This mostly flat, grassy country is teeming with wildlife, including more than 100 species of mammals and over 300 species of birds. Here, a catfish known as the *lau-lau* weighs up to 330 pounds and is considered a culinary delicacy.

Pampas is a word of Quechua origin that means "a plain without trees." This flat land is Argentina's agricultural heartland, home of the gaucho (cowboy) and is famed for its many cattle ranches.

Patagonia is the area between the Andes Mountains and the Atlantic Ocean. It stretches south from the Rio Negro River in southern Argentina to Tierra del Fuego and the Strait of Magellan and is one of the less populated regions in the world. Its mostly rugged, barren land is not suitable for extensive farming, but is compatible with sheep raising.

History

In the sixteenth century, Spanish explorers in the Americas encountered two great civilizations, one in Mesoamerica (the territory controlled by the Aztecs and the Mayas at the time of the conquest) and the other in South America (the territory in the central Andean region under Inca rule). The people of these regions included many tribes and nations, with achievements that included art, cities, and strong foundations of economic, political, and social organization.

The Inca empire, with its capital at Cuzco (in modern-day Peru), covered a large portion of South America in the fifteenth century and the first quarter of the sixteenth century. The empire stretched nearly 2,500 miles down the west coast of South America, and covered coastal desert, high mountains, and low-lying jungle. It covered most of modern-day Peru, part of Ecuador, and Bolivia, northwest Argentina, and the greater part of Chile. To control such a huge area, the Incas built roads, including both mountainous and coastal routes. This road system was key to farming success since it allowed distribution of foodstuffs over long distances. Agriculture was an important part of Incan life and farmers used sophisticated methods of cultivation. By the time of the Spanish conquest, the ancient Americans were some of the greatest plant cultivators in the world. Maize from Mesoamerica and potatoes from the Andes were some of their contributions to the European diet. To get the highest yield from their crops, the Incas used terracing and irrigation methods on hillsides in the highlands. Building terraces meant that they could use more land for cultivation, and it also helped to resist erosion of the land by wind and rain.

Caribbean Sea

Cartagena

Caracas

VENEZUELA

Georgetown
Paramaribo
SURINAME
Cayenne
Fr. G.

Orinoco

GUYANA

Guyana Highlands

Magdalena

BOGOTÁ

COLOMBIA

Negro

Quito

ECUADOR

Japurá

Amazon

P E R U

Purus

Amazon

Madeira

Tapajós

B R A Z I L

Porto
Velho

Xingu

Araguaia

Tocantins

LIMA

Juruá

Guaporé

L. Titicaca

BOLIVIA

La Paz

São Francisco

Brasília

Potosí

Brazilian
Highlands

PARAGUAY

Pilcomayo

PACIFIC

OCEAN

CHILE

Valparaíso
Santiago

Asunción

SÃO PAULO

RIO DE
JANEIRO

Paraná

Colorado

Uruguay

BUENOS
AIRES

URUGUAY

Montevideo

A R G E N T I N A

Colorado

ANDES

ATLANTIC

OCEAN

P A T A G O N I A

Falkland Is.
Stanley

Tierra del Fuego

Scotia Sea

South Georgia I.

Drake Passage

King George I.

South Orkney Is.

South
Sandwich
Is.

Antarctic
Peninsula

Joinville I.

Alexander I.

South America

51

By the sixteenth century, rumors of gold and other riches attracted the Spanish to the area. Spanish conquistadors, led by Francisco Pizarro, explored south from Panama, reaching Inca territory. It was clear that they had reached a wealthy land with prospects of great treasure, and after one more expedition in 1529, Pizarro traveled to Spain and received royal approval to conquer the region and be its viceroy.

Pedros Alvares Cabral set sail from Portugal in 1500 to sail to the eastern side of South America. He arrived on the coast of Brazil and claimed the region for Portugal. Finding the warm climate and rich soil ideal for planting sugarcane, the Portuguese built large plantations and brought slaves from West Africa. Shiploads of Euorpean settlers poured in to make their fortune. Many grew coffee in the rich soil around São Paulo, and Brazil became the foremost coffee producer in the world at that time. Gold mines flourished in the interior, and a new industry to produce rubber emerged up along the Amazon. Cattle ranches sprang up to feed developing mining centers. Brazil soon began exporting coffee, rubber, cocoa, and cattle.

Today these are countries of great contrasts. In each one, there are wealthy and cosmopolitan cities, but there are also areas where many people live in conditions of great poverty. Significant ecological and environmental issues, such as the destruction of the rain forest, loss of plant and animal species, and air and water pollution, are being addressed. Rich in natural resources with growing economies, there is great potential for the future.

The Food

The inhabitants of the Andean region developed more than half the agricultural products that the world eats today. Among these are more than 20 varieties of corn, 240 varieties of potato, as well as one or more varieties of squash, beans, peppers, peanuts, and cassava (a starchy root). Quinoa (which in the language of Incans means "mother of cereals") is a cereal grain crop domesticated in the high plains area around Lake Titicaca (on the border of Peru and Bolivia).

By far the most important of the crops was the potato. The Incas planted the potato, which is able to withstand heavy frosts, in elevations as high as 15,000 feet. At these heights the Incas could use the freezing night temperatures and the heat of the day to alternately freeze and dry harvested potatoes until all the moisture had been removed. The Incas then reduced the potato to a light flour. Corn could also be grown up to an altitude of 13,500 feet; it was consumed fresh, dried, or popped. They also made it into an alcoholic beverage known as *saraiaka* or *chicha*.

The manioc tuber, or cassava root, was another important staple of the natives. This carbohydrate-rich food was easy to propagate but difficult to process, at least for the bitter variety, which is poisonous when raw. To detoxify manioc, the tubers had to be peeled and grated and the pulp put into long, supple cylinders—called *tipitis*—made of woven plant fibers. Each tube was then hung with a heavy weight at the bottom, which compressed the pulp and expressed the poisonous juice. The pulp could then be removed, washed, and roasted, rendering it safe to eat. The product was toasted into coarse meal or flour known as *farinha de mandioc*. Starch settling out from the extracted juice was heated on a flat surface, causing individual starch grains to pop open and clump together into small, round granules called tapioca. The extracted juice, boiled down to remove the poison, was used as the basis of the sauce known as *tucupi*.

Manioc meal became many things in the hands of the Indian women. Pulverized meal was mixed with ground fish to produce a concoction called *paçoka*, or *paçoca*. For the children, small, sun-dried cakes called *carimã* were prepared. There was a porridge or paste known as *mingau*, and thin, crisp snacks called *beijus*, made of either tapioca flour or dough from a nonpoisonous, or sweet variety of manioc known as *macaxeira* or *aipim*. These sweet manioc tubers, which are somewhat fibrous but considerably easier to prepare, were also pared, boiled for several hours to soften them, and eaten like potatoes.

Soups are an indispensable part of the main meal and frequently are a meal in themselves. Most South American soups originated in European kitchens; a few date back to pre-Hispanic times. In the Andean countries there are the *mazamorroas* or *coladoas*, creamlike soups made with ground dried corn and ground dried beans, quinoa, amaranth, or squash. Variations of this type of soup, called *sangos*, are probably the oldest Indian food. *Sango* was the sacred dish of the Incas. The Spaniards introduced *potajes* (hearty soups), *pucheros* (*pot-au-feu*-type soups), and *cocidos* (meat and vegetables soups) that are popular in the southern countries of South America. Chile, Argentina, Uruguay, Bolivia, and Paraguay have *locros*—thick soups made with hominy, beans, squash, and sweet potatoes. *Chupes*, popular in Bolivia, Chile, Peru, and Ecuador, are stewlike soups prepared with fish, chicken, or other meat along with potatoes, cheese, vegetables, and may include eggs.

VENEZUELA

Venezuela is located on the northern edge of South America, bordered by Guyana, Brazil, Colombia, and the southern waters of the Caribbean Sea. The explorer Christopher Columbus, on his third voyage sailing from Spain, landed on its coast in 1498. Venezuela declared itself independent of Spain in 1811 but retains a strong Spanish influence.

The country is one of the world's top ten producers of oil, which has helped it to develop its economy. Due to the diversity in the landscape, Venezuela has an ability to grow a wide variety of crops. Its main crop is sugarcane, followed by fruits such as bananas, oranges, pineapple, papayas, strawberries, passion fruit, watermelons, limes, and avocados. Because of its long Caribbean coastline Venezuela is as much a Caribbean country as it is a South American one. Venezuela has a strong fishing industry, famous for sardines, shrimp, clams, mussels, crabs, and tuna.

Arepas, thick, flattened balls of fried or baked corn or wheat flour, are the main staple of Venezuelan cuisine. These flatbreads can be filled with meats, cheeses, jelly, or vegetables. Favorite fillings include tuna or chicken salad, shredded beef, or ham and cheese. *Arepas* usually accompany Venezuela's national dish, *pabellon criollo*. This is a hearty dish that includes black beans and shredded beef seasoned with onions, garlic, green peppers, tomatoes, and cilantro. This is served atop a mound of rice alongside a fried egg and strips of fried plantain. White cheese is grated over the top. *Hallaca* is a special dish served only during the holidays. A packet of cornmeal dough is steamed in a wrapping of palm leaves with a filling of pork, chicken, and beef, and mixed with olives, capers, raisins, tomatoes, peppers, nuts, and spices. *Hallaca* were first made by servants trying to use up leftovers from their plantation master's tables. Among the unusual foods in this country are *logarto sancocho* (lizard soup) and fried ants, considered a special treat.

BRAZIL

Brazil covers nearly half of South America and both the equator and the Tropic of Capricorn run through the country. Brazil is bordered by Argentina, Paraguay, Uruguay, Bolivia, Peru, Colombia, Venezuela, Guyana, Suriname, and French Guiana, as well as the Atlantic Ocean. The country's main regions are the Amazon Basin, the dry northeast where farmers raise cattle, and the southeast, Brazil's most populated region.

Brazil's population is the largest in Latin America and constitutes about half the population of South America. With nearly all of the people living in cities and towns, Brazil is one of the most urbanized and industrialized countries in Latin America. São Paulo and Rio de Janeiro are among the ten largest cities in the world. Yet parts of Brazil's Amazon region, which has some of the world's most extensive wilderness areas, are sparsely inhabited by indigenous peoples who rarely come into contact with the modern world.

Until 1822 the country was a Portuguese colony and even today its official language is Portuguese. The Portuguese and Spanish brought African slaves to South America, and nowhere is their influence stronger than in Brazil. Dendê (palm oil), peppers, okra, and coconut milk, staples of West African cooking, are firmly established on the Brazilian palate. Brazil's national dish, *feijoada* (literally "big bean" stew), is said to have originated during slave times. Originally *feijoada* contained inexpensive and less desirable cuts of meat such as tripe and pigs feet, as slaves had only the leftovers of the master's table for themselves. Today *feijoada* consists of a variety of meats slowly cooked with black beans and condiments. A *feijoada completa*, or "complete feijoada," is accompanied by rice, fresh orange slices, a side dish of peppery onion sauce, chopped greens such as collards, and *farinha* (toasted manioc flour).

The Portuguese influence shows in the rich, sweet egg breads that are served at nearly every meal, and in the seafood dishes that blend assorted seafoods with coconut and other native fruits and vegetables. Seafood stews predominate in the north, while the south is the land of *churrascos*. *Churrasco* is a Brazilian word that means "to barbecue" and stems from the pampas of Brazil, where ranchers cook large portions of marinated meats on long skewers over an open fire pit. The range of barbecued meats includes pork, beef, chicken, goat, and the very special *galinha do coracao*, or chicken hearts. The meats are cut straight from the skewer with large butcher knives directly onto the plate. They make great use of their rich assortment of tubers, squash, and beans. Manioc is at the heart of Brazilian vegetable consumption. It is the "flour" of the region, and is eaten in one form or another at nearly every meal. Brazilian food, unlike the cuisines of many of the surrounding countries, favors the sweet rather than the hot.

THE GUIANAS

Guyana (formerly British Guiana), Suriname (formerly Dutch Guiana), and French Guiana (an overseas department of France) are situated in northeastern South America. Together they are called the Guianas and the influences are varied.

The Dutch were among the first to settle in Guyana. With the Dutch, many Germans and Austrians also settled in the area, which added to the cuisine of this region. Peas, rice, and bread are staples in the diet of many Guyanese. Locally grown vegetables such as manioc, plantains, and breadfruit are widely consumed, but are available only in season. A popular festive food is *cook-up*, which is any kind of meat prepared in coconut milk and served with rice and beans. There are influences from India and many traditional dishes are very spicy, made with curries and habanero peppers, or Scotch bonnet, which is native to the region.

Suriname is more prosperous than Guyana and has a diversity of ethnic influences. The Indonesian population has contributed a number of spicy meat and vegetable side dishes, including *nasi goring* (fried rice) and *bami goring* (fried noodles). From the Creole population has come *pom* (ground tayer roots, which are a relative of the cassava, mixed with poultry), and *pastei* (chicken pie with vegetables). The African influence is found in the popular peanut soup.

French Guiana is the only remaining nonindependent country on the South American mainland. The French used it as a penal colony between 1852 and 1939, and it is the location of the infamous Devil's Island. In 1947 it became an overseas department of France. It is governed by French law and the French constitution, and enjoys French customs, currency, and holidays. Most of the food here is imported and people in French Guiana enjoy an international cuisine, including Chinese, Vietnamese, and Indonesian dishes.

COLOMBIA

Located in the northwest corner of South America, Columbia is the only country in South America with both Caribbean and Pacific coastlines. Colombia also shares its borders with Panama, Venezuela, Brazil, Peru, and Ecuador. Coffee is Colombia's leading agricultural crop. With its two coastlines, seafood makes a major impact on the cuisine, along with chicken, pork, potatoes, rice, beans, and soup. Columbia's cuisine also has a strong Spanish influence. Interesting regional dishes include *ajiaco*, a specialty from Bogota that is a potato-based soup accompanied by chicken and maize and served with cream, capers, and chunks of avocado; the famous *hormiga culona*, a large ant that is fried and eaten; and *lechona*, a whole suckling pig, spit-roasted and stuffed with rice, which is a specialty of Tolima.

ECUADOR

This county's name comes from the Spanish word meaning "equator" as it sits directly on the equator. It is bordered by Colombia, Peru, and the Pacific Ocean and includes the Galápagos Islands. Ecuador is renowned for its *ceviche*, made with bitter orange juice and chilies. Afro-Ecuadorians along the northern coast enjoy seafood seasoned with coconut milk. Peanuts and bananas are found on the lower-coastal regions. Corn and potato pancakes and soups, as well as grilled *cuy* (guinea pig), are popular further inland along the Andes. Ecuador is also known for its fabulous exotic fruits that include cherimoya (custard apple), physalis (cape gooseberry), tamarillo (tree tomato), babaco (mountain papaya), granadilla (passion fruit), baby bananas, and red bananas. There is also high-quality fish and seafood, and the countless varieties of Andean potatoes. Across the country national and regional dishes include lemon-marinated shrimp, toasted corn, and pastries stuffed with spiced meats. The core of the Ecuadorian diet is rice, potatoes, and meat (beef and chicken throughout the country and pork in the Sierra region). Foods are cooked in *achiote* oil or lard. *Refrito*, a fried mixture containing chopped onions, green peppers, tomato, *achiote*, and salt and/or garlic, is added to many cooked dishes. Meats are often seasoned with a spicy *aji* sauce. The *aji* sauce (made from a spicy red pepper) is a national delicacy and is found on most tables. Ecuador's specialties are fresh soups such as *Locro* soup (cheese, avocado, and potato). *Fanesca* is a soup made of many ingredients including twelve different grains and salted cod served during Lent. Other popular dishes include *lomo salteado* (thin sliced steak, covered with onions and tomatoes) and *chocio* (grilled Andean corn) sold by street vendors.

PERU

Peru, just south of the equator, is located on the western coast of South America. It is bordered by Ecuador, Colombia, Brazil, Bolivia, Chile, and the Pacific Ocean. East of the dry coastal plain of Peru lie the Andes Mountains, which contain active volcanoes and high plateaus between the ranges. East of the Andes are plains covered by rain forests.

This "land of the Incas" is the world's potato capital, with more than three hundred varieties and colors (including purple, blue, yellow, and shades of brown to pink), as well as various sizes, textures, and flavors. This tuber, in addition to rice, chicken, pork, lamb, and fish, comprise the basic ingredient from which most Peruvian dishes originate. Most corn and beans cannot grow in the Andes Mountains because of the cold and the short growing season; thus, the potato was the main staple grown by the Incas and Indians. The Indians also grew quinoa and the grain *kiwicha*, which grows at high altitudes and produces small seeds that are very rich in protein. These were used by the Incas to supplement their diet. The areas surrounding the Pacific Ocean, the Amazon River, and Lake Titicaca have abundant seafood and turtles. *Ceviche* comes in many variations, and is typically served with boiled potato, sweet potato, or *cancha* (toasted corn kernels). Meats are served in a variety of ways. *Butifarras* is a sandwich with Peruvian ham and spicy sauce. *Carapulcra* is a stew made with pork, chicken, yellow potatoes, chiles, peanuts, and cumin. *Aji de gallina* is a peppery chicken served in a creamy, yellow, spicy nut-based sauce. *Seco de cabrito* is goat marinated with *chichi de jora* (a fermented maize drink) or beer, cilantro, and garlic. *Chaiona* is cured lamb, alpaca, or llama. Grilled or fried guinea pig (*cuy*) is a favorite in the highlands. The cuisine's flavor is spicy and sweet and it varies by region. Some Peruvian chile peppers are not spicy but give color to sauces. In Peru rice production is significant and today rice often accompanies Peruvian dishes rather than potatoes.

BOLIVIA

The landlocked country of Bolivia is located in west-central South America and is bordered by Peru, Brazil, Paraguay, Argentina, and Chile. Due to the number of mountains with elevations of 18,000 to 20,000 feet, many people refer to the country as the "Tibet of the Americas." The portion of the Andes Mountains that runs through Bolivia includes some of the highest peaks and most remote regions found anywhere in South America. Lake Titicaca and surrounding streams and rivers offer fresh trout and other fishes. Bolivia is known for its *saltenas* and *empanadas*, which are meat or vegetable pies. Other traditional dishes include *majao*, a rice dish with eggs, beef, and fried banana; *silpancho*, meat served with rice and potatoes; and *pacumutu*, a rice dish with grilled beef, fried yuca, and cheese. Spicy sauces and condiments made with ajis are served with stews and soups such as *chairo* (with cured lamb or alpaca), *chuno* (freeze-dried potatoes), or *saice* (meat soup with onions and tomatoes). Bolivian beer is popular, but the most favored local drink is *chicha cochabambina*, a very potent alcohol made from corn.

PARAGUAY

Although landlocked, Paraguay is bordered and crisscrossed by navigable rivers. Corn and manioc are the cornerstones of the cuisine in Paraguay. Other principal food crops include beans, peanuts, sorghum, sweet potatoes, and rice. Many types of beans are grown in Paraguay, including lima beans, French beans, and peas. The most popular dishes are based on corn, meat, milk, and cheese. *Yerba mate* is a national drink made from the green dried leaves and stemlets of the tree *Ilex paraguarensis* and is an important ritualistic process among the people of Paraguay and Argentina. It is served in a hollow gourd that is filled two-thirds of the way with the moistened mate herb. Hot water is then poured into the gourd. The person sucks the *mate* water out of the gourd with a *bombilla* (a metal filter straw with a strainer at the end, which can range from the functional to the elaborately crafted). When the water is gone, the gourd is refilled by the server with hot water and passed to the next person in the group. When that person finishes, the gourd is handed back to the server for another refill and this rotating process of sharing is what makes the act of mate drinking a moment of intimacy for those present. *Yerba mate* is supposed to have powers that include mental stimulation, fatigue reduction, and stress reduction. Another local drink preferred by Paraguayans is locally produced dark rum made from sugarcane.

CHILE

More than 2600 miles long and only 110 miles at its widest point, the terrain of Chile ranges from the desert in the north to the Antarctic in the south. Chile is located on the western coast of South America and bordered by Argentina, Bolivia, and Peru, as well as the Pacific Ocean. Chile's agriculture is well established in North American and European supermarkets, with major exports of fruit and wine. Spanish priests first introduced vines to Chile in the sixteenth century because they needed wine for religious celebrations. Vines were planted in the central valley around Santiago and grew well. In the 1850s, the Spanish vines were replaced by French varieties and winemaking became a serious industry. Historically, Chile has grown mostly the Cabernet Sauvignon grape, but recent successes with Merlot, Carmenere, and Syrah grapes make a wider range of wines available. Muscatel grapes are grown in the northern region, but mainly for the production of *pisco*, the national drink. During the nineteenth century, the newly independent government sought to stimulate European immigration. Beginning in 1845, it had some success in attracting primarily German migrants to the Chilean south, principally to the lake district. For this reason, that area of the country still shows a German influence in its architecture and cuisine, and German (peppered with archaic expressions and intonations) is still spoken by some descendants of these migrants.

Because of its location in the Southern Hemisphere, the fruits grown there are ready for export in the Northern Hemisphere's winter season. Fruits exported to the United States include apples, avocados, peaches, nectarines, kiwifruits, plums, pears, blueberries, and cherries, and the main vegetables are garlic, asparagus, and onions.

A typical Chilean dish is *cazuela de ave*, a thick stew of chicken, potatoes, rice, green peppers, and, occasionally, onions. *Humitas* are a national favorite, and they come from the Amerindians who are native to Chile. Humitas are made with grated fresh corn, mixed into a paste with fried onions, basil, salt, and pepper. The mixture is then wrapped in corn husks and cooked in boiling water.

Chile's long coastline makes it a natural for seafood such as abalone, eel, scallops, turbot, king crab, sea urchin, and algae. The Juan Fernadez Islands are known for their huge lobsters. Seafood is an ingredient prepared in almost every technique, including stews, *ceviches*, *escabeches*, or snacks with potatoes, corn, squash, and other vegetables. Many of Chile's lamb dishes, such as lamb ribs or lamb shish kebabs, as well as baked deer dishes and cakes, stem from Welsh influence. Chile's most distinctive desserts trace their origins to the southern lake region, where German immigrants left a legacy of *kuchen*—a delicious pastry loaded with fresh fruits like raspberries and apricots. A more common Chilean pastry is the *alfajor*, which consists of *dulce de leche* (caramelized milk) sandwiched between thin pastries and rolled in powdered sugar. Another favorite is *macedonia*, diced fruit with a fruit syrup topping. There is also *arroz con leche*, or chilled rice with milk, sugar, and cinnamon. *Semola con leche* is a flan made of sweet corn flour topped with caramel.

ARGENTINA

Argentina, which means "land of silver," is a rich and vast land—the second largest country (after Brazil) in South America and eighth largest in the world. Located in southern South America, it is bordered by Chile, Bolivia, Paraguay, Brazil, Uruguay, and the Atlantic Ocean.

Argentina's heartland is a broad grassy plain known as the Pampas. The cuisine has been influenced by waves of European immigration. Italian immigrants have had considerable influence, and Italian standards like lasagna, pizza, pasta, and ravioli are commonly seen on the Argentine table, at least in the country's major cities.

Argentina is the beef capital of the world. The rich grassland of the Pampas are home to cattle and sheep, raised by gauchos (Argentine cowboys). The national dish is *matambre*, made from thin flank steak rolled with fillings that include spinach, whole hard-boiled eggs, other vegetables, herbs, and spices. The steak is then tied with a string and either poached in broth or baked. Its name is derived from *mata hambre*, which means "kill your hunger." Probably the most famous Argentine dish is the *parrillada*, a mixed grill plate of different meats and sausages (chorizos). The meat is cooked on a very large grill called a *parilla*. Spit roasting is also very popular. For this the meat to be roasted is placed on spits that look like swords and are placed tip down into and around hot coals. Classic Argentinean cuisine includes *chimichurri* sauce (a cross between Mexican salsa and Italian vinaigrette) and the empanada. Here tortillas are made with potato dough, in contrast to the traditional Mexican corn or flour tortilla.

Argentina is the world's fifth largest producer of wine. The grape varieties are almost entirely of European derivation: Chardonnay, Riesling, Cabernet Sauvignon, Merlot, and Malbec are only a few of some 60 different varieties cultivated. Almost 75 percent of the total wine production originates in the province of Mendoza found in the Andean foothills. Mendoza cultivates its vines on desert flatlands made fertile by irrigated water, which descends from the Andes. Although made from European grapes, Argentine wines have their own flavor because of the climate and soil conditions and irrigation methods. There are two varieties that can be considered exclusively Argentinean in quality if not in origin. The first is Malbec, a grape not considered particularly distinguished in France, but considered by many in Argentina to make fine red wine. The second is the Torrontes, a grape of Spanish origin, which makes a full, fruity, rich white wine.

URUGUAY

Uruguay is located on the southeastern coast of South America, bordered by Brazil, Argentina, and the Atlantic Ocean. It is a land of grassy plains and hills. Sheep and cattle ranches make up 80 percent of the land. Uruguayan cuisine is the result of many influences, including gaucho, Spanish, and Italian. In Uruguay, food and meat are almost synonymous. Most restaurants in Uruguay are *parrillada* (grill-rooms), which specialize in *asado* (barbecued beef), the country's most famous dish. Besides beef, pork, sausage, and grilled chicken are popular. *Chivito* (a sandwich filled with slices of meat, lettuce, and egg) and *puchero* (beef with vegetables, bacon, beans, and sausages) are local favorites. With the arrival of large numbers of Italian immigrants in the twentieth century, many businesses opened by Italians were pasta-making factories. They also imported Parmesan cheese and prosciutto ham into Uruguay and these foods have made their way into the national cuisine.

Glossary

Aji (a'hee) Spicy chili or seasoning: very hot Andean chili pepper, malagueta.

Aji Caco de Cabra Fresh red pepper, long, thin, and very hot, used to make Chile hot pepper sauce.

Ají de Gallina Shredded chicken in a piquant cream sauce (Peru).

Aji Mirasol, aji Amarillo A common pepper in Peruvian and Bolivian cuisine, bright yellow and hot.

Aji Verde Milder variety of *aji caco de cabra*, with a thicker flesh and a waxy, lime green skin. Used in Chile to make condiments.

Alfajores Wafer-thin spirals of shortbread dusted with icing sugar, served with *manjar blanco* (a caramel sauce) (Peru).

Amaranth Tiny ancient seeds cultivated in the Americas for several millennia. One of the staple grains of the Incas and other pre-Columbian Indians. They are rich in protein and calcium, and have a pleasant, peppery flavor. Substitutes: millet, quinoa, buckwheat groats.

Anticuchos Strips of beef or fish marinated in vinegar and spices, then barbecued on skewers (Peru).

Arepa Flour A precooked corn flour used to make *arepas* and tamales in Colombia and Venezuela. It has a grainy texture. It should not be confused with Mexican *masa harina*.

Arepas The native bread made from primitive ground corn, water, and salt (Venezuela).

Arroz Brasileiro or *Arroz Simples* Rice, Brazilian style. Long-grained rice briefly sautéed in garlic and oil before the addition of boiling water. In addition to garlic, some Brazilian cooks add small amounts of onion, diced tomato, or sliced black olives for additional flavor. Properly done, each grain is fluffy and separate from others.

Asada (Asado) Spanish for roasted or broiled. A roast cooked on an open fire or grill. Often served with chimichurri sauce.

Asador A Spanish word for a wire-mesh stovetop grill that can be used to roast vegetables over an outdoor fire or on the stovetop.

Babaco A member of the papaya family. Looks like a papaya but is smaller in diameter and has a tougher skin. The fruit has a delicate white flesh and seeds that are like those of passion fruit.

Bacalao Dried, salted codfish. Introduced by Spanish and Portuguese settlers, it is very popular in Latin America. The whiter *bacalao* is the better quality.

Batida These tropical fruits cocktails are a mixture of fresh fruit juice and *cachaça*, the potent sugarcane liquor from Brazil. Sometimes the recipe will also call for *leite condensado* (sweetened condensed milk) and/or other liquor. They are usually prepared in a blender and served with crushed ice in tiny glasses.

Bedidas Calientes Hot beverages. Hot drinks are as common as cold ones in South America.

Bouillon d'Aoura A dish of smoked fish, crab, prawns, vegetables, and chicken served with aoura (the fruit of Savana trees) (French Guiana).

Breadfruit Resembling a melon with bumpy green scales, breadfruit weighs 2 to 4 pounds. When green, it tastes like a raw potato. When partially ripened, it resembles eggplant and has the sticky consistency of a ripe plantain. When fully ripe it has the texture of soft Brie cheese. It is cooked like potatoes and is never eaten raw.

Café Coffee.

Café con Leche Coffee with warm milk, the preferred South American style.

Camarao Seco Dried shrimp. In various sizes, dried shrimp are utilized in many dishes. Before use they are covered with cold water and soaked overnight. The water is discarded before the shrimp are used. The residual salt is usually enough that more is not added to a recipe.

Carbonada An Argentine stew with meats, vegetables, and fruits.

Cassava People in Hispanic countries use cassavas much like Americans use potatoes. There are sweet and bitter varieties of cassava. The sweet can be eaten raw, but the bitter variety requires cooking to destroy the harmful prussic acid it contains. Cassava played a major role in the expansion by Spanish and Portuguese explorers. Cassava could be prepared in large quantities, it was cheap, and it kept well. Explorers also exported cassava to Africa, the Philippines, and Southeast Asia, where it has become a significant ingredient in those regions' cuisines. It's often best to buy frozen cassava, since the fresh kind is hard to peel. Look for it in Hispanic markets. Unprepared cassava doesn't store well, so use it within a day or two of purchase. Malanga, dasheen, or potato (not as gluey) can be used as substitutes.

Cau Cau Tripe cooked with potato, peppers, and parsley (Peru).

Cazuela A stew made with beef, chicken, or seafood along with various vegetables.

Ceviche Marinated foods, also spelled *seviche* or *cebiche*.

Cheese (Quesos)

Queso Blanco or Queso Fresco (white cheese) The primary cheese used in South America. A fresh, moist, lightly salted, unripened cheese made from cow's milk.

Quesillo A cheese used the same day it is made or within a few days. *Quesillo* is refreshing, similar to ricotta cheese, but it is molded and can be cut into slices. For crumbling use *queso fresco*.

Queso Blanco Also called *queso de mesa*. A firmer cheese because it is pressed and left to mature for weeks. In areas of South American, *queso blanco* comes in various degrees of maturation, from ricotta type to hard cheese.

Queso de Cabra Goat cheese.

Cherimoya A species of *Annona* native to the Andean-highland valleys of Peru, Ecuador, Colombia, and Bolivia. The fruit is fleshy, soft and sweet, white in color, with a custard-like texture, which gives it its secondary name, custard apple. Some characterize the flavor as a blend of pineapple, mango, and strawberry. Similar in size to a grapefruit, it has large, glossy, dark seeds that are easily removed. The seeds are poisonous if crushed open; one should also avoid eating the skin. It is green when ripe and gives slightly to pressure, similar to the avocado.

Chichas Beerlike drink made from many types of seeds, roots, or fruits, such as quinoa, peanuts, grapes, oca, yuca, corn, rice, and the berries of the mulli tree (pink peppercorns).

Chimichurri Sauce Vinegar-based mixture of herbs, vegetables, and spices, traditionally used as the marinade or main sauce with grilled meats (Argentina).

Chocolate A preparation made from cocoa seeds that have been roasted, husked, and ground. Chocolate today is often sweetened and flavored with vanilla. Aztec king Montezuma drank 50 goblets a day in the belief that it was an aphrodisiac.

Ceviche, Seviche, or Cebiche

MARINATED FOODS

Ceviche is seafood prepared in a centuries-old method of cooking by contact with the acidic juice of citrus juice instead of heat. *Ceviche* dates back to the Incas, who seasoned fish with sea salt and *aji* (chile peppers) and cured it in the acidic juice of *tumbo*, a tart tropical fruit. Ceviche's origin is somewhat disputed—either the invention of the pre-Columbians who, food historians tell us, ate their raw fish laced with dried chiles, salt, and foraged herbs; or ceviche as we know it was the creation of Moorish cooks who were brought to South America as Spanish slaves, and who, it is believed, were responsible for the addition of citrus juice to the earlier cooks' traditional salt/spice/herb mix. Traditionally, the citrus marinade was made with *naranja agria* (sour or bitter orange); however, today lemon, lime, and orange juices are used to prepare most ceviche. It can be eaten as a first course or main dish, depending on what is served with it.

Every Latin American country has given ceviche its own touch of individuality by adding particular garnishes. In Peru, it is served on lettuce leaves, without the marinade, garnished with slices of cold sweet potatoes, corn-on-the-cob, slices of hard-cooked egg and cheese, with a bowl of *cancaha* (toasted dried corn) on the side. Peruvians also prefer ceviche spicy. In Ecuador, the hot sauce is normally served on the side, the marinade is served in small bowl, and the ceviche is accompanied by popcorn, French bread, or *cancaha* (toasted dried corn). In Mexico, ceviche is accompanied by slices of raw onions and served on toasted tortillas.

The most famous ceviche comes from Ecuador and Peru, and Ecuadorian ceviche may enjoy the reputation of being the best in South America. In Peru and Ecuador, ceviches are popular snack foods. Ceviche can be made with just about any type of seafood: fish, shrimp, scallops, clams, mussels, squid, langostinos, or lobster. The common denominators among the countries are the lemon and lime juices used as the basis for the marinade. The acid in the marinade "cooks" the fish. Depending on the type of fish and the thickness of the pieces, this "cooking" takes anywhere from three to six hours. Shellfish is usually cooked or blanched first before adding to the marinade.

Colombian ceviches use citrus juices and tomato sauce for the marinade and are served on lettuce leaves, as in Peru. Colombians also have a unique ceviche made with coconut milk, an African contribution.

Chuchoca Corn that is boiled and sun-dried for two to three days.

Chupe de Camarones Chowder-type soup made with shrimp, milk, eggs, potatoes, and peppers (Peru).

Churrascaria A Brazilian or Portuguese steakhouse.

Cochayuyo Seaweed found along the coast of Chile; very important in the Chilean diet.

Cocoa The fruit of the cocoa plant. These beans are fermented, dried, roasted, cracked, and ground. After extracting half the fat, it is again dried into unsweetened cocoa. Dutch cocoa is treated with alkali to neutralize acidity.

Coconut Cream Made by combining one part water and four parts shredded fresh or desiccated coconut meat and simmering until foamy. The coconut is then discarded. It is particularly used in curry dishes.

Coconut Milk Made by combining equal parts water and shredded fresh or desiccated coconut meat and simmering until foamy. The coconut is then discarded. It is particularly used in curry dishes.

Coconut Water The opaque white liquid in the unripe coconut that serves as a beverage for those living near the coconut palm.

Corvina Sea bass.

Creole Style of cooking melding Incan and Spanish culinary techniques and ingredients.

Dendê Oil (Palm Oil) A form of edible vegetable oil obtained from the fruit of the oil palm tree.

Dulce de Leche Caramel-like candy popular in Argentina, Brazil, Chile, Paraguay, Peru, Uruguay, and other parts of the Americas. Its most basic recipe mixes boiled milk and sugar, or it may also be prepared with sweetened condensed milk cooked for several hours.

Empanada Salteña A Bolivian national specialty that is a mixture of diced meat, chicken, chives, raisins, diced potatoes, hot sauce, and pepper baked in dough.

Ensaladas Salads. The most popular salads are cooked vegetable salads and those that include fresh beans. A common characteristic of South American salads is the sparse use of dressing.

Tossed salad (*ensalada mixta*) is generally made with lettuce and tomatoes, thinly sliced onions, shredded carrots, radishes, or watercress and usually tossed with oil and vinegar. South American cuisines also include main course salads, seasoned with a vinaigrette or a mayonnaise dressing (popular in the southern countries, especially during hot months). Potato and rice salads, simple or complex, can be found throughout South America.

Escabeches Escabeches is a very popular technique of pickling food used throughout South America. The technique is of Arab origin introduced by Spanish explorers and traders, adopted as a way of preserving foods, such as fish, poultry, meat, and vegetables.

Fritada Called *chicharron* in the areas around the Andes, usually made with different cuts of pork. In Argentina it is made with beef. This dish requires the meat to be cooked in beer until tender and then browned in its own fat.

Guinea Pigs Called *cuy* or *curi* in the Andean regions, these vegetarian rodents are raised for food in native Indian homes.

Hallaca Cornmeal combined with beef, pork, ham, and green peppers, wrapped in individual pieces of banana leaves and cooked in boiling water. Traditionally eaten at Christmas and New Year's (Colombia and Venezuela).

Hearts of Palm Tender, ivory-colored buds of a particular palm tree. They can be used in salads, soups, as a vegetable, or with *ceviche*.

Ilajhua A hot sauce consisting of tomatoes and pepper pods, used to add spice and flavor (Bolivia).

Jugos Fruit juice drinks that can be made from any fruit mixed with water and sugar.

Kaniwa A nutritious grain that grows at high altitudes, thriving in places where quinoa cannot survive. A prominent early grain used by the Indians of Bolivia and the Peruvian altiplano.

Lingüica Brazilian garlic pork sausage of Portuguese origin. Polish sausage may be substituted.

Llapingachos Pancakes stuffed with mashed potato and cheese (Ecuador).

Lomo Montado Fried tenderloin steak with two fried eggs on top, rice, and fried banana (Bolivia).

Malagueta Small green, yellow, or red pepper from Brazil. This pepper is extremely hot and an essential ingredient in the kitchen. They come preserved in jars or as a table sauce. They are pickled in a 2:1 oil to grain alcohol ratio and then rested for one month before using. Tabasco sauce can be used as a substitute.

Manioc (see Cassava)

Manioc Flour Widely used in Brazil as a breading for chicken. Manioc is not a grain; it comes from the tropical cassava root. When seasoned with spices, roasted manioc flour has a texture and flavor similar to a cornflake crumb breading.

Matambre Rolled stuffed flank steak (Argentina).

Empanadas

In Spain, Portugal, the Caribbean, Latin America, and the Philippines, an empanada (Portuguese empada) is basically a stuffed pastry. The name comes from the Spanish verb *empanar*, meaning to wrap or coat in bread. Empanadas are also known by a wide variety of regional names.

It is likely that the Latin American empanadas were originally from Galicia, Spain, where an empanada is prepared similar to a pie that is cut in pieces, making it a portable and hearty meal for working people. The Galician empanada is usually prepared with codfish or chicken. The addition of the empanada to the cuisine may be due to the influence of the Moors, who occupied Spain for eight hundred years. Middle Eastern cuisine to this day has similar foods, like simbusak (a fried, chickpea-filled "empanada") from Iraq.

Varieties by Country

Argentina	The filling is ground beef, perhaps spiced with cumin and with onion, green olive, chopped boiled egg, and even raisins. While empanadas are usually baked, they can also be fried. They may also contain cheese, ham and cheese, chicken, tuna, *humita* (sweet corn with bechamel sauce) or spinach; a fruit filling is used to create a dessert empanada. Empanadas of the interior can be spiced with peppers. In restaurants where several types are served, a *repulgue*, or pattern, is added to the pastry fold. These patterns, which can be quite elaborate, distinguish the filling.
Bolivia	Widely known as *salteÃas* (after an Argentine province bordering the country to the south), they are made with beef or chicken and usually contain potatoes, peas, and carrots. They are customarily seamed along the top of the pastry and are generally sweeter than the Chilean variety.
Brazil	Empanadas are a common ready-to-go lunch item available at fast-food counters. A wide variety of different fillings and combinations are available, with the most common being chicken, beef, shrimp, cheese, olives, and palmito (heart of palm).
Chile	The dough for these empanadas is wheat flour based, but the meat filling is slightly different and often contains more onion. There are two types of Chilean empanadas: baked and fried. The baked empanadas are much larger than the fried variety. There are three main types of fillings: *pino*, cheese, and seafood. *Pino* contain chopped (or sometimes minced) meat, onion, chopped boiled egg, olives, and raisins. Fried empanadas containing shrimp and cheese are prevalent along the coastal areas. Seafood empanadas are essentially the same as *pino*, but with seafood instead of meat. Sweet empanadas, sugarcoated and filled with jam, are popular during September 18 Independence Day celebrations.
Colombia	Empanadas are either baked or fried. Fillings can vary according to the region, but they usually contain ingredients such as salt, rice, beef or ground beef, boiled potatoes, hard-boiled eggs, and peas. However, variations can also be found (cheese empanadas, chicken-only empanadas, and even *trucha*—trout—empanadas). The pastry is mostly corn based, although potato flour is commonly used. They are usually served with *aji* (*picante*), a sauce made of cilantro, green onions, vinegar, salt, lemon juice, and bottled hot sauces.

Cuba	These empanadas are typically filled with seasoned meats (usually ground beef or chicken) folded into dough and deep-fried. These are not to be confused with Cuban *pastelitos*, which are very similar but use lighter pastry dough and may or may not be fried. Cubans eat empanadas at any meal, but usually during lunch or as a snack.
Dominican Republic	Very similar in preparation and consumption as Cuban empanadas, but modern versions, promoted by some specialty food chains, include stuffing like pepperoni and cheese, conch, Danish cheese, and chicken. A variety in which the dough is made from cassava flour is called *catibías*.
Iraq	Iraq has a traditional "ancestor" to the empanada called *simbusak* or *sambusac*, prepared with a basic bread dough and a variety of fillings, baked or fried. The most traditional simbusak is filled with garbanzo beans, onions, and parsley, and shallow fried. Others have meat or cheese (*jibun*) as a filling.
Mexico	Mexican empanadas are most commonly a dessert or a breakfast item. Sweetened fillings include pumpkin, yams, sweet potato, and cream, as well as a wide variety of fruit fillings. Meat, cheese, and vegetable fillings are not as popular. Particular regions such as Hidalgo are famous for their empanadas.
Peru	Peruvian empanadas are similar to Argentine empanadas, but slightly smaller and eaten with lime juice.
Philippines	Filipino empanadas usually contain a filling flavored with soy sauce and consisting of ground beef or chicken, chopped onion, and raisins in a wheat flour dough. Empanadas in the northern Ilocos region are made of a savory filling of green papaya and, upon request, chopped Ilocano sausage (*longganisa*) and/or an egg. Rather than the soft, sweet dough favored in the Tagalog region, the dough is thin and crisp, mostly because Ilocano empanada is deep-fried rather than baked.
Portugal	In Portugal, empanadas are a common option for a small meal, found universally in patisseries. They are normally smaller than others, about the size of a golf ball; size and shape vary depending on establishment. The most common fillings are chicken, beef, tuna, codfish, or mushrooms, and vegetables. They are usually served hot.
Puerto Rico and the Dominican Republic	Puerto Rican empanadas, called *pastelillos*, are made of flour dough and fried. Fillings are typically ground beef, chicken, guava, cheese, or both guava and cheese.
Venezuela	Venezuelan empanadas use cornstarch-based dough and are deep-fried. Stuffing varies according to region; most common are cheese and ground beef. Other types use fish, *caraotas negras* (black beans), oysters, clams, and other types of seafood popular in the coastal areas, especially in Margarita Island.

Milanesas Breaded cutlets brought to South America by Italian immigrants. They are especially popular in Argentina and Uruguay.

Morcilla Dulce Sweet black sausage made from blood, orange peel, and walnuts.

Pabellón Criollo Hash made with shredded meat and served with fried plantains and black beans on rice (Venezuela).

Pachamanca Typical dish from the desert. It consists of lamb, pork, potatoes, sweet potatoes, and tamales. The food is placed inside a sack and buried in hot rocks to cook. It has to be repeatedly checked to see when it is done because the temperature is unstable. An important part of Peruvian cuisine.

Parrillada A selection of meat grilled over hot coals, often including delicacies such as intestines, udders, and blood sausages (Argentina and Chile).

Postres y Dulces (Desserts and Sweets) Before the arrival of the Portuguese in 1502, South America Indians did not have sugar. They did have honey and a few fruit and vegetable sweeteners. Most early sweets or desserts were fresh fruit, and fruit-based sweets remain the South Americans' favorite desserts.

Quimbolitos Sweet tamales of Ecuador, served for dessert or as a snack with coffee.

Quinoa This ancient seed was a staple of the Incas. It cooks quickly, has a mild flavor, and a slightly crunchy texture. High in the amino acid lysine, it provides a more complete protein than many other cereal grains. It comes in different colors, ranging from pale yellow to red to black. Rinse quinoa before using to remove its bitter natural coating. Couscous, rice, bulgur, millet, buckwheat groats, or amaranth can be substituted.

Refrescos (Refreshments) A term used for all cold nonalcoholic beverages, including *jugos*, sorbets, *licuados*, and *batidos*, all of which are generally made with milk and sometimes ice cream.

Rocoto Cultivated pepper in the Andes, with a thick flesh similar to bell pepper. It is a hotter pepper than other *ajies*. The Mexican *manzano* pepper, though much hotter, is a good substitute.

Rose Water A flavoring used in the preparation of desserts. Brought over by the Spaniards, it is the extract of roses mixed with distilled water.

Shrimp, Dried Tiny shrimp that have been salted and dried, used extensively in Bahian cooking and some Peruvian specialties. They come in two varieties, head and shell on or peeled. Normally, dried shrimp are ground before using.

Tacacá A thick yellow soup with shrimp and garlic (Brazil).

Tamales An important food that has sustained cultures in Central and South America, as well as the southwestern region of North America for millennia.

Tostones Twice-fried slices of plantain that are pounded thin before the second frying.

Tamales

The word *tamale* comes from *tamalli* in Nahuatl, the language of the Aztecs. The word for corn tamale in the Inca language (Quechua) is *choclotanda*, which means "cornbread." We have no record of which culture actually created it, but the tamale is recorded as early as 5000 B.C., possibly 7000 B.C. in pre-Columbian history. Initially, women were taken along in battle as army cooks to make the masa for the tortillas and the meats, stews, and drinks. As the warring tribes of the Aztec, Mayan, and Incan cultures grew, the demand of readying the *nixtamal* (corn) itself became so overwhelming a process, a need arose to have a more portable sustaining foodstuff, creating the tamale.

No history of the tamale would be complete without discussing the process of "nixtamalization," which is the processing of field corn with wood ashes (pre-Colombian) or now with *cal*, or slaked lime. This processing softens the corn for easier grinding and also aids in digestibility and increases the nutrients absorbed by the human body. Nixtamalization dates back to around 1200–1500 B.C. on the southern coast of Guatemala, where kitchens were found equipped with the necessities of nixtamal making.

In South America, tamales are found in Andean countries where there is a concentrated Indian population. The Amazonian Indians also make tamales with corn, yuca, or plantains. Each of the Andean countries has a variety of tamales both savory and sweet. They also go by different names depending not only on the country but also on the region. In Venezuela, they are called *ayacas* or *hallacas*, *bolos*, and *cachapas*; in Colombia *tamales*, *envueltos*, *hallacas*, and *bolos*; and in Ecuador *humitas*, *tamales*, *quimobolitos*, *hallacas*, and *chiguiles*. Peruvians have *tamales*, *humitas*, *juanes*, and *chapanas*; Bolivians *humintas* and *tamales*; Chileans and Argentines *humitas*; and Brazilians *pamonhas*.

In pre-Columbian times tamales were made only from corn and quinoa. Now they are made from potatoes, yuca, plantains, rice, squash, eggplant, sweet potatoes, and a variety of flours. Fillings usually include cheese, chicken, pork, beef, or fish. Raisins, prunes, hard-cooked eggs, hot peppers, almonds, and olives are the traditional garnish. The wrappings were corn husks, banana leaves, fabric, avocado leaves, soft tree bark, and other edible, nontoxic leaves. Tamales were steamed, grilled on the *comal* (grill) over the fire, or put directly on top of the coals to warm, or they were eaten cold.

Superstition has it that a chef must be in a good mood when cooking tamales or they will come out raw.

Vatapá A rich puree that can be made with fish, dried shrimp, cod, or chicken. Thought to have been brought from the Iberian peninsula and modified by African slaves, who added *dendê* (palm oil) and coconut milk. It can be thickened with bread, the Portuguese way of thickening stews, or with rice flour or manioc meal. Groundnuts, peanuts, almonds, or cashews, as well as dried shrimp, are essential to the dish. *Dendê* gives the *Vatapá* its characteristic taste and color. Cooks all have their own preparation of this dish (Brazil).

Yuca Root Although there are many varieties of yuca root, there are only two main categories: bitter and sweet. Used as a thickener in the making of tapioca. Bitter yuca root must be cooked to be edible.

Yuca Flour Made from the bitter cassava (yuca). Once grated and sun-dried, it is also called yuca root meal. It has a texture similar to that of cornstarch and is used to make breads, cookies, cakes, and tapioca.

Menus and Recipes from South America

Sopa de Palmito
Hearts of Palm Soup (Brazi)   SERVES 4

AMOUNT	MEASURE	INGREDIENT
2 tablespoons	1 ounce, 28 ml	Butter
1 cup	4 ounces, 112 g	Leeks, thinly sliced, white parts and 1 inch (2.5 cm) green, washed well
1 tablespoon	7 g	All-purpose flour
1 tablespoon	7 g	Cornstarch
$\frac{1}{4}$ teaspoon	1 g	White pepper
	14 ounces, 392 g	Hearts of palm
2 cups	16 ounces, 470 ml	Chicken stock
1 cup	8 ounces 235 ml	Milk
To taste		Salt and pepper
For garnish		Sweet paprika or cayenne pepper

PROCEDURE

1   Heat butter over low to medium heat; sauté leeks 3 minutes; do not color.

2   Add flour, cornstarch, and white pepper; toss to coat.

3   Add hearts of palm and stock; bring to simmer and cook 25 minutes or until hearts of palm are tender.

4   Puree mixture until smooth.

5   Strain using a small-hole china cap and return to a clean pan.

6   Add milk and bring to boil; reduce to simmer and cook 3 minutes.

7   Correct seasoning and serve with a sprinkling of paprika or cayenne on top.

Ceviche de Champiñones
Mushroom Ceviche (Peru) SERVES 4

AMOUNT	MEASURE	INGREDIENT
3 cups	12 ounces, 336 g	Fresh, firm cremini or white button mushrooms, cleaned, dry, quartered or sliced ($\frac{1}{4}$ inch, .6 cm)
1/3 cup	$\frac{1}{2}$ ounce, 42 g	Celery, $\frac{1}{4}$ inch (.6 cm) dice
1/3 cup	$\frac{1}{2}$ ounce, 42 g	Red onion, 1 inch (2.4 cm) dice, soaked in hot water for 5 minutes and drained
2		Garlic cloves, minced
$\frac{1}{2}$ teaspoon	2 g	Salt
$\frac{1}{4}$ teaspoon	1 g	White pepper
$\frac{1}{2}$ teaspoon	2 ml	Hot pepper sauce
$\frac{1}{2}$ teaspoon	2 g	Dried oregano
$\frac{1}{2}$ cup	4 ounces, 118 ml	Fresh lime or lemon juice
1 tablespoon	$\frac{1}{2}$ ounce, 14 ml	Olive oil
$\frac{1}{4}$ cup	1 ounce, 28 g	Red bell pepper, julienned
$\frac{1}{4}$ cup	1 ounce, 28 g	Green bell pepper, julienned
1		Jalapeño, seeded, minced
For garnish		Alfonso or kalamata olives

PROCEDURE

1 Blanch mushrooms in boiling water for 30 seconds and drain well.

2 Combine celery, onion, and blanched mushrooms.

3 Puree, garlic, salt, pepper, hot sauce, oregano, lime juice, and olive oil until well mixed.

4 Toss with mushroom mixture.

5 Adjust salt and pepper to taste. Refrigerate for 2 hours.

6 Drain well and toss with bell peppers and jalapeño.

7 Garnish with black olives.

Vatapá de Galinha
Chicken in Nut and Dried Shrimp Sauce
(Brazil)   SERVES 4

This classic Bahia dish is considered to be one of the best representations of Afro-Brazilian cuisine. The Portuguese thicken their soups and stews with bread, rice flour, or manioc meal. Groundnuts, dried shrimp, and *dendê* give the *vatapá* its characteristic taste and color. Vatapá can be made with fish, shrimp, dried cod, or chicken.

AMOUNT	MEASURE	INGREDIENT
I cup	4 ounces, 112 g	Onion, $\frac{1}{4}$ inch (.6 cm) dice
2		Garlic cloves, minced
I tablespoon	I ounce, 28 g	Fresh ginger, peeled, minced
I tablespoon	$\frac{1}{2}$ ounce, 14 g	Serrano pepper or to taste
2 cups	12 ounces, 336 g	Tomato, peeled, chopped, seeded, $\frac{1}{4}$ inch (.6 cm) dice
$\frac{1}{2}$ cup	2 ounces, 56 g	Green bell pepper, deveined and seeded, $\frac{1}{4}$ inch (.6 cm) dice
$\frac{1}{2}$ cup	I ounce, 28 g	Cilantro, leaves only, chopped
3 tablespoons	$\frac{1}{2}$ ounce, 45 ml	Dendê oil
I	$2\frac{1}{2}$ pounds, 1.13 kg	Chicken, cut into eight pieces, skinned and patted dry
I teaspoon	5 g	Salt
$\frac{1}{2}$ teaspoon	3 g	Freshly ground black pepper
$\frac{1}{2}$ cup	$\frac{1}{2}$ ounce, 14 g	Bread, day-old, $\frac{1}{2}$ inch (1.2 cm) cubes
$\frac{1}{2}$ cup	4 ounces, 120 ml	Water
$\frac{1}{4}$ cup	$\frac{1}{2}$ ounce, 14 g	Dried peeled shrimp, ground
$\frac{1}{2}$ cup	$\frac{1}{2}$ ounces, 42 g	Peanuts, almonds, or cashews, toasted and ground
I tablespoon	$\frac{1}{2}$ ounce, 15 ml	Fresh lime juice
$\frac{3}{4}$ cup	14 ounces, 420 ml	Unsweetened coconut milk
To taste		Salt and black pepper

PROCEDURE

1 Puree first seven ingredients until smooth.

2 Heat dendê oil over medium heat, add puree and cook, stirring occasionally, 10 minutes.

3 Season chicken pieces with salt and pepper.

4 Add to sauce and toss to coat; bring to simmer.

Vatapá de Galinha – Chicken in Nut and Dried Shrimp Sauce, Ensalada de Tomate y Cebolla – Tomato and Onion Salad, Couve à Mineira – Shredded Kale

5 Cover and cook, 15 to 20 minutes.

6 Remove chicken, cut meat into $\frac{1}{2}$ inch (1.2 cm) wide by $1\frac{1}{2}$ inch (3.8 cm) long boneless pieces.

7 Return to sauce with all remaining ingredients; simmer until sauce thickens.

8 Correct seasoning and serve with Pirão de Arroz (recipe follows).

Pirão de Arroz
Rice Flour Pudding (Brazil)   SERVES 4–6

Pirãos are very thick, savory porridges or mushes, like polenta but of African origin. They may be served either hot or at room temperature.

AMOUNT	MEASURE	INGREDIENT
$\frac{3}{4}$ cup	$3\frac{1}{3}$ ounces, 95 g	Rice flour
I teaspoon		Salt
4 cups	32 ounces, I liter	Unsweetened coconut milk

PROCEDURE

I Scald 3 cups (24 ounces, 720 ml) coconut milk over medium heat.

2 Mix remaining milk with the rice flour and salt.

3 Add flour mixture and stir until mixture is smooth, reduce heat to medium low and cook stirring often until mixture is very thick and smooth, 15 to 20 minutes.

4 Fill lightly oiled molds, let cool to room temperature.

5 Refrigerate until firm, 2 to 3 hours, unmold, and serve.

Couve à Mineira
Shredded Kale   SERVES 4

AMOUNT	MEASURE	INGREDIENT
2 pounds	907 g	Fresh kale,
$\frac{1}{4}$ cup	2 ounces, 60 ml	Olive oil or bacon fat
$\frac{1}{2}$ cup	2 ounces, 56 g	Onions, $\frac{1}{4}$ inch (.6 cm) dice
1		Garlic clove, minced
To taste		Salt and pepper

PROCEDURE

1 Trim blemishes and tough stems from kale leaves. Rinse thoroughly under running water.

2 Layer leaves on top of each other, and slice crosswise into very thin strips.

3 Heat oil over medium high heat; add onion and garlic and cook 3 to 5 minutes until softened.

4 Add kale and cook about 5 to 7 minutes, stirring often, until kale is softened but not discolored or browned. Season to taste.

Ensalada de Tomate y Cebolla
Tomato and Onion Salad (Chile)   SERVES 4

AMOUNT	MEASURE	INGREDIENT
1 cup	4 ounces, 112 g	Sweet onion, julienned
1 pound	16 ounces, 448 g	Tomatoes, firm, peeled, sliced $\frac{1}{4}$ inch (.6 cm) thick
1 tablespoon	3 g	Fresh cilantro, chopped
1 tablespoon	$\frac{1}{2}$ ounce, 15 ml	Fresh lemon juice
2 tablespoons	1 ounce, 30 ml	Olive oil
To taste		Salt and pepper

PROCEDURE

1   Soak onion in cold water to cover 20 minutes; drain and rinse well.

2   Drain and rinse the onions, squeeze, and drain well again.

3   Combine all ingredients, toss, and correct seasoning.

Crepas con Salsa de Dulce de Leche Crepes with Dulce De Leche Sauce SERVES 4

AMOUNT	MEASURE	INGREDIENT
I cup	8 ounces, 240 ml	Dulce de leche sauce
I cup	8 ounces, 240 ml	Heavy cream
$\frac{1}{4}$ cup	2 ounces, 60 ml	Rum
8		Crepes, cooked
$\frac{1}{2}$ cup	2 ounces, 56 g	Pistachios, chopped
2 tablespoons	I ounce, 28 g	Butter

PROCEDURE

1   Add heavy cream to sauce and return to simmer; stir in rum.

2   Place crepe brown-side down, spread 1 tablespoon ($\frac{1}{2}$ ounce, 15 ml) sauce over half, and sprinkle with 1 teaspoon pistachios.

3   Fold in half, then fold in half again; set aside. Repeat with remaining crepes.

4   Arrange crepes in a lightly buttered ovenproof pan and cover. Bake for 10 minutes in a 375°F (190°C) oven.

5   Serve two crepes; top with additional sauce and chopped nuts.

Dulce de Leche Sauce   YIELD: I CUP (8 OUNCES, 240 ML)

AMOUNT	MEASURE	INGREDIENT
I quart	32 ounces, 960 ml	Milk
$\frac{1}{4}$ cups	9 ounces, 252 g	Granulated sugar
$\frac{1}{4}$ teaspoon		Baking soda
I teaspoon		Vanilla extract

PROCEDURE

1   Over medium high heat, combine milk, sugar, and baking soda. Bring to a boil.

2   Reduce heat to low and simmer, stirring occasionally. As it begins to thicken, stir period-ically and cook until caramel-colored and very thick (caramel sauce), about 1 hour.

3   Stir in vanilla extract.

Ceviche de Pescado
Fish Ceviche   SERVES 4

Fish must be extremely fresh. The classic fish for this dish is corvina in Ecuador and tuna in Peru, but any white-fleshed fish, such as sea bass, flounder, red snapper, tilapia, or sole, may be used.

AMOUNT	MEASURE	INGREDIENT
12 ounces	336 g	White-fleshed lean fish fillets, cut $\frac{1}{4}$ inch (.6 cm) thick and 1 inch (2.4 cm) long
Marinade		
$\frac{1}{2}$ cup	4 ounces, 118 ml	Fresh lemon juice
$\frac{1}{4}$ cup	2 ounces, 59 ml	Fresh lime juice
$\frac{1}{2}$ cup	4 ounces, 118 ml	Fresh orange juice
1 tablespoon	$\frac{1}{2}$ ounce, 14 ml	Olive oil
$\frac{1}{2}$ teaspoon	3 g	Salt
1		Garlic clove, minced
1		Ali Amarillo (yellow Peruvian chile), seeded and minced, or canned aji or serrano chile
To taste		Hot pepper sauce
1 teaspoon	1 g	Parsley, chopped
1 teaspoon	1 g	Cilantro, chopped
$\frac{1}{3}$ cup	$1\frac{1}{2}$ ounces, 42 g	Green onions (white part and 1 inch of green), minced
Garnish		
4		Bib, romaine, or green leaf lettuce leaves
2		Corn ears, cut into 2 inch (4.8 cm) pieces
8 ounces	224 g	Sweet potatoes, roasted in the skin, peeled, $\frac{1}{2}$ inch (1.2 cm) thick rounds
8 ounces	224 g	Yuca, peeled, cut into batonnets, boiled soft, cooled

PROCEDURE

1 Soak the fish for 1 hour in lightly salted water; drain and rise well.

2 Combine the citrus juices, salt, garlic, chile, and fish; mix well, cover, and let marinate in refrigerator until it is "cooked" (milky white throughout), 3 to 6 hours. Start checking at 3 hours.

3 Add all remaining marinade ingredients and correct seasoning.

4 To serve, line serving platter with lettuce. Place ceviche in center and display garnish around.

Tamales de Espinaca con Queso Spinach and Cheese Tamales

YIELD: ABOUT 12, DEPENDING ON SIZE OF CORN HUSKS

Basic Tamales

AMOUNT	MEASURE	INGREDIENT
12		Dried corn husks
I cup	8 ounces, 224 g	Lard or vegetable shortening
2/3 cup	6 ounces, 176 ml	Chicken stock or water
3 cups	18 ounces, 504 g	Masa harina or fresh masa (I $\frac{1}{2}$ pounds)
2 teaspoons	10 g	Salt
I teaspoon	4 g	Baking powder

PROCEDURE

1   Place corn husks in warm water to cover and soak 2 hours. Remove, drain, and pat dry.

2   Beat the lard by hand or in mixer until soft and light.

3   Gradually add stock to the masa harina and knead until the dough is no longer sticky. Add salt and baking powder.

4   Move masa harina mixture to mixer and beat lard into the dough, a little at a time, until the dough is light and fluffy. Test for lightness by pinching off a small piece and dropping into a glass of cold water. It should float when ready; if not, continue to beat and test again. The lighter the dough, the better; it results in moist and fluffy tamales. It is impossible to overmix this dough.

Tamales

Spinach and Cheese Filling

YIELD: ABOUT 12, DEPENDING ON SIZE OF CORN HUSKS

AMOUNT	MEASURE	INGREDIENT
$\frac{1}{2}$ tablespoon	$\frac{3}{4}$ ounce, 21 ml	Vegetable oil
$\frac{1}{2}$ cup	2 ounces, 56 g	Onion, $\frac{1}{4}$ inch (.6 cm) dice
$\frac{1}{2}$ cup	3 ounces, 84 g	Tomato, peeled, seeded, $\frac{1}{4}$ inch (.6 cm) dice
4 cups	8 ounces, 224 g	Fresh spinach, or 8 ounces frozen chopped
I cup	4 ounces, 112 g	Adobera, Asadero, or Monterey Jack cheese, shredded
To taste		Salt and pepper

PROCEDURE

1 Heat oil and sauté onions until translucent. Add tomatoes and cook until almost dry.

2 Add spinach and wilt.

3 Let cool and mix well with cheese.

4 Adjust seasoning.

5 Combine spinach and cheese filling with Basic Tamales (masa harina mixture); mix well and check seasoning again.

TO MAKE TAMALES

1 Place an unbroken corn husk on a work surface in front of you with the small tapering end of the husk facing you.

2 Using a spatula or masa spreader, spread approximately $\frac{1}{4}$ cup of dough onto the husk, leaving a border of at least $1\frac{1}{2}$ inches of husk at the tapered end.

3 Fold the two long sides of the corn husk in over the corn mixture.

4 Fold the tapered end up, leaving the top open.

5 Secure the tamale by tying with a strip of husk or a string.

6 Line the steamer with husks. Stand the tamales up in a row around the edge of the steamer.

7 Cover and steam, checking water level frequently and replenishing with boiling water as needed, until tamales easily come free from husks, about 1 hour for tamales made with fresh masa or $1\frac{1}{4}$ to $1\frac{1}{2}$ hours if made with masa harina mixture.

Chifles Green Plantain Chips   SERVES 4

AMOUNT	MEASURE	INGREDIENT
2		Green plantains
As needed		Peanut oil for frying
To taste		Salt

PROCEDURE

1   Peel plantains by trimming both ends with a sharp knife, cutting incisions along the natural ridges and then pulling away the skin. Cut into very thin slices and place in ice-cold water for 15 minutes (this helps keep them crisp). Drain well and dry on paper towels.

2   Heat oil to 375°F (190°C) or until a cube of dried bread added to the oil floats and turns golden after 1 minute.

3   Fry in batches, until golden, about 2 minutes. Drain well on paper towels.

4   Season with salt and serve when cool.

Pabellón Criollo
Shredded Beef with Beans, Rice, and Plantains (Venezuela)   SERVES 4

Pabellón means "flag," and the finished dish resembles a Venezuelan flag.

AMOUNT	MEASURE	INGREDIENT
1½ pounds	672 g	Flank steak; cut in 3 or 4 pieces
1		Bay leaf
1 quart	32 ounces, 960 ml	Beef stock; to cover
2 tablespoons	1 ounces, 30 ml	Olive oil
1 cup	4 ounces, 112	Onion, ¼ inch (.6 cm) dice
2		Garlic cloves; minced
1½ cups	9 ounces, 252 g	Tomatoes, peeled, seeded, ¼ inch (.6 cm) dice
½ teaspoon		Cumin seeds; crushed
1 teaspoon		Oregano
To taste		Salt and pepper
2 tablespoons	1 ounce, 40 ml	Vegetable oil
4 cups		Arroz blanco (see recipe on page 31)
4 cups		Caraotas negras (see recipe on page 41 for Frijoles de Olla; use black beans)
1		Plantain (use ripe plantains with black skins for this dish; green plantains will be too dry). Cut into 2 inch (5 cm), pieces
As needed		Vegetable oil for frying plantain

PROCEDURE

1 Combine flank steak, bay leaf, and stock, bring to simmer, and cook 1 to 1½ hours until very tender.

2 Cool in stock. When cool, shred meat and set aside.

3 Heat olive oil over medium high heat; add onions and cook until translucent.

4 Add garlic, tomatoes, cumin, oregano, salt, and pepper; cook until almost dry.

5 Add shredded beef; cook 5 minutes and correct seasoning.

6 Heat vegetable oil over medium heat and sauté plantains until they are browned all over. Drain on paper towels.

7 To assemble the "flag," arrange beef, rice, and beans on a rectangular platter in three rows with the rice in the center. Garnish with chifles.

In some recipes, fried eggs are placed on top of the meat—one per person.

Chupe de Quinua Quinoa Chowder

SERVES 4

AMOUNT	MEASURE	INGREDIENT
2 tablespoons	I ounce, 60 ml	Butter
I cup	4 ounces, 112 g	Onion, $\frac{1}{4}$ inch (.6 cm) dice
2		Garlic cloves, chopped
I teaspoon	5 g	Salt
$\frac{1}{2}$ teaspoon	2 g	Pepper, freshly ground
$\frac{1}{2}$ teaspoon	2 g	Cumin, ground
$\frac{1}{2}$ teaspoon	2 g	Sweet paprika
3 cups	24 ounces, 720 ml	Hot chicken or vegetable stock
$\frac{1}{2}$ cup	9 ounces, 252 g	Quinoa, cooked
I cup	6 ounces, 168 g	All-purpose potatoes, peeled, cooked, 1-inch (2.5 cm) cubes
$\frac{3}{4}$ cup	6 ounces, 180 ml	Milk
$\frac{1}{2}$ cup	2 ounces, 56 g	Fresh or frozen corn kernels
$\frac{1}{2}$ cup	3 ounces, 84 g	Fava beans or peas, blanched and peeled
$\frac{1}{2}$ cup	2 ounces, 56 g	Manchego: or Cheddar cheese, shredded
2		Large eggs, beaten
To taste		Salt and pepper
I tablespoon	3 g	Fresh mint, chopped
I tablespoon	3 g	Fresh cilantro, chopped
$\frac{1}{2}$ cup	2 ounces, 56 g	Avocado, peeled, pitted $\frac{1}{4}$ inch (.6 cm) dice

PROCEDURE

1   Heat butter over low heat, add onions, and cook for 10 minutes without coloring.

2   Make a paste with garlic, salt, and pepper.

3   Add garlic paste, cumin, and paprika to onions; cook 1 minute.

4   Add stock, quinoa, and potatoes; simmer 15 minutes or until potatoes are tender.

5   Add milk, corn, and beans; simmer until tender, 5 minutes. Do not boil after adding the milk. Adjust the consistency with more hot stock if necessary.

6   Add cheese and eggs, stirring constantly, until cheese has melted and eggs have set.

7   Correct seasoning and serve hot, garnished with mint, cilantro, and avocado.

Salada de Chuchu
Chayote Salad (Brazil) SERVES 4

AMOUNT	MEASURE	INGREDIENT
2		Preserved malagueta peppers, minced, or 1 teaspoon Tabasco sauce
1 teaspoon	3 g	Salt
$\frac{1}{2}$ cup	2 ounces	White onions, minced
1		Garlic clove, minced
1 tablespoon	$\frac{1}{2}$ ounce, 15 ml	Lemon juice, fresh
To taste		Salt and pepper
2 tablespoons	1 ounce, 30 ml	Olive oil
2 cups	12 ounces, 336 g	Chayote, peeled, seeded, $\frac{1}{4}$ inch (.6 cm) slices
4		Romaine or green leaf lettuce leaves

PROCEDURE

1 In a mortar and pestle, blender, or food processor, combine the peppers and salt; process to a paste.

2 Gradually add onions and garlic and process to a paste.

3 Add lemon juice and oil to make dressing, correct seasoning.

4 Cook chayote in boiling salted water until just tender.

5 Drain and toss with half the dressing, cool.

6 Arrange on lettuce leaf and drizzle with remaining dressing.

Patata y Carne de vaca Empanadas

Potato and Beef Empanadas with Chimichurri Sauce (Argentina)   **SERVES 4–6**

Dough
YIELD: 20–24 ROUNDS

AMOUNT	MEASURE	INGREDIENT
2 teaspoons	6 g	Salt
$\frac{3}{4}$ cup	6 ounces, 180 ml	Warm water
$4\frac{1}{2}$ cups	18 ounces, 510 g	All purpose flour
$\frac{1}{4}$ teaspoon		Paprika
$\frac{3}{4}$ cup	6 ounces, 170 g	Lard or vegetable shortening

PROCEDURE

1   Dissolve salt in warm water.

2   Sift together flour and paprika. Add lard or vegetable shortening, blend fat and flour to a fine meal.

3   Add salted water until mixture forms a ball. Add more flour a tablespoon at a time if the dough is too sticky.

4   Shape dough into a ball; knead vigorously for 10 minutes on a lightly floured surface or until smooth and elastic. Reshape into a ball, refrigerate to let rest covered for at least 30 minutes (preferably 2 hours).

5   Roll dough to 1/8 inch (.3 cm) thickness on lightly floured surface and cut into 5-inch (12 cm) rounds. Stack rounds and cover to prevent drying.

Salada de Chuchu – Chayote Salad, Patata y Carne de vaca
Empanadas – Potato & Beef Empanadas

Filling

AMOUNT	MEASURE	INGREDIENT
3 tablespoons	$1\frac{1}{2}$ ounce, 45 ml	Olive oil
I cup	4 ounces, 112 g	Onion, minced
$\frac{1}{2}$ cup	2 ounces, 56 g	Red bell pepper, cored, seeded, $\frac{1}{4}$ inch (.6 cm) dice
$\frac{1}{2}$ teaspoon	2 g	Red pepper flakes
$\frac{1}{2}$ teaspoon	2 g	Paprika
$\frac{1}{2}$ teaspoon	2 g	White pepper
$\frac{1}{2}$ teaspoon	2 g	Ground cumin
I cup	6 ounces, 168 g	Beef shoulder, minced
To taste		Salt and pepper
$\frac{1}{2}$ cup	2 ounces, 56 g	Potato, russet, peeled, $\frac{1}{4}$ inch (.6 cm) dice, boiled, drained, and cooled
$\frac{1}{4}$ cup	I ounce, 28 g	Raisins
$\frac{1}{4}$ cup	2 ounces, 56 g	Green Spanish olives, pitted, $\frac{1}{4}$ inch (.6 cm) dice
$\frac{1}{4}$ cup	I ounce, 28 g	Green onions, white part and I inch green, finely chopped
I		Hard-boiled egg, peeled and chopped

PROCEDURE

1   Heat oil over medium heat and add onion, bell pepper, red pepper flakes, paprika, white pepper, and cumin, cook 6 to 7 minutes or until onions are soft.

2   Add beef and cook, stirring, until meat is brown and cooked.

3   Correct seasoning; set aside to cool.

4   To cooled meat mixture, add cooked potatoes, raisins, olives, green onions, and egg; combine well.

5   Correct seasoning.

6   Preheat oven to 400°F (204°C).

7   To assemble empanadas, place about 3 tablespoons of filling in the center of each dough circle. Fold over and press the edges firmly to seal, starting from the middle and working out to the edges. Curve the ends of the empanada to form a crescent. To make the "rope"

around edge, pinch $\frac{1}{2}$ inch of one corner edge between your thumb and index finger and fold edge over onto itself. Pinch and pull another $\frac{1}{2}$ inch of the edge and fold again, making a rough triangle over the first fold. Repeat this folding around edge, pressing each fold tight.

8   Bake until golden brown, 15 to 20 minutes.

9   Serve warm with chimichurri sauce.

Chimichurri Sauce

SERVES 4–6

AMOUNT	MEASURE	INGREDIENT
$\frac{1}{2}$ cup	4 ounces, 120 ml	Olive oil
$\frac{1}{4}$ cup	2 ounces, 60 ml	Lemon juice, fresh
$\frac{1}{4}$ cup	2 ounces, 60 ml	Sherry or red wine vinegar
$\frac{1}{2}$ cup	2 ounces, 56 g	Onion; finely minced
I tablespoon	6 g	Garlic, finely minced
$\frac{1}{2}$ cup	I ounce, 28 g	Flat-leaf parsley; chopped
I tablespoon	3 g	Fresh oregano leaves, chopped
$\frac{1}{2}$ teaspoon		Dried red chile pepper
I $\frac{1}{2}$ teaspoons		Salt
I teaspoon		Black pepper, freshly ground

PROCEDURE

I   Combine all ingredients; rest for at least 2 hours. This is best if prepared overnight. The parsley may be added just before serving to preserve the color.

Ceviche Mixto
Shellfish Ceviche   SERVES 4

AMOUNT	MEASURE	INGREDIENT
1 quart	32 ounces, 938 ml	Water
1		Green onion, white part and 1 inch green, sliced
12 ounces	340 g	Shrimp (16–20 count), peeled and deveined
6 ounces	168 g	Scallops, rinsed
$\frac{1}{4}$ cup	2 ounces, 60 ml	Dry white wine
12 ounces	340 g	Mussels, scrubbed and debearded
12		Baby clams
		Marinade (recipe follows)
		Garnishes (recipe follows)

PROCEDURE

1   Bring water and green onion to boil; let simmer 5 minutes. Add shrimp, remove from heat, and let stand 1 minute or until shrimp are just cooked. Remove from hot water (reserving the cooking liquid) and cool shrimp so they do not become rubbery.

2   Return cooking liquid to boil, add scallops, remove from heat, and let stand for 3 minutes, depending on size. Cut a scallop in half to see if it is cooked through (it should be milky white in the center). Drain and rinse under cold running water.

3   Bring wine, mussels, and clams to a boil over high heat. Cover and let cook until the shells are open, 3 to 5 minutes. Discard any clams or mussels that do not open. Remove clams and mussels from shells and discard shells. Cool shellfish.

4   Combine cooked shellfish with marinade and refrigerate for at least 2 hours.

5   Before serving, check seasoning for salt, sugar, and hot pepper sauce.

6   Divide seafood equally between four serving containers. Garnish each in the center with 1 teaspoon each chopped tomato, bell pepper, onion, cilantro, and parsley.

7   Serve with the side dishes.

Marinade

AMOUNT	MEASURE	INGREDIENT
$\frac{1}{4}$ cup	2 ounces, 60 ml	Fresh lemon juice
$\frac{1}{4}$ cup	2 ounces, 60 ml	Fresh lime juice
$\frac{1}{2}$ cup	4 ounces, 120 ml	Fresh orange juice
$\frac{1}{2}$ cup	4 ounces, 120 ml	Fish or chicken stock
1 tablespoon	$\frac{1}{2}$ ounce, 14 ml	Olive oil
$\frac{1}{2}$ teaspoon	3 g	Sugar
$\frac{1}{2}$ teaspoon	3 g	Salt
$\frac{1}{4}$ teaspoon	2 g	Black pepper, freshly ground
To taste		Hot pepper sauce

PROCEDURE

1 Combine all ingredients and mix well.

Garnishes

AMOUNT	MEASURE	INGREDIENT
$\frac{1}{2}$ cup	3 ounces, 84 g	Tomato, peeled, seeded, $\frac{1}{4}$ inch (.6 cm) dice
$\frac{1}{2}$ cup	2 ounces, 56 g	Green bell pepper, seeded, $\frac{1}{8}$ inch (.3 cm) dice
$\frac{1}{2}$ cup	2 ounces, 56 g	White onion, $\frac{1}{8}$ inch (.3 cm) dice, rinsed with hot water, and drained
2 tablespoons	6 g	Cilantro, leaves only, minced
2 tablespoons	6 g	Parsley, minced

SIDE DISHES

Popcorn

Tostado (corn nuts)

Feijoada Bean Stew with Beef and Pork (Brazil) SERVES 4-6

Reputedly introduced in Brazil by black slaves as early as the sixteenth century, *feijoada*—a bean potpourri type dish—is the Brazilian equivalent of American "soul food." It is considered the Brazilian national dish. In *uma feijoada legitima*, the real *feijoada*, every part of the pig is used: ears, tail, and snout.

AMOUNT	MEASURE	INGREDIENT
I cup	7 ounces, 196 g	Dried black beans, washed and sorted, soaked overnight, or 2 cups cooked black beans
I piece	5 ounces, 140 g	Ham hock, smoked, 1 inch (2.4 cm) dice
I		Pork foot, ear, tail, tongue (optional)
I cup	5 ounces, 140 g	Chorizo, pepperoni, or Brazilian *lingüica*, $\frac{1}{2}$ inch (1.2 cm) dice
$\frac{1}{2}$ cup	3 ounces, 84 g	Lean Canadian bacon or Brazilian *carne seca*, cut $\frac{1}{2}$ inch (1.2 cm) dice
4 ounces	112 g	Smoked pork or beef ribs
$\frac{1}{2}$ cup	3 ounces, 84 g	Lean pork, 1 inch (2.4 cm) dice
$\frac{1}{2}$ cup	3 ounces, 84 g	Lean beef, 1 inch (2.4 cm) dice
I tablespoon	$\frac{1}{2}$ ounce, 15 ml	Olive oil
I ounce	56 g	Smoked bacon, $\frac{1}{2}$ inch (1.2 cm) dice
I cup	4 ounces, 112 g	Onion, $\frac{1}{2}$ inch (1.2 cm) dice
2		Garlic cloves, minced
I tablespoon	$\frac{1}{2}$ ounce, 15 ml	Sherry vinegar
I		Bay leaf
To taste		Salt and pepper
To taste		Hot sauce
4 cups		Arroz blanco (see recipe on page 31)
2 cups		Couve à Mineira (see recipe on page 77)

PROCEDURE

1   Place the beans in a large saucepot and cover with cold water. Bring to a boil and turn the heat down to simmer. Simmer until soft.

2   Combine ham hock, pork parts, chorizo, Canadian bacon, ribs, lean pork, and beef in saucepot; Add cold water just to cover; bring to a boil and cook 10 minutes or until meat is cooked.

3   Strain meat and retain liquid.

4   Heat oil over medium high heat and render diced bacon.

5   Add onion, garlic, and vinegar; cook until onions are caramelized.

6   Add $\frac{1}{2}$ cup cooked black beans to onion mixture and mash together.

7   Add bay leaf and fry for two minutes remove bay leaf.

8   Combine cooked beans, onion mixture, and cooked meats.

9   Add one cup or more retained liquid from meat.

10 Cook meat and beans together, adding liquid as needed, until meat is tender.

11 Correct seasoning and hot sauce.

12 Serve over rice with Couve à Mineira.

Cuscuz de Tapioca Molho de Chocolate Tapioca and Coconut Cake with Chocolate Sauce SERVES 4

AMOUNT	MEASURE	INGREDIENT
I cup	8 ounces, 240 ml	Unsweetened coconut milk
I cup	8 ounces, 240 ml	Milk
$\frac{1}{2}$ cup	$3\frac{1}{2}$ ounces, 98 g	Sugar
$\frac{1}{2}$ teaspoon		Salt
I cup	$2\frac{1}{2}$ ounces, 42 g	Coconut, grated
I cup	$5\frac{1}{2}$ ounces, 154 g	Quick-cooking tapioca

PROCEDURE

1 Over medium-high heat, combine coconut milk, milk, sugar, and salt.

2 Stir to dissolve sugar and bring to a boil.

3 Combine tapioca and coconut.

4 Add tapioca mixture to milk mixture and simmer until tapioca is clear, 2 minutes.

5 Pour into molds or serving containers; let set up.

6 Serve with chocolate sauce.

Chocolate Sauce

AMOUNT	MEASURE	INGREDIENT
$1\frac{3}{4}$ cups	14 ounce, 420 ml	Sweetened condensed milk
2 tablespoons	$\frac{3}{4}$ ounce, 21 g	Unsweetened cocoa powder
I tablespoon	$\frac{1}{2}$ ounce, 15 ml	Unsalted butter
I tablespoon	$\frac{1}{2}$ ounce, 15 ml	Water
Pinch		Salt

PROCEDURE

1 Combine all ingredients over low heat; cook, stirring, until smooth and hot.

2 Let cool to room temperature.

Truchas à la Parrilla
Grilled Trout   SERVES 4

AMOUNT	MEASURE	INGREDIENT
4	8 ounce, 224 g	Pan-dressed trout
2 tablespoons	1 ounce, 30 ml	Fresh lemon juice
2 tablespoons	1 ounce, 30 ml	Fresh lime juice
2 teaspoons	6 g	Salt
1 teaspoon	3 g	Black pepper, freshly ground
1 teaspoon	3 g	Ground cumin
2		Garlic cloves, minced
1 cup	8 ounces, 240 ml	Unsalted butter, melted

PROCEDURE

1 Make 3 deep incisions in both sides of each trout.

2 Combine lemon juice, lime juice, salt, pepper, cumin, and garlic and coat the trout with it, making sure it gets into the incisions. Cover and refrigerate for at least 1 hour.

3 Grill trout on a oiled perforated grill rack over low heat, basting frequently with melted butter, until just cooked through, about 5 minutes per side.

4 Serve with rice and a salad.

Bobó de Camarão
Shrimp with Yuca Sauce   SERVES 4

AMOUNT	MEASURE	INGREDIENT
I pound	448 g	16–20 ct shrimp, unpeeled
2 tablespoons	I ounce, 30 ml	Fresh lime juice
I $\frac{1}{2}$ cups	9 ounces, 252 g	Yuca, fresh or frozen, peeled, cut $\frac{1}{2}$ inch (1.2 cm) dice
2 cups	16 ounces, 480 ml	Water
I tablespoon	$\frac{1}{2}$ ounce, 15 ml	Olive oil
2 tablespoons	I ounce, 30 ml	Dendê or palm oil
I cup	4 ounces, 112 g	Onions, $\frac{1}{4}$ inch (.6 cm) dice
3		Garlic cloves, minced
$\frac{1}{2}$ cup	2 ounces, 56 g	Green bell pepper, seeded, $\frac{1}{4}$ inch (.6 cm) dice
$\frac{1}{2}$ cup	2 ounces, 56 g	Red bell pepper, seeded, $\frac{1}{4}$ inch (.6 cm) dice
I cup	6 ounces, 168 g	Tomatoes, peeled, seeded, $\frac{1}{4}$ inch (.6 cm) dice
2 tablespoons	6 g	Parsley, chopped
2 tablespoons	6 g	Cilantro, chopped
2 tablespoons	$\frac{1}{2}$ ounce, 14 g	Fresh ginger, peeled, grated
$\frac{1}{2}$ teaspoon	2 g	Salt
$\frac{1}{2}$ teaspoon	2 g	White pepper
I cup	8 ounces, 240 ml	Unsweetened coconut milk,
To taste		Salt, pepper, and hot pepper sauce

PROCEDURE

1 Peel and devein shrimp, reserving the shells; rinse and toss with lime juice.

2 Add water just to cover shrimp shells. Bring to boil, reduce heat, and simmer 10 minutes. Strain the broth and discard the shells.

3 Bring shrimp stock to boil and add yuca, and if necessary enough boiling water to cover. Cook over low heat until tender, about 20 minutes.

4 Drain and reserve liquid.

5 Mash yuca with potato masher or fork, add enough cooking liquid to make a coarse puree (it should not be smooth).

6 Heat oil and dendê over medium heat; add onion and cook, stirring, until softened, 5 minutes.

7 Add garlic, green and red bell peppers, tomatoes, parsley, cilantro, ginger, salt, and pepper. Cover and cook to reduce to a saucelike consistency, 10 minutes.

8 Add coconut milk and cook 5 minutes.

9 Add shrimp and cook 1 minute.

10 Add yuca puree; cook 1 minute.

11 Correct seasoning with salt, pepper, and hot sauce.

12 Add cooking liquid as needed to reach the consistency of heavy cream.

13 Serve with white rice.

Cuñapès Yuca Flour Rolls YIELD: 24 ROLLS

AMOUNT	MEASURE	INGREDIENT
$\frac{3}{4}$ cup, more if necessary	5 ounces, 140 g	Yuca flour
$\frac{3}{4}$ teaspoon	2 g	Baking powder
2		Medium eggs
$1\frac{1}{2}$ cups	6 ounces, 170 g	Queso fresco, crumbled
As needed		Milk

PROCEDURE

1 Sift flour and baking powder until well mixed.

2 Add eggs and cheese; mix—preferably with a food processor—until a dough is formed.

3 If dough is too dry, add a little milk.

4 Shape dough and let rest for 30 minutes.

5 Preheat oven to 375°F (190°C).

6 Bake rolls until lightly colored, about 20 minutes. Serve warm.

Escabeche de Pescado
Pickled Fish   SERVES 4

The most commonly used fish for escabeche is tuna, corvina, red snapper, trout, and catfish. This escabeche can be served warm or at room temperature.

AMOUNT	MEASURE	INGREDIENT
I pound	448 g	Firm white-fish fillets, lean flesh, skinless, all bones removed
I tablespoon	$\frac{1}{2}$ ounce, 14 ml	Fresh lemon juice
$\frac{1}{2}$ teaspoon	2 g	Salt
$\frac{1}{4}$ teaspoon	I g	Black pepper, freshly ground
$\frac{1}{4}$ cup	2 ounces, 60 ml	Olive oil
$\frac{1}{2}$ cup	2 ounces, 56 g	Red onions, julienne
$\frac{1}{4}$ cup	I ounce, 28 g	Red bell pepper, julienne
$\frac{1}{4}$ cup	I ounce, 28 g	Green bell pepper, julienne
		Garlic cloves, minced
I tablespoon	$\frac{1}{2}$ ounce, 14 g	Capers, washed and drained
I		Bouquet garni (I sprig fresh thyme, 2 sprigs fresh parsley, I bay leaf, $\frac{1}{4}$ teaspoon black peppercorns, tied up in cheesecloth)
$\frac{1}{4}$ cup	2 ounces, 60 ml	Dry white wine
$\frac{1}{4}$ cup	2 ounces, 60 ml	Sherry vinegar
$\frac{1}{4}$ cup	2 ounces, 60 ml	Fish or chicken stock
		Lettuce leaves for garnish

PROCEDURE

1   Rub fish with lemon juice and half the salt and black pepper. Let marinate in refrigerator for 1 hour. Cut into 1 inch (2.4 cm) by 2 inch (4.8 cm) pieces and set aside.

2   Heat oil over medium heat; sauté onion, bell peppers, and garlic for 5 minutes or until soft.

3   Add capers and remaining salt and pepper, bouquet garni, wine, vinegar, and stock; bring to simmer.

4   Add fish, baste with sauce, cover, and simmer until opaque in center, 2 to 4 minutes or less. Do not overcook.

5 Discard bouquet garni and correct seasoning.

6 Transfer fish to clean container; pour sauce over and let cool.

7 Before serving, refrigerate 1 to 2 hours or overnight.

8 Arrange on lettuce leaves to serve.

Ají Colombiano

Colombian Sauce   YIELD: 2 CUPS

Ají is as important to Colombians as *chimichurri* is to Argentines

AMOUNT	MEASURE	INGREDIENT
$\frac{1}{2}$ cup	2 ounces, 56 g	Green onions, white and light green parts, thinly sliced
$\frac{1}{2}$ cup	3 ounces, 84 g	Tomatoes, peeled, seeded, $\frac{1}{4}$ inch (.6 cm) dice
$\frac{1}{2}$ cup	2 ounces, 56 g	Red onion, $\frac{1}{4}$ inch (.6 cm) dice
$\frac{1}{4}$ cup	$\frac{1}{2}$ ounce, 14 g	Cilantro, stemmed, chopped
3		Hard-cooked egg whites, chopped
1 tablespoons	3 g	Fresh chives, chopped
$\frac{1}{2}$ cup	4 ounces, 120 ml	Olive oil
1 teaspoon		Tabasco sauce
$\frac{1}{4}$ cup	2 ounces, 60 ml	White wine vinegar
1 tablespoon	$\frac{1}{2}$ ounce, 15 ml	Fresh lime juice
To taste		Kosher salt and freshly ground pepper

PROCEDURE

1 Combine green onions, tomatoes, and red onions. Stir to blend.

2 Add the cilantro, egg whites, and chives. Stir to blend. Gradually stir in the olive oil.

3 Add the Tabasco, vinegar, lime juice, salt, and pepper. Stir to blend.

Humitas Ecuatorianas
Ecuadorian Humitas

YIELD: ABOUT 12, DEPENDING ON SIZE OF CORN HUSKS

Humitas **are the South American cousin of tamale. Made with grated tender corn, the dough is wrapped and tied in corn husks, which are then steamed.** *Humitas* **can be found throughout the Andes from Ecuador down to Argentina. Each country has its own version.**

Chef Tip Ecuadorian cooks place a coin in the bottom of the pot before adding the steamer filled with *humitas*. The coin vibrates noisily on the bottom of the pot as the water simmers. The coin stops making noise when all the water has evaporated. This tells the cook that additional boiling water is needed.

AMOUNT	MEASURE	INGREDIENT
12		Corn husks
4 cups	20 ounces, 560 g	Corn kernels
$\frac{1}{4}$ cup	1 ounce, 28 g	Onion, $\frac{1}{4}$ inch (.6 cm) dice
$\frac{1}{2}$ cup	4 ounces, 112 g	Butter, melted or vegetable oil
3		Large eggs, separated
$\frac{1}{2}$ cup (approximately)	3 ounces, 84 g	Cornmeal
1 teaspoon	4 g	Baking powder
1 teaspoon	8 g	Salt
1 teaspoon	8 g	Sugar
$1\frac{1}{2}$ cups	6 ounces, 168 g	Chihuahua, mozzarella, or Muenster cheese, shredded
		Kitchen twine, cut into twelve 15 inch lengths
2 cups	16 ounces, 469 ml	Water
		Aji Criollo (recipe follows)

PROCEDURE

1   If using dried corn husks, soak them in water for at least 2 hours. Separate them one by one and stack them ready for use. If using fresh, blanch in boiling water for 2 to 3 minutes to make pliable; remove, drain, and cool.

2   Puree corn kernels and onion until finely ground.

3   Add butter, egg yolks, cornmeal, baking powder, salt, sugar, and cheese to corn and onion mixture. Pulse until well incorporated and smooth. The mixture should not be runny; add more cornmeal if necessary.

4   Whip egg whites to soft peaks and fold into mixture.

5   ASSEMBLY: Dry corn husks and place 2 overlapping; place $\frac{1}{2}$ cup (3 ounces, 84 g) corn batter on the lower half of the husks. Fold the two long sides of the corn husk in over the corn mixture. Fold the tapered end up, leaving the top open. Secure the tamale by tying with a strip of husk or a string.

6   Set up a steamer in a large saucepot with an elevated bottom and tight-fitting lid. Add water to reach just under the elevated bottom. Place *humitas* on the elevated bottom, standing up or laying down. Cover with any leftover husks and place the cover on the steamer. Steam until the *humitas* feel firm to the touch, about 30 minutes if small, 45 minutes if large. Add more water if needed.

7   To serve, remove the twine and place on a plate with the husks open to expose the *humitas*. Serve *aji criollo* on the side.

Aji Criollo   Creole Hot Pepper Salsa
YIELD: 3/4 CUP

AMOUNT	MEASURE	INGREDIENT
4		Red or green serranos, or jalapeños peppers, seeded and minced (1/8 inch, 3 cm)
6 tablespoons	3 ounces, 90 ml	Water
$\frac{1}{2}$ teaspoon	3 g	Salt
$\frac{1}{4}$ cup	1 ounce, 28 g	Green onion, white part only, minced
2 tablespoons	6 g	Cilantro or parsley leaves, minced

PROCEDURE

1   Combine peppers, 2 tablespoons water, and salt. Puree in blender.

2   Combine puree with green onion, cilantro and remaining water and mix well. This is best served the same day it's made.

The Caribbean

The Land

The West Indian archipelago forms a massive breakwater 2,000 miles long consisting of thousands of islands and reefs that protect the Caribbean Sea against the Atlantic Ocean. This barrier provides the Caribbean its calm and clear waters.

This area is known by a variety of names. The earliest name, and the one most frequently used, is West Indies. Christopher Columbus gave the region that name erroneously when he arrived in 1492. He thought that he had circumnavigated the earth and that the islands were off the coast of India.

Spain and France called the islands the Antilles, after the mythological Atlantic island of Antilia. The larger islands (Cuba, Jamaica, Hispaniola, and Puerto Rico) came to be known as the Greater Antilles, while the remaining smaller islands were called the Lesser Antilles. Today the area is broken into four island chains: the Bahamas, the Greater Antilles, and the eastern and southern islands of the Lesser Antilles. Together, these islands cover more than 91,000 square miles of land area.

The northernmost island chain is the Bahamas, which include 29 inhabited islands and nearly 3,000 islets stretching southeastward from Florida. Most of them are flat islands formed from coral and limestone.

The Greater Antilles is the largest and westernmost chain. It includes Cuba, Hispaniola, Jamaica, and Puerto Rico. The four main islands comprise nine-tenths of the entire land area of the West Indies. Cuba alone has almost half this area. The main island of Cuba covers 40,543 square miles. Much of the landmass of the Greater Antilles is formed by a partially submerged mountain range, which forms the Sierra Maestras and Sierra de Nipe on Cuba, the Blue Mountains on Jamaica, the Cordillera Central on Hispaniola, and the mountainous core of Puerto Rico farther to the east. The western three-fourths of the island is a vast limestone platform similar to the limestone platforms of Florida and Mexico's Yucatán Peninsula.

The third island chain includes the eastern islands of the Lesser Antilles, which curve north from the coast of Venezuela toward Puerto Rico. The islands along this arc fall into two distinct geographic groups. Some islands formed as a result of volcanic activity, while others emerged from the ocean as low-lying coral islands. Saint Vincent, Saint Lucia, Martinique, Dominica, the western half of Guadeloupe, Montserrat, Nevis, Saint Kitts, and the Virgin Islands are mountainous with rims of coastal plain. There are many active volcanoes in the West Indies, including Montagne Pelée on Martinique and Soufrière on Saint Vincent. The Soufrière Hills volcano on Montserrat erupted during the mid-1990s, destroying the island's capital of Plymouth. The islands of Barbados, Antigua, Barbuda, Anguilla, and the eastern half of Guadeloupe generally have low elevations and more level terrain.

The fourth island chain, the southern islands of the Lesser Antilles, follows the coast of Venezuela, from Lake Maracaibo to the mouth of the Orinoco River. These islands are extreme northeastern extensions of the Andes Mountains and have complex geologic structures. They include Aruba, Bonaire, Curaçao, Margarita, and Trinidad and Tobago. One of the smallest inhabited islands is Saba, part of the Netherlands Antilles. A volcanic cone, Saba towers 2,854 feet above the ocean. Its capital, the Bottom, is built at the bottom of the extinct crater—the only patch of level land on the island. Many smaller uninhabited coral islets are found in the region.

History

The English word *Caribbean*, its Spanish equivalent *Caribe*, and its French version *Caraïbe* comes from the name of an Indian tribe that, in pre-Columbian time, inhabited the northwest portion of South America, Central America, and the southeast islands of the region now known as the Caribbean Basin. The Carib people left their name behind as a symbol of the region they inhabited. On land, they lived in small settlements, farmed and fished, and hunted game with blowguns and bows and arrows and were noted for their ferocity. However the most dominant culture was that of the Tainos or Arawack. These people practiced a highly productive form of agriculture and had an advanced social and material culture.

The arrival of Christopher Columbus was the beginning of the end of the indigenous people of the Caribbean and beginning of the European conquest and domination. The

Caribbean became the most precious jewel in the crown of Spain. They began to settle the Greater Antilles soon after Christopher Columbus landed in the Bahamas in 1492. For the Arawak/Tainos, the Spanish conquest was disaster. Aside of the pressure exerted on them through the destruction of social structures and the disruption of their food supply the Arawaks had to face European diseases for which they were not immunologically prepared.

Spanish control of the region was not undisputed, and other European colonial powers constantly challenged it. The British, French, and Dutch encouraged and at times even licensed their citizens to attack Spanish merchant ships, fleets, and ports. They harassed the Spaniards with some success for nearly two hundred years, most intensively between the mid-1500s and mid-1600s.

The history of the years of massive colonial prosperity of the West Indies, especially in Jamaica (English rule) and St. Domingue (French rule, today Haiti) is centered around the economics of sugarcane production. When the Arawak population disappeared, the lack of manpower resulted in the introduction of African slaves. The flow of slaves to the West Indies was at first a trickle but became a flood in the eighteenth century. At that time, an increase of the demand for sugar in Europe triggered the astronomic growth of production by the West Indian sugar plantations. According to some historians the estimated number of people uprooted from Africa varies between sixty and one hundred million. Though many died during the Middle Passage, many also survived. And, after nearly three hundred years of struggle, the people of African descent became the inheritors of the lands of the Caribbean.

Politically the islands of the West Indies are made up of thirteen independent nations and a number of colonial dependencies, territories, and possessions. The Republic of Cuba, consisting of the island of Cuba and several nearby islands, is the largest West Indian nation. Haiti and the Dominican Republic, two other independent nations, occupy Hispaniola, the second largest island in the archipelago. Jamaica, Barbados, the Bahamas, Trinidad and Tobago, Dominica, Grenada, the Federation of Saint Kitts and Nevis, Saint Lucia, Saint Vincent and the Grenadines, and Antigua and Barbuda are the other sovereign nations.

Rule over nearly all the other West Indies islands is distributed among the United States, France, the Netherlands, Venezuela, and the United Kingdom. Puerto Rico, the fourth largest island of the archipelago, is a U.S. commonwealth and several of the Virgin Islands are United States territories. The French West Indies includes Martinique, Guadeloupe, and a number of smaller dependencies of Guadeloupe. Martinique and Guadeloupe and its dependencies are overseas departments of France. The Dutch possessions consist of the Netherlands Antilles (Curaçao and Bonaire), Aruba, and smaller Lesser Antilles islands. Venezuela controls about seventy Lesser Antilles islands, including Margarita Island. Dependencies of the United Kingdom are Anguilla, the Cayman Islands, Montserrat, Turks and Caicos Islands, and some of the Virgin Islands.

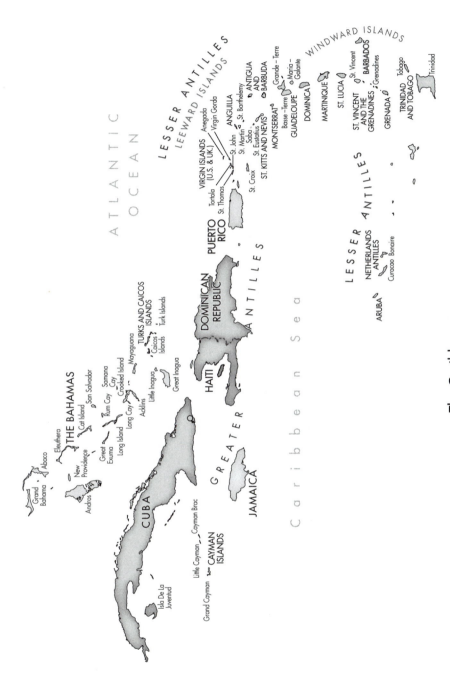

The Caribbean

The People

The roots of the vast majority of Caribbean island people can be traced to Europe, Africa, and Asia. During the seventeenth century the English, Dutch, and French joined the Spanish in settling and exploring the Caribbean islands. At first, the English and French met their needs for labor by bringing Europeans to the islands as indentured servants, individuals who agreed to work for a specific number of years in exchange for passage to the colonies, food, and shelter. Eventually, all the colonizing countries imported slaves from Africa to provide labor. The number of slaves increased dramatically after the sugar plantations were established in the seventeenth century, making slavery the dominant economic institution on many islands.

The African people soon became the majority on most of the islands. Their culture and customs influence much of the religious worship, artistic expression, rhythmic dancing, singing, and even ways of thinking in the Caribbean. Spiritual practices such as Junkanoo in the Bahamas, Santeria in Cuba, Voodun in Haiti, and Rastafari in Jamaica are African-influenced movements that have Caribbean origin and a worldwide following. Reggae music and jerk cooking are also Africa-inspired contributions to the world from the Caribbean.

After the abolition of slave trade in the British West Indies during the early nineteenth century, Asian workers arrived in Cuba and Jamaica and indentured workers from India came to the Lesser Antilles.

Today, an estimated 70 percent of the people of the region are of African descent or *mulatto* (mixed African and European descent), 25 percent European descent, and 5 percent Asian descent. The racial composition of individual islands, however, differs widely. Most of the Caucasians live in Cuba, the Dominican Republic, and Puerto Rico. Most of the Asians live in Trinidad. The inhabitants of the other islands and the third of Hispaniola occupied by Haiti are overwhelmingly of African descent. Jamaica is typical of the older plantation islands, with 76 percent of its population of African descent, 15 percent mulatto, 1 percent of European descent, and 8 percent of Chinese, Indian, or other heritage.

The Food

The islands originally inhabited by the Arawak and Carib Indian tribes had established a varied combination of foodstuffs and cooking techniques. The Caribs were cannibalistic but are credited by food historians to be the people who began ritually spicing their food with chile peppers. The Arawaks, on the other hand, devised a method of slow-cooking their meat by placing it over an open fire on a makeshift grate or grill made out of thin green sticks. They called this a *barbacoa*, which gave rise in both method and name to what is known today as a barbecue.

After Christopher Columbus arrived in the area in 1492, other Europeans followed Spain in colonizing the islands and brought with them their culinary trademarks. Some of the ingredients the Spanish and Europeans introduced included not only sugarcane, but varieties of coconut, chickpeas, cilantro, eggplant, onions, garlic, oranges, limes, mangoes, rice, and coffee.

The Caribbean's close proximity to Mexico and South America encouraged trade between the early settlers. Mexico traded papaya, avocado, chayote, and cocoa. Potatoes and passion fruit came from South America. Later breadfruit was introduced by Polynesians and corn, beans, and chile by Americans. Beginning in the early 1600s the slave trade brought foods from West Africa to the islands. The Africans brought crops of okra, callaloo, and *ackee*. Cuisine is similar from island to island, but each island has its specialties.

Typical Cuban foods include black beans, white rice, yellow rice, citrus marinades, garlic, and fried sliced banana (plantain). Olive oil and garlic marinades are often used as sauces. Popular spices include cumin, cayenne, and cilantro. Meat is often prepared roasted and in a *creola* style marinade. Two things not often seen in Cuban food are cream and milk products and cheeses in heavy sauces. These products, popular in Europe and North America, are expensive to purchase and often difficult to store. Pork and chicken are relatively plentiful, fresh and inexpensive. *Ajiaco*, a thick soup made with pork along with different kinds of edible vegetable roots and stems, is the national dish of Cuba. The taste depends on the vegetables and the seasonings chosen by the cook. Other typical Cuban dishes include *moros y cristianos* (white rice and black beans), *congrí* (a combination of rice and red kidney beans), and *picadillo à la habanera* (a mincemeat dish, Havana style).

Jamaica's national dish is said to be *ackee and saltfish*, usually served at breakfast, but can also be a main dish. *Ackee* is a fruit whose color and flavor when cooked are said to resemble scrambled eggs. A "closed" ackee is unripe and poisonous and is only safe to consume when it ripens and is thus "open." Saltfish is fish (usually cod) that has been heavily immersed in salt for preservation, drying, and curing purposes. Saltfish is usually soaked overnight in cold water to remove most of the salt before eating. Jamaica's saltfish (or codfish) fritters, called *Stamp and Go*, an island form of fast food, are made from a batter of soaked, cooked, skinned, and flaked saltfish, with scallions, chiles, and tomato, fried in coconut oil until golden brown. The long lasting Oriental and Indian influences in Caribbean cooking are represented by curries and rice. Curried goat is a favorite, usually reserved for special occasions. Jamaican *jerk* is another signature dish of the island. It can be either a dry seasoning mixture that is rubbed directly into the meat or it can be combined with water to create a marinade. *Jerk* recipes have passed through generations but the basic ingredients involve allspice, hot chiles (scotch bonnet), salt, and a mixture of up to thirty or more herbs and spices that blend to create one of the hottest and spiciest foods known. The Blue Mountains of Jamaica lend their name to the famous Blue Mountain Coffee, renowned for being smooth and full flavored. Coffee beans were first introduced to Jamaica in 1728 from the country of Martinique. The climatic conditions of the island ensured that the seedlings flourished, which triggered the cultivation of coffee bean crops in the region.

From Puerto Rico come *adobo* and *sofrito*—blends of herbs and spices that give many of the native foods their distinctive taste and color. *Adobo*, made by crushing together peppercorns, oregano, garlic, salt, olive oil, and lime juice or vinegar, is rubbed into meats before they are roasted. *Sofrito*, a potpourri of onions, garlic, and peppers browned in either olive oil or lard and colored with achiote (annatto seeds), imparts the bright yellow color to the island's rice, soups and stews. Soups include *sopón de pollo con arroz* (chicken soup with rice), which tastes different across the island's regions; *sopón de pescado* (fish soup), which is prepared with the head and tail intact; and *sopón de garbanzos con patas de cerdo* (chickpea soup with pig's feet), which is made with pumpkin, chorizo (Spanish sausage), salt pork, chile peppers, cabbage, potatoes, tomatoes, and fresh cilantro. The most traditional Puerto Rican dish is *asopao*, a hearty gumbo made with either chicken or shellfish. One well-known and low-budget version is *asopao de gandules* (pigeon peas). Another is *asopao de pollo* (chicken), which adds a whole chicken flavored with oregano, garlic, and paprika to a rich gumbo of salt pork, cured ham, green peppers, chile peppers, onions, cilantro, olives, tomatoes, chorizo, and pimientos. Stews, which are usually cooked in heavy kettles called *calderas*, are a large part of the Puerto Rican diet. A popular one is *carne guisada puertorriqueña* (Puerto Rican beef stew). The ingredients that flavor the beef vary but might include green peppers, sweet chile peppers, onions, garlic, cilantro, potatoes, pimento-stuffed olives, capers, and raisins. *Pastelón de carne*, or meat pie filled with salt pork, ham, and spices, is a staple of many Puerto Rican dinners. Other typical dishes include *carne frita con cebolla* (fried beefsteak with onions), *ternera a la parmesana* (veal parmesan) and roast leg of pork, fresh ham, lamb, or veal, which are prepared Creole style and flavored with adobo. Exotic fare, such as *Cabrito en Fricasé* (goat meat fricasse,) *Carne Mechada* (larded pork or beef loin with chorizo sausage,) and *Cuajito* and *Mollejas Guisadas* (stews popular during Christmas season) are also enjoyed by locals.

A festive island dish is *lechón asado* (barbecued pig). A recipe dating back to the Taino Indians, it is traditional for picnics and outdoor parties. The pig is basted with *jugo de naranja agria* (sour orange juice) and achiote coloring. Green plantains are peeled and roasted over hot stones, then served as a side dish. The traditional dressing served with the pig is *aji -li-mojili*, a sour garlic sauce consisting of garlic, whole black peppercorns, and sweet seeded chile peppers, flavored further with vinegar, lime juice, salt, and olive oil. Chicken is a Puerto Rican staple, *arroz con pollo* (chicken with rice) being the most common dish. Other preparations include *pollo al Jérez* (chicken in sherry), *pollo agridulce* (sweet-and-sour chicken) and *pollitos asados a la parrilla* (broiled chicken). Fish specialties include *mojo isleño*, fried fish in a typical sauce of olives, olive oil, onions, pimientos, capers, tomato sauce, vinegar, garlic, and bay leaves. Puerto Ricans often cook *camarones en cerveza* (shrimp in beer) and *jueyes hervidos* (boiled crab). Rice and plantains are prepared in dozens of ways and accompany nearly every meal. Rice (*arroz*) is simmered slowly with sofrito and generally served with *habichuelas* (beans) or *gandules* (pigeon peas). Another typical rice specialty is *pegao*, which is rice that is prepared so that it sticks to the bottom of the pan and gets crispy. Plantains also are served in many forms. *Amarillos* are ripe plantains fried with sugar to enhance their sweetness. Green plantains are either mashed into discs and deep fried to make *tostones* or mashed into balls of *mofongo* and mixed with pork or seafood and spices.

In St. Vincent the national dish is roasted breadfruit and jackfish. Seafood is abundant, including lobster, crab, conch (pronounced conk), shrimp, whelk, and mahimahi. A favorite delicacy is *tri tri*, a tiny fish seasoned with spices and curry powder and fried into cakes. Other popular dishes include callaloo stew, *souse* (a soupy stew made with pigs feet), pumpkin soup, *roti*, and *buljol* (salted fish, tomatoes, sweet peppers, and onions served with roasted breadfruit). A favorite dessert, *duckanoo*, originally from Africa, is made with cornmeal, coconut, spices, and brown sugar. The ingredients are tied up in a banana leaf (hence its other name, *Tie-a-Leaf*), and slowly cooked in boiling water.

Native cooking in the Dominican Republic combines Spanish influences with local produce. Beef is expensive (Dominicans raise fine cattle, but mostly for export) and local favorites are pork and goat meat. Breakfast typically calls for a serving of *mangu*, a mix of plantains, cheese, and bacon. *Mangu* has been called "mashed potatoes" of the Dominican Republic. A foundation of the native diet, '*La Bandera Dominicana*, or the Dominican flag meal, is eaten by nearly everyone at lunchtime. The most important meal of the day, *La Bandera* consists of rice, beans, meat, vegetables, and fried plantains. Another popular dish is *Sancocho*, a Spanish-style stew usually served with rice. Ingredients include various roots, green plantains, avocado, and typically chicken or beef, although it sometimes includes a combination of seven different types of meat (*Sancocho prieto*). Goat meat, a staple in many Dominican homes, may also be used in this recipe. It offers a unique addition to the character of any dish since these animals graze on wild oregano. *Locrio*, or Dominican rice, varies. An adaptation of the Spanish paella, *locrio* is made with achiote (a colored dye produced from the seeds of the achiote plant), because saffron spice is unavailable. *Casabe* (a round flat cassava bread) and *catibias* (cassava flour fritters filled with meat) are the only culinary legacy of the Taino Indians. Desserts here are very sweet, made with sugar and condensed milk in various flavors (coconut, papaya, banana, pineapple, soursop, ginger), prepared as flans, puddings, and creams. Tropical fruits are abundant and are used in desserts throughout the year, but many different varieties are found depending on the altitude (for example, cherries, plums, and strawberries grow in the central regions).

Barbados is distinguished for its *flying fish/coo-coo* dinners. Sleek, silver-blue fish with fins that resemble dragonfly wings, flying fish are able to propel themselves in the air at speeds up to thirty miles an hour to escape predators. *Coo-coo* is a polenta-like porridge made from yellow cornmeal, water, salt, pepper, butter, and okra. Other specialties include *conkies*, from Ghana, which are steamed sweet or savory preparations with mixtures of cornmeal, coconut, pumpkin, raisins, sweet potato, and spices, in preboiled banana leaf pieces. *Eddo*, sometimes called *coco*, is a hairy root vegetable with the size and flavor of a potato that is used in soups.

Peas and rice, or pigeon peas are a mainstay of the diet. The peas are cooked with rice and flavored with coconut. The peas are also known as *congo* or *gongo* peas on other islands. *Jug-jug* is a stew made from corned beef, pork, pigeon peas, and guinea corn. Lamb in Barbados is from a breed of black-bellied sheep that look like goats.

Antigua's national dish is *fungi and pepperpot*, a thick vegetable stew with salted meat. *Ducana* (sweet potato dumpling) is served with saltfish and *chop up* (mashed eggplant, okra and seasoning). *Black pineapples* from Antigua are famous throughout the East Caribbean for their unique, extra-sweet flavor.

The signature dish of Curaçao is *keshi yená*, or "stuffed cheese." This dish is traditionally made with chicken, vegetables, seasonings, and raisins, which are stuffed into a scooped-out Edam or Gouda cheese shell. The "top" of the cheese is replaced and the whole is baked for at least an hour. In Colonial times, the Dutch masters would eat the cheese and "generously" donate the shell to their workers. Having to make due with what they had, the poor people of the island came up with this specialty. Two very popular dishes are *funchi* and *tutu*. Both based on cornmeal, they are commonly served as side dishes or appetizers. Taken directly from African cuisine, these two dishes are still cooked in the traditional manner. Funchi is much like polenta, in that cornmeal is poured into boiling water seasoned with butter and salt. It is stirred with a spoonlike utensil called a *mealie* or *funchi stick*. It is most often left mushy and served in a mound, although sometimes it is allowed to stiffen and then shaped into dumplings, much like hushpuppies. Some fancy eateries will shape the *funchi* into ramekins or other molds. *Tutu* is like *funchi* but with the addition of mashed black-eyed peas and is mixed with a *lélé* (a stick with three points, used like a whisk.) *Bitterbal*, another popular Dutch-inspired dish, is sausage meat formed into balls, coated in bread crumbs and fried. It is eaten for breakfast, lunch, and snacks.

Rotis in Trinidad are as common as hamburgers in the United States. This unofficial national dish consists of a curry meal wrapped in thin pastry; its prototype was brought to the Caribbean by Indian immigrants some decades ago. The little packets of food have turned into a top seller for a quick snack.

Glossary

Ackee The fruit of a West African tree, named in honor of Captain Bligh, who introduced it to Jamaica. The ackee fruit is bright red. When ripe it bursts open to reveal three large black seeds and bright yellow flesh. It is popular as a breakfast food throughout Jamaica. Ackee is poisonous if eaten before it is fully mature and because of its toxicity, it is subject to import restrictions and may be hard to obtain in some countries. Never open an ackee pod; it will open itself when it ceases to be deadly. The edible part is the aril, sometimes called Vegetable

Brains; it looks like a small brain or scrambled eggs, with a delicate flavor. It is best known in the Jamaican dish saltfish and ackee.

Allspice, Pimienta Dark-brown berry, similar to peppercorns, that combines the flavors of cinnamon, clove, and nutmeg.

Annatto This slightly musky-flavored reddish yellow spice, ground from the seeds of a flowering tree, is native to the West Indies and the Latin tropics. Islanders store their annatto seeds in oil, giving the oil a beautiful color. Saffron or turmeric can be substituted. The Spanish name *achiote* is sometimes referred to as achote. Available in Latin American and some Oriental markets.

Bay Rum The bay rum tree is related to the evergreen that produces allspice and the West African tree that produces melgueta pepper. Used to flavor soups, stews, and, particularly, *blaff*.

Beans, Peas Interchangeable terms for beans. Kidney beans in Jamaica are called peas. In Trinidad pigeon peas are referred to as peas. The French islands use the term *pois* for kidney beans. Cuba calls beans *frijoles*. Puerto Rico uses the term *habichuelas*, and in the Dominican Republic both terms are used. Often combined with rice, used in soups and stews, or pulped and made into fritters.

Bitter or Seville Orange Also called sour and bigarade orange. It is large, with a rough, reddish-orange skin. The pulp is too acid to be eaten raw, but the juice is used in meat and poultry dishes. The oranges are also used to make marmalade. A mixture of lime or lemon juice and sweet orange juice can be used as a substitute.

Blaff A broth infused with whole Scotch bonnet peppers and bay rum leaves in which whole or filleted fish is poached.

Boniato Tropical sweet potato.

Boudin, Black Pudding Sausage that may include pig's blood, thyme, and Scotch bonnet peppers. Frequently served with souse, a pork dish that can include any part of the pig.

Breadfruit Large green fruits, usually about 10 inches in diameter, with a potato-like flesh. It was introduced to Jamaica from its native Tahiti in 1793 by Captain Bligh. Breadfruit is not edible until cooked; when cooked the flesh is yellowish-white, like a dense potato. Breadfruit is picked and eaten before it ripens and is typically served like squash: baked, grilled, fried, boiled, or roasted after being stuffed with meat, or in place of any starch vegetable, rice, or pasta. It makes an excellent soup.

Calabaza A squash, also called West Indian or green pumpkin. It comes in a variety of sizes and shapes. The best substitutes are Hubbard or butternut squash.

Callaloo The principal ingredient in the most famous of all the island soups. The term applies to the leaves of two distinct types of plant that are used interchangeably. The first are the elephant-ear leaves of the taro plant. The other is Chinese spinach, a leafy vegetable typically prepared as one would prepare turnip or collard greens.

Carambola, Star Fruit Tart or acidy-sweet star-shaped fruit used in desserts, as a garnish for drinks, tossed into salads, or cooked together with seafood.

Cassareep The boiled down juice of grated cassava root, flavored with cinnamon, cloves, and sugar. It is the essential ingredient in pepperpot, the Caribbean island stew. It may be purchased bottled in West Indian markets.

Cassava This tuber, also known as manioc and yuca, is a rather large root vegetable, 6–12 inches length and 2–3 inches in diameter. Cassava has a tough brown skin with a very firm white flesh. Tapioca and cassareep are both made from cassava. There are two varieties of the plant: sweet and bitter. Sweet cassava is boiled and eaten as a starch vegetable. Bitter cassava contains a poisonous acid that can be deadly and must be processed before it can be eaten. This is done by boiling the root in water for at least 45 minutes; discard the water. Alternatively, grate the cassava and place it in a muslin cloth, then squeeze out as much of the acid as possible before cooking. Bitter cassava is used commercially but is not sold unprocessed in some countries.

Chayote, Christophine, Cho-cho, Mirliton A small pear-shaped vegetable, light green or cream colored, and often covered with a prickly skin. Bland, similar in texture to squash, and used primarily in Island cuisine as a side dish or in gratins and soufflés. Like pawpaw (papaya), it is also a meat tenderizer.

Cherimoya Pale-green fruit with white sweet flesh that has the texture of flan. Used for mousse and fruit sauces, the fruit is best when fully ripe, well chilled and eaten with a spoon.

Chorizo Spanish sausage that combines pork, hot peppers, and garlic.

Coo-coo (or cou-cou) The Caribbean equivalent of polenta or grits. Once based on cassava or manioc meal it is now made almost exclusively with cornmeal. Coo-coo can be baked, fried, or rolled into little balls and poached in soups or stews.

Conch Also known as *lambi* or *concha*. These large mollusks from the gastropod family are up to a foot long, with a heavy spiral shell with yellow that shades to pink inside. When preparing conch soup, conch salad or conch fritters, the tough conch flesh must be tenderized by pounding.

Crapaud Very large frogs, known as mountain chicken, found on the islands of Dominica and Monserrat. Fried or stewed legs are considered a national delicacy.

Creole, Criolla Creole refers to the cooking of the French-speaking West Indies, as well as to southern Louisiana and the U.S. Gulf states. Criolla refers to the cuisine of Spanish-speaking islands. Both terms encompass a melding of ingredients and cooking methods from France, Spain, Africa, the Caribbean, and the Americas.

Dhal Hindu name for legumes; in the Caribbean, it refers only to split peas or lentils.

Darne The Caribbean name for kingfish.

Dasheen Also known a coco, taro, and tannia, dasheen is a starchy tuber usually served boiled or cut up and used as a thickener in hearty soups. They are considered by some to have a texture and flavor superior to that of a Jerusalem artichoke or potato, but potatoes can often be used as a substitute for dasheen in recipes. Dasheen is often called coco, but coco is actually a slightly smaller relative of dasheen.

Escabeche The Spanish word for "pickled." It usually refers to fresh fish (and sometimes poultry) that is cooked in oil and vinegar, or cooked and then pickled in an oil and vinegar marinade.

Guava, Guayaba Tropical fruit that has over one hundred species. It is pear-shaped, yellow to green skinned, with creamy yellow, pink, or red granular flesh and rows of small hard seeds. Ripe guava have a perfume-like scent. Guava is used green or ripe in punches, syrups, jams, chutneys, and ice creams.

Hearts of Palm Ivory-colored core of some varieties of palm trees. They are used fresh or canned in salads and as a vegetable.

Hibiscus Also known as sorrel, rosell, or flor de Jamaica, this tropical flower is used for drinks, jams, and sauces. The flower blooms in December, after which it is dried and used to make a bright red drink that has a slightly tart taste and is the color of cranberry juice. It should not be confused with the American hibiscus found in the garden.

Jack A fish family of over two hundred species, these colorful saltwater fish are also known as yellowtail, greenback, burnfin, black, and amber jack. These delicately flavored fish tend to be large, weighing as much as 150 pounds, and readily available in waters around the world. Tuna and swordfish may be substituted.

Lobster Caribbean rock lobster. Unlike the Maine variety, this lobster has no claws.

Malanga, Yautia A relative of dasheen or taro, this tuber is prevalent throughout the Caribbean.

Mamey Apple The large tropical fruit, native to the New World, yields edible pulp that is tangerine in color. The flavor is similar to a peach.

Mango A native of India, this fruit is known as "the fruit of the tropics." Green mangoes are used in hot sauces and condiments, while ripe mangoes appear in desserts, candies, and drinks.

Name This giant tuber is called by a variety of different names. The Spanish translation of the word *ñame* is *yam*. The outer skin is brown and coarsely textured, while the inside is porous and very moist. The ñame grows to enormous size and is considered to be the "king" of tubers.

Otaheite Apple This pear-shaped apple ranges from pink to ruby red in color. This fruit is usually eaten fresh, but also poached in wine, or juiced and served as a beverage.

Papaya Also known as "pawpaw" in Jamaica. Green papaya is often used as an ingredient in chutney or relishes and as a main dish when stuffed. When ripe, it is yellow or orange and eaten as a melon, or served in fruit salad.

Passion Fruit, Maracudja, Granadilla Oval-shaped fruit that has a tough shell and a color range from yellow-purple to eggplant to deep chocolate. The golden-yellow pulp is sweet and it must be strained to remove the seeds. Used in juices, desserts, drinks, and sauces.

Picadillo Spicy Cuban hash, made of ground beef and cooked with olives and raisins.

Pickapeppa Sauce This sauce, manufactured in Jamaica at Shooters Hill near Mandeville, is a secret combination of tamarind, onions, tomatoes, sugar, cane vinegar, mangoes, raisins, and spices. Since 1921 the company has produced this savory sauce, which has won many awards and is distributed throughout North America. The sauce is aged in oak barrels for a minimum of one year.

Saltfish Saltfish is any fried, salted fish, but most often cod. With the increasing availability of fresh fish all over Jamaica, some cooks are moving away from this preserved fish, which originated in the days before refrigeration. Still, Jamaicans have a soft place in their hearts for the taste of this salted cod (sold around the world in Italian, Spanish, and Portuguese markets under some variant of the name *bacalao*). Ackee and saltfish is the preferred breakfast of Jamaicans. When imported saltfish is unavailable, Jamaicans have been known to make their own from fresh fish.

Sofrito A seasoning staple, there are many variations. Most contain pork, lard, green peppers, tomatoes, onions, and coriander. Typically they are prepared in advance and stored under refrigeration. The word comes from a Spanish verb that means "to fry lightly."

Soursop, Corossol, Guanabana Elongated, spike-covered fruit, slightly tart and delicately flavored. It is used mainly in drinks, punches, sherbets, and ice cream.

Stamp and Go, Accra, or Baclaitos Spicy-hot fritters popular throughout the Caribbean. Methods, ingredients, and names vary from island to island.

Star Apple The local fruit is the main ingredient in a popular holiday dish called matrimony, a mix of star apple and oranges. It is similar to an orange but is made up of clear segments. The eight-pointed star that gives the name can be seen when the fruit is sliced.

Stinking Toe A pod that resembles a human toe, this fruit possesses a foul smelling rough exterior. The sugary power inside is eaten, or used in custards or beverages.

Sugar Apple, Sweetsop The flesh of the sweetsop is actually black seeds surrounded by sweet white pulp. The sweetsop is native to the tropical Americas.

Tamarind A large, decorative tree that produces brown pods containing a sweet and tangy pulp used for flavoring curries, sauces, and even beverages.

Yam Similar in size and color to the potato, but nuttier in flavor, it is not to be confused with the Southern sweet yam or sweet potato. Caribbean yams are served boiled, mashed, or baked.

Yautía A member of the taro root family, the yautía is the size of a potato, but more pear-shaped. It has a brown fuzzy outer skin. The flesh is white and slimy and is custard-like when cooked. It is one of the most natural thickeners, used to thicken soups, stews, and bean dishes. There is also a purple yautía, also called *mora*.

Yuca Root vegetable similar in length and shape to a turnip, with scaly yam-like skin. Universally made into flour for breads and cakes, and used as a base for tapioca.

Menus and Recipes from the Caribbean

Buljol

Flaked Saltfish (Trinidad) SERVES 4

The name is from the French *brule gueule*, meaning "to burn your mouth."

AMOUNT	MEASURE	INGREDIENT
$\frac{1}{2}$ pound	8 ounce, 224 g	Saltfish, boneless
2 tablespoons	1 ounce, 30 ml	Fresh lime juice
1 cup	6 ounces, 168 g	Cucumber, peeled and seeded, $\frac{1}{4}$ inch (.6 cm) dice
1 cup	4 ounces, 112 g	Onion, $\frac{1}{4}$ inch dice (.6 cm)
2 teaspoons		Garlic, minced
1 cup	6 ounces, 168 g	Tomato, peeled, seeded, $\frac{1}{4}$ inch (.6 cm) dice
2 tablespoons		Green onion, tops, minced
$\frac{1}{2}$		Scotch bonnet chile, seeded, minced
3 tablespoons	$1\frac{1}{2}$ ounce, 45 ml	Olive oil
1		Avocado, peeled and cut into 12 slices

PROCEDURE

1   Desalt the salt fish: cover with boiling water and allow to cool in the water. Drain. Remove any skin and bones. Shred the fish and cover again with boiling water, let cool. Drain and press out all the water.

2   Combine all the other ingredients except the avocado and mix well.

3   Add fish and toss well, refrigerate for at least two hours.

4   Serve with sliced avocado.

Yuca Mufongo with Cilantro Aioli Sauce (Puerto Rico)

SERVES 4

Yuca is also known as manioc or cassava.

AMOUNT	MEASURE	INGREDIENT
I pound	448 g	Fresh yuca
$\frac{1}{2}$ cup	$2\frac{1}{2}$ ounces, 70 g	Bacon, $\frac{1}{4}$ inch (.6 cm) dice
$\frac{1}{3}$ cup	$1\frac{1}{2}$ ounces, 42 g	Onion, $\frac{1}{4}$ inch (.6 cm) dice
I		Garlic clove, minced
I teaspoon		Oregano, dried ground
I tablespoon		Cilantro, minced
2		Eggs, beaten
I teaspoon		Adobo
To taste		Salt and pepper
As needed		All purpose flour
As needed		Oil for frying

PROCEDURE

1 Trim ends from fresh yuca and peel remainder, removing all waxy brown skin and pinkish layer underneath. Cut yuca into 3 inch thick pieces. Cover with salted water by 2 inches and boil until soft, but firm and almost translucent. Drain. Carefully halve hot yuca pieces lengthwise and remove thin woody cores. Mash until smooth.

2 Over medium heat, render the bacon until crisp.

3 Add the onions and garlic to bacon and cook 2 to 3 minutes or until soft.

4 Add mashed yuca, oregano, cilantro, and eggs; mix well.

5 Season with adobo, salt and pepper to taste.

6 Chill for 1 hour or until firm.

7 Preheat deep fat fryer to 350°F (175°C).

8 Shape two tablespoons of the mixture into balls. Roll in flour, shake off excess, and fry until golden brown. Drain on paper towels.

9 Serve hot or warm with Cilantro Aioli Sauce.

Adobo Spice Mix 1

YIELD: 2 OUNCES

AMOUNT	MEASURE	INGREDIENT
1 teaspoon	4 g	Coriander seeds, toasted and ground
1 teaspoon		Ground ginger
1½ teaspoons		Red pepper flakes, crushed
1 teaspoon		Turmeric, ground
1 tablespoon		Dry mustard
1 teaspoon		Nutmeg, freshly grated
1½ teaspoons		Cayenne pepper
1 teaspoon		Black pepper, freshly ground
1½ tablespoons		Kosher salt
1 tablespoon		Paprika
1 tablespoon		Sugar

PROCEDURE

1 Mix all ingredients together.

Adobo Spice Mix 2

YIELD: 2 OUNCES

AMOUNT	MEASURE	INGREDIENT
1 tablespoon	6 g	Garlic powder
1 tablespoon		Onion powder
1 tablespoon		Dried oregano, ground
½ teaspoon		Ground cumin
½ tablespoon		Salt
1 teaspoon		White pepper, freshly ground

PROCEDURE

1 Mix all ingredients together.

Cilantro Aioli Sauce

SERVES 4

AMOUNT	MEASURE	INGREDIENT
4		Garlic cloves, chopped
$\frac{1}{4}$ teaspoon		Salt
I cup	8 ounces, 240 ml	Mayonnaise, commercial or made with pasteurized eggs
2 tablespoons	I ounces, 30 ml	Fresh lime juice
2 tablespoons		Cilantro, leaves only, minced
To taste		Salt and pepper

PROCEDURE

1 Combine garlic and $\frac{1}{4}$ teaspoon salt; mash to a paste.

2 Combine garlic, mayonnaise, lime juice, and cilantro. Adjust seasoning.

3 Chill for 1 hour to blend flavors.

Jamaican Jerk Beef Steak

SERVES 4

AMOUNT	MEASURE	INGREDIENT
I $\frac{1}{2}$ pounds	24 ounces, 672 g	Skirt or flank steak
To taste		Salt and black pepper, freshly ground
2 tablespoons		Adobo spice mix I
I tablespoon		Fresh thyme, fresh, chopped
2 tablespoons	I ounce, 30 ml	White vinegar
$\frac{1}{4}$ cup	2 ounces, 60 ml	Olive oil

PROCEDURE

1 Season the meat with salt and pepper to taste.

2 Combine the adobo spice, thyme, vinegar and oil; whisk to combine well. Add meat and marinate 1 hour at room temperate or 2 to 3 hours under refrigeration.

3 Grill over high heat to desired temperature.

4 Slice and serve hot with *arroz mamposteao* and *mojo de amarilos*.

Jamaican Jerk Chicken

SERVES 4

AMOUNT	MEASURE	INGREDIENT
$\frac{1}{4}$ cup	2 ounces, 60 ml	Fresh lime juice
$\frac{1}{4}$ cup	2 ounces, 60 ml	Water
$3\frac{1}{2}$ pounds		Whole chicken, cut in half
2		Garlic cloves, minced
Jerk Marinade		
2 teaspoons		Jamaican pimiento, ground
$\frac{1}{2}$ teaspoon		Nutmeg, grated
$\frac{1}{2}$ teaspoon		Mace, ground
I teaspoon		Salt
I teaspoon		Sugar
2 teaspoons		Dried thyme
I teaspoon		Black pepper
I cup	4 ounces, 112 g	Green onions, chopped
I cup	4 ounces, 112 g	Yellow onion, chopped
I		Whole Scotch bonnet
2 tablespoons	I ounce, 30 ml	Vegetable oil

PROCEDURE

1 Preheat grill.

2 Combine lime juice and water and use to rinse chicken. Pat dry and rub with garlic.

3 Combine remaining ingredients in a blender, mortar, or food processor. Process ingredients to almost smooth and pour over chicken; marinate in refrigerator for at least 2 hours.

4 Remove chicken from marinade.

5 Grill, turning often, until fully cooked. Cut chicken into 8 to 12 pieces.

Arroz Mamposteao
Rice and Beans (Puerto Rico)   SERVES 4

AMOUNT	MEASURE	INGREDIENT
Green Sofrito Mix		
I cup	4 ounces, 112 g	Onion, $\frac{1}{2}$ inch (1.2 cm) dice
I cup	4 ounces, 112 g	Cubanelle pepper (Italian), $\frac{1}{2}$ inch (1.2 cm) dice
I cup	4 ounce, 112 g	Green bell pepper, $\frac{1}{2}$ inch (1.2 cm) dice
6		Garlic cloves, chopped
$\frac{1}{2}$ cup	I ounce, 28 g	Fresh cilantro, leaves only
2 tablespoons	I ounce, 30 ml	Water

PROCEDURE

1 Using a food processor, blender, or mortar and pestle, process all ingredients into a loose puree paste. Add additional water if necessary.

Bean Stew		
I cup	6 ounces, 168 g	Pink beans or red kidney beans (dried)
I cups	6 ounces, 168 g	Corned pork or smoked ham, I inch (2.4 cm) cubes
3 cups	24 ounces, 720 ml	Water

PROCEDURE

1 Soak the beans overnight in water. Drain.

2 Combine beans, pork, and water; bring to a boil, cover, and simmer gently until the beans are just tender, about 1 hour.

3 Drain, retaining beans and pork.

Garnish for Bean Stew		
2 tablespoons	I ounce, 30 ml	Oil
$\frac{1}{2}$ cup	2 ounces, 56 g	Onion, $\frac{1}{4}$ inch (.6 cm) dice
2		Garlic cloves, minced
I		Small hot red or green pepper, seeded, minced

3 tablespoons	$\frac{1}{2}$ ounce, 45 ml	Green sofrito
$\frac{1}{4}$ cup	6 ounces, 180 ml	Tomato sauce
I cup	8 ounces, 240 ml	Water
I cup	6 ounces, 168 g	West Indian pumpkin (calabaza) or Hubbard squash
2 teaspoons		Adobo spice mix (I or 2)

PROCEDURE

1 Heat the oil over medium heat, sauté onion and garlic until soft but not brown, 2 to 3 minutes.

2 Add pepper and sofrito; cook 2 minutes.

3 Add tomato sauce; cook 2 minutes.

4 Add cooked beans and pork mixture, water, squash, and adobo spice mix. Cook, uncovered, 15 to 20 minutes or until squash is cooked and sauce has thickened. Remove from heat and reserve.

Mamposteao Rice

2 tablespoons	I ounce, 30 ml	Corn oil
$\frac{1}{4}$ cup	2 ounces, 56 g	Chorizo, chopped
$\frac{1}{2}$ cup	2 ounces, 56 g	Bacon, chopped fine
$\frac{1}{3}$ cup	2 ounces, 56 g	Onion, $\frac{1}{4}$ inch (.6 cm) dice
2		Garlic cloves, minced
I tablespoon		Cilantro, minced
2 tablespoons		Green bell pepper, $\frac{1}{8}$ inch (.3 cm) dice
2 tablespoons		Red bell pepper, $\frac{1}{8}$ inch (.3 cm) dice
I cup	6 ounces, 180 ml	Bean stew
2 cups	8 ounces, 224 g	Cooked rice

PROCEDURE

1 Heat oil over medium heat; sauté chorizo and bacon for 2 to 3 minutes, until cooked.

2 Add onion and garlic; sauté for 3 minute or until soft.

3 Add cilantro and peppers; sauté for 3 minutes or until soft.

4 Add bean stew; cook 2 minutes.

5 Add rice, stirring constantly; cook 4 minutes until the consistency of a wet risotto.

Mojo de Amarilos

Ripe Plantain Chutney (Puerto Rico) SERVES 4

Chef Tip When peeling plantains (plátanos), moisten your hands and rub with salt to prevent the juices from sticking to your hands.

AMOUNT	MEASURE	INGREDIENT
2 tablespoons	1 ounce, 30 ml	Vegetable oil
1 cup	6 ounces, 168 g	Very ripe plantain, very yellow, almost orange, with black spots, peeled, $\frac{1}{2}$ inch (1.2 cm) dice
10		Cherry tomato cut in half
$\frac{1}{4}$ cup	1 ounce, 28 g	Red onion, 1 inch (2.4 cm) julienne
$\frac{1}{4}$ cup	1 ounce, 28 g	Red bell pepper, 1 inch (2.4 cm) julienne
$\frac{1}{4}$ cup	1 ounce, 28 g	Yellow bell pepper, 1 inch (2.4 cm) julienne
1		Garlic clove, thinly sliced
2 teaspoons		Golden raisins
$\frac{1}{4}$ cup	2 ounces, 60 ml	Olive oil
2 tablespoons		Fresh cilantro, leaves only
To taste		Salt and pepper

PROCEDURE

1 Heat oil over medium heat and sauté plantain until tender and brown.

2 Combine remaining ingredients except cilantro, salt, and pepper; simmer together for 5 to 6 minutes.

3 Add cilantro and correct seasoning. Serve warm to hot about 160°F (71°C).

Coo-Coo (Barbados)   SERVES 4

AMOUNT	MEASURE	INGREDIENT
3 cups	24 ounces, 720 ml	Water
To taste		Salt
1 cup	4 ounces, 112 g	Young okras, cut $\frac{1}{4}$ inch (.6 cm) thick
1 cup	$6\frac{1}{4}$ ounces, 175 g	Yellow cornmeal
2 tablespoons	1 ounce, 30 ml	Butter

PROCEDURE

1　Bring water and salt to a boil. Add okras and simmer, covered for 10 minutes.

2　Add cornmeal in a slow, steady stream, stirring constantly with a wooden spoon.

3　Cook over medium heat until mixture is thick and smooth, stirring constantly, 5 minutes.

4　Remove from heat and let stand 3 to 5 minutes.

5　Place on serving dish and spread butter on top.

Coco Quemado
Coconut Pudding (Cuba)   SERVES 4

AMOUNT	MEASURE	INGREDIENT
1½ cups	12 ounces, 336 g	Granulated sugar
¾ cup	6 ounces, 180 ml	Water
3 cups	9 ounces, 252 g	Grated coconut
3		Egg yolks, lightly beaten
1 teaspoon		Ground cinnamon
6 tablespoons	3 ounces, 180 ml	Dry sherry

PROCEDURE

1   Cook the sugar and water to syrup at the thread stage. When sugar syrup reaches this stage, a drop of boiling syrup forms a soft 2-inch thread when immersed in cold water. On a candy thermometer, the thread stage is between 230–234°F (110–112°C).

2   Add coconut, and then stir in egg yolks, cinnamon and sherry. Cook over low heat, stirring constantly until mixture is thick.

3   Pour into serving dish and brown the top under a broiler or with a torch.

4   Serve warm or chilled.

Run Down (Jamaica)   SERVES 4

AMOUNT	MEASURE	INGREDIENT
I pound	16 ounces, 448 g	Mackerel or shad fillets, or other oily fish, such as bluefish, mullet or pompano
$\frac{1}{4}$ cup	2 ounces, 60 ml	Fresh lime juice
I $\frac{1}{2}$ cups	12 ounces, 360 ml	Coconut milk
$\frac{1}{2}$ cup	2 ounces, 56 g	Onion, minced
$\frac{1}{2}$, or to taste		Scotch bonnet chile, seeded and minced
2		Garlic cloves, minced
I cup	6 ounces, 168 g	Tomato, peeled, seeded, $\frac{1}{2}$ inch (.6 cm) dice
2 teaspoons	10 ml	Apple-cider vinegar
I teaspoon		Fresh thyme leaves
To taste		Salt and black pepper

PROCEDURE

1 Marinate fish in the lime juice for 15 minutes.

2 Cook coconut milk over medium heat for 5 to 8 minutes or until it begins to turn oily.

3 Add onion, chile and garlic, cook 5 minutes or until onions are soft.

4 Add tomatoes, vinegar, and thyme and season with salt and pepper.

5 Drain the fish and add to the mixture. Cover and cook over low heat 8 to 10 minutes or until the fish flakes easily.

6 Serve hot with boiled bananas or roasted breadfruit.

Ensalada de Aguacate y Piña

Avocado and Pineapple Salad (Cuba)

SERVES 4

AMOUNT	MEASURE	INGREDIENT
$\frac{1}{4}$ cup	2 ounces, 60 ml	Olive oil
$\frac{1}{4}$ cup	2 ounces, 60 ml	Cider vinegar
$\frac{1}{4}$ cup	2 ounces, 60 ml	Fresh orange juice
$\frac{1}{4}$ cup	2 ounces, 56 g	Granulated sugar
To taste		Salt and pepper
4 cups	8 ounces, 224 g	Iceberg or Boston lettuce, shredded
I cup	6 ounces, 168 g	Fresh pineapple, $\frac{1}{2}$ inch (1.2 cm) cubes
I cup	4 ounces, 112 g	Sweet red onions, thinly sliced
I		Avocado, peeled, sliced $\frac{1}{4}$ inch (.6 cm) thick
4		Fresh lime wedges

PROCEDURE

1 Combine olive oil, vinegar, orange juice, and sugar in a blender until smooth. Season with salt and pepper.

2 Lightly toss together the lettuce, pineapple, and red onions. Dress with oil and vinegar mixture; adjust the amount used to taste.

3 Garnish individual salads with several avocado slices lightly seasoned with salt and pepper and a squeeze of lime juice. Serve with lime wedges.

Ensalada de Aguacate y Piña – Avocado and Pineapple Salad

Arroz con Pollo
Chicken and Rice (Puerto Rico)   SERVES 4

AMOUNT	MEASURE	INGREDIENT
1 $2\frac{1}{2}$ to 3 pound	1 1.12 to 1.34 kg	Chicken, cut into 8 pieces
2		Garlic cloves, minced
$\frac{1}{2}$ teaspoon		Ground oregano
2 teaspoons		Salt
$\frac{3}{4}$ teaspoon		Freshly ground black pepper
2 tablespoons	1 ounce, 30 ml	Red wine vinegar
2 tablespoons	1 ounce, 30 ml	Annatto oil (see recipe)
$\frac{1}{2}$ cup	3 ounces, 84 g	Longaniza (Puerto Rican pork or sausage) or ham, sliced $\frac{1}{4}$ inch (.6 cm) thick
$\frac{1}{2}$ cup	3 ounces, 84 g	Bacon, $\frac{1}{2}$ inch (1.2 cm) dice
1 cup	4 ounces, 112 g	Onion, $\frac{3}{4}$ inch (.6 cm) dice
1 cup	4 ounces, 112 g	Red bell pepper, $\frac{3}{4}$ inch (.6 cm) dice
2 tablespoons	1 ounce, 30 ml	Green sofrito
$\frac{1}{2}$ cup	4 ounces, 120 ml	Tomato sauce
1 cup	4 ounces, 112 g	Banana peppers, $\frac{3}{4}$ inch (.6 cm) dice
2 cups	14 ounces, 392 g	Long grain rice
2 tablespoons	$\frac{1}{2}$ ounce, 15 ml	Capers, rinsed
$4\frac{1}{2}$ cups	36 ounces, 1.08 l	Chicken stock

PROCEDURE

1   Wash the chicken and pat dry.

2   Mix together the garlic, oregano, salt, pepper, and vinegar; rub into the chicken pieces. Let stand 45 minutes.

3   Brown the chicken in the annatto oil until golden; remove and set aside.

4   Brown the longaniza and bacon. Drain off all but approximately 3 tablespoons ($1\frac{1}{2}$ ounces, 45 ml) fat.

5   Add onions and cook until soft, 3 minutes. Add red pepper sofrito, tomato sauce, and banana peppers; stir well and cook 2 minutes.

6   Add rice and stir to coat; cook stirring 2 minutes.

7   Add chicken pieces, capers, stock, and salt to taste. Bring to a boil. Lower heat to a simmer; cover and cook for 20 minutes or until the liquid has been absorbed and the rice and chicken are tender. Serve hot.

Annatto Oil

1 cup	8 ounces, 240 ml	Vegetable oil
$\frac{1}{2}$ cup	2 ounces, 56 g	Achiote seeds

PROCEDURE

1   Heat the oil over low heat, add seeds, and cook for 5 minutes, stirring occasionally, until a rich orange color. Cool, strain, and store, covered, in the refrigerator.

Arroz con Pollo – Chicken and Rice

Pepperpot Soup
(Jamaica) SERVES 4

AMOUNT	MEASURE	INGREDIENT
1 1/4 cup	8 ounces, 224 g	Lean beef stew meat, 1/2 inch (1.2 cm) dice
1/2 cup	3 ounces, 84 g	Corned beef or salt pork, 1/2 inch (1.2 cm) dice
1 quart	32 ounces, 960 ml	Water
4 cups	8 ounces, 224 g	Kale or collard greens, chopped
4 cups	8 ounces, 224 g	Callaloo or spinach, chopped
1/2 cup	2 ounces, 56 g	Onion, 1/4 inch (.6 cm) dice
1		Garlic clove, minced
1/2 cup	2 ounces, 56 g	Green onions, white and green parts, minced
1 teaspoon		Fresh thyme leaves
1		Green hot pepper, seedless, minced
1 cup	4 ounces, 112 g	Yam, peeled, 1/2 inch (1.2 cm) dice
1/2 cup	2 ounces, 56 g	Taro root, peeled, 1/2 inch (1.2 cm) dice
To taste		Salt and pepper
1 tablespoon	1/2 ounce, 15 ml	Butter
1 cup	4 ounces, 112 ml	Okra, sliced 3/4 inch (.6 cm) thick
1/2 cup	2 ounces, 56 g	Small cooked shrimp
1/2 cup	4 ounces, 120 ml	Coconut milk

PROCEDURE

1 Combine meat and water; simmer, covered for 1 hour.

2 Combine kale and callaloo with 2 cups (16 ounces, 480 ml) water in a separate pan and cook until tender, about 30 minutes. Puree kale, callallo and liquid, add to the cooked meat.

3 Add onion, garlic, green onions, thyme, pepper, yam, and taro root and season with salt and pepper. Cover and simmer until meats are tender and yam and taro are cooked, 30 to 45 minutes.

4 Heat butter over medium heat and sauté okra until lightly brown. Add to soup.

5 Add shrimp and coconut milk and simmer 3 to 5 minutes. Correct seasoning.

Sweet Potato Cake
(Martinique)   SERVES 4

AMOUNT	MEASURE	INGREDIENT
2 pounds	896 g	Sweet potatoes, peeled, thickly sliced
2 tablespoons	I ounce, 30 ml	Butter
¾ cup	6 ounces, 168 g	Brown sugar
¼ cup	2 ounces, 60 ml	Dark rum
4		Eggs
½ cup	4 ounces, 120 ml	Milk
2 teaspoons		Lime rind, grated
I tablespoon	½ ounce, 15 ml	Lime juice
½ teaspoon		Ground cinnamon
½ teaspoon		Ground nutmeg
½ teaspoon		Salt
2 teaspoons		Baking powder

PROCEDURE

1 Preheat oven at 350°F (176°C)

2 Cook sweet potatoes in just enough water to cover until tender, 20 to 25 minutes. Drain and mash.

3 While still warm mix in butter, sugar, and rum.

4 Beat in eggs, one at a time.

5 Add milk, grated rind, and lime juice.

6 Sift together cinnamon, nutmeg, salt, and baking powder. Add to sweet potatoes and mix thoroughly.

7 Pour into a greased 9 × 5-inch (22.5 × 12.5 cm) loaf pan.

8 Bake at 350°F (176°C) 1 hour or until a cake tester comes out clean.

9 Let cool 5 minutes, then turn onto a rack to cool.

Camarones Sofrito Shrimp in
Green Sofrito (Dominican Republic) SERVES 4

AMOUNT	MEASURE	INGREDIENT
$\frac{1}{4}$ cup	2 ounces, 60 ml	Butter
I cup	4 ounces, 112 g	Onion, $\frac{1}{4}$ inch (.6 cm) dice
I		Garlic clove, minced
I, or to taste		Scotch bonnet chile, seeded and minced
$\frac{1}{2}$ cup	2 ounces, 56 g	Celery, $\frac{1}{4}$ inch (.6 cm) dice
I cup	6 ounces, 168 g	Tomato, peeled, seeded, $\frac{1}{4}$ inch (.6 cm) dice
To Taste		Salt and pepper
$\frac{1}{2}$ teaspoon		Sugar
I tablespoon	$\frac{1}{2}$ ounce, 15 ml	Lime juice
I		Bay leaf
I tablespoon		Parsley, minced
$\frac{1}{2}$ cup	4 ounces, 120 ml	Green Sofrito (see *Arroz Mamposteao*)
I pound	448 g	Shrimp, 16–20 ct, shelled and deveined

PROCEDURE

1 Heat butter over medium heat, add the onion and garlic, and cook 2 minutes. Add chile and celery, cook 3 minutes, until celery is soft.

2 Add tomatoes, salt, pepper, sugar, lime juice, bay leaf, and parsley; simmer uncovered, until sauce is well blended and slightly reduced, 10 to 15 minutes.

3 In a separate pan heat the sofrito and stir in the shrimp; cook until the shrimp lose their translucency, about 3 minutes.

4 Serve shrimp on top of tomato sauce.

Sopa de Frijol Negro
Black Bean Soup (Cuba) SERVES 4

AMOUNT	MEASURE	INGREDIENT
Sofrito		
$\frac{1}{2}$ cup	2 ounces, 56 g	Green bell pepper, seeded, chopped
$\frac{1}{2}$ cup	3 ounces, 56 g	Tomatoes, peeled, seeded, chopped
$\frac{1}{2}$ cup	2 ounces, 56 g	Onion, chopped
2		Garlic cloves, chopped
2 tablespoons		Fresh cilantro leaves, chopped
I tablespoon		Fresh parsley, chopped
I $\frac{1}{2}$ tablespoons	$\frac{3}{4}$ ounce, 23 ml	Annatto oil
Soup		
2 ounces	56 g	Salt pork, minced
2 ounces	56 g	Lean Virginia ham, trimmed, minced
I teaspoon		Dried oregano, crushed
I $\frac{1}{2}$ cup	9 ounces, 252 g	Dried black beans, picked over and soaked
I teaspoon		Ground cumin
3 $\frac{1}{2}$ cups	28 ounces, 840 ml	Chicken or beef stock
To taste		Salt and pepper
Garnish		
$\frac{1}{4}$ cup		White onions, minced

PROCEDURE

1 Pound or process peppers, tomatoes, onions, garlic, cilantro and parsley to a paste.

2 Heat annatto oil and render the salt pork until crisp. Drain, reserve the oil and salt pork.

3 Return fat to medium-low heat, add the vegetable paste, and sauté 2 to 3 minutes, until vegetables are cooked but not brown. Add ham and cook 1 minute.

4 Drain and rinse beans. Add to sofrito along with the oregano, cumin, stock and seasoning. Stock should cover beans by 1 to 2 inches (2.4 to 4.8 cm).

5 Bring to a boil, lower heat, cover and simmer for $1\frac{1}{2}$ to 2 hours, until beans are very tender. Add additional stock if necessary.

6 Puree half the soup, combine and simmer 5 minutes.

7 Correct seasoning and serve with minced white onions.

Salad of Hearts of Palm with Passion Fruit Vinaigrette (Puerto Rico)   SERVES 4

Fresh hearts of palm are available in Cryovac bags and will last up to two weeks in a refrigerator. Canned hearts of palm may be substituted for fresh.

AMOUNT	MEASURE	INGREDIENT
1 tablespoon	$\frac{1}{2}$ ounce, 15 ml	Passion fruit puree
$\frac{1}{4}$ cup	2 ounces, 60 ml	Red wine vinegar
$\frac{1}{8}$ teaspoon		Dijon-style mustard
$\frac{1}{2}$ cup	4 ounces, 120 ml	Olive oil
To taste		Salt and pepper

PROCEDURE

1   Combine puree, vinegar, and Dijon mustard. Gradually add olive oil, whisking continuously. Correct seasoning.

AMOUNT	MEASURE	INGREDIENT
12		Tomato wedges, peeled
2 cups	12 ounces, 336 g	Fresh hearts of palm, $\frac{1}{2}$ inch (1.2 cm) dice
$\frac{1}{2}$ cup	2 ounces, 56 g	Red bell pepper, $\frac{1}{4}$ inch (.6 cm) dice
$\frac{1}{2}$ cup	2 ounces, 56 g	Green bell pepper, $\frac{1}{4}$ inch (.6 cm) dice
3 cups	6 ounces, 168 g	Boston lettuce leaves, washed, dried, torn
$\frac{1}{2}$ cup	2 ounces, 56 g	Red onion, cut into very thin rings, soaked in ice water for 30 minutes, drained, and patted dry
$\frac{1}{3}$ cup	2 ounces, 56 g	Queso fresco

PROCEDURE

1   Toss tomato wedges with 2 tablespoons of vinaigrette and let stand at least 30 minutes.

2   When ready to assemble salad, combine hearts of palm and red and green bell pepper; toss with a little vinaigrette.

3   Toss lettuce with dressing and place on salad plate. Arrange 3 tomato wedges on each plate. Top lettuce with hearts of palm mixture. Arrange a few sliced onions over salad and sprinkle with queso fresco.

Tamarind Balls (Jamaica) SERVES 4

Tamarind is one of the legacies brought to the Caribbean region by the indentured Indian servants, who replaced the enslaved Africans.

AMOUNT	MEASURE	INGREDIENT
$\frac{1}{2}$ cup	4 ounces, 120 ml	Tamarind paste with seeds
$3\frac{1}{4}$ cups	23 ounces, 644 g	Granulated sugar

PROCEDURE

1 Combine the tamarind paste and 1 pound ($2\frac{1}{4}$ cups, 448 g) sugar on a worktable and knead to together until the mixture is light in color and the majority of the sugar is absorbed.

2 Roll 1 tablespoon ($\frac{1}{2}$ ounce, 15 ml) of the mixture into a ball around one or two of the tamarind seeds (if using). Proceed until all the paste has been used.

3 Spread the remaining sugar on the worktable and roll each ball in sugar until coated.

4 Store in an airtight container.

Stuffed Dates (Curacao) SERVES 4

AMOUNT	MEASURE	INGREDIENT
$\frac{1}{2}$ cup	$2\frac{1}{2}$ ounces, 70 g	Walnuts, chopped fine
$\frac{1}{2}$ cup	3 ounces, 84 g	Dried apricots, minced
1 to 2 tablespoons	$\frac{1}{2}$ to 1 ounce, 15 to 30 ml	Water
24		Dates (Medjool), pitted

PROCEDURE

1 Mix together the walnuts, apricots, and water and spoon 1 teaspoon of the mixture into each date. Do not overfill.

2 Serve at room temperature.

Curried Kid or Lamb
(Trinidad) SERVES 4

AMOUNT	MEASURE	INGREDIENT
1 tablespoon	$\frac{1}{2}$ ounce, 15 ml	Lime juice
1		Lime, cut into quarters
1 tablespoon		Coarse salt
1$\frac{1}{2}$ pounds	24 ounces, 672 g	Boneless lean lamb or goat, 1$\frac{1}{2}$ inch (3.6 cm) cubes
2 tablespoons	1 ounce, 30 ml	Vegetable oil
1 cup	4 ounces, 112 g	Onion, $\frac{3}{4}$ inch (.6 cm) dice
2		Garlic cloves, minced
2 teaspoons	10 ml	Tarmarind pulp
1 cup	4 ounces, 112 g	Green mango, peeled, $\frac{1}{2}$ inch (1.2 cm) dice (optional)
1 tablespoon		Curry powder
1 or $\frac{1}{2}$, to taste		Habanera pepper, seeded and minced
1 cup	6 ounces, 168 g	Tomatoes peeled, seeded, $\frac{1}{2}$ inch (1.2 cm) dice
1 cup	8 ounces, 240 ml	Vegetable or chicken stock
1 cup	6 ounces, 168 g	Potatoes, peeled, $\frac{1}{2}$ inch (1.2 cm) dice
1 cup	6 ounces, 168 g	West Indian pumpkin (calabaza) or Hubbard squash, peeled, $\frac{1}{2}$ inch (1.2 cm) dice
$\frac{1}{2}$ cup	3 ounces, 84 g	Chayote, peeled, $\frac{1}{2}$ inch (1.2 cm) dice
1 tablespoon		Fresh thyme, chopped
1 teaspoon		Lime juice
To taste		Salt and pepper
As needed		White rice, cooked
As needed		Fried ripe plantains (recipe follows)

PROCEDURE

1 Combine the 1 tablespoon lime juice, lime quarters, coarse salt, and meat with 1 cup of water. Cover and allow to stand for 30 minutes. Drain and pat dry.

2 Heat oil over medium-high heat and brown the meat on all sides. Remove meat.

3 Add onions; cook 3 to 4 minutes until golden brown. Add garlic, tamarind pulp, mango, curry powder, and habanera pepper. Cook, stirring, for 3 to 4 minutes. Add tomatoes and

cook 2 minutes. Return meat to mixture; cook 2 to 3 minutes to make sure the meat is coated with spice mixture. Add the stock.

4   Bring to a boil, reduce to a simmer, cover, and cook 30 minutes.

5   Add potatoes, calabaza, and chayote; correct salt. Cover and simmer 30 minutes or until meat and vegetables are tender. Stir in the fresh thyme, 1 teaspoon lime juice and correct seasoning.

6   Serve hot with rice and fried ripe plantains.

Fried Ripe Plantains
(All Islands) SERVES 4

Ripe plantain skins are quite black. If bananas are used as a substitute, use ripe but still firm bananas and be sure the skins are yellow, not black.

AMOUNT	MEASURE	INGREDIENT
2 large		Ripe plantains
As needed		Butter or oil

PROCEDURE

1. Cut off ends of the plantains, peel, and halve lengthwise.
2. Slice in half crosswise, yielding 8 slices.
3. Heat butter or oil over medium heat. Add slices and sauté until browned on both sides. Drain on paper towels and serve hot.

Tostones Twice-Fried Plantains
(All Islands) YIELD: 12 TO 16 TOSTONES

AMOUNT	MEASURE	INGREDIENT
2		Large green plantains
As needed		Salted water
As needed		Oil for frying
To taste		Kosher salt and freshly ground black pepper

PROCEDURE

1 Cut off about 1 inch (2.4 cm) from both ends of plantains. Make 2 lengthwise cuts at opposite ends.

2 Cover with very hot water for 5 to 10 minutes to help loosen the peel. Drain.

3 Hold the plantain steady with one hand and use the other hand to slide the tip of the knife under the skin and begin to pull it away, going from top to bottom.

4 Cut into diagonal slices 1 to $1\frac{1}{2}$ inch (2.4 to 4.8 cm) thick. Soak the slices in salted water for 30 minutes. Drain and pat dry.

5 Heat 2 inches (4.8 cm) oil over medium heat to 350°F (176°C) and sauté the pieces until tender, 3 to 4 minutes; do not let them get crusty on the outside. Drain on absorbent paper.

6 While they are still warm, lay a sheet of parchment paper, waxed paper, or a clean towel over the slices and flatten until half as thick.

7 When ready to serve, refry at 375°F (190°C) until golden. Drain on absorbent paper, season, and serve.

Roasted Breadfruit
(Barbados)   SERVES 4

Chef Tip **Breadfruit is cooked and handled like a potato.**

AMOUNT	MEASURE	INGREDIENT
1 medium		**Breadfruit**

PROCEDURE

1   Roast breadfruit over charcoal grill or directly over a gas burner.

2   Turn the fruit as it begins to char. Cook on all sides till brownish black. This process can take up to 1 hour.

3   When steam starts to escape from the stem end, the breadfruit is done. Or use skewer to check if cooked.

4   Remove from grill and peel off skin.

5   Cut in half.

6   Cut out the "heart" (inedible portion in the middle).

7   Cut breadfruit into appropriate size pieces. Serve hot.

8   To bake, place breadfruit in a baking pan, with water covering the pan bottom. Bake at 350°F (176°C) one hour or until tender.

Stewed Conch
(Cayman Islands)   SERVES 4

AMOUNT	MEASURE	INGREDIENT
1 pound	448 g	Conch meat, fresh or frozen
$\frac{3}{4}$ cup	2 ounces, 60 ml	Lime juice
To taste		Salt and pepper
8 ounces	224 g	Salt pork, $\frac{1}{2}$ inch (1.2 cm) cubes
3 cups	24 ounces, 720 ml	Coconut milk
1 cup	6 ounces, 168 g	Green plantain, peeled, sliced $\frac{1}{2}$ inch (1.2 cm) slices
1 cup	6 ounces, 168 g	Yuca, peeled, 1 inch (2.4 cm) cubes
1 cup	6 ounces, 168 g	Yam, peeled, 1 inch (2.4 cm) cubes
1 cup	6 ounces, 168 g	Sweet potato, peeled, $\frac{1}{2}$ inch (1.2 cm) cubes
$\frac{1}{2}$ cup	3 ounces, 112 84	Breadfruit, peeled, 1 inch (2.4 cm) cubes (optional)
1 tablespoon		Fresh thyme, minced
2 teaspoons		Fresh basil, minced

PROCEDURE

1   Marinate conch in the lime juice for 30 minutes. Drain, rinse, and then tenderize the conch meat by pounding it with a meat mallet. Cover with water, season with salt and pepper, and simmer for 10 minutes. Drain and cut into 1 to $1\frac{1}{2}$-inch (2.4 to 3.6 cm) pieces.

2   In a separate pan, cook salt pork in water to cover for 20 minutes to remove the salt.

3   Combine conch, salt pork, and coconut milk over medium heat; bring to a boil, then lower to a simmer.

4   Add plantain, yuca, yam, and sweet potato; cook 25 minutes. Add breadfruit, adjust seasoning, and cook until everything is tender, about 20 minutes.

5   Add thyme and basil, stir, and adjust seasonings. Serve hot.

Japan

The Land

Japan is a small nation of more than 3,000 scattered islands off the eastern coast of mainland Asia. The Japanese call it *Nippon,* which means "source of the sun"; others call it "Land of the Rising Sun." It is an archipelago, or chain of islands, including four major islands—Hokkaido, Honshu, Shikoku, and Kyusha—and thousands of smaller ones that lie scattered along a southwest to northeast axis of nearly 3,000 miles. Historically, its location isolated the country from the rest of the world. Considering the country's physical geography, its history, and its huge population, Japan has had to overcome many obstacles to achieve its present-day place among major world nations.

Japan is located in a region of geologic instability known as the Pacific Ring of Fire. This region includes approximately 100 active volcanoes and as a result it averages about 1,500 earthquakes each year. Japan is also subject to floods, blizzards, and typhoons that sweep over the islands each year. And volcanic events occurring on the ocean floor can cause devastating tsunamis. Although no longer active, the most recognized of Japan's volcanoes is Mount Fuji. This cone-shaped peak rises 12,388 feet above the Kanto Plain, about 70 miles southwest of Tokyo.

The small valleys of flat land and narrow coastal plains support much of Japan's population and economy. Japan's population is over 127 million people, all of whom occupy an area slightly smaller than the state of California.

History

In 1543, Portuguese traders arrived at one of the small islands of Japan and offered to exchange "what they had for what they did not have." The Japanese were eager for trade and soon Portuguese traders and Jesuit missionaries arrived in increasing numbers, followed by the Dutch and the English. During this time the Shogun (the emperor's commander in chief) Tokugawa Ieyaso, with the aid of the English sailor Will Adams as naval advisor, worked to unify the country.

More than a hundred years later, the Shogun, fearing too much Western influence, closed Japan to "foreigners." During this time Japan was able to develop in its own way. Two hundred years later, when Commodore Matthew Perry of the U.S. Navy demanded reopening of trade in 1853, Japan was again ready to face the West.

Under the modern thinking of Emperor Meiji, Japan soon became a power in the Far East, defeating imperial China and Russia in the late nineteenth and early twentieth centuries. Then an expanding need for raw materials not available set Japan on a course of conquest of Asia and the islands of the Pacific, ultimately leading to their role in World War II. In 1945, Japan was defeated by the United States and its Allies, and occupying American troops helped rebuild its cities and industries.

Today, Japan has one of the most successful economies of any non-Western nation.

The People

Few places in the world are as crowded as Japanese cities. Over 98 percent of the country's inhabitants are ethnic Japanese. Koreans make up the largest group of immigrants and there are small numbers of Chinese, Brazilians, Filipinos, and Americans living in the country.

Religious beliefs and practices in Japan primarily revolve around two faiths: Shintoism and Buddism. Originating in ancient times, Shinto is the polytheistic (believing in many gods) religion of Japan. Followers of Shinto worship their ancestors, offer prayers, and observe various rituals. They believe that *kami* (the many gods of Shinto) control the forces of nature and the human condition, including creativity, sickness, and healing. Because the followers of Shinto believe that the *kami* live in shrines, they erect places of worship in their homes as well as in public places. These structures are often quite extensive, involving several buildings and gardens, to which people make pilgrimages. Buddhism, which originated in India and reached Japan from Korea in the sixth century A.D., focuses on enlightenment and meditation.

Chanoyu has been referred to as the "Japanese Tea Ceremony" for many years but the word literally means hot water for tea. The simple art of Chanoyu is really a synthesis of many Japanese arts with the focus of preparing and serving a bowl of tea with a pure heart. Tea was first introduced to Japan from China with Buddhism in the sixth century. It wasn't until 1191 that tea really took hold in Japan with the return from China of the Zen priest Eisai (1141–1215). Eisai, the founder of the Rinzai sect of Zen Buddhism in Japan, introduced powdered tea and tea seeds that he brought back with him from China. The tea seeds were planted at the Kozanji temple in the hills northwest of Kyoto. The tea master Sen Rikyu developed *wabicha,* or the style of tea that reflects a simple and quiet taste. It is this simple style of tea that is practiced and taught in Japan and throughout the world today. The principles of *Wa Kei Sei Jaku* (harmony, respect, purity, and tranquility) are the principles that practitioners of Chanoyu integrate into their study of tea and into their daily lives. The tea ceremony varies according to the seasons, with tea bowls, types of tea, flowers, and scrolls carefully chosen.

The Food

Rice is Japan's most important crop and has been cultivated by the Japanese for over 2000 years. Japanese rice is short grain rice that becomes sticky when cooked. Most rice is sold as *hakumai* ("white rice"), with the outer portion of the grains (*nuka*) polished away. Unpolished rice (*gemmai*) is considered less desirable. A second major rice variety used in Japan is *mochi* rice. Cooked mochi rice is more sticky than conventional Japanese rice, and it is commonly used for *sekihan* (cooked mochi rice with red beans) or pounded into rice cakes. The rice cakes are traditionally eaten on New Year's day and are usually grilled and then served in a soup or wrapped in nori seaweed. Rice flour is used in various Japanese sweets (*wagashi*) and rice crackers (*sembei*). Daifuku is sweetened red bean paste wrapped in rice flour dough, and *kushi-dango* are rice flour dumplings on skewers. Rice is also used to produce vinegar. Rice wine is commonly known as sake which is the general term for "alcohol" in Japanese.

The importance of rice in the daily diet is revealed in the word *gohan,* which means both "cooked rice" and "meal." This word is extended to *asagohan* (breakfast), *hirugohan* (lunch), and *bangohan* (dinner). A traditional Japanese breakfast is a bowl of rice, *miso* (fermented soy paste) soup, a plain omelet, some dried fish, and pickled vegetables. Lunches are light, often consisting of noodles (*soba* made from buckwheat or *udon* made from wheat), *domburi mono* (a bowl of rice with vegetables, meat, or eggs on top), or a *bento box.* Dinner is a bowl of rice, *miso* or *dashi* soup (a stock made from kelp and dried bonito flakes), a small portion of protein, vegetables, pickled vegetables, and a dessert (usually a seasonal fruit).

Japan

So close to the sea where warm (*kurosio*) currents meet with cold (*oyashio*), the area is home to some of the world's richest fishing grounds. Fish is a main element in the Japanese diet and is eaten in a variety of preparations: steamed, fried, boiled, broiled, and raw.

Preserving fish also became popular and sushi originated as a means of preserving fish by fermenting it in boiled rice. Salted fish was placed in rice and preserved by lactic acid fermentation, which prevents growth of the bacteria that bring about putrefaction. This older type of sushi is still produced in the areas surrounding Lake Biwa in western Japan, and similar types are also known in Korea, southwestern China, and Southeast Asia. A unique fifteenth-century development shortened the fermentation period of sushi to one or two weeks and made both the fish and the rice edible. As a result, sushi became a popular snack food. Sushi without fermentation appeared during the 1600s, and sushi was finally united with sashimi at the end of the eighteenth century, when the hand-rolled type, *nigiri-sushi,* was devised.

In the thirteenth century, Zen monks from China popularized a form of vegetarian cuisine known in Japan as *shojin ryori.* The practice of preparing meals with seasonal vegetables and wild plants from the mountains, served with seaweed, fresh soybean curd (or dehydrated forms), and seeds (such as walnuts, pine nuts and peanuts) is a tradition that is still alive at Zen temples today. Stemming from the Buddhist precept that it is wrong to kill animals, including fish, *shojin ryori* is completely vegetarian. Buddhism prescribes partaking of a simple diet every day and abstaining from drinking alcohol or eating meat. Such a lifestyle, it is thought, together with physical training, clears the mind of confusion and leads to understanding.

In the sixteenth century the Portuguese traders, followed by the Dutch, began to introduce foods such as sugar and corn that were adopted by the Japanese. The use of fried foods such as tempura might seem to be unusual since a scarcity of meat and dairy products in the Japanese diet meant that oil was not commonly used for cooking. However, tempura was enjoyed by many people and is now used for a wide variety of seafood, meats, and vegetables.

Buddhist influences and cultural factors caused Japanese emperors to ban consumption of beef and meat from other hoofed animals in Japan for more than a thousand years until the Meiji Restoration in 1868. It is thought that before this time, Japanese soldiers, involved in many armed conflicts over the years, were fed beef to strengthen them for battle. When the soldiers came home from war, they brought their appetite for beef with them. Village elders believed that consuming beef inside the house was a sacrilege, a desecration of the house, and an insult to their ancestors. Thus young men were forced to cook their beef outside on plowshares (this process became known as *sukiyaki,* which literally means *plow cooking*) until the Meijii Restoration finally relaxed the restriction against eating beef. During the Meiji Restoration the new emperor went as far as staging a New Year's feast in 1872 designed to embrace the Western world. It had a European emphasis and for the first time in over a thousand years, people publicly ate meat.

Kobe beef is a legendary delicacy of Japan that comes from the capital city of Kobe in the Hyogo prefecture (province) of Japan. Cattle were first introduced into Japan around the second century, brought in from the Asian mainland via the Korean Peninsula. The *stop here*

cattle provided a much-needed source of agricultural power, power to pull the plows for the cultivation of rice, power for the growth of a nation. The Shikoku region received the first imports, but because of rugged terrain and difficult traveling in the region, further migration of the cattle was slow. The cattle were in isolated areas, each essentially a closed population. These herds were developed with an emphasis on quality.

Very protective of the breed, Japan went so far as to have the Wagyu classified as a national treasure. Wagyu produce consistently marbled, low-cholesterol carcasses, recognized as the world's finest, unmatched for flavor, tenderness, and overall eating quality. Wagyu is the Japanese breed of cattle used to produce Kobe, Matzukya, and Hokkido beef and is similar to the Hereford, Holstein, and Angus breeds. In order to earn the designation "Kobe beef," the Wagyu beef must come from the Hyogo province and meet strict production standards imposed by the industry. In Japan, Kobe beef is occasionally eaten as sushi, but is more frequently eaten as sukiyaki or steak. To cook a Kobe steak properly one should use high heat to sear the steak for a short amount of time. Since the fat is what gives Kobe beef its exquisite flavor, it is important to cook the steak only to medium rare (at most), since anything more would cause all of the fat to melt away. Most recipes recommend cooking a Kobe steak on the grill or a cast-iron pan, and seasoning only with salt and pepper.

Nabemono dishes are a hearty wintertime specialty, prepared from fish, seafood, chicken, meat and/or vegetables in a bubbling cauldron at the table. Serving trays piled high with raw ingredients arrive at the table, then everyone begins cooking, finally eating together out of the communal pot. There are many different types of nabemono, depending on the ingredients used. Oysters, scallops, cod, salmon, and chicken are all popular. *Chanko-nabe*, a variety made with chicken, seafood, potatoes, and other vegetables, is the staple diet of Japan's sumo wrestlers. Another special type of nabemono is beef sukiyaki.

Grilled *unagi* (eel) is a delicacy in Japan. The cooking process is what makes the eel both crisp and tender: the eels are first grilled over hot charcoal, then steamed to remove excess fat, then seasoned with a sweetish sauce and grilled a second time. The ingredients in the sweet basting sauce differs depending on the family or restaurant. Fancy unagi restaurants keep tanks full of live eels.

Yakitori itself means broiled chicken. Various cuts of chicken, including heart, liver, and cartilage are cooked on skewers over a charcoal grill. Also cooked this way are an assortment of vegetables such as green peppers (*piman*), garlic cloves (*ninniku*) and onions (*negi*). They are flavored using either a tangy sauce (*tare*) or salt (*shio*).

Okonomiyaki restaurants serve large, savory pancakes made with diced seafood, meat, and vegetables. It is topped with a special sauce and mayonnaise and sprinkled with nori and dried fish flakes (*katsuobushi*). Variations include adding a fried egg or soba. The okonomiyaki style of cooking originated in Osaka and is very popular around the country,

Oden is a very simple stew made by simmering fish dumplings, fried tofu, eggs, and vegetables in a kelp based stock for several hours. Sides include daikon (white radish), potatoes, kelp, transparent cakes made from *kon'nyaku* (devil's tongue starch) and *fukuro* (fried tofu pouches stuffed with chopped mushrooms and noodles). There is also a selection of fish cakes such as *chijuwaw*—made by molding fish paste into a tubular shape, steaming it, and finally grilling it. The fish cakes are made from fish that are not popular on their own, such as shark, flying fish, and pollack. *Kaiseki ryouri* is Japanese formal cuisine. Today it is considered an art form that celebrates the harmony between food and nature, with an emphasis on flavors, textures, and colors. A traditional *kaiseki* meal consists of a set sequence of courses based on preparation techniques. One meal can consist of as many as 15 different courses featuring sashimi, tempura, fish and meat dishes, and tofu prepared in diverse traditional style and designed to please all of the senses. Everything, down to the timing of each course and the choice of ceramics is planned to perfection. An example of this meal would be: *sakitsuke* (hors d'ouvre), *zensai* (appetizer), *suimono* (clear soup), *sashimi* (slices of raw fish), *nimono* (stewed seafood and vegetables), *yakimono* (broiled fish), agemono (deep-fried seafood and vegetables), *sunomono* (vinegared seafood and vegetables) *gohan* (cooked rice), *tomewan* (miso soup), konomono (pickled vegetables) and *kudamono* or *mizugashi* (fruit). *Senscha* (green tea) is served before the meal. During and after the meal *hojicha* (roasted tea) is served. Dishes focus on seasonal ingredients, and *kaiseki* chefs give zealous attention to presentation.

Shippoku ryouri, the specialty cuisine of the city of Nagasaki, combines European, Chinese, and Japanese tastes. Although *shippoku* benefited from Chinese, Dutch, and Portuguese culinary influences, it was the original creation of the Chinese living in Nagasaki's Chinese quarters. While it was intended to entertain Japanese and Western visitors, it spread to common households and evolved into a feast that is presented in traditional Japanese restaurants even today. The primary characteristic of Shippoku cuisine is *jikabashi,* the seating of the diners around a lacquered round table on which the food is served in one dish, with all diners serving themselves. This creates an atmosphere of *omoyai* (sharing) and contributes to a harmonious atmosphere. In addition, even before the toast, it is customary for the host to signal the start of the meal with one phrase: "Please help yourself to the *ohire* broth." Varying according to the season, the menu includes *ohire* (clear fish soup); *sashimi* (raw fish); vinegared, cooked, fried, and boiled vegetables and meat; and at the end *umewan* (sweet red bean soup with a salted cherry blossom).

Glossary

Aburage Deep-fried tofu pouch. Before being deep-fried, the tofu is cut into thin sheets.

Akatogarashi Japanese dried red chile pepper, one of the hottest chile varieties in the world. It is sold in a powdered form, called *ichimi togarashi.*

The Bento Box

A *bento* box is a compact container designed to hold a single serving of rice and several side dishes. The earliest records of packed lunches in Japan date back to around the fifth century, when people going out to hunt, farm, or wage war took food along with them. They typically carried dried rice, which was eaten either in its dried state or after being rehydrated with cold or hot water, or rice balls.

Traditionally, people working outdoors—whether in the fields, in the mountains, on fishing boats, or in town—carried their lunches with them because they did not have time to go home for meals. These box lunches were built around such staples as white rice, rice mixed with millet, or potatoes, depending on the region.

During the Edo period (1603–1868), people considered *bento* an essential accompaniment to any outdoor excursions, including the theater. The *makunouchi bento,* which typically contains small rice balls sprinkled with sesame seeds and a rich assortment of side dishes, made its first appearance during this era. *Makunouchi* refers to the interval between the acts of a play, and the *bento* is said to have gotten its name from the fact that spectators ate it during intermission.

In the Meiji period (1868–1912), with the introduction of Japan's railway system, the *ekiben* ("station *bento,*" or box lunches sold at train stations) appeared. The first *ekiben*—rice balls with pickled apricots inside—was reportedly sold in 1885. *Ekiben* are still sold at Japanese train stations today in vast quantities.

Aji-no-moto Monosodium glutamate (MSG).

Atsuage Regular or firm tofu, deep-fried until the outside is crisp and golden brown; the inside remains white.

Azuki beans Tiny, reddish, purplish dried beans, cooked to a sweetened paste and used in a variety of ways; often used in Japanese sweets.

Beni shoga Red pickled ginger.

Bonito Tuna, also known as skipjack tuna.

Buta Pork.

Chutoro The belly area of the tuna.

Daikon A large white radish, crisp, juicy, and refreshing. Available year-round, daikon becomes sweeter during the cold season. The flavor differs slightly depending on the part of the root used. The upper part is sweeter and without bitterness, typically used for *daikon oroshi* (peeled and grated daikon), which accompanies deep-fried foods such as tempura and grilled oily fish and meat. The top part is also used in salads. The bottom half of the root has a mild and pleasant bitter taste. It is usually simmered until soft enough to be broken with chopsticks. Simmered daikon (*furofuki daikon*) is served very hot, with a flavored *miso* sauce.

Dashi Basic Japanese stock made with *kombu* and *katsuoboshi*.

Ebi Cooked shrimp. *Ami Ebi* shrimp is prepared by "curing" the shrimp in a mixture of citrus juices.

Edamame Green soybeans.

Fugu Puffer fish, considered a delicacy, though its innards and blood contain the extremely poisonous neurotoxin *tetrodotoxin*. In Japan only licensed fugu chefs are allowed to prepare fugu.

Futo-Maki Big, oversized sushi rolls.

Gari Pickled ginger (pink or white) served with sushi.

Ginnan Gingko nuts. Asian cooks like to use ginnan in desserts and stir-fries. They're available fresh (in the fall), canned, or dried in Asian markets. To prepare fresh nuts, remove the soft pale yellow nutmeat from the hard shell. Simmer the nuts in salted boiling water. The meat will turn a bright green color. Drain and peel off the skins; refresh under cold water. Ginnan are used in stir-fry, deep-fried, or added to simmered or steamed dishes or soups. Canned nuts have already been shelled, skinned, and boiled, but they're mealier than fresh nuts. Rinse them before using. Substitute blanched almonds or pine nuts.

Goma Sesame seeds, found in two colors: white and black. White sesame seeds contain more oil than black seeds and are used to produce sesame oil. Black sesame seeds have a stronger, nuttier flavor than the white variety. Sesame seeds are sold untoasted, toasted, toasted and roughly ground, and toasted and ground to a smooth paste, with a little oil from the seeds floating on top. Japanese sesame paste is similar to Middle Eastern *tahini*.

Goma Abura Sesame oil. Introduced to Japan by China during the eighth century. There are two types of sesame oil, one made with toasted seeds and the other with raw seeds. Sesame oil made with toasted seeds has a golden brown color and a rich, nutty flavor. It is the preferred type used in Japan. Sesame oil made with raw seeds is clear and milder in flavor. Japanese have also adopted a chile-flavored sesame oil, called *rayu*.

Hakusai Chinese cabbage, about ten inches in length and six inches across the base. The lower parts of the leaves are white and quite thick. The upper parts are light green, thin and wrinkled. Hakusai does not have a strong flavor, making it a very good match with rich flavored stocks. When cooked for only a short amount of time it has a crisp texture.

Hamachi Young yellowtail tuna, or amberjack.

Hanakatsuo Dried bonito, shaved or flaked.

Ichiban Dashi "First fish stock." This stock extracts the best flavor and nutrients from the *kombu* (kelp) and *katsuobushi* (bonito flake). A very short cooking time prevents the stock from becoming strongly flavored or yellowish.

Japan Green Teas First brought to Japan from China in the ninth century by Buddhist Monks, tea has become the beverage of choice in all of Japan. Tea may be divided into three groups, according to how the leaves are processed: unfermented, partially fermented, or fully fermented. Japanese tea is an unfermented type, also called green tea. In Japan, fresh-picked tea leaves are steamed, quickly cooled, and rolled by hand or machine while hot air blows them dry. This process helps to preserve the leaves' maximum flavor, to be released only when the tea is brewed.

Kabocha A winter squash shaped like a pumpkin, six to seven inches in diameter, with a thick, tough, dark green skin. It has a deep orange flesh; when cooked it becomes very sweet and creamy. As with other winter squash it is a versatile vegetable. Substitute pumpkin or butter nut squash.

Kaiware (Daikon Sprouts) These have a pleasantly bitter, refreshing taste and are eaten raw. Used in salads, rolled sushi, or as a condiment for sashimi or noodle dishes.

Kaki Persimmon, native to China and cultivated in Japan for centuries. Both sweet and astringent varieties are grown in Japan. Sweet *kaki* contains chemicals called tannins that produce the astringency in unripe persimmons. The ripening process inactivates the tannins, so the astringency disappears. These sweet varieties have a round and slightly flattened shape. Astringent *kaki,* which is shaped like an acorn, becomes less astringent when the fruit becomes very soft and mushy.

Kamaboko Imitation crab meat, used in California rolls and other *maki.*

Kanten (Agar-Agar) When *kanten* is cooked with liquid and cooled, it forms a gel that is very stable at relatively high temperatures.

Karashi General word for mustard; *wa-garashi* is the expression for Japanese mustard, which is hotter than Western mustard. *Wa-garashi* has a dark yellow color and a pleasant bitter flavor. Colman's English mustard can be a substitute.

Katsuobushi Dried bonito fish flakes. Bonito is a type of tuna, which is a member of the mackerel family, and one of the most important fish in Japanese cuisine. To make *katsuobushi* the tuna is filleted, boned, boiled, smoked, and dried in the sun to make a hard, woodlike block with a concentrated, rich, and smoky flavor. A special tool is used to flake the extremely hard chunks. Bonito shavings form the base for many Japanese sauces and stocks (such as dashi, made with bonito and seaweed). The flakes are frequently sprinkled over boiled or steamed vegetables and into soups.

Kinoko Mushrooms, literally meaning "child of a tree." Various mushrooms are used in Japanese cuisine. Some of the most popular ones are introduced below.

Bunashimeji. A firm-textured cultivated mushroom that is suitable for Japanese, Chinese, and Western-style cooking

Enokitake. Pale yellow mushrooms with long, slender stems and tiny caps, both of which are edible. Enokitake mushrooms have a faint but distinctive flavor: raw they have a pleasant, crisp bite; blanched they have a chewy texture.

Hiratake The Japanese name for oyster mushrooms. This mushroom looks, smells, and tastes like oysters,

Maitake Mushrooms popular in Japanese cuisine. They have a wonderful taste, crisp texture, and excellent aroma. Appearing to be a clump of small suspicious-looking fronds or petals, the *maitake* mushroom is firm and fleshy. Its aroma is somewhat similar to that of the oyster mushroom. Entirely edible, the flavor is mild and deliciously pleasant.

Matsutake Highly priced gourmet mushrooms that grow only in red pine forests. The mushrooms have a firm, chewy texture, and a spicy, clean smell and taste.

Shiitake Large meaty mushrooms with a distinctive, appealing "woody-fruity" flavor and a spongy, chewy texture, which allows it to partner with stronger flavors like beef, pork, and soy sauce.

Kombu A dark green long thick sea vegetable from the kelp family. Used frequently in Japanese cooking, it is an essential ingredient of *dashi.* Never wash or rinse before using. The speckled surface of the kelp is just natural salts and minerals, resulting in great flavor. *Kombu* contains significant amounts of glutamic acid, the basis of monosodium glutamate (MSG).

Kome Rice. More than 300 varieties of rice are grown in Japan. Japanese cuisine typically uses short-grain types that, when cooked, are faintly sweet and slightly sticky. Rice is the most important crop and has been cultivated by the Japanese for over 2000 years and it was once used as a currency. The Japanese word for cooked rice *(gohan)* also has the general meaning of "meal" and the literal meaning of breakfast *(asagohan)* is "morning rice."

There are three major types of *kome* typically used in Japanese cuisine:

Genmai Unpolished brown rice.

Haigamai Partially polished white rice.

Seihakumai Highly polished white rice, the most common type.

In addition to ordinary table rice, short-grain *mochigome,* glutinous rice or sweet rice, is popular.

Komezu Rice vinegar. A light and mild-tasting Japanese vinegar. An essential ingredient for making sushi rice and *sunomono* (vinegary salads). It has a lower acid level than Western vinegars. Vinegar is also known for its antibacterial properties and this is one reason komezu is often used in Japanese dishes that include raw fish, seafood, or meat.

Kyuri Japanese cucumber. This is a slender and long cucumber, about 8 inches, with a bumpy skin that is thick and dark green. Kyuri is very crispy to the bite, with very few seeds.

Menrui Japanese noodles, made from wheat and buckwheat flours, and mung-bean and potato starch. In Japan, rice flour is not used to make noodles.

Mirin A golden yellow, sweet, rich-textured rice wine with an alcohol content of about 14 percent. When used in cooking, it is frequently heated to cook off the alcohol before other flavoring ingredients are added. This technique is called *nikirimirin. Mirin* contributes a rich flavor and an attractive, glossy brown appearance.

Miso A fermented soybean paste made from a starter culture that includes either steamed rice or barley mixed with cooked beans and salt. When the beans ferment the taste is somewhat meaty or mushroom-like, with a texture of nut butters, but is not oily. Miso is used in a variety of ways: to flavor soups or stews, in marinades, and spread on items before cooking. The different types of grains used in production process yield three different kinds of *miso: komemiso* is made of rice and soybeans, *mugimiso* of barley and soybeans, and *mamemiso* nearly entirely of soybeans. The lighter-colored misos, called "white miso"(*shiro miso*), are made from soybeans. They are sweeter, milder, and more delicate than the darker misos. The darker-colored misos (*aka miso*) are made from red adzuki beans (*aka* means "red" in Japanese). It has a richer, saltier taste because it is allowed to ferment longer. *Aka miso* is a specialty of Hokkaido, the northern island of Japan. *Kuro miso* is a dark, almost black miso that is strong tasting and usually aged the longest. *Hinsu miso* is yellow miso that is readily available. *Mugi miso* is made with all barley and no soybeans, usually a medium brown color. All miso is nutrient dense and high in protein, containing live enzymes that aid in digestion.

Mitsuba Literally, "three leaves," often translated as "trefoil." This member of the parsley family has a flavor somewhere between sorrel and celery. Used in soups, eggs, custards, hot stews, and salads.

Mizuna A member of the mustard family, it grows in bunches of thin, snow-white stalks with light green leaves. Each leaf is about the size of an arugula leaf, but is deeply serrated. One of the few indigenous vegetables of Japan, *mizuna* means "water greens" because it is grown in fields that are shallowly flooded with water. May be pickled, eaten raw in salads, stir-fried, simmered, and used in hot-pot dishes.

Moyashi Bean sprouts. Sprouts grown from many different kinds of legume seeds—soybeans, mung beans, azuki beans, alfalfa, peas, and lentils—are generally known as moyashi. Japanese cuisine predominantly uses soybean sprouts, which have yellow heads and thick, snow-white stems. Mung bean sprouts have small green heads and thinner, longer stems and have become more commonplace. Neither soybean nor mung bean sprouts have a distinctive flavor; they are used more for their crisp texture. Bean sprouts are used in soups, stir-fries, and simmered preparations. Generally they are added at the very last preparation step.

Naganegi Literally, "long onion." These are nonbulbing onions 12–16 inches long and 1 inch at the base. Both the white and green parts are used in cooking. The white stem has a strong onion flavor when eaten raw, but becomes very mild and sweet when cooked. It is typically grilled or used in simmered dishes.

Nasu Japanese eggplant. A distinctive eggplant variety, it is short—about 4–5 inches–and slender. Less seedy than other eggplant varieties, it becomes very creamy when cooked. Eggplant is pickled, stir-fried, deep-fried, steamed, grilled, or simmered.

Niban Dashi A "second fish stock" prepared by simmering the kelp and dried bonito flakes used in preparing ichiban *dashi* in the same volume of fresh water. It will have a less refined flavor and a cloudy appearance, but is still good in everyday miso soups and simmered dishes where strong-flavored condiments or ingredients are incorporated.

Nira Chinese chives, also called garlic chives, for their mixed flavor of garlic and chives. These chives have long (up to 16 inches), flat, thin, dark green leaves. When quickly stir-fried, they become bright green and crisp in texture, with a garlicky flavor.

Nori Dried or roasted seaweed. Nori seaweed grows around bamboo stakes placed under water. When harvested it is washed, laid out in thin sheets, and dried. The best quality nori seaweed is glossy black-purple. It is typically toasted before using, which improves flavor and texture. To toast, simply pass the sheet of nori several inches over the heat until it turns from dark green to an even darker green. It only takes a few seconds to toast both sides. In Japan it is eaten for breakfast with a little soup and rice. Nori has two sides: one shinier than the other. When using to make *makizushi* (sushi rolls), roll them with the shiny side facing out.

Panko Japanese bread crumbs that are extremely crunchy.

Okara A by-product of the tofu making process, It is like a moist, white, crumbly sawdust. It is used in soups, stews, or as a side dish.

Renkon This is the root of the lotus or water lily plant, *hasu*. The root grows in sausage-like links and has longitudinal tubular channels, usually ten. When cut crosswise, the root has an attractive flowerlike pattern. Mild flavored when raw; when briefly cooked, it has a pleasant crunchy texture.

Sake Rice wine. The premiere Japanese alcoholic drink. Sake is often used in marinades for meat and fish to soften them as well as to mask their smell. In cooking, it is often used to add body and flavor to various *dashi* (soup stocks) and sauces, or to make *nimono* (simmered dishes) and *yakimono* (grilled dishes).

Sashimi Raw fish fillets.

Sato-Imo Taro is the root of a perennial plant that is found everywhere in tropical Asia. The shape varies from small and round to long and sticklike, with a snow-white flesh. It has no distinctive flavor, but has a pleasant, soft texture. Taro is traditionally simmered in a flavored broth, stewed with proteins, or added to soups. Taro will absorb the flavor it is cooked with. Taro must be washed, peeled, and parboiled before final preparation.

Satsuma-Imo Sweet potato. Originally from Central and South America, sweet potatoes were introduced by Spanish conquistadors to the Philippines; from there they reached China. They were introduced to Japan from China in the seventeenth century. The Japanese produce a very sweet and creamy sweet potato, with a bright, reddish purple skin. The meat is creamy white when uncooked and a bright yellow when cooked. North American sweet potatoes are less sweet and creamy; when cooked they are more watery. Yams may be the best substitute.

Shichimi-Tōgarashi A Japanese spice mixture made from seven spices. *Shichimi* means "seven flavors." It is not the same as Chinese five-spice mixture. The ingredients and proportions used will vary but usually include red pepper flakes, ground roasted orange or mandarin peel, yellow (aka white) sesame seed, black sesame seed or black hemp seeds or poppy seeds, sansho (Japanese pepper also known as Szechuan peppercorns), dark green dried seaweed flakes (nori), rapeseed, or chipi (dried mikan peel).

Shishitogarashi Small green pepper, literally "Chinese lion pepper." A 3-inch-long pepper resembling a miniature Chinese lion head. This pepper has been hybridized to remove most of the heat; it is a uniquely Japanese pepper variety. Shishitogarashi peppers are best when stir-fried or deep-fried. When not available, substitute green bell peppers.

Shiso Herb, a member of the mint family, tasting of cumin and cinnamon. The leaves are used to wrap sushi and as a garnish for sashimi.

Shoga Ginger. One of the oldest seasonings in Japan. It has a pleasant, sharp bite and fragrant bouquet, said to stimulate the appetite. Ginger suppresses undesirable odors from other foods. It is an important condiment for sashimi and sushi because of its antiseptic properties.

Shoyu (see Soy Sauce)

Shungiku Chrysanthemum leaves. These leaves are cultivated to be edible. They are slightly bitter and can be used raw or cooked. Substitute spinach, turnip greens, or mustard greens.

Soba These noodles, which were first called *sobakiri,* are now simply called soba. They are linguine-sized noodles that are hearty, healthy, and served both hot and cold. The quality of the soba noodle is dependent on how much other starchy material, such as wheat flour or yam flour, has been added to the buckwheat flour. Buckwheat, which is not a grain, lacks the gluten needed to form dough. A 100-percent buckwheat flour noodle would lack the "bite" of good pasta. Soba noodles are a regional food. The cooler the climate, the more fragrant and rich-tasting the buckwheat.

Chukasoba Literally, "Chinese-style soba noodles." They are a type of wheat noodle that contains no buckwheat flour, mixed with water and a naturally obtained alkaline agent called *kansui*. The *kansui* provides the noodles with their distinctive elasticity. These noodles are creamy yellow (although they contain no eggs), curly, and resilient in texture. They are served hot, with a richly flavored broth made from chicken and pork bones. The most famous dish made from these noodles and broth is *ramen*.

Harusame Potato starch noodles, slender and transparent, as thin and straight as angel-hair pasta.

Kishimen Flat wheat noodles similar to fettuccini, with a distinctive chewy bite. They are also served both hot and cold.

Ryokuto Harusame Mung bean noodles, clear, thin, wrinkled starch noodles.

Somen and Hiyamugi Thin wheat noodles. *Somen* are as thin as vermicelli, and *hiyamugi* are slightly thicker than *somen*. Both are summertime noodles, usually served cold, with a dipping sauce.

Udon The most popular of the wheat noodles. They are a thick, long, cream-colored, noodle that may be served hot or cold.

Soy Sauce Three types of soy sauce are used in Japanese cooking, which differ in color, flavor, and degree of saltiness.

Koikuchi shoyu, or simply *shoyu,* means brewed with wheat. It has a dark brown color, rich flavor, and complex aroma, with a salt content around 17 to 18 percent. Used in all types of preparations, it gives foods a dark brown color and rich flavor.

Tamari is made nearly entirely from soybeans, and only a small amount of water is added to the fermenting mixture. Tamari is thicker, with a dark brown color, rich in bean flavor and about as salty as regular *shoyu*. Tamari is preferred as a condiment or flavor enhancer rather than a basic cooking ingredient. Follow these key points when cooking with *shoyu:* cook it only for a short time. Brief cooking preserves its natural fragrance, flavor, and color. Because of its high salt content, it should be added toward the end of the cooking process. In stir-frying, *shoyu* is added at the end of the cooking.

Usukuchi shoyu, light-colored soy sauce, is produced by not roasting the wheat as much, and more salt is added to slow the fermentation. The resulting *shoyu* is lighter in color, less flavorful, and has a slightly higher salt content, about 19 percent. *Usukuchi shoyu* is used in recipes where a refined color and weak flavor are required.

Sushi The term is actually sweetened, pickled rice. Raw fish (*sashimi*) wrapped together with a portion of sushi rice is sold as *"sushi." Sushi* is the term for the special rice; in Japanese it is modified to *zushi* when coupled with modifiers that describe the different styles.

Takenoko Bamboo shoots. It is a member of the grass family. Bamboo shoots are young, new canes that are harvested for food before they are two weeks old or one-foot tall. Bamboo shoots are crisp and tender, comparable to asparagus, with a flavor similar to corn. However, fresh bamboo shoots are very difficult to find. Fresh shoots need to be peeled and cooked before using. Raw shoots are bitter tasting and hard to digest.

Tofu Soybean curd. This soft, cheeselike food is made by curdling fresh hot soy milk with a coagulant. Traditionally, the curdling agent used to make tofu is *nigari,* a compound found in natural ocean water, or calcium sulfate, a naturally occurring mineral. The curds then are generally pressed into a solid block.

> **Firm tofu** is dense and solid and holds up well in stir-fry dishes, soups, or on the grill—anywhere you want the tofu to maintain its shape. Firm tofu also is higher in protein, fat, and calcium than other forms of tofu.

> **Kōya-dofu** is freeze-dried tofu, which comes in flat, creamy white squares. When soaked in warm water it absorbs a large amount of liquid and takes on a slightly spongy texture. It has a mild but distinctive flavor. Reconstituted dried tofu has no resemblance to fresh tofu.

> **Silken tofu** is a Japanese-style tofu, with a mild, light, delicate taste. Unlike other types of tofu, the water is not pressed out of it, nor is it strained. A slightly different process that results in a creamy, custardlike product makes silken tofu higher in water content, so it does not hold its shape as well as firm tofu. Silken tofu works well in pureed or blended dishes and soups. In Japan, silken tofu is enjoyed "as is," with a touch of soy sauce and topped with chopped scallions.

> **Yaki-dofu** is tofu that has been grilled on both sides over charcoal, producing a firm texture.

Umami The elusive fifth flavor, translated from Japanese as "delicious," "savory," or "brothy." It refers to a synergy of intricate, balanced flavors. Umami is a taste that occurs when foods with glutamate (like MSG) are eaten.

Ume Japanese green plum. Typically pickled, ume is used as a base for preserves, or for *umeshu* (plum wine).

Wakame One of the most popular sea vegetables in the Japanese diet.

Wasabi Japanese horseradish, pale green in color with a delicate aroma; milder tasting than Western horseradish. *Wasabi* is similar to horseradish in its taste and culinary function but is unrelated. Wasabi grows in the water while horseradish grows in soil. Like ginger, wasabi has antiseptic properties, so it has traditionally been served with sushi and sashimi dishes. Wasabi also helps to promote digestion. Fresh wasabi root should be grated just before consumption; however, fresh is hard to obtain outside of Japan. Powdered or paste *wasabi* is more pungent than freshly grated root, and it is also less fragrant and flavorful. The paste form of wasabi, *neriwasabi,* comes in a tube ready to serve. Powdered wasabi, *konawasabi,* is a mixture of wasabi and horseradish powder; frequently mustard powder is added to increase the pungency and an artificial green color is added to simulate real wasabi.

Yuzu A tangerine-size variety of citron (citrus fruit), with a thick, bumpy rind. Like a lemon, yuzu is valued for both its juice and its rind, which has a pleasant tart and bitter flavor. Substitute lime or lemon rind and equal parts lime, orange, and grapefruit juice for *yuzu* juice.

KITCHEN TOOLS

Deba bocho A heavy-duty knife, similar to the chef's knife, with a thicker blade and a pointed tip. Used to chop fish heads and chicken bones.

Donabe Earthenware pot with lid, used directly for stovetop cooking (on a gas stove) or at the dinner table with a portable stove. It should not be used in an oven. Often used for *sukiyaki, oden,* and *shabu shabu.*

Fukin A thin, rectangular cotton cloth, 12 to 16 inches in length and 10 inches in width. Like cheesecloth, a *fukin* is used for a variety of purposes, including wrapping and forming cooked rice into shapes, lining a colander to strain stock, and squeezing excess water from tofu. A larger version of this is *daifukin.*

Hangiri Wooden sushi tub usually made of cypress wood, in the shape of a large circular plate with high sides. The large surface area cools the rice quickly, and the wood absorbs excess moisture. Used to mix rice with sugar and vinegar to make sushi rice.

Hocho Japanese knives. Most Japanese knives are made for cutting fish and green leafy vegetables only. They are thin-bladed knives not intended to cut root vegetables, winter squash, carrots, or anything else that might chip the blade. Except for *nakkiri bocho* and *bunka bocho,* only one side of the Japanese blade is ground to form the cutting edge, which is straight, not curved. These characteristics give Japanese knives a cleaner, quicker cut.

   Burka bocho All-purpose knives.

   Deba bocho A heavy knife with a sharp tip, used for fish.

   Nakkiri bocho Knives specifically for vegetables. The name derives from its function: *na* refers to "vegetable" and *giri* means "cut."

Ryuba Used to cut fish. *Ryuba* means "willow blade cutting edge."

Sashimi bocho Long, thin blade a bit more than an inch wide. Used to cut filleted fish for sushi and sashimi.

Takobiki Very long and thin blunt-tipped knife, traditional tool of the sushi chef, perfect for accurate slicing.

Usuba bocho A light and efficient knife designed for cutting vegetables, it resembles a basic cleaver, with a slightly rounded end. The straight blade edge is suitable for cutting all the way to the cutting board without the need for a horizontal pull or push.

Kushi Bamboo skewers used for preparing certain grilled Japanese dishes, such as *yakitori*. The cook continually turns the skewers so that the meat is evenly cooked and basted. For this reason, bamboo skewers are essential; steel skewers would become too hot to handle. The skewers are soaked in water for 30 minutes before use so they won't burn during cooking.

Makisu Bamboo rolling mats, made from thin pieces of bamboo tied together. Makisu are used to make sushi rolls (*makizushi*).

Oroshigane A steel grater with very fine spikes, used to grate *wasabi,* ginger, and *daikon* radish.

Oroshiki Porcelain grater, considered better than the metal grater (*oroshigane*), because it does not impart any metallic flavor to the food and is safer on the hands.

Oshizushi no kata Wooden sushi mold. Used when making pressed sushi, such as *oshizushi*. The rice and toppings placed in an *oshizushi no kata* are pressed, resulting in a pressed "cake."

Otoshibuta Literally "drop lid"—a lightweight round lid used to keep foods submerged. It ensures heat is evenly distributed and reduces the tendency of liquid to boil with large bubbles, thus preventing fragile ingredients from losing their original shape. Typically made from wood.

Ryoribashi Cooking chopsticks, typically 14 inches long. Normally, *ryoribashi* have a string at the top to tie the chopsticks together.

Shamoji A paddle made from wood or plastic, used to serve rice. Also used to stir sushi rice after adding sweetened vinegar and cooling. Nowadays, *shamoji* are usually made from plastic, since they are much easier to clean than their wooden counterparts.

Suribachi A bowl with a corrugated pattern on the inside, used as a mortar along with the *surikogi* (pestle) to grind sesame seeds into a paste. It is glazed ceramic on the outside and unglazed on the inside, often brown and beige in color.

Surikogi A wooden pestle, often made from cypress wood, shaped like a big cucumber. The grinder part to *suribachi* (bowl), which makes up the Japanese version of the mortar and pestle.

Wok For stir-frying. Japanese cuisine uses the traditional, round-bottomed Chinese wok.

Zaru A shallow bamboo basket used to drain, rinse, or dry foods. In the summer, cold soba noodles are served in a *zaru,* accompanied by a small bowl filled with dipping sauce, called *zaru soba.*

COOKING TERMS

Agemono Fish or vegetables fried in vegetable oil. The first cooking oil used in Japan was probably sesame oil, goma abura, introduced by the Chinese during the eighth century. However, the majority of deep-frying is now accomplished using refined, flavorless vegetables oils such as canola, soybean, cottonseed, or corn oils, or a combination of these.

There are two styles of deep-frying: tempura and *kara-age.* Tempura is batter frying, while kara-age uses no batter. Instead, ingredients are breaded or dusted with cornstarch and fried. The word *kara* refers to China, meaning that this method originated in Chinese cooking (*age* means deep-fried).

Daikon Oroshi Grated daikon. Many fried dishes, including tempura and grilled or broiled oily fish, are almost always served with grated daikon. Choose a radish that is heavy for its size, so it will be juicy. Grate only the top part, which is sweeter than the lower part.

Hana Ninjin Floral-cut carrots.

Hiya-Gohan Day-old rice, used in stir-frying or rice soup.

Itameru Stir-frying.

Katsura Muki A technique used with daikon, cucumber, and carrots to cut a continuous paper-thin sheet of flesh.

Mizukiri The process of removing excess water from tofu before it is used.

Momiji Oroshi Spicy grated daikon. *Momiji* means "autumn leaf color." To prepare *momiji oroshi,* make two deep holes on the cut surface of a disk of daikon, Insert one *skatog arashi* (Japanese dried red chile) into each hole. Grate the daikon and chile together, producing a slightly red, spicy *oroshi.*

Nabemono One-pot cooking, a specific style of Japanese preparation, with ingredients added in succession to a pot to cook and ultimately to be served from the cooking pot. The term is also used for simmered dishes. The technique is often applied to vegetables, chicken, and fish. Foods are typically cut into manageable pieces with chopsticks before they are simmered. The basic liquids used include *dashi* (fish stock), *kombu dashi* (kelp stock), water, or sake (rice wine). *Otoshibuta,* or "drop-lid," is frequently used in simmering.

Shiraga Negi Literally, "gray-hair long onion," the white part of Japanese long onion *(naganegi),* cut into very thin strips. These thin strips are soaked in ice water so they are crisp and curly. Used as a garnish.

Tamagoyaki Egg omelet, sweet and light. In Japan it is the trademark of each sushi chef.

Yakimono Foods (usually meat) that are grilled, broiled, or pan-fried. The ingredients are generally marinated in sauce or salted then skewered so they retain their shape and grilled over a hot fire so the skin (if any) is very crisp while the meat stays tender and juicy. *Yakitori* is a type of *yakimono.*

SUSHI TERMS

Chirashi-zushi Translates as "scattered sushi." A bowl or box of sushi rice topped with a variety of sashimi (usually nine, which is considered a lucky number).

Gunkam-maki Battleship roll. The maki is rolled to form a container for the liquid of an item, such as oysters, *uni,* quail eggs, *ikora,* and *tobiko.*

Inari-zushi *Aburage* (simmered with sweet sake, shoyu, and water), then stuffed with sushi rice.

Kaiten-zushi A sushi restaurant where the plates with the sushi are placed on a rotating conveyor belt that winds through the restaurant and moves past every table and counter seat. Customers may place special orders, but most simply pick their selections from a steady stream of fresh sushi moving along the conveyor belt. The final bill is calculated based on the number and type of plates of the consumed sushi. Besides conveyor belts, some restaurants use a fancier form of presentation such as miniature wooden "sushi boats" traveling small canals, or miniature locomotive cars.

Maki-zushi Rice and seaweed rolls with fish and/or vegetables made with a makisu mat made from thin pieces of bamboo that facilitates the rolling process. Most rolls are made with the rice inside the *nori,* a few—like the California roll—place the rice on the outside of the *nori.*

Ana-kyu Maki Conger eel and cucumber rolls.

Chutoro Maki Marbled tuna roll.

Futo Maki Large rolls with nori on the outside.

Hosomaki Thin rolls, similar to *futomaki* but about half the size in diameter.

Kaiware Maki Daikon sprout roll.

Kanpyo Maki Pickled gourd rolls.

Kappa Maki Cucumber-filled *maki zuchi.*

Maguro Temaki Tuna *temaki.*

Maki Mono Vinegared rice and fish (or other ingredient) rolled in nori.

Natto Maki Sticky, strong-tasting fermented soybean rolls.

Negitoro Maki Scallion and tuna roll.

Nori Maki Same as *kanpyo maki;* in Osada, same as *futo maki.*

Oshinko Maki Pickled daikon rolls.

Otoro Maki Fatty tuna roll.

Tekka Maki Tuna filled *maki zushi.*

Tekkappa Maki Selection of both tuna and cucumber rolls.

Temaki Hand-rolled cones made from nori.

Uramaki Inside-out rolls; the rice is on the outside with the nori and filling inside.

Neta The piece of fish that is placed on top of the sushi rice for *nigiri.*

Nigiri-zushi The little fingers of rice topped with wasabi and a filet of raw or cooked fish or shellfish. This is the most common form of sushi.

Oshinko Japanese pickles.

Oshi-zushi Sushi made from rice pressed in a box or mold.

Sashimi Raw fish without rice.

Tamaki-zushi Hand-rolled cones of sushi rice, fish, and vegetables wrapped in seaweed.

Menus and Recipes from Japan

Gyoza
Japanese Pot-Stickers

YIELD: 4 SERVINGS OR 40 SMALL DUMPLINGS

The primary difference between packaged gyoza skins and packaged wonton skins is the shape (round for gyoza skins, square for wonton skins) this is a matter of preference. The dough can be made but it is a time-consuming process and the dough must be rolled quite thin.

AMOUNT	MEASURE	INGREDIENT
2 cups	9 ounces, 252 g	All-purpose flour, plus extra for dusting
1 teaspoon		Salt
1½ cups	12 ounces, 360 ml	Boiling water
2½ cups	7 ounces, 196 g	Chinese cabbage, upper leafy parts only, or bib lettuce, minced
1 cup	8 ounces, 224 g	Ground pork, or ½ cup (4 ounces, 112 g) ground pork and ½ cup (4 ounces, 112 g) ground shrimp
2 teaspoons	10 ml	Shoyu
1 teaspoon	5 ml	Grated ginger
1		Garlic clove
1 tablespoon		Green onions, green part only, minced
Pinch		Sugar
½ teaspoon		Black pepper, fresh ground
40		Gyoza or Wonton skins
3 tablespoons	1½ ounces, 45 ml	Sesame oil mixed with vegetable oil
3 tablespoons	1½ ounces, 45 ml	Vegetable oil
1 cup	8 ounces, 240 ml	Boiling water
As needed		Hot mustard paste
As needed		Shoyu

PROCEDURE

1 Sift flour and ½ teaspoon salt together.

2 Add 1½ cups boiling water to flour little by little, stirring with chopsticks, until mixture is shaped into a ball. Cover and let stand 1 hour.

3   On floured work surface, knead the dough for 6 minutes or until smooth. Form the dough into a long log, and cut the log crosswise into 40 disks. Dust each cut side with additional flour to prevent the surfaces from drying out.

4   Roll each piece of dough into a 3-inch disk, making the rim thinner than the center. Dust liberally with additional flour; stack and wrap in plastic. Set aside.

5   Toss Chinese cabbage with remaining salt. Let stand for 10 minutes. Squeeze the cabbage to remove excess water.

6   Combine ground pork with shoyu and mix until the pork is sticky. Mix in the cabbage, ginger, garlic, green onion, sugar, and black pepper.

7   Have a small bowl of water at hand. Place a wrapper in one hand, wet half the rim of the wrapper with water, and place a little stuffing in the center of the wrapper. Fold the wrapper in half by placing the dry edge over the wet edge. While sealing the dumpling, make six to eight pleats in the top, dry edge, starting at one side and continuing around the rim.

8   Over medium heat, heat a pan large enough to hold 20 dumplings; add 2 tablespoons (1 ounce, 30 ml) oil. When hot, add dumplings to the skillet, pleated sides up, and cook until the bottoms are golden and crisp.

9   Combine 1 cup boiling water and 2 tablespoons (1 ounce, 30 ml) oil. When dumplings are golden, add enough of the liquid mixture to reach to $\frac{1}{4}$ the height of the dumplings. Immediately cover and steam dumplings over medium to low heat for 4 to 5 minutes.

10   Remove lid, turn heat up to high, and cook away any remaining liquid.

11   Remove dumplings from the pan and keep warm. Repeat with remaining dumplings.

12   Serve hot with mustard paste and shoyu.

Miso-Shiru

Miso Soup   SERVES 4

This is a traditional soup, which can be served at any meal.

AMOUNT	MEASURE	INGREDIENT
4 cups	32 ounces, 950 ml	Ichiban dashi (recipe follows)
$\frac{1}{2}$ cup	$1\frac{1}{3}$ ounces, 37 g	Wakeme seaweed or shiitake mushrooms, thinly sliced
3 tablespoons	$1\frac{1}{2}$ ounces, 45 ml	Shiro miso (sweet white miso)
1 cup ($\frac{1}{2}$ block)	7 ounces, 196 g	Firm or soft tofu, $\frac{1}{2}$ inch (1.27 cm) dice
3 tablespoons	$\frac{1}{2}$ ounce, 14 g	Green onion, green and white parts, $\frac{1}{8}$ inch (.3 cm) thin diagonal cut

PROCEDURE

1   Combine dashi and mushrooms; simmer over medium heat 3 minutes.

2   Soften the miso with a little stock and stir into the dashi until miso is dissolved. Do not boil: miso's flavor changes when boiled. Add the tofu and heat 30 seconds.

3   Divide the green onion, mushrooms, and tofu equally among serving bowls.

4   Ladle in dashi. Serve immediately, as hot as possible.

Dashi
Japanese Basic Stock

Dashi is indispensable in Japanese cooking. Although chicken stock can be a suitable substitute, to cook truly "Japanese," *dashi* should always be used when a recipe calls for stock or broth.

Ichiban Dashi (First Fish Stock)

YIELD: 1 QUART

AMOUNT	MEASURE	INGREDIENT
1 quart	32 ounces, 1 liter	Water
1	1 x 4 inch (10 cm)	Kombu (kelp), wiped clean
$\frac{1}{2}$ cup	$\frac{1}{2}$ ounce, 14 g	Katsuobushi (bonito fish flakes), tightly packed

PROCEDURE

1 Combine water with *kombu* over medium heat; bring almost to a boil but do not let the *kombu* boil or the stock will become stronger than desired.

2 Immediately remove *kombu*; save.

3 Bring back to boiling point; remove from heat and stir in bonito flakes. Let sit for 1 to 2 minutes; flakes will settle to the bottom.

4 Strain the stock through a cheesecloth-lined strainer. Store in an airtight container for up to 4 days.

Kyuri No Sunome
Japanese Cucumber Salad SERVES 4

AMOUNT	MEASURE	INGREDIENT
2 cups	8 ounces, 224 g	Cucumber, peeled, seeded, cut lengthwise in half and sliced very thin
$\frac{1}{2}$ cup	1 ounce, 28g	Green onions, chopped $\frac{1}{4}$ inch (.6 cm)
2 tablespoons	1 ounce, 30 ml	Shoyu
1 tablespoon	$\frac{1}{2}$ ounce, 15 ml	Sesame oil
1 tablespoon	$\frac{1}{2}$ ounce, 14 g	Granulated sugar
4 tablespoons	2 ounces, 120 ml	Rice vinegar
To taste		Salt
2 teaspoons		Mixture of black and white sesame seeds, toasted

PROCEDURE

1 Combine all ingredients except sesame seeds and let stand for 1 hour.

2 Sprinkle with toasted sesame seeds.

Sashimi
Sliced Raw Fish   SERVES 4

AMOUNT	MEASURE	INGREDIENT
$1\frac{1}{2}$ pounds	672 g	Impeccably fresh sea bass, tuna, or other saltwater fish, filleted
2 cups	6 ounces, 168 g	Daikon, shredded
$\frac{1}{2}$ cup	1 ounce, 28 g	Carrot, shredded
$\frac{1}{2}$ cup	2 ounces, 56 g	Green onion, white and green parts, minced
1 tablespoon	$\frac{1}{2}$ ounce, 14 g	Wasabi
To taste		Shoyu
1 tablespoon	$\frac{1}{2}$ ounce, 14 g	Ginger, grated

PROCEDURE

1 Remove any skin, blood, and dark sections from the fish.

2 Cut diagonally into slices 1 inch (2.5 cm) long and $\frac{1}{4}$ inch (5 mm) thick.

3 Arrange shredded *daikon,* carrot, and green onion in mounds on a serving platter.

4 Arrange raw fish slices on platter.

5 Mix wasabi to a thick paste with a little water and place on platter.

6 To serve, pour shoyu into individual bowls, then allow diners to add wasabi and ginger to their own bowls.

7 Serve with rice, if desired. Dip fish and vegetables into sauce before eating.

Sushi
Basic Vinegared Rice

Chef Tip **Keys** to success: Use white short-grain Japanese rice or medium-grain California rice.

Wash rice thoroughly under cold running water, rubbing it well between the palms of the hands. Drain and repeat the process 3 times until the water is clear. Drain and set in a colander to air dry for 30 minutes, tossing once or twice for even air circulation, before cooking. This produces firmly cooked rice, perfect for tossing with vinegar dressing. Rice for sushi should not be soaked.

Use good-quality rice vinegar.

Mix cooked rice and vinegar dressing in a *hangiri* tub. Because the wood absorbs moisture and retains heat, the rice doesn't become watery, nor does it cool too quickly. An unfinished wooden salad bowl is a good substitute for a *hangiri*. Soak wood bowls and spatula in cold water for at least 20 minutes so the rice will not stick.

Never refrigerate sushi rice; it will become unpleasantly firm.

Gohan (Rice)

YIELD: 8–9 CUPS

AMOUNT	MEASURE	INGREDIENT
3 cups	19 ounces, 532 g	Rice
4 cups	32 ounces, 960 ml	Water
2 tablespoons	1 ounce, 30 ml	Sake
1	2 inch (4.8 cm) square	Kombu
Vinegar Dressing		
3 tablespoons	1$\frac{1}{2}$ ounces, 42 g	Sugar
2 teaspoons	$\frac{1}{2}$ ounce, 14 g	Salt
$\frac{1}{2}$ cup	4 ounces, 120 ml	Rice vinegar

PROCEDURE

1 Prepare rice for cooking.

2 Combine rice, water, and sake in correct-size pot (three times deeper than water level). Place the *kombu* on top, bring to a boil, and then immediately remove the *kombu*.

3 Cook, uncovered, until the water level is almost level with the rice.

4 Reduce heat to low and cover with a tight-fitting lid. Cook for another 10 to 15 minutes.

5 Remove from heat and let stand, covered, for 10 minutes. This resting makes the rice easier to toss.

6 Dissolve the sugar and salt in the vinegar. Do not allow to boil vigorously or the flavor of the vinegar will be compromised. Cool slightly.

7 Transfer the hot rice to a *hangiri,* wooden bowl, or sheet pan. Spread into a thin layer.

8 Pour the vinegar dressing over the cooling rice and cut into the rice with a wooden spatula, while fanning the rice to cool it. Do not use all the dressing right away or the rice may get mushy. Keep fanning, stirring, and adding vinegar dressing until the rice is at room temperature. Taste as you go; you may not need all the dressing.

9 The rice is ready to make sushi when it has cooled to room temperature.

Chef Tip To prevent cooked sushi rice from becoming sticky when handling, keep your hands damp with *tezu* ("hand-vinegar"), which is a combination of water and vinegar that can be used to dip your fingers into while making sushi. To create *tezu*, combine 1 tablespoon sushi dressing with 3 tablespoons cold water.

Nigiri-Zushi

YIELD: 24 PIECES

AMOUNT	MEASURE	INGREDIENT
Tezu		
$\frac{3}{4}$ cup	6 ounces, 180 ml	**Water**
$1\frac{1}{2}$ tablespoons	$\frac{3}{4}$ ounce, 23 ml	**Rice vinegar**
1 tablespoon		**Wasabi powder**
1 tablespoon	$\frac{1}{2}$ ounce, 15 ml	**Warm water**
2 cups	14 ounces, 418 g	**Cooked sushi rice**
12 ounces	336 g	**24 assorted pieces raw fish cut for sushi—$1\frac{1}{2}$ inches (3.6 cm) long by 2 inches (4.8 cm) wide by $\frac{1}{4}$ inch (.6 cm) thick**
As needed		**Pickled ginger**
As needed		**Shoyu**

PROCEDURE

1   Make the tezu by stirring together the water and rice vinegar.

2   Mix wasabi powder with the warm water to make a paste; set aside to rest for 30 minutes.

3   Dip fingers in the tezu and clasp your hands together to dampen palms. Take about $1\frac{1}{2}$ tablespoons of rice in your fingers and gently compress into the shape of a finger, about $\frac{3}{4}$ inch (1.8 cm) wide, $1\frac{1}{2}$ inches (3.6 cm) long, and $\frac{3}{4}$ inch (1.8 cm) high.

4   Smear a bit of wasabi paste down the center of one flat side of a piece of fish. Holding the rice in one hand and the fish in the other, press the two together. The fish should completely cover the top of the rice.

5   Repeat with remaining rice and fish and place on a serving platter.

6   Mound a small amount of wasabi on the platter and serve with shoyu and pickled ginger.

Yakitori
Grilled Chicken   SERVES 4

AMOUNT	MEASURE	INGREDIENT
4	16 ounces, 448 g	Chicken thighs, skinned, boned, and cut into 1 inch (2.4 cm) by $1\frac{1}{4}$ inch (3 cm) pieces
2		Green onion, cut diagonally to match the size of chicken
8		Bamboo skewers, soaked in water for 1 hour
As needed		Salt
As needed		Yakitori Basting Sauce (recipe follows)

PROCEDURE

1 Preheat broiler or grill.

2 Thread chicken and green onions alternately onto skewers. Salt chicken and green onions.

3 Cook the skewered chicken and onions for 4 minutes, turning the skewers several times. Remove from heat and baste with *tare* (basting sauce).

4 Return to heat and cook 2 minutes, turning several times. Remove from heat and baste.

5 Return to heat and cook 2 minutes, turning once. Remove from heat and baste once more. Serve hot.

Yakitori Tare
Yakitori Basting Sauce   YIELD: ½ CUP, 4 OUNCES, 120 ML

AMOUNT	MEASURE	INGREDIENT
8		Chicken wings
¾ cup	6 ounces, 180 ml	Sake
1⅓ cups	10½ ounces, 315 ml	Mirin
3 tablespoons	1½ ounces, 42 g	Granulated sugar
1⅓ cups	10½ ounces, 315 ml	Shoyu

PROCEDURE

1 Char chicken wings over about half their surfaces.

2 Over medium heat, bring sake and mirin to boil; add sugar and cook to dissolve. Add shoyu and chicken wings; bring to a boil and reduce heat to low.

3 Cook over low heat for 30 minutes, until sauce is thick and glossy.

4 Strain through cheesecloth; serve warm to hot.

Hiyashi Chukasoba
Summertime Chilled Chukasoba   SERVES: 4

Chef Tip   To make ginger juice, peel and grate ginger. Wrap grated ginger in cheesecloth and squeeze the juice through the cheesecloth.

Sauce

AMOUNT	MEASURE	INGREDIENT
$\frac{1}{4}$ cup	2 ounces, 60 ml	Mirin
1 tablespoon	$\frac{1}{2}$ ounce, 14 g	Granulated sugar
1$\frac{1}{2}$ cups	12 ounces, 360 ml	Chicken stock or ramen stock
$\frac{1}{2}$ cup	4 ounces, 120 ml	Shoyu
3 tablespoons	1$\frac{1}{2}$ ounces, 45 ml	Rice vinegar
1 tablespoon	$\frac{1}{2}$ ounce, 15 ml	Sesame oil
1–2 teaspoons		Ginger juice, to taste

PROCEDURE

1   Over high heat bring mirin to a boil; add sugar and chicken stock and return to a boil.

2   Add shoyu, return to boil, remove from heat, and transfer to a clean, cooled container.

3   Add rice vinegar, sesame oil, and ginger juice. Let cool and refrigerate for at least 1 hour.

Toppings

AMOUNT	MEASURE	INGREDIENT
3 cups	12 ounces, 336 g	Soybean or mung bean sprouts
2 ounces	48 g	Mung bean noodles, soaked in boiling water for 6 minutes

PROCEDURE

1   Blanch sprouts in boiling water for 30 seconds. Drain and set aside.

2   Drain soaked mung-bean noodles, cool under cold running water, and cut into 6-inch (14.4 cm) lengths.

Thin Omelet

AMOUNT	MEASURE	INGREDIENT
Pinch		Salt
1 teaspoon	5 g	Granulated sugar
4		Eggs, lightly beaten
1½ tablespoons	¾ ounce, 23 ml	Vegetable oil
Noodles		
13 ounces		Dried chukasoba noodles
2 teaspoons	10 ml	Sesame oil
Plating		
1 cup	6 ounces, 168 g	Japanese or salad cucumber, julienned in 2½ inch (6 cm) lengths
8		Cherry tomatoes, cut in half
8		Shrimp (16–20 count), cooked, peeled, and cut in half
Garnish		
2 tablespoons		White or black sesame seeds, toasted
To taste		Hot mustard paste or smooth French-style mustard

PROCEDURE

1   Combine salt, sugar, and eggs.

2   Use oil and eggs to make 8 small very thin omelets. Cut into 2-inch (4.8 cm) julienne strips.

3   Cook noodles in large amount of boiling water until al dente, 3 to 5 minutes or as instructed on package.

4   Drain and rinse under cold running water. Drain again, toss with sesame oil.

5   Divide the noodles among 4 individual shallow bowls. Top noodles with cucumber, tomatoes, shrimp, sprouts, mung bean noodles, and omelets strips. In traditional presentations, the items are placed in separate mounds like the colorful spokes of a wheel. Pour some of the sauce over each dish, garnish with sesame seeds on top, and place a dab of mustard on the rim of the bowl.

Asari no Ushio-jiru
Asari Clam Soup   YIELD: 16 PIECES

AMOUNT	MEASURE	INGREDIENT
12	24 ounces, 672 g	Asari clams, or littleneck or New Zealand cockles
4 cups	32 ounces, 960 ml	Water
1	3 inch (7.2 cm)	Square kombu (kelp)
1 tablespoon	$\frac{1}{2}$ ounce, 15 ml	Sake
To taste	$\frac{1}{2}$ ounce, 15 ml	Light soy sauce
To taste		Salt
To taste		Lemon juice
To taste		Sugar
Garnish		
$\frac{1}{2}$ cup	2 ounces, 48 g	Daikon sprouts, roots removed, or watercress leaves
$\frac{1}{4}$		Yuzu citron or lemon rind, julienned

PROCEDURE

1. Place clams into a colander, and place the colander in a large bowl of salted cold water (1 tablespoon salt to 1 quart water). Let clams stand in a cool place for 2 hours to expel any sand, then rub and rinse under cold running water.

2. Combine clams, water, and *kombu* and bring almost to a boil over medium heat, skimming any foam. Remove and discard the *kombu*.

3. Add the sake and cook clams, covered, until they open, 3 to 4 minutes. Discard any unopened clams.

4. Strain soup through a sieve lined with cheesecloth. Reserve clams, and return both clams and soup broth to pot. Season to taste with soy sauce, salt, lemon juice, and sugar.

5. Serve each portion with equal amounts of clams and broth.

6. Top each serving with daikon sprouts and julienned lemon rind.

Maki Sushi
Futomaki: Seasoned Vegetables

YIELD: 16 PIECES

AMOUNT	MEASURE	INGREDIENT
1 tablespoon		Wasabi powder
1 tablespoon	$\frac{1}{2}$ ounce, 15 ml	Warm water
1 cup	6 ounces, 168 g	Vegetables, julienned—(suitable vegetables include bamboo shoots, carrot, celery, daikon, spinach (squeeze especially well), green beans, asparagus, snow peas)
1 cup	8 ounces, 240 ml	Dashi
$1\frac{1}{2}$ tablespoons		Sugar
$1\frac{1}{2}$ tablespoons	$\frac{3}{4}$ ounce, 22.5 ml	Mirin
$1\frac{1}{2}$ tablespoons	$\frac{3}{4}$ ounce, 22.5 ml	Soy sauce
$\frac{3}{4}$ cup	6 ounces, 180 ml	Water
2 tablespoons	1 ounce, 30 ml	Rice vinegar
2		Full sheet nori, toasted
3 cups	21 ounces, 588 g	Cooked sushi rice
As needed		Soy sauce
As needed		Pickled ginger

PROCEDURE

1   Mix wasabi with warm water to make a paste and set aside to rest for 30 minutes.

2   Combine vegetables, dashi, sugar, mirin, and $1\frac{1}{2}$ tablespoons soy sauce. Simmer over medium heat until the vegetables are just tender.

3   Remove from heat, cool, and squeeze to remove excess liquid.

4   Make the tezu by stirring together the water and rice vinegar.

5   Place the rolling mat in front so the bamboo pieces are horizontal. Cover with film, if desired.

6   Place the nori shiny side down (textured side up) on top of the mat, with the shorter edge near you. Align the edge of the nori with the edge of the rolling mat so that the nori is squared off.

7   Dip fingers in to tezu and spread the rice over the nori, covering the surface from edge to edge but leaving a 1-inch (2.4 cm) portion of nori bare at the top. The rice should be about $\frac{1}{4}$ inch (.6 cm) thick.

8   Use your finger to make a shallow indentation in the center of the rice that runs horizontally across.

9   Smear wasabi in the indentation and add half the vegetables down the center line.

10 Place your fingers on top of the filling to help keep it in place and use your thumbs to lift the bamboo mat up and over, rolling it forward. Bring the bottom edge of the nori and rice up and over the filling to meet the end of the rice.

11 Squeeze your fingers back toward you, tucking under the bottom and far side of the roll. Doing so compresses the filling and rice to make a tight roll.

12 Remove the mat and gently squeeze the roll to firm it and round out its shape.

13 Moisten the blade of a thin, sharp knife and slice each roll into $8 \times \frac{3}{4}$ inch (19.2 × 1.8 cm) pieces. Wipe the blade with a clean, warm cloth between slices.

14 Arrange on a serving plate; serve with soy sauce, wasabi, and pickled ginger on the side.

Horenso Goma-ae
Spinach with Sesame Dressing   SERVES 4

AMOUNT	MEASURE	INGREDIENT
5 tablespoons	$1\frac{1}{4}$ ounces, 35 g	Sesame seeds, toasted
1 tablespoon	$\frac{1}{3}$ ounce, 10 g	Granulated sugar
2 tablespoons	1 ounce, 30 ml	Dashi
$\frac{1}{2}$ teaspoon		Tamari
$3\frac{1}{4}$ cups	7 ounces, 196 g	Spinach, washed
As needed		Yuzu citron or lime rind

PROCEDURE

1   Grind toasted sesame seeds with a mortar and pestle until an oily paste. Add sugar, blending thoroughly. Add dashi a little at a time, mixing until smooth. Use additional dashi, if necessary, to make a smooth paste. Blend in tamari. (A food processor or blender can also be used to make the dressing.)

2   Cook spinach in salted boiling water for 45 seconds.

3   Drain spinach and cool under running water. Squeeze tightly to remove excess water.

4   Cut spinach into $1\frac{1}{2}$ inch (3.6 cm) lengths.

5   Just before serving, toss the spinach with sesame dressing and garnish with yuzu citron or lime rind.

Chawan Mushi Savory Custard

SERVES 4 (6 OUNCES EACH)

AMOUNT	MEASURE	INGREDIENT
$\frac{1}{2}$ cup	2 ounces, 56 g	Chicken breast fillet
As needed		Salt
4	4 ounces, 112 g	Shrimp, headed, peeled, deveined, cut in $\frac{1}{4}$ inch (.6 cm) pieces
2	2 ounces, 56 g	Shiitake mushrooms, stems removed, quartered
2 teaspoons	7 ml	Light soy sauce
4		Large eggs
$1\frac{1}{2}$ cups	12 ounces, 360 ml	Dashi
Pinch		Salt
1 teaspoon	5 ml	Mirin
8		Watercress leaves, stems removed
Garnish		Yuzu citron or lemon rind, julienned

PROCEDURE

1 Remove any sinew from the chicken breast, lightly salt, and let stand 15 minutes.

2 Wipe chicken with a paper towel to remove the salt and exuded juice.

3 Cut the fillet in half diagonally, then halve the two pieces crosswise into $\frac{1}{2}$-inch (1.2 cm) pieces.

4 Blanch chicken and shrimp in salted boiling water for about 10 seconds. Drain and wipe dry.

5 Toss shrimp, chicken, and mushrooms with $1\frac{1}{2}$ teaspoon soy sauce. Let stand 15 minutes.

6 Wipe dry with paper towel and divide equally among four custard cups or ramekins.

7 Beat eggs lightly, add remaining soy sauce, dashi, salt, and mirin, and mix again.

8 Strain egg mixture through a fine sieve; divide among ramekins.

9 Wrap the ramekins with film and steam custard for 2 minutes over high heat; reduce heat to medium and continue to steam for 13 minutes or until clear liquid runs out when a wooden skewer is inserted. It is important that the steam temperature is not too high; the custard should be silky and smooth, similar to soft tofu.

10 Remove film and place a watercress leaf on top of each ramekin; steam for 30 seconds. Remove from steamer and cover with a lid to keep warm.

11 Serve the custard with a spoon. Garnish with yuzu or lemon rind.

Buta Teriyaki
Pork on Skewers   SERVES 4

AMOUNT	MEASURE	INGREDIENT
$\frac{1}{2}$ cup	4 ounces, 120 ml	Mirin
$\frac{1}{4}$ cup	2 ounces, 60 ml	Sake
$\frac{1}{4}$ cup	2 ounces, 60 ml	Shoyu
2 tablespoons	1 ounce, 28 g	Granulated sugar
2 pounds	896 g	Pork tenderloin, cleaned and thinly sliced $\frac{1}{4}$ inch (.6 cm) thick
1 teaspoon	5 g	Fresh ginger root, grated
1 cup	4 ounces, 112 g	Onion, minced

PROCEDURE

1   To make teriyaki sauce, over medium heat, combine the mirin and sake for 5 minutes. Add shoyu and sugar; stir to dissolve the sugar.

2   Cook over low heat for 25 minutes; cool before using.

3   Combine remaining ingredients with teriyaki sauce and marinate for 1 hour.

4   Thread the pork on 4 skewers, reserving marinade.

5   Grill (broil) for 3 minutes on each side, basting frequently with the marinade. Serve immediately with plain white rice.

Nasu No Karashi
Mustard-Pickled Eggplant   SERVES 4

AMOUNT	MEASURE	INGREDIENT
6		Small Japanese elongated eggplants
3 cups	24 ounces, 720 ml	Water
I tablespoon	$\frac{1}{2}$ ounce, 15 g	Salt
Dressing		
I$\frac{1}{2}$ teaspoons	7 g	Dry mustard or wasabi
3 tablespoons	I$\frac{1}{2}$ ounces, 45 ml	Shoyu
4 tablespoons	2 ounces, 60 ml	Mirin
2 tablespoons	I ounce, 28 g	Granulated sugar

PROCEDURE

1   Cut eggplant crossways into slices about $\frac{1}{8}$ inch (2.5 mm) thick, then cut into quarters.

2   Combine water and salt; add eggplant and soak for 1 hour.

3   Drain eggplant and pat dry.

4   Combine remaining ingredients to make the dressing, mix well.

5   Combine eggplant and dressing. Chill for 2 hours or longer to combine flavors before serving.

Kamonanban Soba
Soba with Duck and Long Onions SERVES 4

AMOUNT	MEASURE	INGREDIENT
2	8 ounces, 224 g	Duck breast, excess fat removed and reserved
14 ounces	392 g	Dried soba noodles
1		Naganegi long onion, or 4 thick scallions
$\frac{1}{4}$ cup	2 ounces, 60 ml	Sake
6 cups	48 ounces, 1440 ml	Kakejiru, warm to hot (recipe follows)
1 cup	2 ounces, 56 g	Watercress leaves
As needed		Seven-spice powder

PROCEDURE

1 Slice duck breast diagonally into $\frac{1}{4}$ inch (.6 cm) thick slices.

2 Cook noodles al dente; drain and rinse under cold running water, rubbing them between your hands until they are cold and no longer starchy. Drain well.

3 Heat reserved duck fat over medium heat; cook until fat covers the bottom of the pan. Remove the solid duck fat.

4 Add duck and long onion or scallion; cover and cook until the surface of the duck turns whitish and the bottom is slightly golden.

5 Turn the duck and long onion, sprinkle with sake, cover, and continue to cook 2 more minutes.

6 Add duck and onions to the *kakejiru*.

7 Add noodles and reheat for 1 to 2 minutes.

8 Divide noodles among the serving bowls and pour over hot broth.

9 Serve noodles topped with duck, onion, and watercress.

10 Sprinkle with seven-spice powder.

Kakejiru
Broth for Hot Noodles

YIELD: 1 QUART, 32 OUNCES, 960 ML

AMOUNT	MEASURE	INGREDIENT
1 quart	32 ounces, 960 ml	Ichiban dashi
1½ tablespoons	¾ ounce, 21 g	Granulated sugar
1½ teaspoons	10 g	Salt
1 tablespoon	½ ounce, 15 ml	Shoyu
1½ teaspoons	8 ml	Light soy sauce

PROCEDURE

1 Bring all ingredients to a slow boil over low heat.

Tempura

Portuguese missionaries first brought tempura to Japan in the sixteenth century, but there are many legends about its origins. One is that it was named after the Buddhist curator who, centuries ago, invented the dish to please his noble lord. Another explanation is that the word *tempura* is broken down into three *kanji,* or picture characters: *tem,* signifying heaven; *pu,* signifying woman; and *ra,* meaning silken gauze; the combination means something like "woman veiled in silken gauze, giving a glimpse of heaven."

Tempura refers to vegetables or seafood that have been battered and deep-fried. Tempura reflects many qualities of the Japanese cuisine; absolutely fresh ingredients, artful presentation, and the perfection of a technique. When correctly executed, tempura results in a fried food that is light and fresh tasting, a triumph of Japanese cooking.

The secret to tempura's crispiness is in its batter coating, or more precisely, the lumps, which are apt to form in the tenuous mixture of egg, ice water, and flour. Because these ingredients remain unmixed, each morsel dipped to the bottom of the batter is coated in an egg-water-flour sequence. The batter must be made in small batches and not left to stand. If the batter is overmixed, the result will be armorlike pancake casing, rather than the crispy coating the Japanese call a *koromo,* or "cloak." The Japanese claim that they can tell the difference between tempura made by a five-year "novice" and a twenty-year veteran, so subtle is the chemistry at work in the tempura chef's powdery-ringed batter bowl.

Traditional Tempura Batter

YIELD: 4

AMOUNT	MEASURE	INGREDIENT
1		Large egg
$\frac{1}{2}$ cup	4 ounces, 120 ml	Ice cold club soda or water
1 cup	4 ounces, 112 g	Rice flour

PROCEDURE

1   Combine egg and club soda or water.

2   Add the flour to the liquid and stir together with chopsticks. Do not overmix; the batter should be a bit lumpy.

3   Let rest at least 15 minutes but no more than 1 hour before using.

4   If too thick, add water to achieve the consistency of whipping cream; stir with chopsticks.

Shrimp and Vegetable Tempura

Shrimp and Vegetables

AMOUNT	MEASURE	INGREDIENT
8	8 ounces, 224 g	Shrimp (16–20 count)
As needed		All-purpose flour
Oil for frying		80/20 blend of vegetable oil and sesame oil, minimum 2 inches deep, heated to 350°F (180°C)
8		Small button mushrooms, stems removed
1	8 ounces, 224 g	Zucchini, cut diagonally into 8 slices, $\frac{1}{3}$ inch (.8 cm) thick
8 slices		Lotus root, cut into $\frac{1}{4}$ inch (.6 cm) rings
8 ounces	224 g	Sweet potato, peeled, cut diagonally into eight slices $\frac{1}{4}$ inch (.6 cm) thick
As needed		Tentsuyu (dipping sauce; recipe follows)
Garnish		
$\frac{1}{2}$ cup	3 ounces, 84 g	Daikon, grated
2 tablespoons	1 ounce, 28 g	Fresh ginger root, grated

PROCEDURE

1 Peel shrimp, being careful to retain the tails for handling. Cut the back of the shrimp along the vein and wash in cold water to remove.

2 Spread the shrimp out flat with the tail end toward you.

3 Make two shallow vertical cuts the length of each half. This cuts the muscles to prevent curling during frying.

4 Using the side of your hand tap shrimp, cut side up, gently pushing out and away with lengthwise strokes from tail to blunt end of the shrimp, being careful not to destroy the shrimp. The object is to spread it to $1\frac{1}{2}$–2 times its original size.

5 Dip shrimp in flour and let set for 5 to 10 minutes to assure a good adhesion of batter to shrimp in frying.

6 Prepare oil for frying; be sure to maintain heat while frying.

7 Have all the vegetables and shrimp ingredients ready: coat with batter, and cook similar ingredients together for even cooking, frying until light golden. Fry in small batches, turning frequently with clean chopsticks. The pieces should move freely.

8 Remove from oil and drain on paper towels. Serve immediately. Between batches, skim off the small bits of batter (*tenkasu*) that float in the oil. The Japanese save these bits of *tenkasu* to use as croutons in soup or over rice.

9 Serve with dipping sauce and garnish. Diners should mix together dipping sauce and garnish according to taste.

Tentsuyu

Tentsuyu **is a dipping sauce served with fresh hot fried foods, such as tempura. Dipping hot foods in** *tentsuyu* **cools them a little and provides additional flavor. The sauce is served warm or at room temperature.**

AMOUNT	MEASURE	INGREDIENT
I cup	8 ounces, 240 ml	Ichiban dashi
3 tablespoons	I$\frac{1}{2}$ ounces, 458 ml	Light soy sauce
I teaspoon	5 ml	Shoyu
2 tablespoons	I ounce, 30 ml	Mirin

PROCEDURE

I Combine all and bring to a boil. Remove from heat.

2 Serve in individual serving bowls, warm or at room temperature.

Goma-anko Manju
Steamed Dumplings with Sweet Azuki
Paste and Sesame Seeds   YIELD: 12 DUMPLINGS

AMOUNT	MEASURE	INGREDIENT
$\frac{1}{2}$ cup	4$\frac{1}{2}$ ounces, 135 ml	Anko (sweet azuki bean paste; recipe follows)
2 tablespoons	2 ounces, 60 ml	Water
1 teaspoon		Black sesame seeds, toasted
$\frac{3}{4}$ cup plus 2 tsp	3 ounces, 84 g	Cake flour
$\frac{1}{2}$ teaspoon		Baking powder
5 tablespoons	2$\frac{1}{2}$ ounces, 70 ml	Water
4$\frac{1}{2}$ tablespoons	2$\frac{1}{4}$ ounces, 63 g	Granulated sugar

PROCEDURE

1   Combine anko and 2 tablespoons water. Cook over medium heat, stirring, until thoroughly mixed. Add sesame seeds and stir to mix. Cool to room temperature. Divide into 12 portions.

2   Sift together flour and baking powder.

3   Combine 5 tablespoons water and the sugar; cook mixture to dissolve sugar; cool to room temperature.

4   Combine flour and sugar water to form a ball. Let stand, covered, for 30 minutes.

5   Line a bamboo or metal steamer basket with parchment paper and place steamer on boiling water.

6   On a floured counter, knead the dough briefly, 10 to 20 times. The dough should be somewhat soft. Roll the dough into a long, thin log, and cut the log into 12 equal pieces. Flatten dough with palms into a 1-inch (2.4 cm) disk, $\frac{1}{8}$ inch (.3 cm) thick.

7   Wrap the dough around each portion of bean paste (about 1 teaspoon), so you have 12 dumplings (shao mai style). To fill each dumpling, place a wrapper on the palm of your hand and cup it loosely. Place one filling in the cup. Then, with the other hand, gather the sides of the wrapper around the filling, letting the wrapper pleat naturally. Squeeze the middle gently to make sure the wrapper fits firmly against the filling, and to give the cylinder a wasp-waisted look. Tap the dumpling to flatten the bottom so it can stand upright.

8   Transfer to steamer and cook over high steam for 8 to 10 minutes. Serve with green tea.

Anko

Sweet Azuki Bean Paste   YIELD: 19 OUNCES

Sweet bean paste is available at most Asian markets.

AMOUNT	MEASURE	INGREDIENT
I cup	7 ounces, 196 g	Dried azuki beans
I cup	7 ounces, 196 g	Granulated sugar

PROCEDURE

1 Over medium heat, combine dried beans and 4 cups (32 ounces, 960 ml) water. Bring to a boil, drain, and discard the water.

2 Repeat with 4 cups (32 ounces, 960 ml) water and bring to boil over medium heat. Reduce heat to low and cook, uncovered, until tender, 60 minutes. Add more water, if necessary; at the end of the cooking time the beans should barely be covered with liquid.

3 In a food processor or blender, blend the beans with some of the cooking liquid to a smooth puree. Press the puree through a fine sieve; yield should be about $2\frac{1}{4}$ cups.

4 Transfer pureed beans to cheesecloth, make a sachet, close the ends, and grip tightly.

5 Plunge the cloth into a bowl of cold water, enough to completely cover and rinse the beans by squeezing the cloth in the water.

6 Discard the water and rinse again using fresh cold water. Remove and squeeze the cloth to remove excess water.

7 Combine pureed beans, sugar, and $\frac{1}{3}$ cup (80 ml) water over medium-low heat; bring to boil and reduce heat to low.

8 Cook until the mixture resembles soft peanut butter, about 20 minutes. cool quickly. Use a shallow pan to spread the mixture out and expose maximum surface, or use and ice bath (place the bean spread over in a container into an ice bath and stir frequently to avoid hot spots and to enhance cooling.

The Land

China shares its border with twelve countries. To the north is Mongolia, the east North Korea, and the northeast and northwest, Russia. Afghanistan, Pakistan, India, Nepal, Sikkim, and Bhutan are to the west and southwest, and to the south are Myanmar, Laos, and Vietnam. China's coastline is bounded by the Bohai, Yellow, East, and South China seas. With a population of 1.3 billion and a land area of 3.7 million square miles, China dominates not only Asia, but the entire world. It has about 22 percent of the total world population, but only some 6.5 percent of the world's land area.

The diversity of China is best recognized in the features of the landscape. China is a rugged country, with mountains, hills, and plateaus occupying about 65 percent of the total land area. The highest peak in the world, Mount Everest, stands on the border between China and Nepal. Moving north, the terrain drops to between 3,280 and 6,560 feet above sea level. Here are the famous grasslands of Mongolia, important to cattle breeding, and the Gobi Desert. In the northwest is the largest desert in China, the Taklamakan Desert, through which the ancient Silk Road passed. Nearby, bordered by the Tian Mountains, is the Turfan Depression; known as the Oasis of Fire, its temperatures can reach 120°F. In central China is the Yang Zi river delta, an important agricultural area, heavily populated. Further south, the geography changes more dramatically, with unusually shaped cliffs, gorges, and waterfalls.

The growth of civilization in China has centered on three great river systems, all of which flow from west to east. The northern quarter is drained by the Huang He (Yellow River); the middle half of the country is drained by the Chang Jiang (Yangtze River, the third longest in the world); and the southern quarter of China is dominated by the Xi Jiang (West River). The two noted cities of Guangzhou (formerly Canton) and Hong Kong are situated at the mouth of the West River. These river systems were the cheapest and most practical form of transportation, and were an important source for irrigation and energy. The river valleys also provided fertile soils for the surrounding level land. As a result, much of China's population is concentrated along these rivers and reaches its highest and most extensive density at their mouths.

History

China has one of the world's oldest continuous civilizations. It is thought that some form of organized society began around 2000 B.C., and throughout the centuries, China has made significant world contributions in philosophy, religion, science, math, politics, agriculture, writing, and the arts. Confucius, whose teachings and writing still influence Chinese thought, lived during the Zhou Dynasty, about 2,500 years ago. The Confucian classics were the guide for Chinese civilization, highlighting education and family as the foundation of society. Taoists believed that people should renounce worldly ambitions and turn to nature and the Tao, the eternal force that permeates everything in nature. Buddhism has become a very powerful belief system for the Chinese. It provided a refuge in the political chaos that followed the fall of the Han Dynasty (206 B.C.–A.D. 220). By the fifth century A.D., Buddhism was widely embraced throughout China. Over the centuries, openness to new ideas fostered the emergence of many Chinese inventions and discoveries.

The ancient Silk Road was established over 2,000 years ago. It started at the Han capital of Changan (today's Xian) and stretched west for 4,350 miles. Crossing mountains and deserts, it branched into two routes, one going through central and western Asia to the eastern shore of the Mediterranean, the other crossing the Aral and Caspian Seas to Constantinople (Turkey). From here, silk was carried on to Rome and Venice. Chinese silk and the four great Chinese inventions—paper, printing, gunpowder, and the compass—made their way to the rest of Asia and to Europe along this route. In return, merchants brought religion, and the art and culture of these foreign regions to China. Trade along the route brought and enriched the northern provinces with herbs, fruits, vegetables, and spices. Coriander, sesame seeds, grapes, walnuts, peas, and garlic were imported from the west and became a hallmark of much of northern Chinese cooking.

The Chinese government has always been characterized by some form of central authority, dating as far back as the Xia Dynasty of 2200 B.C. Subsequent dynasties reinforced cultural unity and continuity for the Chinese civilization. One dynasty succeeded another through warfare, but with only occasional intrusion by forces outside of China. The lack of outside contacts allowed the Chinese to develop one culture across many regions with a strong sense of national identity. A series of emperors served as political leaders supported by well-equipped armies. The Chinese people believed their emperors ruled by "Mandate of Heaven." These dynasties continued over the centuries until the opening of China to the West in the 1800s.

The twentieth century saw dynamic forces change the political landscape of China. Shortly after the century began, the ages-old imperial dynastic system was swept away. Along the way, the country survived occupation by foreign troops, a short-lived republican government, a failed attempt at monarchical restoration, a war against Japan, and five years of civil war. The People's Republic of China emerged on October 1, 1949, a Communist government under the authoritarian Chairman Mao Zedong. By century's end, global realities forced China to experiment with forms of capitalism. Over the last half century, there has been major land and social reform, the Great Leap Forward Campaign, the Cultural Revolution, famine, the market reforms of Deng Xiaoping, and the move to put China on the world political and economic map. Through it all, Chinese culture has endured and even thrived. A strong sense of unity has held the Chinese nation together through 4,000 years. Its stable territorial boundaries, borders that defy easy penetration, culture, language, rich philosophy, and political institutions have allowed China to remain unified through dynastic changes and periodic social upheavals. The country has proved resilient and enduring.

The People

China is a united multi-ethnic nation of 56 ethnic groups. According to the fourth national census, taken in 1990, the Han people made up 92 percent of the country's total population, and the other 55 ethnic groups, 8 percent. China's ethnic groups include Zhuang, Uygurs, Mongols, Tibetans, and others scattered over vast areas, mainly in the border regions.

The peasants of China make up 80 percent of the population and are the backbone of the economy. They alone make up one-third of all the farmers in the world. *Feng shui*, or "wind and water," is about living in harmony with the natural environment and tapping the goodness of nature for good fortune and health. It was first practiced in ancient China by farmers, to whom wind and water were the important natural forces that could either destroy or nurture their crops. Feng shui has developed into an art of locating buildings and other man-made structures (for example, fountains and bridges) to harmonize with and benefit from the surrounding physical environment.

Yin and yang is a concept in Chinese philosophy that consists of two opposing yet complementary forces. Yin is the female, passive, cool force. Yang is the male, active, hot force. These forces are engaged in an endless cycle of movement and change. This is best illustrated

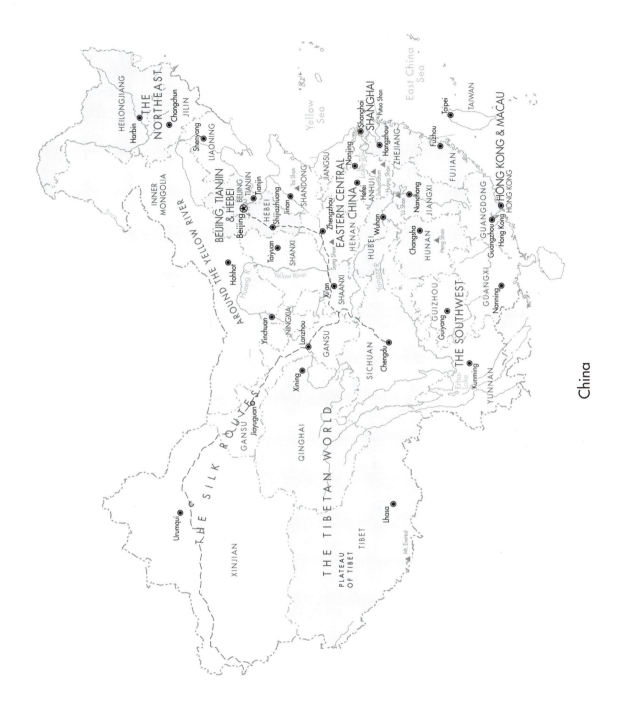

China

by the *taiji*, a symbol that shows a light patch and a dark patch winding around each other. This symbol illustrates how each of the two forces contains some of the opposing force. As yang reaches its peak, it changes into yin. As the cycle continues and yin peaks, it changes into yang. This never-ending cycle of peaks and valley expresses the Chinese view of life, history, and everything else in the world.

The Food

Not surprisingly, given China's size, there are a number of distinct regional cooking styles that can be divided into four major traditions: the northern plains, including Beijing; the fertile east, watered by the Yangtze River; the south, famous for the Cantonese cooking of the Guangdong Province; and the luxuriant west of Szechwan and Hunan Provinces. Some observers characterize those regional cuisines as salty in north, sweet in south, hot in east, and sour in west.

NORTH CHINA

Severe winters, a short growing season, and arid climate shape the hearty cuisine of China's north. The staples are wheat, barley, millet, potatoes, and soybeans, as opposed to rice, which characterizes the other regions. Noodles such as cellophane noodles (made from mung bean flour), rice ribbon noodles (made from rice flour), and breads such as steamed wheat buns, pancakes, and dumplings are the base of the meal. Soy milk is extracted from soybean paste and used to make bean curd, commonly known as tofu. Tofu is used in a variety of ways because it absorbs the flavor of sauces and seasonings, readily resulting in very tasty dishes. The most commonly eaten vegetable is Chinese cabbage, or bok choy. Salted and pickled vegetables such as turnips and white radish are common. The food is flavored with onions, garlic, and dark soy sauce. Soybean paste is the basis of many other pastes like hoisin (also known as Chinese barbeque sauce or plum sauce) and yellow bean, usually used to thicken sauces or as a marinade or seasoning. The northern portion of China also has a distinct Mongolian influence, characterized by the nomadic simplicity of the fire pot. Fuel being scarce in this region, the Mongols would huddle around the fire pot warming their hands while a tureen of broth was heating. Paper-thin slices of lamb or beef were dipped into the boiling broth until cooked and then dipped in spicy sauces. After the meal, the then richly seasoned broth was poured into bowls and served as soup. Northern cooking is known also as *Mandarin* or *Beijing* cooking and was influenced by the imperial court, where royal haute cuisine was developed. Peking duck is a traditional delicacy where thin slices of barbecued duck skin, wrapped in thin pancakes, are eaten with hoisin sauce. Beijing is known for *jiaozi*, the traditional Chinese dumpling filled with pork and vegetables, but variations may include sweet fruits or chestnuts during the holidays.

CENTRAL CHINA

The central coast provinces are known as "The Land of Fish and Rice" and produce the eastern style of cooking, based on fresh seafood and river fish. Wheat, barley, rice, corn, sweet potatoes, and soybeans are the major staple crops. Sugar cane is grown in the humid valleys. Numerous varieties of bamboo shoots, beans, melons, gourds, squashes, and leafy vegetables are found here, and peaches, plums, and grapes flourish. Based around the cities of Shanghai, Zhejiang, and Fujian, as well as the Yangtze River, eastern Chinese cuisine includes careful preparation and fine knife skills, delicate forms, and light, fresh, sweet flavors based on the use of stocks and slow cooking. Stir-fried dishes and steaming are also common cooking methods. Dried and salted meats and preserved vegetables are commonly used to flavor dishes. It was in this region that Chinese vegetarian cuisine was elevated to sophisticated heights, as a result of the wealth of ingredients and the expertise of the regional chefs.

One of the most striking features in eastern cooking is the quantity of sugar included in both vegetable and meat cooking. Sugar combined with a dark soy sauce creates perhaps the most fundamental eastern flavor. Rice wine appears in regional specialties such as Drunken Chicken, Drunken Spare Ribs, and Drunken Prawns. Regional specialties include soy-braised duck and goose and Beggar's Chicken, a dish wrapped in lotus leaves, covered in clay, and oven baked. Century egg is also known as a preserved egg, or thousand-year egg. It is made by preserving duck, chicken, or quail egg in clay, ash, salt, or lime, for several weeks or months. The yolk of the egg turns pale and dark green, while the egg white turns dark brown and translucent. The egg white has a gelatinous texture, similar to that of a cooked egg, but has very little taste. *Wuxi* spare ribs features the common eastern technique of "red cooking," in a stock of soy sauce and rice wine to produce a flavorful stew. Hangzhou and the West Lake area boast the delicate ham known as *jinhua*, a type of cured ham known for its smoky flavor and scarlet color, and the world-famous Dragon Tea Well, for which only the top three leaves of each branch are considered worthy. Shanghai is known for its unusual "soup inject" dishes (*xiao long bao, or xiao long tang bao*), which are meatballs, dumplings, or buns filled with a gelatin and stock mixture and cooked until the inside is soupy.

WESTERN CHINA

Western China is known for Sichuan, or Szechuan, cooking. A basin in the southwestern part of the country, Sichuan is one of the most agriculturally productive areas in China. Broken by small hills, the countryside is cut into squares, each an irrigated paddy field. Rice is grown during the summer, and after it has been harvested in the late autumn, wheat is planted in its place to be harvested six months later. The government, which controls all the supplies of grain in China, uses the surplus to help feed the big cities further east. On the lower slopes of the hills are an abundance of citrus fruit orchards (tangerines in particular) and bamboo groves, while on the higher forested mountainsides the people collect various kinds of edible fungi, such as *muer* (wood-ears) and silver fungi. The western half of Sichuan is very mountainous and sparsely populated. The people, mainly of Tibetan origin, keep sheep, cows, and horses.

The tea plant has long been of great agricultural importance for China. Its origins trace to the second century A.D., when it was grown in plantations in the uplands of central China and the ranges of the coastal provinces. Tea is also important in the interior Sichuan province. Green tea accounts for 45 percent of tea production. Black and brick tea comprise another 45 percent, and *wulung*, chrysanthemum, and jasmine tea are other varieties. Yunnan grows magnificent teas, especially the exotic *pu-erh*, that is sometimes aged for up to a hundred years before being served at banquets. Another well-known product is Yunnan ham (similar to Spanish serrano). China's west also grows some of the world's hottest chile peppers, which have given Sichuan a reputation for heat. There are several thoughts behind this; one is that the fire will stimulate the palate to distinguish the flavors beneath; another is that the heat induces perspiration and helps people to keep cool; and some say the spices are used to mask the taste of foods that rot quickly in the heat.

The texture of different ingredients in a dish is important to western Chinese cooking and care is taken to produce "chewy" and "crunchy" results. Unlike dishes in eastern China, many western dishes are accompanied by only the minimum of sauce to convey the seasonings; the sauce itself is not an important feature in the dish. The resulting dishes are drier. Similar to the southern regional cuisine, it is usual to find garlic, chiles, vinegar, sugar, and soy sauce in one dish. Because of the region's humidity, the preservation of food takes top priority. Salting, drying, pickling, and smoking are traditionally all employed. Pungent vegetables like onions, garlic, and ginger are used, as well as aromatic sesame, peanuts, soybean products, fermented black soybeans, orange peel, aniseed, ginger, and spring onions. Also known as pepper flower, Chinese pepper, and *fagara*, Szechuan pepper is not a pepper at all. Instead, the reddish-brown fruit, one of the ingredients in five-spice power, is a berry that comes from the prickly ash tree. While not as hot as chile pepper, it has a unique flavor, famous for its numbing effect on the tongue. Some notable Szechuan dishes include *kung pao chicken*, tea-smoked duck, *chengdu chicken* (chicken cubes with hot bean paste), and *mapo tofu*, a snow-white bean curd with fried, minced beef and green garlic shoots flavored with crushed peppercorns.

SOUTH CHINA

Hunan (south of the river) cuisine is less well known and descriptions of Chinese cuisine often lump the two together. Hunan cuisine is often even hotter than Szechuan cooking.

While Szechuan recipes often call for chile paste, Hunan dishes frequently use fresh chile peppers, including the seeds and membranes, where most of the heat is contained. Simmering, steaming, stewing, and frying are popular cooking techniques in Hunan Province. Hunan cooks have a great variety of ingredients to work with and they tend to have several steps in preparation. For example, a classic Hunan dish is orange beef, where the beef is marinated overnight, then washed and marinated again with a mixture including egg white, wine, and white pepper. In braised soy sauce beef, the meat is simmered in an aromatic mixture including star anise, sugar, ginger, soy sauce, and sherry. Another popular dish is crispy duck, where the duck is seasoned with peppercorns, star anise, fennel, and other spices, then steamed and finally deep fried.

China's southernmost province, Guangdong (formerly Canton), is the home of the most famous of the Chinese regional cuisines. Though densely populated, this is very fertile land with mild winters. Rice is the main staple, but the farmers grow a profusion of fruit and green vegetables throughout the year. The subtropical climate is perfect for fruits such as pineapple, lychee, oranges, and bananas. Subtler than other Chinese cuisines, Cantonese is best known for its freshness and emphasis on natural flavors. As an example of the high standard for freshness in Cantonese meals, cows and pigs used for meat are usually killed earlier the same day. Chickens are often killed just hours beforehand, and fish are displayed in tanks for customers to choose for immediate preparation. The spices used in Cantonese cooking tend to be light and natural: ginger, salt, soy sauce, white pepper, spring onion, and rice wine or fresh citrus. Fish is quickly steamed with minimal touches of ginger and soy sauce; soups are slow-cooked; pork and duck are barbecued or roasted; and virtually everything that walks, crawls, or flies with "its back to heaven" (as the Cantonese saying goes) is quickly stir-fried in blazing-hot woks. The people of this region are known to eat nearly everything: fish maw, snake liver, dog, and guinea pig are some of the more unusual ingredients.

Guangdong is also praised for its perfected tradition of presentation. Cantonese cooks often make artistic and colorful presentational accents, such as radish roses or scallion flowers. Seafood flavors are incorporated into meat cookery, such as oyster sauce, made from a distillation of the oysters grown in the shallow waters of the Pear River, or shrimp sauce. Salted black beans are used to impart a highly savory taste; ginger is used to counteract fishiness; and garlic is used as an aromatic. Barbecue-roasted duck, chicken, and pork dishes are important here. Fruit is often included in Cantonese cooking, especially lemon, plum, tangerine, and orange, which are evident in the tangy, sweet-and-sour sauces. The tradition of *dim sum* ("touching the heart" or "little eats") originated here. It is usually eaten in the mornings and early afternoons. Popular dim sum items are *ha gau* (shrimp dumpling), *siu mai* (prawn and pork dumpling), *pai gwat* (steamed spareribs), *chun guen* (spring rolls), *cha siu pau* (steamed barbecued pork buns), and *cheung fun* (steamed rice flour rolls with barbecue pork, beef, or shrimp). Other well-known Cantonese dishes include shark's fin soup, roasted suckling pig, barbecued pork or *char siu*, lo mein, and the omelets known as *fu young*.

Glossary

Agar-Agar A Japanese seaweed product sold in the form of 8-inch long bars with 1-inch-square cross section or thin sticks $\frac{1}{8}$ inch in diameter. Usually colorless but sometimes dyed a deep red, it is used much like clear gelatin, but has a different texture. While gelatin gels are resilient, gels made of agar-agar liquid break cleanly on the bite. For best results, pass the boiled agar-agar liquid through a sieve to remove the undissolved particles before gelling. Agar-agar sticks, cut into 2-inch lengths, are often mixed with fresh cucumber shreds and soy sauce in a northern Chinese salad. A favorite agar-agar dessert is almond bean curd, which is agar-agar gel flavored with milk, sugar, and almond essence, but no bean curd.

Amaranth Young leaves and stems of this decorative plant are a common vegetable (*xiancai*) in east and south China. Salt-preserved amaranth stems, thick as a thumb, is an east China specialty.

Aniseeds Seeds from the anise plant, similar to fennel in both taste and appearance.

Bacon, Chinese Meat from the belly of the pig, with lean and fat layers interlaced and skin attached, is called five-flower meat in China, and is used extensively, especially in braised dishes in which $\frac{1}{4}$-inch-thick slices are separated by slices of starchy vegetables, such as taro. Winter-preserved meat (laro), often called Chinese bacon, also uses this cut, and is marinated first, then dried in the winter sun.

Bamboo Fungi Often mistakenly thought to be the lining of the hollow bamboo stem, these are a relative of the North American stinkhorn. The unique crisp texture is similar to bamboo shoots. This is one of the most expensive edible fungi in China, often three times more the price of French truffles.

Bamboo Shoots Bamboo plants propagate by issuing shoots from below the ground. The texture of the shoots changes with the seasons. Winter shoots, stubby and firm, have a meatlike chewiness; spring shoots are slender and tender; most commonly available are summer shoots, looser in texture, succulent, though inclined to be bitter. In North America fresh shoots are a rarity and the quality of canned shoots varies greatly with the brand. Winter and spring shoots are so specified on cans; unspecified ones are summer shoots, which should be ivory-white rather than yellow, and firm rather than mushy.

Bean Cheese Also called fermented bean cake, or *furu*. A fermented soybean product in the form of tiny yellow bricks, it is soft, salty, and pungent. It is used to accompany congee and oil-strips for breakfast. Subtle-tasting red bean cheese (*nanru*) is used extensively to flavor pork dishes and Cantonese snacks.

Bean Curd The process of making bean curd from soybeans has much in common with making cheese. Known as *doufu* in China and *tofu* in Japan and commonly called "meat without bones," it is extremely high in protein. Although quite bland in taste, it absorbs the flavors of the food it is cooked with and is used in a number of dishes, from soups and sauces to stir-fries. It is offered in three texture grades; **Soft**—Soft and smooth, used mostly for soups and steamed dishes; **Semi-soft**; and **Hard**—More substantial, used mostly for cutting into slices and cubes, or pressed and then shredded.

Bean Sprouts Sprouts from both soybeans and mung beans are used extensively in Chinese cooking. Mung bean sprouts have a fresh taste and a crisp, almost crystalline texture. This is true also of the stems of soybean sprouts. However, the large, yellow head of the latter is chewy and meatlike.

Bird Chiles Tiny chiles, extremely hot.

Bird's Nest Nests formed on sheer cliffs made of dried swallow saliva, found in Malaysia, Thailand, and Indonesia. The best ones are crystalline white, sometimes tinged with pink. Lower grades may be gray with adhered swallow down. Very expensive and getting rarer every year.

Bitter Melon or Foo Gwa Also known as balsam pear, this is a very strange-looking gourd, shaped something like a cucumber with a rough, pockmarked skin. The flavor is unusual as well; like cilantro, it's an acquired taste.

Black Beans, Fermented These beans come already cooked, fermented, and seasoned with salt and ginger. They are widely used in stir-frying and steaming in country cooking all over south China.

Blackfish Roe Dried roe of the blackfish (*wu* fish); thin slices are roasted and consumed as a snack in Fujian and Taiwan.

Broad Beans (Fava Beans) A very common vegetable, especially in north China. The pods are poisonous and must be removed. Served as a vegetable in stir-fries, in soups, as a paste, or as a snack.

Brown Sugar Chinese brown sugar comes in slabs like an elongated domino. Each slab looks like a sandwich, brown and solid top and bottom, and lightly yellow and powdery in between. Common brown sugar serves the same purpose except for the appearance.

Cassia Blossoms, Preserved (Guihua) Tiny yellow flowers of the osmanthus preserved in sugar or salt. They are used extensively in east and north China for their sweet fragrance in dumplings, pastries, and sauces.

Caul or Lace Fat (Wangyou, "Net-fat") This is a net of stringy fat that forms a casing, used for wrapping food before cooking for a self-braising effect, to improve external appearance, and to add special chewiness.

Cellophane Noodles (Fensi, Flour Threads, Bean Threads) Dried white threads made of the flour of the mung bean, they turn translucent and resilient when cooked, and are important in country cooking. A related product is *fenpi* (flour skin), which is a platter-size sheet of the same material.

Chestnuts Considered one of the best companions to chicken, available fresh or dried. The Chinese chestnut is easy to peel and has a smooth surface. Dried chestnuts should be soaked for hours before use. Chestnut paste is used commonly in North China for cakes and fillings of pastries or puddings.

Chile Pepper Products Chile pepper oil is red and very hot. It is a common table condiment and comes in two types: those made of ground chiles are orange red, somewhat like Tabasco sauce, but are thicker in consistency and are not vinegary; those made of crushed chiles often contain added ingredients such as ginger, fermented black beans, and shallots. Dried chile peppers are used liberally in Sichuan and Hunan cooking. Chile pepper powder is not found in Cantonese kitchens.

Chinese Almonds Not really almonds at all, Chinese almonds are seeds of the apricot, and come in two varieties. Southern almonds are mild, interchangeable in taste with American almonds; northern almonds are more bitter. A soup recipe may call for both types. American almonds are known to the herbist as flatpeach seed.

Chinese Cabbage (Sui Choy) or Napa Cabbage Several types of Chinese cabbage exist. The variety most commonly associated with Chinese cabbage is Napa cabbage, the large-headed cabbage with firmly packed, pale green leaves. It is also known as Peking cabbage and celery cabbage. Lining a bamboo steamer with cabbage helps prevent food from sticking to the bottom.

Chinese Sausage or Lop Cheong Smaller (up to 6 inches in length) and thinner than western sausages, these are usually made from pork or liver. The taste varies somewhat depending on the ingredients used, but they generally have a sweet-salty flavor.

Chinese White Radish or Lo Bak Also known simply as white radish and in Japan as daikon, this popular Asian vegetable has no resemblance to the round red radishes. Chinese cooks use it for soups and stir-fries.

Chives, Chinese and Yellow Chinese chives, often called Chinese leeks, have the shape of chives and the odor of leeks. They are used for stir-frying, for making egg pancakes, and for stuffing dumplings in north China cuisine. Yellow chives are grown in the dark; they are pale yellow and tender. Both Chinese chives and yellow chives are available in large Western Chinatowns.

Chrysanthemums Fresh white chrysanthemum petals are edible. They are used as a garnish for a number of banquet dishes or dried and used for tea. Chrysanthemum tea is popular with

Cantonese people when eating dim sum and it is often sweetened with rock sugar. As with all edible flowers, they should not be exposed to pesticides.

Cilantro or Chinese Parsley An aromatic herb with flat leaves, cilantro is the leaf of the coriander plant. Featured prominently in Asian and Latin cuisines, Chinese cooks use cilantro in soups, stir-fries, and frequently as a garnish. Although a member of the parsley family, cilantro has a much stronger flavor, which its detractors have described as "soapy."

Cloud Ear, Black Ruffle-edged, thin, black mushrooms. Cloud ears are similar in appearance to wood ears except wood ears are black with a brownish-tan inner color, whereas cloud ears are black with a slightly lighter shade of black as their inner color. Cloud ears have a more delicate, milder flavor and are much smaller than wood ears. Cloud ears reconstitute to a puffy, soft, smooth texture and delicate flavor.

Congee Boiled rice porridge. Plain congee with oil-strips, bean cheese, and pickles is a standard breakfast for many Chinese. Common in South China is congee with meat, chicken, roast duck, animal organs, and/or peanuts.

Cornstarch (Cornflour) A powdery "flour," nearly all starch, obtained from the endosperm of corn. Mixed with water to form a paste, it is often added to stir-fries as a thickening agent near the final cooking stages, as overcooked cornstarch loses its power as a thickener. If necessary, cornstarch can be used as a substitute for tapioca starch.

CUTTING TECHNIQUES

Slicing Hold the knife vertical or horizontal to the cutting board and cut straight across the ingredient.

Julienne and Shredding To get narrow strips, slice the ingredient into pieces of roughly $\frac{1}{8}$-inch (.3 cm) thickness, stack two or three of these pieces, and cut them again into $\frac{1}{8}$-inch (.3 cm) sticks.

Dicing Make the julienne sticks above, line the sticks up perpendicular to the knife blade, and cut straight down to get the size cubes called for in your recipe, usually $\frac{1}{4}$- to $\frac{1}{2}$-inch (.6 to 1.2 cm).

Mincing Slice or dice the ingredient into small pieces, then using the tip of the knife as a pivot, move only the lower blade in a chopping motion, from side to side across the ingredient until it is finely minced.

Roll-cutting For carrots, zucchini, and other cylindrical vegetables, hold the knife perpendicular to the board and slice down on a diagonal angle, then roll the vegetable a quarter turn and slice at the same angle; keep rolling and slicing a quarter turn at a time.

Crushing A fast, easy way to smash ginger, garlic, and lemongrass, place the knife flat on the ingredient with the blade facing away and press down hard on the blade with the palm of your hand.

Dates, Chinese Red Also called jujube dates, these are sold in dried form. They are used in soups, steamed chicken as garnish, and also as a filling for pastries.

Dragon Well Tea This is the most well-known green tea, grown in Hangzhou Province near Dragon Well Spring, the water of which is almost as famous.

Dried Bean Curd Sticks Made from soybeans and water, bean curd sticks resemble long yellowish icicles. They feel like thin plastic and break apart quite easily. They must be soaked overnight in cold water before use, or boiled for 20 minutes, or soaked in warm water for 1–2 hours.

Dried Lily Buds Also known as golden needles and tiger lilies, dried lily buds are the unopened flowers of day lilies. Dried lily buds are yellow-gold in color, with a musky or earthy taste. Before using, cut off about $\frac{1}{4}$ inch at the bottom to get rid of the woody stem. Like many other "woodsy" Chinese vegetables, lily buds must be soaked in warm water before use, for about 30 minutes.

Dried Shrimps Made from small shrimp tails, usually sun-dried.

Dried Tangerine Peel Soak the tangerine peel in warm water to soften it before using.

Duck, Preserved (Laya, Winter-Preserved Duck) A salted whole duck, flattened into a roughly circular disc and dried. The best ones come from Nanan in Jiangxi Province, just north of the border with Guangdong. Preserved duck from Nanking is called *banya* (board duck).

Eggs, Thousand-Year-Old Duck eggs that have been preserved in potash, they acquire a blue-black yolk and a translucent brown egg white.

Fennel An important ingredient in five-spice powder and in *lu*, the south China simmering sauce. Aniseed is often substituted.

Fish Lips and Fish Maws Fish lips are the meaty part of the shark near the mouth and fins. Fish maws are dried, deep-fried bladders of a large fish, usually cod.

Fish Sauce Fish sauce is a thin, salty liquid used in place of salt as a seasoning in many Asian recipes. It is also used as a dipping sauce. Chinese brands are often labeled "fish gravy" or "fish sauce," while it is called *nuoc mam* in Vietnam and *nam pla* in Thailand. However, they are all basically the same product, although the Thai and Vietnamese brands are considered superior.

Five-Spice Powder A common ingredient in Chinese cooking, this delicious mixture of five ground spices usually consists of equal parts of cinnamon, cloves, fennel seed, star anise, and Szechwan peppercorns.

Fuzzy Melon (Mo Gwa) Looks like a zucchini covered with fuzz. While zucchini is a type of squash, fuzzy melon is a gourd, related to winter melon. Peel off the skin or scrub well to remove the fuzz before using.

Gingko Nuts or White Nuts Typically used in desserts and stir-fries. Substitute blanched almonds or pine nuts.

Ginger The roots of the ginger plant, an indispensable ingredient in Chinese cuisine. Valued for its clean, sharp flavor, ginger is used in soups, stir-fries, and marinades. It is especially good with seafood, as it can cover up strong fish odors.

Green Onion, Spring Onion, or Scallion An immature onion with a white base (not yet a bulb) and long green leaves. Both parts are edible.

Hair Vegetable (Facai) Freshwater algae, with the appearance of course, dull, black human hair. Valued in vegetarian cuisine.

Hoisin Sauce A thick sauce valued for its unique combination of sweet and spicy flavors. It is made from soybean paste and flavored with garlic, sugar, chiles, and other spices and ingredients.

Hot Mustard A popular condiment served with Chinese appetizers; you'll also often find it added to sauces in Japanese dishes. It is made by mixing dry mustard powder with water, causing a chemical reaction that produces a sharp, hot taste.

Hua Diao ("Flower-Engraved") The best yellow wine from Xiaoxing Province.

Lo Mein In this dish, boiled and drained noodles are added to the other ingredients and stir-fried briefly during the final stages of cooking. This gives the noodles more flavor than is the case with chow mein, where the meat and vegetables are served over noodles that have been cooked separately.

Lotus root Grows underwater. It is starchy when cooked, but crispy and refreshing when raw. Slices of the lotus root have a beautiful pattern. Substitute water chestnuts or jicama.

Lychee Also called litchi, lichee, lichi, leeched, and laichee. Popular Chinese fruit about the size of a walnut, with a bumpy red shell encasing white translucent pulp that's similar in texture to a grape. The flavor is sweet, exotic, and very juicy.

Lychee Nuts Also called litchi nut, lichee nut, lichi nut, and leechee nut. These are sun-dried litchis. The outer shells are brown and the meat inside looks like a large raisin.

Marinade In Chinese cooking the primary reason meat is marinated before cooking is to improve flavor. The amount of marinade should be just sufficient to coat the meat or fish. Red meat is typically marinated with a little oil to prevent them from becoming dry and sticking together during the cooking process. Dark meat is marinated with whole egg and white meat and fish with egg white.

Monosodium Glutamate (MSG) A white crystalline compound used to enhance flavor. Note that MSG may not be suitable for everyone.

Mushrooms, Chinese Black Dried mushrooms. The name is a bit of a misnomer, since Chinese black mushrooms can be light brown, dark brown, and even gray. They are frequently speckled. Chinese black mushrooms (also known as shiitake mushrooms) range in price from moderate to quite expensive. The more costly are often called flower mushrooms because they have a thick cap and a nice curl. The drying process gives them a stronger flavor. Before use, soak them in warm water for 20 to 30 minutes, and remove the stems.

Mushroom Soy Sauce Soy sauce that has been infused with the flavor of straw mushrooms.

Oil (Dipping) Poaching A technique used to give the meat a more tender texture, oil poaching (also called velveting) seals the meat.

Oyster Sauce A rich sauce made from boiled oysters and seasonings, it does not have a fishy taste. Its savory flavor is used in meat and vegetable dishes, and is an important ingredient in Cantonese cooking.

Red Cooking Similar to Western braising, the cooking liquid is a soy sauce–based liquid.

Rice Vinegar Chinese rice vinegars are milder and less acidic than regular vinegar (as are Japanese vinegars). There are three basic types—black, red, and white—as well as sweetened black vinegars. The black variety is somewhat similar to balsamic vinegar, while red vinegar has both a sweet and tart taste. White vinegar is the closest in acidity and flavor to cider vinegar. There are no hard and fast rules, but black vinegar is generally recommended for braised dishes and as a dipping sauce; red vinegar for soups, noodle, and seafood dishes; and white for sweet and sour dishes and for pickling. In recipes, rice vinegar is sometimes also called rice wine vinegar.

Rice Wine Known colloquially as yellow wine, rice wine is a rich-flavored liquid made from fermented glutinous rice or millet and has a relatively low alcohol content. Aged for ten years or more, rice wine is used both in drinking and cooking. Pale dry sherry is the most acceptable substitute.

Sesame Oil Amber-colored, aromatic oil, made from pressed and toasted sesame seeds. Not for use as a cooking oil. Has an intense flavor and very low smoke point.

Sesame Seed Paste Roasted sesame seeds ground to a thick aromatic paste.

Shark's Fin The pale yellow, translucent ligaments within the fins of the shark.

Snow Peas Also known as *mangetout*, French for "eat it all." The French name comes from the fact that the whole pea including the pod is eaten.

Snow Pea Shoots The tips of the vines and the top set of leaves of the pea plant are an Oriental delicacy. They can be served raw in salads, quickly cooked in stir-fries, or blanched and used in soups.

Soy Sauce Invented by the Chinese approximately 3,000 years ago, soy sauce is made from fermented soybeans, wheat flour, water, and salt. The two main types of soy sauce are light and dark. As the name implies, light soy sauce is lighter in color, and also sweeter than dark soy sauce. Aged for a longer period of time, dark soy sauce is thicker and blacker in color. It is also less salty than light soy. It is used in certain recipes to add color, and as a dipping sauce.

Star Anise Whole star anise looks like an eight-pointed star about 1 inch (2.5 cm) across. It gives a licorice flavor to savory dishes, particularly those with pork and poultry.

Straw Mushrooms Delicate meaty texture and fine flavor, used for many soups and vegetable dishes.

Sugar, Rock Comes in chunks that look like crystals, has a subtle taste, and is used in most braised or "red-cooked" dishes.

Szechuan (Sichuan) Peppercorn Also called anise pepper, brown peppercorn, Chinese aromatic pepper, Chinese pepper, flower pepper, sancho, Japanese pepper, Japan pepper, wild pepper, and fagara pepper. Reddish-brown peppercorns, native to Szechuan Province. Much stronger and more fragrant than black peppercorns. These aren't true peppercorns, but rather dried flower buds.

Tapioca Made from the starch of the cassava root, tapioca comes in several forms, including granules and flour, as well as the pellets that are called pearl tapioca. Tapioca starch is often used to make dumpling dough, or as a thickening agent.

Water Chestnuts A knobby vegetable with papery brown skin, it is an aquatic vegetable that grows in marshes. Indigenous to Southeast Asia, the water chestnut is valued both for its sweetness and its ability to maintain a crisp texture when cooked.

White-Cooking A typical Cantonese technique to cook a whole fowl or fish by immersing it in boiling water. The heat is then turned off and the pot is covered until the item is done. The word for "white" in Chinese means "plain."

Winter Melon (Dong Gua) Resembles a large watermelon with dark green skin. The flesh inside is white, looking much like it has been lightly covered with snow, and the seeds are white as well. Winter melon has a very mild, sweet taste. It is used in soups and stir-fries, where it absorbs the flavors of the ingredients it is cooked with.

Wok The most important piece of Chinese cooking equipment, a wok can be used for stir-frying, deep-frying, steaming, and roasting. While a frying pan can be used in place of a wok for stir-frying (cast iron is particularly good), a wok has numerous advantages in shape, design, and material. It distributes heat more evenly, and requires less oil to cook with. There are two instruments traditionally used for cooking with a wok: a long-handled spoon and a long-handled perforated scoop with a slightly rounded edge.

Wonton Wrappers Made of flour, water, salt, and eggs; sold fresh or frozen. The dough is cut in $3\frac{1}{2}$ inch (8.75 cm) squares.

Wood Ear Mushroom A distant relative of the cloud ear fungus. Larger and somewhat tougher, they lack the delicate taste of cloud ears. They can be soaked in cold instead of warm water.

Menus and Recipes from China

Pungent and Hot Soup
Hot and Sour Soup   SERVES 4

Different versions of this soup are found in northern, eastern, central, and even southern China. This northern version has the lightest color.

Chinese black mushrooms are the dried mushrooms sold in Asian grocery stores. The name is a bit of a misnomer, since Chinese black mushrooms can be light brown, dark brown, and even gray. They are frequently speckled.

AMOUNT	MEASURE	INGREDIENT
Seasoning		
1 teaspoon		Tapioca powder or cornstarch
$1\frac{1}{2}$ teaspoons		Soy sauce
$\frac{1}{4}$ teaspoon		Sugar
$\frac{1}{2}$ cup	3 ounces, 84 g	Pork, lean boneless, julienned $\frac{1}{8} \times \frac{1}{8} \times 2$ inches (.3 × .3 × 5 cm)
Hot and Sour Mixture		
$1\frac{1}{2}$ teaspoons	7 ml	Sesame oil
1 tablespoon	$\frac{1}{2}$ ounce, 15 ml	Soy sauce
$\frac{1}{2}$ teaspoon		White pepper
1 tablespoon	$\frac{1}{2}$ ounce, 15 ml	Black or rice vinegar
$\frac{1}{2}$ teaspoon		Sugar
3 cups		Chicken stock
3		Medium dried black mushrooms, soaked in hot water 5 minutes, or until soft, rinsed thoroughly, tough ends trimmed; cut into $\frac{1}{8} \times \frac{1}{8} \times 2$ inch (.3 × .3 × 5 cm) pieces
	$\frac{1}{4}$ ounce, 4 g	Dried black cloud ears, soaked in hot water 20 minutes, cut into $\frac{1}{8} \times \frac{1}{8} \times 2$ inch (.3 × .3 × 5 cm) pieces
$\frac{1}{2}$ cup	3 ounces, 84 g	Bamboo shoots, $\frac{1}{8} \times \frac{1}{8} \times 2$ inches (.3 × .3 × 5 cm)
$1\frac{1}{2}$ tablespoons		Tapioca powder or cornstarch
1 tablespoon	$\frac{1}{2}$ ounce, 15 ml	Water
1 cup	6 ounces, 168 g	Soft bean curd, $\frac{1}{8} \times \frac{1}{8} \times 2$ inches (.3 × .3 × 5 cm)
1		Egg, lightly beaten
1 tablespoon		Green onion, minced
2 tablespoon		Cilantro leaves and short stems, 2 inches (5 cm)

PROCEDURE

1   Mix seasoning ingredients and combine with julienne pork; mix well.

2   Combine hot and sour mixture ingredients.

3   Bring chicken stock to a boil; add mushrooms, bamboo shoots, and pork shreds. Bring back to a boil; reduce heat to medium. Stir to separate pork shreds and cook for 5 minutes.

4   Reduce heat to low. Mix $1\frac{1}{2}$ tablespoons tapioca powder with the water and add gradually to soup, stirring constantly until thickened. Add bean curd.

5   Add hot and sour mixture to soup. Stir, correct seasoning.

6   Return to a boil, using a ladle float the eggs in very thin petals. Immediately remove from heat. Allow soup to set for 15 seconds. Garnish with green onion and cilantro.

Mandarin Pancakes

SERVES 4

Chef Tip Cooking pancakes in pairs makes the inside moist and assures a paper-thin pancake.

AMOUNT	MEASURE	INGREDIENT
2 cups	8 ounces, 224 g	All-purpose flour
$\frac{3}{4}$ cup	6 ounces, 180 ml	Boiling water
As needed		Sesame oil

PROCEDURE

1. Place the flour in a mixing bowl, making a well in the center. Add water to the flour, incorporating the flour by stirring it into the water with a wooden spoon or chopsticks. Let the dough cool slightly and turn onto a floured surface.

2. Knead for about 10 to 12 minutes or until smooth. Cover the dough and allow it to rest for 30 minutes. Knead an additional 1 to 2 minutes.

3. Roll the dough into a sausage shape, about $1\frac{1}{2}$ inches (3.6 cm) in diameter. Measure the cylinder and cut into 16 equal size pieces. Roll each piece into a smooth ball. Grease an area of the kneading board about 10 inches (24 cm) square with oil to prevent sticking. Moisten fingers with a bit of sesame oil. Flatten each ball into a 2-inch (4.8 cm) round and brush evenly with sesame oil on the surface. Place another round on top, forming a 2-layered round. Using a rolling pin, roll out this double-layered disk into a circle about 6 inches (14.4 cm) in diameter and $\frac{1}{8}$ inch (.3 cm) thick. Grease the board with more oil if needed.

4. Roll 2 pancakes, then proceed with the cooking. Continue to roll and cook, 2 pancakes at a time, until all the dough is used up.

5. To cook, heat a griddle or heavy pan over medium heat until hot. Cook the pancake on an ungreased surface for 1 minute or until the surface puffs up and brown spots appear on the bottom side. Turn to brown on the other side for about 30 seconds to 1 minute.

6. Transfer pancakes to a clean plate and cover with foil or a lightly dampened cloth to keep moist and warm.

7. Separate the two layers carefully; fold into quarters, with the cooked side on the inside. Serve warm.

Jiao Zi or Guo-tieh

Pot-Stickers   YIELD: 25 TO 30 POT-STICKERS

Chef Tip The additional chicken stock is to insure a moist filling, and adds intensity.

Dough

AMOUNT	MEASURE	INGREDIENT
2 cups	8 ounces, 224 g	All-purpose flour
$\frac{1}{8}$ teaspoon		Salt
$\frac{1}{2}$ cup	4 ounces, 120 ml	Boiling water
2 tablespoons	1 ounce, 30 ml	Cold water

PROCEDURE

1   Sift together the flour and salt. Make a well in the center add the boiling water. Mix together with a wood spoon or spatula.

2   Cover and let set for 5 minutes, and then add the cold water and mix to combine. Cover and let set for 15 minutes.

3   Turn out onto a floured board and knead until smooth, sprinkling additional flour as needed, for about 15 minutes.

4   Divide dough into two parts and roll each out 1 inch (2.4 cm) in diameter and about 12 inches (29 cm) long. Cut the rolls into $\frac{1}{2}$-inch (1.2 cm) slices. Lightly flour, then flatten and roll out each piece to a 3-inch (7.2 cm) diameter circle, $\frac{1}{8}$ inch (.3 cm) thick. The wrappers can be dusted with tapioca powder and stacked.

Chinese Egg Noodle

This dough may also be used for wonton and egg-roll wrappers.

Dough (optional dough)

AMOUNT	MEASURE	INGREDIENT
$1\frac{3}{4}$ cups	$9\frac{1}{4}$ ounces, 260 g	All-purpose flour
4 tablespoons	$1\frac{1}{3}$ ounce, 37 g	Bread flour
$\frac{1}{2}$ teaspoon		Salt
1		Egg
7 tablespoons		Water
$\frac{1}{8}$ teaspoon	$3\frac{1}{2}$ ounces, 105 ml	Sesame oil
$\frac{1}{3}$ cup	$1\frac{1}{2}$ ounces, 42 g	Cornstarch

PROCEDURE

1 In a food processor fitted with a metal blade, process the flours and salt together.

2 Beat the egg with 5 tablespoons ($2\frac{1}{2}$ ounces, 75 ml) water and sesame oil. Gradually add egg mixture, processing just until the dough begins to form a ball; add additional water if necessary. Process 10 seconds if using a pasta machine; process 30 seconds longer if rolling by hand.

3 Turn the dough, which should be barely sticky, onto a lightly floured board, and knead for 1 minute. Dough should be satiny and not stick to the palm of the hand. Cover and let rest 30 minutes to 1 hour.

4 To roll out with a pasta machine, roll the dough into a sausage shape $1\frac{1}{2}$ inch (3.6 cm) in diameter and cut into thirds. Flatten each piece to a rectangle about $\frac{1}{4}$ inches (.6 cm) thick and lightly coat both sides with cornstarch. Pass the dough through the thickest setting. Then fold the dough into thirds, flatten, dust with cornstarch, and run it through the rollers again, feeding in the unfolded end first. Repeat the procedure three times. Turn the machine to the next thinnest setting, dust the dough, and roll it though unfolded. Repeat this procedure with each setting until it is $\frac{1}{16}$ inch (.15 cm) thick for pot-stickers.

5 Cut the dough, allow the cut pieces to dry about 10 minutes, then dust them with cornstarch and stack them.

Filling

AMOUNT	MEASURE	INGREDIENT
2 cups	8 ounces, 224 g	Napa cabbage, $\frac{1}{4}$ inch (.6 cm) dice
1 teaspoon		Salt
1 cup	8 ounces, 224 g	Ground pork
$\frac{1}{4}$ cup	1 ounce, 28 g	Green onion, minced
2 teaspoons		Ginger, grated
1 tablespoon		Garlic clove, minced
1 tablespoon	$\frac{1}{2}$ ounce, 15 ml	Soy sauce
1 tablespoon	$\frac{1}{2}$ ounce, 15 ml	Dry sherry
2 tablespoons	1 ounce, 30 ml	Sesame oil
2 teaspoons		Rice vinegar
$\frac{1}{2}$ cup	4 ounces, 120 ml	Chicken Stock, depending on the moisture content of the mixture
2 teaspoons		Tapioca or cornstarch powder
For Frying		
3 tablespoons	$\frac{3}{4}$ ounce, 20 ml	Vegetable oil
$\frac{1}{2}$ cup	4 ounces, 120 ml	Water
1 teaspoon		Vinegar
Ginger and Vinegar Sauce		
2 tablespoons	1 ounce, 28 ml	Ginger, finely shredded
$\frac{1}{4}$ cup	2 ounces, 60 ml	Chinese black (Chinkiang) or rice vinegar
1 tablespoon	$\frac{1}{2}$ ounce, 15 ml	Sesame oil

PROCEDURE

1 Mix cabbage with the 1 teaspoon salt. Allow to sit for 30 minutes, then wrap in cheesecloth and squeeze to remove as much moisture as possible.

2 Combine cabbage with remaining filling ingredients. It should bind together; if not, add a little more cornstarch.

3 To assemble the dumplings, place about 1 tablespoon filling in the center of each wrapper and shape the filling into a strip.

4 Fold the wrapper over to make a half-moon shape and pinch the edges together at the center of the arc, leaving the two ends open.

5 With your fingers, make about 3 to 4 pleats in one side of the opening at each end. Pinch all along the edges to seal.

6   Remove the finished pot-sticker to a tray dusted with flour or cornstarch; keep covered with a cloth.

7   To cook, heat a heavy 10-inch (24 cm) skillet over high heat until drops of water sprinkled into it sizzle and dry up. Add oil to coat the bottom evenly.

8   Add enough pot-stickers to fill the pan, arranging them closely together with pleated sides up. Pan-fry over medium heat for 2 minutes, or until the bottoms are lightly browned.

9   Mix water with vinegar and add to skillet. Cover the skillet and cook for 6 to 8 minutes or until the liquid is evaporated.

10   Remove cover and continue to pan-fry until they can be moved around easily. Remove from the heat and transfer to a serving platter, brown side up.

11   Combine sauce ingredients. Serve pot-stickers hot with ginger and vinegar sauce on the side.

Chef Tip   **Boiled dumplings (*jiaozi*) are made with the same filling. However, the dough is made with only cold water. Assembly of the *jiaozi* is made simple by pinching the edges together instead of pleating. They are then boiled in salted water in the following manner: bring water to a boil and add the dumplings and stir immediately. When the water returns to the boil, add cold water to reduce the temperature. Cook for 5 minutes or until the *jiaozi* float to the top.**

Stir-Fried Bok Choy

SERVES 4

AMOUNT	MEASURE	INGREDIENT
Sauce		
1 teaspoon		Cornstarch
2 tablespoons	1 ounce, 30 ml	Chicken stock.
$\frac{1}{4}$ teaspoon		Sesame oil
3 tablespoons	$1\frac{1}{2}$ ounces, 45 ml	Oil
To taste		Salt and white pepper
Bok Choy		
3 tablespoons	$1\frac{1}{2}$ ounces, 45 ml	Vegetable oil
2 slices		Ginger root
1 cup	4 ounces, 112 g	Onions, thinly sliced
2 cups	4 ounces, 112 g	Mushrooms, washed, $\frac{1}{2}$ inch (1.2 cm) sliced
2 cups	12 ounces, 336 g	Bok choy, washed, $\frac{1}{2}$ inch (1.2 cm) sliced on the bias
2 tablespoons	1 ounce, 30 ml	Chicken stock

PROCEDURE

1 Combine the sauce ingredients.

2 Set a wok over high heat until the bottom turns a dull red. Add 3 tablespoons ($1\frac{1}{2}$ ounces, 45 ml) oil. When oil is hot and smoky, add ginger briefly to flavor oil, and then discard when brown.

3 Add onions, stirring and turning, for 30 seconds. Add mushrooms, stirring and turning, for 30 seconds.

4 And bok choy, stirring and turning until each piece is well coated with oil.

5 Whirl in stock along edge of wok and cover immediately. Cook for two minutes.

6 Add the sauce; stir until thickened, season with salt and white pepper to taste, cover.

7 Keep wok covered for one minute. Serve immediately.

Vinegar-Slipped Fish Chunks

SERVES 4

Made from the starch of the cassava root, tapioca powder thickens at a lower temperature than cornstarch, remains stable when frozen, and imparts a glossy sheen. With the exception of dumpling dough, in most cases cornstarch can be used as a substitute.

Chef Tip Ginger juice is often used as a seasoning, along with wine. The best process to maximize the ginger is to grate as much ginger as needed into a small bowl, and then add the wine and mix well. Pour the mixture through a small strainer and squeeze the grated ginger against the wall of the strainer to extract all the juice. A normal-size slice of gingerroot is the size and thickness of an American quarter.

AMOUNT	MEASURE	INGREDIENT
1 pound	16 ounces, 448 g	Boneless, skinless fish fillet (cod, red snapper, or sole)
2		Green onions, white and green parts, separated
3 cups	24 ounces, 720 ml	Oil
1		Garlic clove, crushed
1 tablespoon	$\frac{1}{2}$ ounce, 15 ml	Dry sherry
2 teaspoons		Sesame oil
Marinade		
2		Egg whites
2 tablespoons		Tapioca powder or cornstarch
1 tablespoon	$\frac{1}{2}$ ounce, 15 ml	Dry sherry
$\frac{1}{2}$ teaspoon		Salt
2 slices		Ginger juice (see Chef Tip)

AMOUNT	MEASURE	INGREDIENT
Vinegar Sauce		
$\frac{3}{4}$ cup	6 ounces, 180 ml	Chicken stock
2 tablespoons	1 ounce, 30 ml	Red rice vinegar
2 tablespoons	1 ounce, 28 g	Sugar, granulated
2 teaspoons		Tapioca powder or cornstarch
$\frac{1}{4}$ teaspoon		Salt

PROCEDURE

1 Cut fillets lengthwise into strips 1 inch (2.4 cm) wide. Cut each strip into chunks about 1 × 1$\frac{1}{2}$ inches (2.4 cm × 3.6 cm).

2 Mix ingredients for marinade and add to the fish. Mix well, using your fingers or chopsticks.

3 Cut white parts of green onion into 4-inch (9.6 cm) lengths, then flatten with a cleaver. Add them to the marinating fish.

4 Chop the green onion greens very fine and set aside.

5 Mix ingredients for sauce and set aside.

6 When ready to cook, remove green onion whites and chop fine. Combine with green parts.

To Cook

1 Set wok over medium heat. When hot, add the oil. Wait 2 to 3 minutes, heat to 325°F (163°C) or until a piece of green onion dropped in oil bubbles, sizzles, and moves around.

2 Add the fish chunks to the oil. Lightly stir in a spading manner to separate (30 seconds). Cook fish 2 minutes, then turn heat up and continue to cook 1 minute longer, at 375°F (190°C). Drain fish and oil into a colander or strainer-lined container. Leave about 1 tablespoon ($\frac{1}{2}$ ounce, 15 ml) oil in wok.

3 Return wok to high heat. When very hot add the garlic, stirring 10 seconds. Sizzle in the wine along the sides of the wok, and then add the sauce mixture. Turn heat to low; stir sauce until thickened.

4 Glaze sauce with sesame oil, and then slip in the fish chunks. Add the chopped green onions and mix together. Correct seasoning and serve.

Mo Shu, Moshu, Moo Shu, or Mu Shu Pork

Wood Shavings Pork   SERVES 4

Chef Tip Nappa cabbage may have a high moisture content, green cabbage has a lower moisture content.

AMOUNT	MEASURE	INGREDIENT
		Mandarin pancakes (see p. 218)
6 tablespoons	3 ounces, 90 ml	Vegetable oil
2		Eggs

PROCEDURE

1   Prepare mandarin pancakes. Cover finished pancakes with a clean cloth to prevent condensation from dropping onto the surface. Cover and keep warm until ready to serve.

2   Set a wok over high heat. Add one tablespoon ($\frac{1}{2}$ ounce, 15 ml) oil, swirl around wok.

3   Beat eggs lightly. When oil is hot, pour in eggs, and tilt the wok so that the whole surface is covered with a thin coat of eggs. Flip the egg sheet over and cook for a few seconds. Transfer to plate; when cool, shred into narrow strips 2 inches (4.8 cm) long.

AMOUNT	MEASURE	INGREDIENT
$\frac{1}{2}$ pound		Lean pork
Marinade		
To taste		Freshly ground pepper
$\frac{1}{4}$ teaspoon		Fresh ginger, minced
2 teaspoons		Cornstarch
1 teaspoon		Dry sherry
1 tablespoon	$\frac{1}{2}$ ounce, 15 ml	Soy sauce

PROCEDURE

1   Shred pork by slicing it $\frac{1}{8}$ inch (.3 cm) thick across the grain, then cut the slices into strips about $\frac{1}{8}$ inch × $\frac{1}{8}$ inch × 2 inches (.3 cm × .3 cm × 4.8 cm).

2   Combine marinade ingredients; mix with shredded pork. Toss to coat thoroughly; let stand at least 30 minutes.

AMOUNT	MEASURE	INGREDIENT
6		Chinese dried mushrooms
$\frac{1}{4}$ cup		Dried black cloud ears
25		Dried tiger lily buds
I cup	4 ounces, 112 g	Cabbage, $\frac{1}{8}$ × $\frac{1}{8}$ × 2 inches (.3 × .3 × 5 cm)

PROCEDURE

I   Soak mushrooms and black cloud ears in 2 cups (16 ounces, 480 ml) hot water for 20 minutes. Discard the water. Remove stems; shred mushrooms into thin strips.

2   Soak tiger lily buds in 1 cup (8 ounces, 240 ml) hot water for 10 minutes. Discard the water. Snap off hard ends of the buds. Rinse and cut each bud in half. Combine with mushrooms and black cloud ears.

AMOUNT	MEASURE	INGREDIENT
Sauce		
I teaspoon		Tapioca powder or cornstarch
I tablespoon	$\frac{1}{2}$ ounce, 15 ml	Light soy sauce
4 tablespoons	2 ounces, 60 ml	Chicken stock or water
$\frac{1}{2}$ teaspoon		Sesame oil

PROCEDURE

I   Mix all ingredients to combine.

AMOUNT	MEASURE	INGREDIENT
2		Garlic cloves, crushed
I teaspoon		Garlic cloves, minced
$\frac{1}{2}$ teaspoon		Salt
2		Green onions, minced

PROCEDURE

I   Return wok to high heat. When very hot, add 2 tablespoons (1 ounce, 30 ml) of oil. Flavor the oil with crushed garlic and discard the garlic when browned. Add the tiger lilies, wood ears black mushrooms, and cabbage, stirring for 3 to 4 minutes. Toss and season. Remove from wok.

2   Rinse wok and reset over high heat. When very hot, add two (1 ounce, 30 ml) tablespoons oil. Flavor with minced garlic for 10 seconds, then add the meat and green onions, stirring continuously until the shreds separate.

3   Push ingredients to the side of wok and restir sauce mixture. Add sauce mixture to the center of the wok, stirring sauce until it thickens. Return the tiger lilies, mushrooms, bean sprouts, and eggs to wok; mix well and remove.

4   Serve with steamed mandarin pancakes as wrappers. Serve with Hoisin dipping sauce to be spread on the pancakes before wrapping filling.

Hoisin Dipping Sauce

AMOUNT	MEASURE	INGREDIENT
$\frac{1}{4}$ cup	2 ounce, 60 ml	Hoisin sauce
2 tablespoons	1 ounce, 30 ml	Water

PROCEDURE

1   Combine to a smooth sauce.

Fortune Cookies   SERVES 4

Before making the cookies, prepare the fortunes on small slips of paper.

AMOUNT	MEASURE	INGREDIENT
3		Eggs
$\frac{3}{4}$ cup	6 ounces, 168 g	Sugar
$\frac{1}{2}$ cup	4 ounces, 112 g	Butter, melted
$\frac{1}{4}$ teaspoon		Vanilla extract
1 cup	4 ounces, 112 g	All-purpose flour
2 tablespoon	1 ounce, 30 ml	Water

PROCEDURE

1 Preheat oven to 350°F (176°C).

2 Combine ingredients in order listed, mixing well after each addition.

3 Chill for 20 minutes.

4 On a nonstick baking pad or parchment paper, fill a 3-inch (7.2 cm) circle mold with cookie butter and spread to $\frac{1}{8}$-inch (.3 cm) thickness. Bake two cookies at a time

5 Bake 4 to 5 minutes, until edges are lightly browned.

6 Working quickly, place a fortune paper slip in the center of each cookie. Fold cookie in half, enclosing the fortune slip and forming a semicircle.

7 Grasp the rounded edges of the semicircle between thumb and forefinger with both hands. Push the fortune cookie down over a dowel, making certain the solid sides of cookie puff out.

8 Place each cookie in small muffin tin, open end up, until cookies are set.

9 Return to oven to finish baking until golden brown, about 1 to 2 minutes.

Lamb on Rice Sticks   SERVES 4

Lamb is a tradition in Peking.

When marinating meats be sure to add oil or the meat will stick together when cooking.

AMOUNT	MEASURE	INGREDIENT
	12 ounces	Lamb, trimmed of all visible fat and all gristle removed, cut $\frac{1}{8} \times \frac{1}{8} \times 1\frac{1}{2}$ inch (.3 × .3 × 3.6 cm) shreds
1 teaspoon		Ginger juice
$\frac{1}{2}$ cup	3 ounces, 84 g	Bamboo shoots
2 cups plus 1 tablespoon	16.5 ounces, 495 ml	Vegetable oil
1 ounce		Rice sticks
2 cups	8 ounces, 224 g	Leeks, white part only, washed well, $\frac{1}{8} \times \frac{1}{8} \times 1\frac{1}{2}$ inch (.3 × .3 × 3.6 cm) shreds
4 medium		Black mushrooms, soaked in warm water until soft, stems trimmed; squeeze to extract moisture, $\frac{1}{8} \times \frac{1}{8} \times 1\frac{1}{2}$ inch (.3 × .3 × 3.6 cm) shreds
1		Garlic clove, minced
1 cup	4 ounces, 112 g	Carrots, peeled, $\frac{1}{8} \times \frac{1}{8} \times 1\frac{1}{2}$ inch (.3 × .3 × 3.6 cm) shreds
3, or to taste		Hot chiles, seeds and pulp removed, shredded finely
$\frac{1}{2}$ teaspoon		Salt
1 teaspoon		Granulated sugar
1 tablespoon	$\frac{1}{2}$ ounce, 15 ml	Dry sherry
1 teaspoon		Tapioca powder or cornstarch mixed with 1 tablespoon ($\frac{1}{2}$ ounce, 15 ml) chicken stock
1 teaspoon		Sesame oil
Marinade		
1		Egg
1 tablespoon		Tapioca powder or cornstarch
1 tablespoon	$\frac{1}{2}$ ounce, 15 ml	Soy sauce
1 tablespoon		Ginger juice
$\frac{1}{4}$ teaspoon		Salt
$\frac{1}{8}$ teaspoon		White pepper
1 tablespoon	$\frac{1}{2}$ ounce, 15 ml	Vegetable oil

PROCEDURE

1   Combine all marinade ingredients and add to lamb. Mix until well blended; refrigerate 30 minutes.

2   Blanch bamboo shoots in boiling water 1 minute; rinse with cold water. Shred finely, $\frac{1}{8}$ × $\frac{1}{8}$ × $1\frac{1}{2}$ inch (.3 × .3 × 3.6 cm) shreds; drain and pat dry with paper towels.

3   Set wok over high heat. When very hot, add 2 cups (16 ounces, 480 ml) oil and heat to 400°F (204°C). Test temperature by dropping a few inches of rice stick into the oil. If it puffs up immediately, the oil is hot enough.

4   Add the rice sticks, turning over quickly when puffed up. Deep-fry for 5 more seconds and remove; drain on paper towels. The rice sticks should be creamy white in color.

5   Remove wok from heat, strain sediments from oil, and return to 400°F (204°C). Add the lamb shreds to the wok, stirring to separate. Cook 1 to 2 minutes, then pour oil and lamb into a strainer-lined container to drain.

6   Return wok and two tablespoons (1 ounce, 30 ml) oil to high heat. When hot, add the leeks and garlic to the oil, stir-fry until limp. Add mushrooms, carrots, bamboo shoots, and chiles, in that order, stirring after each is added. Season with salt.

7   Return lamb to wok. Stir and sizzle in the sherry along the edge. Push all the ingredients to the side, restir thicking mixture, and add to center of wok. Stir until thickened, then add sesame oil. Mix all ingredients.

8   Line a serving platter with rice sticks, pressing down to break sticks into smaller pieces. Place the lamb shreds on top. Serve hot.

Wonton Soup
SERVES 4

AMOUNT	MEASURE	INGREDIENT
40		Wonton Wrappers, packaged
Filling		
$\frac{1}{2}$ pound	8 ounces, 224 g	Ground pork, chicken or shrimp
2 tablespoons	1 ounce, 30 ml	Soy Sauce
1 tablespoon	$\frac{1}{2}$ ounce, 15 ml	Rice wine or dry sherry
$\frac{1}{2}$ teaspoon		Salt
1		Egg
2 tablespoons	1 ounce, 30 ml	Sesame oil
$\frac{1}{4}$ cup	1 ounce, 28 g	Green onions, minced
$\frac{1}{2}$ cup	3 ounces, 84 g	Chinese cabbage or bamboo shoots, minced
Dash		White pepper
Soup		
6 cups	48 ounces, 1.4 L	Chicken or beef stock
2 tablespoons	1 ounce, 30 ml	Soy sauce
To taste		Salt
2 tablespoons		Green onions, minced

PROCEDURE

1 Mix filling ingredients, chill until needed.

2 Place 1 teaspoon filling in the center of each wrapper.

3 Fold over at the center, wet the edges with water and press to seal.

4 Fold in half lengthwise at the open side, bring the two ends over the other and press together with a little water.

5 Bring 3 quarts (96 ounces, 2.8 L) of water to a boil. Add wontons, stir. Cover and return to boil.

6 Add 1 cup (8 ounces, 240 ml) of cold water, cover and return to boil. When cooked the wontons will float.

7 Drain and rinse with cold water to stop cooking.

8 Combine stock, soy sauce and salt, bring to a boil.

9 Add wontons and return to a boil. Add minced green onions, serve hot.

Pavo con Salsa de Achiote a la Yucataneca— Yucatán-Style Steamed Turkey in Achiote Sauce (Mexico)

Pabellón Criollo— Venezuelan Shredded Beef with Beans, Rice and Plantains (South America)

Ceviche de Pescado—Fish Ceviche (South America)

(Bottom left) Camarones Sofrito—Shrimp in Green Sofrito (Dominican Republic); (Top right) Curried Lamb, Salad of Hearts of Palm, with Passion Fruit Vinaigrette and Fried Ripe Plantains (Caribbean)

Jamaican Jerk Beef Steak on Arroz Mamposteao—Rice and Beans

Yakitori—Grilled Chicken, Maki Sushi, Horenso Goma-ae—Spinach in Sesame Dressing (Japan)

Gyoza—Japanese Pot-Stickers, Kyuri No Sunome—Japanese Cucumber Salad, and Nigiri-Zushi (Japan)

Kamonanban Soba—Soba with Duck and Long Onions (Japan)

Emerald Shrimp and Shanghai Sweet and Sour Spareribs (China)

Red Cooked Duck and Yangchow (Yangzhou) Fried Rice (China)

Hacmul Jungol—
Seafood Hot Pot
and Bibim Naeng
Myun—Garden's
Cold Mixed Noodles
(Korea)

Dwaeji Galbi—Spicy
Pork Ribs and
Bibimbap –
Garnished Rice
(Korea)

ssorted spices and
erbs—Bottom platter,
ockwise from bottom left:
ine nuts, ground cayenne,
enugreek, walnut pieces,
araway seeds, white
ardamom. Between the
atters, clockwise from the
ottom: Green onions,
mon grass, red chile de
bol, mint leaf, lime,
allots, curry leaf, kaffir
ne leaves, habanero, garlic
oves, ginger, red onion;
p platter, clockwise from
ottom left: cloves, chives,
intaka chile, dried red chili
akes, árbol, chile basil,
mpkin seeds, cinnamon
icks (Southeast Asia)

Goi Cuon—Fresh
Spring Rolls and Cha
Gio—Fried Spring
Rolls (Vietnam,
Southeast Asia)

Laksa Lemak—
Chicken, Shrimp and
Rice Noodles in
Coconut Sauce;
Pepes Ikan—Grilled
Fish in Banana Leaf
(Indonesia,
Southeast Asia)

Dia Rau Song—
Vegetable Platter;
Ga Xao Sa Ot—
Lemon Grass
Chicken (Vietnam,
Southeast Asia)

Jellyfish and White Radish Salad SERVES 4

Chef Tip It is best to soak the jellyfish overnight. Keep it as dry as possible so the dressing will not be diluted.

AMOUNT	MEASURE	INGREDIENT
	4 ounces, 112 g	Precut jellyfish shreds, soaked overnight
$1\frac{1}{2}$ cup	8 ounces, 224 g	Chinese white radish (daikon), peeled, $\frac{1}{8} \times \frac{1}{8} \times 1\frac{1}{2}$ inch (.3 × .3 × 3.6 cm) shreds
		Salt
$\frac{1}{2}$ cup	2 ounces, 56	Carrot, peeled, $\frac{1}{8} \times \frac{1}{8} \times 1\frac{1}{2}$ inch (.3 × .3 × 3.6 cm) shreds
1		Green onion, trimmed, white part and 2-in. (4.8 cm) green part, minced
2		Chinese parsley (cilantro) sprigs, cut into 2-in. (4.8 cm) pieces
Dressing		
2 teaspoons		Rice vinegar
2 teaspoons		Sesame oil
2 tablespoons	1 ounce, 30 ml	Peanut oil
2 teaspoons		Granulated sugar
To taste		White pepper and cayenne

PROCEDURE

1 Rinse jellyfish with cold water, squeezing and rubbing to remove salt. Cover in cold water and soak, preferably overnight, then rinse thoroughly. Drain in colander for 1 hour, or until most moisture is gone. Pat dry and wrap with a towel. Chill and refrigerate.

2 Rub radish with 1 tablespoon salt and let stand at room temperature for 2–3 hours or until limp. Rinse radish with cold water to remove salt, then squeeze shreds by hand to remove excess moisture. Repeat until all shreds are squeezed dry.

3 Process carrot in the same manner as radish.

4 One hour before serving, mix dressing, and combine with all ingredients. Toss well. Serve chilled.

Pearl Balls
Porcupine Meatballs   SERVES 4 AS AN APPETIZER

Chef Tip Make sure the egg is well incorporated, it is a binding agent. If rice is not sticking to the pearl balls, wet with a little cold water.

AMOUNT	MEASURE	INGREDIENT
$\frac{1}{2}$ cup	$3\frac{1}{2}$ ounces, 98 g	Glutinous rice
1 cup	8 ounces, 224 g	Lean ground pork
$\frac{1}{4}$ teaspoon		Salt
1 tablespoon	$\frac{1}{2}$ ounce, 15 ml	Light soy sauce
1		Egg
2 teaspoons		Dry sherry
$\frac{1}{4}$ teaspoon		Granulated sugar
1 teaspoon		Ginger, grated
2 teaspoons		Sesame oil
2 teaspoons		Tapioca powder or cornstarch
To taste		White pepper
$\frac{1}{2}$ cup	3 ounces, 84 g	Bamboo shoots
2 tablespoons		Green onion, white parts only, minced
$\frac{1}{4}$ cup	2 ounces, 60 ml	Rice vinegar
1 tablespoon		Ginger, minced

PROCEDURE

1   Rinse the rice and soak in cold water for a least 1 hour. Drain thoroughly and spread in one layer on pan lined with paper towels. Make sure the rice is dry before using.

2   Combine pork, salt, and soy sauce. Mix with your fingers and scoop up pork mixture by the hand, beating it back into the bowl several times until firm. Add the egg, sherry, sugar, ginger, sesame oil, tapioca powder and pepper to the meat, scooping and beating several more times.

3   Blanch the bamboo shoots in boiling water for two minutes. Run cold water over to stop the cooking process; shred into bite sized bits. Squeeze out as much moisture as possible.

4 Add the green onion to the pork together with bamboo shoots. Mix well; chill for at least 2 hours or until ready to use.

5 Scoop up a handful of pork mixture and squeeze out through the fist until it reaches the size of a walnut (1 tablespoon is 1 ounce). Scrape off with a wet spoon.

6 Drop pork balls onto the rice, rolling around until the surface is evenly covered with the rice. Place on a greased container that can be used in a steamer; or on a lettuce leaf (banana leaf, bamboo leaf, napa cabbage) allow $\frac{1}{2}$ inch (1.2 cm) separation between each pearly ball.

7 Place the meatballs in a steamer; steam over high heat 25 to 30 minutes or until the rice is cooked and turns shiny and translucent.

8 Combine vinegar and ginger to make sauce. Serve meatballs hot or warm with sauce.

Emerald Shrimp

SERVES 4

AMOUNT	MEASURE	INGREDIENT
12 ounces		Shrimp (16–20 count), shelled, deveined, and cut down the middle from the back
4 cups	8 ounces, 224 g	Flat leaf spinach, washed well, stems removed, coarsely chopped
2 tablespoons		Green onion, white part only, roll-cut in $\frac{1}{2}$ inch (1.2 cm) cuts
	$\frac{1}{2}$ ounce, 14 g	Smithfield ham, $\frac{1}{2}$ inch (1.2 cm) dice
2 cups	16 ounces, 480 ml	Water
$1\frac{1}{2}$ cup	12 ounces, 360 ml	Vegetable oil
1		Garlic clove
2 teaspoons		Mirin
Marinade		
1		Egg white
$\frac{1}{2}$ teaspoon		Salt
2 teaspoons		Tapioca powder or cornstarch
$\frac{1}{4}$ teaspoon		Sesame oil
$\frac{1}{4}$ teaspoon		Sugar
Dash		White pepper

PROCEDURE

1 Arrange the shrimp in one layer on double paper towels. Roll up like a jelly roll and chill for at least two hours. The shrimp need to be very dry.

2 In a blender, combine 1 cup (8 ounces, 240 ml) water with the spinach. Process until reduced to a puree. Pour the puree into a very fine-mesh strainer; press the pureed spinach to extract liquid. Reserve strained liquid and spinach.

3 Transfer spinach puree to a bowl and thin with remaining water. Pour it through the strainer again to combine liquid with the previously extracted spinach juice.

4 Heat the spinach juice over high heat until small bubbles start to appear gradually along the sides of the pan and the liquid begins to foam. Remove immediately from heat.

5 Set a coffee filter into a cone and skim the spinach foam from the pan into the filter. Let it drain thoroughly and squeeze to extract all the liquid; there should be about 1 tablespoon of very fine spinach paste. Cover and chill until ready to use. Discard the juice in the pan.

6 Pat shrimp with paper towel; they must be very dry for the green spinach coloring to adhere. Combine shrimp and 1 teaspoon spinach paste, mixing it well by hand. Continue to add $\frac{1}{2}$ teaspoon at a time, mixing well after each addition until shrimp is tinted evenly with green coloring. You need at least 2 teaspoons of spinach paste; avoid over-coloring.

7 Mix marinade with wire whisk until smooth. Add to the green shrimp, mixing well by hand until evenly coated. Chill for 1 to 2 hours.

8 Set a wok over high heat. When very hot, add about $\frac{1}{4}$ cup (2 ounces, 60 ml) oil, swish around the wok to grease the surface, and remove that oil from the wok. Add remaining oil, heat to 325°F (163°C) or until a piece of green onion dropped in oil bubbles, sizzles, and moves around.

9 Stir shrimp mixture, and then add the whole batch to the oil at once. Stir to separate shrimp quickly, about 20 seconds. Pour shrimp and oil into a strainer-lined container to drain oil, leaving about 1 tablespoon ($\frac{1}{2}$ ounce, 15 ml) of oil in wok.

10 Return wok to high heat. Add garlic. Remove wok quickly from heat, let garlic cook in hot oil for 10 seconds, then discard. (This ensures the oil in wok is clear.)

11 Reset wok on high heat. Return the shrimp to wok and stir-fry 15 to 20 seconds. Sizzle in the mirin, then add green onions and ham. Stir 20 seconds and serve immediately.

Red-Cooked Duck   SERVES 4

Chef Tip   **Cold Red-Cooked Duck is outstanding, should be served garnished with cilantro.**

AMOUNT	MEASURE	INGREDIENT
3½ pound	1.5 kg	Young duck, cut in quarters
2 tablespoons	1 ounce, 30 ml	Vegetable oil
1		Garlic clove, flattened
2		Green onions, ¼ inch (.6 cm) lengths
1		Star anise
2 teaspoons		Tapioca powder or cornstarch
1 tablespoon	½ ounce, 15 ml	Water
1 teaspoon		Sesame oil
To taste		Salt
Marinade		
2 teaspoons		Ginger juice
2 tablespoons	1 ounce, 30 ml	Dry sherry
2 tablespoons	1 ounce, 30 ml	Dark soy sauce
½ teaspoon		Salt
Braising Mixture		
2 cups	16 ounces, 480 ml	Chicken stock
1 tablespoon	½ ounce, 15 ml	Oyster sauce
1 tablespoon	½ ounce, 14 g	Rock sugar or granulated sugar
1		Thai bird chile (small red)

PROCEDURE

1   Remove excess loose fat from duck, then flatten the duck. Rinse and pat dry. Prick the skin.

2   Combine marinade ingredients, mix well, and rub evenly on the skin and cavity. Let marinate at room temperature for at least 1 hour, turning occasionally.

3 Drain duck, reserving excess marinade. Set wok over high heat; when hot, add 2 (1 ounce, 30 ml) tablespoons oil. Swish oil around and then place duck in wok. Turn heat to medium and brown the duck slowly and evenly on all sides.

4 Mix together the braising mixture and bring to boil over high heat, then add the duck. Return to a boil; add reserved marinade, garlic, green onion, and star anise. Cover and reduce to a simmer; cook 1 to $1\frac{1}{2}$ hours or until a chopstick pierces through the thigh easily. Remove duck and chile; degrease the sauce.

5 Return braising liquid to a boil, add duck to reheat, remove, drain, cut into serving pieces, and place on serving platter.

6 Mix tapioca powder with the water and add to the liquid in the wok, stirring constantly until thickened. Correct seasoning, then glaze sauce with sesame oil. Pour over duck. Serve hot or cold.

Yangchow (Yangzhou) Fried Rice   SERVES 4

This colorful fried rice may have started in Yangzhou, a city famous for Eastern cuisine, but many versions are found all over China. The original version was said to have at least eight ingredients and each grain of rice coated with egg!

Chef Tip Always marinate dark meat with whole egg.

AMOUNT	MEASURE	INGREDIENT
I cup	6 ounces, 168 g	Boneless, skinless chicken thigh meat, cut $\frac{1}{2}$ inch (1.2 cm) dice
9 tablespoons	$3\frac{1}{2}$ ounces, 105 ml	Vegetable oil
$\frac{3}{4}$ cup	4 ounces, 112 g	Shrimp, raw, dice $\frac{1}{2}$ inch (1.2 cm).
$\frac{3}{4}$ cup	4 ounces, 112 g	Cantonese roast pork (*char siu*), dice $\frac{1}{2}$ inch (1.2 cm).
$\frac{3}{4}$ cup	4 ounces, 112 g	Chinese Ham
3		Black mushrooms, soaked in hot water until soft. Trim stems and squeeze to extract moisture, dice $\frac{1}{2}$ inch (1.2 cm).
2		Eggs and I egg yolk, beaten with a pinch of salt
2 tablespoons	I ounce, 28 g	Carrots, $\frac{1}{2}$ inch (1.2 cm) dice, blanched
$\frac{1}{4}$ cup	2 ounces, 56 g	Green peas, cooked
3 cups	12 ounces, 336 g	Cold cooked rice, grains separated
4		Green onions, $\frac{1}{4}$ inch (.6 cm) lengths
Marinade for Chicken		
2 tablespoons	I ounce, 30 ml	Water
$\frac{1}{2}$ teaspoon		Salt
I		Egg whole
I tablespoon	$\frac{1}{2}$ ounce, 15 ml	Dry, sherry
To taste		White pepper
I tablespoon		Tapioca powder or cornstarch
I tablespoon		Oil
I teaspoon		Sesame oil

AMOUNT	MEASURE	INGREDIENT
Marinade for Shrimp		
2 tablespoons	I ounce, 30 ml	Water
$\frac{1}{2}$ teaspoon		Salt
I		Egg white
I tablespoon	$\frac{1}{2}$ ounce, 15 ml	Sherry, dry
I tablespoon	$\frac{1}{2}$ ounce, 15 ml	Vegetable oil
I tablespoon	$\frac{1}{2}$ ounce, 15 ml	Sesame oil
To taste		White pepper
I tablespoon		Tapioca powder or cornstarch
I tablespoon		Oil

PROCEDURE

1 In separate containers, combine the ingredients for the chicken marinade and shrimp marinade; mix well. Add the diced chicken thigh meat to the chicken marinade; toss to coat, chill for 30 minutes. Add the shrimp to the shrimp marinade; toss to coat, chill 30 minutes.

2 Set wok over high heat. When very hot, add two tablespoons (1 ounce, 30 ml) oil. Add chicken, stirring constantly until separated and just cooked (no longer pink). Remove and reserve.

3 Heat one tablespoon oil in wok, over high heat. When oil is hot, add the pork and mushrooms. Stir 1 minute, add ham, stir 30 seconds. Add green peas and carrots, stir-fry 15 seconds. Remove and reserve with chicken and shrimp.

4 Rinse wok and wipe dry. Set over high heat; when wok is hot, add remaining oil. Scramble the eggs until set, and turn heat to medium. Break the scrambled eggs in the wok into small pieces; about the same size as the chicken. Add the rice and sprinkle with salt. Stir-fry the rice, about 5 to 7 minutes.

5 Return all cooked items to the wok and stir-fry to mix with rice.

6 Add green onions, and correct seasoning with $\frac{1}{4}$ teaspoon sesame oil, white pepper and salt.

Shanghai Sweet-and-Sour Spareribs

SERVES 4

AMOUNT	MEASURE	INGREDIENT
$\frac{1}{2}$ teaspoon		Salt
I tablespoon	$\frac{1}{2}$ ounce, 15 ml	Dry sherry or rice wine
I teaspoon		Tapioca powder or cornstarch
I pound	448 g	Pork spareribs cut $\frac{1}{2}$ inch wide by I inch in length (1.2 cm x 2.4 cm), silver skin removed (or substitute pork chops)
$\frac{1}{4}$ cup	2 ounces, 60 ml	Vegetable oil
Sauce		
$\frac{1}{3}$ cup	2.3 ounces, 64 g	Granulated sugar
3 tablespoons	$1\frac{1}{2}$ ounces, 45 ml	Rice wine vinegar
2 tablespoons	I ounce, 30 ml	Soy sauce
I tablespoon	$\frac{1}{2}$ ounce, 15 ml	Tomato catsup
I teaspoon		Tapioca powder or cornstarch

PROCEDURE

1   Combine salt, sherry, and tapioca powder, and mix well. Add sparerib pieces, toss to coat, and marinate for minimum of 30 minutes.

2   Heat oil in a wok over medium heat to about 350°F (176°C) or until a piece of green onion dropped in oil bubbles, sizzles, and moves around.

3   Add the spareribs and deep-fry until crisp, stirring to keep them from sticking together, 5 to 7 minutes. Remove from oil and drain on paper towels.

4   Reset empty wok on medium high heat. Stir sauce ingredients to blend, pour into wok, and cook, stirring, until thickened. Return pork to wok and stir well until each piece is coated with sauce. Serve hot.

Bean Curd in Oyster Sauce

SERVES 4

AMOUNT	MEASURE	INGREDIENT
2 tablespoons	1 ounce, 30 ml	Oil
2		Green onion, white and greens separated, minced
1¼ cups	8 ounces, 224	Semi-firm bean curd (tofu), soaked in hot water 15 minutes, drained, dried, cut into 1 inch (2.4 cm) cubes
Sauce		
1 tablespoon	½ ounce, 15 ml	Oyster sauce
½ tablespoon	¼ ounce, 8 ml	Soy sauce
1 tablespoon	½ ounce, 15 ml	Dry sherry
To taste		Salt
2 tablespoons	1 ounce, 30 ml	Chicken stock

PROCEDURE

1 Combine sauce ingredients.

2 Heat wok over high heat; when hot add oil and swirl. When the oil is just below the smoke point, add the white parts of the green onions; stir-fry 10 seconds.

3 Add the tofu and stir-fry 1 minute, turning gently to coat with oil and onions.

4 Add sauce ingredients; Bring to boil, reduce to simmer and cook 2 minutes.

5 Add green onions tops; toss and serve.

Tea and Spice Smoked Quail with Sweet-and-Sour Cucumbers

SERVES 4

AMOUNT	MEASURE	INGREDIENT
2		Quail, semi-boneless
		Sweet-and-sour cucumbers (recipe follows)
Seasoning Salt		
I tablespoon	10 g	Sea salt
$\frac{1}{2}$ teaspoon	2 g	Toasted Sechuan pepper, ground
I $\frac{1}{2}$ teaspoons	5 g	Five-spice powder
I cup	8 ounces, 240 ml	Vegetable oil
Smoking Mixture		
$\frac{1}{2}$ cup	3 $\frac{1}{2}$ ounces, 98 g	Long-grain rice
3 pieces		Dry mandarin peel
I piece		Cassia bark
I ounce	28 g	Jasmine tea leaves
I $\frac{1}{2}$ ounces	42 g	Brown sugar
3		Star anise

PROCEDURE

1 Combine seasoning salt ingredients and rub on quail; marinate 30 minutes.

2 Combine smoking mixture ingredients. Line bottom of a wok with foil. Place smoking mixture on foil and place over high heat.

3 Place a rack in the wok and cover until it begins to smoke. Reduce heat and place quail on rack. Cover and smoke quail, 2–3 minutes. Watch to ensure quail is cooked only to rare. Remove quail and hold until ready to serve.

4 Set wok over high heat. Heat oil to 350°F (176°C°). Deep-fry quail until golden brown and crispy, 3–4 minutes. Serve with sweet-and-sour cucumbers.

Tea and Spice Smoked Quail with Sweet and Sour Cucumbers

Sweet-and-Sour Cucumbers

SERVES 4

AMOUNT	MEASURE	INGREDIENT
2 cups	12 ounces, 336 g	English cucumber, julienned
Dressing		
2		Thai bird chile (small red), finely slice
2		Garlic clove, minced
3 tablespoons	1 $\frac{1}{2}$ ounces, 45 ml	Rice wine vinegar
4 teaspoons	40 ml	Water
2 teaspoons	20 g	Granulated sugar
$\frac{1}{2}$ teaspoon		Salt

PROCEDURE

1 Combine all dressing ingredients; mix well to dissolve sugar. Toss cucumbers with dressing; let sit 30 minutes before serving.

Ma-Puo (Mapo) Doufu

SERVES 4

AMOUNT	MEASURE	INGREDIENT
2 tablespoons	1 ounce, 30 ml	Dark soy sauce
2 tablespoons	1 ounce, 30 ml	Shaoxing wine or dry sherry
2 tablespoons	1 ounce, 30 ml	Fermented chile bean paste
1 cup	8 ounces, 224 g	Pork, lean ground
1 $\frac{1}{4}$ cups	10 ounces, 300 ml	Chicken stock
4 tablespoons	2 ounces, 60 ml	Vegetable oil
2 tablespoons		Ginger, grated
2		Garlic cloves, minced
2		Green onions, white part, sliced thinly
1 pound	448 g	Tofu, semi-firm, blanch in hot water for 3 minutes, then cut $\frac{1}{2}$ inch (1.2 cm) cubes
1 teaspoon		Sichuan peppercorns, toasted and cracked finely, or 1 teaspoon ground in spice mill
2 tablespoons	1 ounce, 30 ml	Water
1 tablespoon		Tapioca powder or cornstarch
1 teaspon		Sesame oil
1 tablespoon		Cilantro, chopped

PROCEDURE

1 Combine half the soy sauce, half the wine, bean paste, and pork. Mix well.

2 Combine remaining soy sauce and wine with chicken stock.

3 Set wok over high heat; when very hot, add oil. Add pork mixture; cook, stirring, to separate the grains of meat, about 30 seconds. Add ginger, garlic, and green onion; stir-fry 1 minute. Add chicken stock; cook 1 minute.

4 Add bean curd. Stir mixture gently; the bean curd breaks easily. Cook just to heat through, about 1 minute. Sprinkle Sichuan peppercorns over the mixture.

5 Blend water and tapioca powder and add, stirring gently to thicken. When dish is thickened, add sesame oil and transfer to serving dish and garnish with cilantro.

Sichuan Stuffed Eggplant

SERVES 4

Chef tip   **The cornstarch between the eggplant slices helps to maintain the positioning of the ground pork.**

AMOUNT	MEASURE	INGREDIENT
$\frac{1}{2}$ cup	4 ounces, 112 g	Lean ground pork
1 tablespoon	$\frac{1}{2}$ ounce, 15 ml	Soy sauce
As needed for coating		Cornstarch
2		Eggs
$\frac{1}{8}$ teaspoon		White pepper
3		Japanese eggplant, 6 ounces (168 g) each
2		Eggs
$\frac{1}{8}$ teaspoon		Salt
4 cups plus 1 tablespoon	$32\frac{1}{2}$ ounces, 975 ml	Vegetable oil
1 teaspoon		Sesame oil
Seasoning		
1 tablespoon	$\frac{1}{2}$ ounce, 15 ml	Soy sauce
1 teaspoon		Dry sherry
$\frac{1}{4}$ teaspoon		Granulated sugar
2 tablespoons		Ginger, grated
1 tablespoon		Garlic, minced
2 teaspoons		Tapioca powder or cornstarch
2 tablespoons		Green onion, white part, minced
1 teaspoon		Sesame oil
Sauce for glazing		
$\frac{1}{2}$ cup	4 ounces, 120 ml	Chicken stock
1 tablespoon	$\frac{1}{2}$ ounce, 15 ml	Sichuan hot bean paste
2 teaspoons	10 ml	Dark soy sauce
1 tablespoon	$\frac{1}{2}$ ounce, 15 ml	Rice vinegar
1 tablespoon	$\frac{1}{2}$ ounce, 15 ml	Brown sugar

PROCEDURE

1 Combine pork with the soy sauce from the seasoning. Mix with your fingers, scooping up pork mixture with your hand and beating it back into the bowl several times until firm. Add the remaining seasoning and mix well.

2 Cut eggplant into $\frac{3}{4}$- to 1-inch (1.8 cm to 2.4 cm) pieces using a vertical slope-cut. Make a slit down the center of each slice and cut two thirds of the way down, forming double-layer slices with skin side not cut all the way through. Gently open up the double layer and brush the inside surface lightly with cornstarch. Slice and brush the remaining pieces the same way, noting that they are not uniform in size but in thickness only.

3 Stuff about one tablespoon of pork mixture into each piece of eggplant. Then dip the back of a spoon in a little water and smooth the pork mixture.

4 Mix the glazing sauce ingredients; set aside.

5 About 10 minutes before cooking, beat eggs with $\frac{1}{8}$ teaspoon salt until smooth. Dip each piece of stuffed eggplant into the egg mixture, then coat with cornstarch. Shake off excess cornstarch.

6 Set a wok over high heat. When hot, add 4 cups oil. Heat oil to 375°F (190°C), or until a piece of green onion or ginger sizzles noisily and quickly turns brown.

7 Add the eggplant pieces in succession to the oil; deep-fry until the coating is set, then remove. Reheat oil to very hot 400°F (204°C) and return all eggplant pieces to the oil. Deep-fry until golden, then remove and drain on paper towels.

8 Set in a separate wok or pan over high heat. When hot, add remaining tablespoon oil. Stir the glazing sauce and add it to the wok. Bring to a boil, glaze sauce with sesame oil.

9 Plate hot eggplant and glaze with sauce. Eggplant should be glazed within a minute or two after frying.

Kung Pao Chicken

SERVES 4

AMOUNT	MEASURE	INGREDIENT
Marinade		
I tablespoon	$\frac{1}{2}$ ounce, 15 ml	Soy sauce
I teaspoon		Chinese rice wine or dry sherry
2 teaspoons		Cold water
I		Egg
I tablespoon	$\frac{1}{2}$ ounce, 15 ml	Vegetable oil
2 teaspoons		Tapioca powder or cornstarch
Sauce		
I tablespoon	$\frac{1}{2}$ ounce, 15 ml	Dark soy sauce
2 teaspoons		Light soy sauce
I tablespoon	$\frac{1}{2}$ ounce, 15 ml	Rice vinegar
I tablespoon	$\frac{1}{2}$ ounce, 15 ml	Chicken stock
I tablespoon	$\frac{1}{2}$ ounce, 14 g	Granulated sugar
$\frac{1}{2}$ teaspoon		Salt
$\frac{1}{2}$ teaspoon		Sesame oil
I teaspoon		Tapioca powder or cornstarch
Other ingredients		
2 cups	12 ounces, 336 g	Chicken thigh meat, cut $\frac{1}{2}$ inch (1.2 cm) cubes
3 cups	24 ounces, 720 ml	Vegetable oil
12		Dried red chile peppers, whole
2		Garlic cloves, minced
$\frac{1}{8}$ teaspoon		Sichuan peppercorns, ground
$\frac{1}{2}$ cup	$2\frac{1}{2}$ ounces, 70 g	Unsalted peanuts

PROCEDURE

1 Combine marinade ingredients; mix well. Add chicken pieces and marinate 30 minutes.

2 Combine all sauce ingredients, whisking in tapioca powder last.

3 Set a wok over high heat. Heat the 3 cups oil to 350°F (176°C) or until a piece of green onion dropped in oil bubbles, sizzles, and moves around. Carefully slide the chicken into the wok; fry for 3–4 minute, until the cubes separate and turn white. Remove and drain on paper towels. Remove all but one tablespoons ($\frac{1}{2}$ ounce, 315 ml) of oil from the wok.

4 Heat oil, add chiles, and stir-fry until the skin starts turn dark red and chilies plump. Add garlic; stir-fry until you smell the garlic aroma, 10 seconds, add Sichuan peppercorn.

5 Return chicken to wok; stir-fry 30 seconds. Stir the sauce, and pour into the center. Toss with chicken, cook until sauce thickens, add the peanuts, and mix well. Serve hot.

Stir-Fried Long Beans

SERVES 4

AMOUNT	MEASURE	INGREDIENT
I pound	16 ounces, 448 g	Long beans, cut 2 inch (5 cm) pieces
4 tablespoons	2 ounces, 60 ml	Vegetable oil
I tablespoon		Garlic, minced
I tablespoon		Ginger, grated
$\frac{1}{2}$ teaspoon		Sesame oil
$\frac{1}{2}$ teaspoon		Rice vinegar
To taste		Salt and white pepper

PROCEDURE

I Wash beans, trim the ends, and cut diagonally into 2 inch (2 cm) pieces.

2 Blanch the beans in boiling salted water, remove, shock in ice water, drain, and set aside.

3 Set wok over high heat; when very hot, add oil. Swirl around wok, add garlic and ginger, and stir-fry 30 seconds.

4 Add long beans and stir-fry 1 to 2 minutes. Glaze with sesame oil, add vinegar, and correct seasoning.

Dan Dan Mian Spicy Noodles

SERVES 4

AMOUNT	MEASURE	INGREDIENT
1 tablespoon	$\frac{1}{2}$ ounce, 14 g	**Dried shrimp**
$\frac{3}{4}$ cup	6 ounces, 180 ml	**Hot water**
$\frac{1}{4}$ cup	2 ounces, 56 g	**Sichuan preserved vegetables**
6 tablespoons	3 ounces, 90 ml	**Vegetable oil**
4 cups	32 ounces, 960 ml	**Chicken stock**
1 pound		**Asian noodles, or 12 ounces dried Asian noodles (width between linguine and fettuccine), or 12 ounces linguine**
4		**Green onions, whole**
1 tablespoon		**Sesame seeds**
Dan Dan Sauce		
2 tablespoons	1 ounce, 30 ml	**Dark soy sauce**
2 tablespoons	1 ounce, 30 ml	**Light soy sauce**
1 tablespoon	$\frac{1}{2}$ ounce, 15 ml	**Rice vinegar**
2 tablespoons	1 ounce, 30 ml	**Sesame paste**
1 tablespoon	$\frac{1}{2}$ ounce, 15 ml	**Chile oil**
2 tablespoons	1 ounce, 30 ml	**Sesame oil**
1 tablespoon	$\frac{1}{2}$ ounce, 14 g	**Granulated sugar**

PROCEDURE

1   Soak shrimp in hot water 20 minutes. Chop finely and reserve soaking liquid.

2   Rinse chile and spices off the preserved vegetables; chop finely.

3   Toast the sesame seeds until golden; set aside.

4   Mix ingredients for the dan dan sauce until smooth.

5   Set wok or heavy saucepan over medium high heat. When very hot, add one tablespoon ($\frac{1}{2}$ ounce, 15 ml) oil. Add shrimp; stir for 2 minutes or until oil is well flavored. Add the preserved vegetables; stir-fry 1 minute. Remove from heat.

6   Combine the dan dan sauce ingredients, the shrimp mixture, and 2 tablespoons (1 ounce, 30 ml) oil. Set aside.

7   Heat chicken stock and shrimp soaking liquid over very low heat.

8 Cook noodles following directions. Strain, shake the colander to drain excess water, and toss with remaining oil.

9 Serve the dan dan sauce in 4 separate bowls and place $\frac{1}{4}$ of the hot noodles on sauce. Sprinkle chopped green onions and sesame seeds on top. Serve with chicken/shrimp stock in separate bowls.

Dan Dan Mian – Spicy Noodle and Stir-Fried Long Beans

Fish-Flavored Pork Shreds

SERVES 4

There is no fish in this dish from fish-starved Sichuan. The flavor is adapted from the sauce used in braising fish.

AMOUNT	MEASURE	INGREDIENT
1½ cups	12 ounces, 336 g	Pork, cut from loin, trimmed of excess fat, $\frac{1}{8}$ × $\frac{1}{8}$ × 2 inch (.3 × .3 × 4.8 cm) shreds
2 cups plus 2 tablespoons	17 ounces, 510 ml	Vegetable oil
8 medium		Wood ears, soaked in warm water 30 minutes until soft, tough ends trimmed; cut into strips, about $\frac{1}{8}$ inch (.3 cm) wide
$\frac{1}{4}$ cup	2 ounces, 56 g	Water chestnuts, $\frac{1}{8}$ inch (.3 cm) strips
$\frac{1}{4}$ cup	2 ounces, 56 g	Bamboo shoots, $\frac{1}{8}$ inch (.3 cm) strip
1 tablespoon		Carrots, $\frac{1}{8}$ inch (.3 cm) strips
To taste		Salt
2 tablespoons		Green onions, white part, minced
1 tablespoon		Ginger, grated
1 tablespoon		Garlic clove, minced
1 tablespoon	$\frac{1}{2}$ ounce, 15 ml	Dry sherry
2 teaspoons		Sesame oil
Seasoning		
2 tablespoons	1 ounce, 30 ml	Dark soy sauce
1 tablespoon		Tapioca powder or cornstarch
Sauce mixture		
1 tablespoon	$\frac{1}{2}$ ounce, 15 ml	Sichuan hot bean paste
1 tablespoon	$\frac{1}{2}$ ounce, 15 ml	Rice vinegar
1 tablespoon	$\frac{1}{2}$ ounce, 15 ml	Dark soy sauce
2 teaspoons	10 ml	Granulated sugar
1 teaspoon		Tapioca powder or cornstarch

PROCEDURE

1 Mix ingredients for sauce mixture; set aside. Mix seasoning ingredients and combine with pork.

2 Set wok over high heat; when very hot, add 2 cups (16 ounces, 360 ml) oil. Heat oil to 375°F (190°C), or until a piece of green onion or ginger sizzles noisily and quickly turns brown. Add the pork shreds, stirring to separate; stir-fry 1 minute. Pour both meat and oil into strainer-lined bowl to drain, leaving about 1 tablespoon ($\frac{1}{2}$ ounce, 15 ml) oil in wok.

3 Place wok over medium high heat and add the wood ears, water chestnuts, bamboo shoots and carrots stirring for 1 minute. Season with salt, stir, and remove.

4 Add remaining two tablespoons (1 ounce, 30 ml) oil to the wok. When the oil is hot, add green onions, ginger, and garlic. Stir for 10 seconds, then return pork to wok. Sizzle in the sherry along the edge of the wok, stirring constantly. Add wood ears, water chestnuts, bamboo shoots, and carrots.

5 Stir sauce mixture and add to the center of the wok, stirring until thickened. Glaze sauce with sesame oil, mix well, and serve.

Sichuan Spicy Fired Beef Shreds

SERVES 4

AMOUNT	MEASURE	INGREDIENT
I pound	16 ounces, 448 g	Flank steak, $\frac{1}{8}$ × $\frac{1}{8}$ × 1$\frac{1}{2}$ inch (.3 × .3 × 3.6 cm) shreds
$\frac{1}{2}$ cup/1 tablespoon	4$\frac{1}{2}$ ounces, 135 ml	Vegetable oil
2		Garlic cloves, flattened
3		Dried hot chiles, seeds removed
I cup	4 ounces, 112 g	Celery, $\frac{1}{8}$ × $\frac{1}{8}$ × 1$\frac{1}{2}$ inch (.3 × .3 × 3.6 cm) shreds
$\frac{1}{2}$ cup	2 ounces, 56 g	Carrot, peeled, $\frac{1}{8}$ × $\frac{1}{8}$ × 1$\frac{1}{2}$ inch (.3 × .3 × 3.6 cm) shreds
3		Fresh hot chiles, $\frac{1}{8}$ × $\frac{1}{8}$ × 1$\frac{1}{2}$ inch (.3 × .3 × 3.6 cm) shreds
To taste		Salt
I tablespoon		Sesame oil
Marinade		
4 tablespoons	2 ounces, 60 ml	Dark soy sauce
		Juice of 3 slices gingerroot
I tablespoon	$\frac{1}{2}$ ounce, 15 ml	Dry sherry
2 teaspoons	10 g	Granulated sugar

PROCEDURE

1   Mix marinade ingredients, add the meat, and toss. Let sit at room temperature for at least 30 minutes. Turn the meat occasionally.

2   Set wok over high heat; when very hot add $\frac{1}{2}$ cup (4 ounces, 120 ml) oil. Flavor the oil with the garlic; remove the garlic when it turns brown.

3   Add meat; stir-fry 1 to 2 minutes, or until strips separate. Turn heat to medium low; continue to stir-fry until strips turn brown, 1 to 2 minutes; remove from wok.

4   Rinse wok and wipe dry. Set on medium high heat; when hot, add sesame oil. Flavor oil with dried chile until brown. Add celery, carrots, and fresh chiles, stirring 30 seconds to 1 minute; season with salt.

5   Return meat and mix with vegetables. Glaze the meat with sesame oil and serve with rice.

Spinach Velvet Soup SERVES 4

This soup does not reheat well. Do not prepare too far in advance or it will lose its beautiful bright green color.

AMOUNT	MEASURE	INGREDIENT
3 cups	6 ounces, 180 g	Spinach, leaves loosely packed
2 teaspoons		Granulated sugar
2		Egg whites
1 tablespoon	$\frac{1}{2}$ ounce, 15 ml	Water
3 tablespoons		Tapioca powder or cornstarch
$3\frac{1}{2}$ cups	28 ounces, 840 ml	Chicken stock
1 tablespoon		Ginger juice
2 tablespoons		Smithfield ham, $\frac{1}{4}$ inch (.6 cm) dice
1 teaspoon		Sesame oil
$1\frac{1}{2}$ tablespoons	$\frac{3}{4}$ ounce, 20 ml	Vegetable oil
To taste		Salt and white pepper

PROCEDURE

1 Remove stems from spinach, rinse thoroughly, and drain.

2 Heat 2 quarts (1.9 l) water to a boil; add sugar and spinach, stirring until water boils again. Immediately drain in a colander, running cold water over the spinach to stop the cooking process.

3 Squeeze spinach leaves to extract as much water as possible. Julienne finely; do not use a blender.

4 Beat egg whites with water until smooth but not foamy.

5 Mix tapioca powder and $\frac{1}{4}$ cup (2 ounces, 60 ml) stock.

6 Heat remaining stock over high heat, bring to a boil, and reduce heat to medium. Add half the ham and ginger juice and cook 4 minutes. Turn heat to high and add the spinach, stirring until it returns to a boil.

7 Season soup and add the tapioca powder mixture. Stir until the soup thickens (creamy).

8 Remove from heat and whirl in the egg whites. Do not stir for 30 seconds, then stir to mix. Add sesame oil and vegetable oil.

9 Pour soup into bowls and garnish with remaining ham. Adjust seasoning. Serve immediately.

Char Siu Cantonese Roast Pork

SERVES 4

AMOUNT	MEASURE	INGREDIENT
1½ pounds	672 g	Lean pork butt (trimmed weight)
1		Carrot, cut into 2 inch (4.8 cm) lengths, then cut in half vertically
¼ cup	2 ounces, 60 ml	Honey
2 tablespoon	1 ounce, 30	Mirin wine
1 tablespoon	½ ounce, 15 ml	Sesame oil
Marinade		
¼ cup	2 ounces, 60 ml	Dry sherry
2		Garlic cloves, crushed
3 tablespoons	1½ ounces, 45 ml	Light soy sauce
1 tablespoon	½ ounce, 15 ml	Sesame paste
1 tablespoon	1 ounce, 30 ml	Brown bean paste
2 tablespoons	1 ounce, 30 ml	Hoisin sauce
1 teaspoon		Salt
½ teaspoon		Five-spice powder
¼ cup	2 ounces, 56 g	Granulated sugar

PROCEDURE

1   Trim fat from meat and cut into 1 × 1 × 8 inch strips (2.4 × 2.4 × 20 cm).

2   Combine all marinade, ingredients; mix well. Add pork and toss to cover with marinade. Cover and set at room temperature for at least 1 hour or refrigerate 3 hours or overnight. Turn every 30 minutes or so.

3   Thread pieces of pork lengthwise on skewers, using pieces of carrots as the end pieces to keep the pork from sliding off.

4   Preheat oven to 375°F (190°C). Fill a shallow roasting pan with 1 inch (2.4 cm) boiling water to catch dripping and to prevent smoking. Place pan on the lowest rack in the oven and hook skewers to the highest rack, each 2 inches (4.8 cm) apart. Roast meat for 40 minutes.

5   Turn oven to 450°F (232°C). Mix the honey and mirin. Remove skewers from oven and brush with honey mixture, then sesame oil.

6   Empty the water from the roasting pan and return to the oven. Hang the skewers as before and roast 10 minutes. Remove.

Char Sui Bau Steamed Pork Buns

YIELD: 12 BUNS (DOUGH FOR UP TO 24 BUNS)

AMOUNT	MEASURE	INGREDIENT
1 cup	8 ounces, 224 g	Char sui, $\frac{1}{4}$ inch (.6 cm) dice
Seasoning		
1 tablespoon	$\frac{1}{2}$ ounce, 15 ml	Oyster sauce
2 tablespoons	1 ounce, 28 g	Granulated sugar
$1\frac{1}{2}$ tablespoons	$1\frac{1}{2}$ ounce, 45 ml	Peanut oil
1 teaspoon		Sesame oil
Bun Dough		
1 tablespoon	$\frac{1}{2}$ ounce, 14 g	Granulated sugar
$\frac{1}{4}$ cup	2 ounces, 60 ml	Warm water (105°F, 40.5°C)
$2\frac{1}{4}$ teaspoons	$\frac{1}{4}$ ounce, 7 g	Active dry yeast
4 cups	16 ounces, 448 g	All-purpose flour
2 tablespoons	1 ounce, 28 g	Lard or shortening
$\frac{1}{2}$ cup	4 ounces, 112 g	Extra-fine granulated sugar
1 cup	8 ounces, 240 ml	Milk, warm (105°F, 40.5°C)
1 tablespoon	$\frac{1}{2}$ ounce, 15 ml	Oil
1 tablespoon		Baking powder mixed with $1\frac{1}{2}$ tablespoons ($\frac{3}{4}$ ounce, 23 ml) water
Filling Base		
2 tablespoons	1 ounce, 30 ml	Peanut oil
2 teaspoons		Shallots, minced
$1\frac{1}{2}$ tablespoons		All-purpose flour
6 tablespoons	3 ounces, 90 ml	Chicken stock
1 tablespoon	$\frac{1}{2}$ ounce, 15 ml	Dark soy sauce

PROCEDURE

Filling

1 Heat the oil over medium heat and sauté the shallots 2 minutes or until light brown. Add the flour, stir to combine, and cook 1 minute.

2 Add the chicken stock, stir well, and cook 2 minutes. Add soy sauce and cook one minute.

3 Remove from heat and stir in cut pork and seasoning ingredients. Chill until very firm.

Dough

1   Dissolve sugar in warm water, sprinkle yeast over; let stand for 2 to 3 minutes, and then stir to mix well. Let set until it starts of foam, 10 minutes.

2   Sift flour and make a well in the center. Combine lard, extra-fine sugar, yeast mixture, and milk; mix well. Combine liquid mixture with the flour; gradually incorporate the flour with the liquid to make dough.

3   Knead the dough for 10 minutes, sprinkling with flour as necessary.

4   Use the oil to grease the dough; cover and let rest in a warm area $1\frac{1}{2}$ hours or until double in size.

5   Punch dough down and flatten out to about $\frac{3}{4}$ inch (1.8 cm) thick. Spread the baking powder mixture evenly on the dough (this acts as a stabilizer). Roll dough up and knead about 15 minutes, or until smooth and satiny. The dough should be firmer than regular white bread dough.

6   Cover and let rest 30 minutes.

Dough Breaking

1   Divide dough into four equal parts. Roll one part by hand to form a rope approximately 9 (22.5 cm) inches long and $1\frac{1}{4}$ inchs in (3.12 cm) diameter.

2   Mark into 6 equal parts, $1\frac{1}{2}$-inch (3.75 cm) long.

3   Holding the dough with one hand, grip at the first mark with the thumb and index finger of the other hand and tear away briskly to break off a small dough piece. Continue breaking off until you have 12 pieces.

Dough Rolling

1   Flatten each piece of dough with your palm.

2   Using a rolling pin, roll each into a round disc, making a quarter turn with each roll.

3   Roll to leave the center thick; thinner edges are easier to pleat.

Assembling

1   Place about $1\frac{1}{2}$ tablespoons ($\frac{3}{4}$ ounce, 21 g) of filling at the center of each dough round, flat side up.

2   Gather the edges by first pleating counterclockwise, then twisting to seal securely.

3   Let rest, covered, for at least 30 minutes.

Cooking

1   Steam on high heat for 8 to 10 minutes. Do not uncover the steamer any time during the steaming. If a flat-lid steamer is used, wrap the lid with a kitchen towel to prevent condensed steam from dripping on the buns.

Chef Tip Dough breaking instead of cutting is a traditional Cantonese practice in dim sum restaurants. The breaking leaves no sharp cutting edges, which would require longer time for the dough to round out.

Char Sui Bau – Chinese Steamed Pork Buns, and Tea Leaf Eggs

Stir-Fried Squid with Fermented Black Bean Paste　SERVES 4

Chef Tip　**Squid** is cut (scored) because as it cooks it rolls up, and the crosshatching cuts will catch and hold the sauce.

AMOUNT	MEASURE	INGREDIENT
14 ounces	392 g	Squid body meat, scored and cut into 1 inch (2.4 cm x 2.4 cm) cubes
1 tablespoon		Salt
2 tablespoons		Vegetable oil
1 tablespoon		Ginger, grated
1 tablespoon		Garlic clove, minced
1		Red chile (hot) seeded, sliced thinly
3 tablespoons	$1\frac{1}{2}$ ounces, 45 ml	Fermented black bean paste
1 cup	4 ounces, 112 g	Red bell peppers, seeded, 1 inch (2.4 cm) cubes
1 cup	4 ounces, 112 g	Onion, 1 inch (2.4 cm) cubes
1 cup	4 ounces, 112 g	Green bell peppers, seeded, 1 inch (2.4 cm) cubes
2 tablespoons	1 ounce, 30 ml	Shaoxing wine or dry sherry
2 teaspoons		Sesame oil
1 tablespoon		Cilantro, chopped
Sauce		
2 tablespoons	1 ounce, 30 ml	Chicken stock
2 teaspoons		Tapioca powder or cornstarch
1 tablespoon	$\frac{1}{2}$ ounce, 15 ml	Light soy sauce

PROCEDURE

1 To clean squid, grip the head in one hand and the body in the other. Gently pull the head away from the body. The ink sac will come out at the same time. Pull out the yellow jelly pouch and the translucent center bone inside the body.

2 Reserve only the body for this recipe and discard the rest or keep the tentacles for some other use. Open up the body cavity and under running water rub the purplish outer skin with fingers, peeling it off. On larger squid, the skin tends to be tough when cooked.

3 Rub and squeeze the squid with salt; rinse and drain well.

4 Turn the inner side of a piece of squid up, scoring gently on the diagonal at $\frac{1}{4}$ inch (.6 cm) intervals, forming a diamond pattern.

5 Bring 6 cups (1.4 l) water to a boil. Remove from the heat and add the squid immediately. Stir once and pour into a colander to drain. Arrange in a single layer on paper towels and pat dry.

6 Prepare ingredients for sauce and set aside.

7 Set wok over high heat; when very hot; add the oil. Add the ginger, garlic, and chile; stir-fry for 10 seconds. Add the bean paste and cook 10 seconds. Add the bell peppers and onions; stir-fry 1 minute.

8 Add squid and stir-fry 45 seconds. Push squid and vegetables to the side, restir the sauce mixture, and add to the center of the wok, stirring until thickened. Sizzle in the wine along the edges, stir to mix all ingredients, and glaze with sesame oil.

9 Sprinkle with chopped cilantro, mix well, and serve.

Buddha's Delight   SERVES 4

Adapted from *Louhan Zhai*, the vegetarian dish for the five hundred disciples sworn to protect the Buddhist way.

AMOUNT	MEASURE	INGREDIENT
8		Medium dried shiitake mushrooms or fresh
$\frac{1}{2}$ cup	3 ounces, 84 g	Bamboo shoots
$\frac{1}{2}$ cup	2.5 ounces, 70 g	Firm tofu, 1 inch (2.4 cm) cubes
1 slice		Ginger
$\frac{1}{2}$ cup	2 ounces, 56 g	Snow peas or sugar snap beans, strings removed, rinsed
$\frac{1}{2}$ cup	2 ounces, 56 g	Carrots, julienned
$\frac{1}{4}$ cup	2 ounces, 56 g	Water chestnuts, sliced thin
1 cup	4 ounces, 112 g	Napa cabbage, julienned
$\frac{1}{2}$ cup	3 ounces, 84 g	Baby corn
$\frac{1}{2}$ cup	2 ounces, 56 g	Red pepper, diamond cut
$\frac{1}{4}$ cup	2 ounces, 56 g	Gingko nuts, drained and rinsed
1 teaspoon		Sesame oil
Seasoning		
$1\frac{1}{2}$ teaspoons		Granulated sugar
$\frac{1}{2}$ cup	4 ounces, 120 ml	Chicken stock, vegetable stock, or water
$\frac{1}{2}$ teaspoon		White pepper
1 teaspoon		Salt
Slurry		
2 tablespoons	1 ounce, 30 ml	Water
1 tablespoon		Cornstarch

PROCEDURE

1 If using dried mushrooms, soak them in $\frac{1}{2}$ cup (4 ounce, 120 ml) of warm water for about 15 minutes or until soft. Trim the stems and tough ends. Squeeze to extract moisture from shiitake. Reserve mushroom liquid; strain through cheesecloth.

2 Blanch all the vegetables individually in boiling water, rinse with cold water and reserve.

3 Cut the bamboo shoots finely into $\frac{1}{8} \times \frac{1}{8} \times 1\frac{1}{2}$ inch (.3 × .3 × 3.6 cm) shreds. Drain and pat dry with paper towel.

4   Set wok or heavy-bottomed pot over medium high heat. When hot, add 2 tablespoons (1 ounce, 30 ml) oil. Flavor oil with 1 garlic clove; remove garlic when brown. Add the shiitake, stirring for 1 minute.

5   Add remaining blanched vegetables, stir fry for 3 to 4 minutes

6   Add mushroom liquid and all seasoning and bring to boil.

7   Make a slurry by mixing water and cornstarch and add 1 to 2 tablespoons to vegetable mixture.

8   Add sesame oil and serve hot.

Buddha's Delight

Fried Chicken Hong Kong Style   SERVES 4

AMOUNT	MEASURE	INGREDIENT
I pound	16 ounces, 448 g	Boneless, skinless chicken thighs
6 cups plus 2 tablespoons	49 ounces, 1.47 l	Vegetable oil
I		Egg, lightly beaten
As needed		Cornstarch and all-purpose flour mixed in 50:50 ratio
I cup	4 ounces, 112 g	Onions, julienned
I tablespoon		Garlic clove, minced
Marinade		
2 tablespoons	I ounce, 30 ml	Light soy sauce
I tablespoon	$\frac{1}{2}$ ounce, 15 ml	Dry sherry
I teaspoon		Ginger juice
Sauce		
$\frac{1}{2}$ cup	4 ounces, 120 ml	Chicken stock
2 tablespoons	I ounce, 30 ml	Tomato catsup
2 tablespoons	I ounce, 30 ml	Worcestershire sauce
I tablespoon	$\frac{1}{2}$ ounce, 15 ml	Lemon juice
I teaspoon		Lemon zest
I tablespoon		Tapioca powder or cornstarch
$\frac{1}{4}$ teaspoon		Salt
2 tablespoons	I ounce, 28 g	Brown sugar

PROCEDURE

1   Remove any yellow film on chicken thighs; rinse and pat dry. Prick with a fork so marinade can penetrate.

2   Mix marinade ingredients, combine with chicken, and allow to rest at room temperature for 30 minutes or in refrigerator 2 to 3 hours. Drain and reserve marinade.

3   Combine marinade with sauce ingredients and set aside.

4   Heat 6 cups (48 ounces, 1.4 l) oil to 375°F (190°C), or until a piece of green onion or ginger sizzles noisily and quickly turns brown. While waiting on the oil, dip the chicken in egg and dredge in cornstarch-flour mixture. Shake off excess.

Fried Chicken – Hong Kong Style

5   Add chicken to hot oil and deep fry until the coating sets and is lightly browned. Remove and drain.

6   Use a fine-mesh strainer to remove sediment from the oil. Reheat oil 400°F (204°C). Return chicken pieces and deep-fry until golden brown; remove and drain on paper towels.

7   Using a basket, add onions to hot oil. Fry onions 1 minute, until soft and translucent. Remove onions. Pour out oil and wipe wok clean.

8   Set wok over high heat and add 1 tablespoon ($\frac{1}{2}$ ounce, 15 ml) oil. Flavor oil with garlic; stir-fry 10 seconds. Mix sauce ingredients again and add to wok, stirring constantly until thickened. Turn heat to low, glaze the sauce with remaining oil, and turn off heat.

9   Arrange thighs in single layer on serving platter, top with fried onions, pour sauce over, and serve immediately.

Steamed Whole Fish

SERVES 4

AMOUNT	MEASURE	INGREDIENT
I each I $\frac{1}{2}$ pound	673 g	Whole firm fish, head and tail on (any firm, white fish such as rock cod, striped bass, snapper, perch, sole, or tilapia)
2		Whole green onions
$\frac{1}{8}$ teaspoon		White pepper
$\frac{1}{4}$ teaspoon		Salt
I tablespoon		Ginger, grated
2		Green onions, thinly sliced
$\frac{1}{4}$ cup	2 ounces, 60 ml	Vegetable oil
2 teaspoons		Sesame oil
3 tablespoons	I $\frac{1}{2}$ ounces, 45 ml	Light soy sauce
2		Cilantro sprigs, 2 inch lengths

PROCEDURE

1. Clean and scale the fish; rinse well and pat dry.

2. Arrange green onions lengthwise on a heatproof fish platter; the platter should be large enough to hold the fish and be placed in the steamer. Place the fish on the green onions, so the steam will flow under and over the fish.

3. Steam fish for approximately 10 minutes or until a chopstick can go easily into the thickest part of the fish. Remove from steamer; drain excess liquid. Discard green onions.

4. Sprinkle the white pepper and salt over the fish. Spread ginger and green onions on top of the fish.

5. Heat the oil and sesame oil to very hot and pour over the fish. Add the soy sauce to the bottom of the serving platter. Garnish with cilantro sprigs and serve.

Steamed Whole Fish

Tea Leaf Eggs

SERVES 4

AMOUNT	MEASURE	INGREDIENT
4		Large eggs
Tea Leaf Mixture		
3 cups	24 ounces, 720 ml	Water
1 tablespoon	$\frac{1}{2}$ ounce, 15 ml	Dark soy sauce
1		Star anise, whole
2 teaspoon		Salt
2 tablespoons		Green tea leaves
1 tablespoon	$\frac{1}{2}$ ounce, 15 ml	Rock sugar

PROCEDURE

1 Combine eggs and enough cold water to cover. Bring to a boil and cook 10 minutes.

2 Remove eggs and immerse in ice water until cool.

3 Using a tablespoon, tap the shells gently to make fine cracks.

4 Combine tea-leaf ingredients and bring to a boil. Add the cracked eggs and bring back to a boil. Turn heat to low and simmer for 30 minutes.

5 Remove pan from heat and let eggs cool to room temperature.

6 Shell the eggs and serve cold.

The Land

Korea is a rugged peninsula lying between China on the west and north and Japan to the east. It shares a very small border with Russia to the extreme northeast. Korea is surrounded by water on three sides: the Korea Bay and the Yellow Sea to the west, the Korea Strait to the south, and the East Sea (also known as the Sea of Japan) to the east. There are more than 3,400 islands along the coast. Mountains and hills make up about 70 percent of the country. The Korean peninsula is divided by two political states: the Democratic People's Republic of Korea (North Korea) and the Republic of Korea (South Korea). The counties are separated by a line 38 degrees north of the equator. North Korea occupies about 55 percent of the peninsula's 84,402 square miles of land. To the west and south of the peninsula are broad coastal plains where the larger cities are located and where most of the agricultural land is found. With a combined population of nearly 72 million Koreans, in a country the size of Great Britain or New Zealand, the land is well used. The land gently slopes from the south and western coastal plains toward the mountains and drops steeply from the mountains to the East Sea.

History

The Korean Peninsula's first inhabitants migrated from the northwestern regions of Asia. Some of these peoples also populated parts of northeast China (Manchuria); Koreans and Manchurians still show physical similarities.

According to legend, the god-king Tangun founded the Korean nation in 2333 B.C. By the first century A.D., the Korean peninsula was divided into the kingdoms of Silla, Koguryo, and Paekche. In A.D. 668, the Silla kingdom unified the peninsula. The Koryo dynasty—from which Portuguese missionaries in the sixteenth century derived the Western name *Korea*—succeeded the Silla kingdom in 935. The Choson dynasty, ruled by members of the Yi clan, replaced Koryo in 1392 and lasted until the Japanese annexed Korea in 1910.

Throughout most of its history, Korea has been invaded, influenced, and fought over by its larger neighbors. Korea was under Mongolian occupation from 1231 until the early fourteenth century and was plundered by Japanese pirates in 1359 and 1361. The unifier of Japan, Hideyoshi, launched major invasions of Korea in 1592 and 1597. When Western powers focused "gunboat" diplomacy on Korea in the mid-nineteenth century, Korea's rulers adopted a closed-door policy, earning Korea the title of "Hermit Kingdom."

Though the Choson dynasty paid loyalty to the Chinese court and recognized China's control in East Asia, Korea was independent until the late nineteenth century. At that time, China sought to block growing Japanese influence on the Korean peninsula and Russian pressure for commercial gains there. This competition resulted in the Sino-Japanese War of 1894–95 and the Russo-Japanese War of 1904–05. Japan emerged victorious from both wars and in 1910 annexed Korea as part of its growing empire.

Japanese colonial administration was characterized by tight control from Tokyo and ruthless efforts to supplant Korean language and culture. Organized Korean resistance during this era—such as the March 1, 1919, Independence Movement—was unsuccessful, and Japan remained firmly in control until the end of World War II in 1945.

Japan surrendered to the Allied Forces in August 1945, and Korea was liberated. However, the unexpectedly early surrender of Japan led to the immediate division of Korea into two occupation zones, with the United States administering the southern half of the peninsula and the U.S.S.R taking over the area to the north of the 38th parallel. This division was meant to be temporary and to facilitate the Japanese surrender until the U.S., Britain, the Soviet Union, and China could arrange a trusteeship administration.

At a meeting in Cairo, it was agreed that Korea would be free "in due course." At a later meeting in Yalta, it was agreed to establish a four-power trusteeship over Korea. In December 1945, a conference convened in Moscow to discuss the future of Korea. A five-year trusteeship was discussed, and a joint Soviet-American commission was established. The commission met intermittently in Seoul but deadlocked over the issue of establishing a national government.

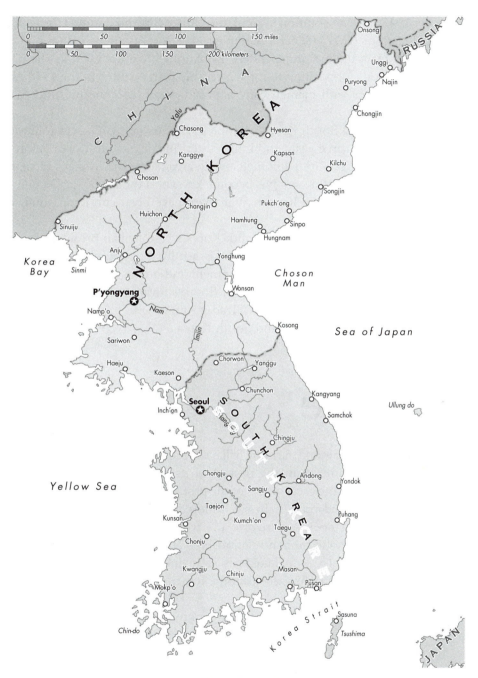

North and South Korea

In September 1947, with no solution in sight, the United States submitted the Korean question to the United Nations (U.N.) General Assembly.

Initial hopes for a unified, independent Korea quickly evaporated as the politics of the Cold War and domestic opposition to the trusteeship plan resulted in the 1948 establishment of two separate nations with diametrically opposed political, economic, and social systems. War broke out in 1950.

North Korea invaded South Korea on June 25, 1950. The U.N. sent military assistance. The Korean War lasted three years and inflicted terrible damage to Korea before a cease-fire ended the war in 1953. The four-kilometer-wide area along the Military Demarcation Line that divides North and South Korea has become known as the DMZ, or Demilitarized Zone. In the forty-five years since the Korean War there have been continual conflicts along the DMZ.

In 1993, Kim Young Sam became South Korea's first civilian president following thirty-two years of military rule. South Korea today is a fully functioning modern democracy. By contrast, North Korea is a communist government and one of the most isolated countries in the world. In June 2000, a historic first North-South summit took place between the South's President Kim Tae-chung and the North's leader Kim Jong Il.

Efforts continue to unify North and South Korea.

The People

Korea's markets, its fishing and farming villages, modern though the buildings might be, remain very much the same as in the past. And its artisans—celadon pottery makers, for example—have re-created the great works of the past. All are traditional expressions of Korean culture, which is still based on certain six-hundred-year-old Confucian principles. Unlike a religion, Confucianism does not involve the worship of a higher being. But like some religions, it attempts to guide human relationships and improve social and ethical conduct. The fundamental thrust of Confucianism is to maintain peace and order. It has rules for familial relationships that emphasize harmony. It stresses the importance of education and respect for authority.

The Korean family structure is part of a larger kinship structure that is defined by specific obligations. Multigenerational households are quite common in rural areas and in a Korean home, the head of the family—usually the oldest male—holds the position of authority and every family member is expected to do as he says. Large families have been prized and over many centuries families intermarried within the regions of Korea to form large clans. Family names reflect this. A dozen family names predominate, especially Kim, Park, Lee, Kang, and Cho. But Kims from the city of Pusan in the south are not the Kims from Seoul and all the Kims know exactly to which group they belong. Custom forbids people marrying within their own clan, no matter how distant the cousin might be. In order to know who is who, families and clans keep detailed genealogical records that might go back many hundreds of years. Even in today's Westernized Korea, many people can still recite the history of their clans and take pride in it.

The oldest religious ideas in Korea are called shamanism. These are beliefs that the natural world is filled with spirits, both helpful and harmful, that can be addressed by people with special powers called shamans. Herbal medicines, dances, chants, and other ceremonies mark the work of shamans, most of whom are women. Though few people believe in the religious teachings today, they do accept old ideas about the natural world and use many ancient herbal remedies. Buddhism is one of the most popular religions in South Korea. The religion is based on the teachings of the Buddha; the basic idea is that salvation can come from giving up worldly desires and living in moderation. By living according to the Buddha's teachings, a Buddhist believes that he or she can reach the state of nirvana—ultimate peace—wherein a person experiences no pain or worry.

Taoism came from China and is similar to shamanism in its worship of many equally important gods. Taoism's main principle is to create harmony between humans and nature. The many gods are used as ideals toward which humans can strive and Taoists believe that spiritual perfections can be attained in this life through patience, purity, and peace.

Christianity was brought to Korea in the sixteenth century by Confucian intellectuals who learned about it in the Chinese capital of Peking. The first half of the nineteenth century was a difficult time for Korean Christians; thousands were persecuted and many were killed. Today South Korea is second in Asia only to the Philippines in its percentage of Christians.

The Food

The climate of the Korean peninsula resembles the north central region of the United States: cold winters, warm summers, and long, pleasant autumns. Because the land is made up mostly of mountains and extends from the North Asian landmass into warmer seas in the south, Korea has many microenvironments. In the mountainous northeastern part of the country the most famous dishes have wild ferns, mushrooms, and native roots in them. *Namul* (raw or cooked vegetable or wild green dishes) is one of the most basic side dishes in the Korean diet. In the rice-growing valleys of the south, in the region of Chonju city, the best known dish, *pibimpap* (*bibimpap*), is a large bowl of rice covered in a variety of finely sliced vegetables, meats, and a fiery red pepper sauce. The basic flavors of Korean food include garlic, ginger, black pepper, spring onions, soy sauce, sesame oil, and toasted sesame seed. The chile, a native to Central and South America, was spread across the world by Portuguese and Spanish merchants. Chiles and chile paste has become an important part of all Korean tables and many food preparations.

Its peninsular location gives Koreans three different seas from which to gather fish: the Yellow Sea, the East Sea, and the unique microenvironment where the two seas come together at the south end of the peninsula, the Korea Strait. Fish from the Yellow Sea differ from those of the Eastern Sea (Sea of Japan) and those of the south coast differ from the others. Koreans are seafood connoisseurs and seek out the specialties of each region. But three types of seafood are served all the time. One kind is a small dried sardine, used not as a main dish but as condiments to be eaten with others and bowls of these appear at every meal, including breakfast. Another is dried cuttlefish (similar to squid or octopus), which is the most popular snack food. All along the road and streets near fishing ports are lines of these cephalopods hanging out to dry. Seaweed and seaweed products are known for numerous health benefits and are prepared to keep well in a climate that endures long winters. Pregnant women, new mothers, and babies are fed seaweed soups. *Miyeok guk* is a brown seaweed soup known as birthday soup.

Koreans eat many preserved foods, prepared to keep over wintertime. *Kimchi* is Korea's signature dish of spicy, pickled vegetables and is served every day at every meal. *Kimchi* is characterized by its sour, sweet, and carbonated taste, yet is very different from sauerkraut, which is a popular fermented vegetable product in the West. The first written description of making *kimchi* dates to about A.D. 1250. Many different recipes were published and fermentation methods "invented" for making *kimchi*, so it is not surprising that the tastes are quite different from one another. Despite the uniqueness of every *kimchi*, the basic taste is derived from salt, lactic acid fermentation of vegetables, spices (including hot red pepper, garlic, ginger, and green onion), and pickled fish or fresh seafood. There are about 170 different varieties and two or three kinds are served with meals. It is also used as a seasoning in soups and stews. In summer, *kimchi* is prepared weekly, since the vegetables are in season. But when winter sets in, no crops can be produced until late spring. The approach of winter marks the start of a long *kimchee*-making time called *gimjang*. During *gimjang*, Koreans gather in groups to cut, wash, and salt hundreds of pounds of the vegetables. After it is prepared, it is stored in the yard in large earthenware crocks. In the countryside, the crocks are buried up to their necks to keep the pickled vegetables from freezing.

Bulgogi is one of Korea's most famous grilled dishes. It is made from sirloin or another prime cut of beef (such as top round), cut into thin strips. For an outside barbecue, the meat is marinated in a mixture of sesame oil, soy sauce, black pepper, garlic, sugar, onions, ginger, and wine for at least four hours to enhance the flavor and to tenderize it. The marinated beef is cooked on a metal dish over the burner. Whole cloves of garlic, sliced onions, and chopped green peppers are often grilled at the same time. To eat, a piece of cooked beef is wrapped in lettuce with rice, *kimchi*, and shredded vegetables.

There are no real "courses" in a Korean meal. Generally, all food is laid out on the table at the same time and eaten in any order. Dessert is not a Korean tradition; seasonal fruit is normally served with hot tea or coffee.

Glossary

An-ju Appetizers or bar snacks, like tapas, usually savory, pungent, and strong-flavored foods intended to promote thirst.

Baechu (Napa Cabbage) The most popular vegetable used in traditional kimchi.

Bap (pab)-or (Ssal) Rice; Koreans eat short-grain rice.

Bokeum Stir-fried or sautéed dish.

Boo Long white radish resembling a parsnip in appearance, with a mild flavor. Tender white turnips can be substituted.

Buchu Korean chives, resembling a bundle of long grass rather than ordinary chives. They are highly perishable.

Bulgogi Grilled, marinated beef or other meat.

Busut Mushrooms.

Cellophane Noodles See Mung Bean Threads.

Chang Gilum A strongly flavored sesame oil used for seasoning; made from roasted sesame seeds.

Chongol (Jongol) Korean one-pot stew, similar to Japanese sukiyaki.

Dalaji White bellflower roots. Crunchy with a slightly sweet flavor, used both fresh and dried.

Dang-myun Sweet potato noodles that are distinctly Korean. Made from potato and sweet potato starch, they must be soaked in boiling water for 10 minutes before using.

Dubu Tofu or soybean curd.

Dwenjang Fermented soybean paste, brownish yellow in color and chunky in texture, different from the Japanese miso.

Gam Persimmons.

Gochu A chile pepper, introduced by Portuguese and Spanish traders in the seventeenth century.

Gochu Galu Korean chile powder made from sun-dried thin red peppers.

Gooksu, Myon or Kuksu Noodles.

Gui Barbecued or grilled food.

Jajang-myeon Korean noodle dish, black bean sauce, minced pork, and vegetables.

Jjigae Jungol Liquid-based hot-pot main courses for everyone to share.

Jjim, Jolim Simmered or stewed foods.

Jook Porridge.

Jon, Jun, Buchingae Batter-fried vegetables, meat, or fish.

Kalbi Short ribs, either barbecued or braised in soy sauce.

Kimchi Essentially the national dish of Korea, it combines countless varieties of pickled (fermented) vegetables. Most common kimchi consists of salted Korean cabbage, layered with garlic, ginger, chile paste, and salt or fermented fish, shrimp, or oysters.

Kochujang (Gochujang) Hot chile and bean curd paste, a staple of the Korean kitchen.

Kochukaru (Gochu Galu) Korean chile powder. Dried, powdered spicy red pepper.

Kong-namul (Kohng Namool) Soybean sprouts.

Laver (Gim) Edible seaweed.

Mae un Tang *Mae un* means spicy; *tang* is a meat-based soup boiled for a long time. It has been described as a "Korean bouillabaisse"—hot and spicy fish soup with chiles and kochujang.

Malt Powder (Yut Gilum) Beige-colored powder made from dried barley. Malt powder made from dried soybeans is called *meju galu*.

Mandu Korean dumplings, filled with ground pork, kimchi, spring onions, and bean curd, usually poached in a rich beef broth.

Manul Korea is number one in the world for garlic consumption per capita. Three major types of *manul* are grown in Korea: *soinpyun*, which has three or four large cloves; *dainpyun*, with many small cloves; and *jangsun*, grown mostly for its stems.

Miwon Pure MSG in white crystal form.

Miyuk or Dashima Kelp, sold dry. When soaked for about 10 minutes, it softens and expands, becoming slightly slimy and flowing.

Mu Radish, Asian or daikon.

Mung Bean (Nokdu) Dried mung beans are very small and green in color, yellow if the green husks have been removed. Dried split peas may be used as a substitute.

Mung Bean Sprouts (Nokdu Namool) or Green Bean Sprouts (Sookju Namool) Mung bean sprouts and green bean sprouts are interchangeable. Smaller than soybean sprouts, they do not have the large yellow bean head.

Mung Bean Threads Very fine dried noodles made from mung bean flour. Soak in water for 10 minutes before using.

Myuichi Anchovies. Dried anchovies are commonly used in Korean cooking; salted anchovies (paste) are also used. Korean brands are usually less salty and pungent than those of other Asian countries.

Naeng myon Literally, "cold noodle." Korean noodles made from buckwheat flour and potato starch. They are brownish in color with a translucent appearance, most often eaten cold.

Naju Bae An Asian pear that looks like a large brown apple with tough skin. It is very crispy and juicy, often peeled.

Namool Vegetables.

Oi Cucumbers; small pickling varieties are used in Korean cooking.

Pa Green onions.

Panchan Side dishes.

Pibimbap One-dish meal of rice, vegetables, meat, fried egg, and kochujang.

Pindaettok Mung bean pancake.

Pokkum Stir-fried or braised dish.

Saengsonhoe Raw fish.

Saewu Jut Salted shrimp; tiny salted shrimp (krill) is one of the major ingredients in making *kimchi*. Not to be confused with the more salty and pungent Southeast Asian shrimp paste.

Sang-chi-sam Lettuce-wrapped meal accompanied by many side dishes.

Sesame Seeds (Ggae) Used raw and toasted. There are two types, white and black.

Shil Gochu These chile pepper threads are a traditional garnish. The hair-thin threads, which resemble saffron, are machine-cut from dried red chile peppers.

Shinsollo Korean hot pot.

Soybean Paste Known as miso in Japan, a basic seasoning made from cooked soybeans, malt, and salt.

Tang Meat-based soup.

Toen Jang Miso-like fermented soybean paste used in soups and stews.

Twoenjangtchigae Pungent soybean paste soup, the soul of Korean cuisine.

Wun Tun Skins Called wonton skins in North America, paper-thin squares or circles of dough.

Menus and Recipes from Korea

Pa Jon Korean-Style Pancake   SERVES 4

Chef Tip **For crispy pancakes, use very cold water in the batter.**

AMOUNT	MEASURE	INGREDIENT
I teaspoon		**Salt**
¾ cup	3 ounces, 84 g	**All-purpose flour**
¼ cup	I ounce, 28 g	**Rice flour**
¾ cup	6 ounces, 180 ml	**Ice cold water**
I cup	4 ounces, 112 g	**Green onions, 1½ inch (3.75 cm) long, julienned**
¼ cup	I ounce, 28 g	**Zucchini (skin on), seeded, julienned**
¼ cup	I ounce, 28 g	**Red bell pepper, julienned**
4 tablespoons	2 ounces, 60 ml	**Vegetable oil**
		***Yangnyum Ganjang* or *Cho Ganjang* (recipes follow)**

PROCEDURE

1 Sift salt and flours together; add water a little at time, mixing until it is the consistency of thin pancake batter.

2 Add vegetables and mix.

3 Over medium-high heat, coat griddle or frying pan with just enough oil to thinly cover.

4 Cook batter in two batches, creating two large flat circles. Distribute the batter and vegetables evenly around the pan. Cook to golden brown, 3 minutes. Flip and cook other side, 2–3 minutes. Adjust heat if necessary to prevent burning; add oil as needed. Smaller pancakes are acceptable.

5 Cut pancake into 4 or 8 pieces and serve hot with *Yangnyum Ganjang* (seasoned soy sauce) or *Cho Ganjang* (vinegar soy sauce).

Yangnyum Ganjang

Seasoned Soy Sauce   YIELD: $\frac{1}{2}$ CUP (4 OUNCES, 120 ML)

AMOUNT	MEASURE	INGREDIENT
4 tablespoons	2 ounces, 60 ml	Soy sauce
$\frac{1}{4}$ cup	1 ounce, 28 g	Green onion, minced
1 tablespoon		Toasted sesame seeds
1 tablespoon	$\frac{1}{2}$ ounce, 15 ml	Sesame oil
$\frac{1}{2}$ tablespoon		*Kochukaru* (Korean chile powder)
$\frac{1}{2}$ teaspoon		Black pepper

PROCEDURE

1 Combine all ingredients.

Cho Ganjang   Vinegar Soy Sauce

YIELD: $\frac{1}{2}$ CUP (4 OUNCES, 120 ML)

AMOUNT	MEASURE	INGREDIENT
4 tablespoons	2 ounces, 60 ml	Soy sauce
2 tablespoons	2 ounces, 60 ml	Rice vinegar
2 tablespoons	1 ounce, 30 ml	Sesame oil
1 tablespoon		Toasted sesame seeds
1 teaspoon		Black pepper

PROCEDURE

1 Combine all ingredients.

Mu Sangchae
Spicy Radish Salad   SERVES 4–6

AMOUNT	MEASURE	INGREDIENT
1 teaspoon		*Kochukaru* (Korean chile powder)
2 tablespoons	1 ounce, 30 ml	Rice or white vinegar
1 tablespoon		Sugar
1 tablespoon		Salt
2 cups	12 ounces, 336	Daikon, peeled and julienned

PROCEDURE

1   Combine chile powder vinegar, sugar, and salt, stir to dissolve completely. Mix vinegar with daikon, let marinate under refrigeration for 2 hours before serving.

2   Serve chilled.

Buhsut Namool
Seasoned Mushrooms   SERVES 4

AMOUNT	MEASURE	INGREDIENT
1 tablespoon	$\frac{1}{2}$ ounce, 15 ml	Sesame oil
1		Garlic clove, minced
2 cups	5 ounces, 140 g	Shiitake mushrooms, $\frac{1}{4}$ inch (.6 cm) slices
1 teaspoon		Soy sauce
1 teaspoon		Sesame seeds, toasted

PROCEDURE

1   Heat sesame oil over medium-high heat; add garlic and mushrooms and stir-fry 2–3 minutes. Add soy sauce, toss, and remove from heat.

2   Serve warm or cold, sprinkled with toasted sesame seeds.

Twigim Mandu
Fried Meat Dumplings   YIELD: 24 DUMPLINGS

AMOUNT	MEASURE	INGREDIENT
$\frac{1}{2}$ cup	2 ounces, 56 g	Mung bean or green bean sprouts
	4 ounces, 112 g	Ground pork
$\frac{1}{4}$ cup	1 ounce, 28 g	Onion, minced
$\frac{1}{4}$ cup	1 ounce, 28 g	Green onion, white and green top, minced
2		Garlic cloves, minced
$\frac{1}{2}$ tablespoon	$\frac{1}{2}$ ounce, 14 g	Ginger, peeled and minced
1		Small egg
$\frac{1}{2}$ teaspoon		Sesame oil
$\frac{1}{4}$ teaspoon		Salt
$\frac{1}{4}$ teaspoon		White pepper
24		Round or square dumpling (wonton) wrappers, fresh (recipe follows) or purchased
As needed		Vegetable oil, for frying

PROCEDURE

1   Blanch mung bean sprouts in boiling water, shock in ice water, and squeeze out all excess moisture. Chop fine.

2   Combine chopped sprouts and remaining ingredients except dumpling wrappers and vegetable oil; mix well.

3   To make each dumpling, place $1\frac{1}{2}$ teaspoons (7.5 ml) filling in the center of a wrapper. Fold the wrapper over the filling in a semicircle for a round wrapper or a triangle for a square wrapper. Seal the edges by moistening them with a little water and pinching them. (To form a hat-shaped *mandu*, moisten the corners for the semicircular dumplings and bring them together, pinching them so that the dumpling forms a sort of fat tortellini.) Keep both wonton skins and dumplings moist under plastic or damp towels as you work. Repeat until all filling or wrappers are used.

4   Over medium-high heat, added enough oil to a frying pan to cover the bottom surface. Place dumpling in hot pan, filling but not crowding; you don't want the dumplings to touch and stick together.

5   Fry until golden brown and crispy on one side. Flip (long wooden chopsticks work great), cooking on all sides until golden and crispy all over. Continue cooking, adding oil as needed.

6   Serve with warm *Cho Ganjang*.

Mandu Pi   Fresh Dumpling Skins

YIELD: 50 SKINS

AMOUNT	MEASURE	INGREDIENT
3 cups	12 ounces, 336 g	All-purpose flour
$\frac{1}{4}$ teaspoon		Salt
$\frac{2}{3}$ cup	5.25 ounces, 158 ml	Water

PROCEDURE

1   Sift together flour and salt. Add water to a bowl; add flour a little at a time, mixing with each addition. Continue kneading until dough is well mixed and stiff. Cover and let rest 30 minutes.

2   Roll out on a floured surface or use a pasta machine. Pinch off small pieces and make them into round balls to roll out flat with a rolling pin. Alternately, roll the dough into small sausage-shaped rolls and slice them before rolling them into flat thin circles.

Bibim Naeng Myun

Garden's Cold Mixed Noodles   SERVES 4

After serving, the dish is eaten by stirring everything into the sauce with chopsticks. Note: the sauce is very hot and spicy.

AMOUNT	MEASURE	INGREDIENT
$\frac{1}{2}$ cup	4 ounces, 120 ml	Red pepper paste (recipe follows)
$\frac{1}{3}$ cup	2.66 ounces, 80 ml	Soy sauce
2 tablespoons		Granulated sugar
$1\frac{1}{4}$ tablespoons		Garlic, minced
$2\frac{1}{4}$ tablespoons		Green onions, minced, white part
1 tablespoon		Sesame seeds, toasted and crushed
$\frac{1}{4}$ cup	2 ounces, 60 ml	Sesame oil
3 tablespoons	$1\frac{1}{2}$ ounces, 45 ml	Beef broth
$1\frac{1}{2}$ pounds		Fresh-frozen buckwheat noodles (*naeng myun*), or 12 ounces dried, or 9 ounces bean threads
1		Asian pear or other hard pear, peel, cored, and sliced lengthwise, $\frac{1}{4}$ inch (.6 cm)
1 cup	8 ounces, 224 g	Marinated cucumbers (recipe follows)
2		Hard-cooked eggs

PROCEDURE

1   Combine red pepper paste, soy sauce, sugar, garlic, onion, sesame seeds, sesame oil, and broth. Mix or process until well blended and almost smooth.

2   Cook frozen noodles about 45 seconds in boiling water or until they are chewy but tender. Rinse with cold water, drain well, and chill. Or, if using dried noodles or bean threads, soak in water to cover 20 minutes, boil 1 minute; drain, rinse, and chill.

3   Divide the sauce among 4 bowls. Mound a fourth of the noodles in each bowl in the center of the sauce with a border of red sauce showing.

4   Arrange the pear slices and cucumbers on noodles.

5   Top with half a hard-cooked egg.

Red Pepper Paste

AMOUNT	MEASURE	INGREDIENT
¾ cup plus 1 tablespoon		Crushed red hot Korean peppers, or New Mexico or *Guajillo* chile peppers
¾ cup plus 1 tablespoon	6½ ounces, 195 ml	Water

PROCEDURE

1 Combine water and crushed peppers; let soak 30 minutes.

2 Process in a blender or food processor, or use a mortar and pestle to get a thick, slightly textured paste. Adjust thickness with water.

Marinated Cucumbers
SERVES 4

AMOUNT	MEASURE	INGREDIENT
2 tablespoons	1 ounce, 30 ml	Rice vinegar
1 tablespoon		Granulated sugar
1½ teaspoons		Salt
1½ cups	8 ounces, 224 g	European cucumber, unpeeled, sliced lengthwise ⅛ inch (.3 cm) thick and 2½ inches (6.25 cm) long

PROCEDURE

1 Combine vinegar, sugar, and salt; stir to dissolve.

2 Add cucumbers; cover and marinate at least 2 hours at room temperature. Refrigerate until ready to use.

Hacmul Jungol
Seafood Hot Pot SERVES 4

AMOUNT	MEASURE	INGREDIENT
1 cup	5 ounces, 140 g	Onion, $\frac{1}{4}$ inch (.6 cm) slices
$\frac{1}{2}$ cup	2 ounces, 56 g	Shiitake mushrooms, $\frac{1}{4}$ inch (.6 cm) slice
2 cups	8 ounces, 224 g	Napa cabbage, (5 cm) 2-inch-long strips
1 $\frac{1}{2}$ teaspoons		Garlic, minced
1 $\frac{1}{2}$ teaspoons		Ginger, minced
3 cups	24 ounces, 720 ml	Chicken broth (stock)
$\frac{3}{4}$ cup	4 ounces, 112 g	Squid, cleaned, sliced into thin (5 cm) 2-inch-long strips
4 ounces	112 g	16–20 shrimp
4 ounces	112 g	Fresh oysters, shelled, cleaned
4		Medium clams, shelled, cleaned
1 tablespoon		Chile paste (red pepper paste)
1 tablespoon		Kochukaru (Korean chile powder)
$\frac{1}{2}$ cup	2 ounces, 56 g	Green onion, cut on the diagonal, 2 inch (5 cm) long
3		Chrysanthemum leaves (optional)
To taste		Salt and pepper

PROCEDURE

1 Combine onion, mushroom, cabbage, garlic, and ginger with stock. Bring to boil and reduce to simmer.

2 Add seafood, chile paste, and chile powder to taste. Let cook until seafood is just done, 2 to 3 minutes.

3 Add green onions and chrysanthemum leaves; simmer 1 minute.

4 Correct seasoning.

5 Serve by placing the hot pot in middle of the table.

Kalbi-Kui
Barbecue Beef Ribs   SERVES 4

AMOUNT	MEASURE	INGREDIENT
$\frac{1}{2}$ cup	4 ounces, 120 ml	Soy sauce
2 tablespoons	1 ounce, 28 g	Granulated sugar
$\frac{1}{4}$ teaspoon		Dry mustard
$\frac{1}{4}$ teaspoon		Black pepper, freshly ground
1 teaspoon		Sesame seeds
2 tablespoons	1 ounce, 30 ml	Rice vinegar
2 tablespoons	1 ounce, 30 ml	Sesame oil
1 teaspoon		Ginger, minced
4		Garlic cloves, minced
$\frac{1}{4}$ cup	1 ounce, 28 g	Green onions, chopped
$2\frac{1}{2}$ pounds	1.12 kg	Korean-style short ribs (beef chuck flanken), cut $\frac{1}{3}$ to $\frac{1}{2}$ inch (.83 cm to 1.2 cm) thick across the bones, about 8 to 10 pieces

PROCEDURE

1 Combine all ingredients except short ribs; whisk well.

2 Trim the excess fat from the ribs. Score the meat deeply every $\frac{1}{2}$ inch (1.2 cm), almost to the bone.

3 Add short ribs to the marinade and coat evenly, turning the meat so the scored side is face-down in the marinade. Cover and let stand at least 3 hours, or refrigerate overnight, if possible.

4 Broil over charcoal, grill, or cook under a broiler. Look for outside to become crisp.

Kimchi
Traditional Napa Cabbage   YIELD: 1 GALLON

AMOUNT	MEASURE	INGREDIENT
1 cup plus 1 tablespoon	$8\frac{1}{2}$ ounces, 238 g	Salt
$\frac{1}{2}$ gallon	64 ounces, 1.92 l	Water
2		Napa cabbage heads, cut into 2 inch (5 cm) wedges
1		Garlic head, cloves separated and peeled
2	1-inch (2.4 cm) pieces	Ginger root
$\frac{1}{4}$ cup	2 ounces, 60 ml	Fish sauce or Korean salted shrimp
1 bunch		Green onion, 1 inch (2.4 cm) pieces
$\frac{1}{2}$ cup	4 ounces, 112 g	Korean ground chile
1 teaspoon		Granulated sugar

PROCEDURE

1   Dissolve 1 cup (8 ounces, 224 g) salt in water. Soak cabbage in salt water 3 to 4 hours.

2   Combine garlic, ginger, and fish sauce and process until almost smooth.

3   Combine green onions, garlic mixture, chile, 1 tablespoon ($\frac{1}{2}$ ounce, 14 g) salt, and sugar.

4   Drain cabbage and rinse thoroughly. Drain well in colander, squeezing as much water from the leaves as possible.

5   Spread green onion/chile mixture between cabbage leaves, making sure to fill each leaf adequately.

6   When all the cabbage has been stuffed, wrap a few of the larger leaves tightly around the rest of the cabbage, making tight bundles.

7   Divide cabbage among four 1-quart (960 ml) jars or one 1-gallon (1.28 l) jar, pressing down firmly to remove any air bubbles.

8   Let stand 2 to 3 days in the refrigerator to ferment.

Soo Jeung Kwa

Persimmon Punch YIELD: 1 QUART

AMOUNT	MEASURE	INGREDIENT
1 quart	32 ounces, 960 ml	Cold water
¼ cup	1 ounce, 28 g	Ginger, peeled, sliced thin
2		Cinnamon sticks
½ cup	4 ounces, 112 g	Granulated sugar
2		Dried persimmons, sliced, or 4 fresh or 10 dried apricots, 1 inch (2.5 cm) dice
¼ cup	1 ounce, 28 g	Pine nuts

PROCEDURE

1 Simmer water, ginger, and cinnamon sticks for 30 minutes or until water turns slightly red.

2 Strain, add sugar and persimmons, and let cool.

3 Serve well chilled with a teaspoon of pine nuts floating in each cup.

Jahb Chae
Mung Bean Noodles   SERVES 4

AMOUNT	MEASURE	INGREDIENT
3 cups	6 ounces, 168 g	Spinach
2 tablespoons	1 ounce, 30 ml	Sesame oil
1 tablespoon		Minced garlic
As needed		Salt
1 cup	4 ounces, 112 g	Onion, julienned
1 cup	4 ounces, 112 g	Green onions, bias cut into 2 inch (5 cm) pieces
$\frac{1}{2}$ cup	2 ounces, 56 g	Carrots, peeled, julienned
1 cup	3 ounces, 84 g	Shiitake mushrooms, thinly sliced
As needed		Soy sauce
As needed		Granulated sugar
As needed		Vegetable oil
6 ounces	168 g	*Dang myun* (Korean starch noodles), cover with boiling water, let stand 15 to 20 minutes or until softened, drained
As needed		Pepper
As needed		Sesame seeds, toasted

PROCEDURE

1   Blanch spinach in boiling salted water; cool under cold running water. Squeeze out as much moisture as possible. Cut into 3 inch (7.2 cm) lengths.

2   Combine sesame oil, minced garlic, and a pinch of salt. Toss with spinach and set aside.

3   Over medium high heat sauté all the vegetables separately with vegetable oil. To use the same pan, start with light-colored vegetables: onions, green onions, carrots, then shiitake mushrooms. The vegetables do not need to take on color, they just need to be softened.

4   Toss the sautéed shiitake mushrooms with $\frac{1}{2}$ teaspoon (2.5 ml) soy sauce, 1 teaspoon (5 ml) sugar, and 1 teaspoon (5 ml) sesame oil mix together.

5   Combine $1\frac{1}{2}$ cups (12 ounces, 360 ml) water, $\frac{1}{4}$ cup (2 ounces, 56 g) sugar, 2 tablespoons (1 ounce, 30 ml) soy sauce, and $\frac{1}{4}$ cup (2 ounces, 60 ml) vegetable oil to make *dang myon* seasoning.

6   In correct size pan, combine *dang myon* seasoning and soaked noodles. Bring to a boil, stirring occasionally for a few minutes until liquid is absorbed, then stir constantly until noodles are soft and translucent. Remove from heat, let cool, and cut into manageable length.

7   Toss noodles and vegetables; correct seasoning with salt and pepper. Transfer to a shallow serving dish and serve warm or at room temperature. Sprinkle with sesame seeds.

Jahb Chae – Mung Bean Noodles

Dak Chochu Jang Boekum
Chicken in Hot Chile Sauce   SERVES 4

AMOUNT	MEASURE	INGREDIENT
1 $\frac{1}{2}$ pounds	672 g	Chicken, cut into 3 inch (7.2 cm) pieces
4 tablespoons	2 ounces, 56 g	Granulated sugar
2		Garlic cloves, minced
$\frac{1}{4}$ cup	1 ounce, 28 g	Green onions, chopped
1 tablespoon	$\frac{1}{2}$ ounce, 15 ml	Fresh ginger, peeled, minced
2 tablespoons	1 ounce, 30 ml	Soy sauce
4 tablespoons	2 ounces, 60 ml	*Gochu jang* (Korean hot fermented chile paste)
2 tablespoons	1 ounce, 30 ml	Sesame oil
2 tablespoons	$\frac{1}{3}$ ounce, 10 g	Sesame seeds, toasted
$\frac{1}{2}$ cup	4 ounces, 120 ml	Water

PROCEDURE

1   Toss chicken pieces with sugar and let stand 1 hour.

2   Combine all other ingredients except water.

3   Toss chicken pieces with mixture and let stand 1 hour.

4   Bring water to a boil, add chicken and marinade, and bring to a simmer. Cover and simmer 30 minutes, or until chicken is cooked and most of the liquid has evaporated. Stir to prevent burning.

Dubu Jolim Simmered Tofu

SERVES 4

AMOUNT	MEASURE	INGREDIENT
18 ounces	504 g	Firm tofu
2 tablespoons	1 ounce, 30 ml	Soy sauce
1		Garlic clove, minced
$\frac{1}{2}$ cup	2 ounces, 56 g	Green onion, sliced thin
$\frac{1}{4}$ cup	1 ounce, 28 g	Red bell pepper, minced
1 tablespoon	$\frac{1}{2}$ ounce, 15 ml	Vegetable oil

PROCEDURE

1 Rinse tofu in cold water. Cut into $\frac{1}{2}$ inch (1.2 cm) cubes. Set aside to drain on paper towels.

2 Combine soy sauce, garlic, green onions, and red bell pepper. Set aside.

3 Heat oil over medium high heat and add tofu; make sure a flat side of each piece is in contact with the pan. The tofu will still have moisture, so be careful of splatters. Cook until first side is light brown, 2 to 4 minutes. Turn over and brown the opposite side, 2 to 4 minutes.

4 Reduce heat to medium; add soy mixture, spooning over the top. Cover and cook 2 to 3 minutes until infused with the seasoning.

Dan Kim Kui Crispy Seaweed

SERVES 4

AMOUNT	MEASURE	INGREDIENT
As needed		Sesame oil
10		Nori (seaweed) sheets
As needed		Salt

PROCEDURE

1   Using a pastry brush, brush a thin layer of oil onto the seaweed. Sprinkle a little salt over the entire sheet. Turn over and repeat on the other side.

2   In a large fry pan over medium heat, toast the nori until they turn brownish dark green; flip and toast the other side.

3   Cut toasted nori sheets down the middle lengthwise, then cut twice crosswise to make 6 small pieces.

Kohng Namool
Seasoned Soybean Sprouts   SERVES 4

AMOUNT	MEASURE	INGREDIENT
4 cups	16 ounces, 448 g	Soybean sprouts
½ cup	2 ounces, 56 g	Green onions, thinly sliced
1½ tablespoons		Garlic cloves, minced
1 tablespoon		Toasted sesame seeds, crushed
1 tablespoon	½ ounce, 15 ml	Sesame oil
1 teaspoon		White vinegar
1 teaspoon		Salt
1 teaspoon		*Kochukaru* (Korean chile powder)

PROCEDURE

1   Wash bean sprouts in cold water, removing any bean husks.

2   Combine sprouts and 1 cup (8 ounces, 240 ml) water in a pot with lid. Bring to a boil and cook 3 minutes. Do not lift lid. Remove from heat.

3   Rinse in cold water and drain.

4   Combine remaining ingredients, mix well, and toss with sprouts. Correct seasoning with salt and chile powder.

Bulgogi (Boolgogi)

Fire Meat SERVES 4

While literally translated as "fire meat," *bulgogi* is a nonspicy dish. Traditionally, it is eaten wrapped in green lettuce with *gochujang* (bean-paste hot sauce), but it may also simply be placed over a bowl of rice.

AMOUNT	MEASURE	INGREDIENT
$\frac{1}{2}$ cup	4 ounces, 112 g	Asian or hard pear, peeled, cored, and grated
2 tablespoons	$\frac{1}{2}$ ounce, 14 g	Onion, minced
$\frac{1}{4}$ cup	1 ounce, 28 g	Green onion, sliced thin
2 tablespoons	1 ounce, 30 ml	Sake
$\frac{1}{2}$ cup	4 ounces, 120 ml	Water
1 tablespoon		Garlic, minced
2 tablespoons	1 ounce, 30 ml	Sesame oil
2 teaspoons		Sesame seeds
1 teaspoon		Black pepper, freshly ground
2 tablespoons	1 ounce, 28 g	Granulated sugar
1 pound	448 g	Beef top round, partially frozen, cut very thin into 2 inch (5 cm) squares.
As needed		*Bulgogi* sauce (recipe follows)

PROCEDURE

1 Combine all ingredients except the beef; stir well to dissolve.

2 Add beef to marinade and toss; marinate for at least 3 hours.

3 Drain meat, discarding marinade.

4 Cook beef on a *bulgogi* grill pan or grill over hot charcoal or stir-fry over high heat.

5 Dip broiled, grilled, or stir-fried meat slices in *bulgogi* sauce.

Ojingo Pokum – Squid with Vegetables in Chili-Hot Sweet Sauce, Dubu Jolim – Simmered Tofu, Bulgogi (Boolgogi) – Fire Meat, Kimchi, Rice

Bulgogi Sauce

SERVES 4

AMOUNT	MEASURE	INGREDIENT
1		Garlic clove
1 tablespoon	$\frac{1}{2}$ ounce, 14 g	Granulated sugar
To taste		Salt
3 tablespoons	$1\frac{1}{2}$ ounces, 45 ml	Dark soy sauce
1 tablespoon	$\frac{1}{2}$ ounce, 15 ml	Sesame oil
1 teaspoon		Chinese bean paste
1 teaspoon		Sesame seeds, toasted
2 tablespoons	1 ounce, 30 ml	Sake or dry sherry
1 teaspoon		Green onion, white part, minced
1 tablespoon	$\frac{1}{2}$ ounce, 15 ml	Oil
$\frac{1}{4}$ teaspoon		Cayenne pepper

PROCEDURE

1 Crush garlic with sugar and salt to make a smooth paste.

2 Combine remaining ingredients.

Ojingo Pokum
Squid with Vegetables in Chile
Hot-Sweet Sauce SERVES 4

AMOUNT	MEASURE	INGREDIENT
2 tablespoons	1 ounce, 30 ml	Vegetable oil
1 cup	4 ounces, 112 g	Green onions, cut into 1 inch (2.4 cm) lengths
1 cup	4 ounces, 112 g	Spicy Korean red peppers, or red bell peppers, julienned
1 cup	4 ounces, 112 g	Carrots, julienned
1 cup	4 ounces, 112 g	Onions, julienned
1 cup	4 ounces, 112 g	Mushrooms, sliced thin
1 pound	448 g	Squid, cleaned and cut into flat 1 x 2 inch (2.4 x 4.8 cm) inch pieces
2 teaspoons		Garlic, minced
2 teaspoons		Granulated sugar
1 tablespoon		Red pepper flakes or *kochukaru* (Korean chile powder)

PROCEDURE

1   Heat the oil, add the vegetables, and stir-fry 2 minutes.
2   Remove from heat and add squid, garlic, and sugar. Stir-fry 2 minutes.
3   Add chile powder and cook over high heat 1 minute. Serve hot.

Bibimbap Garnished Rice SERVES 4

This is a one-dish meal with rice and an assortment of seasonal vegetables, and often a small bit of meat may be added. It is traditionally served in a heated stone pot, garnished with a raw egg yolk on top. When eaten, everything is mixed together, and the raw yolk is fully cooked by the heated stone.

Red Pepper Paste

AMOUNT	MEASURE	INGREDIENT
2 tablespoons	I ounce, 30 ml	Red pepper paste
2 tablespoons	I ounce, 30 ml	Soy sauce
I tablespoon		Garlic, minced
2 tablespoons	$\frac{1}{2}$ ounce, 14 g	Green onion, white part, minced
I tablespoon	$\frac{1}{2}$ ounce, 14 g	Granulated sugar
I tablespoon		Sesame seed, toasted
2 tablespoons	I ounce, 30 ml	Sesame oil

PROCEDURE

I Combine all ingredients and simmer on low heat until thick.

Seasoning Sauce

AMOUNT	MEASURE	INGREDIENT
4 tablespoons	2 ounces, 60 ml	Soy sauce
2 tablespoons	I ounce, 30 ml	Granulated sugar
I tablespoon	$\frac{1}{2}$ ounce, 15 ml	Rice wine
I tablespoon		Green onion, minced
I tablespoon		Garlic, minced
I tablespoon	$\frac{1}{2}$ ounce, 15 ml	Sesame oil
I tablespoon		Sesame seeds, toasted
$\frac{1}{2}$ teaspoon		Black pepper

PROCEDURE

I Combine all ingredients.

AMOUNT	MEASURE	INGREDIENT
3 cups	18 ounces, 504 g	White rice, cooked
1 cup	4 ounces, 112 g	Carrots, julienned blanched
1 teaspoon		Soy sauce
1 tablespoon		Sesame seeds
Pinch		Salt

PROCEDURE

Stir-fry rice and carrots with 1 teaspoon (5 ml) soy sauce, $\frac{1}{2}$ teaspoon (2.5 ml) sesame oil, 1 tablespoon (5 ml) sesame seed, and a pinch of salt.

AMOUNT	MEASURE	INGREDIENT
1 cup	6 ounces, 168 g	English cucumber, julienned
2 teaspoons		Salt
$\frac{1}{2}$ teaspoon		Sesame oil

PROCEDURE

Sprinkle cucumber with 1 teaspoon salt; toss and let stand 10 minutes. Squeeze out the moisture and stir-fry in 1 teaspoon salt and $\frac{1}{2}$ teaspoon sesame oil until hot.

AMOUNT	MEASURE	INGREDIENT
2 cups	8 ounces, 224 g	Bean sprouts
$\frac{1}{2}$ cup	4 ounces, 120 ml	Boiling water, salted
1 teaspoon		Salt
1 teaspoon		Sesame oil
1 teaspoon		Green onion
$\frac{1}{2}$ teaspoon		Garlic

PROCEDURE

Scald bean sprouts in boiling salted water. Drain and mix with remaining ingredients.

AMOUNT	MEASURE	INGREDIENT
I cup	6 ounces, 168 g	Spinach, blanched, moisture squeezed out
I teaspoon		Soy sauce
$\frac{1}{2}$ teaspoon		Sesame oil
$\frac{1}{2}$ teaspoon		Sesame seeds
I teaspoon		Green onion
$\frac{1}{2}$ teaspoon		Garlic
To taste		Black pepper

PROCEDURE

I   Stir-fry spinach with soy sauce, sesame oil, sesame seed, green onion, garlic, and black pepper.

AMOUNT	MEASURE	INGREDIENT
4		Whole eggs

PROCEDURE

I   Fry egg to taste.

Serving

I   Place $\frac{1}{4}$ of the rice in 4 warm bowls. Arrange vegetables in separate mounds around the rice. Top each serving with 1 egg. Serve with red pepper paste, which is normally mixed together with the rice and vegetables. Serve the seasoning sauce on the side.

Dwaeji Galbi

Spicy Pork Ribs   SERVES 4

AMOUNT	MEASURE	INGREDIENT
1 inch (2.4 cm)		Ginger root, peeled, minced
1		Garlic clove, minced
$\frac{1}{4}$ cup	2 ounces, 60 ml	Chile paste
2 tablespoons	1 ounce, 30 ml	Korean malt syrup (*mool yut*) or corn syrup or honey
2 tablespoons	1 ounce, 28 g	Granulated sugar
1 tablespoon	$\frac{1}{2}$ ounce, 15 ml	Soy sauce
1 tablespoon	$\frac{1}{2}$ ounce, 15 ml	Sesame oil
$\frac{1}{2}$ teaspoon		Black pepper
$1\frac{1}{4}$ pound	560 g	Pork back ribs, trimmed and cut into serving pieces

PROCEDURE

1 Preheat oven to 350°F (176°C)

2 Combine ginger, garlic, chile paste, malt syrup, sugar, soy sauce, sesame oil, and black pepper. Rub marinade generously over meat. Cover and refrigerate 2 hours or longer.

3 Arrange ribs, slightly overlapping in roasting pan. Cover with foil; bake 1 hour or until ribs are tender. Set aside and reserve roasting juices.

4 When ready to serve, heat grill to medium-high heat and grill 5 to 6 minutes per side. Baste with roasting juices.

Bibim Gooksu
Spicy Summer Noodles   SERVES 4

AMOUNT	MEASURE	INGREDIENT
I cup	8 ounces, 224 g	Kimchi, chopped
I $\frac{1}{2}$ cup	9 ounces, 252 g	Cucumber, peeled, seeded, julienned
I tablespoon	$\frac{1}{2}$ ounce, 15 ml	Soy sauce
I tablespoon	$\frac{1}{2}$ ounce, 15 ml	Sesame oil
I		Garlic clove, minced
I tablespoon	$\frac{1}{2}$ ounce, 15 ml	Rice vinegar
I tablespoon	$\frac{1}{2}$ ounce, 14 g	Granulated sugar
10 ounces	280 g	Dried buckwheat noodles (*naeng myun*), cooked and cooled in ice water

PROCEDURE

1 Combine kimchi and cucumbers.

2 Combine soy sauce, sesame oil, garlic, vinegar, and sugar; stir to dissolve.

3 Toss dressing with vegetables.

4 Drain the noodles thoroughly and divide among four shallow bowls. Top each portion with the vegetable mixture and serve immediately.

Bibim Gooksu – Spicy Summer Noodles

Maeum Tang Spiced Fish Soup

SERVES 4

AMOUNT	MEASURE	INGREDIENT
1 pound	448 g	Cod fillets, skinned, boned, $1\frac{1}{2}$ inch (3.6 cm) cubes
$2\frac{1}{2}$ cups	20 ounces, 600 ml	Water or light fish stock
2 tablespoons	1 ounces, 30 ml	Vegetable oil
1 cup	4 ounces, 112 g	Onion, $\frac{1}{4}$ inch (.6 cm) dice
2 tablespoons	$\frac{1}{2}$ ounce, 14 g	Green onion, white part, minced
2		Garlic cloves, minced
1 teaspoon		Ginger, minced
2–4 teaspoons		Chile powder, to taste
2 teaspoons		Salt
1 cup	4 ounces, 112 g	Zucchini, halved lengthwise and sliced thin
$\frac{1}{2}$ cup	2 ounces, 56 g	Green pepper, julienne cut

PROCEDURE

1   Combine cod and water; bring to a simmer and cook 3–4 minutes or until just cooked. Remove from heat and set aside.

2   Heat oil over medium high heat; stir-fry onions, green onions, garlic, ginger, and chile powder for 1 minute. Add salt, zucchini, and green peppers; stir-fry one minute.

3   Combine vegetables with soup, bring back to simmer, and serve hot.

Kaji Namul
Marinated Eggplant   SERVES 4

AMOUNT	MEASURE	INGREDIENT
2 or 3	8 ounces, 224 g	Japanese eggplants, ends trimmed
$\frac{1}{2}$ cup	2 ounces, 56 g	Green onions, green and white parts, minced
2 tablespoons	I ounce, 30 ml	Soy sauce
I		Garlic clove, minced
I teaspoon		Sesame seeds
2 teaspoon		Sesame oil
I teaspoon		Rice vinegar

PROCEDURE

1   Steam eggplant in a Chinese-style steamer until tender, 8 to 10 minutes. Let cool and cut into 3-inch (7.2 cm) strips.

2   Combine remaining ingredients; whisk together. Toss dressing with eggplant and refrigerate until ready to serve. Serve at room temperature.

Oi Bok Kum Namul
Cooked Cucumbers   SERVES 4

AMOUNT	MEASURE	INGREDIENT
2 cups	8 ounces, 224 g	Cucumber, peeled, seeded, cut $\frac{1}{4}$ × $\frac{1}{4}$ × $2\frac{1}{2}$ inches (.6 cm × .6 cm × .6 cm) long
$1\frac{1}{4}$ teaspoons		Salt
$1\frac{1}{2}$ tablespoons	$\frac{3}{4}$ ounce, 20 ml	Sesame seed oil
2 tablespoons	$\frac{1}{2}$ ounce, 14 g	Green onions, minced
2 tablespoons	1 ounce, 30 ml	Soy sauce
2 teaspoons		Chile powder
$1\frac{1}{2}$ teaspoon		Granulated sugar
1 tablespoon		Sesame seeds, toasted

PROCEDURE

1   Toss cucumber with salt and let stand 10 minutes. Rinse and dry thoroughly.

2   Heat oil over medium heat and sauté cucumbers and green onions until they begin to soften, 2 to 3 minutes.

3   Add soy sauce, chile powder, and sugar; toss to distribute evenly. Transfer to serving dish and sprinkle with sesame seeds.

4   Serve warm or slightly chilled.

Seng Sun Bulgogi
Barbecued Spiced Fish SERVES 4

AMOUNT	MEASURE	INGREDIENT
1 teaspoons		Salt
1½ pounds	5 ounces each, 140 g each	Fillet of fish, sea bass, red snapper, flounder, or similar fish, skin on
2 teaspoons		*Kochujang (Gochujang)* paste
1 teaspoon		Granulated sugar
½ teaspoon		Black pepper
1 teaspoon		Toasted sesame seeds
1 teaspoon		Sesame oil
1 teaspoon		Rice wine
2 tablespoons		Green onions, minced
1		Garlic clove, minced
1 teaspoon		Ginger root, minced

PROCEDURE

1 Sprinkle salt over fish fillet and let stand under refrigeration for at least 3 hours, preferably overnight, to dry out. Turn the pieces over a few times.

2 Mix remaining ingredients to a paste. Rub paste into fish fillets. Let stand 30 minutes.

3 Grill or broil filets until just done, 3 to 5 minutes per side, according to thickness. Do not overcook. Serve hot or warm.

Yak Sik Steamed Rice Pudding

SERVES 4

AMOUNT	MEASURE	INGREDIENT
1¾ cup	12¼ ounces, 343 g	Glutinous rice
2 tablespoons	1 ounce, 30 ml	Sesame oil
½ teaspoon		Ground cinnamon
½ cup	2½ ounces, 70 g	Raisins
½ cup	3½ ounces, 98 g	Dates, pitted, cut in half
1 cup	7 ounces, 196 g	Packaged chestnuts, peeled, cut in half
¼ cup	2 ounces, 60 ml	Honey
2 tablespoons		Pine nuts
Seasoning Mix		
1½ tablespoons	¾ ounce, 22.5 ml	Soy sauce
¼ cup	2 ounces, 56 g	Brown sugar
¾ cup	5¼ ounces, 147 g	Granulated sugar

PROCEDURE

1 Wash rice and soak in cold water 4 hours, if possible. Drain and steam 30 minutes. Transfer hot cooked rice to a large bowl.

2 Combine seasoning mix ingredients and fold into the hot rice until well mixed. Add sesame oil and cinnamon and mix again. Gently add the raisins, dates, and chestnuts while stirring.

3 Return mixture to steamer and steam for one hour. Test one of the chestnuts to make sure everything is cooked. Sprinkle with honey and mix while steaming. Serve topped with pine nuts.

4 For an alternative serving presentation, press the hot steamed rice pudding into a form lined with film or foil. Make at least three layers, sprinkling pine nuts on each layer. Let cool enough to slice into squares. Serve warm or at room temperature.

Southeast Asia

The Land

Southeast Asia, a region of Asia of over 1,740,000 square miles, is bordered by the Indian subcontinent on the west, China on the north, and the Pacific Ocean on the east. The name "Southeast Asia" came into popular use after World War II and has replaced such phrases as "Further India," "East Indies," "Indo-China," and "Malay Peninsula," which formerly designated all or part of the region. Southeast Asia includes the Indochina Peninsula, which juts into the South China Sea, the Malay Peninsula, and the Indonesian and Philippine archipelagos. The region has ten independent countries: Brunei, Cambodia, Indonesia, Laos, Malaysia, Myanmar, the Philippines, Singapore, Thailand, and Vietnam.

Peninsular Southeast Asia is a rugged region traversed by many mountains and drained by great rivers such as the Thanlwin, Ayeyarwady, Chao Phraya, and Mekong. Insular Southeast Asia is made up of numerous volcanic and coral islands. Overall, the region has a generally tropical rainy climate, with the exception of the northwestern part, which has a humid subtropical climate. The wet monsoon winds are vital for the economic well-being of the region. Tropical forests cover most of the area. Rice is the chief crop of the region; rubber, tea, spices, and coconuts are also important. The region has a great variety of minerals and produces most of the world's tin.

History

Throughout the early human history of Southeast Asia, one group after another was displaced and pushed southward by successive waves of immigrants from China and Tibet. Only the inhabitants of the highlands retained their traditional culture.

By the first century A.D., traders from India and China were vying for a foothold in the region, drawn there by its rich abundance of minerals, spices, and forest products. For the next thirteen or fourteen centuries, India's influence dominated, except in what is now Vietnam. Although there is some small Indian influence seen in the cuisine, China maintained a political foothold in Vietnam for a thousand years. Even after it lost control over the area during the 900s, Chinese migrants and merchants continued to make a strong impact on the region.

Throughout this long period, local kingdoms, such as the Khmer empire, rose and fell, but the peoples of the region were never unified culturally. Frequently, they were caught up in savage wars with one another. Even today, there is a legacy of distrust among groups of differing ancestries in Southeast Asia.

In the late fifteenth century Islamic influences grew strong but were overshadowed by the arrival of Europeans, who established their power throughout Southeast Asia; only Thailand remained free of colonial occupation. Because of Southeast Asia's strategic location between Japan and India, and the importance of shipping routes that traverse it, the region became the scene of battles between Allied and Japanese forces during World War II.

Since the war the countries of Southeast Asia have reemerged as independent nations. They have been plagued by political turmoil, weak economies, ethnic strife, and social inequities, although the situation for most Southeast Asian nations improved in the 1980s and 1990s. Throughout the 1960s and early 1970s, however, there were open conflicts between communist and non-Communist factions, especially in Vietnam, Laos, and Cambodia. In 1967 Indonesia, Malaysia, the Philippines, Singapore, and Thailand created the Association of Southeast Asian Nations (ASEAN), the objectives of which are to promote regional economic growth, political stability, social progress, and cultural developments. Since then, Brunei (1984), Vietnam (1995), Laos (1997), and Myanmar and Cambodia (1999) have joined ASEAN. In 1997 a monetary collapse in Thailand sparked a general economic crisis in several nations in the region; the results were most severe in Indonesia, which underwent economic, political, and social turmoil in the late 1990s.

Religion, ethnicity, and language are diverse throughout Southeast Asia. There are dozens of religions, including Buddhism, Confucianism, Hinduism, Islam, and Roman Catholicism. Hundreds of languages are spoken throughout.

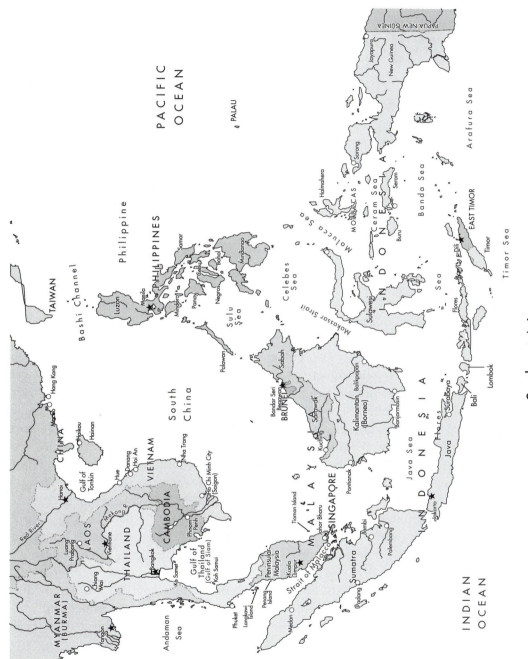

Southeast Asia

The People

Southeast Asia is one of the world's great melting pots. Its diverse peoples moved into the region in search of a better life and greater security. The original inhabitants of Southeast Asia can be found in the highland regions of the Philippines, Indonesia, and Malaysia. Around 2500 B.C., the first major wave of migrating peoples entered the area. They were the Malays, or Indonesians, and it is their descendants who form the great majority of the populations of the Philippines and Indonesia today. The Malays formerly lived in what is now southern China, but pressure from the Chinese population in the north forced other peoples southward. These people in turn pressed upon the Malays, who moved through the mountain passes into mainland Southeast Asia, down the Malay Peninsula, and out into the Indonesian and Philippine islands. Skilled sailors, the Malays expanded eastward through these islands.

Others followed, principally the Cambodians, the Vietnamese, the Myanmar (Burmese), and the Thai moving south out of China, to settle in mainland Southeast Asia. The Thai were the last of the major groups to settle in here, establishing their first important kingdom during the 1200s.

These various groups brought with them their own customs, cultures, and living patterns, but they were to be strongly influenced by still other people. Traders from India brought Indian philosophies to Southeast Asia, especially the Hindu and Buddhist religions. Myanmar, Thailand, Laos, and Cambodia are today Buddhist countries as a result. Later, Muslim traders brought Islam to Malaysia and Indonesia, which are now predominantly Muslim. The culture and religion of Vietnam were influenced by China.

This process of infusion of both people and ideas has continued into modern times. The European powers began their colonization of the region (except for Thailand, which was never colonized) during the 1500s, bringing with them Western ideas of government, culture, and religion. The Philippines, colonized by Spain, became largely Roman Catholic. During the late 1700s and early 1800s large numbers of Chinese and Indians came to Southeast Asia to take advantage of the economic opportunities during the height of the European colonial period.

More than three-quarters of the Southeast Asia population is agriculture-based. Much fish is consumed in this region, reflecting the long coastlines and river environments of Southeast Asia. The staple food throughout the region is rice, which has been cultivated for thousands of years.

In Asia, there are different styles of eating food. In India and the Middle East, as well as Southeast Asia, people typically eat food with their hands. It is a very direct way to experience the texture of the food, and people wash their hands before and after each meal. Normally, only the right hand is used, so that one knows to keep it especially clean. Generally, the foods to be eaten are placed on plates in the center of the mat or table, and people take food in small portions as they eat. The exception to this pattern is Vietnam, where the influence of China was much stronger than anywhere else in Southeast Asia. Here, chopsticks are the utensil of choice, and food is served onto individual plates or into individual bowls. Today, the influence of Western cultures is found not only in the use of tables and chairs in many modern Southeast Asian households, but also in the use of spoons and forks. Knives are not necessary, since meat and vegetables are chopped into smaller portions before cooking or serving. A large spoon is held in the right hand, while the left hand is used to scoop food into the spoon.

The Food

Due to the close proximity of the borders between countries in Southeast Asia, and to combined influences from India and China that have affected indigenous taste and cooking styles, the ingredients are similar throughout most of the region, while they are individualized by each culture to suit their palate and taste. Indian cooking has influenced much of Southeast Asia. However, Indian cooking traditions vary throughout the region and according to ethnic and religious preference. Muslims do not eat pork, and the month of Ramadan (the ninth month of the Muslim lunar calendar) is a time of fasting for Muslims all over the world, during which time they may neither eat nor drink during the daylight hours. Hindus, in contrast, believe that cows are sacred and the eating of beef is forbidden. Others from the south of India are vegetarians. Buddhists, too, are expected not to eat meat, as the killing of any animal is against Buddhist beliefs. However, many Buddhists do eat meat as well as fish, and this belief tends to be most closely observed by monks or ascetics rather than by ordinary people today. Curries originated in India, with the milk and butter from cows being included in the recipes. In Southeast Asia, coconut milk is substituted for cow's milk, which gives a very different taste to the curries. Noodles are popular throughout Southeast Asia, and reflect Chinese as well as Indian influence in the spices and methods of preparation.

Europeans have had their culinary influence in Southeast Asia. In the Philippines, for example, Spanish influence is clearly present not only in the languages of the country but in their love of such dishes as *pan de sal* (a type of bread), *kilawin* (marinated raw seafood with chile), *paella* (a seafood, meat, and rice stir fry dish), empanadas (turnovers), and a variety of other seasoned meat dishes. Conventional dishes in the Philippines reflect more influence from a blend of Chinese, Spanish, and indigenous Southeast Asian traditions than is found anywhere else in Southeast Asia.

Popular meals in Southeast Asia consist of rice, fish, vegetables, fruits, and spices. Curry, *satay* (spiced or marinated meat on a stick that is barbecued), *sour fish soup*, noodles, and soy products are popular. Common flavorings include ginger, pepper, chile peppers, onions, garlic, soy sauce, fish sauce, fermented fish paste, turmeric, candlenut, lemongrass, cloves, nutmeg, cinnamon, as well as tamarind and lime (for a sour taste). Coconut milk is often used to bind sharp flavors, while palm sugar is used to balance the spices. Unique combinations of sweet and sour, hot and sour, or hot and sweet are common in various regions. Fish paste and prawn paste is spicy-sour, and is popularly consumed with green mangoes, fresh fish, or in stews. Fish sauce is used in almost all Southeast Asian curries as well as in various forms of cooking fish and pork. Popular vegetables are sweet potatoes, maize, taro, tapioca, legumes, blossoms, and the leaves of many green plants. Popular fruits are pineapple, coconut, star fruit, jackfruit, papaya, bananas, rambutan, mangosteen, and the somewhat foul-smelling durian. Tea and coffee are abundant throughout the region, although the popular drink with a meal is water.

The islands of Indonesia support the fourth most populous nation in the world, a population that is 90 percent Muslim, with hundreds of tribes, subcultures, and languages. *Satay*—pieces of grilled meat, poultry, or seafood served with spicy peanut sauce—is Indonesia's best-known dish. One of the region's most unique foods is the vegetarian *tempeh* or *tempe*. This is made from soybeans and was originally produced to be a food similar to China's tofu. *Gado-gado*, a dish of mixed vegetables and salad with both tofu and tempeh, topped with a spicy peanut sauce, is one of the typical ways in which it is used. *Sambal*, a spicy sauce made from chiles, shrimp paste, and tomatoes, is available everywhere and is eaten with main dishes and snacks.

In Bali the cuisine and culture are distinctively different due to the predominance of the Hindu religion on the island. *Babi guling*, a dish of spit-roast suckling pig stuffed with herbs, is one of the most distinctive Balinese dishes, and often accompanied by the local version of black pudding. Along with rice, proximity to the Pacific Islands means other sources of starch; sago, cassava, and taro are popular staples. There is a large variety of fresh fish to choose from, including eels, squid, barracuda, crab, and shrimp.

Cambodian and Laotian dishes rely on the original ingredients for the core of the flavoring. The most frequent methods of cooking are steaming, grilling over a charcoal fire, or a quick stir-fry in a wok. One of the most popular flavorings is *tik marij*, a mixture of ground black pepper, salt, and lime juice. A main course in the Cambodian diet is simply cooked meat or fish with *tik marij*. Banana leaves are used for wrapping food during grilling or steaming. The leaves retain liquid while adding some flavor to a dish. A favorite Cambodian dessert consists of grilling sticky rice balls with coconut and jackfruit inside a banana leaf.

A combination of different Asian culinary tastes, Lao cuisine combines a love of sticky rice, raw greens, and spicy dipping sauce. Their national dish, *larb*, is a mixture of marinated meat or fish, sometimes served raw, and offered with a combination of vegetables, herbs, and spices. Another popular dish is *tam mak houng*, green papaya salad. Except for crisp green vegetables, Lao foods favor sour over sweet. Galangal, lemongrass, shallots, and garlic are also herbs and vegetables seen as a necessity.

Malaysia has been influenced by Chinese, Indian, and Arabic roots. A majority of Malays are Muslims who consume rice, but not pork or alcohol. However, similar to its Thai neighbors in the north, Malay cooking extensively uses chile peppers and thick coconut milk. East Asian spices contribute flavor to many of the sauces. Malaysian dishes are typically seasoned with curry, shallots, garlic, shrimp paste, tamarind, lemongrass, or coconut milk.

For almost four hundred years, the Spanish had control in the Philippines, leaving a lasting effect that is apparent in Filipino cooking today. Many dishes have Spanish names, regardless of a Spanish connection. A basic technique to start off many Filipino dishes was introduced by the Spaniards: sautéing tomatoes, garlic, and onions in olive oil. The Spaniards also introduced sausages and dishes using meat and dairy. Beef was initially brought to the Philippines by Spanish ships, so many beef entrees are of Spanish origin. In the Philippines, four meals a day are served: breakfast, lunch, *merienda* (snack), and dinner. *Pancit*, or noodles, is considered a *merienda* dish and is served with a sponge cake called *puto* and a glutinous rice cake called *cuchinta*. Lunch is the heaviest meal and consists of rice, a vegetable, a meat, and sometimes fish as well. Vegetables include *kangkung* (a local spinach), broccoli, Chinese broccoli, bitter melon, mung bean, bean sprouts, eggplant, and okra. Beef, pork, and chicken are eaten often, and water buffalo are eaten in the provinces. Other important foods include rice, corn, coconuts, sugarcane, bananas, coffee, mangoes, and pineapples.

In Singapore, cooking—known as Straits Chinese, Baba, or Peranakan cuisine, or Nonya cooking—is a mixture of Chinese and Malay traditions. Described as a fusion of Chinese techniques and tropical produce, Nonya cooking tends to be spicier and tangier than Chinese food but, unlike indigenous Malay cuisines, features the use of pork and noodles. The result is highly refined but also boldly flavored. *Laksa*, the rich coconut soup-noodle dish, is one of the best-known Nonya dishes. *Otak otak* is mashed fish with coconut milk and chile, wrapped in banana leaf and grilled over coals. Singapore is particularly famous for its crab dishes. *Chile crab* features pieces of shellfish smothered in tangy chile and tomato sauce, while black pepper crabs are seasoned in a thick black pepper and soy sauce. The European influence can be seen in curry puffs (pastry parcels filled with curried potato and chicken or lamb), which are similar to England's pasties, and *kaya*, which is a sweet preserve most likely based on Europe's imported jams, but made of coconut and egg. It is usually served with bread.

Thailand can be broken into four regions. The influences of neighboring Laos are reflected strongly in the northeastern region food, with glutinous rice being the staple food, eaten both as a base for a meal and also as a dessert, steamed with coconut milk and black beans. Herbs such as dill are widely used, and a popular regional dish is *Khanom Buang*, a thin crispy egg omelette stuffed with shrimp and bean sprouts. Northeastern food is highly spiced, with regional specialties like *lap*, spicy minced meat or chicken, or the famous *som tam* (papaya salad) and *kai yang* (barbecued chicken). Freshwater fish and shrimp are the main sources of protein in northeastern dishes, as meat is a scarce commodity.

The central plains area is considered to be the cultural and economic heart of Thailand due to the fertility of the land. A vast number of paddy fields have traditionally provided the country with its principal source of food, hence the Thai expression *kin khao* ("to eat"), which literally translates as "to eat rice." Unlike the north and northeast, the central plains use plain rice, traditionally steamed, but sometimes boiled or fried. The central region provided much of what is known as traditional Thai cuisine: rice, fish, and vegetables flavored with garlic, fish sauce, and black pepper, along with an abundance of fresh fruits. When Ayutthaya became the capital of Thailand, the increase in the use of chiles occurred, along with coriander, lime, and tomato. As well as freshwater fish from the river, the central plains have access to the nearby Gulf and so the cuisine features much seafood. A wide range of vegetables grows in the fertile soils, along with fruit such as mango, durian, custard apple, pomelos, and guavas. The north of Thailand is a region of wild, densely forested mountains and temple filled towns. Rice tends to be of the glutinous variety, eaten after being kneaded into small balls with the fingers and using it to scoop up more liquid dishes.

Northern curries are generally milder than elsewhere in Thailand, with the influence of neighboring countries such as Myanmar evident in dishes such as *kaeng hang le*, a pork curry with ginger, tamarind, and turmeric, and *khao soi*, a curry broth with egg noodles. Another northern specialty is a spicy pork sausage, called *name*. The south of Thailand has vast plantations of pineapple, coconut, and rubber, and due to the large Muslim influence along the Malaysian border, a distinctive culture. Southern food is characterized by local produce. Coconut has a prominent role in most dishes—its milk to cool the chiles in curries and soups, its flesh when grated to serve as a condiment, or its oil for frying. Fresh seafood is featured prominently. The cashew nuts from local plantations are used as starters or stir-fried—particularly with chicken and chiles—and an exotic, bitter flavor is provided by the pungent flat bean called *sato*. A variety of cultural influences can be seen in southern Thai cuisine; several Malaysian dishes such as fish curries are found. *Kaeng massaman* is a mild Indian-style curry with cardamom, cloves, and cinnamon; *satay*—originally an Indonesian dish—is widely eaten with a spicy peanut sauce. Probably most famous is the influence of the large Chinese community, who hold a ten-day vegetarian festival in Phuket every October.

Vietnamese cuisine can be divided into three regional varieties. In the cool, mountainous north, in the city of Hanoi, a history of Chinese rule is evident in Cantonese-style stir-fries and simple, brothy soups. The flat, arid central region serves up heartier, more refined dishes. In the hot, steamy south, including the city of Ho Chi Minh City (formerly Saigon), tropical abundance is the rule: seafood, pork, and numerous fruits and vegetables are found in bold and spicy dishes, including curries influenced from nearby India. And throughout the country, *banh mi* (a kind of Vietnamese po'boy with meat, pâté, hot peppers, and pickled vegetables) and strong, sweet coffee serve as reminders of Vietnam's French colonial past.

The presence of fresh herbs is one of the most distinctive elements in Vietnamese cooking. Collectively called *rau thom*, Vietnamese herbs include mint; purplish Thai basil (also called holy or Asian basil); aniselike red perilla (also known as shiso); lemony green perilla; floral, cilantro-like saw leaf herb; and spicy, sharp Vietnamese coriander. A table salad known as *rau song* includes a plateful of herbs, along with lettuces, cucumbers, mung bean sprouts, and sometimes pickled vegetables; it is served at every meal. It is also tucked inside leaves of lettuce and wrapped around grilled meats and fried spring rolls, lending a clean, crisp dimension to foods that might otherwise taste heavy in Vietnam's hot climate.

Vietnamese food does not include large amounts of meat and fish; instead, rice is supplemented with vegetables and eggs. Similar to Chinese cooking, Vietnamese cooking uses little fat or oil for frying. Instead of using soy sauce for seasoning, *nuoc mam* (fish sauce) is used as the main flavoring in almost every dish. *Pho* is a type of soup in which noodles, beef, chicken, or pork are added, and the soup is then garnished with basil, bean sprouts, and other seasonings. Vietnamese spring rolls are an alternative to Chinese egg rolls. These wraps are characterized by their rice paper packaging. *Bahn trang* are paper-thin, white crepes that have a criss-cross pattern from the trays on which they are dried. Rice flour is a crucial item in a Vietnamese kitchen. The flour is the main element of a Vietnamese pancake/crepe, bánh Xèo. These pancakes are stuffed with minced pork, shrimp, and bean sprouts. They are garnished with mint and served with a spicy, sweet dipping sauce. Fruits are an integral part of each meal—bananas, mangoes, papayas, oranges, coconuts, and pineapple are all popular. Vietnamese coffee is made with condensed milk to make the drink sweet. Hot green tea is very popular as well.

Glossary

Bac ha Eaten as a vegetable, the long, strong, bright green stem of the giant taro plant looks like a smooth stalk of celery but does not have thick fibers. It is frequently used in Vietnamese sour soup.

Banh Pho Short, flat, white Vietnamese rice stick noodle about $\frac{1}{8}$ inch wide. They cook in minutes in boiling water or soup and should not be overdone. They are used in soup noodle dishes, particularly the Hanoi soup that goes by the common name of *pho*.

Banh Trang The Vietnamese equivalent of ravioli skins. It is round, semitransparent, thin, hard, and dry rice paper and is used as the wrapping on Vietnamese spring rolls and broiled meats, along with salad and herbs. It is made from a dough of finely ground rice, water, and salt, with tapioca (cassava) flour as a binding agent. The dough is passed through rollers and then cut into circles 7 to 14 inches in diameter. These are then put on bamboo mats to dry in the sun. Once dry, they will keep indefinitely. To use, they must be moistened by covering with a damp cloth until soft or by dipping quickly into warm water. To get a crisp, golden-brown color, the wrappers can be brushed lightly with a sugar-water solution before frying.

Basil, Asian Basil, Thai Basil This medium to dark green basil with purple flowers has a sharp anise taste that handles heat better than sweet basil. It has little taste or aroma when raw; the strong flavor emerges when it is cooked.

Bean Curd Made from dried soybeans soaked, pureed, and boiled with water. The resulting milky liquid is strained and then mixed with a coagulant or natural solidifier, which causes curds to form. These are then taken to wooden tubs lined with cloth and pressed until they form bean curd.

Bean Sprouts The tender young sprouts of the germinating mung bean are used in Asia as a vegetable and fried in cooked dishes. They are also often used raw in salads.

Black Vinegar A dark, mild, almost sweet vinegar that has only one equivalent: balsamic vinegar. It is usually made from glutinous rice or sorghum, which gives it its distinctive taste.

Cabbage There are many varieties of cabbages; the white or pale green cabbages are popular in South East Asia.

Candlenut A round, cream-colored nut with an oily consistency used to add texture and a faint flavor to many dishes. Substitute macadamia nuts or raw cashews.

Chiles (Cabai Cabe, or Lombok) There are several types of chile pepper used in Indonesia. The amount of heat of a chile pepper increases as the size of the chile pepper decreases. Green chiles are the unripe fruit, with a flavor different from red chiles. Fresh, finger-length red chiles are the most commonly used types in Southeast Asia. Dried chiles are also used in some dishes; they should be torn into pieces and soaked in hot water to soften before grinding or blending. Hottest of all chiles are the tiny fiery bird's-eye chiles (*cabe* or *rawit*). To reduce the heat of the dish while retaining the flavor, remove some or all the chile's seeds.

Chile Sauce Usually a fairly thick, hot sauce. Chile sauce is prepared from pulped peppers, flavored with garlic and vinegar, and thickened with cornstarch.

Chinese Five-spice Powder A blend of spices consisting of anise-pepper, star anise, cassia, cloves, and fennel seed. A licorice flavor predominates.

Chinese Mushroom Also called shiitake mushroom, these are the most widely used mushrooms in east Asian cooking and are grown in China and Japan on the wood of dead deciduous trees. Dried mushrooms should be soaked in warm water for 20 minutes before cooking.

Coconut Milk and Coconut Cream These are two of the most important ingredients in this region's cooking and are used in both curries and desserts, as well as beverages. Coconut milk is the liquid squeezed from the grated flesh of mature coconut after the flesh has been soaked in lukewarm water. Coconut cream is a richer version. Coconut milk uses 3 cups of grated coconut to 5 cups of water, whereas coconut cream uses just 2 cups of water. Both must be soaked for 15 minutes, mixed, and then poured through muslin lined strainer; all of the liquid must be squeezed out of the muslin.

Cup Leaves (Daun Mangkok) The shape of the leaf is like a cup. Also known as *tapak leman* (*Nothopanax scutellarium*), it is usually used to cook stew dishes. A good substitute is curly kale.

Curry Paste Red curry paste is the most common of all the curry pastes. It is a mixture of dried chile pepper, shallot, garlic, galangal, lemongrass, cilantro root, peppercorn, coriander, salt, shrimp paste, and kaffir lime zest. Green curry paste has the same ingredients as the red, except that fresh green pepper is substituted for the dried chile pepper. Yellow curry paste comes from southern Thailand and is similar to red or green curry, but it is made with yellow peppers and turmeric.

Fermented Black Beans Oxidized soybeans that are salt-dried, with a savory, salty, and slightly bitter flavor. They are used in stir-fries, marinades, and sauces. Before using, they should be soaked in water for 10 to 30 minutes to get rid of excess salt. When purchasing fermented black beans, look for shiny and firm beans, rather than dull and dry ones with salt spots. Once open, store in plastic in the refrigerator for up to one year.

Noodles

While noodles are known by an assortment of names, they are made from just four basic four groups: wheat, rice, mung bean, and buckwheat. Noodles also come in a variety of shapes and width, but are customarily served long and uncut. The noodle's length symbolized longevity in the Asian culture; according to this belief, the longer the noodle, the longer the life.

- Egg noodles, udon, kishimen, hiyanmugi, somen, and ramen noodles are all made from wheat flour. These noodles are similar to American noodles. Their sizes range from fine to coarse and they can be pale yellow in color, the result of an egg and wheat mixture, or white if made without eggs. Egg noodles are commonly used in chow mein, which translates to "fried noodles." Udon noodles are thick wheat noodles eaten in Japan. Usually round in shape and white in color, they are used in soups like *kake udon*, a hot broth topped with thin slices of green onions, and in dishes such as *yakiudon*, which is udon stir-fried in soy-based sauce. *Japanese* somen noodles are fine white noodles made from wheat flour, water, and a small bit of oil. Like soba noodles, they're often served cold with a dipping sauce. Ramen are curly, long, brick-shaped noodles often purchased as instant noodles. In the Philippines, *Filipino noodles*, or *pancit*, is made from wheat flour and coconut oil and is often used in soups and salads. Indonesians use noodles made from wheat flour and eggs in a local fried noodle dish called *bami goring*.

- Rice vermicelli, rice sticks, and bun noodles are made from rice flour. The noodles are named for their shape and thickness, which can range in diameter from 1 cm to almost threadlike. *Rice vermicelli* is fine, while *rice sticks* are thicker and can be round or flat. Rice noodles are opaque and the texture resembles that of rice.

- Cellophane noodles are made from mung beans. Also called glass noodles, bean threads, bean noodles, or cellophane vermicelli, these noodles are aptly named because of their transparent appearance when cooked. Cellophane noodles are long, slippery, and soft, and because they are flavorless on their own, will readily absorb the flavors of the ingredients they are prepared with. They do not need to be cooked, but merely heated and softened in warm water for best results.

- Buckwheat, or soba, noodles are made from buckwheat flour. These thin noodles are slightly brown in color. They are often served chilled with a dipping sauce or as a noodle soup.

Fermented Soya Beans (Tao Jiaw) These are available whole and fermented from either yellow or black beans; in English they are most commonly known as black bean and yellow bean sauce. They are nutritious, strongly flavored, and salty, replacing salt completely in some Thai dishes.

Fish Sauce Fish sauce, called *nam pla* in Thai (the salt of Thai cuisine) or *nuoc mam* in Vietnamese, is used much like salt or soy sauce as a flavor enhancer. Made from the liquid drained from fermented anchovies, it is very is potent. It is usually combined with other ingredients when used as a dipping sauce. For cooking it can be used straight, but never add it to a dry pan or the smell will be overpowering. Like olive oil, there are several grades of fish sauce. High-quality fish sauce, which is the first to be drained off the fermented fish, is usually pale amber, like clear brewed tea, and used in dipping sauces. For cooking usually stronger-flavored, lower-grade brands, which are made from a secondary draining, are used.

Galangal A member of the ginger family, galangal is used in many countries as a substitute for ginger. It has a hot, peppery taste and is used mainly as flavoring and as a pungent ingredient in ground curry pastes. Galangal can be found in fresh root, frozen, dry, and powdered form in most Asian grocery stores. If using dried slices of galangal, soak them in warm water for at least 30 minutes. Substitute the fresh galangal with half the amount of dry galangal in the recipe.

Ground Coriander One of the essential ingredients in curry powders. The whole spice is ground when needed. To get the best out of the coriander seed, it is advisable to toast first in an oven and then finely grind it.

Hoisin Sauce The barbecue sauce of Vietnam. Made from red rice colored with a natural food dye, usually from annatto seeds, it is a sweet-tasting, thick, reddish brown sauce best used as a condiment for roast pork and poultry.

Holy Basil, or Sacred Basil (Bai Gkaprow) Often called hot basil because of its peppery taste, especially when very fresh, with a hint of mint and cloves. Since its exotic flavor becomes fully released with cooking, it is not eaten raw, but added in generous amounts to stir-fried dishes and some spicy soups. Holy basil is so called because it is a sacred herb in India where it is frequently planted around Hindu shrines.

Kaffir Lime leaves, Makrut, Thai Lime Leaves One of the signature flavors in Thai cooking, lemony and floral. If not available, substitute regular lime leaves and fruit. Kaffir limes, however, are used for their rind, since they are very dry inside. The zest is highly aromatic. Kaffir lime leaves may be frozen or dried for future use, or even kept green by standing leafy twigs in water on a sunny windowsill.

Kangkon Green, smooth-leafed vegetable native to the Philippines. It has a flavor that is milder than spinach and a texture similar to watercress.

Rice

Deriving originally from wild grasses, rice is a staple food in Asia. Historians believe that it was first domesticated in the area covering the foothills of the eastern Himalayas (northeastern India), and stretching through Burma, Thailand, Laos, Vietnam, and southern China. From here, it spread in all directions and human cultivation created numerous varieties. Different types of rice cross-breed easily. According to the International Rice Research Institute (IRRI), based in the Philippines, there are 120,000 varieties of rice worldwide. Over the centuries, three main types of rice developed in Asia, depending on the amylose content of the grain. They are *indica* (high in amylose and cooking to fluffy grains to be eaten with the fingers), *japonica* (low in amylase and cooking to sticky masses suitable for eating as clumps with chopsticks), and *javanica* (intermediate amylose content and stickiness). Rice is further divided into long-, medium-, and short-grained varieties, and in the subcontinent different populations grow and consume different varieties.

Rice grains are grown in a variety of colors and textures. Brown rice grains, unlike white, still have an outer coating of bran. This bran carries twice as much fiber and increased levels of vitamin E and magnesium as enriched white rice does. Usually produced as long or medium grains, brown rice takes more time to cook, tastes chewier, and retains a mild, nutty bran flavor.

Black sticky rice, often called forbidden rice, is a nutty, medium-grain rice. When cooked, the brown-black rice turns a shade of purple-black. It may also be labeled "black

Kare-Kare Philippine meat-vegetable stew with oxtail, beef, or tripe; eggplant, banana buds, and other vegetables cooked in peanut sauce and ground toasted rice.

Lemongrass An essential ingredient in Southeast Asian cooking, it is a long, thin, pale green edible grass with bright lemon fragrance and taste. To use a lemongrass stalk, cut off the grassy top and root end. Peel and remove the large, tough outer leaves of the stalk until you reach a light purple color. Chop it very fine to use in salads and grind into curry pastes if eating them directly. Or cut into 2-inch portions and bruise them to extract the flavor before boiling with soup broth. Lemongrass can be found fresh in most grocery stores because it has a very long shelf life. Dry and frozen forms are also available in most Asian stores.

Lumpia Philippine egg rolls.

Nuoc Mam A fish sauce that is a powerfully flavored, pungent seasoning sauce, used extensively in Southeast Asia. It is made by layering fish and salt into large barrels and allowing the fish to ferment for three or more months before the accumulated liquid is siphoned off, filtered, and

glutinous rice" or "black sweet rice." Cultivated in Indonesia and the Philippines, stickier varieties of black rice are often used for sweets such as rice pudding in countries throughout Southeast Asia including Thailand, Malaysia, and Singapore.

Thailand originated the planting of the aromatic jasmine rice. This fragrant long-grain rice has a soft texture due to a special water-milling process. When cooked, this rice comes out moist and tender like medium grains. Available in brown and white, jasmine rice is a staple of Thai cooking.

In medium-grain rice, the length of the grain is less than twice its width. High in starch, the cooked grains come out moist and tender with a bit of stickiness. Medium grains are harvested in Italy and Spain; they tend to grow in regions farther from the equator. This rice, known as arborio, is found in European dishes such as risotto and paella.

Short-grain rice also has a length that is less than twice its width. When cooked, the grains are softer and stickier than medium grain. In Japan, sushi is only as good as the short-grain sticky rice that is used. Sticky rice has numerous uses. While it is also used for desserts, it is an integral part of every meal in the regions of Laos, Cambodia, and Vietnam. In addition, sticky rice is a primary source for brewing rice-based alcohol like sake.

Another type of rice essential to this region is glutinous rice. Although it does not contain any gluten, this short-grain, starchy rice becomes quite sticky and dense when cooked. This rice is labeled as sticky, waxy, and sweet. Generally used for desserts, glutinous rice is used for making little cakes in Japan, Thailand, Malaysia, and Indonesia.

bottled. In Vietnam *nuoc mam* is made into different dipping sauces by adding chiles, ground roasted peanuts, sugar, and other ingredients.

Oyster Sauce One of the most popular bottled sauces in Vietnam. Made from dried oysters, it is thick and richly flavored. The cheaper brands tend to be saltier. The original sauce was much thinner and contained fragments of fermented, dried oysters. It is mostly used in stir-fried dishes.

Palm Sugar An unrefined sweetener similar in flavor to brown sugar. Used in sweet and savory Asian dishes. Commonly available in podlike cakes, it is also sold in paste form at Asian markets. Store as you would other sugar.

Paprika Derived from bell peppers. In Vietnam it is used as a vegetable and as a spice. In its latter guise, it is dried and ground to a powder.

Pomelo A large fruit that resembles a grapefruit. It tapers slightly at the stem end and has a thick, sweet, slightly rough-textured skin, and a dry, semi-sweet flesh.

Sambal A spicy condiment used especially in Indonesia and Malaysia, made with chile peppers and other ingredients, such as sugar or coconut.

Satay or Saté or Sateh Pieces of meat or fish threaded onto skewers and grilled. Meat satay is typically served with a spicy peanut sauce.

Shallots Like the French, Vietnamese cooks use shallots rather than onions as a major flavoring ingredient, prizing their sweeter, more aromatic quality. Shallots, along with garlic and lemongrass, are among the few seasonings that are typically cooked, rather than added to dishes raw. Fried shallots, along with crushed, roasted peanuts, also appear on the Vietnamese table as a garnish for noodle dishes and soups.

Shrimp Paste Shrimp paste adds depth to noodle dishes, soups, and curries. It comes in bottled form and is available at most Asian grocery stores. As it is salty and highly concentrated, it is used sparingly.

Sinigang Sour soup dish of meat or fish with vegetables, seasoned with tomatoes, onions, and lemon juice.

Soy Sauce Made from fermented soybeans mixed with a roasted grain, normally wheat. It is infected with a yeast mold and after fermentation begins, salt is added. Yeast is added for further fermentation and the liquid is left in vats for several months and then filtered.

Star Anise The seedpods of one type of magnolia tree. The tan eight-pointed pods resemble stars, hence the name. When dried, a shiny, flat, light brown seed is revealed in each point.

Straw Mushrooms Grown on paddy straw, left over from harvested wheat, which gives them a distinctly earthy taste. Generally, they are packed in water and canned.

Sugarcane The sugarcane bought for cooking consists of the stem, the leaves being chopped off in the cane fields. The cane should be very carefully peeled with a strong, sharp knife. Reasonably easy to obtain from large grocers.

Szechwan Peppercorns Aromatic, small, red-brown seeds from the prickly ash tree known as fagara. The whole peppercorns can be kept for years without loss of flavor if stored in a tightly sealed jar.

Tamarind The dark brown pod of the tamarind tree contains a sour fleshy pulp, which adds a fruity sourness to many dishes. Packets of pulp usually contain the seeds and fibers. To make tamarind juice, measure the pulp and soak it in hot water for 5 minutes before squeezing it to extract the juice, discarding the seeds, fiber, and any skin.

Tausi Black soybeans, salted and fermented.

Turmeric A native of Southeast Asia, it belongs to the same family as ginger and galangal. It has a bright orange yellow flesh with a strong, earthy smell and a slightly bitter taste. The flesh is responsible for the yellow color we associate with curry powder and it overpowers all other spices.

Wood Ear Fungus Perhaps the most common is derived from its habitat of decayed wood. It is valued for its subtle, delicate flavor and slightly crunchy "bite."

Yellow Bean Sauce Made according to the ancient recipe for *jiang*, or pickled yellow soybeans in a salty liquid. It is normally bought in cans and jars but it is best transferred to a jar in which it can be stored in a refrigerator almost indefinitely.

Menus and Recipes from Southeast Asia

Krupuk Udang Shrimp Chips

SERVES 4

Uncooked shrimp chips come in many shapes and sizes. Most are Indonesian, pale-pink in color with a distinct shrimp flavor. When deep-fried in hot oil, they become light, crisp, and crunchy, and swell to more than twice their size within seconds.

AMOUNT	MEASURE	INGREDIENT
As needed		Oil for deep frying
12		Dried shrimp chips

PROCEDURE

1 Heat oil in a wok or deep-fat fryer to 360°F (182°C). Fry the chips, a few at a time, if the oil is hot enough; they will puff up within 2 to 3 seconds. Fry until lightly colored, approximately 15 seconds. Remove and drain on paper towels.

Sambal Ulek Chile Sauce

YIELD: $\frac{3}{4}$ CUP (6 OUNCES, 180 ML)

This is served during most meals to allow each person to season soup, meat, and fish dishes.

AMOUNT	MEASURE	INGREDIENT
$\frac{1}{2}$ teaspoon		Salt
10		Hot red chiles, thinly sliced
$\frac{1}{2}$ teaspoon		Shrimp paste (*terasi*)
$\frac{1}{2}$ teaspoon		Granulated sugar
$\frac{3}{4}$ cup	5 ounces, 140 ml	Tomatoes, peeled, seeded, $\frac{1}{4}$ inch (.6 cm) dice

PROCEDURE

1 Pound or process salt, chiles, shrimp paste, and sugar in a mortar or processor to form a coarse paste. Add tomatoes and crush slightly to blend flavors.

Serundeng Kacang

Toasted Spiced Coconut with Peanuts

YIELD: 1–1½ CUPS

Serve this sprinkled over practically any dish.

AMOUNT	MEASURE	INGREDIENT
5		Shallots, chopped
3		Garlic cloves, chopped
2 tablespoons	1 ounce, 30 ml	Vegetable oil
1 teaspoon		Coriander, ground
½ teaspoon		Cumin, ground
½ teaspoon		Galangal, ground
1 tablespoon	½ ounce, 15 ml	Tamarind water
1 teaspoon		Brown sugar
½ teaspoon		Salt
1 cup	6 ounces, 168 g	Coconut, freshly grated, or ½ cup dried coconut flakes soaked 5 minutes in 1 cup (8 ounces, 240 ml) water
½ cup	2½ ounces, 70 g	Unsalted peanuts, roasted

PROCEDURE

1 Pound or process shallots and garlic to a smooth paste; heat oil and stir-fry paste over medium heat for approximately 2 minutes or until translucent. Do not brown.

2 Add coriander, cumin, galangal, tamarind water, brown sugar, and salt. Stir-fry 1 minute on low heat to blend flavors.

3 Add coconut (if using rehydrated, let simmer until all the water has been soaked up by the coconut before stirring). Cook over low heat, stirring until coconut is nearly dry and medium brown in color, about 20 to 30 minutes.

4 Add peanuts and toast 5 minutes, stirring constantly until coconut is golden brown. Be careful not to let it burn.

5 Remove from heat and let cool before serving.

Tahu Telur
Spicy Tofu Omelet SERVES 4

AMOUNT	MEASURE	INGREDIENT
I cup	2 ounces, 56 g	Fresh bean sprouts
I cup	8 ounces, 224 g	Fresh tofu, drained, $\frac{1}{4}$ inch (.6 cm) dice
4		Eggs, beaten with $\frac{1}{4}$ teaspoon salt
$\frac{1}{2}$ teaspoon		Salt
I teaspoon		Vegetable oil
2		Green hot chiles, seeds removed, finely sliced
2 tablespoons	I ounce, 30 ml	Sweet soy sauce (*kecap manis*) (recipe follows)
I tablespoon	$\frac{1}{2}$ ounce, 15 ml	White vinegar
3 tablespoons		Fried peanuts, crushed
3 tablespoons		Fried shallot flakes (recipe follows)
I tablespoon		Parsley leaves

PROCEDURE

1 Blanch bean sprouts in boiling water 30 seconds. Drain, refresh with cold water, and drain again.

2 Combine tofu, eggs, and salt.

3 Heat oil in a 10-inch omelet pan. Add half the egg mixture, tilting the pan to make a thin omelet. Cook over medium heat until set and lightly browned. Remove and keep warm. Repeat to make a second omelet.

4 Evenly spread bean sprouts and chiles over omelets.

5 Combine *kecap manis* and vinegar; drizzle over omelets.

6 Garnish with peanuts, fried shallot flakes, and parsley leaves.

7 To serve, cut in wedges.

Kecap Manis　Indonesian Sweet Soy Sauce

YIELD: $1\frac{1}{2}$ CUPS (12 OUNCES, 360 ML)

AMOUNT	MEASURE	INGREDIENT
1 cup	8 ounces, 224 g	Dark brown sugar, packed
1 cup	8 ounces, 240 ml	Water
$\frac{3}{4}$ cup	6 ounces, 180 ml	Soy sauce
7 tablespoons	$3\frac{1}{2}$ ounces, 105 ml	Dark molasses
$\frac{1}{2}$ teaspoon		Laos (galangal) ground
$\frac{1}{4}$ teaspoon		Coriander, ground
$\frac{1}{4}$ teaspoon		Black pepper, freshly ground
1		Star anise

PROCEDURE

1　Combine the sugar and water; simmer over low heat, stirring frequently, until the sugar dissolves. Bring to a boil and cook to 200°F (93°C) on a sugar thermometer, approximately 5 minutes. Reduce heat to low, add remaining ingredients, and simmer 5 minutes.

2　Remove from heat and let cool.

Fried Shallot Flakes

AMOUNT	MEASURE	INGREDIENT
10		Shallots
1 tablespoon	$\frac{1}{2}$ ounce, 15 ml	Vegetable oil

PROCEDURE

1　Slice shallots very thin.

2　Lightly oil a small skillet. Heat pan over medium heat and add shallots.

3　Cook for approximately 5 to 7 minutes, shaking the pan so they brown slowly and evenly.

4　When golden brown, remove from the oil and drain on paper towels until cool. They will crisp and turn darker brown as they stand.

Satay Babi Pork Satay   SERVES 4

AMOUNT	MEASURE	INGREDIENT
I pound	448 g	Boneless, skinless pork tenderloin or loin
I tablespoon	$\frac{1}{2}$ ounce, 15 ml	Butter
I		Garlic clove, crushed
2 teaspoons		Dark soy sauce
2 teaspoons		Fresh lemon juice
Marinade		
2 tablespoons	I ounce, 30 ml	Soy sauce
2		Garlic clove, crushed
I teaspoon		Ginger, ground
I teaspoon		Five-spice powder
I tablespoon	$\frac{1}{2}$ ounce, 15 ml	Honey
$\frac{1}{2}$ teaspoon		White pepper
As needed		*Sambal Kecap* (recipe follows)

PROCEDURE

1 Slice pork across the grain into thin slices, $\frac{1}{4}$ inch (.6 cm) wide by 3 to 4 inches (7.2 to 9.6 cm) long.

2 Combine marinade ingredients and mix well. Add pork, mix well, and let stand 2 hours.

3 Remove from marinade and thread onto skewers.

4 Melt butter and add remaining ingredients. Before placing on the grill, brush with this mixture.

5 Grill 2 to 3 minutes or until just done.

6 Serve hot or warm with Sambal Kecap (Chile and Soy Sauce).

Sambal Kecap Chile and Soy Sauce SERVES 4

AMOUNT	MEASURE	INGREDIENT
6 tablespoons	3 ounces, 90 ml	Dark soy sauce
I teaspoon		Chile powder
3		Serrano chiles, sliced very thin
½ cup	2 ounces, 56 g	Onions, minced
2 tablespoons	I ounce, 30 ml	Fresh lime juice
2		Garlic cloves, minced.

PROCEDURE

1 Place all the ingredients in a small saucepan and cook over a medium to low heat for about 5 minutes, stirring constantly. Let cool.

Satay Ayam Chicken Satay SERVES 4

AMOUNT	MEASURE	INGREDIENT
I pound	448 g	Chicken thigh meat, boneless, skinless
I stalk		Lemongrass, finely minced
2		Garlic cloves, minced
½ teaspoon		Turmeric, ground
½ teaspoon		Fennel, ground
½ teaspoon		Cumin, ground
2 tablespoons	I ounce, 30 ml	Vegetable oil
To taste		Salt
		12-inch bamboo skewers, soaked in water for I hour

PROCEDURE

1 Slice chicken across the grain into thin slices $\frac{1}{4}$ inch (.6 cm) wide by 3 to 4 inches (7.2 to 9.6 cm) long.

2 Combine lemongrass, garlic, turmeric, fennel, cumin, and oil to a paste. Add chicken, mix well, and let stand 2 hours.

3 Remove from marinate and thread on to skewers. Season with salt before cooking.

4 Grill or broil, basting occasionally with oil.

5 Serve hot or warm with peanut sauce and cucumber salad.

Krupuk Udang – Shrimp Chips, Satay Babi (Pork) and Satay Ayam (Chicken)

Gado Gado
Cooked Vegetable Salad, Sumatran Style   SERVES 4

AMOUNT	MEASURE	INGREDIENT
4 ounces	112 g	Firm tofu
1 teaspoon		*Kecap manis* (Sweet soy sauce)
3 tablespoons	1½ ounces, 45 ml	Vegetable oil
½ cup	2½ ounces, 70 g	Boiling potatoes, cooked, ¼ inch (.6 cm) slice
½ cup	2 ounces, 56 g	Carrots, 2 inch (4.8 cm) julienne
½ cup	2 ounces, 56 g	Green beans, 2 inch (4.8 cm) julienne
1 cup	4 ounces, 112 g	Cabbage, shredded, 2 inch (4.8 cm)
1 cup	4 ounces, 112 g	Bean sprouts
½ cup	3 ounces, 84 g	Cucumber, peeled, halved, seeded, ¼ inch (.6 cm) slice
2		Eggs, hard-boiled, sliced
Garnish		
As needed		*Sambal kacang* (peanut sauce)
¼ cup		Fried shallots flakes (see recipe on page 334)
As needed		Shrimp chips
As needed		Soy sauce

PROCEDURE

1 Drain tofu. Rinse and cut into two pieces. Place on a plate. Top with another plate and put 1 to 2 pounds (448 to 896 g) on top (heavy canned goods work well as a weight). Let stand 30 minutes. Discard liquid. Pat tofu dry. Sprinkle with *kecap manis.*

2 Set wok over high heat. When hot, add the oil. When the oil is hot but not smoking, add the tofu. Stir-fry 3 to 4 minutes or until golden. Transfer to paper towels to drain. Cut the tofu into ½ inch (1.2 cm) pieces. Heat oil in wok to 350°F (176°C). Return tofu and fry until golden brown and puffy, about 3 to 4 minutes. Remove and drain on paper towels.

3 Boil the potatoes; peel and cut into ¼ inch (.6 cm) slices.

4 Blanch carrots, green beans, and cabbage separately for 1 to 2 minutes. Drain and refresh with cold water; drain again.

5 Blanch bean sprouts in boiling water 30 seconds. Rinse under cold water; drain well.

6 Arrange vegetables and tofu in separate sections on a platter, with the egg in the center.

7 Serve with warm peanut sauce, spooning a little on the salad and the rest on the side.

8   Sprinkle with fried shallot flakes.

9   Serve at room temperature with shrimp chips and soy sauce.

Sambal Kacang (Bumbu Sate) Peanut Sauce

YIELD: 1 CUP(8 OUNCES, 240 ML)

AMOUNT	MEASURE	INGREDIENT
2 teaspoons		Coriander seed, toasted
1 teaspoon		Fennel seed, toasted
1 teaspoon		Cumin seed, toasted
6		Dry red chiles, seeded and soaked
$\frac{1}{2}$ teaspoon		Shrimp paste
5		Shallots, sliced thin
2		Garlic clove, sliced thin
1 tablespoon	$\frac{1}{2}$ ounce, 15 ml	Vegetable oil
$\frac{1}{2}$ cup	$2\frac{1}{2}$ ounces, 75 g	Peanuts, roasted, roughly ground (crunchy peanut butter)
$\frac{3}{4}$ cup	6 ounces, 180 ml	Coconut milk
1 tablespoon		Tamarind paste, dissolved in 4 tablespoons (2 ounces, 60 ml) water
1 teaspoon		Palm sugar
To taste		Salt and pepper

PROCEDURE

1   Grind the dry spices in a spice grinder or mortar and pestle.

2   Pound or process the chiles, shrimp paste, shallots, and garlic into a paste.

3   Over low heat, sauté the paste lightly until fragrant in oil, 1 minute. Add the dry spices and cook 1 minute. Be careful not to burn the paste after adding the dry spices.

4   Add the peanuts, coconut milk, tamarind, and sugar. Simmer about 10 minutes, adding water if the sauce thickens too fast.

5   Adjust seasoning and serve warm.

Laksa Lemak Chicken, Shrimp, and Rice Noodles in Coconut Sauce SERVES 4

AMOUNT	MEASURE	INGREDIENT
Paste		
2		Garlic cloves, chopped
1 tablespoon		Ginger, grated
4		Dried red chiles, soaked in hot water until softened, minced
1 stalk		Lemongrass, sliced, bottom 6 inches only, or thinly peeled rind of 1 lemon
4		Shallots, peeled, chopped
3		Candlenuts or macadamia nuts, minced
2 teaspoons		Turmeric, ground
1 teaspoon		Coriander, ground
2 teaspoons		Dried shrimp, soaked in hot water until soft, about 10 minutes
4 tablespoons	2 ounces, 60 ml	Vegetable oil
1 cup	6 ounces, 168 g	Shrimp, shelled, deveined
1¾ cups	14 ounces, 420 ml	Chicken stock
1 cup	6 ounces, 168 g	Chicken meat, cooked, skinless, boneless, 1½ inch (3.6 cm) pieces
10 ounces	280 g	Dried rice noodles (rice vermicelli), soaked in hot water to soften, 15 minutes, drained
¾ cup	6 ounces, 180 ml	Coconut milk, thick
1 cup	4 ounces, 112 g	Bean sprouts (optional)
Garnish		
1 tablespoon		Cilantro, chopped
¼ cup		Green or red hot chiles, sliced thin
¼ cup	1 ounce, 28 g	Green onions, chopped
8		Lime wedges

PROCEDURE

1. Pound or blend garlic, ginger, chiles, lemongrass, shallots, nuts, turmeric, and coriander to a fine paste.

2. Pound or blend dried shrimp separately until smooth; if necessary, add 1 to 2 tablespoons coconut milk.

3. Heat half the oil and add the dried shrimp paste; cook 1 minute. Add spice paste and cook 1 to 2 minutes.

4. Add remaining oil, heat, add raw shrimp, and stir-fry 1 minute.

5. Add chicken stock and chicken pieces; cook 5 minutes.

6. Add drained rice noodles and coconut milk; bring to a boil slowly, stirring gently to prevent milk from curdling.

7. Add bean sprouts and simmer 3 minutes or until hot. Sprinkle with cilantro.

8. Serve with separate bowls of chiles, green onions, and lime wedges.

Pepes Ikan

Grilled Fish in Banana Leaf SERVES 4

AMOUNT	MEASURE	INGREDIENT
6		Shallots, peeled and sliced
3		Garlic cloves, chopped fine
1 tablespoon		Ginger, grated
3		Red chiles fresh, seeded, sliced thin
$\frac{1}{4}$ cup		Holy basil (hot basil) leaves, shredded
$\frac{1}{2}$ cup		Green onion, green only, julienned on the bias
2		Whole trout, cleaned, boned, head and tail removed
1 tablespoon	$\frac{1}{2}$ ounce, 15 ml	Light soy sauce
1 tablespoon	$\frac{1}{2}$ ounce, 15 ml	Fresh lime juice
As needed		Banana leaf for wrapping
12 slices		Lemon, very thin
6		Cilantro sprigs

PROCEDURE

1 Pound or process shallots, garlic, ginger, chiles, basil, and green onion to a paste. Spread paste on the inside of the fish, sprinkle with soy sauce and lime juice, and marinate 30 minutes.

2 Cut the banana leaf in pieces to fit the width of the fish less the head and tail, and long enough to wrap the fish once. Pour boiling water over the banana leaf to soften and prevent splitting.

3 Place each fish in the middle of a leaf and wrap each fish in a leaf, making two packages. Place lemon slices and cilantro sprigs on top of fish. Wrap envelope style into a neat parcel, keeping seam side on top. Secure with a metal skewer, toothpick, or staples.

4 Grill over a very low grill until the leaf begins to brown; allow 10 minutes per inch thickness of fish.

5 Cut open the banana leaves. Serve fish in banana leaves with rice, and a sambal on the side.

Tumis Terong
Sautéed Eggplant   SERVES 4

AMOUNT	MEASURE	INGREDIENT
2 cups	8 ounces, 240 g	Eggplant, 2 inch (4.8 cm) thick slices
2 tablespoons	1 ounce, 30 ml	Vegetable oil
3 tablespoons	1½ ounces, 45 ml	Sweet soy sauce (kecap manis) (optional)
½ cup	2 ounces, 56 g	Onions, sliced thin
1		Garlic clove, minced
1 teaspoon		Shrimp paste
To taste		Salt and pepper

PROCEDURE

1   Heat deep fryer to 375°F (190°C). Deep-fry eggplant for 30 seconds; remove and drain.

2   Set a wok over high heat. When very hot, add the oil, onion, garlic, and shrimp paste. Stir-fry two minutes.

3   Add eggplant; pour in soy sauce, stir and cover pan. Simmer 10 minutes. If there is no juice from steaming the eggplant, add ¼ cup (2 ounces, 60 ml) water.

4   Correct seasoning and serve hot.

Lapis Daging

Stir-Fried Beef SERVES 4

AMOUNT	MEASURE	INGREDIENT
$\frac{1}{2}$ teaspoon		Nutmeg
1		Egg, beaten
8 ounces	224 g	Flank steak, cut $\frac{1}{4}$ inch (.6 cm) wide and 2 to 3 inches (4.8 to 7.2 cm) in length
1 tablespoon	$\frac{1}{2}$ ounce, 15 ml	Vegetable oil
$\frac{1}{4}$ cup	1 ounce, 28 g	Onion, sliced thin
1		Garlic clove, sliced thin
1 tablespoon	$\frac{1}{2}$ ounce, 15 ml	Sweet soy sauce (kecap manis)
1		Cinnamon stick, 1 inch (2.4 cm) long
2		Whole cloves
To taste		Pepper
$\frac{1}{2}$ cup	3 ounces, 84 g	Tomato, peeled, seeded, chopped
As needed		Fried shallot flakes (see recipe on page 334)
As needed		Sambal tomat (recipe follows)

PROCEDURE

1 Combine nutmeg and egg. Coat the steak slices with the egg mixture.

2 Heat the oil over medium heat and sauté the onion and garlic, 2 to 3 minutes or until soft.

3 Drain the egg from the meat and sauté until medium.

4 Combine sweet soy sauce, cinnamon, cloves, pepper, and tomato. Add to the cooked steak. Mix well and cook 3 to 5 minutes or until the sauce has thickened slightly. If necessary, add a little water.

5 Sprinkle with fried shallot flakes. Serve immediately with rice and sambal tomat.

Sambal Tomat   SERVES 4

AMOUNT	MEASURE	INGREDIENT
2 cups	12 ounces, 336 g	Tomato, peeled, seeded, chopped
3		Shallots, minced
1		Red chile fresh, seeded, sliced
To taste		Salt
1 tablespoon	$\frac{1}{2}$ ounce, 15 ml	Fresh lime juice
1 tablespoon		Basil, shredded

PROCEDURE

1 Combine tomato, shallots, and chile; season with salt and lime juice.

2 Let stand 1 hour, add basil, and serve.

Naam Prik   Chile Sauce   YIELD: $\frac{3}{4}$ CUP

AMOUNT	MEASURE	INGREDIENT
4 tablespoons	2 ounces, 30 ml	Palm sugar
7 tablespoons	$3\frac{1}{2}$ ounces, 105 ml	Hot water
2 tablespoons	1 ounce, 30 ml	Fish sauce (*nam pla*)
	100 ml	Water, hot
2 tablespoons		Fish sauce
1		Red chile, fresh, thinly sliced
2 tablespoons	1 ounce, 30 ml	Fresh lime juice

PROCEDURE

1 Dissolve the sugar in the hot water. Let cool.

2 Combine remaining ingredients.

Ma Hor Galloping Horses SERVES 4

AMOUNT	MEASURE	INGREDIENT
1 tablespoon	$\frac{1}{2}$ ounce, 15 ml	Vegetable oil
2 teaspoons		Garlic, minced
1 cup	6 ounces, 168 g	Pork, ground
1 tablespoon	$\frac{1}{2}$ ounce, 15 ml	Fish sauce (*nam pla*)
2 tablespoons	1 ounce, 28 g	Brown sugar
$\frac{1}{8}$ teaspoon		Black pepper, freshly ground
$\frac{1}{4}$ cup	$1\frac{1}{2}$ ounces, 42 g	Peanuts, roasted, coarsely chopped
1		Butter lettuce, head, separated into leaves
2		Tangerines, peeled, pith and white fibers removed, cut horizontally into $\frac{1}{3}$ inch (.8 cm) thick, or pineapple wedges
Garnish		
$\frac{1}{4}$ cup		Mint leaves
$\frac{1}{4}$ cup		Cilantro leaves
2		Red chiles, fresh, seeded, cut into thin shreds

PROCEDURE

1 Heat wok over medium heat. When hot, add oil. Add garlic, and stir-fry 30 seconds.

2 Add pork, fish sauce, brown sugar, and black pepper. Stir-fry until pork is cooked.

3 Stir in peanuts; mix. Remove from heat and let cool.

4 Place lettuce leaves on serving platter. Arrange tangerine slices on lettuce. Put a heaping teaspoon of the cooked meat on each slice.

5 Garnish with mint and cilantro leaves.

6 Serve chilled or room temperature with chiles on the side.

Tord Man Pla Fried Fish Cakes   SERVES 4

AMOUNT	MEASURE	INGREDIENT
$\frac{3}{4}$ pound	12 ounces, 336 g	Catfish or any white-fleshed fish fillet
1 $\frac{1}{2}$ tablespoons	$\frac{3}{4}$ ounce, 22 ml	Fish sauce (*nam pla*)
1 tablespoon	$\frac{1}{2}$ ounce, 15 ml	Red curry paste
1 tablespoon		Galangal or ginger
1		Egg, lightly beaten
4		Kaffir lime leaves, stems removed, finely shredded
$\frac{1}{4}$ cup	2 ounces, 60 ml	Vegetable oil

PROCEDURE

1 Pound or process fish, fish sauce, curry paste, galangal, and egg to a smooth paste. Do not overprocess.

2 Add kaffir leaves and mix well. Moisten hands with water and shape mixture into small cakes, about 3 inches (7.2 cm) by $\frac{1}{4}$ inch (.6 cm) thick.

3 Heat oil to 350°F (176°C). Fry cakes until both sides are light brown, pressing down on the cakes. Drain on paper towels.

Nam Prik Kaeng Ped   Red Curry Paste
YIELD: 3 TABLESPOONS

AMOUNT	MEASURE	INGREDIENT
14		Red chiles, dried, seeded soaked in water 10 minutes to soften
2 teaspoons		Galangal, chopped
1		Lemongrass stalk, bottom 6 inches (14.4 cm) only
1 teaspoon		Lime zest
2 tablespoons		Cilantro roots, chopped
1		Shallot, chopped
1 teaspoon		Shrimp paste
10		Peppercorns, black
2 tablespoons	1 ounce, 30 ml	Vegetable oil

PROCEDURE

1 Pound or process all ingredients in a mortar, blender, or processor to a smooth paste. Add a little more oil if necessary.

Tom Yam Goong
Hot and Spicy Shrimp Soup YIELD: SERVES 4

AMOUNT	MEASURE	INGREDIENT
1 pound	448 g	Shrimp, 30-count size
1 tablespoon	$\frac{1}{2}$ ounce, 15 ml	Vegetable oil
5 cups	40 ounces, 1.2 l	Chicken stock
2		Lemongrass stalks
1$\frac{1}{2}$ tablespoons		Cilantro stems, minced
2		Garlic cloves, minced
2		Green hot chiles, seeds removed, minced
4		Kaffir lime leaves, chopped
$\frac{1}{2}$ teaspoon		Lime zest
$\frac{1}{2}$ teaspoon		White pepper
15 ounce	420 g	Straw mushrooms, drained
1 tablespoon	$\frac{1}{2}$ ounce, 15 ml	Fish sauce (*nam pla*)
2 tablespoons	1 ounce, 30 ml	Lime juice
2		Red chiles, seeds removed, julienned
2 tablespoons		Cilantro, leaves only, chopped
2 tablespoons		Green onion, sliced on the thin on the bias

PROCEDURE

1 Peel, wash, and devein shrimp; reserve the shells. Cut shrimp in half lengthwise.

2 Heat the oil and sauté the shrimp shells until they turn pink, 2 to 3 minutes.

3 Add chicken stock. Cut off the top of the lemongrass; reserve the bottom 5 inches (12 cm). Bruise the lemongrass stalks with the side of a cleaver or knife. Add to stock. Slice the remaining bottom inches into paper-thin slices.

4 Pound or process the sliced lemongrass, cilantro stems, garlic, green chiles, Kaffir leaves, lime zest, and white pepper to a paste.

5 Add the paste to the stock and stir to combine. Bring to a boil. Cover, reduce to a simmer, and cook 20 minutes. Strain.

6 Return stock to heat and bring back to a boil.

7 Add shrimp and mushrooms; cook 2 to 3 minutes, or until shrimp are just cooked.

8 Remove from heat; add fish sauce and lime juice, and correct seasoning.

9 Serve hot, with red chiles, cilantro leaves, and green onions on the side.

Mun Tot
Fried Sweet Potatoes   SERVES 4

AMOUNT	MEASURE	INGREDIENT
$\frac{3}{4}$ cup	$5\frac{1}{4}$ ounces, 147 g	Rice Flour
$\frac{1}{4}$ cup	1 ounce, 28 g	Unsweetened coconut, grated
$\frac{1}{4}$ cup	2 ounces, 56 g	Granulated sugar
1 teaspoon		Red curry paste
6 tablespoons	3 ounces, 90 ml	Coconut cream, thick
2 cups	8 ounces, 224 g	Sweet potatoes, peeled, $\frac{1}{4}$ inch (.6 cm) pieces, rounds, bias cuts, or sticks
As needed		Peanut sauce (see recipe on page 339)

PROCEDURE

1 Combine all ingredients except sweet potatoes and stir to a paste. Do not overmix.

2 Heat deep fryer to 375°F (190°C).

3 Dip sweet potato pieces into batter and fry until golden. Drain on paper towels.

4 Serve with peanut sauce.

Yam Makeua Issaan
Grilled Eggplant Salad   SERVES 4

AMOUNT	MEASURE	INGREDIENT
1 pound	448 g	Eggplant
3		Shallots, unpeeled
5		Garlic cloves, unpeeled
2		Anaheim or banana chiles
2		Green onions, minced
$\frac{1}{2}$ cup		Cilantro leaves, chopped
$\frac{1}{4}$ cup		Mint leaves, chopped
2 tablespoons	1 ounce, 30 ml	Fresh lime juice
3 tablespoons	$1\frac{1}{2}$ ounces, 45 ml	Fish sauce (nam pla)
2 tablespoons		Sesame seeds, dry roasted
As needed		Crispy rice crackers (recipe follows)

PROCEDURE

1. Prick the eggplant all over with a small knife or fork. Grill or broil until well softened and browned, 10 to 15 minutes, or oven-roast. Remove from heat and cool.

2. Broil or roast shallots, garlic, and chiles until soft and covered with a few black spots. Remove from heat and cool. Peel and coarsely chop.

3. Pound or process shallots, garlic, and chiles to a coarse paste.

4. Remove skin from the eggplants and coarsely chop. Mash to a lumpy mixture; add chile paste and mix.

5. Stir in the green onions, cilantro, mint, lime juice, and fish sauce.

6. Garnish with sesame seeds. Serve with Crispy Rice Crackers.

Khao Tang
Crispy Rice Crackers   SERVES 4

AMOUNT	MEASURE	INGREDIENT
2 cups	12 ounces, 336 g	Cooked jasmine rice, warm or hot
As needed		Peanut or other oil

PROCEDURE

1 Preheat oven to 350°F (176°C).

2 With a rice paddle or wooden spoon, spread the rice onto a lightly oiled baking sheet to make a layer about $\frac{1}{2}$ inch (1.2 cm) thick. Press down to compact the rice so that it sticks together.

3 Place sheet pan into oven and turn down the temperature to 250°F (121°C). Let dry 3 to 4 hours; the bottom will be a light brown.

4 Heat 2 inches (4.8 cm) oil to 350°F (176°C) or use a deep fryer. To test the temperature, drop a small piece of dried rice cake into the oil. It should sink to the bottom and immediately float back to the surface without burning or crisping. Adjust the heat as necessary.

5 Break off rice cakes and fry in the hot oil. When the first side stops swelling, turn over and cook on the other side until well puffed and just starting to brown, 30 seconds. Remove and drain on a paper towels.

Pad Thai Thai Fried Noodles SERVES 4

Chef Tip Noodles for Pad Thai should be soaked with warm, not boiling, water. Noodles should be somewhat flexible and solid, not completely expanded and soft.

AMOUNT	MEASURE	INGREDIENT
2 tablespoons	1 ounce, 30 ml	Tamarind water or white vinegar
2 tablespoons	1 ounce, 28 g	Granulated sugar
4 teaspoons	20 ml	Fish sauce
$\frac{1}{2}$ teaspoon		Dried chile peppers
1 tablespoon	$\frac{1}{2}$ ounce, 15 ml	Preserved turnips (optional)
2 tablespoons	1 ounce, 30 ml	Peanut oil
2 tablespoons	$\frac{3}{4}$ ounce, 20 g	Peanuts
1		Shallot, minced
3		Garlic cloves, minced
$\frac{3}{4}$ cup	4 ounces, 112 g	Extra-firm tofu, 1 inch (2.4 cm) julienned
5 ounces	140 g	Thai rice noodles, soaked in lukewarm water for 5 to 10 minutes, drained
1		Egg
$\frac{1}{2}$ pound	8 ounces, 224 g	Shrimp, peeled, washed, and deveined
$\frac{1}{2}$ pound	8 ounces, 224 g	Lean-cut pork, $\frac{1}{4}$ inch (.6 cm) wide and 2 to 3 inches (4.8 to 7.2 cm) long
1 cup	4 ounces, 112 g	Bean sprouts, washed and drained
1 cup	2 ounces, 56 g	Green onions, 2 inch (4.8 cm) pieces
4		Lime wedges

PROCEDURE

1 Mix together tamarind, sugar, fish sauce, chile peppers, and preserved turnip, set aside.

2 Heat wok over high heat; when hot, add oil. Fry the peanuts until toasted and remove from wok.

3 Add shallot, garlic, and tofu; stir-fry until they start to brown, 2 to 3 minutes.

4 Add drained noodles; they should be flexible but not expanded.

5 Stir-fry to prevent sticking. Add tamarind mixture; stir. If the wok is not hot enough you will see a lot of juice; if so, turn up the heat.

6   Move the ingredients to one side and crack the egg into the wok. Scramble until it is almost set. Fold the egg into the noodles.

7   Add shrimp and pork and stir-fry until cooked.

8   Add half the bean sprouts and chives. Stir and cook 30 seconds. The noodles should be soft and very tangled.

9   Serve sprinkled with peanuts, the remaining bean sprouts, and chives, and lime wedge on the side.

Pad Thai, Khao Tang – Crispy Rice Crackers

Kaeng Kiew Warn Kai
Green Curry with Chicken SERVES 4

AMOUNT	MEASURE	INGREDIENT
$\frac{1}{2}$ cup	4 ounces, 120 ml	Coconut milk, thick
$\frac{1}{4}$ cup	2 ounces, 56 g	Green curry paste (recipe follows)
3 cups	24 ounces, 720 ml	Coconut milk
1	$2\frac{1}{2}$ pound, 1.12 kg each	Whole chicken, cut into 8 pieces
1		Japanese eggplant, 1 inch (2.4 cm) sections
2 tablespoons	1 ounce, 30 ml	Fish sauce (nam pla)
1 tablespoon	$\frac{1}{2}$ ounce, 14 g	Brown sugar
$\frac{1}{2}$ teaspoon		Salt
1 teaspoon		Lime zest
$\frac{1}{2}$ cup	1 ounce, 14 g	Sweet basil
4		Kaffir lime leaves, shredded
$\frac{1}{2}$ cup	2 ounces, 56 g	Red bell pepper, julienned
As needed		Jasmine rice

PROCEDURE

1 Over medium heat, bring the $\frac{1}{2}$ cup (4 ounces, 120 ml) thick coconut milk to a boil, stirring until it thickens and has an oily surface.

2 Add the curry paste. Continue cooking and stirring until the oil has separated from the curry, about 3 to 5 minutes. Be careful not to burn it.

3 Add the chicken and stir-fry until the chicken is firm, 3 to 5 minutes.

4 Add the 3 cups coconut milk; gradually stirring, return to a low boil. Reduce heat, add eggplant, fish sauce, brown sugar, salt, lime zest, half the basil leaves, and Kaffir lime; and simmer 5 to 10 minutes until the chicken and eggplant are tender.

5 Add red bell pepper and cook 1 minute.

6 Garnish with remaining basil leaves and serve with jasmine rice.

Kaeng Kiew Warn Kai – Green Curry with Chicken and Mun Tot –
Fried Sweet Potato

Green Curry Paste

AMOUNT	MEASURE	INGREDIENT
I tablespoon		Coriander seeds, dry roasted and ground
2 teaspoons		Cumin seeds, dry roasted and ground
I teaspoon		Black peppercorns, ground
$\frac{1}{4}$ cup		Cilantro stems, minced
I $\frac{1}{2}$ teaspoons		Salt
$\frac{1}{2}$ cup		Lemongrass, minced
$\frac{1}{4}$ cup		Garlic, chopped
$\frac{1}{4}$ cup		Shallots, chopped
I tablespoon		Ginger, minced
I tablespoon	$\frac{1}{2}$ ounce, 15 ml	Fresh lime juice
I tablespoon		Lime zest
$\frac{1}{2}$ cup	I ounce, 28 g	Green bird chiles, stemmed and coarsely chopped
I tablespoon		Shrimp paste

PROCEDURE

1   Combine coriander, cumin, and peppercorns.

2   Pound or process to reduce ingredients to a paste. Place cilantro stems in a mortar with a pinch of salt and pound until well soft and breaking down. Add the lemongrass and work to mash. Add garlic and another pinch of salt and continue to work. Once the garlic is mashed, add the shallots, then the ginger and lime juice mash. Add the lime zest and another pinch of salt; work to a coarse paste.

3   Add the spice blend and mash and pound until well combined. Add chopped chiles and remaining salt, work until broken down and somewhat smooth. Set aside.

4   Place the shrimp paste on a piece of aluminum foil about 8 × 4 9. (19.2 × 6 cm) inches. Spread it out in a thin layer; fold to a flat package. Place in a pan over high heat and cook 3 minutes on the first side, pressing it down. Turn over and repeat. You should smell the hot shrimp paste. Remove and work into the curry while hot.

Khao Niew Mam Uang
Mangoes and Sticky Rice   SERVES 4

AMOUNT	MEASURE	INGREDIENT
2 cups	13 ounces, 364 g	Rice, glutinous (sticky or sweet rice), washed, soaked overnight (8 hours), and drained
$\frac{1}{2}$ cup	4 ounces, 112 g	Granulated sugar
1 teaspoon		Salt
1 cup	8 ounces, 240 ml	Coconut milk, thick
Topping		
1 cup	8 ounces, 230 ml	Coconut milk
$\frac{1}{2}$ teaspoon		Salt
$\frac{1}{4}$ cup	2 ounces, 56 g	Granulated sugar
2 cups	12 ounces, 336 g	Mangoes, peeled, halved, stone removed, $\frac{1}{2}$ inch (1.2 cm) thick slices

PROCEDURE

1 Place the rice on cheesecloth and steam over water 20 to 25 minutes or until the rice is soft.

2 Dissolve the $\frac{1}{2}$ cup (4 ounces, 112 g) sugar, salt, and thick coconut milk together over medium heat. Bring to a slow boil and remove from heat immediately.

3 Add the rice to the hot milk; stir until completely mixed. Cover and let stand 30 minutes.

4 Bring the remaining coconut milk to a boil, add the salt and $\frac{1}{4}$ cup (4 ounces, 112 g) sugar. Stir to dissolve the sugar.

5 Serve the sliced mangoes with sticky rice and coconut topping.

Cha Yen Thai Iced Tea SERVES 4

AMOUNT	MEASURE	INGREDIENT
$\frac{1}{2}$ cup	4 ounces, 120 ml	Thai tea
3 cups	24 ounces, 720 ml	Water
$1\frac{3}{4}$ cups	14 ounces, 420 ml	Sweetened condensed milk
$1\frac{1}{2}$ cups	12 ounces, 360 ml	Milk

PROCEDURE

1 Place tea in a coffee filter in a drip cone set over a pot.

2 Bring water to a boil and pour over the tea. Allow tea to drip through. Repeat this procedure 5 times, until the tea is a deep reddish orange color and very strong.

3 Add the condensed milk to the tea and allow the mixture to come to room temperature.

4 To serve, fill tall glasses with ice; fill half full with the tea/condensed milk mixture, then fill the other half with milk. Stir.

Banh Hoi Thit Nuong
Shrimp Toast   YIELD: 20 SHRIMP TOASTS

AMOUNT	MEASURE	INGREDIENT
8 ounces	224 g	Shrimp, peeled and deveined
4		Garlic cloves, chopped
6		Shallots, chopped
$\frac{1}{2}$ teaspoon		Ginger, grated
$\frac{1}{2}$ teaspoon		Salt
$1\frac{1}{2}$ teaspoons		Granulated sugar
1 tablespoon		Cornstarch
To taste		Black pepper, freshly ground
1 tablespoon	$\frac{1}{2}$ ounce, 15 ml	Vietnamese fish sauce (*Nuoc mam*)
1		Baguette, $\frac{1}{2}$ inch (1.2 cm) thick slices
1 cup	2 ounces, 56 g	Fresh bread crumbs
As needed		Oil for frying
As needed		Nuoc cham (see recipe on page 369)

PROCEDURE

1 Pound or puree the shrimp, garlic, shallots, ginger, salt, sugar, cornstarch, and pepper. Process to a coarse paste. Add fish sauce and mix well.

2 Spread about 1 tablespoon of the shrimp paste on each slice of bread; round off the top. Dip the shrimp-coated side in the bread crumbs. Refrigerate.

3 Heat $\frac{1}{2}$ inch (.6 cm) of oil to 360°F (182°C) or until bubbles form around a dry wooden chopstick when inserted in the oil. Working in batches, add the shrimp toast, shrimp side down. Fry 1 minute or until golden brown. Turn over, bread side down, and fry 1 minute. Drain on paper towels.

4 Serve hot with *nuoc cham*.

Cha Gio Fried Spring Rolls SERVES 4

AMOUNT	MEASURE	INGREDIENT
1 ounce	28 g	Fine bean threads, soaked/cooked, drained, and cooled
2 tablespoons		Cloud ears or shiitake, dried, soaked in warm water 20 minutes to soften, drained, chopped into 2 inch (4.8 cm) strips
$\frac{1}{4}$ cup	1 ounce, 28 g	Water chestnuts (or jicama), $\frac{1}{4}$ inch (.6 cm) dice
1 cup	6 ounces, 168 g	Chicken breast, raw, skinned, boned, minced
$\frac{1}{2}$ cup	3 ounces, 84 g	Crabmeat, picked over and flaked
$\frac{1}{2}$ cup	3 ounces, 84 g	Shrimp, raw, peeled, deveined, minced
2		Garlic cloves, minced
2 tablespoons		Shallots, minced
$\frac{1}{4}$ cup	1 ounce, 28 g	Red onions, minced
1 tablespoon	$\frac{1}{2}$ ounce, 15 ml	Vietnamese fish sauce (nuoc mam)
2 tablespoons	1 ounce, 28 g	Granulated sugar
$\frac{1}{2}$ teaspoon		Black pepper, freshly ground
4 cups	32 ounces, 960 ml	Water, warm (110°F, 43°C)
4 tablespoons	2 ounces, 56 g	Granulated sugar
14		Rice paper, $6\frac{1}{2}$ inches (15.6 cm) (banh trang)
2		Egg whites, beaten
As needed		Oil for frying
Garnish		
As needed		Dia rau song (vegetable platter; see recipe on page 363)

PROCEDURE

1 Combine bean threads, cloud ears, water chestnuts, chicken, crab, shrimp, garlic, shallots, onions, fish sauce, 2 tablespoons sugar, and pepper; mix well.

2 Combine warm water with 4 tablespoons sugar; stir to dissolve.

3 Dip 3 or 4 rice papers separately into the water for 3 to 4 seconds. Remove and place on a flat work surface. Allow rice paper to soften, 1 to 2 minutes, until soft and transparent.

4 Fold up the bottom third of each wrapper. Center 1 to 2 teaspoons (.5 to 1.0 ml) filling near curved end of the wrappers, leaving space on both ends. Press filling into a compact rectangle. Fold one side of the wrapper over the mixture, then the other. Roll from

bottom to top to completely enclose. Seal with egg white. Continue making packages until wrappers are filled.

5   Heat $1\frac{1}{2}$ to 2 inches (3.6 to 4.8 cm) oil to 325°F (163°C). Add rolls but do not crowd or let them touch; they will stick together. Fry over medium heat 10 to 12 minutes, turning often, until golden and crisp. Drain on paper towels. Keep warm while frying the remaining rolls.

6   To eat, each diner wraps a roll in a lettuce leaf along with a few strands of noodles and a variety of other ingredients from the vegetable platter before dipping it in the *nuoc cham*.

Cha Bo   Grilled Beef Patties   SERVES 4

AMOUNT	MEASURE	INGREDIENT
2 tablespoons	$\frac{1}{3}$ ounce, 9 g	Peanuts, roasted, ground
$1\frac{1}{2}$ cups	9 ounces, 252 g	Lean ground beef
2 tablespoons		Shallots, minced
2 teaspoons		Vietnamese fish sauce (*nuoc mam*)
2 tablespoons	I ounce, 30 ml	Coconut milk
$\frac{1}{2}$ teaspoon		Cumin, ground
$\frac{1}{2}$ teaspoon		Granulated sugar
To taste		Salt and pepper
8		Bamboo skewers, soaked in water 30 minutes

PROCEDURE

1   Combine all ingredients; mix well. Divide into 16 portions.

2   Shape into a ball and then flatten to form a $1\frac{1}{2}$ inch (3.6 cm) patty.

3   Thread 2 patties on each skewer.

4   Grill or broil over high heat until desired temperature, 4 to 5 minutes. Turn only once.

5   Serve immediately with *nuoc cham*.

Goi Cuon Fresh Spring Rolls   YIELD: 4–8 ROLLS

AMOUNT	MEASURE	INGREDIENT
I cup	4 ounces, 112 g	Carrots, shredded
I teaspoon		Granulated sugar
8		Rice paper (*banh trang*), $8\frac{1}{2}$ inches (20.4 cm) in diameter
4		Red leaf or Boston lettuce leaves, thick stem ends removed, cut in half
2 ounces	56 g	Rice vermicelli or Japanese alimentary paste noodles (*somen*), soaked/cooked, drained, and cooled
12 ounces	336 g	Pork loin, thinly sliced 1 x 2 inch (2.4 x 4.8 cm) pieces
I cup	4 ounces, 112 g	Bean sprouts, washed and drained
$\frac{1}{2}$ cup		Mint leaves
8		Shrimp (16–20 ct), cooked, cooled, shelled, deveined, and cut lengthwise in half
$\frac{1}{2}$ cup		Cilantro leaves
I tablespoon		Peanuts, roasted, chopped
As needed		Peanut sauce
As needed		Nuoc cham with shredded carrot and daikon

PROCEDURE

1   Combine shredded carrots and sugar; let stand 10 minutes to soften.

2   Fill a container of warm water (110°F, 43°C) large enough to hold the rice paper. Work with only 2 sheets of rice paper at a time; keep the remaining sheets covered with a damp cloth to prevent curling.

3   Immerse each sheet individually into the warm water, 5 seconds. Remove and spread out flat; do not let the sheets touch each other. Allow the rice paper to soften 2 to 3 minutes. When soft and transparent, assemble the rolls.

4   Lay one piece of lettuce over the bottom third of the rice paper. On the lettuce, place 1 tablespoon of noodles, 1 tablespoon (14 g) carrots, 2 to 3 pieces of pork, a few bean sprouts and several mint leaves. Roll up the paper halfway into a cylinder. Fold in the sides in an envelope pattern. Lay 2 shrimp halves, cut side down, along the crease. Place a few cilantro leaves next to the shrimp. Keep rolling the paper into a tight cylinder to seal. Repeat with remaining wrappers. Store with seam side down.

5   Sprinkle the chopped nuts over the dipping sauce and serve.

Dia Rau Song
Vegetable Platter SERVES 4

AMOUNT	MEASURE	INGREDIENT
1		Head of Boston or other soft lettuce, separated into individual leaves (approximately 3 leaves per person)
1 cup	4 ounces, 112 g	Green onions, cut into 2-inch lengths
1 cup	2 ounces, 56 g	Cilantro leaves
1 cup	2 ounces, 56 g	Mint leaves
1 cup	2 ounces, 56 g	Basil leaves
1½ cups	9 ounces, 252 g	Seedless cucumber, peeled in alternating strips, halved lengthwise, sliced thinly crosswise
1 cup	4 ounces, 112 g	Bean sprouts, washed, drained
½ cup	2 ounces, 56 g	Carrots, julienned
As needed		Lime slices

PROCEDURE

1 Arrange ingredients in separate groups.

Pho Bo
Vietnamese Beef and Noodle Soup

YIELD: 3 TO 4 QUARTS

AMOUNT	MEASURE	INGREDIENTS
I pound	448 g	Oxtail, cut 3 inch (7.2 cm) pieces
I pound	448 g	Beef bones
2 quarts	64 ounces, 1.92 l	Beef stock
I tablespoon	$\frac{1}{2}$ ounce, 15 ml	Vegetable oil
2		Onions, cut in $\frac{1}{4}$ inch (.6 cm) slices
8 ounces	224 g	Daikon, chopped
I $\frac{1}{2}$ ounces	42 g	Ginger, peeled, sliced
3		Green onions, crushed
3		Garlic cloves
I		Cinnamon stick, 2 inch (4.8 cm)
I piece		Star anise
I teaspoon		Black pepper
Garnish		
4 ounces	112 g	Dried rice sticks (*bahn pho*), soaked in hot water for 30 minutes, drained
8 ounces	224 g	Flank steak, cut very thin
I cup	4 ounces, 112 g	Bean sprouts
I cup	4 ounces, 112 g	Red onions, thinly sliced
I		Green chili pepper (jalapeño), sliced thinly
$\frac{1}{2}$ cup	2 ounces, 56 g	Green onions, $\frac{1}{2}$ inch pieces
$\frac{1}{2}$ cup	I ounce, 28 g	Cilantro leaves, fresh
$\frac{1}{2}$ cup	I ounce, 28 g	Mint leaves, fresh
$\frac{1}{2}$ cup	I ounce, 28 g	Basil leaves, fresh
2 tablespoons	I ounce, 30 ml	Vietnamese fish sauce (*nuoc mam*)
8		Lime wedges

PROCEDURE

1. Rinse the oxtail and beef bones. Cover with cold stock and additional water if necessary, bring to a slow boil. Reduce heat and simmer, skim as necessary for the first 30 minutes.

2. Heat oil and add sliced onions; cook, stirring until the onions are browned. Remove and drain the fat.

3. After the stock has stopped foaming add the browned onions, daikon, ginger, green onions, garlic, cinnamon, star anise and black pepper. Simmer and continue to skim for 2 hours. Strain the stock using two layers of cheese cloth. Remove oxtail and shred the meat; serve with the soup.

4. Blanch the bean sprouts in boiling water for 3 seconds. Drain, rinse with cold water and drain.

5. Arrange the sliced beef on a platter. Garnish with red onions, sliced chilies, lime wedges, mint leaves, and basil.

6. At serving time, cook rice sticks in boiling water to heat. Drain.

7. Divide rice sticks equally among 4 serving bowls.

8. Season hot beef stock with fish sauce and black pepper.

9. Each person adds cooked beef, raw flank steak and red onions to their noodles; ladle hot stock over the meat, stirring to cook the meat.

10. Add green chili, bean sprouts, cilantro, mint, basil, and lime to taste.

Dua Chua
Pickled Carrot and Daikon Salad SERVES 4

AMOUNT	MEASURE	INGREDIENTS
2 cups	8 ounces, 224 g	Carrots, julienned
2 cups	8 ounces, 224 g	Daikon, julienned
1 teaspoon		Salt
$\frac{1}{2}$ cup	4 ounces, 120 ml	Water
11 tablespoons	$5\frac{1}{2}$ ounces, 165 ml	Rice wine vinegar
$\frac{1}{4}$ cup	2 ounces, 56 g	Granulated sugar
$\frac{1}{2}$ teaspoon		Vietnamese fish sauce (*nuoc mam*)
1 tablespoon		Cilantro leaves, shredded
1 tablespoon		Mint leaves, shredded
1 tablespoon		Basil leaves, shredded

PROCEDURE

1 Combine carrots, daikon, and salt; toss to coat. Place in a colander to drain for 30 minutes. Rinse and squeeze dry.

2 Combine water, vinegar, sugar, and fish sauce, bring to a boil, and cool to room temperature.

3 Add vegetables to cool vinegar mixture and let marinate 1 hour.

4 Just before serving, toss with herbs.

Ga Xao Sa Ot

Lemongrass Chicken SERVES 4

AMOUNT	MEASURE	INGREDIENT
2		Lemongrass stalks, bottom 6 inches, only, minced
3 tablespoons	1½ ounces, 45 ml	Vietnamese fish sauce (*nuoc mam*)
¼ teaspoon		Black pepper, ground
1 tablespoon		Garlic, minced
1 pound	16 ounces, 448 g	Chicken thigh meat, boned, skinned, cut into 1-inch (2.4 cm) cubes
1 tablespoon	½ ounce, 15 ml	Vegetable oil
2		Red chile, fresh, seeded, shredded into 1½ inch (3.6 cm) lengths
½ cup	2 ounces, 56 g	Green onions, shredded into 1½ inch (3.6 cm) lengths
1 teaspoon		Granulated sugar
2 tablespoons		Basil leaves
1 tablespoon		Mint leaves
Garnish		
¼ cup	1 ounce, 28 g	Peanuts, unsalted roasted
		Dia Rau Song (vegetable platter; see recipe on page 363)

PROCEDURE

1 Combine lemongrass, 2 tablespoons (1 ounce, 30 ml) fish sauce, pepper, and garlic; mix well. Add chicken and toss to combine, let marinate for 1 hour.

2 Heat a wok over medium heat. Add oil; stir-fry chicken, 2 to 3 minutes, until chicken is no longer pink. Add a little water if mixture is too dry.

3 Add remaining fish sauce, chiles, green onions, and sugar. Stir for 30 seconds. Add basil and mint leaves; toss to combine.

4 Serve garnished with peanuts and vegetable platter or rice.

Bo Nuong Grilled Beef SERVES 4

AMOUNT	MEASURE	INGREDIENT
2		Lemongrass stalks, bottom 6 inches only, sliced thin, or 2 tablespoons dried lemongrass, soaked in warm water 1 hour
$\frac{1}{4}$ cup	1 ounce, 28 g	Shallots, sliced thin
4		Garlic cloves, crushed
1 tablespoon	$\frac{1}{2}$ ounce, 14 g	Granulated sugar
1		Fresh red chile peppers, seeded
2 tablespoons	1 ounce, 30 ml	Vietnamese fish sauce (*nuoc mam*)
1 tablespoon	$\frac{1}{2}$ ounce, 15 ml	Sesame oil
1 tablespoon	$\frac{1}{2}$ ounce, 15 ml	Peanut oil
2 tablespoons		Sesame seeds
1 pound		Beef, sirloin or flat iron steak, very cold, cut into thin strips, $1\frac{1}{2}$ (3.6 cm) inches by 4 to 5 (9.6 to 12 cm) long.
24		Bamboo skewers, 8 inches (19.2 cm), soaked in water 30 minutes
Garnish		
4 ounces	112 g	Rice vermicelli, thin, soaked/cooked, drained, and cooled
As needed		*Dia Rau Song* (Vegetable Platter; see recipe on page 363)
As needed		*Nuoc cham* with shredded carrots and daikon (recipe folllows)

PROCEDURE

1 Combine lemongrass, shallots, garlic, sugar, and chiles in a mortar; pound to a fine paste. Move to a bowl and stir in fish sauce, sesame oil, peanut oil, and sesame seeds; blend well.

2 Add beef strips to the paste; toss to coat well. Let marinate for 30 minutes.

3 Weave a skewer through each strip of meat.

4 Grill or pan sear, 1 minute per side. Serve at room temperature with cooked noodles, vegetable platter, and *nuoc cham*.

5 Each diner fills a lettuce leaf with vegetables, noodles, and barbecued beef. The leaf is wrapped into a neat roll and dipped in individual bowls of *nuoc cham* and eaten by hand.

Nuoc Cham with Shredded Carrots and Daikon

YIELD: $1\frac{1}{2}$ CUP

AMOUNT	MEASURE	INGREDIENT
2 tablespoons	1 ounce, 30 ml	Rice vinegar
3 tablespoons	$1\frac{1}{2}$ ounces, 45 l	Fresh lime juice
$\frac{1}{4}$ cup	2 ounces, 60 ml	Vietnamese fish sauce (*nuoc mam*)
$\frac{1}{4}$ cup	2 ounces, 60 ml	Water
2 tablespoons	1 ounce, 28 g	Granulated sugar
1		Garlic clove, minced
$\frac{1}{2}$ teaspoon		Red pepper flakes
$\frac{1}{2}$ cup	2 ounces, 56 g	Carrot, shredded
$\frac{1}{2}$ cup	2 ounces, 56 g	Daikon or turnip, peeled, shredded
1 teaspoon		Granulated sugar
As needed		*Nuoc cham* (recipe follows)

PROCEDURE

1   Combine rice vinegar, lime juice, fish sauce, water, and sugar; stir to dissolve. Add garlic and red pepper flakes. Stir. Cover and let stand for at least 1 hour.

2   Toss the carrot and daikon shreds with the 1 teaspoon of sugar. Let stand 15 minutes to soften. Combine with the *nuoc cham*.

Nuoc Cham   YIELD: 1 CUP

AMOUNT	MEASURE	INGREDIENT
2		Garlic cloves, crushed
1		Fresh red chile pepper, seeded, minced
2 tablespoons	1 ounce, 28 g	Granulated sugar
2 tablespoons	1 ounce, 30 ml	Fresh lime or lemon juice
$\frac{1}{4}$ cup	2 ounces, 60 ml	Rice vinegar
$\frac{1}{4}$ cup	2 ounces, 60 ml	Nuoc mam (Vietnamese fish sauce)
$\frac{1}{4}$ cup	2 ounces, 60 ml	Water

PROCEDURE

1   Using a mortar, make a paste of the garlic, chile, and sugar. Add remaining ingredients; stir to blend.

Suon Rang

Glazed Spareribs   SERVES 4

AMOUNT	MEASURE	INGREDIENT
1 tablespoon	$\frac{1}{2}$ ounce, 15 ml	Vegetable oil
2 pounds	32 ounces, 896 g	Spareribs, lean, cut into 2 inch (4.8 cm) pieces
2 tablespoons	1 ounce, 28 g	Granulated sugar
2 tablespoons	1 ounce, 30 ml	Vietnamese fish sauce (*nuoc mam*)
1 tablespoon	$\frac{1}{2}$ ounce, 15 ml	Soy sauce
6		Garlic cloves, mashed
1 $\frac{1}{2}$ cups	6 ounces, 168 g	Onions, 1 inch (2.4 cm) cubes
1 $\frac{1}{2}$ cups	6 ounces, 168 g	Red bell peppers, 1 $\frac{1}{2}$ inch (3.6 cm) cubes
$\frac{1}{2}$ cup	2 ounces, 56 g	Green onions, 2 inch (4.8 cm) lengths
To taste		Black pepper, freshly ground
As needed		Cilantro sprigs

PROCEDURE

1   Heat wok over medium heat; add oil. Add ribs and cook on both sides until browned, about 15 to 20 minutes.

2   Add sugar and stir. Cook 10 minutes.

3   Pour off all but 1 tablespoon ($\frac{1}{2}$ ounce, 15 ml) fat. Add fish sauce and soy sauce and stir-fry 3 to 4 minutes. Add garlic, onions, bell peppers, and green onions. Stir-fry 3 to 4 minutes or until onions are lightly browned and peppers are tender but firm. Transfer to serving dish.

4   Sprinkle with black pepper and garnish with cilantro sprigs. Serve with rice.

Spain

The Land

Spain is Europe's third largest nation and occupies most of the Iberian Peninsula at the southwestern edge of the continent. It borders France and Andorra in the north and Portugal in the west. Spain's rule once extended all over the world, but today it has been reduced to the mainland, the Balearic Islands in the Mediterranean Sea, the Canary Islands off the northwestern coast of Africa, the Spanish free ports of Ceuta and Melilla on the northern coast of Africa in Morocco, and several other small islands off the coast of Morocco. Spain's physical geography comprises a large peninsula protected by a ring of mountains on nearly all sides. These mountains make Spain the second highest country in Europe, after Switzerland. Continental Spain consists of the Meseta or central plateau, the largest plateau of its kind in Europe, which is surrounded by the Baetic, Andalusian, and Iberian Mountains to the south and southeast, and the Pyrenees to the north, as well as the Cordillera Cantabrica (Catabrian Mountains) to the northwest. The eastern and southern coasts of Spain border the Mediterranean Sea. The varied topography makes for diversity in both climate and natural resources.

History

Around 1100 B.C., Phoenicians from the area that is now present-day Lebanon set up trading colonies along the Spanish coast. Greeks also traded along the northeastern coast. After the fall of Phoenecia it was occupied by Rome for six centuries, laying such important foundations as the Latin language, Roman law, the municipality structure, and the Christian religion.

After the Roman Empire fell, the Suevi, Vandals, and Alans came to Spain but were defeated by the Visigoths, who, by the end of the sixth century, had occupied most of the peninsula. The Arabs entered from the south at the beginning of the eighth century. They conquered the country quickly except for a small area in the north that would become the initial springboard for the reconquest that would occur eight centuries later. The era of Muslim rule is divided into three periods: the Emirate (711–756), the Caliphate (756–1031), and the Reinos de Taifas (small independent kingdoms, 1031–1492).

In 1469, two Catholic monarchs were married: Isabella of Castile and Ferdinand of Aragon. The marriage prepared the way for the two kingdoms to be united. This union marked the opening of a period of growing success for Spain. The year 1492 heralded the discovery of the Americas under the command of Christopher Columbus. During the sixteenth and seventeenth centuries the Spanish Empire became the world's foremost power, and a huge presence in European politics. In 1808 Joseph Bonaparte was installed on the Spanish throne, following the Napoleonic invasion. A fierce resistance followed and Spanish rule was restored with Fernando VII occupying the throne. The Spanish overseas empire finally dissolved in 1898 when, after a brief war with the United States, Spain lost Cuba, Puerto Rico, and the Philippines.

During elections in 1931, it became clear that the people no longer wanted the monarchy ruling over them. In all the large towns of Spain the candidates who supported the monarchy were defeated heavily. However, many smaller country towns supported the monarchy, and thus it was able to keep power. The cities held much power, however, and within them support for Republicans was enormous. Great crowds gathered in Madrid, and the king's most trusted friends advised him to leave. He did so, and the Republic was established on April 14, 1931. During the five-year lifetime of the Republic, it was riddled with political, economic, and social conflicts, which split opinion into two irreconcilable sides: those who still supported a republic and those who did not. The climate of violence grew and on July 18, 1936, a military uprising turned into a tragic three-year civil war.

On October 1, 1936, General Francisco Franco took over as head of state and commander-in-chief of the armed forces. Spain began a period of forty years' dictatorship. The early years were years of economic privation and political repression. Later in Franco's rule, steps toward modernizing Spain's economy began, and increased external influence began to be felt both from the burgeoning tourist trade and industrial investments in Spain.

Franco died in 1975, bringing to an end a significant period of modern Spanish history and opening the way to the restoration of the monarchy with the rise to the throne of Juan Carlos I. Once in power, the young king pushed for change to a western-style democracy. Adolfo Suarez, the prime minister of the second monarchy government, carried out the transition

Spain

to democracy, which culminated in the first democratic parliamentary elections in forty-one years, on June 15, 1977. The years since have been years of rapid change, politically, economically, and socially. In 1982, Spain became a member of the North Atlantic Treaty Organization (NATO). In 1995, Spain joined the European Union. Spain's economy has grown at a rapid pace, and now has reached near parity with the northern European industrialized democracies. Socially, Spain also has moved toward the European mean, with the younger generation more urban and more cosmopolitan than generations before.

On March 11, 2004, Spain was the victim of a massive terrorist attack when Islamic extremists exploded a series of bombs on trains in the crowded Atocha train station in central Madrid. Nearly three hundred died, and hundreds more were injured. In an election a few days later, voters angry at a lack of transparency in the government's handling of the attack—and especially angry at apparently politically-motivated government attempts to link the bombings to Basque terrorists and denial of any Al Queda involvement—led to a surprise victory for the Socialists and their regional allies after eight years of right-wing Partido Popular rule.

The People

Spain's land-bridge location between Europe and Africa and its long history of invasion and settlement by many different groups have resulted in a great mixing of peoples and cultures, particularly the strong influences of the Roman, Jewish, Moorish, and Muslim cultures.

The language of Spain reflects this inherent diversity. Even though Spanish is the official language, other languages in Spain are highly dominant in parts of the country and have been officially recognized. Catalan is spoken in the regions of Catalonia and the Balearic Islands. In Valencia both Castilian and a dialect called Valencian are spoken. Gallego, or Galician, is popular in northwest Spain. The native language of the Basque region is called Euskera. It is not a form of Spanish, and its origins are unknown.

Most Spaniards are baptized, married, and buried as members of the Roman Catholic Church. Under the 1978 constitution the church is no longer Spain's official faith, though financial support is still provided by the state. Among non-Catholic Spaniards, Muslims from Morocco form the largest community. Many other non-Catholics are Protestants, and Spain is also home to small Jewish and Eastern Orthodox congregations. One long-standing minority group is the Roma (Gypsies), who are known as Gitanos. Some of the Roma follow a traditional nomadic lifestyle, while others have assimilated into mainstream Spanish society. Some Basques also claim an ethnic or racial uniqueness from other Spaniards, in addition to a language difference. In the late twentieth century, Spain began receiving large numbers of immigrants for the first time since the sixteenth century. Most of the country's foreign populations are from Latin America, elsewhere in Europe, or North Africa.

The discussion of Spanish culture would not be complete without mentioning two of the most popular customs of Spain: flamenco and bullfighting. These customs are synonymous with Spain throughout the world and hence have become a part of its culture. They are an important part of any fiesta or carnival in Spain. Traditionally, flamenco is an intense artistic expression that originated in southern Spain. Song, dance, and guitar are blended into passionate rhythms that are often improvised and spontaneous. Bullfighting had its first mention as a sport during the Greek and Roman periods. Many northern Europeans are critical of bullfighting and condemn it as a cruel blood sport. Most Spaniards, however, do not see it this way. To them bullfighting is an exciting test of bravery, skill, and grace.

The Spanish are known for eating late. Breakfast often consists of rolls, butter or preserves, and coffee. Lunch, served between 2 and 3 p.m., is the main meal of the day. Dinner is eaten after 9 p.m., often as late as midnight, and is lighter.

The Food

The Moors' occupation of Spain for 750 years greatly influenced Spanish culinary development. The Moorish invaders introduced the cultivation of rice; spices such as saffron, cumin, and anise; nuts (especially almonds); and fruit such as figs, citrus, and bananas. The Moors also introduced their own methods of food preparation. For example, the technique of marinating fish in a strong, vinegary sauce and the combination of sweet and spicy foods are of Arab origin. From the Spanish conquests in the New World in the sixteenth century came eggplant, tomatoes, potatoes, red and green peppers (both hot and sweet), and chocolate.

The Spanish mainland can be broadly divided into five distinct regions: Green Spain, Central Spain, the Pyrenees, Mediterranean Spain, and Andalusia.

Green Spain is located in the north and northwest and includes the regions of Galicia, Asturias, Cantabria, and the Basque provinces. Galicia is known for its abundance of seafood, especially scallops, hake, salmon, and trout. An elegant fan-shaped sea scallop that the Galacians call *vieira* has flavor and history. Travelers from the south kept the shells as proof of their journey through the rocky coastlines. The Asturias is known for its abundance of fish and vegetables. Known for contented cows and mountain ranges full of forests, Asturias and Cantabria are cheese and apple country. *Arroz con leche* is a simple rice pudding made with famous rich and creamy milk. The milk not used for bottling is used for some of the best cheeses in Spain. Cow, sheep, and goat's milk is used to make a soft creamy cheese known as Cabrales Blue that is wrapped in chestnut leaves and stored in humid caves. Light green-blue veins develop to intensify its taste and aroma. Also famous in this region is a blood sausage made with cow's blood, bacon, and onions.

Basque cuisine has agriculture, pastoral, and fishery influences. Peas, beans, green and red peppers, tomatoes, onions, and other mixed vegetables are the stars of many Basque dishes. The Basque district curves around the Bay of Biscay and these waters provide many varieties of fish and shellfish that include crab, hake, tuna, cod, mussels, oysters, lobsters, edible sea barnacles, and baby eels, or angulas. Octopus that inhabit the deep bay waters also find their way to the table as *pulpo gallega*. In Basque country the people enjoy *pintxos* (tapas) twice during the day. One is the *aperitivo* in the morning, and the other is the *txikiteo*, in the evening. Examples of pintxos include tiny rolls filled with ham, grilled eggplant, red peppers, various omelets, fish, sausage, fresh anchovies, as well as croquettes and towering creations of potato salad, egg, mayonnaise, and shrimp supported by a toothpick and topped by an olive. *Bacalao*, or dried salted cod, is a staple food that is affordable and can be stored for days. All salt cod needs to be refreshed in water to remove the salt that has preserved the cod. Cooks will first slap the fish against a hard surface to break down the fibers and then leave it to soak for at least 24 hours, changing the water frequently. It is then simmered, or cooked with vegetables, or pureed with cream, olive oil, and spices.

Central Spain is located on the vast Meseta plateau and includes the provinces of La Rioja, Castile-Leon, Castile-LaMancha, Extremadura, and the country's capital, Madrid. Food here is a blend of Jewish, Muslim, and Christian traditions producing a rustic style of cooking. Dishes range from simple broths such as warm garlic soup (*sopas de ajo*) to more complex winter dishes. *Cocido Madrileno*, or simply *cocido*, is one of Spain's notable dishes. Cocido is based on a large cauldron, which simmers all day. The meats used are chosen for their diversity; salt meat, fresh meat, and sausage are used, as well as meat bones and trotters to add richness to the stock. *Caldo* is a clear stock to which sherry is added. The pot also contains vegetables, the first being chickpeas, then onion, garlic, and leek, and finally fresh vegetables. The order and manner of serving is governed by family tradition. Some families like a large display, with everything served at the same time on different platters, or it may be served in courses. The region is also well known for its roasts; lamb, veal, suckling pig, young goat, and other meats are slowly cooked in wood ovens. The Manchegos have great meat roasting traditions and have produced numerous recipes for cooking game, such as the *gazpacho manchego* (a stew of partridge, hare, rabbit, and pheasant). This region produces some of the finest iberico pork and cheese products in Spain. The foods are reminiscent of those described in *Don Quixote*, prepared with saffron, honey, and manchego cheese. The Castile–La Mancha district produces a range of fine foods and drink, including Spain's best sheep cheese (manchego), excellent table wines (*Valdepenas*), honey, asparagus, strawberries, and saffron. The city of Toledo is renowned for its *yemas* (egg yolk sweets) and marzipans; Madrid is known for its *chocolate con churros*, *orejuelas* (honey fritters); and Ciudad Real for its *bizcochos*, *borrachos* or wine-soaked cakes. The cool Mediterranean climate, semi-arid conditions, and high altitude of central Spain provide the perfect environment for growing olive trees. In the slopes of the Sierras (Montes de Toledo, Sierra de Alcaraz, La Alcarria) the trees are protected from frost. The olive oils of this region have been appreciated for their quality and taste with the cultivation of the first olive trees dating back to the twelfth century. Central Spain is also where one of their most precious products is produced, saffron. The Moors brought with them the spice *az-zafaran* over a thousand years ago. Today over 70 percent of the world's saffron is grown on the high Castilian plateau known as La Mancha. Every October the crocus flowers open at night. The people from Toledo to Albacete rush to the fields at dawn, the opening of the crocus creating a purple blanket as far as the eye can see. All the saffron crocuses must be gathered before dusk; otherwise they lose their flavor. The La Vera region of Spain produces a particularly high quality smoked paprika. Over the centuries, the Yuste monks shared their secrets for growing and processing the chile with local farmers. But it was not until the mid-nineteenth century that the farmers began growing their pimientos on a large scale and processing them into pimentón. These days the pimenton is the region's main source of income. The pimientos are slowly dried over smoldering oak logs for ten to fifteen days and are hand-turned twenty-four hours a day before they are ready to be processed. The smoke-dried pods are then ground into powder and packed in bulk containers. The majority of the pimenton goes to the sausage factories to flavor chorizo. But it is also packed in tins for the consumer market. There are three varieties of pimenton—sweet (dulce), hot (picante), and bittersweet (agridulce).

The rugged mountain chain of the Pyrenees extends along the Spanish-French border from the Bay of Biscay to the Gulf of Valencia. Throughout this mountainous region there are upper meadows, pasture land, glacial lakes, and streams. At the foot of the mountains lie a series of valleys that turn to fertile orchards and vineyards at the Ebro river basin. The cuisine of this region is typically mountain cuisine. Trout and other fish from mountain streams are cooked *a la llosa:* on a slate slab over hot coals. Beef can also be prepared this way. Dishes made with rabbit, quail, partridge, venison, and duck are popular as well. Wild mushrooms are also a local delicacy.

Mediterranean Spain includes the regions of Catalonia, Valencia, and Murcia. The coastal or irrigated plains are home to citrus orchards and produce. Rice fields, vineyards, olive groves, almond, fig, and citrus orchards are characteristic of this area. Seafood and shellfish are abundant here. Catalan cuisine is the oldest, most well-known, most individual, and most traditional cuisine in Spain. It is made up of seven primary ingredients: olive oil, garlic, onions, tomatoes, nuts (almonds, hazelnuts, and pine nuts), dried fruits (raisins and prunes), and herbs (oregano, rosemary, thyme, and bay leaves). There are seventeen officially recognized varieties of chorizo in Catalonia. It is usually made from lean pork, garlic, paprika, red bell peppers and red chile pepper flakes. This region's cuisine is as varied as that of most Spanish regions, but it is a rice-growing land. The short-grain rice was mass-produced around the city of Valencia as a result of the sophisticated irrigation system introduced by the Moors. It was the poor peasant people of the Valencian region who first prepared *paella,* Spain's most famous dish. The original recipe combined homegrown vegetables (usually green and broad beans) with off-cuts of rabbit. Today paella has many variations, most commonly rice cooked with both seafood and chicken or rabbit and then scented and colored with saffron. Another variation is the *paella negra* (black paella), which is colored by the ink from the squid. The region of Valencia produces a wide variety of oranges, mandarins, and lemons. Valencia is also the birthplace of the soft drink *horchata,* made from something called a *chufa,* which translates as "tiger nut," grown all over eastern Spain. *Horchata* looks like an off-white milk, with a toffeelike aroma, and is served cold. Valencia is the home of the famous Spanish candy, *turron,* thought to have been introduced by the Moors. It is traditionally eaten at Christmas. Turron is made by roasting almonds and slow-cooking them with honey and egg white.

Andalusia in southern Spain is the largest of the country's provinces. Andalusia is the world's largest producer of olive oil and its flavor is the foundation of the region's cooking. Black and green olives are grown on the same tree; green olives are simply unripe black olives and are picked in October. Remaining olives ripen and turn black, ready for picking in January or February. In Spain black olives are hardly ever eaten, being used mostly for making oil. Green olives are harvested for eating as tapas or for use as cooking ingredients. Tapas, the age-old custom in Spain originated in Andalusia. The word *tapa* literally means "cover" or "lid" and it is said that the first tapas was simply a hunk of bread placed over the glass to keep out the fruit flies. As the tradition developed, tapas became more elaborate small portions of foods, both hot and cold, served in bars, bodegas, and tascas to accompany a *copa of fino* (dry Spanish sherry), or draught beer. Tapas recipes vary according to the taste and gastronomic traditions of each region. But the tapas most often served are usually those including the many varieties of olives: green, Manzanilla, *machacadas* (crushed), *goradales* (big), *rellenas* (stuffed), *aliñadas* (flavored), and *deshuesadas* (stoneless), dry nuts, as well as many kinds of cold cuts.

Andalusia's most famous contribution to world gastronomy is said to be gazpacho. Traditionally gazpacho is known as peasant food consisting of bread, olive oil, and crushed garlic. None of those forerunners of gazpacho contained tomatoes, as tomatoes were unknown in Spain until after the discovery of the New World. The Moorish influence is evident in some of the variations on the basic theme, such as *ajo blanco*, made with ground almonds. The mountainous province of Huelva in western Andalusia is famous for producing cured hams from pigs fed partially or entirely on a diet of acorns. The hams hang from the ceilings of most establishments, most with hooves still attached and a small container attached at the bottom to catch draining fluids. The hams are taken down and placed on special clamps and very thin slices are carved using a flexible and very sharp knife.

Sherry is a fortified wine, made in and around the town of Jerez. According to Spanish law, Sherry must come from the triangular area of the province of Cadiz, between Jerez, Sanlucar de Barrameda, and El Puerto de Santa Maria. In earlier times Sherry was known as sack, a rendering of the Spanish *saca*, meaning a removal (from the *solera*, or barrel). Sherry differs from other wines by how it is treated after fermentation. After fermentation is complete, it is fortified with brandy. Sherry vinegar can only be made from wines produced in the "sherry triangle." Not only must sherry vinegar be made from wines from this small area but it has to be aged in one of these sherry towns.

Spain is the world leader in the production of air-dried hams, about 190,000 tons per year, which represents some 30 million hams, produced by 1,700 companies. The hams spend a short period of time in salt and then at least three months curing in the mountain air. Most are produced from white pigs but the darker Iberian pigs produce the most expensive hams. All these hams are subject to stringent quality control and are awarded certain classes depending on their production methods. They are best eaten on their own, without bread. A significant amount of Spanish hams are exported each year, mainly to Germany and France.

Glossary

Aioli Garlic flavored mayonnaise, typical of Catalonia and the Balearic Islands.

Anisette A digestive, the flavoring for many liqueurs (anisette or anise). Its flavor varies according to which seeds are used—aniseed or star anise.

Bacalao Preserved salt cod.

Capaplanas Traditional domed clam cookers from the Algarve region in southern Portugal.

Chorizo Brick-colored sausage prepared with light variations in various parts of Spain. Normally made with pork, fat, and pimentón, which gives it its characteristic color and smokiness. In Spain chorizo comes in three varieties. *Fully cured dry chorizo* has a texture similar to pepperoni. *Semi-cured, fully cooked soft chorizo* has a consistency similar to kielbasa. *Fresh chorizo* is raw, uncooked sausage.

Churro Choux pastry dough deep-fried in olive oil, spiral shaped, and similar to a doughnut. *Churros* are made from dough extruded into thin tubes; these have a star-shaped cross section and are several inches long. Traditionally eaten at breakfast with hot chocolate.

Cocido Stews, famous in northern and central Spain. More than just a stew, they are elaborate creations, an event, usually prepared to feed a large group of friends and family.

Empanada In Spanish the word *empanada* means "in dough" and describes pies with savory fillings enclosed in bread dough, short pastry, or puff pastry.

Flan Baked custard dessert, usually served with caramel sauce.

Gazpacho Cold vegetable soup, the best-known version of which is from the southern Spanish region of Andalusia. It is made of ripe tomatoes, bell peppers, cucumbers, garlic, and bread moistened with water that is blended with olive oil, vinegar, and ice water and is served cold.

Jambon Serrano Cured ham similar to the prosciutto of Italy, with a sweet-salty flavor.

Paella Traditional rice dish originating from Valencia, an authentic *paella valenciana* contains chicken, rabbit, sometimes duck, and the land snails called *vaquetes*, for which a rosemary sprig can be substituted. The only permissible vegetables are flat green beans, artichokes, and butter beans. The star of this dish is rice. Other authentic ingredients include a *sofrito* of tomatoes, garlic, saffron, and pimiento. The Valencian word *paella*, meaning "pan," comes from the Latin *patella*, which also means "pan."

Paella Pan Thin, round, shallow, flat-bottomed, two-handled pan. The wide, shallow shape allows the largest area of rice to come in contact with the bottom of the pan, where the flavor of the ingredients is concentrated. It also helps liquid evaporate rapidly.

Pimentón Smoked paprika. It differs from other European paprikas because of the characteristic smoked aroma that it gives off during processing from being dried by means of wood smoke.

Piquillo Peppers Spanish wood-roasted sweet peppers.

Queso (Cheese) PDO Status The governments in most European countries have instituted a government-controlled quality program known as PDO (Protected Designation of Origin) for

About Olive Oil

Spain is the largest producer of olive oil in the world, followed closely by Italy. Greece is the third-largest producer, though it uses more olive oil per capita than any other country. No two olive oils are exactly alike. Just as with wine, each oil is distinct, a unique product of soil, climate, olive type (there are at least 60 varieties of olives), and processing method.

The olive tree is a hearty evergreen with silver-green leaves that thrives in the mild winters and long hot summers of the Mediterranean and does well in dry, arid climates. In many cases olive trees, which start bearing usable fruit after five to eight years, can be hundreds of years old and still produce fruit. Olive trees planted near the sea can produce up to 20 times more fruit than those planted inland. A mature olive tree will produce only 15 to 20 kilograms (33 to 44 pounds) of olives each year. Since it takes about 5 kilograms of olives to make a liter of oil, one tree is capable of producing only about 3 to 4 liters of oil per year.

Picked olives are taken to an olive oil mill, where they are pressed for their oil. This is done the same day, or at most a day later, before they start to oxidize and ferment. The actual fruit of the tree—the just-picked olives—is far too bitter and acrid to eat and it must be washed and soaked and then either brined or salted and allowed to age before it is edible.

Virgin olive oil is extracted without heat, additives, or solvents from the freshly picked bitter olives, and should have a lush, rich taste and velvety texture. The oil from olives is ready to use immediately after extraction.

Olive oil that is "cold-pressed" is made from olives that have been crushed with a traditional millstone or stainless steel grindstone. No heat or chemicals are added during the process, which produces a heavy olive paste. The paste is then spread over thick, round straw or plastic mats that are placed in a press. This press extracts the liquid from the paste—a combination of oil and water. The oil is separated from the water either by decanting or by centrifuge and then filtered to remove any large particles. The resulting oil is then graded and classified, according to standards established by the IOOC. The finest olive oils are those that have the lowest acidity, which is measured as a percentage per 100 grams of oil.

TYPES OF OLIVE OIL

- **Extra-Virgin Olive Oil:** Any olive oil that is less than 1 percent acidity, produced by the first cold pressing of the olive fruit. Most olive oils today are extra virgin in name only, meeting only the minimum requirements. Extra virgin is a chemical requirement that does not indicate quality and taste.

- **Virgin Olive Oil:** It is made from olives that are slightly riper than those used for extra-virgin oil and is produced in exactly the same manner but has a slightly higher level of acidity ($1\frac{1}{2}$ percent).

- **Unfiltered Olive Oil:** This oil contains small particles of olive flesh. Some claim this adds additional flavor. Unfortunately, it causes a sediment to form at the bottom of the bottle, which can become rancid, negatively impacting flavor and shelf life. It is recommended that this oil not be used for cooking. Unfiltered oil should be carefully stored and used within three to six months of bottling.

- **Early Harvest (Fall Harvest Olive Oil):** Olives reach their full size in the fall but may not fully ripen from green to black until late winter. Green olives have slightly less oil and more bitterness and can be higher in polyphenols. The oil tends to be more expensive because it takes more olives to make a bottle of oil. This oil has a more peppery and bitter flavor.

- **Late Harvest (Winter Harvest Olive Oil):** The fruit is picked ripe and the olives have a little more oil. It has a light, mellow taste with little bitterness and more floral flavors.

- **Refined Olive Oil:** This olive oil is obtained from refining virgin olive oil that has defects (the result is an essentially tasteless olive oil). Among the defects are a natural acidity higher than 3.3 percent, poor flavor, and an unpleasant odor. This product is also known as "A" refined olive oil.

- **Refined Olive-Pomace Oil:** Oil obtained by treating olive pomace with solvents and refined using methods that do not lead to alterations in the initial glyceridic structure.

- **Olive-Pomace Oil:** Olive oil that consists of a blend of refined olive-pomace oil and virgin olive oil.

- **Light and Extra Light Olive Oil:** The olive oil advertised as "light" or as "extra light" olive oil contains the exact same number of calories as regular olive oil and is a mixture of refined olive oils that are derived from the lowest-quality olive oils available through chemical processing.

- **First Press:** This is no longer an official definition for olive oil. A century ago, oil was pressed in screw or hydraulic presses. The paste was subjected to increasingly high pressures with subsequent degradation in the flavor of the oil. Today the vast majority of oil is made in continuous centrifugal presses. There is no second pressing.

many agricultural and food products. Often called DO, this program means the government guarantees the origin, preparation methods, and production within a certain location in the country, and the quality of a product.

Spanish DO Cheeses

Cabrales One of the great blue cheeses of the world, produced from raw milk, mainly cow's milk. The rind is sticky and yellow, with an intense smell. The interior is compact but very open, with lots of holes and blue veins. The taste is strong, although not as strong as the smell, slightly piquant, acid, and creamy.

Cantabria Also called queso de nata or cantabrian cream cheese. Aged cheese from soft to semi-cured to cured, made from pasteurized cow's milk, it has a smooth flavor, ranging from sweet and slightly acidic to buttery.

Ibores Made with unpasteurized milk from the serrata goat breed of Verata and Retinta, using mixed coagulation (lactic and enzymatic) techniques. It is a semi-soft paste of medium aging. The rind is rubbed with olive oil or smoked paprika from Vera. Its flavor is creamy and very buttery, with aromas of unpasteurized milk.

Idiazábal Aged cheese, from semi-cured to cured, made exclusively from whole raw sheep's milk. Idiazábal is a robust and sharp cheese, made to be ripened for a long period, with a dry and crumbly paste.

L'Alt Urgell y la Cerdanya Made with pasteurized whole milk from frisona cows. It has a soft and creamy texture, with sweet aroma.

L'Alt Urgell A very aromatic soft cheese cured for a short time, with a buttery taste, although intense and persistent.

La Serena Cheese aged for at least eight weeks, from soft to semi-cured, made with unpasteurized whole milk, from merino sheep. The flavor is very buttery, thick, and creamy. It is full flavored with an underlying tart flavor and a spreadable texture. This is a cheese almost always made in an artisanal way, of a very small production, difficult to find and expensive.

Mahón Also known as Menorquín cheese. Fresh to much-cured cheese, depending on the state of aging, made from raw or pasteurized cow's milk. The taste is very particular, slightly acidic and salty, but not buttery. It can be milky and humid when fresh, and dry, strong, and piquant as it ages.

Majorero Also called queso de fuerteventura. Aged cheese, from aired to very cured. Made with goat's milk, it has a compact but open interior, and a slightly gummy texture. The taste of the little-cured variety is acidic, a little piquant, and buttery but not salty. Aged cheese is rubbed with oil, paprika, and gofio (a local sweet wheat flour) in order to avoid excessive drying.

Manchego Aged cheese, with a firm interior, compact and closed. The color is ivory to pale yellow. The taste is very characteristic, well developed but not too strong, buttery and slightly piquant, with a sheep's milk aftertaste. Semi-cured to cured cheese is made exclusively with raw or pasteurized sheep's milk and has a crumbly texture. The shape is cylindrical, with a flat top and bottom surfaces engraved with the typical "flower" left by the wooden presses. The sides show a zigzag pattern produced by the mat-weed (esparto) of the molds.

Murcia al Vino Aged cheese, from soft to semi-cured, made with pasteurized goat's milk, and aged by applying external washes with red wine. It has a mild aroma, and the flavor is pleasantly acid and a little salty.

Picón Also known as Queso de los Picos de Europa. Aged for at least three months, cured, made of a mixture of unpasteurized cow's, goat's, and sheep's milk. A type of blue cheese, it is robust and full flavored, cylindrical in shape. It is an artisanal cheese limited in production and aged in natural caves in the Picos de Europa in northern Spain.

Quesucos de Liebana Fresh cheese or aged and soft, produced mainly with cow's milk, although sometimes mixed with sheep's and goat's milk. Cylindrical in shape, smoked or with a natural rind, the unsmoked cheese has a smooth and buttery flavor, while the smoked variety has a more acidic and cured flavor.

Roncal Also queso del valle del roncal. Aged for at least four months, and cured, made from sheep's milk from Laxta or Aragonese breeds. Its flavor is well developed and structured, buttery with an aroma of straw, dried fruit, and mushrooms.

Tetilla Aged, from soft to semi-cured, made with cow's milk. The soft paste, thick and smooth with few air pockets, is very creamy on the palate. The flavor is clean and smooth. The word *tetilla*, meaning "nipple," clearly defines the traditional shape of this cheese: a flattened pear-shaped cone with a small nipple on the top.

Zamorano The rind is dark gray and oily. The inside is closed and compact, with tiny crystal-like dots spread evenly throughout. The cheese is compact, not easy to melt, and has a straw-yellow color. The taste is intense although not too strong, slightly piquant, and buttery.

Saffron The stigma of the purple crocus flower, intensely fragrant, slightly bitter in taste. By soaking saffron in warm water, the result is a bright yellow-orange solution.

Sangria Red wine mixed with fruit juices.

Sherry Sherry is a fortified wine from a small region of Spain, made from the Muscat, Palomino, and Pedro Ximenez grapes.

Menus and Recipes
from Spain

Aceitunas Verdes Rellenas de Pimiento y Anchoa

Green Olives Filled with Piquillo Peppers and Anchovy SERVES 4

AMOUNT	MEASURE	INGREDIENT
8		Extra-large green olives unpitted
4		Anchovy fillets, oil-packed, cut in half lengthwise
2		Piquillo pepper, cut into 8, $\frac{1}{2}$ inch (1.2 cm) wide strips
1		Garlic clove, rough chopped
3 tablespoons	$1\frac{1}{2}$ ounces, 45 ml	Spanish extra-virgin olive oil
1 tablespoon		Orange zest, grated
1 tablespoon	$\frac{1}{2}$ ounce, 15 ml	Sherry vinegar
To taste		Sea salt

PROCEDURE

1 Using the flat side of a chef knife, press each olive until the pit pops out; do not split the olive in half.

2 Place one slice anchovy and pepper in each olive.

3 Combine garlic, olive oil, orange zest, and sherry vinegar to make a dressing.

4 Marinate stuffed olives in dressing for 30 minutes.

5 Serve sprinkled with sea salt.

Queso Idiazábal
Cheese with Fresh Herbs   SERVES 4

Chef Tip Any semi-hard cheese can be substituted.

AMOUNT	MEASURE	INGREDIENT
3		Garlic cloves, split in half, crushed
2 cups	12 ounces, 336 g	Idiazábal cheese, cut into 1 inch (2.5 cm) cubes
1 tablespoon		Whole black peppercorns
2		Fresh rosemary sprigs, rough chopped
2		Fresh thyme sprigs, rough chopped
1 cup	8 ounces, 240 ml	Spanish extra-virgin olive oil

PROCEDURE

1 Combine all ingredients and coat the cheese thoroughly.

2 Marinate at room temperature, for as long as overnight.

Pan Con Tomate Tomato Toast   SERVES 4

AMOUNT	MEASURE	INGREDIENT
4		Rustic bread, $\frac{1}{2}$ inch (1.2 cm) thick slices
2		Ripe tomatoes, cut in half
$\frac{1}{2}$ cup	4 ounces, 120 ml	Spanish extra-virgin olive oil
To taste		Sea salt
Optional		Garum (recipe follows)
Optional		Jamón serrano (Spanish cured ham)

PROCEDURE

1 Toast or grill bread.

2 Rub the open face of the tomato into one side of each piece of toast until all the flesh is grated. Discard skin.

3 Drizzle olive oil over tomato and season with salt.

4 Serve with garum, if desired, or a thin slice of jamón serrano.

Calamares Encebollados
Squid with Caramelized Onions SERVES 4

AMOUNT	MEASURE	INGREDIENT
$\frac{1}{4}$ cup	2 ounces, 60 ml	Spanish extra-virgin olive oil
1		Garlic clove
2 cups	8 ounces, 224 g	Spanish sweet onions, sliced thin
1		Bay leaf
To taste		Salt
2 cups	12 ounces, 336 g	Fresh squid, $\frac{1}{2}$ inch (1.2 cm) pieces
$\frac{1}{2}$ cup	4 ounces, 120 ml	Dry white wine
2 teaspoons		Flat-leaf parsley, chopped

PROCEDURE

1 Heat the olive oil over medium heat in a medium sauté pan.

2 Add garlic and cook 2 minutes or until brown; remove.

3 Add onions and bay leaf; cook over medium-low heat until lightly brown, about 10 minutes.

4 Reduce heat to low and continue cooking until onions are soft and caramelized, about 20 minutes longer.

5 Remove onions from pan and set aside, leaving the oil in pan.

6 Return heat to high and sprinkle pan with salt. Add squid, making sure not to overcrowd the pan; there must be ample space so the squid does not boil. Sauté 15 to 20 seconds on each side. Remove from pan and repeat the process with remaining squid.

7 Return all the squid to the pan, add caramelized onions, and stir to mix. Add wine around sides and boil for 20 seconds.

8 Sprinkle with parsley and serve.

Garum Black Olive, Anchovy, and Caper Spread YIELD: ¾ CUP

In ancient Rome, garum was a pungent all-purpose condiment made from fermented anchovies, similar to Asian fish sauce. This current version, from Catalonia, is closer to the French tapenade and works well with grilled meat, chicken, or fish. Try to find olives that are pungent, but not vinegary and briny.

AMOUNT	MEASURE	INGREDIENT
I cup	6 ounces, 168 g	Pitted black olives, Niçoise
2		Anchovy fillets, chopped and mashed to a paste
I tablespoon	½ ounce, 14 g	Capers, drained and rinsed
I		Garlic clove, smashed
I		Hard-cooked egg yolk, smashed
I tablespoon	½ ounce, 15 ml	Rum, brandy, or water
¼ teaspoon		Dijon mustard
2 tablespoons	I ounce, 30 ml	Olive oil

PROCEDURE

1 Combine olives, anchovy, capers, garlic, egg yolk, rum, and mustard in a food processor or mortar; process to a medium-fine paste.

2 Gradually add olive oil.

3 Let stand 1 hour at room temperature to allow flavors to develop.

4 Serve with grilled bread or tomato toast.

Croquetas de Jamón
Serrano Ham Fritters   YIELD: 15 FRITTERS

AMOUNT	MEASURE	INGREDIENT
4 tablespoons	2 ounces, 56 g	Butter
$\frac{1}{4}$ cup	1 ounce, 28 g	Spanish onion, $\frac{1}{4}$ inch (.6 cm) diced
$1\frac{1}{4}$ cups	6 ounces, 168 g	All-purpose flour
2 cups	16 ounces, 480 ml	Milk
$\frac{1}{2}$ cup	3 ounces, 84 g	Jamón serrano (Spanish cured ham), finely chopped
To taste		Salt
Pinch		Nutmeg
1		Large egg, beaten with teaspoon of water
1 cup	1 ounce, 28 g	Dry bread crumbs
2 cups	16 ounces, 480 ml	Olive oil, for frying

PROCEDURE

1. Heat butter over medium heat; add onion and sauté until translucent, 3 minutes.

2. Add 1 cup ($4\frac{1}{2}$ ounces, 126 g) flour and mix well. Cook to a blond roux, about 5 minutes.

3. Add milk gradually, stirring continuously; cook 3 to 4 minutes, until a thick béchamel.

4. Add ham, salt, and nutmeg; cook 2 minutes. The mixture should be thick enough to mold by hand. Test for correct consistency by carefully picking up a tablespoon-size bit and balling it with your hands. It should not be very sticky. If mixture sticks to your hands, return to heat and cook 2 more minutes; recheck.

5. Spread mixture out on a half sheet pan and cool to room temperature.

6. Form the mixture into small cylinders the size of a wine cork, using about a tablespoon of mixture for each.

7. Roll each fritter in remaining flour, the egg, and breadcrumbs.

8. Refrigerate for 30 minutes before frying.

9. Heat oil to 375°F (190°C).

10. Deep-fry fritters in small batches. Fry until golden color, about 1 minute; turn as needed.

11. Transfer to absorbent towels to drain. Repeat with all fritters and serve hot.

Bacalad al Ajo Arriero
Bacalao Hash SERVES 4

Chef Tip Cooked with care, desalted reconstituted bacalao is moist, plump, and falling apart in big, luxurious flakes. Depending on the grade of the fish and the salting method used, bacalao can take anywhere from 24 hours to 2 days to desalt properly. To desalt, cover with 2 inches of cold water and refrigerate, changing water every 4–5 hours if possible. Taste a small piece and if it is still too salty, soak longer, changing water as needed. It can also be cooked in milk instead of water to draw out some of the salt. It is important to cook salt cod very gently or it will become tough and rubbery; never boil it. The fish is cooked when it flakes easily with the point of a knife. There are small bones that need to be removed.

AMOUNT	MEASURE	INGREDIENT
	3 ounces, 84 g	Salt cod, soaked, cooked, drained
2 tablespoons	1 ounce, 30 ml	Olive oil
$\frac{1}{2}$ cup	2 ounces, 56 g	Onion, $\frac{1}{4}$ inch (.6 cm) dice
2		Garlic cloves, minced
$\frac{1}{4}$ cup	1 ounce, 28 g	Green bell pepper, $\frac{1}{4}$ inch (.6 cm) dice
$\frac{1}{2}$ cup	2 ounces	Piquillo peppers (from can or jar) or pimientos, or Red bell pepper, julienne cut
1 cup	6 ounces, 168 g	Boiling potatoes (Yukon gold), peeled, boiled, drained, $\frac{1}{4}$ inch (.6 cm) dice
$\frac{1}{4}$ teaspoon		Sweet (not smoked) paprika
2 tablespoons	1 ounce, 30 ml	Tomato sauce
$\frac{1}{4}$ teaspoon		White wine or sherry vinegar
To taste		Coarse salt and freshly ground black pepper
1 tablespoon		Flat-leaf parsley, minced
For serving		Sliced crusty baguette

PROCEDURE

1   Flake salt cod finely, discard bones, skin, and any tough bits.

2   Heat olive over medium-low heat. Add onion and sauté until translucent, 3 minutes. Add garlic; cook 2 minutes.

3   Add green pepper and cook until pepper and onions are very soft, 5–6 minutes. Do not brown.

4   If pan looks dry add a little more oil, stir in cod, piquillo peppers, and potatoes; mix well, cover, and cook 5 minutes. Stir only 2–3 times.

5   Add paprika and stir for a few seconds. Add tomato sauce and wine, reduce heat to very low, re-cover, and simmer 7–8 minutes. Hash should still be moist; if not, add a little water and simmer 1 or 2 minutes.

6   Let hash cool to warm or room temperature; the flavor will develop as it cools.

7   Stir in parsley, adjust seasoning, and serve on or with bread.

Tortilla de Patatas
Potato Omelet   SERVES 4

AMOUNT	MEASURE	INGREDIENT
1½ cups	10 ounces, 300 ml	Olive oil
2 cups	8 ounces, 224 g	All-purpose potatoes, peeled, very thin slices
1 teaspoon	5 g	Salt
½ cup	3 ounces, 84 g	Spanish onion thinly sliced
4		Eggs, lightly beaten

PROCEDURE

1   Heat olive oil over medium heat, until a piece of potato dropped in the oil jumps, 275°F (135°C).

2   Add potatoes to hot oil and cook until lightly browned and crispy around edges, 10 minutes. Remove from heat, strain potatoes from oil, and reserve oil.

3   Season potatoes with half the salt and set aside.

4   Reheat oil and add onions; cook over medium heat until golden brown, 8 minutes.

5   Strain onions, set aside, and reserve oil.

6   Combine egg, potatoes, and onions.

7   Add reserved oil to a 6-inch (15 cm) sauté pan over medium heat.

8   Heat oil until it just begins to smoke, add egg mixture. Shake pan 10 to 15 seconds, then cook 30 seconds without moving pan. Lower heat and cook 2 to 3 minutes until a crust has formed.

9   Flip tortilla when edges are cooked but the center is not completely set. Place a plate on top of the pan and gently flip tortilla onto the plate. Slide tortilla back into pan and continue cooking over low heat for 1 minute longer. Pan may need additional oil before returning tortilla.

10   Serve hot, at room temperature, or cold.

Gambas al Ajillo
Sizzling Garlic Shrimp   SERVES 4

AMOUNT	MEASURE	INGREDIENT
I pound	16 ounces, 448 g	Large shrimp (26 to 30 ct), in shell
To taste		Coarse salt
I cup	8 ounces, 240 ml	Olive oil
5		Garlic cloves, finely chopped
$\frac{1}{2}$		Small dry red chile (arbol), crumbled
2 tablespoons		Flat-leaf parsley, minced
For serving		Bread

PROCEDURE

1   Pat shrimp dry and sprinkle with salt.

2   Combine olive oil and garlic over medium-low heat until oil is hot and garlic begins to sizzle gently. Cook until garlic is very fragrant but not colored, 2–3 minutes; reduce heat if necessary.

3   Add chile and stir for 30 seconds.

4   Add shrimp; cook, stirring, until shrimp are just cooked, about 3 minutes.

5   Season with salt to taste, stir in parsley, and cook 15 seconds.

6   Serve with bread.

Rape con Romesco

Monkfish with Romesco Sauce   SERVES 4

AMOUNT	MEASURE	INGREDIENT
	12 ounces, 336 g	Monkfish fillet or any meaty fish
5		Bay leaves, dry or fresh
2 tablespoons	1 ounce, 30 ml	Olive oil
To taste		Salt and white pepper
2 cups	16 ounces, 480 ml	Romesco sauce (recipe follows)

PROCEDURE

1 Clean fish of any membrane and cut 5 incisions about 1 inch apart in the fillet; do not cut all the way through.

2 Insert a bay leaf into each slot.

3 Heat oil over medium high heat and sauté fillet until lightly browned on each side, 3 to 4 minutes. Set fish aside to cool.

4 Remove bay leaves and discard. Slice fillet into 1-inch (2.5 cm) medallions; season with salt and white pepper.

5 Place medallions on romesco sauce and drizzle with olive oil to serve.

Romesco Sauce

Catalan roasted-vegetable sauce.

YIELD: 2 CUPS

AMOUNT	MEASURE	INGREDIENT
I		**Red bell pepper**
I pound	16 ounces, 448 g	**Ripe plum tomatoes**
I		**Garlic head, halved**
I	6 ounces, 180 g	**Whole Spanish onion**
½ cup plus 2 tablespoons	5 ounces, 150 ml	**Olive oil**
3		**Ñora chile peppers or any dried sweet chili pepper**
¼ cup	I ounce, 28 g	**Blanched almonds**
½ cup	I ounce, 28 g	**White bread, crust removed**
I tablespoon	½ ounce, 15 ml	**Sherry vinegar**
I teaspoon		**Pimentón (Spanish sweet paprika)**
To taste		**Salt**

PROCEDURE

1   Heat oven to 350°F (176°C).

2   Toss red bell pepper, tomatoes, garlic, and onion with 2 tablespoons (1 ounce, 30 ml) olive oil; place on baking sheet and roast until all are soft, 25 minutes. Let vegetables cool; peel and seed pepper; peel onion; seed tomatoes; peel garlic.

3   Cover ñora chile peppers with enough hot water to cover; soak 15 minutes. Strain and remove seeds.

4   Puree chiles until smooth. Pass the puree through a fine-mesh sieve and set aside.

5   Heat 1 tablespoon (½ ounce, 15 ml) oil over medium low heat, sauté almonds 1 minute or until lightly toasted; remove from pan to stop the cooking.

6   Toast the bread until it is a nice brown color.

7   Sauté the pureed ñora over medium heat 30 seconds; remove from heat

8   Place cooled peeled vegetables, almonds, toasted bread, pureed ñora, vinegar, pimentón, and remaining oil in a blender. Blend to a thick sauce; add salt.

Sopa de Ajo

Castilian Garlic Soup   SERVES 4

Chef Tip Traditionally the eggs are poached right in the soup, but they can be poached ahead of time.

AMOUNT	MEASURE	INGREDIENT
6 tablespoons	3 ounces, 90 ml	Olive oil
6		Garlic cloves, sliced thin
$\frac{1}{2}$ cup	2 ounces, 56 g	Serrano ham or prosciutto, minced
2 cups	4 ounces, 112 g	Day-old country bread without crusts, $1\frac{1}{2}$ inch (3.75 cm) dice
2 teaspoons		Smoked sweet Spanish paprika
5 cups	40 ounces, 1.2 l	Chicken stock
To taste		Salt and pepper
4		Garlic cloves, smashed to a paste
4		Poached eggs
1 tablespoon		Flat-leaf parsley, minced

PROCEDURE

1 Heat olive oil over low heat; add garlic and ham. Cook, stirring, until garlic is very fragrant but not brown, 4 to 5 minutes.

2 Add bread, stirring to coat with oil; cook 2 to 3 minutes. Add more oil if the pan is dry.

3 Remove from heat and add paprika; toss the bread to coat evenly.

4 Return pan to heat and add stock. Increase heat to medium and simmer about 7 minutes or until bread swells but still holds its shape.

5 Season with salt and pepper, add garlic paste, and cook 1 minute.

6 Ladle soup into warm bowls, top each with a warm poached egg and parsley.

7 To eat, break the poached egg, stirring the yolk into the soup; the egg will cook slightly from the heat and thicken the broth.

Fabes con Almejas
Asturian Bean Stew with Clams   SERVES 4

AMOUNT	MEASURE	INGREDIENT
I cup	7 ounces, 196 g	Asturian beans or other large dried white beans such as cannellini, dried, sorted, soaked overnight
1½ quarts	48 ounces, 1.44 l	Water
I		Spanish onion, peeled
I		Roma tomato
2 inch (5 cm)		Carrot piece, peeled
3		Fresh parsley sprigs
4 tablespoons	2 ounces, 60 ml	Olive oil
To taste		Salt
16		Littleneck clams, cleaned

PROCEDURE

1   Combine soaked beans and water; bring to a boil. Reduce heat to low and simmer 10 minutes, occasionally removing any foam that comes to the surface.

2   Add onion, tomato, carrot; and parsley; simmer 2 hours. Every 15 minutes, add $\frac{1}{4}$ cup (2 ounces, 60 ml) cold water to slow the simmering. Beans should always be covered with liquid. By the end of the cooking time the beans should be just covered with liquid.

3   Remove the vegetables and place in a food processor or blender with a $\frac{1}{2}$ cup (4 ounces) of beans that are split or broken and 1 tablespoon ($\frac{1}{2}$ ounce, 15 ml) cooking liquid. Blend until somewhat smooth, pass through a fine strainer, and return to the bean mixture.

4   Add 2 tablespoons (1 ounce, 30 ml) olive oil to beans and season with salt. Beans should be very soft and broth creamy and starchy. Return to a simmer.

5   Heat 1 quart of water to a boil. Add 4 clams at a time until they just open, 5 to 10 seconds. Remove from water. Repeat with remaining clams.

6   Working over a bowl to collect any clam juice, use a paring or clam knife to remove clams from shell.

7   Strain juices and add to the beans.

8   Serve beans topped with clams and drizzle clams with remaining olive oil.

Paella Valenciana   SERVES 4

Chef Tip **According to Valencian traditionalists, this is the only legitimate paella. This dish evolved from a range of simpler rices prepared by laborers in the Levantine rice paddies and *huertas* (vegetable plots) with whatever could be hunted and gathered.**

Paella is not a pilaf or risotto; the rice is never washed or the barley stirred. It should have a crispy, caramelized, toasted bottom (called socarrat).

AMOUNT	MEASURE	INGREDIENT
1½ cups	10 ounces, 280 g	Skinless, boneless chicken thighs, 1½ inch (3.75 cm) chunks
	16 ounce, 448 g	Rabbit, bone-in, cut into small pieces
1½ teaspoons		Smoked sweet Spanish paprika
To taste		Salt and fresh black pepper
6		Garlic cloves, minced or crushed with a garlic press
4 cups	32 ounces, 960 ml	Chicken stock
Pinch		Saffron, pulverized in a mortar
5 tablespoons	2½ ounces, 75 ml	Olive oil
1 cup	6 ounces, 168 g	Spanish chorizo, 1½ inch (3.75 cm) pieces
¼ cup	2 ounces, 56 g	Green beans (Italian flat beans), trimmed, 1½ inch (3.75 cm) lengths
½ cup	3 ounces, 84 g	Cooked butter beans or baby lima beans
1 cup	6 ounces, 168 g	Frozen artichoke hearts, thawed, patted dry
½ cup	3 ounces, 90 ml	Tomato, cut in half and grated on box grater, skin discarded
Pinch		Cayenne
2 cups	14 ounces, 392 g	Short- to medium-grain rice
12 large		Snails (optional)
½ cup	3 ounces, 84 g	Red bell pepper, roasted, peeled, julienned

PROCEDURE

1 Preheat oven to 425°F (218°C).

2 Combine chicken, rabbit, ½ teaspoon paprika, salt, pepper, and half the garlic; toss well and set aside for 15 minutes.

3 Bring chicken stock to a simmer. Add the saffron and continue to keep hot.

4   Using only one burner, place 4 tablespoons (2 ounces, 60 ml) olive oil in a 14-inch (53.6 cm) paella pan over medium heat until oil begins to smoke.

5   Add chicken and rabbit; brown, 6 to 7 minutes.

6   Add chorizo; cook 2 minutes.

7   Add green beans, butter beans, and artichokes; toss until vegetables begin to take on color, 5 minutes. Move all items to the edge of pan.

8   Add remaining oil to center of paella pan, add remaining garlic, and cook until fragrant, about 30 seconds.

9   Add tomatoes to center of the pan, reduce heat to low, and cook, stirring, until tomato is thickened and reduced, 5 to 6 minutes.

10 Toss tomato mixture with meat and vegetables, add remaining paprika and cayenne; stir to combine.

11 Add rice to pan and stir to coat. Add hot stock.

12 Place pan over two burners, stir in snails if using, and shake pan to distribute rice evenly. Cook over medium low heat until the cooking liquid is almost level with the rice, 6–8 minutes; rice will still be soupy. Move and rotate pan so the liquid cooks evenly. If liquid is absorbed too fast and the rice seems raw, add a little more stock.

13 Transfer paella pan to oven and bake until the rice is tender but still al dente, about 15 minutes. Check and sprinkle with more stock if necessary.

14 Remove paella from the oven, cover with aluminum foil, and let stand 5 minutes. Uncover and let stand 10 minutes; flavors will develop as it rests.

15 Garnish with roasted peppers and serve.

Espinacas à la Catalana

Spinach Catalan-Style SERVES 4

Catalans enjoy cooking with dried fruits.

AMOUNT	MEASURE	INGREDIENT
2 tablespoons	1 ounce, 30 ml	Olive oil
1 cup	4 ounces, 112 g	Sweet apple (golden delicious), peeled, $\frac{1}{4}$ inch (.6 cm) dice
$\frac{1}{4}$ cup	$\frac{1}{2}$ ounce, 14 g	Pine nuts
$\frac{1}{4}$ cup	1 ounce, 28 g	Dark raisins
5 cups	10 ounces, 280 g	Baby spinach, washed
To taste		Salt and white pepper

PROCEDURE

1 Heat oil over high heat; add apples and brown lightly, about 1 minute.

2 Add pine nuts and cook until they are light brown, 30 seconds, stirring constantly. Add raisins.

3 Add spinach and toss; sauté until it begins to wilt, then remove from heat; it will continue to cook.

4 Correct seasoning and serve.

Pera Salsa de Caramelo al Café

Pears with Caramel-Coffee Sauce SERVES 4

AMOUNT	MEASURE	INGREDIENT
4		Anjou, Bosc, or Comice pears, medium, not too ripe
3 tablespoons		Granulated sugar
2 tablespoons	1 ounce, 28 g	Butter, broken into bits
1 cup	8 ounces, 240 ml	Heavy cream
1 teaspoon		Confectioner's sugar
1 tablespoon		Coffee extract or strong espresso
$\frac{1}{8}$ teaspoon		Vanilla extract

PROCEDURE

1 Preheat oven to 425°F (218°C).

2 Peel and split pears lengthwise, remove seeds, and core.

3 Place flat side down in a gratin dish; do not overlap. Sprinkle with sugar and top with butter.

4 Bake 35 minutes or until tender and sugar has caramelized. Check for tenderness by piercing with the point of a knife. If necessary, cook an additional 5–10 minutes.

5 Add $\frac{3}{4}$ cup (6 ounces, 180 ml) cream, coffee extract or espresso, and continue to cook for 10–15 minutes, basting every 5 minutes. The cream should have reduced to sauce consistency and taken on an ivory color. Remove from oven and cool to lukewarm.

6 Whip remaining cream with confectioner's sugar and vanilla extract.

7 Serve with sauce and whipped cream.

Gazpacho Sevillano

Classic Gazpacho SERVES 4

Chef Tip The original mortar-pounded gazpachos were coarse in texture; modern Spanish cooks prefer a smooth soup.

AMOUNT	MEASURE	INGREDIENT
1 cup	1 ounce, 28 g	Day-old country bread, crust removed, 1 inch (2.5 cm) cubes
1		Garlic clove, minced
Pinch		Ground cumin
To taste		Salt
4 cups	24 ounces, 672 g	Tomatoes, very ripe, peeled, seeded, $\frac{1}{2}$ inch (1.2 cm) dice
1 cup	5 ounces, 140 g	Kirby (pickling) cucumber, peeled, $\frac{1}{2}$ inch (1.2 cm) dice
$\frac{1}{2}$ cup	2 ounces, 56 g	Italian frying pepper, Italianelles or cubanels (long, green peppers, sweet and tender with thin skin), $\frac{1}{4}$ inch (.6 cm) dice
$\frac{1}{2}$ cup	2 ounces, 56 g	Red bell pepper, $\frac{1}{4}$ inch (.6 cm) dice
2 tablespoons	$\frac{1}{2}$ ounce, 14 g	Spanish onion, $\frac{1}{4}$ inch (.6 cm) dice
$\frac{1}{4}$ cup	2 ounces, 60 ml	Olive oil
$\frac{1}{4}$ cup, more if needed	2 ounces, 60 ml	Water
$1\frac{1}{2}$ tablespoons, more to taste	$1\frac{1}{2}$ ounces, 45 ml	Aged sherry vinegar
To taste		Freshly ground pepper
Garnishes		
2 tablespoons	$\frac{1}{2}$ ounce, 14 g	Cucumber, $\frac{1}{8}$ inch (.3 cm) dice
2 tablespoons	$\frac{1}{2}$ ounce, 14 g	Granny Smith apple, $\frac{1}{8}$ inch (.3 cm) dice
2 tablespoons	$\frac{3}{4}$ ounce, 21 g	Underripe tomato, peeled, seeded, $\frac{1}{8}$ inch (.3 cm) dice
2 tablespoons	$\frac{1}{2}$ ounce, 14 g	Green bell pepper, $\frac{1}{8}$ inch (.3 cm) dice
1 tablespoon		Basil, chiffonade

PROCEDURE

1   Cover bread with ice cold water; soak 10 minutes. Drain and squeeze out excess liquid.

2   Mash garlic, cumin, and $\frac{1}{2}$ teaspoon salt with a mortar and pestle.

3   Toss together tomatoes, cucumbers, Italian and red peppers, onion, soaked bread, and garlic paste. Let stand 15 minutes.

4   Using a food processor, process ingredients until smooth; add olive oil while processing.

5   Add water and vinegar, correct seasoning with salt, pepper, and additional vinegar.

6   Cover and chill, 1 hour or more.

7   Serve with garnishes.

Pollo En Pepitoria
Chicken in Almond and Saffron Sauce SERVES 4

AMOUNT	MEASURE	INGREDIENT
1		Chicken (about $2\frac{1}{2}$ pounds; 1.3 kg), cut into 12 pieces, rinsed, patted dry, excess fat trimmed
To taste		Coarse salt and freshly ground black pepper
$\frac{1}{2}$ cup	4 ounces, 120 ml	Olive oil
$\frac{3}{4}$ cup	3 ounces, 84 g	Whole blanched almonds
5		Garlic cloves
6		Whole black peppercorns
$\frac{1}{4}$ cup		Flat-leaf parsley, minced
2 cups	8 ounces, 228	Onion, $\frac{1}{4}$ inch (.6 cm) dice
$1\frac{1}{2}$ inch	1 2.5–5 cm	Cinnamon stick
$\frac{3}{4}$ cup	6 ounces, 180 ml	Dry white wine
$2\frac{1}{4}$ cup	18 ounces, 540 ml	Chicken stock
2 teaspoons		Saffron, pulverized in a mortar and steeped in 3 tablespoons hot water
$\frac{1}{4}$ teaspoon		Ground cloves
$\frac{1}{3}$ cup	1 ounce, 28 g	Lemon slices, paper thin, cut in half, seeds removed
2		Eggs, hard-cooked, yolk and whites separate
$\frac{1}{4}$ cup		Almonds, slivered, toasted

PROCEDURE

1 Season chicken and let stand 10 minutes.

2 Heat oil over medium heat; add whole almonds and cook 2 minutes until lightly colored.

3 Add garlic and cook with almonds until both are golden brown, 2 minutes. Remove from fat onto paper towels to drain, reserve oil.

4 In a mini food processor or mortar, grind almonds, garlic, peppercorns, and $\frac{2}{3}$ of the parley to a paste, set aside.

5 Reheat oil over medium-high heat and brown chicken on all sides, 5–8 minutes. Remove and reserve.

6 Return only two tablespoons of oil to medium-low heat; add onion and cinnamon stick and cook slowly until onions are very soft, 10 minutes.

7 Return chicken to pan, add wine and stock, and bring to simmer over medium-high heat.

8 Add almond paste, saffron, and cloves; cover and reduce heat to medium low and simmer, covered, until chicken is tender, 30 minutes, turning pieces every 10 minutes. At the end of the 30 minutes, stir in lemon slices and cook 10 minutes. Check for tenderness and correct seasoning. Remove chicken pieces and keep hot.

9 Chop egg white for garnish.

10 Mash egg yolks and whisk 3 tablespoons ($1\frac{1}{2}$ ounces, 75 ml) cooking liquid.

11 Return cooking liquid to a boil and reduce to by $\frac{1}{3}$, 2–4 minutes.

12 Stir in mashed egg yolk and cook 3–4 minutes; sauce will thicken somewhat.

13 Return chicken pieces, coat with sauce, and reheat.

14 Serve chicken with sauce on top, garnish with slivered almonds, chopped egg white, and remaining parsley.

Ensalada con Higos, Cabrales, y Granada
Mesclun, Figs, Cabrales, and Pomegranate   SERVES 4

AMOUNT	MEASURE	INGREDIENT
1		Medium-size pomegranate
$\frac{1}{2}$ teaspoon		Honey
$4\frac{1}{2}$ teaspoons	$1\frac{1}{2}$ ounces, 45 ml	Fresh lemon juice
$4\frac{1}{2}$ teaspoons	$1\frac{1}{2}$ ounces, 45 ml	High-quality red wine vinegar
2 tablespoons	$\frac{1}{2}$ ounce, 14 g	Shallots, minced
$\frac{1}{4}$ cup	2 ounces, 60 ml	Olive oil
8		Purple figs, trimmed, quartered lengthwise
4 cups	6 ounces, 168 g	Mesclun, rinsed, dried, loosely packed
$\frac{1}{4}$ cup	1 ounce, 28 g	Pine nuts, toasted
To taste		Coarse salt and freshly ground black pepper
$\frac{1}{3}$ cup	2 ounces, 56 g	Cabrales or other blue cheese, crumbled

PROCEDURE

1 Cut pomegranate into quarters. Remove seeds from 3 of the pieces and place in a bowl; pick out and discarding any membrane.

2 Working over a sieve, press the juice from the remaining pomegranate quarter into a separate bowl. Add honey, lemon juice, vinegar, and shallots; slowly whisk in the olive oil. Correct seasoning.

3 Broil fig quarters cut side up until they look caramelized and lightly charred, 4–5 minutes.

4 Combine figs, pomegranate seeds, mesclun, and toasted pine nuts, toss with dressing, and season with salt and pepper.

5 Toss in cheese and serve.

Merluza en Salsa Verde

Hake in Green Sauce   SERVES 4

If available, use a cazuela that just fits the fish. Cazuelas are terra cotta casserole dishes, and have been used in Spain for thousands of years.

AMOUNT	MEASURE	INGREDIENT
8		Manila clams, medium size
2 tablespoons	I ounce, 30 ml	Olive oil
I		Garlic clove, minced
I teaspoon		All-purpose flour
	12 ounces, 336 g	Hake, skin on, cut into 4 pieces
To taste		Salt
I tablespoon		Flat-leaf parsley, minced
I $\frac{1}{2}$ tablespoons	$\frac{3}{4}$ ounce, 23 ml	Crisp dry white wine

PROCEDURE

1   Bring 1 quart (32 ounces, 960 ml) water to a boil. Add 4 clams at a time and cook 10–15 seconds or until they just open. Remove and repeat with the other four clams. Working over a bowl to collect juices, remove the clams from the shells and discard shells.

2   Heat oil over low heat, add garlic, and cook until it just begins to jump, 45 seconds; do not brown. Add flour.

3   Season fish with salt and place skin side down in pan. Add parsley.

4   Moving pan in a constant circular motion, cook 3 to 4 minutes. Turn fish over and repeat on second side, 3 to 4 minutes. Maintain a low temperature.

5   Add clams, clam juices, and white wine. Cook an additional 3 to 4 minutes; do not boil liquid.

6   The natural gelatins of the fish will emulsify with the oil, making a light green sauce. Correct seasoning and serve 1 piece of fish, 2 clams, and sauce for each portion.

Cerdo Cocido con la Fruta Seca

Braised Pork with Dried Fruit　SERVES 4

AMOUNT	MEASURE	INGREDIENT
2 pounds	896 g	Boneless pork shoulder roast, trimmed of excess fat and tied
To taste		Coarse salt and freshly ground black pepper
2		Garlic cloves, chopped fine
3 tablespoons	$1\frac{1}{2}$ ounce, 45 ml	Olive oil
1 cup	4 ounces, 112 g	Onions, $\frac{1}{4}$ inch (.6 cm) dice
1 cup	4 ounces, 112 g	Carrot, $\frac{1}{4}$ inch (.6 cm) dice
1 cup	4 ounces, 112 g	Pearl onions, peeled
$\frac{1}{4}$ cup	2 ounces, 60 ml	Kirsch or brandy
$1\frac{1}{2}$ cups	10 ounces, 300 ml	Full-bodied dry high-acidity red wine
2 cups	16 ounces, 480ml	Beef or chicken stock
$\frac{3}{4}$ cup	3 ounces, 84 g	Pitted dried sour cherries
$\frac{1}{2}$ cup	2 ounces, 56 g	Dried apricots, quartered
1		Bay leaf
$1\frac{1}{2}$ inch	1 2.5–5 cm	Cinnamon stick
2		Fresh rosemary sprigs
As needed		Saffron rice or boiled potatoes

PROCEDURE

1　Preheat oven to 325°F (162.7°C).

2　Season pork roast with salt and pepper.

3　Heat 2 tablespoons (1 ounce, 30 ml) olive oil over medium-high heat until almost smoking.

4　Add pork and sear to a rich brown color, 8 minutes. Add remaining oil if needed. Transfer to a holding platter.

5　Add diced onions, garlic, carrots, and pearl onions; brown well, 6–7 minutes.

6　Add kirsch and reduce to almost dry, 1 minute.

7   Add wine, stock, cherries, apricots, bay leaf, cinnamon, and rosemary sprigs and bring to a simmer. Return pork to pan. Cover tightly and transfer to oven.

8   Cook until very tender, about 1 hour, turning every 30 minutes.

9   Remove pork from braising liquid; keep warm.

10 Remove and discard bay leaf, cinnamon stick, and rosemary sprigs; bring liquid back to boil and reduce to sauce consistency, 3 to 5 minutes. Correct seasoning.

11 Remove string, slice pork, and serve with the sauce and saffron rice or boiled potatoes.

Arroz con Leche
Rice and Milk   SERVES 4

AMOUNT	MEASURE	INGREDIENT
10 cups	80 ounces, 1.4 l	Milk
1 inch	2.5 cm	Lemon zest
$1\frac{1}{2}$ inch	1 2.5–5 cm	Cinnamon stick
1 cup	$6\frac{1}{4}$ ounces, 175 g	Arborio rice or any short-grain rice
4 tablespoons	2 ounces, 60 ml	Butter
1 cup	7 ounces, 196 g	Granulated sugar

PROCEDURE

1   Combine milk, lemon zest, and cinnamon stick over medium-high heat and bring to a boil.

2   Stir in rice, reduce heat to low, and simmer 30 minutes, stirring constantly so rice does not stick to the bottom of the pan.

3   Add butter and simmer 5 minutes.

4   Add sugar and stir briskly. Remove from heat and spread rice out on a platter. Let rest; as it cools the milk will develop a thin skin on top. Fold back into the rice before serving.

5   Serve at room temperature or cold.

The Middle East

The Land

The Middle East is at the junction of trade routes connecting Europe and China, India and Africa, and all the cultures of the Mediterranean basin. Many of these routes have been documented from as early as five thousand years ago, and the presence of so many different people and products over the years has had a profound effect on the region's culture, politics, and economy. More specifically, the Middle East is a term used to describe the area covering sixteen countries and states: Bahrain, Egypt, Iran, Iraq, Israel, Jordan, Kuwait, Lebanon, Oman, Qatar, Saudi Arabia, Syria, Turkey, United Arab Emirates, West Bank/Gaza Strip, and Yemen. The Middle East region represents an area of over five million square miles.

The physical geography of the Middle East is varied. Vast deserts are common in the region. The Sahara Desert runs across North Africa, essentially limiting settlement to along the Mediterranean coastline and in Egypt along the Nile River. The desert of the Arabian Peninsula is so inhospitable that it has been given the name "Empty Quarter." In areas better served by rainfall and rivers (for example the Tigris-Euphrates river system, the Jordan River, and along the Mediterranean coast), rich agriculture is abundant. Mountain ranges exist throughout the Middle East, with some peaks rising as high as 19,000 feet.

Geography and natural resources have always influenced political power in this region. The Nile River and the rivers of the Mesopotamian region (now modern Iraq, and extending north into Syria and Turkey) can support a rich agricultural base, but only if the water supply is sustained and controlled through irrigation systems. Mesopotamian farmers used Persian Gulf seawater to irrigate for centuries, and, as a result, much of southern Iraq's soil is now too salty to grow crops. Agriculture in the region now relies on modern practices like fresh water irrigation, crop rotation, and technologically sophisticated dam projects.

Today, the wealth in Middle Eastern soil comes not from crops but from petroleum. This region contains about two-thirds of the world's known petroleum reserves. When the United States and Europe increased their consumption of oil drastically during World War II, the oil reserves in the Middle East became critically important to U.S. foreign policy, and have remained so ever since.

History

The Middle East is the most ancient region of human civilization. The rich, fertile soil of the Middle East led early civilizations to settle, domesticate plants and animals, and thrive. The Fertile Crescent between the Tigris and Euphrates Rivers known as Mesopotamia was the home of the world's first urban culture, the Sumer, six thousand years ago. The Sumerians' Egyptian rivals took advantage of the annual flooding of the Nile for their regular harvest, later exporting a large portion of their produce to the Roman Empire. Some time later, the Hittites settled in the rolling hills of Anatolia (modern Turkey) and the Phoenicians off the eastern Mediterranean (modern-day Lebanon, Syria, and northern Israel). Over the years many different great civilizations and cultures developed from or invaded the area. The list of ancient empires includes the Egyptians (c. 2000–1000 B.C.); the Assyrians and Babylonians (c. 1000–500 B.C.); the Persians (c. 550–330 B.C.); and the Romans (c. 60 B.C.–140 A.D.).

During the first millennium B.C. through the middle of the second millennium A.D., a vast network of trade routes known as the Silk Road linked the people and traditions of Asia with those of Europe. These historic routes, covering over five thousand miles of land and sea, were a major conduit for the transport of knowledge, information, and material goods between East and West and resulted in the first global exchange of scientific and cultural traditions.

In modern times the Ottoman Empire (c. 1300–1923) became the largest political entity in Europe and western Asia. The Safavid Empire (1501–1736) dominated the area of modern Iran.

The Middle East has been the center of more than twenty major conflicts from the Persian-Greek Wars to the Crusades to the Iran-Iraq War. After World War I, the decline and disbursement of the Ottoman Empire marked the beginning of a new stage of conflict over territory centering around the lands of Palestine.

While today about 92 percent (292 million) of the people are Muslim, the Middle East is the geographic and emotional center of three of the world's most influential religions: Islam, Christianity, and Judaism.

The Middle East

The People

The people of the Middle East belong to various ethnic groups, which are based largely on culture, language, and history. Ethnically, more than three-fourths of the Middle Eastern people are Arabs. Although they live in different countries, Arabs share a common culture and a common language, Arabic. Iranians and Turks also form major ethnic groups in the region. Smaller groups in the Middle East include Armenians, Copts, Greeks, Jews, Kurds, and various black African groups.

The Food

Originally, Arabic food was the food of the desert nomads—simple and portable. Nomads stopped in oases and settled farming areas to get some of their food, such as flour for bread, fruits, vegetables, and spices. They brought animals with them to provide meat and milk, and they cooked over campfires. During the early Middle Ages, Islamic empires spread from the Atlantic Ocean to India. The world of Islam would continue to expand to other areas of the world in later centuries. It was not uncommon for an exchange of foods from the various territories to occur. As the people settled in villages, towns, and large cities, the food was no longer only that of the desert nomads.

Flat bread was made along the caravan routes and in the nomads' camps. Made from wheat flour, water, and a little salt, the dough can be flattened and shaped by hand and put on a flat pan over a fire. Dates come from the date palm tree, which grows in the hottest desert oases, and are one of the most important foods of the Middle East. Sheep were the most important source of milk, used for cheese and yogurt, and mutton and lamb continue to be the most popular meat in Arabic cuisine. Goats were also raised for meat and milk. Beans and grains such as garbanzo beans, fava beans, and lentils were dried and carried on the nomads' travels. Other dried fruits such as grapes, dried apricots, figs, and nuts were an important part of the diet. Familiar spices and herbs like cinnamon, cloves, black pepper, hot red and green peppers, allspice, ginger, mint, parsley, bay leaves, basil, dill, rosemary, garlic, and onions were and still are used frequently.

It is a shared history, including that of two great world empires, which has brought unity to the kitchens of the Middle East. The spread of Islam and the establishment of an enormous Islamic state stretching across Asia, North Africa, and the Mediterranean was the most important factor in the development of a gastronomic tradition comparable to that of France and China. As the state grew, Arabs brought to each new region their own tastes as well as those of the countries they had already conquered. Cooking styles traveled with the massive migrations of people; large-scale transport brought into the cities, and even into distant parts of the Middle East, local produce from the desert, olive oil from Syria, dates from Iraq, and coffee from Arabia. Crops such as rice, sugar, hard wheat, eggplant, spinach, pomegranates, and even grapes are all part of the Arab heritage. The Ottoman Turks had significant influence in the Balkans, responsible for little cakes called turbans and puff pastry croissants found in the shape of the Turkish crescent. Certain cooking methods, like cooking skewered ingredients over charcoal or long, slow simmering in unglazed covered pots, are typical of the whole region. Skewering meats, chicken, or fish kebabs is believed to have been developed by the Turks on the field of battle.

All the countries have rice and wheat dishes, stuffed vegetables, pies wrapped in paper-thin pastry, meatballs, thick omelets, cold vegetables cooked in oil, scented rice puddings, nut-filled pastries, fritters soaked in syrup, and many other common elements. One of the most important parts of a meal in many parts of the region is the *mezeh*, which can be anything from half a dozen saucers of appetizers to a spread of fifty dishes, a veritable banquet. A basic selection will include raw carrot sticks, radishes, lettuce hearts, cucumber, and green pepper slices along with salted nuts, olives, crumbly goat's cheese, green onions, sprigs of mint and mountain thyme, pickled turnips and peppers, strained yogurt (*labneh*) topped with golden olive oil, and the national specialties: *hummus bi tahini, baba ghannouj*, and *tabbouleh*. In the center, in reach of all, will be a stack of the puffy hollow rounds of flat Arab bread or sheets of the paper-thin mountain bread. Bread is torn to make scoops for the dips and to wrap small pieces of meat and vegetables. It can also serve as a plate, tablecloth, and napkin. *Hummus bi tahini* is a paste of chickpeas flavored with sesame seed oil, lemon juice, and garlic. *Baba ghannouj* is a smoky dip of eggplant that has been charred over a flame and whipped with the same flavorings to a fluffy consistency. These dips are swirled into a saucer and garnished with whole chickpeas, pomegranate seeds, a sprinkling of paprika, or sprigs of cress or mint. *Tabbouleh* is a salad composed of chopped parsley, onions, tomatoes, and mint leaves mixed with softened cracked wheat kernels (bulgur) and dressed with lemon juice and a little oil.

Iranian cuisine is considered to be the most refined. Fragrance during cooking and at the table plays as important a role as taste. Iran was first to use many common herbs such as basil, mint, cumin, cloves, and coriander. The foods of the courts of ancient Persia (as Iran was called until the 1930s) included perfumed stews flavored with cinnamon, mint, and pomegranates; elaborate stuffed fruits and vegetables; and tender roasted meats. Many different foods originated in or were introduced by Iran, such as oranges, pistachios, spinach, saffron, sweet-and-sour sauces, kabobs, and almond pastries. The domesticated goat is believed to have originated in Persia since the goat's ability to subsist in sparse vegetation made it ideal for domestication by nomads. Wheat, barley, and rice are the most important Iranian crops. Long-grain rice, grown in moist areas bordering the Caspian Sea, has a place of honor, often prepared with a golden crust formed from clarified butter, saffron, and yogurt. Lamb and chicken are marinated and grilled as kebabs, or mixed into stews called *khoreshes* with fruit and sour ingredients such as lime juice. Pickles and flatbreads are served at every meal. Desserts feature rose water and pistachios, and refreshing drinks called *sharbats* are made from diluted fruit and herb syrups.

On the Mediterranean shore are the great network of rivers—the Euphrates, Tigris, Orontes, and Jordan—that irrigate the valleys and plains of Syria, Lebanon, Palestine, Jordan, and Iraq. Known as the Fertile Crescent, this region is a vegetarian's paradise, with a seasonal procession of fruits and vegetables, cereals, golden olive oil, and fragrant herbs. Syria, Lebanon, and Jordan have much the same style of cooking. Rice and cracked wheat are the primary grains. Syria's finest food is found in the city of Aleppo. Distinctly local foods are *muhammara*, a spicy paste eaten like *hummus* but made of the city's renowned hot pepper, pomegranate juice, and ground walnuts; a seasonal kebab in a sauce of stewed fresh cherries, called *kababbi-karaz*; and varieties of *kibbe* made with sumac and quince. Aleppo's famous pistachios are used in many sweets—rolled in doughs and smothered with syrup, or embedded in sweet gelatin.

There is a wide variety in the Jordanian style of cooking. The authentic Jordanian cuisine can range from grilling (*shish kababs, shish taouks*) to stuffing of vegetables (grape leaves, eggplants, and so on), meat, and poultry. Also common in the Jordanian style of cooking is roasting, and/or preparing foods with special sauces. Jordan's most distinctive dish is *mansaf,* a Bedouin dish often served for special occasions. *Mansaf* consists of Arabic rice, a rich broth made from dry sour milk (*jameed*), and either lamb or chicken. It is also considered the greatest symbol in Jordanian culture for generosity and the level of generosity is determined by the amount of lamb presented. Utensils are not commonly used when eating *mansaf*. Guests feast from the communal dish using their hands.

Lebanon is nestled along the eastern shore of the Mediterranean Sea at the very crook of the Fertile Crescent. Its contributions to Middle Eastern cuisine are unmistakable. The flavors that spice the foods of all the surrounding lands can be found here in abundance: olive oil, lemon, garlic, and mint. Lebanese cuisine features such staples as *kibbeh* (ground lamb with bulgur wheat) and *tabbouleh*. The food is simply prepared, with the flavors blending together into a complex medley of earthy, fruity tastes and scents.

With so much coastline and varying climatic conditions, Turkey has always had an abundance of fresh produce and fish, making for a varied diet. Turkey's geographical location made it a natural route for traders, travelers, and migrants, all of whom influenced Turkish cuisine. Since the Turkish sultan had complete control over the Spice Road, many spices and seasonings were adapted to flavor traditional dishes. The climatic and geographical differences within the country also heavily influence regional cooking, from desert-like heat in the southeast, where the food tends to be spicier and meat dishes such as kebabs are common, to temperate fertile zones to the west, where seafood and olive oil are frequently used ingredients. Then there is the eastern region, with its long cold winters where dairy, produce, honey, cereals, and meat are popular. Turkey is discussed in more detail in the next chapter.

The modern state of Israel is an ancient land that has been a formal nation only since 1948. Its citizens hail from over eighty countries. It is truly a culinary and ethnic melting pot. The majority of its population arrived from Eastern European countries such as Russia, Poland, and Hungary, and Middle Eastern and North African countries such as Morocco and Syria. There is also a sizable population originally from Greece. Jewish culinary traditions are ancient and strong. From the rituals of the Passover Seder to fasting at Yom Kippur, many of these observances date back to biblical times. Yet while Jews as a people have endured for over three thousand years, the modern state of Israel is still relatively young. That fact, and the uncertainty and instability associated with the Palestinian conflict, have made it difficult for a truly national Israeli cuisine to develop and flourish. Israeli cuisine was formed according to the availability (or lack) of certain foods. Fruits and vegetables are plentiful and are included in virtually every meal. Dairy products, including different types of yogurt and soured milks and creams, are also a major part of the Israeli diet. Red meat is rarely eaten, partly because the lack of quality grazing land for livestock produces a lower grade of meat. Turkey and chicken are a major part of the Israeli diet. *Cholent* is a traditional stew served on the Jewish Sabbath, which is observed from sundown on Friday to sundown on Saturday. Because the oven in a religious home cannot be lit after sundown on Friday, *cholent* simmers overnight in a warm oven turned on before the Sabbath begins. Various types of *cholent* reflect the traditional foods of the different Jewish ethnic groups. Moroccan Jews, for example, use beef, spices, chickpeas, and potatoes, while Sephardic Jews include beans, meat, potatoes, and eggs. *Kugel*, a noodle casserole that is a traditional food among Eastern European Jews, is also a Sabbath favorite because it can be left overnight in a warm oven and be ready for the meal on Saturday.

Another factor that plays a significant role in the Israeli menu is the dietary laws of the Jews and Muslims. Jewish kashrut dietary laws were developed during early times. Food prepared according to these rules is called kosher, or "proper." Jews are prohibited from eating pork, so lamb, mutton, and beef are the preferred meats. The consumption of blood is also forbidden, so meats must be butchered and prepared using a process of salting and curing, in order to remove all traces of blood. Meat and dairy are never mixed in the same dish or even, according to some interpretations, in the same meal. Orthodox homes maintain two separate sets of utensils and dishes, one for meat and one for dairy. The very wealthy may even have two separate kitchens. With regard to seafood, it is forbidden to eat anything without scales. That means no shrimp, shellfish, squid, or octopus. There are varying degrees of adherence to kashrut laws in modern Israel. While one finds strict fidelity among the Orthodox population, it is not uncommon to see only partial or no observation among secular Jews.

Throughout the Mediterranean Middle East, the cultures and people have intermingled, and carried with them their foods and traditions. In no other place in the world is there such a blending of cultures that has mingled so much, yet maintained their distinct, national flavors.

Glossary

Aleppo Pepper Sweet and sharp chile from the Aleppo region of Syria, with moderate heat that doesn't overpower the fruity flavor of the pepper. As a substitute, combine an equal amount of crushed, hot red pepper with Spanish paprika.

Arabic Bread (Khubz Arabi, Pita) Flat, round bread, which can be easily split to make a sandwich, or broken apart and used as a utensil for scooping food.

Ataif (Gatayef, Kataif) Small pancakes stuffed with nuts or cheese and doused with syrup.

Aysh abu Laham Something like pizza, made from leavened dough, egg-rich and flavored with seeds of fennel, and black caraway. It is baked in the shape of a thick-bottomed pie shell, filled with fried mutton, chopped *kurrath*, or spring onion, and topped with a sauce made from tahina (Saudi Arabia).

Baba Ghanoush (Baba Ganouj or Baba Gannoujh) A puree of char-grilled eggplant, *tahina*, olive oil, lemon juice, and garlic, served as a dip.

Baharat (Bjar) Arabic mixed spices; in Egypt a mixture of ground cinnamon, allspice, and cloves often used with meat. In Morocco, a mixture of ground cinnamon and rosebuds.

Baklawa (Baklava) Dessert of layered pastry filled with nuts and steeped in honey-lemon syrup. Usually cut into triangular or diamond shapes.

Bukhari Rice Lamb and rice stir-fried with onion, lemon, carrot, and tomato paste.

Bulgur Also known as *bulghur, burghul, bulger, bulgar, wheat groats* (Arabic, Armenian, Turkish, British), kernels of whole wheat are steamed, dried, and then crushed to make bulgur. The process involved to make bulgur is what gives it a fine, nutty flavor. It requires no or little cooking; it is typically used in tabbouleh and mixed with lamb in kibbeh.

Cardamom Aromatic spice, used to flavor Arabic coffee, yogurt, and stews. Cardamom is an essential ingredient in that ubiquitous symbol of Arab hospitality, coffee. In the Arabian Peninsula, coffee is usually a straw-colored brew, made from lightly roasted beans, lavishly perfumed and flavored with crushed, large green cardamom pods, and served unsweetened in miniature handleless cups in a stream of generosity that ends only when the guest's thirst is satisfied. As it is one of the world's most expensive spices, cardamom's generous use is intended as an honor. In addition, coffee brewed from dark-roasted beans, and usually prepared with sugar, is drunk occasionally. That brew is sometimes spiced with a little ground cardamom seed as well. Cardamom is not limited to coffee; its pleasant, camphor-like flavor combines well with any food or beverage, hot or cold. The seedpods, slightly crushed, are a standard spice in the traditional Arabian dish *kabsah*, a lamb-and-rice stew, and it is a common ingredient in fruit desserts. Native to southern India, the spice traveled the short distance to the Arabian Peninsula along the Silk Road. The plant is a member of the ginger family, grows to a height of six to eight feet, and produces its aromatic seed pods on curly panicles at its base.

Chai Black tea brewed with selected spices and milk. Each ingredient adds subtle flavor changes and brewing methods vary widely.

Chelo Cooked (steamed) rice.

Chelo Kebah Rice, grilled marinated lamb, egg yolk, spices, and yogurt. National dish of Iran.

Cheeses

> **Akawi or Akawieh** Made from sheep's milk, with complex flavor. It is a hard cheese used primarily as a table cheese.

> **Baladi** Soft-white, smooth, creamy cheese with a mild flavor. Eaten for breakfast as well as snacks with fresh bread or crackers.

> **Feta** Curd cheese that dates back thousands of years and is still made by shepherds in the Greek mountains with unpasteurized milk. Originally made with goat's or sheep's milk, but today much is often made commercially with pasteurized cow's milk. The milk, curdled with rennet, is separated and allowed to drain in a special mold or a cloth bag. It is cut into large slices (feta means "slice") that are salted and packed in barrels filled with whey or brine, for a week to several months. Feta cheese is white, usually formed into square cakes, and can range from soft to semi-hard, with a tangy, salty flavor that can range from mild to sharp. Its fat content can range from 30 to 60 percent; most is around 45 percent milk fat.

Halloumi A mild-flavored, creamy-tasting chewy textured cheese that is most often served cooked. Halloumi is usually made with sheep's milk and may be flavored with mint.

Jibneh Arabieh A simple cheese found all over the Middle East. It is particularly popular in Egypt and the Arabian Gulf area. The cheese has an open texture and a mild taste. The heritage of the product started with Bedouins, using goat's or sheep's milk; however, current practice is to use cow's milk to make the cheese. *Jibneh Arabieh* is used for cooking, or simply as a table cheese.

Kenafa An unsalted, very fresh, soft cheese that melts easily and freely. It is used to make the popular *knafe*. It can also be used as a base for other sweet cheese desserts.

Labane A cheese shaped into small balls, very popular in the Middle East. Made of sheep's or goat's milk and is eaten young, almost liquid in form.

Labenah (Labneh) Thick creamy cheese, made from sheep's or goat's milk, made by draining soured milk or yogurt. Soft texture and a tangy flavor, often spiced and used as a dip.

Naboulsi A salty, fresh, brined cheese popular in Syria, Lebanon, and Jordan. The cheese is packed in brine.

Testouri From Egypt shaped like an orange, made from sheep's or goat's milk, eaten fresh and lightly salted. This cheese was introduced into North Africa by the Ottomans after the fifteenth century.

Tzfatit A delicate, salty cheese. One of Israel's most popular cheeses, its flavor is especially delectable when served with slices of fresh vegetables, olive oil, and herbs such as zatar.

Coriander (Cilantro) Lacy, green-leaf relative of the parsley family with an extremely pungent flavor akin to a combination of lemon, sage, and caraway.

Couscous Small, grainlike semolina pasta.

Dibbis Date syrup, an Iraqi sweetening agent made by boiling dates and draining. Resembles thick brown molasses.

Dried Limes Lends a bright tang to stews, some varieties of *kabsah*, and fish dishes. The limes may be used whole and fished out of the dish before serving, or pounded to a fine powder. To make your own dried limes, boil the small round variety of lime vigorously for a few minutes, then dry them in a sunny or otherwise dry and warm place for several weeks until they turn brown and feel hollow.

Falafel Small deep-fried patties made of highly spiced ground chickpeas.

Fatayer Pastry pockets filled with spinach, meat, or cheese.

Fattoush A salad of toasted croutons, cucumbers, tomatoes, and mint.

Fenugreek Leaves Leaves with a pleasant bitter flavor, used fresh or dried, used in soups and stews (Iran; *shambabileh* in Persian).

Fillo Consists of thin sheets of unleavened flour dough. They are layered with butter and baked to make flaky pies and pastries. The layers of fillo dough can be as thin as paper or a millimeter or so thick. Fillo is used in many of the cuisines of the former Ottoman Empire. (*Phyllo* to the Greeks and *yufka* to the Turks.)

Gyros (Sandwich) Meat cooked on a rotisserie, sliced in thin shavings and served traditionally with tomatoes, onions, and tzatziki in pita or plain bread.

Halwa (Halva) Sesame paste; sweet, usually made in a slab and studded with fruit and nuts.

Hamour Red Sea fish from the grouper family.

Hummus (Hommus) Spreadable paste made of chickpeas, tahini, lemon juice, and garlic.

Jarish Crushed wheat and yogurt casserole.

Kabsa Classic Arabian dish of meat mixed with rice.

Kamareddine Apricot nectar used to break the fast during Ramadan.

Kebab Skewered chunks of meat or poultry cooked over charcoal or broiled.

Khubz Marcook Thin, dome-shaped Arabic bread.

Kibbeh (Kibbe) The national dish of Syria, Lebanon, and Jordan; there are countless versions, some widely known throughout the Middle East. It always involves a mixture of minced lamb, grated onion, and fine-ground bulgur pounded to a paste.

Kibbeh Naye Raw *kibbeh*, eaten like steak tartar.

Kofta Fingers, balls, or a flat cake of minced meat and spices. May be baked or charcoal-grilled on skewers. The word *kofta* is derived from the Persian word *kūfta*, meaning "meatball."

Kouzi Whole lamb baked over rice so that the rice absorbs the juice of the meat.

Kunafi (Kunafah) Shoelace-like pastry dessert stuffed with sweet white cheese, nuts, and syrup.

Lahma Bi Ajeen Arabic pizza.

Ma'amul Date cookies shaped in a wooden mould called a *tabi*.

Mahlab Spice obtained from the dark kernels inside the pits of small wild black cherry trees. It has been used for centuries in the Middle East as a sweet/sour, nutty addition to breads, cookies, and pastries.

Kosher and Halal

Kosher and halal describe what is "fit and proper" to eat for two groups of people, Jews and Muslims, according to religious law. Although these terms are used to describe a wide array of foods and beverages that are acceptable to eat, the most significant laws refer to meat. Both of these food laws have their roots in Old Testament scripture, and Torah for kosher and the Quran for halal.

	KOSHER	HALAL
Blessing of animals	Blessing before entering slaughtering area, not of each animal	Blessing of each animal while slaughtering
Preparation of meat	Soaked and salted to drain all blood	No special preparation; blood drained during slaughtering
Gelatin	From kosher animals	From halal bones only
Dry bones	From kosher animals	From halal animals only
Fish	From kosher fish only	From any fish
Pork	Pork is forbidden	Pork is forbidden
Fish and other seafood	Permitted except fish that do not have fins and scales (e.g., catfish, eels, rays, sharks, swordfish) shellfish (e.g., oysters, clams), crustaceans (e.g., crab, lobster), and mollusks (e.g., scallops) not permitted	Permitted
Alcohol	Permitted, except for grape derivatives such as wine, brandy, or some liqueurs; alcohol must be certified kosher before permitted	Not permitted
Combining dairy and meat products	Not permitted	Permitted
Special occasions	Additional restrictions during Passover	Same rules apply all the time

Mastic The resin exuded from the bark of a small evergreen shrub closely related to the pistachio tree; it is best known in the West today for its use in such products as varnish and paint, but cooks in Arabia continue their centuries-old custom of enjoying its unique, fresh, resinous aroma and flavor in meat soups and stews and in puddings. Mastic melts into the food rather than dissolving, so it is best to pulverize the translucent light-yellow lumps before adding them. Mastic is one of the many ingredients used in the popular *shawurma*, an elaborate construction of marinated meat, fat, and flavors, which rotates on a vertical spit placed close to a fire.

Mehshi Means *stuffed*. Eggplant, zucchini, vine leaves, or cabbage may be stuffed with a mixture of minced meat, rice, and onions.

Melokhiyyah Green spinachlike vegetable.

Mezze (Mezza, Meze, Mezzah) The Arabic word for appetizer (small plates).

Mouhammara A mixture of groundnuts, olive oil, cumin, and chiles, eaten with Arabic bread.

Moutabe Eggplant dip made with tahini, olive oil, and lemon juice.

Mutabak Sweet or savory pastry turnovers usually stuffed with cheese, banana, or meat.

Nutmeg The seed of a large evergreen tree native to the Spice Islands (the Moluccas) of what is now Indonesia. The fleshy yellow, peach-like fruit of this tree splits open when ripe, revealing the nutmeg encased in a dark-brown shell, which in turn is wrapped in a bright red net, or aril; this aril is the spice mace. Nutmeg has long been in popular use in Middle Eastern cuisine, as in the rest of the world, both as a flavoring and a medicine; however, its medicinal properties have caused it to be classified officially as a drug and it is therefore banned in Saudi Arabia today. Very large quantities of nutmeg can produce hallucinations followed by ferocious headaches, and an overdose can be lethal.

Orange-Blossom Water *(Mai Qedda)* Produced from the blossom of the sour-orange tree, it contributes a delicate perfume to syrups and pastries.

Pomegranate Seeds The juicy, shiny pink seeds of the fresh fruit, used as garnish.

Pomegranate Syrup (Molasses or Concentrate) Made from the juice of sour (not sweet) pomegranates boiled down to thick syrup. Prominent in Iranian and Syrian cooking.

Rakwi Long-handled coffee pot.

Rose water *(Mai Ward)* Distilled essence of rose petals, used to scent syrups and pastries. Rosewater is one of the earliest distilled products ever made, and its manufacture has been an important industry in the Middle East for about 1,200 years. Rosewater and orange-blossom water are added to food simply for the pleasure their fragrance gives, rather than for flavor.

Saffron The highly prized red saffron threads are the pistils of a particular purple crocus grown in Iran, Kashmir, and Spain. Saffron is used in a variety of ways in Persian and Moroccan cooking. This spice, the world's most expensive, is made up of the stigmas of an autumn-flowering crocus native to the Middle East. The stigmas and parts of their styles are dried to brittle red threads, which, when ground, yield a yellow powder. Each flower has only three tiny stigmas, and as many as 80,000 flowers are needed to produce a pound of spice. Most of the saffron in trade today comes from Spain, where it was introduced by the Arabs in the eighth or ninth century.

Sahlab (Salep) The root tuber of a type of orchid used in powder form to thicken milk and flavor hot drinks and ice cream. *Sahlab* is very expensive.

Sambusek (Sambusak) Triangular pies filled with meat, cheese, or spinach.

Samneh (Ghee) Ghee is the classic shortening of India and the Middle East. It is simple to make and it keeps forever even in the hot climate. In the Middle East it is called samneh. The solids are removed from butter.

Seleek Meat and rice dish in which the rice is cooked in milk rather than the juice of the meat.

Sesame Seeds The pale, small seeds of a tall herb grown in many parts of the Middle East are extremely important to the cuisine of the region. The seeds are pressed to extract a high-quality oil; lightly toasted; they add their nutty flavor to a large number of breads and pastries, or provide a tasty coating for sweet Medina dates stuffed with almonds. *Tahini*, a paste made from sesame, is mixed with mashed chickpeas, garlic, and lemon juice to make *hummus*. Sesame seeds mixed with honey are a nutritious, sweet snack. The seed pods of this plant (except for modern commercial varieties) burst open suddenly and forcefully when the seeds are ripe, scattering them widely.

Shaour Red Sea fish from the emperor family.

Shawarma (Shawerma) A cone of layered pressed lamb, chicken, or beef roasted on a vertical spit where the meat is shaved off from the outside as the spit keeps turning. Saudi Arabia's most popular sandwich is Arabic bread filled with *shawarma* meat, salad, hot sauce, and tahina.

Shaybah Also known as "old man's beard," a tree lichen found in the Arabian Peninsula whose complex, bitter, metallic flavor is popular in meat and vegetable stews. A small piece of curly black-and-silver lichen will flavor a large pot of stew.

Shourba Soup.

Sumac (Sumac) A dark, wine-colored spice with an astringent sour flavor, made from the coarsely ground dried berries of the sumac shrub. Iranians, Iraqis, Lebanese, and Syrians use it frequently. It is often sprinkled on kebabs, salads, and fish dishes. Powdered dark-red *sumac* berries provide a pleasant lemony spice that tastes especially good on meats such as shish kebabs. Although it is produced by a small Mediterranean/Persian tree related to the poisonous sumac of North America, and it is sometimes used in tanning leather, the acid of these berries is in no way harmful. Sumac was mentioned nearly two thousand years ago in the writing of Dioscorides, a Greek physician serving in the Roman army, as having healthful properties; Dioscorides says it was "sprinkled among sauces" and mixed with meat. Modern-day eaters find it excellent on pizza. Sumac is also generally considered an essential ingredient in the spice mixture *za'tar*.

Tabbouleh A salad of bulgur, tomato, mint, and parsley.

Tahini An oily paste made from ground sesame seeds. It is used raw, in dips and salads, and cooked, in sauces.

Tahrini A brass coffee grinder.

Taklia A spice consisting of ground coriander and garlic.

Tamarind (Tamarhendi) The name is derived from the Arabic for "Indian date." The pulp of the long brown seed pods of the tamarind tree yields an extremely viscous syrup with a distinctive sour flavor that is excellent in vegetables, meat, and fish dishes. Tamarind syrup makes a delicious and refreshing cold drink, prepared like lemonade with water and sugar. This spice is not as exotic in the West as it may seem at first; tamarind is an ingredient in Worcestershire sauce.

Tamr Dates.

Taratour A thick mayonnaise (water emulsified) of pureed pine nuts, garlic, and lemon, used as a sauce or dip.

Turmeric The rhizome or underground stem of a ginger-like plant, almost always available ground into a bright yellow, fine powder. Turmeric is used extensively in the East and Middle East as a condiment and culinary dye. It has an earthy and slightly acrid bouquet; its flavor is warm and aromatic with a bitter undertone.

Tzatziki Strained yogurt and cucumbers seasoned with onion and garlic.

Um Ali "Ali's mother" is a pastry pudding with raisins and coconut steeped in milk.

Zattar (Zahtar) Wild thyme. It is also the name of a mixture of this herb with sumac, salt, and toasted sesame seeds. It is made by combining 1 part ground dried thyme, 1 part lightly toasted sesame seeds, $\frac{1}{4}$ part sumac, and salt to taste.

Zereshk Called barberries in English, these are tart red berries used dried in Persian cooking.

Menus and Recipes from the Middle East

Hummus Bi Tahini
Chickpea and Sesame Dip   YIELD: 3 CUPS

AMOUNT	MEASURE	INGREDIENT
2 cups	14 ounces, 392 g	Garbanzos (chickpeas), cooked, separated from their skins; drained and rinsed if canned
$\frac{1}{3}$ cup	2.66 ounces, 80 ml	Tahini
$\frac{1}{2}$ cup	4 ounces, 120 ml	Fresh lemon juice
2		Garlic cloves, crushed
To taste		Salt
For serving		
1 tablespoon	$\frac{1}{2}$ ounce, 15 ml	Olive oil
1 teaspoon		Parsley, chopped
Sprinkle		Cayenne pepper or paprika

PROCEDURE

1   Combine garbanzos (reserve 1 tablespoon), tahini, $\frac{1}{4}$ cup (2 ounces, 60 ml) lemon juice, and garlic in a food processor using a metal blade. Process until thick and smooth. Adjust flavor with lemon juice and salt. Adjust consistency with a little water.

2   Serve in a shallow dish, swirling with back of spoon to cover the dish. Pour olive oil in the center, garnish with reserved chickpeas, chopped parsley, and a sprinkling of paprika or cayenne.

Fatayer Sbanikh

Triangle Spinach Pies   YIELD: ABOUT 15 TRIANGLES

AMOUNT	MEASURE	INGREDIENT
Dough		
1½ teaspoons	8 g	Dry yeast
1 cup	8 ounces, 240 ml	Warm water
1 teaspoon	5 g	Salt
4 cups	16 ounces, 448 g	All-purpose flour
½ cup	4 ounces, 120 ml	Olive oil
Spinach Filling		
6 cups	12 ounces, 336 g	Fresh spinach, leaves and small stems, washed
3 tablespoons	1½ ounces, 45 ml	Olive oil
½ cup	2 ounces, 48 g	Onion, ⅛ inch (.3 cm) dice
¼ cup	1 ounce, 28 g	Pine nuts or chopped walnuts
1 tablespoon	15 g	Sumac*
2 tablespoons	1 ounce, 30 ml	Fresh lemon juice
¼ teaspoon		Nutmeg
To taste		Salt and freshly ground black pepper

*If not using the sumac, increase lemon juice to taste.

PROCEDURE

Dough

1   Soak yeast in warm water for 5 minutes.

2   Combine salt and flour.

3   Add oil to water and yeast mixture; stir to combine.

4   Make a well in the center of the flour mixture and gradually add yeast mixture, combining as you add the liquid.

5   Knead for 10 to 15 minutes until the dough is soft and not sticky.

6   Cover and let rise in a warm place 1 to 1½ hours or until double in size.

Spinach Filling

1　Chop spinach finely.

2　Cook spinach in a dry nonreactive deep pan, uncovered, until wilted and almost dry, about 4 minutes. Stir often.

3　When wilted, turn into a colander and press with the back of a spoon to remove as much moisture as possible.

4　Heat olive oil over medium heat and cook onion until transparent, 2 minutes.

5　Add spinach and cook 2 to 3 minutes longer.

6　Add pine nuts, lemon juice, and seasoning. Cook an additional 5 minutes or until moisture has evaporated. Cool.

7　Punch down dough and roll out on a lightly floured board until $\frac{1}{4}$ inch (.6 cm) thick. Cut into 4 inch (10.2 cm) squares; cover any unused dough.

8　Place a tablespoon of spinach filling in center of each square and fold corner to corner and pinch tightly. Press edges firmly with fingertips to seal pies completely.

9　Place close together on lightly oiled baking pans and brush each parcel with additional olive oil. Bake in a 350°F (180°C) preheated oven 10 to 15 minutes or until golden brown.

10　Serve hot or warm.

Tabbouleh
Cracked Wheat and Herb Salad   SERVES 4

AMOUNT	MEASURE	INGREDIENT
$\frac{1}{2}$ cup	3.5 ounces, 98 g	Bulgur wheat, fine
$1\frac{1}{4}$ cups	10 ounces, 300 ml	Cold water
$1\frac{1}{4}$ cups	2.25 ounces, 63 g	Flat-leaf parsley, coarsely chopped
$\frac{1}{2}$ cup	2 ounces, 48 g	Green onions, coarsely chopped
$\frac{1}{4}$ cup	1 ounce, 28 g	Mint, coarsely chopped
$2\frac{1}{2}$ tablespoons	1.5 ounces, 45 ml	Olive oil
$1\frac{1}{2}$ tablespoons	$\frac{3}{4}$ ounce, 23 ml	Fresh lemon juice
1 teaspoon	5 g	Salt
$\frac{1}{2}$ teaspoon	3 g	Black pepper, freshly ground
$\frac{1}{2}$ cup	3 ounces, 84 g	Tomato, peeled, seeded $\frac{1}{4}$ inch (.6 cm) dice
4		Romaine leaves
$\frac{1}{4}$ cup	2 ounces, 60 ml	Fresh lemon juice
$\frac{1}{2}$ teaspoon		Salt

PROCEDURE

1   Cover bulgur with cold water; soak 30 minutes. Drain through a fine sieve, pressing with back of a spoon to extract moisture. Spread out on a lined pan to dry further.

2   Wash parsley, shake off excess, and remove thick stalks. Wrap in cheesecloth and refrigerate for 30 minutes to dry and crisp.

3   Combine dry bulgur and green onions; squeeze mixture so bulgur absorbs onion flavor.

4   Chop parsley, measure, and add to bulgur with mint.

5   Combine olive oil, $1\frac{1}{2}$ tablespoons ($\frac{3}{4}$ ounce, 23 ml) lemon juice, 1 teaspoon (5 g) salt, and black pepper; add to bulgur and toss well.

6   Gently stir in tomato; cover and chill 1 hour or more.

7   Serve with romaine. Combine remaining lemon juice and salt to serve on the side, to be added according to individual taste.

Khobz
Whole Wheat Flat Bread   YIELD: 6 ROUNDS

Whole wheat: Whole grains that have been milled to a finer texture rather than leaving the grain intact become whole wheat. Whole wheat contains all the components of the grain, so whole wheat foods are also whole grain. Whole wheat bread and rye bread are typical examples of products made with whole wheat.

AMOUNT	MEASURE	INGREDIENT
1½ cups	6 ounces, 168 g	Whole wheat flour
½ teaspoon	3 g	Salt
½ cup		Tepid water
As needed		Oil

PROCEDURE

1   Combine flour and salt.

2   Add water and work to a soft dough.

3   Knead for 10 minutes. Dough will feel slightly sticky at first but will become smooth as it is kneaded.

4   Cover and rest for at least 2 hours.

5   Divide dough into 6 even-sized balls the size of a large egg; roll out to 6-inch (15 cm) diameter rounds. Dough should be shaped without flour; dust lightly with white flour if needed.

6   Cover and rest rounds 20 minutes.

7   Heat a heavy frying pan or flat griddle. Cooking surface is hot enough when a little water sprinkled on bounces off the surface. Rub surface with a little oil.

8   Put in a round of dough and cook for about 1 minute, pressing top lightly with a folded cloth to encourage even bubbling of dough. When browned on the first side, turn and cook 1 minute or until bread looks cooked.

9   As breads are cooked, wrap in a cloth to keep soft and warm. Rub cooking surface occasionally with oil.

Kukuye Mohi
Fish Omelet   SERVES 4

AMOUNT	MEASURE	INGREDIENT
12 ounces	336 g	**White fish fillets, skinless, boneless**
1 teaspoon	5 g	**Salt**
$\frac{1}{4}$ cup	2 ounces, 60 ml	**Samneh (clarified butter)**
$\frac{1}{2}$ cup	3 ounces, 84 g	**Onion, $\frac{1}{4}$ inch (.6 cm) dice**
$\frac{1}{2}$ teaspoon	3 g	**Turmeric**
1 tablespoon	5 g	**Coriander leaves, finely chopped**
1 tablespoon	15 g	**All-purpose flour**
4		**Large eggs**
To taste		**Black pepper, freshly ground**

PROCEDURE

1   Preheat oven to 350°F (180°C).

2   Salt fish fillet and let sit 10 minutes.

3   Heat half the samneh over medium heat and sauté fish until cooked; fish does not have to brown. Remove, flake with a fork, and remove all bones.

4   In the same pan, add the onions and cook 3 minutes until transparent. Stir in turmeric and cook 2 minutes. Mix into fish with coriander and flour.

5   Beat eggs well with a pinch of salt. Add to fish mixture and season with pepper.

6   Heat remaining samneh in an 8-inch (20 cm) nonstick cake pan or casserole dish; swirl to coat base and sides.

7   Pour in egg mixture and bake in preheated oven for 30 minutes. Top should be slightly brown.

8   Unmold onto serving platter and serve hot or cold, cut into wedges.

Bamia Lamb and Okra Casserole

SERVES 4

AMOUNT	MEASURE	INGREDIENT
2 tablespoons	1 ounce, 30 ml	Samneh (clarified butter)
12 ounces	336 g	Boneless stewing lamb, $1\frac{1}{4}$ inch (3 cm) dice
$\frac{3}{4}$ cup	4 ounces, 112 g	Onion, $\frac{1}{8}$ inch (.3 cm) dice
$\frac{1}{2}$ teaspoon	2 g	Cumin, ground
$\frac{2}{3}$ cup	4 ounces, 112 g	Tomato, peeled, seeded, $\frac{1}{4}$ inch (.6 cm) dice
1 tablespoon	$\frac{1}{2}$ ounce, 14 g	Tomato paste
$\frac{1}{2}$ cup	4 ounces, 120 ml	Lamb, beef, or chicken stock
To taste		Salt and black pepper
$\frac{1}{2}$ teaspoon	2 g	Granulated sugar
12 ounces	336 g	Fresh okra
1 tablespoon	$\frac{1}{2}$ ounce, 15 ml	Samneh (clarified butter)
As needed		Ta'leya I (recipe follows)

PROCEDURE

1 Heat 2 tablespoons samneh over medium heat and brown meat on all sides. Transfer to another container as meat browns.

2 Reduce heat and add onions to the same pan the meat was browned in and cook 2 to 3 minutes until transparent. Add cumin, tomatoes, tomato paste, and cook 1 minute.

3 Add stock and stir well to collect browned sediment.

4 Return meat to pan, correct seasoning, and add sugar.

5 Cover and cook in a moderately slow oven or on top of stove for $1\frac{1}{2}$ hour or until meat is almost tender.

6 Prepare okra, remove stem, leave whole.

7 Heat remaining samneh (clarified butter) over medium heat and sauté okra 3 minutes, tossing as needed.

8 Arrange okra on top of meat; cover and cook until okra and meat are tender.

9 Prepare ta'leya and pour while hot over bamia. Serve at the table from the cooking dish.

Muaddas Rice with Lentils SERVES 4

AMOUNT	MEASURE	INGREDIENT
1 cup	7 ounces, 196 g	Basmati (quality long-grain) rice
$\frac{1}{2}$ cup	3.5 ounces, 98 g	Brown or green lentils
2 tablespoons	1 ounce, 30 ml	Samneh (clarified butter)
$\frac{1}{2}$ cup	2 ounces, 56 g	Onion, $\frac{1}{4}$ inch (.6 cm) dice
2 cups	16 ounces, 480 ml	Boiling water
1 teaspoon	5 g	Salt

PROCEDURE

1 Pick over rice and wash in several changes of cold water until water runs clear. Drain well.

2 Pick over lentils to remove small stones and discolored seeds. Put in a bowl of water and remove any that float. Wash lentils well and drain thoroughly.

3 In a heavy, deep pan heat the samneh over medium high heat and sauté the onions until transparent and lightly browned.

4 Add rice and lentils; cook 3 to 4 minutes, stirring often.

5 Add boiling water and salt; return to a boil, stirring occasionally. Reduce heat to low, cover pan, and simmer gently 25 to 30 minutes.

6 Remove cover and cook 5 minutes longer. Fluff the rice with a fork and serve.

Ta'leya I: Garlic Sauce

AMOUNT	MEASURE	INGREDIENT
4		Garlic cloves
$\frac{1}{2}$ teaspoon	3 g	Salt
2 tablespoons	1 ounce, 30 ml	Samneh (clarified butter)
1 teaspoon		Coriander, ground
Pinch		Hot chile pepper

PROCEDURE

1 Crush garlic with salt in a mortar to make a garlic paste.

2 Heat samneh in a small pan and add garlic. Cook, stirring constantly, until golden brown; remove pan from heat and stir in coriander and pepper. Use while sizzling hot.

Khoshaf Dried Fruit Compote

SERVES 4

AMOUNT	MEASURE	INGREDIENT
$\frac{3}{4}$ cup	3 ounces, 84 g	Prunes, pitted, coarse chopped
$\frac{3}{4}$ cup	3 ounces, 84 g	Dried apricots, coarse chopped
$\frac{3}{4}$ cup	3 ounces, 84 g	Sultanas (white raisins)
As needed		Water to cover
$\frac{1}{3}$ cup	2.3 ounces, 9.4 g	Granulated sugar
1		Thin strip of lemon rind
2		Cloves
$\frac{1}{4}$ teaspoon		Allspice, ground
2 tablespoons	$\frac{1}{2}$ ounce, 14 g	Walnuts, chopped

PROCEDURE

1 Wash dried fruits well.

2 Place in a pan with cold water just to cover. Bring to boil, reduce to simmer, and cook over low heat 15 minutes.

3 Add sugar, lemon rind, and spices. Stir to dissolve and add water if necessary. Simmer gently, uncovered, until fruit is soft but not mushy, and syrup is thick. Remove lemon rind and whole spices.

4 Chill well before serving. Serve in dessert glasses sprinkled with chopped nuts.

Qahwah Arabic Coffee

SERVES 4

Chef Tip Cardamom has a very strong flavor, and too much of it can cause a soapy taste.

AMOUNT	MEASURE	INGREDIENT
1		Cardamom pods
1 cup	8 ounces, 240 ml	Water
$\frac{1}{4}$ cup	$\frac{1}{2}$ ounce, 14 g	Dark roast ground coffee beans

PROCEDURE

1 Bruise cardamom pods.

2 Combine all ingredients and bring to boil.

3 Serve in Arabic coffee cups, half filled.

Traditionally a little silver urn of rose water or orange blossom water accompanies the coffee, so a few drops may be added to individual taste. Sugar is not generally served.

Borani Chogondar
Beet and Yogurt Salad

SERVES 4

Chef Tip To make drained yogurt, place yogurt in cheesecloth, tie with string, and suspend from a fixed object over a receptacle to collect draining liquid. Hang for 2 to 4 hours, depending on initial thickness of yogurt. When drained, yogurt should have the consistency of softened cream cheese.

AMOUNT	MEASURE	INGREDIENT
I pound	448 g	Beets, mixed red and golden, if available
I $\frac{1}{2}$ cups	12 ounces, 360 ml	Drained yogurt
To taste		Salt and pepper
To taste		Vinegar or fresh lemon juice (optional)
I tablespoon		Fresh mint, chopped
For garnish		Fresh mint leaves

PROCEDURE

1   Preheat oven to 400°F (205°C).

2   Rinse beets, leaving on roots and 1 inch (2.5 cm) of stems. Bake, covered, with $\frac{1}{4}$ inch (.6 cm) water, 25 to 40 minutes or until beets can be easily pierced with a knife. Cool.

3   When the beets are cool enough to handle, peel and dice $\frac{1}{2}$ inch (1.3 cm).

4   Reserve about $\frac{1}{4}$ cup (2 ounces, 60 ml) diced beets. Mix remainder into yogurt with salt and pepper to taste. Sharpen the flavor with vinegar or lemon if desired.

5   Blend in mint; cover and chill.

6   Serve garnished with reserved beets and mint leaves.

Falafel Dried Bean Croquettes

YIELD: ABOUT 35 CROQUETTES

Chef Tip Favas have a wonderful flavor, but if you can't find them, dried white beans, such as cannellini or navy, can be substituted.

AMOUNT	MEASURE	INGREDIENT
I cup	6 ounces, 168 g	Fava beans (broad beans), dried and shelled, soaked overnight and drained
I cup	6 ounces, 168 g	Garbanzo beans (chickpeas), dried, soaked overnight, and drained
$\frac{1}{2}$ cup	2 ounces, 56 g	Onion, $\frac{1}{4}$ inch (.6 cm) dice
2		Garlic cloves
$\frac{1}{2}$ cup	I ounce, 28 g	Flat-leaf parsley, finely chopped
2 tablespoons	6 g	Cilantro leaves, finely chopped
$\frac{1}{8}$ teaspoon		Hot chile pepper, ground
I teaspoon	4 g	Coriander, ground
$\frac{1}{2}$ teaspoon	2 g	Cumin, ground
I teaspoon	4 g	Baking soda
To taste		Salt and freshly ground black pepper
		Oil for deep-frying
As needed		Taratour bi tahini (recipe follows)
As needed		Khoubiz (Arabic flat bread; see recipe on page 438)

PROCEDURE

1. Combine fava beans, chickpeas, onion, and garlic and grind twice in food grinder using a fine die, or process in food processor to form a coarse paste.

2. Combine with remaining ingredients except oil and tahini. Knead well and let rest for 30 minutes. Correct seasoning.

3. Shape a tablespoon of the mixture at a time into balls, then flatten into thick patties $1\frac{1}{2}$ inches (4 cm) in diameter. Let rest 30 minutes at room temperature.

4. Deep-fry in two inches of oil at 375°F (190°C), 6 to 8 at a time; cook 4 to 5 minutes, turning to brown evenly. Falafel should be toasty brown and crunchy on the outside. Remove and drain on a paper towel.

5. Serve hot as an appetizer with taratour bi tahini or in split khoubiz with the same sauce and salad vegetables.

Taratour bi Tahini   YIELD: ABOUT 1½ CUPS

AMOUNT	MEASURE	INGREDIENT
2		Garlic cloves, crushed with ½ teaspoon salt
½ cup	4 ounces, 120 ml	Tahini
¼–½ cup	2–4 ounces, 60–120 ml	Cold water
½ cup	4 ounces, 120 ml	Fresh lemon juice
To taste		Salt

PROCEDURE

1   Using a food processor, combine garlic and tahini until smooth.

2   Beat in a little water and lemon juice alternately. The water thickens the mixture; lemon juice thins it.

3   Add all the lemon juice and enough water to give a thin or thick consistency, depending on the use. Correct seasoning; flavor should be tart.

Khubz (Khoubiz) Arabic Flat Bread

YIELD: ABOUT 10 6-INCH KHUBZ

Chef Tip To cook in a sauté pan, preheat pan on highest heat with lid on. When heated, oil the base of the pan quickly and slide in the dough. Cover and cook 3 minutes, remove lid, turn bread over, re-cover, and cook 2 minutes.

AMOUNT	MEASURE	INGREDIENT
$\frac{1}{2}$ cup	4 ounces, 120 ml	Warm water
2 teaspoons	8 g	Active dry yeast
4 cups	16 ounces, 448 g	Bread flour
1 teaspoon	5 g	Salt
1 cup	8 ounces, 240 ml	Warm milk
As needed		Olive oil

PROCEDURE

1 Set a pizza stone on the bottom rack of a preheated 500°F (260°C) oven.

2 Combine warm water and yeast; let stand until foamy, about 10 minutes.

3 In a mixer, food processor, or by hand, combine flour and salt.

4 Add yeast mixture and then the warm milk; work to form dough.

5 On a lightly floured surface, knead one minute. Form the dough into a ball.

6 Lightly oil a bowl with olive oil. Transfer the dough to the bowl and turn to coat; cover and let rise in a warm place until doubled in bulk, about 1 hour.

7 Lightly dust a work surface with flour. Punch down dough and cut in half. Cut each half into 5 pieces, roll them into balls, then flatten into 6-inch rounds; cover. Let rise until puffy, 25 minutes.

8 Rub stone with oil and then slide dough rounds a few at a time onto it. Bake for 4 to 5 minutes until it puffs up like a balloon. To brown, turn quickly and leave for one minute. Remove bread and wrap in a cloth to keep warm and soft.

Baba Ghannouj (Moutabal)
Eggplant Dip   SERVES 4

AMOUNT	MEASURE	INGREDIENT
1 medium	12 ounces, 336 g	Eggplant
$\frac{1}{4}$ cup	2 ounces, 60 ml	Fresh lemon juice
$\frac{1}{4}$ cup	2 ounces, 60 ml	Tahini
2		Garlic cloves
2 teaspoons or to taste	10 g	Salt
1 tablespoon	$\frac{1}{2}$ ounce, 15 ml	Olive oil
$\frac{1}{4}$ cup	$\frac{1}{2}$ ounce, 14 g	Flat-leaf parsley, chopped fine
As needed		Khoubiz (Arabic flat bread; see recipe on page 438)

PROCEDURE

1 Grill eggplant or roast in a hot oven, turning often; cook until soft.

2 Peel off skin while hot and remove stem and end if still firm.

3 Chop flesh and pound to a puree in a mortar with pestle, or puree in a blender or food processor.

4 Blend in $\frac{3}{4}$ of the lemon juice and gradually add the tahini.

5 Crush garlic to a paste with 1 teaspoon salt and add to eggplant. Beat well; adjust flavor with more lemon juice and salt.

6 Beat in olive oil and parsley. Do not puree the parsley.

7 Serve with khoubiz as an appetizer.

Morgh Polou Chicken with Rice SERVES 4

AMOUNT	MEASURE	INGREDIENT
2½ to 3 pounds	1.15–1.4 kg	Chicken, cut into 8 pieces
To taste		Salt and black pepper
¼ cup	2 ounces, 60 ml	Samneh (clarified butter)
1 cup	4 ounces, 112 g	Onion, ¼ inch (.6 cm) dice
½ cup	3 ounces, 84 g	Dried apricots, coarsely chopped
½ cup	3 ounces, 84 g	Sultanas (white raisins)
½ teaspoon		Cinnamon, ground
¼ cup	2 ounces, 60 ml	Water
8 cups	64 ounces, 1.89 liters	Water
2 tablespoons	1 ounce, 28 g	Salt
2 cups	14 ounces, 392 g	Basmati (quality-long grain) rice
¼ cup	2 ounces, 30 ml	Samneh (clarified butter)
¼ cup	2 ounces, 30 ml	Water
½ teaspoon		Saffron threads

PROCEDURE

1   Wipe chicken pieces dry with paper towels and season.

2   Heat half the first quantity of samneh and brown chicken well on all sides. Remove.

3   Add remaining samneh to same pan and sauté onion until transparent.

4   Add fruit and cook 5 minutes over low heat.

5   Stir in cinnamon and add ¼ cup (2 ounces, 60 ml) water to deglaze pan.

6   Wash rice until water runs clear; drain.

7   Bring 8 cups of water to a boil, add salt and rice, stir, and return to boil.

8   Boil for 5 minutes. Pour immediately into a large sieve or colander and drain.

9   Combine second quantity of samneh and ¼ cup water; bring to boil. Pour half into pan the rice was cooked in and swirl to coat base and sides.

10   Spread half the partly cooked rice in base of pan, and even out with back of spoon.

11   Place chicken pieces on top of rice. Spread apricot mixture over chicken and top with remaining rice and samneh mixture.

12   Cover top of pan with clean doubled tea towel or 2 paper towels, place lid on tightly, and cook over low heat (or in the oven) for 40 minutes or until chicken is tender. The cloth absorbs the steam and makes the rice fluffy and light.

13   While polou is cooking, boil 2 tablespoons (1 ounce, 30 ml) water and mix with saffron. Leave aside to steep.

14   Just before serving, sprinkle saffron liquid over rice and stir in gently. Serve piled on a platter.

Adas Bis Silq
Lentil and Swiss Chard Soup   SERVES 4

AMOUNT	MEASURE	INGREDIENT
1 cup	6 ounces, 168 g	Brown lentils
4 cups	32 ounces, 960 ml	Cold water
$\frac{1}{4}$ cup	2 ounces, 60 ml	Olive oil
$\frac{1}{2}$ cup	3 ounces, 84 g	Onion, $\frac{1}{4}$ inch (.6 cm) dice
2		Garlic cloves, minced
4 cups	8 ounces, 224 g	Swiss chard leaves, washed, shredded coarsely
$\frac{1}{4}$ cup	$\frac{1}{2}$ ounce, 14 g	Cilantro leaves, coarsely chopped
To taste		Salt and freshly ground black pepper
3 tablespoons	$1\frac{1}{2}$ ounces, 45 ml	Fresh lemon juice

PROCEDURE

1   Pick over lentils to remove small stones and discolored seeds. Put in a bowl of water and remove any that float. Wash lentils well and drain thoroughly.

2   Cover lentils with the cold water; bring to boil, skimming if necessary, then cover and simmer gently for 1 hour or until soft.

3   Heat oil over medium heat and sauté onions until transparent. Stir in garlic and cook for 15 seconds.

4   Add shredded Swiss chard to the onion mixture; cook, stirring often, until wilted.

5   Add onion mixture to cooked lentils, add remaining ingredients, and simmer gently, 15 to 20 minutes.

6   Serve with lemon wedges and khoubiz or other bread.

Baklawa "Be'aj" Fillo and Nut Pastries

YIELD: ABOUT 20 PASTRIES

Chef Tip The butter firms fairly quickly and it could be difficult to shape pastries if the buttered sheets are left for a long time. It is advisable to fill and shape in lots.

AMOUNT	MEASURE	INGREDIENT
$\frac{1}{2}$ pound	8 ounces, 224 g	Fillo pastry
$\frac{1}{2}$ cup	4 ounces, 120 ml	Samneh or unsalted butter, melted
Nut Filling		
1		Egg white
$\frac{1}{4}$ cup	2 ounces, 56 g	Granulated sugar
1 cup	4 ounces, 112 g	Walnuts, coarsely ground
1 cup	4 ounces, 112 g	Almonds, coarsely ground
1 teaspoon	5 ml	Rose water
Atar Syrup		
1 cup	7 ounces, 196 g	Granulated sugar
$\frac{3}{4}$ cup	6 ounces, 180 ml	Water
$\frac{1}{2}$ teaspoon		Fresh lemon juice
$\frac{1}{2}$ teaspoon		Orange flower water
$\frac{1}{2}$ teaspoon		Rose water
Garnish		
$\frac{1}{2}$ cup	2 ounces, 56 g	Pistachio nuts, peeled, chopped

PROCEDURE

1 Stack 10 sheets fillo dough on a flat surface, keeping any reminder covered with a dry towel, then a damp towel on top.

2 Brush top sheet of stack with melted butter, lift sheet, and replace on stack, buttered side down. Brush top with butter, lift top two sheets, and turn over on stack. Repeat until all 10 sheets are buttered, lifting an extra sheet each time. Top and bottom of finished stack should remain unbuttered.

3 Cut stack into 4-inch (10 cm) squares. Stack and cover. Prepare any remaining sheets.

Baklawa 'Be'aj' – Fillo and Nut Pastries and Khoshaf – Dried Fruit Compote

4   Beat egg white until stiff and beat sugar in gradually. Fold in walnuts, almonds, and rose water.

5   Butter top of fillo square and place a tablespoon of nut mixture in the center. Gently squeeze into a lily shape, with four corners of square as petals and filling in center.

6   Place in a buttered baking pan close together.

7   Bake at 350°F (180°C) for 30 minutes; reduce to 300°F (150°C) and cook 15 minutes longer.

8   To make syrup, dissolve sugar in water over high heat, add lemon juice and orange flower water, and bring to boil. Boil 15 minutes, remove from heat, add rose water, and cool.

9   Spoon cool thick syrup over hot pastries. Leave until cool and sprinkle pistachio nuts in center.

Muhammara
Red Pepper and Walnut Dip   SERVES 4

AMOUNT	MEASURE	INGREDIENT
I pound	448 g	Red bell peppers
$\frac{1}{2}$ cup	2 ounces, 56 g	Walnuts, coarsely ground
2 tablespoons		Bread crumbs or sesame cracker crumbs
I tablespoon	$\frac{1}{2}$ ounce, 15 ml	Pomegranate molasses
I tablespoon	$\frac{1}{2}$ ounce, 15 ml	Fresh lemon juice
$\frac{1}{2}$ teaspoon, plus more for dusting		Cumin, ground
$\frac{1}{2}$ teaspoon		Aleppo pepper, or $\frac{1}{4}$ teaspoon crushed red pepper or red chile paste
To taste		Salt and pepper
I tablespoon	$\frac{1}{2}$ ounce, 15 ml	Olive oil

PROCEDURE

1   Roast bell peppers over gas flame or under broiler, turning until blackened and blistered. Wrap with film or place in a bag to steam 10 minutes to loosen the skin. Let cool slightly; remove skin, membranes, stems, and seeds. Allow to drain.

2   Combine walnuts and bread crumbs in a food processor and process until finely ground.

3   Add bell peppers, pomegranate molasses, lemon juice, cumin, and aleppo or crushed red pepper; blend until creamy. Adjust seasoning with salt, pepper, and aleppo or crushed peppers.

4   Chill at least two hours.

5   Serve with a dusting of ground cumin and a drizzle of olive oil.

Besara Broad Bean Puree   SERVES 4

AMOUNT	MEASURE	INGREDIENT
3 cups	18 ounces, 504 g	Broad beans (fava), cooked, skin removed
To taste		Salt and pepper
2 teaspoons		Dried mint
Garnish		
		Ta'leya II (recipe follows)
		Olive oil
		Chopped onion
		Lemon wedges

PROCEDURE

1 Pass the beans through a sieve or puree in a food processor.
2 Add enough hot water to give the beans a dip consistency.
3 Season to taste with salt and pepper and add mint; simmer 5 minutes.
4 Serve hot in small bowls, garnishing each with ta'leya.
5 Serve with a cruet of olive oil, chopped raw onion, and lemon wedges.

Ta'leya II

AMOUNT	MEASURE	INGREDIENT
$\frac{1}{4}$ cup	2 ounces, 60 ml	Olive oil
2 cups	8 ounces, 224 g	Onions, thin semicircle cuts
2		Garlic cloves, minced

PROCEDURE

1 Heat oil over medium heat and sauté onions until golden brown.
2 Add garlic and cook 1 minute.

Samke Harrah al-Sahara
Baked Fish with Hot Chile Sauce SERVES 4

AMOUNT	MEASURE	INGREDIENT
I	4 pound, 1.81 kg	Snapper or other baking fish, cleaned, scaled, head on but eyes removed
As needed		Salt
$\frac{1}{2}$ cup	4 ounces, 120 ml	Olive oil, for frying
4		Garlic cloves
I teaspoon		Salt
$\frac{1}{4}$ cup	$\frac{1}{2}$ ounce, 14 g	Cilantro leaves, finely chopped
$\frac{1}{2}$ cup	4 ounces, 120 ml	Cold water
I cup	8 ounces, 240 ml	Tahini
$\frac{1}{2}$ cup	4 ounces, 120 ml	Fresh lemon juice
$\frac{1}{4}-\frac{1}{2}$ teaspoon		Hot chile pepper
I tablespoon		Pine nuts
For garnish		Lemon wedges and coriander sprigs

PROCEDURE

1 Preheat oven to 350°F (180°C).

2 Slash snapper in 2 places on each side. Sprinkle inside and out with salt; cover and refrigerate 1 hour. Pat dry before cooking.

3 Heat all but 1 tablespoon oil in large sauté pan and fry fish on high heat for 2 to 3 minutes on each side. Do not cook through. Remove from oil and place in baking dish.

4 Mash garlic with 1 teaspoon salt, and mix in cilantro.

5 Remove all but 2 tablespoons fat from sauté pan and reheat. Add garlic mixture; fry until mixture is crisp but not burnt. Cool.

6 Gradually add water to tahini, beating constantly. Mixture will thicken, then add lemon juice gradually and stir in garlic mixture and chile pepper to taste.

7 Pour sauce over fish, covering fish completely. Bake in preheated oven for 30 to 35 minutes or until fish is cooked through and sauce is bubbling.

8 Toast pine nuts in reserved tablespoon oil until golden brown.

9 Lift cooked fish onto platter and spoon sauce on top. Sprinkle with pine nuts and garnish with lemon wedges and coriander sprigs.

Shurabat al Kibbeh
Kibbeh Soup SERVES: 4

Kibbeh

AMOUNT	MEASURE	INGREDIENT
1 cup	4 ounces, 112 g	Bulgur wheat
11 ounces	308 g	Lean lamb
$\frac{1}{3}$ cup	1.5 ounces, 42 g	Onion, chopped
1 teaspoon		Salt
$\frac{1}{2}$ teaspoon		Black pepper
$\frac{1}{3}$ teaspoon		Allspice
		Ice water or ice chips

PROCEDURE

1 Cover bulgur with cold water and let soak 10 minutes. Drain in a sieve and press with back of spoon to remove as much moisture as possible. Lay out flat and chill 1 hour.

2 Trim all fat and fine skin from lamb; cut into cubes. Chill 1 hour.

3 Pass meat through a food grinder twice, using fine die. Grind onion twice and combine with meat, bulgur, salt, pepper, and allspice.

4 Pass through grinder twice, adding a little ice water if necessary to keep mixture cold.

5 Knead to a smooth, light paste with hands, adding ice water when necessary. Cover and chill.

Soup

AMOUNT	MEASURE	INGREDIENT
As needed		Kibbeh mixture
$\frac{1}{4}$ cup	1 ounce, 28 g	Pine nuts
$\frac{1}{4}$ cup	2 ounces, 60 ml	Samneh (clarified butter)
1 cup	4 ounces, 112 g	Onion, $\frac{1}{4}$ inch (.6 cm) dice
4 cups	32 ounces, 960 ml	Water or stock
1 small piece		Cinnamon strck
To taste		Salt and pepper
$\frac{1}{3}$ cup	2 ounces, 56 g	Short-grain rice, washed
$\frac{1}{4}$ cup	$\frac{1}{2}$ ounce, 14 g	Parsley, chopped, for garnish

PROCEDURE

1 Shape kibbeh into balls the size of a walnut. Make a hole in each, insert two pine nuts, and re-form into balls.

2 Heat samneh and brown kibbeh balls, shaking pan so they keep the round shape and brown evenly. Remove and leave fat in pan.

3 Add onion to pan and sauté until soft, 3 to 5 minutes.

4 Add 1 cup water or stock and bring to boil, scraping bottom of the pan to get all the drippings.

5 Remove to a soup pot and add remaining liquid, cinnamon, salt and pepper to taste, and rice.

6 Bring to boil, stirring occasionally; simmer, covered, 10 minutes.

7 Add kibbeh balls; cover and simmer 15 to 20 minutes.

8 Correct seasoning.

9 Serve with parsley sprinkled on top.

Fattoush
Toasted Bread Salad   SERVES 4

AMOUNT	MEASURE	INGREDIENT
1 6-inch		Khoubiz, toasted golden brown, $\frac{1}{2}$ inch (1.2 cm) dice
3 cups	6 ounces, 168 g	Romaine, shredded or broken into small pieces
$\frac{3}{4}$ cup	4 ounces, 112 g	Cucumber, peeled, $\frac{1}{2}$ inch (1.2 cm) dice
1 cup	6 ounces, 168 g	Tomato, peeled, seeded, $\frac{1}{2}$ inch (1.2 cm) dice
$\frac{1}{3}$ cup	1 ounce, 28 g	Green onion, chopped
$\frac{1}{3}$ cup	$\frac{1}{2}$ ounce, 14 g	Flat-leaf parsley, chopped
3 tablespoons		Fresh mint, chopped
$\frac{3}{4}$ cup	3 ounces, 84 g	Green bell pepper, $\frac{1}{2}$ inch (1.2 cm) dice
As needed		Salad dressing (recipe follows)

PROCEDURE

1   Combine all ingredients and toss with salad dressing.

Salad Dressing

AMOUNT	MEASURE	INGREDIENT
1		Garlic clove
1 teaspoon		Salt
$\frac{1}{2}$ cup	4 ounces, 120 ml	Fresh lemon juice
$\frac{1}{2}$ cup	4 ounces, 120 ml	Olive oil
To taste		Black pepper

PROCEDURE

1   Mash garlic with salt and stir in remaining ingredients.

Fattoush – Toasted Bread Salad

Nane Lavash (Taftoon)

Flat Bread   YIELD: 4 ROUNDS

The only difference between the breads is the size. Nane lavash is the better-known Persian bread, but it is very large. Taftoon is the same dough shaped in smaller rounds.

AMOUNT	MEASURE	INGREDIENT
$\frac{2}{3}$ cup	3 ounces, 84 g	All-purpose flour
2 cups	8 ounces, 224 g	Whole wheat flour
2 teaspoon	$\frac{1}{4}$ ounce, 7 g	Active dry yeast
$1\frac{2}{3}$ cups	13 ounces, 390 ml	Water
1 teaspoon	5 g	Salt
		Oil for handling dough

PROCEDURE

1   Preheat oven to 500°F (260°C). Set a pizza stone or griddle on the center rack.

2   Sift flours together; discard any flakes left in sifter.

3   Dissolve yeast in $\frac{1}{4}$ cup (2 ounces, 60 ml) warm water. Combine warm water and yeast; let stand until foamy, about 10 minutes.

4   Add $1\frac{1}{2}$ cups (12 ounces, 360 ml) of the remaining water and the salt.

5   Combine yeast with flour and mix using a dough hook on low speed for 15 to 20 minutes, gradually adding as much of the remaining $\frac{3}{4}$ cup (6 ounces, 180 ml) water as the dough will absorb. As the dough is worked, its ability to absorb water increases.

6   Oil your hands and divide dough into 4 equal-size pieces, shaping each into a ball.

7   Roll out one at a time as thin as possible with an oiled rolling pin. Prick well all over with a fork or pin wheel.

8   Take round and flip across the backs of your hands to stretch it.

9   Oil pizza stone or griddle and press dough on to it. Close oven and cook 1 minute; pat dough down again to prevent bread puffing up.

10 Bake until surface is bubbly, about 3 minutes; turn over and cook 2 minutes more. Remove and wrap in a cloth. Let oven regain heat and continue with remaining dough. Rolled-out dough should not rest before being baked.

Tapauch Ets Im Mits Tapuzim

Apples in Orange Juice SERVES 4

AMOUNT	MEASURE	INGREDIENT
1½ cups	12 ounces, 360 ml	Orange juice, fresh
3 tablespoons	1½ ounces, 42 g	Seedless raisins
3 tablespoons	1½ ounces, 42 g	Butter
4 medium size		Tart-eating apples
2 teaspoons		Cornstarch
2 tablespoons	1 ounce, 30 ml	Water

PROCEDURE

1 Combine orange juice, raisins, and butter; bring to boil.

2 Peel, core, and cut the apples in half.

3 Add apples to orange juice; cover and simmer gently until tender and shape still holds.

4 Blend cornstarch with water and thicken liquid.

5 Serve warm with meal.

Tan Yogurt Drink

Tan accompanies every Armenian meal.

SERVES 4

AMOUNT	MEASURE	INGREDIENT
2 cups	16 ounces, 480 ml	Plain yogurt
1 cup	8 ounces, 240 ml	Water
Salt		Salt

PROCEDURE

1 Process yogurt in blender until smooth.

2 Add water gradually, blending as you add, until mixture reaches a drink consistency. Add salt and chill well before serving.

Turkey, Greece, and Crete

The Land

TURKEY

Turkey is located on two continents, Europe and Asia, and is close to where the three continents of Asia, Europe, and Africa come together. About 3 percent of the country lies within Europe and is called Eastern Thrace. The other 97 percent of Turkey is located in Asia and is called Anatolia, or Asia Minor. Unlike some of the lands that neighbor it, Turkey is not only a Middle Eastern country; it shares a lot of history with Europe and is considered to be one of the world's cradles of civilization. Over the centuries it has given birth to many civilizations, religions, empires, and states.

Turkey is shaped like a rectangle and is similar to a peninsula. To the north is the Black Sea; to the south is the Mediterranean Sea; and to the west is the Aegean Sea. The Bosporus Strait, the Sea of Marmara, and the Dardanelles Strait divide the continents of Europe and Asia from each other within Turkey. Turkey borders the countries of Greece, Bulgaria, Georgia, Armenia, Iran, Iraq, Azerbaijan, and Syria.

Geographically, Turkey can be divided into eight main regions, each with its own landscape and history. The small region of Eastern Thrace has rolling hills and fertile grasslands. This region produces maize, wine, and tobacco. Herds of sheep graze on the hilly slopes. The northern Black Sea region is cattle country and people on the western part of the coast mainly live in noncommercial fishing towns. The Marmara and the Aegean regions are important agricultural markets where groves of olives and other crops thrive. The Aegean coast is home to the historical sites of Troy and Pergamum and is important from an archaeological viewpoint. The Mediterranean region has some of the most beautiful scenery in the entire country with the Taurus Mountains and a rugged coastline in the east. Western Anatolia is covered with mountain ranges. Central Anatolia is considered to be Turkey's heartland because it is where the first Turkish tribes settled in the tenth century. Eastern Anatolia is far more isolated and underdeveloped; the land is barren and poverty is common. Southeastern Anatolia shares borders with Syria, Iraq, and Iran, so there is a Middle Eastern flair to its culture.

As of 1998, Turkey is the world's largest producer of hard-shell nuts, figs, and apricots, a leader in fresh vegetables, grape, and tobacco production, and seventh in the world in wheat and cotton production.

GREECE

Like Turkey, Greece also lies at the crossroads of three continents. The country is located at the southeastern corner of Europe on the southern part of the Balkan Peninsula. Continental Asia lies to the east of Greece across the Aegean Sea, and Africa lies south across the Mediterranean Sea. Greece is famous for its jagged coastline bordered by the Aegean Sea on the east, the Mediterranean Sea on the south, and the Ionian Sea on the west. In the north, Greece shares a boundary with Albania, the former Yugoslav republic of Macedonia, and Bulgaria. Its territory includes more than 2,000 islands in the Aegean and Ionian seas, of which only 170 or so are inhabited.

The geography of Greece exercises an important influence upon the political destinies of its population. Greece is one of the most mountainous countries of Europe. Its surface is occupied by a number of small plains, either entirely surrounded by limestone mountains or open only to the sea. Arcadia was almost the only political division that did not possess some territory upon the coast. Each of the principal Grecian cities was founded in one of these small plains and, since the mountains that separated it from its neighbors were lofty and rugged, each city led solitary independence. Thus shut out from their neighbors by mountains, the Greeks were naturally attracted to the sea, and became a maritime people.

CRETE

Crete is the largest of the Greek islands. A mountainous island, it lies south of the Aegean Sea, a link between Asia, Africa, and Europe. Its unique geographical position between the three continents determined its historical course both throughout antiquity and in modern times.

The island is an elongated shape. To the south it is bordered by the Libyan Sea, to the west the Myrtoon Sea, to the east the Karpathion Sea, and to the north the Sea of Crete. Its coastline, which consists of both sandy beaches and rocky shores, is framed by the small islets of Kouphonisi, Gaidouronisi, Dia, Aghioi Pantes, Spinalonga, and Gavdos in the Libyan Sea. Crete is the southernmost point of Europe.

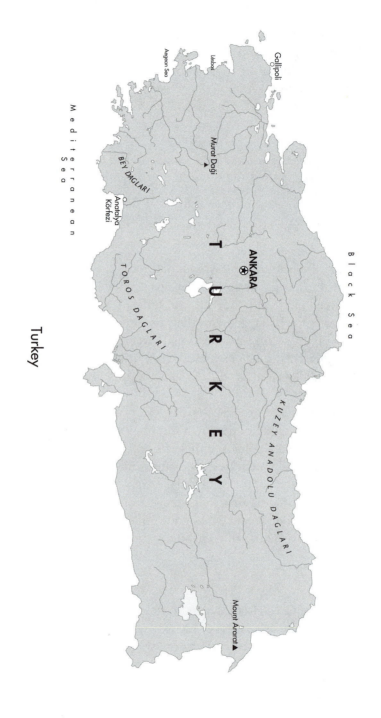

Turkey

Greece and Crete

History

TURKEY

Archaeologists have found evidence of advanced societies living in this part of the world as early as 6000 B.C. As in many countries of the world, the years saw shifting power as one empire after another took control, and then others came along to challenge it. The first to dominate the region were the Hittites, the leading rulers of the Middle East in 1500 B.C. They were followed by the Greeks (eighth century B.C.), and the Persians (sixth century B.C.), and in A.D. 395 it became part of the Byzantine Empire. The area was conquered by the Ottoman Turks between the thirteenth and fifteenth centuries and remained the core of the Ottoman Empire. Its modern history dates to the rise of the Young Turks (after 1908) and the collapse of the empire in 1918. Under the leadership of Kemal Atatürk, a republic was proclaimed in 1923.

GREECE

Greece is one of the cradles of European civilization, whose ancient scholars made great advances in philosophy, medicine, mathematics, and astronomy. Its city-states were pioneers in developing democratic forms of government. The historical and cultural heritage of Greece continues to resonate throughout the world in literature, art, philosophy, and politics.

The first settlement dated from the Paleolithic era (11,000–3,000 B.C.). During the second millennium B.C., Greece gave birth to the great civilizations of the Minoan, the Mycenaean, and the Cycladic on the Greek islands in the Aegean Sea. The classical period of Greek history (sixth to fourth centuries B.C.) was the golden age; during this period lived the great philosophers and mathematicians. Following that period, the history of Greece is a succession of various invasions and dominations; the Macedonians formed a strong empire, followed by the Romans and the Byzantine Empire, which ended with the invasion of the Turks. The Ottoman rule lasted for four hundred years and was a dark period for the inhabitants of Greece. Wanting to finally win their freedom, Greeks started to organize themselves and various revolts exploded against their Turkish oppressors.

The Independence War started in the Peloponnese peninsula in 1821 and ended in March 1831, with the establishment of the new and independent Greek state. Yet despite their illustrious history, the people of Greece are still striving to gain a role in world affairs. After enduring political and cultural oppression for centuries, their deep sense of cultural unity has preserved a rich society through occupation, wars, and political strife. In the last forty years Greece's main economic sectors have grown to include agriculture, tourism, construction, and shipping.

CRETE

Crete's geography defined its historical course down through the ages. Situated between three continents, it was at the junction of the major cultural currents and at the crossroads of conflicting geopolitical interests and bloody clashes. On Cretan soil were hatched and developed features of civilization that mark the history of humankind. At the same time the island paid a heavy price because of its strategic position and was repeatedly invaded and periodically conquered, which contributed to the destruction of Crete's native civilization, the lowering of living standards, and the subsequent misery of the inhabitants. However, through successive restructuring new forms of social coexistence were forged, new intellectual values arose, and new material and cultural creations appeared that left their indelible mark on Crete and the historical role of the Cretans.

The People

TURKEY

The people of Turkey have changed along with their country. Their beginnings were primarily in Asia. About 85 percent of Turks are descended from people who migrated to Anatolia from central Asia during the tenth century A.D. The largest minority group in Turkey is the Kurds. About ten to twelve million Kurds live in the mountainous region of southeast Turkey as well as in the west. Many Kurds would like to form their own independent state, separate from Turkey. This issue has come into direct conflict with Turkey's plans for future development and is an ongoing battle that has yet to be solved. A small portion of the Turkish population consists of Arabs, Armenians, and Greeks. While there is no state religion and people have the freedom to choose, almost everyone who lives in Turkey is Muslim.

GREECE

The Greek people are only partly descended from the ancient Greeks, having mingled through the ages with the numerous invaders of the Balkans. Modern vernacular Greek is the official language. There is a small Turkish-speaking minority, and many Greeks also speak English and French. The Greek Orthodox Church is the established church of the country, and it includes the great majority of the population.

In a country that traditionally has been poor agriculturally, making the most of meager produce has evolved from necessity to a national obsession with food. As necessity breeds innovation, Greek cuisine comprises a rich diversity of cooking styles, ingredients, and flavors. It also has a colorful history dating from antiquity and has incorporated outside elements from Italian, Turkish, and French cuisines. Vegetarianism has a long tradition in Greece and was espoused by Pythagoras, who abstained from meat for moral reasons. Even to this day, the ultra-religious abstain from meat and animal products on Wednesdays and Fridays as well as during the forty days of Lent.

CRETE

The island of Crete has been inhabited since prehistoric times. There is evidence of organized habitation dating back to 8000 B.C., and twentieth-century excavations have revealed a splendid civilization that ruled the island and much of the Aegean region during the Bronze Age. The Minoan civilization is credited as the first civilization of Europe. It began around 2000 B.C. and it lasted for about two millennia before it was replaced on the island by the Mycenaean civilization circa 1375, and then by classical and Hellenistic Greeks, who in turn were replaced by the Romans. The Byzantine Empire and the Venetians controlled the island for a few hundred years before the Ottoman Empire invaded the island.

The Ottoman Empire ruled the island from 1645 until 1898 when the Greeks revolted and finally reunited the island with Greece in 1913.

The Food

TURKEY

In history, the Turks led a nomadic life, dependent on agriculture and on the breeding of domestic animals. The word "yogurt" is Turkish in origin and the fermenting process used in yogurt is thought to have originated among these nomadic tribes. Early Turks cultivated wheat and used it liberally, in several types of leavened and unleavened breads, which are baked in clay ovens, fried on a griddle, or buried in embers. Stuffing not only pastry but also all kinds of vegetables remains common practice, as evidenced by dozens of different types of "dolma." Skewering meat as another way of grilling, what we know as the kebab, was developed by the Turks. Turkish cuisine is full of vegetables, grains, fresh fish, and seemingly infinite varieties of lamb dishes. Fish and meat are typically served grilled or roasted, although often with inordinate amounts of *yag* (oil). The core group of seasonings is garlic, sage, oregano, cumin, mint, dill, lemon, and yogurt. The richness of Turkish cooking originated from Ottoman sultans. During their reign, many of the chefs were trying to create a new dish and taste to please the sultan in order to receive praise and reward. A sultan's palace kitchen might include hundreds of chefs and more than one thousand kitchen staff. As a result, a large variety of dish offerings from meat to many fresh vegetables were developed. The majority of these recipes, recorded in Arabic script, were regrettably lost in the language reforms. Some Ottoman favorites have continued, however, like *hünkar begendi* (the sultan was pleased), *imam bayaldi* (the priest fainted), and *hanim göbegi* (lady's navel), a syrupy dessert with a thumbprint in the middle.

The first meal of the day is breakfast. A typical Turkish breakfast is fresh tomatoes, white cheese, black olives, bread with honey and preserves, and sometimes an egg. Lunch often will include a rice or bulgar pilaf dish, lamb or chicken baked with peppers and eggplant, and fresh fish grilled with lemon. A popular lamb cut is *prizolla*. These are extra-thin-cut lamb chops seasoned with sumac (a tart red berry dried and coarsely ground, often referred to as a "souring agent") and thyme, and then quickly grilled. Other favorites include *sucuk,* a spicy sausage, and *pastirma,* a sun-dried cumin-fenugreek coated preserved beef. It is sliced thin much like pastrami.

Dinners will most commonly start with *mezeler* (singular, *mezze*), or appetizers. These often become a meal in themselves, accompanied by an ample serving of *raki* (a liquorlike anisette,

Pulse & legumes   croissants
pintxos

licorice flavored; when diluted with water it assumes a milky color). Cold mezes include *patli-can salatasi* (roasted eggplant puree flavored with garlic and lemon), *haydari* (a thick yogurt dip made with garlic and dill), *dolma, ezme* (a spicy paste of tomatoes, minced green pepper, onion, and parsley), *kizartma* (deep-fried eggplant, zucchini, or green pepper served with fresh yogurt), *cacik* (a garlicky cold yogurt "soup" with shredded cucumber, mint, or dill), *barbunya pilaki* (kidney beans, tomatoes, and onions cooked in olive oil), and *barbunya pilaki* (slow-roasted baby eggplant topped with olive oil-fried onions and tomatoes and seasoned with garlic). Hot appetizers, usually called *ara sicak,* include *börek* (a deep-fried or oven-baked pastry filled with cheese or meat), *kalamar* (deep-fried calamari served with a special sauce), and *midye tava* (deep-fried mussels). Fresh fish, often a main course, is commonly served grilled and drizzled with olive oil and lemon. Specialties include *alabalik* (trout), *barbunya* (red mullet), *kalkan* (turbot), *kefal* (gray mullet), *kiliç* (swordfish, sometimes served as a kebab), *levrek* (sea bass), *lüfer* (bluefish), and *palamut* (bonito). Grilled quail is most common inland; it's often marinated in tomatoes, yogurt, olive oil, and cinnamon. *Karisik izgara,* a mixed grill, usually combines chicken breast, beef, a lamb chop, and spicy lamb patties, all served with rice pilaf and vegetables.

Soups have traditional importance and are generally served as the first course or starter and can be eaten with any meal, even breakfast. They come in a wide variety and many are are based on meat stock. Lentil soup is the most common, but there are other preferred soups such as *yayla* (a yogurt-based soup), *tarhana* (cracked wheat or flour, yogurt, and vegetables fermented and then dried)*, asiran* (made from bulgur wheat and yogurt), and *guli* (from greens, white beans, and lamb). The well-known "wedding soup" is made with lamb shanks in an egg broth.

One of the pillars of Turkish cooking is *pilavlar,* or pilaf. Generally made of rice, but sometimes with bulgur or *sehriye* (vermicelli), pilaf is one of the mainstays of the Turkish table. The rice should not be sticky but separate into individual grains. The pilaf may include eggplant, chickpeas, beans, or peas. Although pilaf is traditionally a course in its own right, it may also be used as a garnish with meat and chicken dishes.

Börek is a general Turkish term for filled pastries. The filling is often white sheep's milk cheese and a chopped vegetable such as parsley or spinach. Often the dough is paper-thin *yufka* (phyllo) layered, rolled, or folded around the ingredients, then baked, steamed, or fried.

Kebabs are dishes of plain or marinated meat either stewed or grilled. Although the ingredient of choice for Turks is lamb, some kebabs are made with beef, chicken, or fish, usually grilled with vegetables on a skewer. *Doner kebab* is a famous Turkish dish of a roll of lamb on a vertical skewer turning parallel to a hot grill. *Adana kebaps* are spicy ground-lamb patties arranged on a layer of sautéed pita bread, topped with a yogurt-and-garlic sauce. *Iskender kebaps,* also known as *bursa kebaps,* are sliced grilled lamb, smothered in tomato sauce, hot butter, and yogurt. *Sis kebaps* are the traditional skewered cubes of lamb, usually interspersed with peppers and onions. *Kofte* are meatballs, predominantly lamb, and there is a rich variety of kofte recipes within Turkey. Finely minced meat mixed with spices, onions, and other ingredients is shaped by hand, and grilled, fried, boiled, or baked. Some *koftes* are cooked in a sauce; as in the case of the *izmir kofte,* the *koftes* are first grilled and then cooked with green peppers, potato slices, and tomatoes in their own gravy. In southern and southeastern Turkey, bulgur wheat is an essential ingredient of many varieties of meatballs. The stuffed meatballs known as *içli köfte* have an outer shell of bulgur and minced meat and a filling of walnuts and spicy minced meat. Raw *köfte* are a specialty that requires top-quality meat without a trace of fat. This is then minced and kneaded with bulgur and the purplish hot pepper of the region.

Dolmas is family of stuffed vegetable dishes. This applies to tomatoes, peppers, eggplant, potatoes, onions, quince, and even apples; although stuffed mackerel and squid are also called *dolma*. *Dolmas* originated in Turkey, but are also found from the Balkans to Persia. Perhaps the best-known is the grape leaf *dolmas*. The stuffing may include meat or not. Meat *dolmas* are generally served warm, often with sauce; meatless ones are generally served cold.

Bread has major cultural significance in Turkey. It is usually baked twice a day, early in the morning and late in the afternoon. The freshly baked elongated loaf of bread, which looks like French bread, is the bread that most people eat during the day. Then there is flat bread, known as pita bread (*pide* in Turkish) which is good for wrapping; *lavash,* a wafer thin type of bread, is also good for wrapping; and *simit,* which is a round bread much like a bagel, covered with sesame seeds.

Many fresh and dried fruits are stewed into compotes in which the liquid is as important an element as is the fruit itself. Desserts made from apricots or figs are given a topping of fresh clotted cream and sometimes crushed walnuts. The same topping is used on *kabak tatlisi,* an unusual dessert made by cooking pieces of pumpkin in syrup. Milk-based desserts include a wide variety of puddings, some of which are baked. *Keskul* is a milk pudding made with coconut. *Gullac* is a confection of thin sheets of pastry in a milk sauce to which rosewater is added; and pastry-based desserts include baklava, as well as *kadayif* (made from shredded pastry baked in syrup, often filled with pistachio nuts, walnuts, or clotted cream), *revani* (a sweet made from semolina), *hanim göbegi,* and *sekerparee* (two kinds of small sweet cake). Turkish delight and helva are well-known candies. Turkish delight is made from cornstarch or gelatin, sugar, honey, and fruit juice or jelly, and is often tinted pink or green. Chopped almonds, pistachio nuts, pine nuts, or hazelnuts are frequently added. Once the candy becomes firm, it is cut into small squares and coated with confectioners' sugar. Helva is made by pan-sautéing flour or semolina and pine nuts in butter before adding sugar and milk or water, and briefly cooking until these are absorbed. The preparation of helva is conducive to communal cooking. People are invited for "helva conversations" to pass the long winter nights.

Tea (cay) is the national drink. It is served extremely hot and strong in tiny tulip-shaped glasses, accompanied by two sugar cubes. The size of the glass ensures that the tea gets consumed while hot. The coffee culture is a little less prevalent but no less "steeped" in tradition. Early clerics believed it to be an intoxicant and consequently had it banned. But the *kahvehane* (coffeehouse) refused to go away, and now the sharing of a cup of coffee is an excuse to prolong a discussion, plan, negotiate, or simply relax. Turkish coffee is ground to a fine dust, boiled directly in the correct quantity of water, and served as is. There are two national drinks, *raki* and *ayran*. *Raki* is an alcoholic drink distilled from raisins and then redistilled with aniseed. *Ayran* is a refreshing beverage made by diluting yogurt with water.

GREECE

As in every culture of the world, local culinary traditions are the reflection of two interconnected factors, geography and history. The mainland cuisine of Greece is primarily a nomadic shepherd's cuisine. As recently as a generation ago, shepherds moved on foot with their flocks twice a year, in mid-fall and mid-spring, between the low-lying plains (where it was warmer) and the mountains, where they spent their summers. Foraging, not farming, was the norm. Butter and lard were the predominant fats, and cheese, yogurt, and myriad other dairy products played a dominant role in those diets, as did meat. Vegetables were typically wild greens, picked in and around nomadic settlements and often turned into pies, one of the backbones of mainland Greek cooking. For an itinerant shepherd, it was the most efficient food, a dish that could be easily prepared from accessible ingredients, baked in makeshift portable ovens, was satisfyingly filling, and could be carried with ease over long distances.

There are many pies in Greece that fall into several broad categories. *Tiropita* is a cheese pie. The filling is usually a simple combination of local cheese, usually feta, and eggs. Some pies are multilayered; others are very thin, almost like crepes filled with cheese. *Hortopita* is a category of pies, filled with seasonal, usually mild, greens. In some, a little cheese is added. *Kreatopita* translates as meat pie. Pork, lamb, and some beef appear in fillings from various regions. Chicken is also used as a filling for pies. These are called *kotopites.* There are also some unusual pies filled with eggplant (*thesalia*) and with pulses, such as lentils, which is a very old dish from Ipiros. *Bourekakia* are individual, hand-held pies that can be filled with cheese, vegetables, or meat. They are either fried or baked and shapes vary. *Glikes pites* are sweet pies. Baklava falls into this category. Other dessert pies include *galaktoboureko,* a custard-filled pie almost always prepared with commercial phyllo, not homemade and *galatopita,* or milk pie, which is a classic country dish in Roumeli, Thesalia, and Ipiros. Often, *trahana* or rice is added to the filling of milk pies to make it more substantial. There is also an unusual sweet Lenten pie found throughout Ipiros made with rice and raisins.

There are several subcategories of Greek cuisine: cooking large casseroles, stews, grilled meat and seafood specialties, and phyllo items (*pites*). Each type of cooking is represented by a specialty restaurant. *Tavernas* can be found all over Greece and specialize in preprepared casserole items (*moussaka, pastitsio,* vegetables stuffed with rice). *Psistaries* serve only grilled meats. *Pites,* phyllo pastry pies stuffed with greens, are generally considered as *laiko,* or village cuisine, made at home or purchased from either a bakery or a street vendor specializing in one type of pita.

Breakfast, or *proeeno,* is a light meal, usually eaten as early as 7 a.m. Many people have only Greek coffee, which is a strong, thick mixture of fine ground coffee, water, and sometimes sugar, boiled together. This may be accompanied by a roll with butter, honey, or jelly. Lunch, or *mesimeriano,* is the main meal, eaten at home at 2 or 3 p.m. Appetizers, meat or fish, salad, yogurt with honey, and fruit may be served at a typical midday meal. Dinner is *deipnon,* usually eaten in the late evening, as late as 10 p.m. Most Greeks have appetizers, or *mezedakia,* in the early evening, before dinner. The word *meze* describes a form of socializing as much as a group of dishes. Drinking without eating is frowned upon in Greece. People gather in *ouzeries* in the early evening not just for drinks, but also for *mezethes* to tide them over until dinner. *Meze* is eaten throughout the Eastern Mediterranean, and Greek *mezethes* share common flavors with the Turkish, Middle Eastern, and North African varieties (nearly four hundred years of Ottoman rule left a strong mark on the entire area). But this style of eating can be traced to ancient Greece; Plato's writings include descriptions of symposium spreads that would not be out of place in an *ouzerie* today. Greek *mezethes* generally have robust or spicy flavors to stand up to strong drinks. The hallmarks of Greek cuisine since antiquity—olives, fresh vegetables, spit-roasted or grilled meats, dried and fresh fruit, oregano, mint, yogurt, and honey—figure prominently. *Meze* in seaside areas includes dishes like wood-grilled squid and octopus, while the mountainous inland regions are known for pies stuffed with meat and cheese.

Feta cheese and yogurt are the backbone of the Greece's dairy industry. The country produces 150,000 tons of feta per year. Because of Greek emigrations, this brined cheese has become known worldwide. The European Union has granted this cheese a Protected Designation of Origin (PDO) and has prohibited other countries in its domain from using the name "feta." Derived from the milk of both sheep and goats (but never cows), its unique flavors result from these animals grazing on indigenous plants in rather dry pastures.

Whereas Greek mountain cooking is basically rooted in a pastoral tradition, the cuisine of the Peloponnese, the large peninsula joined to the rest of mainland Greece by a narrow strip of land (the Isthmus of Corinth), is rural, farm cuisine at its best. Here is Greece's most important olive grove—the tree grows virtually all over the Peloponnese—and olive oil figures prominently in the cuisine.

Perhaps no other symbol represents Greece as does the olive tree. The Greek poet Homer once described Greece's olive oil as "liquid gold" and for a long time olive groves were protected. Said to be given by the goddess of wisdom, Athena, to the city bearing her name, the olive tree provides two staples of Greek cuisine: table olives and olive oil. Today its production and sale plays a significant role in the economic life of twenty-first-century Greece. Greece is home to 120,000,000 olive trees, about twelve trees for every resident. About 120,000 tons of table olives each year are produced, which is the fifth largest total in the world. Two-thirds of the crop goes to export markets. Of the many varieties grown, three predominate: the *kalamata*, perhaps the best known; the *conservolia*; and the *halkidiki*. It is a point of pride that 80 percent of Greece's olive oil is rated extra virgin, making the country the world's largest producer in this category. Olive oil is used in virtually every method of cooking in Greece and is also used as a condiment, especially with the greener, more herbaceous varieties of oil. Common dishes like the green bean, eggplant, potato, or zucchini stew, cooked in lemon or tomato sauce, are called *ladera* (cooked in olive oil).

Other important elements in the cuisine of the Peloponnese are tomatoes, garlic, onions, spinach, artichokes, fennel, lettuce, cabbage, *horta* (wild greens), zucchini, eggplant, and peppers. Fruits are eaten either fresh, or preserved by drying. Popular varieties include apricots, grapes, dates, cherries, apples, pears, plums, and figs.

The excellent quality of Greek herbs and spices reflects the country's ample sunshine and the variability of its landscape. This special landscape makes Greek flora so rich that of the 7,500 different species of plants growing in Greece, 850 of them are found only there. Some of the best herbs grow there naturally: chamomile, mountain tea, *tilio* (lime blossom), sage, thyme, oregano, and basil are chosen above others by celebrity chefs across Europe. Spices from Greece include sesame, white sesame, *machlepi* (the kernel of a certain cherry; it has a pleasant, sweet and earthy aroma and is used to flavor certain holiday breads), and cumin. The most valuable and expensive spice, red saffron, is cultivated in Greece. There are certain defining flavors and combinations that make a dish unquestionably Greek. Among them are lemon and dill; lemon and olive oil; lemon, olive oil, oregano, and garlic; lemon and eggs (*avgolemono*); tomatoes and cinnamon (in sauces); tomatoes, honey, vinegar, and dill; garlic ground with mint (sometimes with the addition of walnuts); garlic and vinegar; anise (or *ouzo*) and pepper; and olives, orange, and fennel. Garlic is indispensable to Greek cooking and is used in stews and other savory dishes, but it most important in dipping sauces, such as *skordalia* and in yogurt-based dips, such as *tzatziki*. Greeks enjoy the taste of garlic and nuts, and there are several sauces that call for walnuts and garlic or almonds and garlic.

With documented production dating to sixth century B.C., honey has a special resonance in Greece. It's the basic sweetening ingredient in the Mediterranean diet and Greece is one of the primary providers of honey in Europe. The country defines its honey sources in two broad categories. Forest honey, most of which is pine honey, fir honey, and oak honey, accounts for 60 to 70 percent of all production. The balance is considered flower honey and includes sources such as orange, heather, chestnut, and aromatic plants like wild oregano, wild lavender, and salvia. Because Greece's vegetation is sparser than in some other parts of the world, bees must work harder. In Greece a beehive will average 10 kilos (about 22 pounds) production, while in the rest of Europe hives generate over 30 kilos (about 66 pounds). However, the Greek bees that struggle and collect nectar from a wider variety of plants produce a honey that is denser and richer in aromatic substances.

Wheat has been cultivated in Greece for thousands of years and is a staple of Greek cuisine. It's used to make a variety of breads including pita bread and crusty whole-grain peasant bread. Bulgur, which is made from cracked whole wheat, is eaten as an accompaniment to hearty stews or added to soups and salads. Pasta, introduced to the Greeks by the Italians, is also a popular wheat-based food. Another important grain food in the Greek diet is rice, which is used in pilafs and bakes, served with stews, or wrapped in grape leaves to make *dolmades*.

Legumes such as chickpeas, lima beans, split peas, and lentils are used in traditional Greek cooking. They are eaten either whole in stews, bakes, pilafs, soups, and salads, or pureed and used as a dip or spread such as hummus. The most popular dried beans are the *gigantes*, or giant beans, which resemble lima or butter beans but are bigger. These are made into casseroles, baked with tomatoes and other vegetables, and sometimes served up simply boiled with a little olive oil, lemon juice, and oregano. Greeks call the yellow split pea *fava*. The most common way to cook them is to simmer the yellow split peas until they become creamy and dense, like mashed potatoes. This is a classic Greek dish, usually topped with raw olive oil and raw onions. In Santorini, *fava* is "married," that is, it is served with a topping of either stewed capers, another local specialty, or stewed eggplants. Once the puree has been made, it can also sometimes be turned into fritters. Many types of nuts are used in cooking or eaten as snacks, particularly pine nuts, almonds, walnuts, and pistachios.

Meat, particularly large roasts, have been an important part of Greek culinary history. Today, Easter would be incomplete without lamb or kid on a spit, or its *kokoretsi* (innards sausage), skewered and grilled outdoors. On the everyday table, skewered meats are also prominent, in the form of *souvlaki,* sold all over the country. *Souvlaki,* like the kebab, is made by skewering small chunks of meat, usually pork or lamb, and grilling them over coals. *Souvlaki* may be made with or without slices of peppers, tomatoes, and onions on the skewer. A *souvlaki* pita is wrapped in grilled pita bread together with tomatoes, *tzatziki,* and onions. A *gyros* (also spelled *giros*) is like *souvlaki* pita, usually served wrapped in grilled pita bread with one difference: *gyros,* which means round, is made by stacking very thin slices of meat on a vertical skewer and grilling the resulting cone on a rotisserie for hours, until all the slices meld together. To serve it, the *gyro* maker slices off thin pieces and wraps them in pita bread with tomatoes, onions, and *tzatziki.* There are countless stews and stovetop meat preparations in the traditional Greek culinary repertoire. Meat is expensive and so used sparingly, most often in combination with other ingredients, such as vegetables, beans, and rice or pasta.

Moussaka is the best known of all Greek foods. It is a lamb and eggplant casserole covered with a thick layer of béchamel sauce that is baked until golden and crusty. It can be made with other ingredients besides lamb and eggplant, using beef, or vegetables such as zucchini or potatoes.

Greece is surrounded by the sea, so fish and shellfish are an important part of the diet. The most popular types of fish and shellfish include tuna, mullet, bass, halibut, swordfish, anchovies, sardines, shrimp, octopus, squid, and mussels. This fish and seafood is enjoyed in many ways, including grilled and seasoned with garlic and lemon juice, baked with yogurt and herbs, cooked in rich tomato sauce, added to soups, or served cold as a side dish.

Fresh and dried fruit are the usual dessert. Rich desserts and pastries, often sweetened with honey, are mostly reserved for special occasions or eaten in small amounts. Greek sweets made with fruits are a part of the Greek tradition and way of life since they represent a warm welcome for the visitor to the friendly environment of a Greek home. In the near past, these sweets were usually homemade according to the art and secrets of each housewife. They were called "spoon sweets" because the usual serving size was a well-filled teaspoon.

Most sweets were prepared at the time of year each fruit matured: apricots, prunes, grapes, quince, bergamot, citrus, wild cherries, and figs followed each other from early summer to late autumn. Other varieties such as pistachio, walnut, fig, and bitter orange used fruit that was not yet fully ripe. Sometimes spoon sweets were made by using vegetables (such as eggplants or tomatoes) or even flower petals. The Greek seamen and merchants traveling east to Mesopotamia particularly appreciated the Turkish dessert baklava. They brought the recipe to Athens. *Phyllo* was coined by Greeks and means "leaf" in the Greek language. In a relatively short time, in every kitchen of wealthy households in the region, trays of baklava were being baked for all kinds of special occasions from the third century B.C. onward.

Wine is consumed regularly in Greece, but mainly with food, and in moderation. Ouzo is Greece's national drink. Ouzo is made from a precise combination of pressed grapes, herbs, and berries including aniseed, licorice, mint, wintergreen, fennel, and hazelnut. It is usually served as an aperitif, but is also used in some mixed drinks and cocktails. When mixing Ouzo with water it will turn whitish and opaque.

CRETE

Island cooking has always been shaped by the various rites of the Greek Orthodox Church. Christmas, Easter, and the feast of the Dormition of the Virgin Mary on August 15 (corresponding to the feast of the Assumption in the Roman Catholic Church) are the most colorful of the festivals. Easter is preceded by the forty days of Lent, during which people abstain from all foods derived from animals (meat, dairy products, and eggs), as they do every Wednesday and Friday throughout the year. This abstention has inspired cooks to develop a number of exquisite vegetarian dishes that substitute for the more familiar versions made with meat. Lenten grape leaves stuffed with rice; pasta with olive oil, onions, and spices; tomato and onion flatbread, and zucchini; and chickpea fritters are just a few of the flavorful examples. There is plenty of celebration food as well, like roast leg of lamb with potatoes, fragrant with garlic, oregano, and thyme, and baked chicken with orzo.

It is argued that the Cretan diet, based on olive oil, cereals, wine, and fish hasn't really changed since Minoan times. It has created the world's healthiest and long-lived people and is the basis of the famous Mediterranean diet. Research in the 1950s by the international scientific community concluded that Cretans were this healthy due to their diet. Today, it is generally agreed that following the traditional Cretan way of eating leads to less chance of suffering from heart disease compared to other Mediterranean countries. This seems to be due to the fact that Cretans eat twice as much fruit, a quarter less meat, and more pulses than other Europeans. Greek island cuisine is largely free from animal fats, an absence considered healthful. More than anywhere else in Greece, maybe more than anywhere else in the whole Mediterranean, the cooking of the Aegean islands is one in which the basic rule is that food be embellished as little as possible and altered as little as possible from its original state.

Glossary

Avgolemono Egg-lemon sauce prepared by adding fresh lemon juice to whisked eggs.

Baklava Famed Mediterranean pastry whose origin is debatable. Made from many layers of butter-brushed, nut- and sugar-sprinkled layers of phyllo pastry.

Barbouni Red mullet, a favorite fish usually served grilled or fried. The cheeks and liver are considered special delicacies.

Béchamel Sauce By this name, the sauce's origin is attributed to Louis de Béchamel, of the court of King Louis XIV. However, it should be noted that this same sauce—a roux of fat and flour whisked with a liquid, usually milk or cream—was described by Athenaeus in A.D. 200 and widely used in Greek cuisine.

Bourekakia A Turkish name for all the tiny appetizer pastries made from phyllo pastry and filled with a variety of savory fillings, including vegetables, meats, and cheese. In Greece these appetizers commonly take their name from the filling.

Greek Cheeses

Anthotiro A variation of mizithra. It is buttery in texture and comes in two variations, soft and dry.

Feta The most popular and most ancient of the Greek cheeses, the traditional cheese of Greece. It is traditionally made from goat's or sheep's milk and is stored in barrels of brine. Most feta comes from mountainous areas. It is used in salads, baked in pies, crumbled on omelets, or even stuffed into fish. The most popular way to eat feta is to lay a thick slab on a plate, pour on some olive oil, and add a pinch of oregano on top.

Graviera Hard in texture, mild in taste, this cheese resembles Swiss or Gruyère in texture. It is served with meals or used for grating over spaghetti.

Kapnisto Metsovone One of the few smoked cheeses of Greece. It is made from cow's milk, but sometimes with the addition of a little sheep's or goat's milk.

Kaser *(Kasseri)* This mild- to sharp-tasting cheese (depending on variety) is faint yellow in color, oily in texture, and usually eaten on its own. It is made from sheep's milk and is good as a table cheese.

Kefalograviera A cross between Kefalotiri and Graviera, this cheese is made from cow's milk. It is a hard cheese, pale yellow in color with a sharp taste and smell, used as a table cheese and for grating or frying.

Kefalotiri This traditional Greek cheese is very hard in texture. It is made with a combination of sheep's and goat's milk. Salty and sharp tasting, it is similar to regato and Parmesan and is used for grating over spaghetti. It is primarily used for frying. It is ripened for at least three months and so acquires a sharp aroma and a rich, salty, tangy taste.

Ladotyri This is sheep's and goat's milk cheese. It is made in the shape of small spheres and so is sometimes called *kefalaki* (little head). Its proper name refers to olive oil, in which it is aged. It can be aged for as much as a year and emerge richer and tastier.

Manouri Like mizithra, ricotta, and cottage cheeses, manouri is soft in texture and unsalted. It is made from full-fat sheep's milk and is mainly used for sweet pies. In Athens and the islands it is the name of soft cream cheese.

Mizithra It is made from sheep's or goat's milk and comes in two forms. The fresh, ricotta-like mizithra is unsalted. The dried version is salted, aged until hard, and is good for grating and cooking. Mizithra is more often used for sweet pies.

Telemes A variation of feta cheese. The difference is that it is made from cow's milk.

Touloumotiri This sweet, moist, snow-white cheese is stored by hanging in goatskin or sheepskin bags.

Dolmadakia Any stuffed food, this term refers to tiny stuffed foods such as small rolls of cabbage, spinach, or vine leaves or tiny scooped-out vegetables. These are filled with savory mixtures such as béchamel sauce and cheese or rice with seasonings.

Domates Tomatoes.

Fakki Meatless brown lentil soup, a standby for busy days and a staple when meat is scarce.

Fenugreek Pleasantly bittersweet seed generally ground.

Imam Bayaldi Slowly baked eggplants stuffed with tomatoes and sliced onions and flavored with garlic. Literally, "the caliph fainted," so named because the dish was so delicious that the priest was said to have fainted (here the stories differ) either when he tasted it or when he was denied a taste.

Kafes Turkish coffee introduced to Greece, brewed in a long-handled pot called a *briki*. In Greece it is called Greek coffee, but it is still made in thirty-three variations, as is Turkish coffee.

Kataifia Sweetened very fine shreds of a wheat flour pastry rolled up with chopped nuts.

Kefthedes or Keftethes Tiny meatballs prepared with finely minced meat (any kind) blended with bread crumbs and eggs then seasoned with garlic, mint, oregano, and salt and pepper. The mixture is formed into tiny balls and fried in oil until brown.

Kolokythia Called baby marrows in England, courgettes in France, and zucchini in Italy. Greeks enjoy the flowers freshly picked, stuffed, and fried.

Kouloura A Greek bread.

Kourabiedes Rich buttery shortbread-type cookies baked in round balls, liberally sprinkled with rosewater or orange flower water, and dusted with powdered sugar.

Mahlab Used in dessert breads, the spice is actually the pit of a sour cherry.

Mastica Unique to Greek cooking, the powdered resin from a small evergreen grown mostly on the Greek isle of Chios. Like ginger and mahlab, mastic is used as a spice in desserts and sweets, as well as a way to sweeten main entrées. Used for flavoring yeast dough. There is also a liqueur by the same name.

Melitzanosalata A popular Mediterranean appetizer of pureed eggplant seasoned liberally with onion and vinegar and garnished with black olives and tomato wedges.

Moussaka Browned eggplant slices layered with tomatoes, cheese, onions, and ground meat finished with a béchamel sauce. Typically Greek, there is a faint taste of cinnamon.

Nigella Small black seed with a nutty, pepper flavor that looks like black sesame. Most often used to top breads and to flavor salads and vegetables.

Ouzo A Greek anise-flavored alcoholic beverage that turns opaque when mixed with water.

Pastizzio A baked layered casserole of cooked pasta sprinkled with cheese and a layer of seasoned minced meat. The casserole is finished with cheese and béchamel sauce.

Phyllo or Fillo This paper-thin pastry is usually made commercially of egg, flour, and water. The Greek word *phyllo* means "leaf."

Saganaki or Tiraki Any firm cheese cut in squares, dusted with flour, and quickly fried in hot oil and served as an appetizer.

Skordalia or Skorthalia A smooth, thick sauce made with oil, lemon juice, soft white bread, and garlic. There are many variations depending on the region and the family; many versions include potato.

Souvlakia Skewered cubes of lamb with onions, green peppers, and tomato wedges, all marinated then broiled.

Spanakopita A "pie" of buttery layers of phyllo with a center portion of chopped cooked spinach and feta mixed with béchamel.

Stefado A stew.

Sumac Deep red, slightly sour spice with citrus notes. Ground sumac is used in salads, on grilled meats, in soups, and in rice dishes.

Taramosalata Creamy dip made of roe, white bread or potato, garlic, oil, and lemon juice.

Tzatziki A tangy dip of plain yogurt, minced cucumber, garlic, salt, and pepper.

Vasilopita Sweet yeast bread flavored with grated orange rind, cinnamon, and mastic, made especially for Saint Basil's Day.

Menus and Recipes from Greece and Turkey

Spanakopita Peloponniso
Peloponnese Spinach Rolls   SERVES 4

Feta cheese comes packed in brine. Rinse it under cold water, let it drain on a paper towel for a few minutes, then crumble it into the bowl containing the spinach and onions.

AMOUNT	MEASURE	INGREDIENT
8 cups	16 ounces, 448 g	Spinach, washed, coarse stems removed, roughly chopped
$\frac{1}{4}$ cup	2 ounces, 60 ml	Olive oil
$\frac{1}{2}$ cup	2 ounces, 56 g	Onion, $\frac{1}{4}$ inch (.6 cm) dice
$\frac{1}{2}$ cup	2 ounces, 56 g	Leek, white part only, $\frac{1}{4}$ inch (.6 cm) dice
$\frac{1}{2}$ cup	2 ounces, 56 g	Green onion, $\frac{1}{4}$ inch (.6 cm) dice
$\frac{1}{4}$ cup	$\frac{1}{2}$ ounce, 14 g	Flat-leaf parsley, chopped fine
$1\frac{1}{2}$ teaspoons		Fresh dill, chopped
$\frac{1}{8}$ teaspoon		Nutmeg
$\frac{1}{2}$ cup	2 ounces, 56 g	Feta cheese, crumbled
1		Egg, beaten
To taste		Salt and freshly ground black pepper
4		Sheets phyllo pastry
As needed		Olive oil or butter for assembling rolls

PROCEDURE

1 Preheat oven to 350°F (180°C).

2 Wilt spinach over medium heat and drain well in colander, pressing with spoon to remove all moisture.

3 Heat oil over medium heat and sauté onion for 5 minutes until soft. Add leeks and green onion, cook until soft, 5 minutes.

4 Combine the drained spinach, onion mixture, herbs, nutmeg, feta, and egg and season with salt and pepper. Cool.

5 Place a sheet of phyllo on work surface; brush lightly with olive oil or melted butter. Top with remaining sheets, brushing each with oil.

6 Brush top lightly with oil and place 2 ounces (56 g) spinach mixture along the length of the pastry toward one edge; leave $1\frac{1}{2}$ inches (4 cm) clear on each end.

7   Fold bottom edge of pastry over filling, roll once, fold in ends, then roll up. Place a hand at each end of roll and push it in gently, like an accordion.

8   Place roll on a parchment lined or oiled baking dish. Brush top with oil and bake at 350°F (180°C) for 30 minutes or until golden brown.

9   Serve hot, cut in portions.

Elliniki Salata Greek Salad SERVES 4

AMOUNT	MEASURE	INGREDIENT
2 cups	4 ounces, 112 g	Romaine lettuce, $\frac{1}{2}$ inch (1.27 cm) strips
$\frac{1}{4}$ cup	$\frac{1}{2}$ ounce, 14 g	Fresh dill
1 cup	6 ounces, 168 g	Tomatoes, peeled, seeded, $\frac{1}{2}$ inch (1.27 cm) dice
1 cup	6 ounces, 168 g	Cucumber, peeled, seeded, cut in half lengthwise, $\frac{1}{4}$ inch (.6 cm) slices
1 cup	4 ounces, 112 g	Red onion, cut into very thin rings
$\frac{1}{2}$ cup	2 ounces, 56 g	Green Italian or green bell pepper, seeded, $\frac{1}{2}$ inch (1.27 cm) dice
$\frac{1}{2}$ cup	3 ounces, 84 g	Kalamata olives, pitted
$\frac{1}{2}$ cup	3 ounces, 84 g	Feta cheese, crumbled (optional)
Dressing		
$\frac{1}{4}$ cup	2 ounces, 60 ml	Olive oil
1 tablespoon	$\frac{1}{2}$ ounce, 30 ml	Red wine vinegar
1 tablespoon	$\frac{1}{2}$ ounce, 30 ml	Fresh lemon juice
1		Garlic clove, mashed with $\frac{1}{2}$ teaspoon salt
2 teaspoons		Fresh oregano, or 1 teaspoon dried
To taste		Salt and pepper

PROCEDURE

1   Make dressing by whisking together all dressing ingredients.

2   Scatter lettuce on a platter; sprinkle with half the dill.

3   Combine remaining salad ingredients and dressing; toss well.

4   Distribute over lettuce and serve.

Aginares me Avgolemono
Artichokes with Egg and Lemon Sauce   SERVES 4

AMOUNT	MEASURE	INGREDIENT
4		Whole globe artichokes
2 tablespoons	1 ounce, 30 ml	Fresh lemon juice
1		Lemon, sliced
1 tablespoon	$\frac{1}{2}$ ounce, 15 ml	Olive oil
$1\frac{1}{4}$ cups	10 ounces, 300 ml	Chicken stock, boiling
$1\frac{1}{2}$ teaspoons		Cornstarch
2		Eggs, separated
1 tablespoon	$\frac{1}{2}$ ounce, 15 ml	Fresh lemon juice
To taste		Salt and pepper
1 tablespoon		Dill and parsley, chopped fine for garnish

PROCEDURE

1   Wash artichokes well and cut off stem close to base. Add 1 tablespoon (15 ml) lemon juice to enough cold water to cover artichokes.

2   Remove tough outer leaves and trim carefully. Cut off $1\frac{1}{4}$ inches (3 cm) from top and trim remaining leaf ends with scissors. Rub with lemon slices, to prevent discoloration.

3   Cook prepared artichokes in boiling salted water, 1 tablespoon (15 ml) lemon juice, and olive oil for 30 minutes or until tender. Test by pulling a leaf; if it comes away easily the artichokes are done.

4   Remove and invert to drain. Place in serving dish and keep warm.

5   Make avgolemono sauce using chicken stock or half stock and half artichoke water.

6   Mix cornstarch with enough cold water to make a paste and add to stock, stirring until thickened and bubbling. Let cook 1 minute.

7   Beat egg whites until stiff; add egg yolk and continue beating until light and fluffy. Add lemon juice gradually, beating constantly.

8   Gradually pour in thickened hot stock to egg, beating constantly.

9   Return sauce to heat and cook, stirring constantly, over low heat for 1 to 2 minutes to cook egg. Mixture should thicken enough to coat the back of a spoon. Do not boil.

10   Remove from heat and continue stirring; correct seasoning.

11   Serve immediately, pour over artichokes and sprinkle with chopped dill and parsley.

Fasoulatha Bean Soup   SERVES 4 TO 6

AMOUNT	MEASURE	INGREDIENT
2 cups	15 ounces, 420 g	Dried nave, cannellini, lima, or black-eyed beans
8 cups	64 ounces, 1.92 l	Water or stock
$\frac{1}{3}$ cup	$2\frac{1}{2}$ ounces, 75 ml	Olive oil
1 cup	4 ounces, 112 g	Onion, $\frac{1}{4}$ inch (.6 cm) dice
1 cup	4 ounces, 112 g	Celery, including leaves, $\frac{1}{4}$ inch (.6 cm) dice
1 cup	4 ounces, 112 g	Carrots, $\frac{1}{4}$ inch (.6 cm) dice
1 tablespoon	$\frac{1}{2}$ ounce, 14 g	Garlic, minced
$1\frac{1}{2}$ cups	9 ounces, 270 ml	Tomatoes, peeled, seeded, $\frac{1}{4}$ inch (.6 cm) dice
2 tablespoons	1 ounce, 28 g	Tomato paste
$\frac{1}{2}$ teaspoon		Granulated sugar
To taste		Salt and pepper
$\frac{1}{2}$ cup	1 ounce, 28 g	Flat-leaf parsley, chopped
As needed		Cayenne pepper
As needed		Lemon juice

PROCEDURE

1 Soak the beans in water overnight and drain.

2 Combine beans and water or stock; bring to boil.

3 Heat oil and sauté onions until transparent, 3 minutes.

4 Add celery and carrots and cook 3 to 4 minutes; add garlic and cook 1 minute.

5 Add tomatoes and tomato paste, cook 2 to 3 minutes.

6 Combine cooked vegetables with beans, bring to boil, reduce to simmer, and cook until beans are soft. Time depends on type of bean.

7 Add sugar and correct seasoning with salt and pepper.

8 To thicken the soup, mash some of the beans and vegetables against the side of the pot.

9 Stir in the chopped parsley and correct seasoning with toasted cayenne pepper and lemon juice if desired.

Garithes Saganaki
Baked Shrimp   SERVES 4

AMOUNT	MEASURE	INGREDIENT
	1 pound, 448 g	16–20 count uncooked shrimp, peeled and deveined
2 tablespoons	1 ounce, 30 ml	Fresh lemon juice
$\frac{1}{4}$ cup	2 ounces, 60 ml	Olive oil
1 cup	4 ounces, 112 g	Onions, $\frac{1}{4}$ inch (.6 cm) dice
2 tablespoons	1 ounce, 28 g	Pepperoncini, minced
2		Garlic cloves, minced
$\frac{1}{2}$ cup	2 ounces, 56 g	Green onion, minced
1 cup	6 ounces, 240 ml	Tomatoes, peeled, seeded, $\frac{1}{4}$ inch (.6 cm) dice
$\frac{1}{4}$ cup	2 ounces, 60 ml	Dry white wine
$\frac{1}{4}$ cup	$\frac{1}{2}$ ounce, 14 g	Parsley, chopped
$\frac{1}{2}$ teaspoon		Oregano
To taste		Salt and pepper
$\frac{1}{2}$ cup	2 ounces, 56 g	Feta cheese, crumbled

PROCEDURE

1 Sprinkle the cleaned shrimp with lemon juice and let stand until sauce is ready.

2 Heat oil over medium heat and sauté onions until transparent, 2 to 3 minutes. Add pepperoncini and garlic and cook 2 minutes; add green onion and cook 1 minute.

3 Add tomato to onion mixture and cook 5 minutes. Add shrimp, white wine, and half the parsley and oregano; cook 2 minutes. Correct seasoning.

4 Spoon half the tomato sauce into 4 individual oven dishes or 1 large dish. Add shrimp and spoon remaining sauce over shrimp; top with crumbled cheese.

5 Bake in a 450°F (232°C) oven for 6 to 7 minutes or until shrimp are firm (160°F, 71.1°C) and the feta is melted and lightly browned. Do not overcook or the shrimp will be tough.

6 Sprinkle with remaining parsley and serve with crusty bread.

Afelia Fried Pork with Coriander

SERVES 4

AMOUNT	MEASURE	INGREDIENT
1½ pounds	680 g	Pork tenderloin, cut in ½ inch (1.2 cm) cubes
1½ cups	12 ounces, 360 ml	Good-quality dry red wine
1 teaspoon		Salt
2 tablespoons		Coriander seeds, coarsely crushed
1		Cinnamon stick
To taste		Black pepper, freshly ground
6 tablespoons	3 ounces, 180 ml	Olive oil
As needed		Pourgouri pilafi (recipe follows)

PROCEDURE

1 Combine pork with red wine, salt, 1 tablespoon coriander seeds, cinnamon stick, and fresh pepper to taste (this dish requires lots of pepper). Marinate under refrigeration for at least 2 hours, turning pork occasionally.

2 Drain pork, reserving marinade, and pat dry. Do not discard the marinade.

3 Heat oil in pan over medium-high heat. Add pork; turn up heat to high and sauté, stirring frequently, until browned and just cooked through. Remove to serving plate.

4 Discard most of remaining fat, add remaining coriander seeds, and lightly toast until fragrant. Return marinade to pan, reduce until about ¼ cup (2 ounces, 60 ml) remains; should be sauce consistency. Discard cinnamon stick and correct seasoning.

5 Return pork, toss to coat, and reheat pork.

6 Serve immediately with pourgouri pilafi and yogurt.

Pourgouri Pilafi
Pilaf of Cracked Wheat   SERVES 4

AMOUNT	MEASURE	INGREDIENT
2 tablespoons	1 ounce, 30 ml	Olive oil
1 cup	4 ounces, 112 g	Onion, $\frac{1}{4}$ inch (.6 cm) dice
$\frac{1}{2}$ cup	1 ounce, 28 g	Vermicelli, crumbled
2 cups	16 ounces, 480 ml	Chicken stock
1 cup	7 ounces, 196 g	Pourgouri (coarse cracked wheat)
To taste		Salt and pepper

PROCEDURE

1   Heat oil over medium heat and sauté onion until transparent, 3 minutes.

2   Stir in vermicelli; sauté with onion until vermicelli begins to absorb the oil.

3   Add the stock and bring to a boil.

4   Wash the pourgouri under cold running water; add to liquid, and season to taste.

5   Stir until it boils again, reduce heat to a simmer, and cook 8 to 10 minutes or until all the stock is absorbed.

6   Let sit for 10 minutes before serving.

Fresh Fruit

Sweets are not the everyday desert in Greece but are rather reserved for special occasions, holidays, or between-meal treats. Serve fresh fruits such as grapes, figs, melons, pomegranates, or whatever is in season. In Greece, the fruits usually come in a large bowl of ice water. Dried fruits such as figs and raisins are standard winter fare. A bowl of nuts usually accompanies the fruits.

Assorted fresh fruit

Dolmathakia me Rizi
Stuffed Grape Vine Leaves

YIELD: ABOUT 30; SERVES 4–6

AMOUNT	MEASURE	INGREDIENT
8 ounces	240 ml	Preserved vine leaves, or 40 fresh leaves
2 tablespoons	$\frac{1}{2}$ ounce, 14 g	Pine nuts
$\frac{1}{4}$ cup	2 ounces, 60 ml	Olive oil
I cup	4 ounces, 112 g	Onions, $\frac{1}{8}$ inch (.3 cm) dice
$\frac{1}{2}$ cup	$3\frac{1}{2}$ ounces, 98 g	Short-grain rice
$\frac{1}{4}$ cup	$\frac{1}{2}$ ounce, 14 g	Parsley, chopped
I teaspoon		Mint, chopped
I tablespoon		Dill, chopped
$\frac{1}{2}$ cup	2 ounces, 56 g	Green onion, tops included, chopped
$\frac{1}{8}$ teaspoon		Allspice, ground
$\frac{1}{8}$ teaspoon		Cinnamon, ground
I teaspoon		Salt
To taste		Pepper, freshly ground
$1\frac{1}{4}$ cups	10 ounces, 300 ml	Vegetable or chicken stock
2 tablespoons	I ounces, 30 ml	Lemon juice
I cup	8 ounces, 240 ml	Olive oil
As needed		*Tzatziki* (recipe follows)

PROCEDURE

1   Drain brine from the grape leaves, rinse in cold water, and blanch in boiling water 1 minute. Transfer to a cold-water bath and drain in colander until needed. If using fresh leaves, blanch in boiling water for 3 to 4 minutes; shock and drain.

2   Toast pine nuts in oven until they just turn amber.

3   Heat oil over medium heat and sauté onions until transparent, 5 minutes.

4   Add rice; stir until completely coated with oil.

5   Add herbs, allspice, cinnamon, and season with salt and pepper. Add $\frac{1}{2}$ cup (4 ounces, 120 ml) stock.

6   Cover pan and simmer 5 minutes. Remove from heat and stir in pine nuts. Cool.

7   To shape dolma, place a vine leaf, shiny side down, on work surface. Snip off stem if necessary. Place about a tablespoon of mixture near stem end, fold end and sides over stuffing, and roll up firmly. (Do not roll too tightly because the rice will swell).

8   Line base of a shallow pan with vine leaves (use damaged ones) and place dolmas side by side in layers, seam side down and close together. Sprinkle with lemon juice; add 1 cup (8 ounces, 240 ml) olive oil and remaining stock (enough just to cover the dolmas). Cover top rolls with remaining grape vine leave.

9   Place a plate over dolma to prevent them from opening, cover and simmer over a low heat for about 35 to 40 minutes or until rice is completely cooked.

10   Uncover the dolmas so they can cool quickly. As soon as they can be handled, remove with a spatula and arrange on a platter. Serve warm or at room temperature with *tzatziki* and lemon wedges.

Saganaki Fried Cheese SERVES 4

AMOUNT	MEASURE	INGREDIENT
	12 ounces, 336 g	Kefalograviera, kasseri, or graviera cheese, or provolone
As needed		Flour for dredging
½ cup	4 ounces, 120 ml	Olive oil
1		Lemon, cut in wedges

PROCEDURE

1 Cut the cheese into strips 2 inches (4.9 cm) wide and ½ inch (1.2 cm) thick.

2 Run strips under cold running water and dredge lightly with flour. Be sure to cover all surfaces of the cheese with flour.

3 Heat oil over medium-high heat and pan-fry cheese, turning once, until golden brown on both sides.

4 Remove, drain on paper towels, and serve immediately, accompanied by the lemon wedges. Or squeeze lemon juice to taste onto fried cheese, serve cheese in pan. Serve with additional lemon wedges and eat with crusty bread, which is dipped into the lemon-flavored oil in the pan.

Tzatziki
Garlic, Cucumber, and Yogurt Dip   SERVES 4

AMOUNT	MEASURE	INGREDIENT
1 cup	8 ounces, 240 ml	Plain yogurt
1 cup	6 ounces, 180 ml	Cucumber, peeled, seeded, and shredded
3		Garlic cloves, minced
2 tablespoons	1 ounce, 30 ml	Olive oil
1 tablespoon	$\frac{1}{2}$ ounce, 15 ml	Red wine vinegar or lemon juice
To taste		Salt and black pepper
		Mint leaves for garnish

PROCEDURE

1   Drain the yogurt in a colander lined with cheesecloth for at least 1 hour. The yogurt will lose about a third of its volume and will be considerably creamier and thicker.

2   Press the shredded cucumbers in a colander with a dish on top of them to weigh them down, and let drain for one hour. Squeeze the cucumber to remove all excess moisture.

3   Combine yogurt, cucumbers, garlic, olive oil, vinegar, salt, and pepper; mix well. Refrigerate for 1 hour before serving.

4   Serve chilled with crusty bread, garnished with mint leaves.

Salata me Portokalia kai Elies
Orange and Olive Salad

SERVES 4

AMOUNT	MEASURE	INGREDIENT
4		Navel oranges, peeled, pith removed, and sliced into $\frac{1}{4}$ inch (.6 cm) rounds
I cup	4 ounces, 112 g	Red onion, cut into very thin rings
I cup	4 ounces, 112 g	Kalamata olives, pitted, rinsed, and halved
I		Garlic clove, smashed
$\frac{1}{2}$ teaspoon		Dried thyme
$\frac{1}{2}$ teaspoon		Black peppercorns
2 tablespoons	I ounce, 30 ml	Orange juice, fresh strained
2 teaspoons	20 ml	Red wine vinegar
$\frac{1}{4}$ cup	2 ounces, 60 ml	Extra virgin olive oil
I cup	2 ounces, 56 g	Arugula leaves, washed, patted dry, and shredded

PROCEDURE

1   Arrange the oranges, onions, and olives on a platter.

2   Using a mortar and pestle, crush together the garlic, thyme, and peppercorns. Combine spices with orange juice, vinegar, and olive oil; whisk well to combine.

3   Sprinkle the shredded arugula leaves over the oranges, onion slices, and drizzle with the dressing.

4   Serve immediately.

Psari Savoro
Fried Fish with Rosemary and Vinegar

SERVES 4

AMOUNT	MEASURE	INGREDIENT
4	4–5 ounce, 112–140 g	Fish fillets, boneless and skinned
2 tablespoons	1 ounce, 30 ml	Fresh lemon juice
As needed		Salt
As needed		Olive oil, for frying
As needed		All-purpose flour
2		Garlic cloves, minced
1 teaspoon		Rosemary leaves, fresh or dried
3 tablespoons	$1\frac{1}{2}$ ounces, 45 ml	Sherry or red wine vinegar
3 tablespoons	$1\frac{1}{2}$ ounces, 45 ml	White wine
To taste		Salt and fresh pepper

PROCEDURE

1 Sprinkle fish with lemon juice and salt; let sit 30 minutes.

2 Heat oil over medium heat.

3 Flour fish and pan-fry until golden brown on both sides and cooked completely. Drain and place on warm dish.

4 Pour off all but 2 tablespoons (1 ounce, 30 ml) oil. Add garlic and rosemary; cook 1 minute. Sprinkle in 2 teaspoons flour and stir over medium heat until lightly colored.

5 Add vinegar and white wine; cook 1 minute, stirring constantly. Correct seasoning and consistency (thin with water if too thick) and serve over fish.

Fasolakia
Fresh Green Bean Ragout SERVES 4

AMOUNT	MEASURE	INGREDIENT
$\frac{1}{4}$ cup	2 ounces, 60 ml	Olive oil
I cup	6 ounces, 168 g	Red onions, halved, thinly sliced
3		Garlic cloves, minced
I pound	16 ounces, 448 g	Green beans, trimmed
2 cups	10 ounces, 280 g	Potato, peeled, $\frac{1}{2}$ inch (1.2 cm) dice
I		Fresh or dried chile pepper
I cup	6 ounces, 168 g	Tomato, peeled, seeded, $\frac{1}{4}$ inch (.6 cm) dice
To taste		Salt and pepper
$\frac{1}{2}$ cup	I ounce, 28 g	Parsley, chopped
2 tablespoons	I ounce, 30 ml	Red wine vinegar
I cup	6 ounces, 168 g	Feta cheese

PROCEDURE

1 Heat olive oil over medium heat and sauté onions and garlic until soft, 7 minutes.

2 Add green beans and toss to coat. Cover pan, reduce heat, and steam green beans in the oil for 10 minutes.

3 Add potatoes and chile pepper, toss to coat, add tomatoes, and season with salt and pepper.

4 Add enough water just to cover vegetables. Cover pan and simmer until beans and potatoes are tender, 20 to 30 minutes.

5 Add parsley and vinegar, toss to coat, and cook 5 minutes.

6 Adjust seasoning. Serve warm or at room temperature, with feta cheese on the side.

Kataifi Nut-Stuffed Shredded Wheat Rolls

YIELD: 12 ROLLS

AMOUNT	MEASURE	INGREDIENT
1 $\frac{1}{4}$ cups	12 ounces, 360 ml	Butter, melted
$\frac{3}{4}$ cup	3 ounces, 84 g	Walnuts, coarsely ground
$\frac{3}{4}$ cup	3 ounces, 84 g	Almonds, coarsely ground
$\frac{1}{8}$ cup	1 ounce, 28 g	Granulated sugar
$\frac{1}{2}$ teaspoon		Cinnamon, ground
1		Egg, beaten
2 tablespoons	1 ounce, 30 ml	Heavy cream
8 ounces		Kataifi pastry, thawed, room temperature
Galaktoboureko Syrup		
1 cup	7 ounces, 196 g	Granulated sugar
1 cup	8 ounces, 240 ml	Water
1 tablespoon	$\frac{1}{2}$ ounce, 15 ml	Fresh lemon juice
Pinch		Cinnamon, ground

PROCEDURE

1   Brush sheet pan with melted butter and set aside.

2   Combine nuts, sugar, and cinnamon; mix well.

3   Beat egg with cream and 3 tablespoons melted butter.

4   To prepare shredded wheat rolls, spread out a handful of the pastry to about 6 inches long. Brush generously with melted butter, place a tablespoon of nut filling on bottom, and roll up tightly, incorporating the loose ends inward as you go.

5   Place seam side down on buttered pan, and repeat with remaining pastry and filling.

6   Brush the tops of the pastries liberally with remaining butter.

7   Bake at 350°F (180°C), 1 hour.

8   Remove to a rack and let stand for 5 to 10 minutes.

9   Make syrup by combining sugar and water over medium heat; as soon as sugar dissolves, add lemon juice and cinnamon. Bring to a boil, reduce heat, and simmer 10 minutes.

10 Spoon hot syrup over rolls. Cover the pan with a clean towel and let stand 2 to 3 hours before serving, occasionally basting with syrup.

Moussaka Eggplant Moussaka   SERVES 4

AMOUNT	MEASURE	INGREDIENT
1	16 ounce, 448 g	Eggplant, skin on, cut into $\frac{1}{4}$ inch (.6 cm) slices
As needed		Salt
Meat Sauce		
2 tablespoons	1 ounce, 30 ml	Olive oil
1 cup	6 ounces, 168 g	Onion, $\frac{1}{4}$ inch (.6 cm) dice
2		Garlic cloves, minced
2 cups	1 pound, 16 ounces, 448 g	Ground lamb or lean ground beef
1 cup	6 ounces, 180 ml	Tomato, peeled, seeded, $\frac{1}{4}$ inch (.6 cm) dice
2 tablespoons	1 ounce, 30 ml	Tomato paste
$\frac{1}{2}$ cup	4 ounces, 120 ml	White wine
2 tablespoons		Chopped parsley
1 teaspoon		Sugar
$\frac{1}{4}$ teaspoon		Cinnamon, ground
To taste		Salt and pepper
Cream Sauce		
$\frac{1}{4}$ cup	2 ounces, 60 ml	Butter
$\frac{1}{3}$ cup	2.33 ounces, 66 g	Flour, all-purpose
2 cups	16 ounces, 480 ml	Milk
$\frac{1}{8}$ teaspoon		Nutmeg
$\frac{1}{4}$ cup	1 ounce, 28 g	Kefalotiri or Parmesan cheese
To taste		Salt and pepper
1		Egg, lightly beaten

PROCEDURE

1   Sprinkle eggplant slices with salt and let sit 1 hour. Dry with paper towels.

Meat Sauce

1   Heat oil over medium heat and sauté onion, 2 minutes. Add garlic; cook 2 minutes or until onions are soft.

2   Add lamb and brown over high heat, stirring well. Add remaining meat sauce ingredients; cover and cook 20 minutes. Correct seasoning.

Cream Sauce

1 Melt butter over medium heat and stir in flour; cook gently 2 minutes. Add milk, stir to combine, turn heat to high, and bring to a boil. Cook 2 minutes. Remove from heat.

2 Sir in nutmeg and 1 tablespoon cheese; correct seasoning.

Assemble Moussaka

1 Oil an 8 × 8 inch (20 × 20 cm) baking pan. Place a layer of eggplant slices in the base. Top with half the meat sauce, add another layer of eggplant, the remainder of meat sauce, and finish with eggplant.

2 Stir beaten egg into sauce and spread on top. Sprinkle with remaining cheese.

3 Bake at 350°F (180°C), 1 hour. Let stand 10 minutes before cutting into squares to serve.

Moussaka – Eggplant Moussaka

Kabak Kizartmasi and Patlican Kizartmasi
Zucchini and Eggplant Fritters   SERVES 4

AMOUNT	MEASURE	INGREDIENT
2 cups	10 ounces, 280 g	Long slender eggplant
2 cups	10 ounces, 280 g	Zucchini, $\frac{3}{4}$ inch (1.8 cm) slices lengthwise or diagonally
As needed		Oil for pan-frying
1 cup	7 ounce, 196 g	All-purpose flour
1 teaspoon		Salt
$\frac{3}{4}$ cup	6 ounces, 180 ml	Beer
2		Garlic cloves
$\frac{1}{2}$ teaspoon		Salt
1 cup	8 ounces, 240 ml	Yogurt
As needed		Tarator (recipe follows)

PROCEDURE

1 Peel off lengthwise strips of eggplant to give a striped effect, then cut into $\frac{1}{4}$ inch (.6 cm) diagonal slices. Sprinkle liberally with salt and leave for 30 minutes. Wipe off salt and dry with paper towels.

2 Oil eggplant slices on both sides and broil or grill, turning, until brown on both sides. Alternatively, eggplant may be pan-fried. Remove from heat or oil and stack until needed.

3 To make batter, sift flour and salt together; add beer and mix to a smooth batter.

4 Dip eggplant and zucchini into batter and pan-fry until tender and golden brown on both sides, approximately 2 to 3 minutes. Drain on paper towels.

5 Serve hot with *yogurt salcasi* and *tarator*.

Yogurt Salacasi: Yogurt Sauce

1 Mash 2 cloves garlic with salt to a fine paste. Combine with yogurt and chill.

Tarator Hazelnut Sauce   YIELD: 2 CUPS

AMOUNT	MEASURE	INGREDIENT
I cup	4 ounces, 112 g	Hazelnuts, whole and peeled
I cup	3 ounces, 84 g	Fresh white breadcrumbs
2		Garlic cloves, crushed
I tablespoon	$\frac{1}{2}$ ounce, 15 ml	Water
I cup	8 ounces, 240 ml	Olive oil
$\frac{1}{2}$ cup	4 ounces, 120 ml	White vinegar or fresh lemon juice
I teaspoon		Salt

PROCEDURE

1 Grind hazelnuts in a blender or food processor or pound in mortar. If using a mortar, place nuts in a bowl when pulverized.

2 Add breadcrumbs, garlic, and water; process while adding oil.

3 Gradually add vinegar, process until smooth, and add salt.

4 Chill and serve.

Midye Dolmasi
Stuffed Mussels   SERVES 4

AMOUNT	MEASURE	INGREDIENT
$\frac{1}{4}$ cup	2 ounces, 60 ml	Olive oil
I cup	4 ounces, 112 g	Onions, $\frac{1}{4}$ inch (.6 cm) dice
I tablespoon		Pine nuts
$\frac{1}{2}$ cup	4 ounces, 112 g	Long-grain rice, washed
I tablespoon		Parsley, chopped
$\frac{1}{2}$ teaspoon		Allspice, ground
$\frac{1}{2}$ cup	3 ounces, 90 ml	Tomatoes, peeled, seeded, $\frac{1}{4}$ inch (.6 cm) dice
$\frac{1}{2}$ cup	4 ounces, 120 ml	Fish stock or water
To taste		Salt and fresh pepper
20 large		Mussels
$\frac{1}{2}$ cup	4 ounces, 120 ml	Fish stock or water
4		Lemon wedges, for serving
As needed		Tarator (see recipe on page 491)

PROCEDURE

1   Heat oil over medium heat; sauté onions until transparent, 5 minutes. Add pine nuts and cook 2 minutes. Stir in rice, parsley, allspice, tomatoes, and $\frac{1}{2}$ cup (4 ounces, 120 ml) stock; add salt and pepper. Cover and simmer on low 15 minutes until liquid is absorbed.

2   Prepare mussels. Scrub mussels well and tug beard toward pointed end of the mussel to remove. To open, place scrubbed mussels in warm salted water. As they open, insert point of knife between the shells and slice it toward pointed end to sever the closing mechanism. For stuffing do not separate shells.

3   Place 2 teaspoons of filling in each mussel and close the shell as much as possible. Arrange mussels in a even layer, and place a weight on top to keep them closed.

4   Add water or stock, bring to a simmer, cover pan, and simmer 15 to 20 minutes, until mussel meat is cooked. Turn off heat and cool in pan.

5   Carefully remove mussels and wipe shell with paper towel. Shells may be lightly oiled for a more attractive appearance.

6   Serve chilled or at room temperature with lemon wedges and tarator.

Midye Dolmasi – Stuffed Mussels

Sis Kebap
Skewered Lamb and Vegetables   SERVES 4

AMOUNT	MEASURE	INGREDIENT
	20 ounces, 560 g	Lamb meat, boneless from leg, $1\frac{1}{4}$ inch (3.18 cm) cubes
2 tablespoons	1 ounce, 30 ml	Fresh lemon juice
$\frac{1}{4}$ cup	2 ounces, 60 ml	Olive oil
$\frac{3}{4}$ cup	3 ounces, 84 g	Onion, thinly sliced
To taste		Black pepper, freshly ground
1		Bay leaf, crumbled
$\frac{1}{2}$ teaspoon		Thyme, dried
8		Wooden skewers, soaked in water 1 hour
Garnish		
8		Pearl onions, peeled and parboiled in salted water
8 cubes		Red bell pepper, cored, seeded, white membrane removed, cut in $1\frac{1}{4}$ inch (3.18 cm) cubes
8 cubes		Green bell pepper, cored, seeded, white membrane removed, cut in $1\frac{1}{4}$ inch (3.18 cm) cubes

PROCEDURE

1   Combine lamb cubes, lemon juice, olive oil, onions, black pepper, bay leaf, and thyme. Do not add salt, it draws out the meat juices. Mix well and marinate at room temperature 1 hour or refrigerate 2 to 3 hours.

2   Blanch bell peppers in boiling salted water for 30 seconds; let cool.

3   To assemble skewers, remove meat from marinade and thread onto 8 skewers, alternating cubes of meat with onions and peppers.

4   Grill over medium high heat, turning frequently and brushing with marinade when required. After searing meat, move to lower heat to avoid burning vegetables.

5   Serve hot on a bed of Beyaz Pilav, colored with turmeric.

Sis Kebap – Skewered Lamb and Vegetables and Havuc Plakisi – Braised Carrots, Beyaz Pilav

Balik Köftesi Fish Balls   SERVES 4

AMOUNT	MEASURE	INGREDIENT
	12 ounces, 336 g	White fish fillets, skinless, boneless
$\frac{1}{4}$ cup	1 ounce, 28 g	Green onion, white only, minced
1 tablespoon		Parsley, minced
1 teaspoon		Dill, minced
Pinch		Hot red pepper
$\frac{3}{4}$ cup	3 ounces, 84 g	Fresh white breadcrumbs
1		Egg
To taste		Salt and fresh pepper
As needed		All-purpose flour
As needed		Oil for deep-frying
4		Lemon wedges, for serving

PROCEDURE

1   In a food processor combine fish, onion, parsley, dill, and red pepper; process to a smooth paste.

2   Remove to a bowl and work in breadcrumbs and egg; work to a paste and correct seasoning. Do not overwork.

3   With moistened hands, shape into balls the size of walnuts. Chill until firm.

4   Coat with flour and deep-fry for 4 to 6 minutes at 370°F (188°C).

5   Drain on paper towels and serve hot with lemon wedges.

Domates Salatasi
Tomato Salad   SERVES 4

AMOUNT	MEASURE	INGREDIENT
2	10 ounces, 280 g	Tomatoes, firm
I	10 ounces, 280 g	English cucumber
2 tablespoons	I ounce, 30 ml	Lemon juice
I tablespoon	$\frac{1}{2}$ ounce, 15 ml	White vinegar
2 tablespoons	I ounce, 30 ml	Olive oil
I teaspoon		Fresh mint, chopped fine
2 teaspoons		Fresh parsley, chopped fine
To taste		Salt and fresh pepper
$\frac{3}{4}$ cup	3 ounces, 84 g	Black olives, pitted

PROCEDURE

1 Peel tomatoes and slice $\frac{1}{8}$ inch (.3 cm) thick; arrange in a row on platter.

2 Peel cucumber and slice $\frac{1}{8}$ inch (.3 cm) thick; arrange in a row on platter.

3 Combine lemon juice, vinegar, olive oil, mint, and parsley; correct seasoning.

4 Pour over tomatoes and cucumber. Chill 15 minutes.

5 Garnish platter with olives before serving.

Havuc Plakisi Braised Carrots   SERVES 4

AMOUNT	MEASURE	INGREDIENT
$\frac{1}{4}$ cup	2 ounces, 60 ml	Olive oil
I cup	4 ounces, 112 g	Onions, cut in half lengthwise, then sliced into thin semicircles
I pound	16 ounces, 448 g	Carrots, $\frac{1}{4}$ inch (.6 cm) diagonal slices
$\frac{3}{4}$ cup	6 ounces, 180 ml	Water
2 tablespoons		Parsley, chopped
I teaspoon		Granulated sugar
To taste		Salt and freshly ground black pepper
I teaspoon		Fresh lemon juice

PROCEDURE

1 Heat oil over medium heat and sauté onions until transparent, 5 minutes.

2 Add carrots and cook 5 minutes, stirring frequently.

3 Add water, half the parsley and sugar. Season to taste, cover pan tightly, and simmer on low heat until carrots are tender, 15 minutes. Remove from heat, add lemon juice, and correct seasoning. Remove to serving dish to cool to room temperature.

4 Serve sprinkled with remaining parsley.

Beyaz Pilave Plain Pilaf SERVES 4

AMOUNT	MEASURE	INGREDIENT
1 cup	7 ounces, 196 g	Long-grain rice
2 tablespoons	1 ounce, 30 ml	Olive oil
$\frac{1}{4}$ teaspoon		Turmeric
$1\frac{3}{4}$ cups	14 ounces, 420 ml	Chicken stock
To taste		Salt

PROCEDURE

1 Wash rice until water runs clean. Drain well.

2 Heat oil over medium heat and add turmeric; stir to incorporate.

3 Add rice and sauté for 5 minutes.

4 Add stock, salt to taste, and stir occasionally until boiling. Reduce heat, cover, and simmer 20 minutes or until firm to the bite but evenly tender.

5 Remove from heat and let stand, covered, for 5 minutes.

6 Fluff up with a fork and serve.

Íncír Compostu Figs in Syrup

SERVES 4

AMOUNT	MEASURE	INGREDIENT
	12 ounces, 336 g	Dried figs
3 cups	24 ounces, 720 ml	Water
As needed		Blanched almonds
$\frac{1}{2}$ cup	4 ounces, 112 g	Granulated sugar
Thin strip		Lemon rind
2 tablespoons	1 ounce, 30 ml	Fresh lemon juice
3 tablespoons	$1\frac{1}{2}$ ounces, 45 ml	Honey
$\frac{1}{4}$ cup	1 ounce, 28 g	Pistachios, almonds, or walnuts, chopped
$\frac{1}{2}$ cup	4 ounces, 120 ml	Yogurt

PROCEDURE

1   Wash figs and plump in cold water overnight, or simmer gently for 10 minutes. Drain and save liquid.

2   Insert almond in base of each fig; set aside.

3   Add sugar to water; heat to dissolve. Add lemon rind, juice, and honey; bring to a boil.

4   Add prepared figs and return to the boil. Simmer gently for 30 minutes, until figs are tender and syrup is thick. If necessary, remove figs and reduce cooking liquid. Remove lemon rind.

5   Arrange figs and pour syrup over, chill.

6   Sprinkle with chopped nuts and serve with yogurt.

Africa

The Land

The African continent is bordered by the Indian Ocean to the east, the Atlantic Ocean to the west, and the Mediterranean Sea to the north. It was once connected to Asia's land mass in the northeastern corner by the Sinai Peninsula, where the Suez Canal now exists. The Nile River in northeast Africa is the longest river in the world and has been a source of survival for many African people for thousands of years. The river and its tributaries run through nine countries and flow a total of 4,160 miles, providing food, fertile land, and a mode of transportation.

Northern Africa includes Algeria, Morocco, Tunisia, Libya, Egypt, and the Sudan. The Atlas Mountains run from Morocco to Tunisia, covering more than 1,200 miles and providing a route between the coast and the Sahara Desert. Both the High and Middle Atlas slopes have dense forests containing cedar, pine, cork, and oak trees. There are fertile valleys and tracts of pasture where livestock can feed. Within the mountain range, there is a wide variety of mineral deposits that have hardly been touched. The Sahara Desert separates northern Africa from the rest of the continent. All of the regions south of northern Africa are known as sub-Sahara.

Western Africa includes the countries Mali, Burkina Faso, Niger, the Ivory Coast (Cote d'Ivoire), Guinea, Senegal, Mauritania, Benin, Togo, Cameroon, Guinea-Bissau, Sao Tome and Principe, Cape Verde, Equatorial Guinea, Western Sahara, Liberia, Sierra Leone, Gambia, Ghana, and Nigeria. West Africa contains dense forests, vast expanses of desert and grassland, environmentally important wetland areas, and many large, sprawling cities. Virgin rain forests that once covered much of the West African coast have been drastically reduced by logging and agriculture. The southern regions' tropical rain forest grows some of the world's most prized hardwood trees, such as mahogany and iroko. The Niger River flows 2,600 miles and supports rich fish stocks.

Eastern Africa includes Ethiopia, Eritrea, Somalia, Djibouti, Rwanda, Burundi, Uganda, Kenya, Mozambique, Angola, and Tanzania. The Great Rift Valley dominates East Africa and includes Lake Victoria, the mountains of Kilimanjaro, and Mount Kenya. East Africa's coastline is among the finest in the world and includes an almost continuous belt of coral reefs that provide an important habitat for fish and other marine life. The vast expanses of savanna grassland that cover much of the rest of East Africa are home to many of the region's people and much of its rich wildlife. The Serengeti and the Masai Mara contain some of the greatest concentrations of wildlife in the world. In northern Kenya the savanna turns into a semiarid landscape where few people live and very little grows. Nairobi, Mombasa, Dar es Salaam, and Kampala are thriving modern cities in stark contrast to the vast savanna plains of Tanzania, the rain forests of western Uganda, and the remote deserts of northern Kenya. These cities reflect East Africa's relatively advanced development compared with other African countries.

Central Africa includes the Democratic Republic of the Congo (formerly Zaire), the Congo, Gabon, Chad, Central African Republic, Zambia, and Malawi. The great rain forest basin of the Congo River embraces most of Central Africa. Lake Chad is the fourth largest lake in Africa and is located in the Sahel zone of west-central Africa between Chad, Cameroon, Nigeria, and Niger. Lake Chad is a very important asset to the region, because of its contribution to the region's hydrology and because of the diversity of flora and fauna that it attracts. The Lake Chad region is known for its important role in trans-Saharan trade and for important archaeological discoveries that have been made here.

Southern Africa includes the countries of South Africa, Namibia, Lesotho, Swaziland, Botswana, as well as the islands of Madagascar, Mauritius, Seychelles, and Comoros. Like much of the African continent, this region is dominated by a high plateau in the interior, surrounded by a narrow strip of coastal lowlands. Unlike most of Africa, however, the perimeter of South Africa's inland plateau rises abruptly to form a series of mountain ranges before dropping to sea level. These mountains are known as the Great Escarpment. The coastline is fairly regular and has few natural harbors. Each of the dominant land features—the inland plateau, the encircling mountain ranges, and the coastal lowlands—exhibits a wide range of variation in topography and in natural resources, The interior plateau consists of a series of rolling grasslands (*veld* in Afrikaans), arising out of the Kalahari Desert in the north. The largest subregion in the plateau is the 1,200-meter to 1,800-meter-high central area known as the Highveld that stretches from Western Cape province to the northeast. In the north, it rises into a series of rock formations known as the Witwatersrand (literally, "Ridge of White Waters" in Afrikaans, commonly shortened to Rand). The Rand is a ridge of gold-bearing rock that serves as a watershed for numerous rivers and streams. It is also the site of the world's largest proven gold deposits and the country's leading industrial city, Johannesburg. North of the Witwatersrand is a dry savanna subregion known as the Bushveld, characterized by

Africa

open grasslands with scattered trees and bushes. The Bushveld, like the Rand, is a treasure chest of minerals, one of the largest and best known layered igneous (volcanic) mineral complexes in the world. It has extensive deposits of chromium and significant reserves of copper, gold, nickel, and iron. South Africa is rich in diamonds and is the world's biggest supplier of platinum.

History

Until about a thousand years ago, Africa was a land of many different tribes with a few larger kingdoms. It had little contact with the rest of the world. Over the next nine hundred years, it was slowly penetrated by other outside cultures, principally the Arabs of the Middle East and the seafaring nations of northwest Europe. These intruders brought their religions—Islam in the north and east, Christianity in much of the rest—and the slave trade. A few settled in the land, but most were content to take the continent's riches home with them. By the end of the 1800s, most of Africa was formally divided into European colonies, under the direct rule of the European colonial powers.

It was during this period, with the slave trade abolished and most of the continent explored, mapped, and divided, that the European powers began to govern Africa on a daily basis.

This colonial period ended, with a few exceptions, in the late 1950s and early 1960s. In the decade that followed Ghana's independence in 1957 (the first sub-Saharan country to gain independence), the British, French, and Belgians withdrew from almost all their African colonies. Only the Portuguese (in Angola, Mozambique, and Portuguese Guinea) and the white minority government of South Africa clung to colonial power.

After the European administrators went home, most of the newly independent countries set out to develop their economies along free enterprise lines and to establish systems of government. There have been some successes. A few economies have flourished, at least for a while, and there are signs that democracy has taken root in some countries. But mostly there have been failures. Over the last forty years, many African countries have succumbed to brutal dictators, and economic progress has been either minimal or nonexistent. As poverty and hopelessness have spread, violence has erupted both within and between states.

African countries are varied in their levels of economic development; however, the continent as a whole is considered to be a developing region. The most economically developed country is South Africa. Next are the Mediterranean countries in northern Africa as well as Nigeria. Zaire, Kenya, Cameroon, Ghana, Cote d'Ivoire, Zimbabwe, Gabon, Reunion, Namibia, and Mauritius are considered to be partly developed. The remaining countries are considered to be less developed.

The People

The people of Africa belong to several thousand different ethnic groups. At the same time, over the centuries the different groups have also influenced one another and contributed to and enriched one another's culture. There are over fifty countries in Africa, and some have twenty or more different ethnic groups living within their boundaries.

While the majority of the countries in Africa are inhabited by people of African origin, some ethnic groups have been affected by the migration of Arab peoples into northern Africa. There are also Europeans whose families moved to Africa during the colonial period and have stayed on. In some parts of Africa, there are people of Asian origin, such as those from the Indian subcontinent. Some of the more widely known ethnic groups in Africa are Arabs, Ashanti, Bantu, Berbers, Bushmen, Dinka, Fulani, Ganda, Hamites, Hausa, Hottentot, Kikuyu, Luba, Lunda, Malinke, Moors, Nuer, Semites, Swahili, Tuareg, Xhosa, and Yoruba.

Although the majority of the people in Africa lead a rural life, the continent is urbanizing at a fast pace. Over a third of the population now lives in cities. Those who live and work in the major metropolitan areas live in ways similar to most people in the industrialized world. However, they may not always have all the advantages of those who live in the larger, more modern cities. Their schools may have fewer resources, the opportunities for earning a living may not be as varied, and the services available may not be as technologically advanced.

The lifestyle of those living in rural Africa has remained virtually unchanged for centuries. They have rich cultural heritages that they have passed down from generation to generation with very little influence from the outside world.

There is extreme poverty and vast wealth; there are people who suffer from droughts and famine and people who have plentiful food. There are vast, magnificent nature reserves with an abundance of wildlife and there are highly urbanized parts with major cities with high-rise buildings and modern amenities. Much of the economy is based on agriculture in most African countries; and yet only 6 percent of the land mass is arable, while 25 percent is covered with forests, and another 25 percent is used for pasture or rangeland. Approximately 66 percent of the available workforce is involved in farming. Most of the back-country communities practice subsistence farming, growing just enough to feed their villages.

The Food

The prime characteristic of native African meals is the use of starch as a focus, typically accompanied by a stew containing meat or vegetables, or both. Starch filler foods, similar to the rice cuisines of Asia, are a hallmark. Yams, beans, lentils, millet, plantains, green bananas, and cassava are some of the essential foods in Africa. Meat is often used merely as one of a number of flavorings, rather than as a main ingredient in cooking. Other major foods, such as wheat and rice, are imported on a wide scale from Asia, Europe, and North America, especially in countries where the climate does not admit extensive cultivation.

The African taste and use of ingredients has changed a great deal. In the eastern part of the continent (especially in Kenya) Arab explorers brought dried fruits, rice, and spices and expanded the diets of the coastal farmers. They also brought oranges, lemons, and limes from China and India. The British imported new breeds of sheep, goats, and cattle, as well as strawberries and asparagus. Beans, cassava, groundnuts, corn, tomatoes, sweet potatoes, and seasonings like pepper, cinnamon, clove, curry, and nutmeg were introduced to Africa as a direct result of European exploration of the North American continent.

Traditional ways of cooking involve steaming food in leaf wrappers (banana or corn husks), boiling, frying in oil, grilling, roasting in a fire, or baking in ashes.

NORTH AFRICA

The countries of North Africa that border the Mediterranean Sea are largely Muslim. As a result, their diet reflects Islamic traditions, such as not eating pork or any animal product that has not been butchered in accordance with the traditions of the faith. Each North African region has its signature seasonings. Morocco's *ras el hanout* (or "head of the shop") includes twenty-five to forty different ingredients, including cinnamon, black peppercorns, green cardamon, caraway, nutmeg, and rosebuds. As with curry powder, each vendor creates his or her own recipe. *Chermoula*, a Moroccan marinade, contains garlic, onions, mint, paprika, and almonds. Tunisia's *harissa*, a deep-red, hot table condiment with red chilies, cumin, garlic, tomatoes, vinegar, and olive oil is used even at breakfast. Morocco and Algeria have milder versions. Egyptians season meats with *baharat*, made with cinnamon, cumin, allspice, and paprika.

The national dish of Algeria and Tunisia is couscous, which is steamed semolina wheat, served with lamb or chicken, cooked vegetables, and gravy. This is so basic to the diet that its name in Arabic, *ta'am,* translates simply as "food." Common flavorings include onions, turnips, raisins, chickpeas, and red peppers, as well as salt, pepper, cumin, and coriander. Alternatively, couscous can be served sweet, flavored with honey, cinnamon, or almonds. Couscous presentation varies among regions. Algerians serve couscous, meat, and sauce in individual dishes, and mix them together at the table. Tunisians like it very moist with sauced meats or vegetables spooned over it. In Morocco, sauced meat or vegetables are served in a hole formed in a mound of couscous. Lamb is popular and is often prepared over an open fire and served with bread. This dish is called *mechoui.* Other common foods are *chorba,* a spicy soup; *dolma,* a mixture of tomatoes and peppers; and *bourek,* a specialty of Algiers consisting of minced meat with onions and fried eggs, rolled and fried in batter.

The most traditional dish in Morocco is a *tangine* (tanjine), named for the covered conical clay earthenware dish it is cooked in. It may be made with lamb, chicken, or other meat, and is a combination of sweet and sour flavors. It usually includes prunes, almonds, onions, and cinnamon. Pigeons are often included in dishes, particularly the *bastila*, a flaky pastry filled with meat, nuts, and spices and coated with sugar and cinnamon before it is baked. Popular vegetables include okra, *meloukhia* (spinachlike greens), and radishes. Fruits found in this region include oranges, lemons, and pears. Legumes such as broad beans (fava beans), lentils, yellow peas, and black-eyed peas are important staples. Mint tea and coffee are very popular beverages in this region.

The main crops in Egypt are barley and *emmer*, a type of wheat. Nuts such as pistachios, pine nuts, almonds, hazelnuts, and walnuts are cultivated. Apples, apricots, grapes, melons, quinces, figs, and pomegranates grow in this fertile region. Ancient gardens featured lettuce, peas, cucumbers, beets, beans, herbs, and greens. Pharaohs considered mushrooms a delicacy. Egypt has several national dishes. *Koushari* (lentils, macaroni, rice, and chickpeas) *kofta* (spicy, minced lamb), and *kebab* (grilled lamb pieces) are the most popular. *Ful* (pronounced "fool," bean paste), *tahini* (sesame paste), and *aish baladi* (a pitalike bread) are common accompaniments. Egypt's records indicate that bread was made in more than thirty different shapes. They included pita types made either with refined white flour called *aysh shami*, or with coarse, whole wheat *aysh baladi*. Sweet cakes were made by combining honey, dates and other fruits, spices, and nuts with the dough, which was baked in the shapes of animals and birds.

The main staple of the Sudanese diet is a type of bread called *kissra*, which is made of *durra* (sorghum, one of the most important cereal crops in the world) or corn. It is served with the many variety of stews. Dried okra is used in preparing stews like *waika, bussaara,* and *sabaroag*. *Miris* is a stew that is made from sheep's fat, onions, and dried okra. Vegetables like potatoes, eggplants, and others are used in preparing other stews with meat, onions, peanut butter, and spices. *Elmaraara* and *umfitit* are made of sheep lungs, liver, and stomach. To these are added onions, peanut butter, and salt; it is eaten raw. Soups are an important part of Sudanese cuisine; the most popular is *kawari'*, made of cattle's or sheep's hoofs with vegetables and spices. *Elmussalammiya* is a soup made with liver, flour, dates, and spices. These meals are accompanied with porridge (*asseeda*), which is made with wheat flour or corn, and served with *kissra*.

Due to climatic conditions and poor soils, Libya imports most foods. Domestic food production meets only about 25 percent of demand. Typically, grains such as wheat and barley, dates, and soft fruits provide the staple items, along with lamb and some fish.

WESTERN AFRICA

This is the first part of Africa that Europeans explored. Prior to this, main staples included rice, millet, and lentils. Portuguese, British, Dutch, and other European traders introduced several foods that became staples, such as cassava and corn. Yams are an important crop in

West Africa and are served in a variety of dishes, including *amala* (pounded yam) and *egwansi* (melon) sauce. Millet is used for making porridge and beer. The plantain is abundant in the more tropical areas of West Africa. Dates, bananas, guava, melons, passion fruit, figs, jackfruit, mangos, pineapples, cashews, and wild lemons and oranges are also found here. Meat sources include cattle, sheep, chicken, and goat, though beef is normally reserved for holidays and special occasions. Fish is eaten in the coastal areas. Palm oil is the base of stew in the Gambia, southern, and eastern regions. In the Sahara area, peanut butter is the main ingredient for stew. All the stews in this territory are heavily spiced with chiles and tend to be based on okra, beans, sweet potato leaves, and cassava. Other vegetables are eggplant, cabbage, carrots, French beans, lettuce, onions, and cherry tomatoes.

Côte d'Ivoire is the world's leading producer of cocoa, and is the third largest producer of coffee in the world (behind Brazil and Columbia). It is also Africa's leading exporter of pineapples and palm oil. The people of Côte d'Ivoire rely on grains and tubers to sustain their diet. Yams, plantains, rice, millet, corn, and peanuts are typically an ingredient in most dishes. The national dish is *n'voufou* (called *fufu*), which is plantains, cassava, or yams pounded into a sticky dough and served with a seasoned meat (often chicken) and vegetable sauce called *kedjenou*. As with most meals, it is typically eaten with the hands, rather than utensils. *Kedjenou* is a meal prepared from peanuts, eggplant, okra, or tomatoes. *Attiéké* is a popular side dish. Similar to the tiny pasta grains of couscous, it is a porridge made from grated cassava. Habanero peppers are the most widely cultivated pepper. Fresh fruits are the typical dessert, often accompanied by *bangui*, a local white palm wine or ginger beer. Often the best place to sample the country's local cuisine is at an outdoor market, a street vendor, or a *maquis*, a restaurant unique to Côte d'Ivoire. These reasonably priced outdoor restaurants are scattered throughout the country and are growing in popularity. To be considered a *maquis* the restaurant must sell braised food, usually chicken or fish served with onions and tomatoes.

Nigeria has such a variety of people and cultures that it is difficult identify just one national dish. A large part of Nigeria lies in the tropics, where the popular fruits are oranges, melons, grapefruits, limes, mangoes, bananas, and pineapples. People of the northern region (mostly Muslim, whose beliefs prohibit eating pork) have diets based on beans, sorghum, and brown rice. The people from the eastern part of Nigeria, mostly Igbo/Ibo, eat *gari* (cassava powder) dumplings, pumpkins, and yams. The Yoruba people of the southwest and central areas eat *gari* with local varieties of okra and spinach in stews (*efo*) or soups. A common way coastal Nigerians prepare fish is to make a marinade of ginger, tomatoes, and cayenne pepper, and then cook the fish in peanut oil.

EASTERN AFRICA

Extensive trade and migrations with Arabic countries and South Asia has made East African culture unique, particularly along the coast. The main staples include potatoes, rice, *matake* (mashed plantains), and a thick porridge made from corn. Beans or a stew with potatoes, or vegetables often accompany the porridge. Outside of Kenya and the horn of Africa, the stew is not as spicy, but the coastal area has spicy, coconut-based stews. The grain *teff* is used in this area and has a considerably higher iron and nutrient content than other grain staples found in Africa. In East Africa cattle, sheep, and goats are regarded as more a form of currency and status, and so are rarely eaten.

The cuisine of modern-day Somalia and Ethiopia is characterized by very spicy food prepared with chiles and garlic. In addition to flavoring the food, the spices also help to preserve meat in a country where refrigeration is rare. *Berbere* is the name of the special spicy paste that Ethiopians use to preserve and flavor foods. According to Ethiopian culture, the woman with the best *berbere* has the best chance to win a good husband. The national dish of Ethiopia is *wot*, a spicy stew. *Wot* may be made from beef, lamb, chicken, goat, or even lentils or chickpeas, but it always contains spicy *berbere*. *Alecha* is a less-spicy stew seasoned with green ginger. A soft white cheese called *lab* is popular. A common traditional food is *injera*, a spongy flat bread that is eaten by tearing it, then using it to scoop up the meat or stew. Although Ethiopians rarely use sugar, honey is occasionally used as a sweetener. A special Ethiopian treat is *injera* wrapped around a fresh honeycomb with young honeybee grubs still inside.

About half of the Ethiopian population is Orthodox Christian. During Lent, the forty days preceding the Christian holiday of Easter, Orthodox Christians are prohibited from eating any foods from animal products (no meat, cheese, milk, or butter). Instead they eat dishes made from beans, lentils, chickpeas, field peas, and peanuts called *mitin shiro*. The beans are boiled, roasted, ground, and combined with *berbere*. This mixture can be made into a vegetarian *wot* by adding vegetable oil and then shaped like a fish or an egg; it is eaten cold. During festive times such as marriage feasts, *kwalima*, a kind of smoked and dried beef sausage made with onions, pepper, ginger, cumin, basil, cardamom, cinnamon, cloves, and tumeric, is served.

Traditional Kenyan foods reflect the many different lifestyles of the various groups in the country. Staple foods consist mainly of corn, potatoes, and beans. *Ugali*, a corn porridge, is typically eaten inland, while the coastal peoples eat a more varied diet.

The Maasai, cattle-herding peoples who live in Kenya and Tanzania, eat simple foods, relying on cow and goat by-products (such as the animal's meat, milk, and blood). The Maasai do not eat any wild game or fish, depending only on the livestock they raise for food. The Kikuyu and Gikuyu grow corn, beans, potatoes, and greens. They mash all of these vegetables together to make *irio*. They roll *irio* into balls and dip them into meat or vegetable stews. In western Kenya, the people living near Lake Victoria (the second largest freshwater lake in the world) mainly prepare fish stews, vegetable dishes, and rice.

Swahili dishes reflect a history of contact with the Arabs and other Indian Ocean traders. Their dried fruits, rice, and spices expanded the Swahili diet. Here, coconut and spices are used heavily. Although there is not a specific national cuisine, there are two national dishes: *ugali* and *nyama choma*. Corn is a Kenyan staple and the main ingredient of *ugali*, which is thick and similar to porridge. *Nyama choma* is the Kiswahili phrase meaning "roasted meat." Huge chunks of meat are roasted over an open charcoal fire. Typically, the chunks consist of a whole leg, or the ribs making up one half of the chest. Special stoves are used so that the grill holding the meat can be raised or lowered depending on the conditions of the fire, and the temperatures needed to cook the meat. The *nyama choma* challenge is that after the countless raising and the lowering of the grill, the meat is well done but not dry. *Sukuma wiki* is a combination of chopped spinach or kale that is fried with onions, tomatoes, maybe a green pepper, and any leftover meat, if available. Fresh fruits include mangoes, papaya, pineapple, watermelon, oranges, guavas, bananas, coconuts, and passion fruit.

The Portuguese influence upon Angola and Mozambique is pervasive and subtle. They were the first Europeans to colonize Africa south of the Sahara in the fifteenth century. This relatively inconspicuous European country influenced African life more than the more direct and intrusive British, French, and Dutch. The Portuguese brought the European sense of flavoring with spices, and techniques of roasting and marinating to African foods. Catholicism also influenced Portuguese African cuisine in the sense of feast and fast days, and meatless Fridays. The Portuguese brought oranges, lemons, and limes from their Asian colonies. From South America they brought the foods of the new world: chiles, peppers, corn, tomatoes, pineapples, bananas, and the domestic pig. Mozambique is more fish based. Angola is reflective of the west side, with drier climate, and corresponding change in ingredients.

In addition to growing cashews, Mozambique is most known for its *piripiri*, or hot pepper dishes. Using the small, tremendously hot peppers of that country, sieved lemon juice is warmed and red freshly picked chiles are added and simmered exactly five minutes, then salted and pounded to a paste. This pulp is returned to heat with more lemon juice and served over meats, fish, and shellfish.

CENTRAL AFRICA

Very little is known about central African cuisine, due partly to lack of documentation, as most central African languages were not written down until the colonial era of the eighteenth and nineteenth centuries. Slaves, ivory, rubber, and minerals interested most the Europeans and Arabs who went there.

One distinguishing characteristic of central African cooking is the use of edible leaves, collard greens, kale, and mustard greens. Often greens are the main ingredient in the daily stew, cooked with only a little onion, hot pepper, meat, fish, or oil for flavoring. Some of the greens consumed in central Africa are bitterleaf, cassava, okra, pumpkin, sorrel, sweet potato, and taro. People cultivate these greens as well as gather them from the wild. In many tropical areas of the world cassava is grown primarily for its tubers, but Africans have a long tradition of eating both the leaves and the tubers of this plant. Before cooking, women pound greens in a mortar and pestle, or roll them like giant cigars and use a sharp knife to shred them finely. *Saka-saka*, or *pondu*, is a dish made from cassava leaves, onion, and a bit of dried fish.

Saka-madesu contains cassava leaves cooked with beans. Another recipe, variations of which are found all over sub-Saharan Africa, calls for greens to be cooked with tomato, onion, and mashed peanuts.

One of the other distinguishing characteristics of central African cuisine is the use of red palm oil, obtained from the fruit of the African oil palm. Reddish and thick, it has a distinctive flavor for which there is no substitute. The oily pulp is cooked with chicken, onion, tomato, okra, garlic, or sorrel leaves, and chili pepper to produce a stew called *moambé* or *poulet nyembwe* (made with chicken). *Moambé* is also made with other meats.

One of the important central African cooking methods is steaming or grilling food wrapped in packets fashioned from the leaves of banana trees or other plants. This cooking method predates the use of iron and maybe even clay cooking pots. Certain leaves are especially favored because they give a particular flavor to food. *Maboké* (singular *liboké*, also called *ajomba* or *jomba*)—leaf-wrapped packets of meat or fish, with onion, tomato, and okra, seasoned with lemon juice or hot chile pepper—are grilled over hot coals or steamed in a pot. Crushed peanuts or *mbika* (seeds of a small gourd) are sometimes included. Filling the leaf packets with mashed beans (such as black-eyed peas) and sautéed peppers, then steaming, produces *koki* (also called *ekoki* or *gâteau de haricots*).

SOUTH AFRICAN

The first people in South Africa, the San, were hunter-gatherers. The San have lived in Africa for nearly 30,000 years. About two thousand years ago, the Khoikhoi people moved into southern Africa from farther north. They settled in groups, raising sheep and cattle. Around A.D. 300, another group of people settled in what is now eastern South Africa. Known as the Bantu, they raised crops of corn, sweet potato, gem squash, and livestock.

Europeans first came to South Africa in 1488 when the Dutch East India Company established a food supply stop for the company's ships as they made their way around the Cape of Good Hope. Shortly after they arrived, the Dutch were joined by the Huguenots (Protestants from France) and the Germans. *Boerwors* is a homemade farmer's sausage evolved from recipes brought by German immigrants. In the fifteenth century, the Portuguese added traditional fish dishes. The South African waters, then as now, were rich in kingklip, snoek, red roman, hake, cod, and sole as well as abalone, oysters, mussels, calamari, shrimps, and crayfish. Cape Malay cuisine is one of the most flavorful in the country, characterized by a blend of styles and spices brought to South Africa by the Indonesian and Bengalese slaves. A mix of Asian, Indian, and European dishes is peppered with curry, cumin, ginger, and other exotic spices. Some of the best-known Cape Malay dishes include *sosaties* (traditional kebabs), *bobotie* (a curried one-pot meal made of minced meat cooked with brown sugar, apricots and raisins, milk-soaked mashed bread, and curry flavoring), and *bredies* (meat and vegetable casserole, much like a Shepherd's pie). Traditional dishes also include practical stews, such as *potjiekos*. The early hunters and trekkers stewed their game and whatever vegetables they could find from the land in a three-legged cast iron pot. As new animals were hunted, their meat was added to the pot, as were bones to thicken the stew. Today, *potjiekos* are just as popular and annual competitions to create the best are an important way of socializing around the campfire. Another typical South African food is *biltong*. Made of meat that has been dried, *biltong* is similar to meat jerky, made from any kind of meat, even ostrich, antelope, or crocodile.

The *braai* is the South African equivalent to the barbecue. Meat, fish, chicken, potatoes and onions are cooked over coals outdoors. The food may be *biltong* (jerky), *chilli-bites* (small balls of savory curried dough and vegetables deep fried) as a starter while waiting for the *sosaties* (kebabs), or *boerewors*. *Snoek braai* is a fish barbeque using snoek fish (a large game fish similar to a barracuda, a national delicacy, but very bony) caught off the Cape coast marinated in lemon juice, garlic, and herbs and cooked over coals.

Mealies are a very popular food in South Africa. Made from corn, *mealies* are either boiled or cooked over coals in the cob, or made into *mealie bread*. *Mealie pap*, a stiff cornmeal mix, is a staple food of the South African diet, accompanied by a variety of savory foods made from green vegetables and spiced with chili.

A dish called *umngqusho* is famous for being former President Nelson Mandela's favorite dish. It is made of *stamp mealies* (broken dried corn kernels) with sugar beans, butter, onions, potatoes, chiles, and lemons, then simmered. Another traditional dish is *mashonzha*. It is the Mopani caterpillar, cooked with chiles and often eaten with peanuts. *Melktert* is a typical South African dessert, a sour cream pastry filled with a mix of milk, flour, and eggs and flavored with cinnamon sugar.

Glossary

Agbono This ground seed is used for its thickening properties. Like okra and baobab, it gives a sauce the slippery texture.

Akara Popular breakfast dish made from mashed black-eyed peas seasoned with salt, pepper, and onion, then deep-fried.

Akassa Ghanian porridge made from corn flour and hot water.

Ana Ofia Fresh meat from any forest animal. The meat is prepared by first singeing over an open fire, then washing and cutting as preparation for smoking, drying, or cooking. Most African meats are tough and stringy and therefore best prepared by marinating (in beer, wine, fruit juices, or soured milk), then cooking with moisture or used in soups and stews.

Asida Term used for a late morning meal usually consisting of *fufu* and relishes.

Bajias Small seasoned balls of cooked mashed potatoes or yams, flour-coated then deep-fried. A favorite of African Indians.

Balila Term used for the evening meal. In many areas care is taken to eat this before dark so as to avoid evil spirits.

Bamia Also called "ladyfingers." Both are names for okra.

Baobab The dried, powdered leaves of the Baobab tree, added to soups and stews for a slippery texture similar to okra.

Baobab Tree As functional as the coconut palm. Fruit and leaves are edible; ashes of the wood are used as salt; seeds and pods are roasted to make a drink or snack; the tree trunk is a source of water.

Bastila Flaky-crusted pigeon pie, a Moroccan specialty.

Berbere Red pepper spice paste used in Ethiopia.

Biltong Dried and salted raw meat similar to the beef jerky made in the United States. An older Afrikaner delicacy is made of ostrich, beef, kudu, or any other red meat.

Bitterleaf (Ndole) Variety of African greens used for medicinal as well as dietary purposes.

Bobotie A traditional South African dish of spicy-flavored ground lamb or beef (similar to meat loaf) topped with an egg custard; served with yellow rice.

Boerewors A traditional spicy South African sausage made of beef or lamb. Popular at open-air *braais* (barbecues).

Bota Thin gruel often prepared from millet and used as a supplementary food for infants.

Braai A barbecue featuring grilled meat, highly popular form of cooking (South Africa).

Braaivleis Afrikaans (a language derived from Dutch) for a barbecue.

Breadfruit A Malaysian evergreen timber tree (*Artocarpus altilis*) having large, round, yellowish, edible fruits. Breadfruit should be cooked as it begins to become ripe. Fully ripened, mushy breadfruit is not as good.

Bredie Traditional stews made from lamb or tomatoes and vegetables, cooked slowly over coals (South Africa).

Callaloo A casserole of vegetables, various fish, and seafood with meat and seasonings. A popular combination includes spinach, mixed seafood, and cubed lamb seasoned with garlic, chiles, and tomato paste. It thought that the Portuguese traders and explorers brought this recipe back with them. (This is also the name of a Caribbean soup named for the coarse green callaloo leaves from dasheen or taro plant.)

Cardamom Spice, the whole or ground dried fruit of *Elettaria cardamomum,* a plant of the ginger family indigenous to India and Sri Lanka. Used in curries, spiced tea, and coffee.

Cassava Also called manioc; the tuber from which manioc flour and tapioca are made. Slightly fermented and ground into flour, manioc is used to prepare the classic *gari.*

Chapatis Unleavened breads freshly made for a meal from almost any flour; they are rolled flat then deep-fried until they puff and brown. Well known in India and much favored by African Indians.

Chenga A thick milk soup made with rice or corn and thickened with corn flour (cornstarch). Considered one of the chief foods of East Africa.

Cheese The demand for cheese as a protein and vitamin-rich food supplement is growing in Africa, especially in light of an abundance of raw materials by way of cow's and goat's milk. Particular favorites are the Greek, Lebanese, and Italian styles of cheeses.

Chihengi Pineapple.

Chin Chin Deep-fried cookie leavened with Swahili yeast.

Cocoyams Variety of wild yams.

Couscous Cereal product made by moistening wheat flour and rolling it into small pellets, which are then steamed. A traditional staple food in North Africa.

Daddawa Black, fermented paste made from the flat beans of the locust tree. It has a very strong odor, but adds a wonderful flavor to sauces. Maggi sauce can be a substitute.

Dendê oil The Brazilian name for the densely rich palm oil brought to Brazil by West African slaves. Its reddish hue can be imitated by adding paprika to peanut or vegetable oil, though the flavor is not the same.

Dovi Paste of groundnuts (peanut butter).

Duri Mortar and pestle.

Eguisi (Agusi, Agushi, Egushi) Flour ground from seeds of various species of gourds, melons, pumpkins, and squashes, used as a thickener. In western Africa, the plants and seeds, as well as soups and stews made with them, are all called *egusi.*

Fish Dried, smoked, and salted. Drying and smoking were common methods of preservation before refrigeration. Used extensively in African cuisine.

Fufu, Ugali, or Ampesi Staple African food. Thick porridge-like mixture made by pounding then cooking any one of many starchy plant foods or mixtures of them. Corn, millet, rice, cassava, plantain, green bananas, or varieties of yams may be used. For eating, the mixture is formed into small balls with three fingers of the right hand then dipped into sauces or relishes made from fish, meat, or vegetables—almost always spicy hot.

Futari Yams Thick mixture of cooked potatoes flavored with groundnuts, tomatoes, and onions.

Garden Eggs Term for a small green-skinned African eggplants.

Garri, or Gari Slightly fermented cassava flour used in cooking. A favorite of many, especially Ghanians.

Ghada The midday meal.

Groundnuts Peanuts, a staple food.

Guinea Pepper Pepperlike spice made from the seed of a plant native to Africa, used in African cooking as a seasoning before the arrival of Asian black pepper.

Gumbo With a consistency between a soup and a stew, gumbo is derived from the African Bantu word for okra. Simmered gently with spicy seasoning, okra, and other vegetables, gumbos take their name from the main seafood or meat ingredient and are usually served over wild rice. In America, gumbos are a treasured part of Creole cuisine.

Harira Hearty soup with legumes, meat, and vegetables, important during Ramadan.

Hovo or Hobo Bananas.

Lnjera Classic Ethiopian bread prepared like a huge pancake from *teff* (fine millet flour).

Ji Akwukwo Very thick stew of many vegetables plus yams. Favorite in West Africa.

Keuke Corn bread prepared from wet fermented corn flour. Sour in East Africa, sweeter and whiter in West Africa.

Kikwanga Congo name for disc-shaped bread made from cassava flour. The same bread in Jamaica is called *bammy* and in the southern United States, pan bread.

Kola Nuts Brownish-orange, bitter nuts about the size of a chestnut. West Africans enjoy chewing them, and claim they give an extra burst of energy. These nuts contain two to three times the caffeine of coffee beans.

Kuli-Kuli Delicacy made from frying the residual groundnut paste after the oil has been extracted.

Liboke (plural, Miboke) Lingala word, meaning banana, used throughout the Congo region to describe food that is cooked, usually by steaming or grilling, in a packet made from banana leaves. Called *ajomba* or *jomba* along the Atlantic coast of central Africa.

Madafu Immature coconut water, a beverage.

Maggi Cube or Maggi Sauce Brand of bouillon cube and flavoring sauce, similar to soy sauce. Very popular in Africa.

Maheu Traditional drink for women and children; slightly alcoholic sweet liquid left from soaking cooked *fufu*.

Mahshi Almost any available variety of vegetable stuffed with a mix of ground meat or fish and rice and baked with tomato sauce.

Manhanga Term used to refer to many varieties of squash and pumpkin.

Manioc or Cassava General name given to any starch roots from which tapioca and other flours may be made.

Manwiwa Watermelon.

Mealie The South African name for cornmeal.

Milioku Ngozi Also called *blessing soup*. A hot West African soup usually made with a whole chicken and yams. Soup is served first, then sliced meat and vegetables are served afterward. Usually served at planting and harvest celebrations.

Millet The small grains of a cereal grass, used in preparation of some foods.

Mseto Swahili word for rice or lentils; usually cooked into a thick sauce, highly seasoned and served with meat or fish.

Mudumbe The succulent root fibers from the elephant ear plant.

Muriwo Relish or sauces accompanying *fufu*. These are an important part of the diet's nutrients, containing not only a wide variety of vegetables and seasonings (hot), but often meat and fish and bones, when available.

Naarjes South African tangerines, deep in color and rich in flavor.

Nhopi A *fufu* or porridge made from pumpkin.

Niter Kibbeh Clarified butter to which nutmeg, cinnamon, and cardamom seeds are added with turmeric for color, then browned, strained, and used as seasoning and cooking oil in Ethiopia.

Ofe Nsala A fiery pepper sauce made with a base of meat or fish. This is one of the most popular things served to women with new babies and may comprise the main part of the diet, diluted as a soup or gruel, or eaten with *fufu*.

Ogbono Seed kernel of the African wild mango, cooked and crushed to form a cake or powder used to thicken soups and stews.

Ogede Plantain.

Oka Esiri Esi A corn and milk soup.

Okra Generally thought to have originated in the wild in northern and northeastern Africa or western Asia, cultivated for its seedpod fruit.

Olilie One version of the seasoning paste made from dried, fermented, and cooked seeds, used for flavoring.

Olele A baked or steamed Nigerian pudding made from ground cowpeas (or blackeyed peas), onions, and salt.

Palm Butter Thick red paste made from palm nuts.

Palm Oil The reddish-orange oil extracted from the pulp of the fruit of the African palm. It's extremely high in saturated fat (78 percent) and has a distinctive flavor that is popular in West African and Brazilian cooking.

Peanuts Legumes, well suited to the West African climate and a staple food. Know by the English name of groundnuts.

Periperi (Portuguese Hot Sauce) A spicy hot-pepper sauce that goes on almost everything.

Plantain Tropical plant bearing a fruit similar to the banana. Plantains are more starchy than sweet and must be cooked before being eaten. They are staple crop in much of Africa. Used to make *fufu* and various beers or wines.

Pombe Beer made from plantains or bananas.

Rupiza Thin porridge or gruel made from powdered dried beans.

Sabal Palmetto The young sprouting leaves of cocoyams and sweet potatoes, cut and cooked as greens for relishes.

Shea Butter A fat extracted from the nut of the shea tree of West Africa. This butter is used to make margarine and chocolate.

Sorghum Cereal grass grown for grain or fodder, similar to corn, indigenous to Africa.

Sorrel Plant native to West Africa, the leaves have a strong acid flavor. In Africa the leaves and stalks are eaten as a cooked vegetables (greens).

Sosaties Barbecued pieces of meat on a stick, normally marinated in curry sauce (South African).

Suya Cut-up meats marinated in peanut oil then skewered and cooked.

Swahili Yeast Yeast made from the fermentation of ripe plantains, sugar, water, and wheat flour. Used as leavening agent for breads, buns, and fried cookies.

Sweet Potato Food plant, cultivated for its edible tuberous root and, particularly in Africa, for its leaves, which are eaten as greens.

Tamarind The fruit or pulp in the seedpods of *Tamarindus indica*, an evergreen tree native to Africa. It is the only spice of African origin cultivated and used world-wide, especially in Asian and Latin American recipes. The tamarind fruit is a seedpod, brown in color and several inches long, which contains a sour-tasting pulp.

Taro A tuber, similar to potatoes, cooked as a vegetable, and made into breads and porridges. Taro is especially well known as Polynesian Poi, which is made from fermented taro starch. It has a hairy outer skin, similar to a coconut's, which is removed. The large leaves (called *calalu* or *callaloo* in the Caribbean and in some parts of Africa) are cooked as greens. Some varieties of taro are highly toxic. Taro must be thoroughly cooked before it is eaten.

Teff Fine millet flour.

Tomato Native to the American tropics. Today, tomatoes and canned tomato paste are used to such an extent in African sauces, soups, and stews that many Africans might think that tomatoes were native to Africa.

Trio Swahili word for a combination of cooked vegetables, cubed or chopped and seasoned with oil and salt and pepper. Favorite in East Africa.

Tseme or Nhembatemba Special pot used for storing *dovi* (groundnut butter).

Tuwo Spicy okra sauce.

Tuwonsaffe In northern Ghana, the daily *fufu* is allowed to ferment in this "sourpot" and the *fufu* needed for meals is scooped from the *tuwonsaffe*.

Ugali Tanzanian staple cornmeal porridge of *fufu*.

Wors (Vors) Spicy sausages often sold by street vendors like hot dogs; essential at any *braai*. (South African)

Yam The nutritious white yam is a powerfully symbolic staple food frequently staving off malnutrition and starvation, particularly in West Africa. Often of immense size, one African yam can easily feed a family. Feast days are common and yams figure largely in any festive occasion. Because the egg symbolizes fertility and therefore eternity, eggs often accompany yams in these special dishes.

Yassa Traditional Senegalese (West African) marinade of lemon juice, onion, and mustard.

Menus and Recipes from Africa

Harira   Lamb and Vegetable Soup   SERVES 4

This thick, peppery soup is a symbol of the Moroccan way of fasting. It is traditionally served after sundown during the month of Ramadan to break each day's fast.

AMOUNT	MEASURE	INGREDIENT
$\frac{1}{2}$ cup	4 ounces, 120 ml	Ghee
I cup	4 ounces, 112 g	Onions, $\frac{1}{4}$ inch (.6 cm) dice
$\frac{1}{4}$ cup	8 ounces	Lean lamb, $\frac{1}{2}$ inch (1.2 cm) cubes
$\frac{1}{2}$ teaspoon		Turmeric, ground
$\frac{1}{2}$ teaspoon		Black pepper
$\frac{1}{4}$ teaspoon		Cinnamon, ground
$\frac{1}{4}$ teaspoon		Paprika
$\frac{1}{2}$ teaspoon		Fresh ginger, minced
3 cups	24 ounces, 810 ml	White stock
$\frac{1}{2}$ cup	2 ounces, 56 g	Celery, $\frac{1}{4}$ inch, (.6 cm) dice
To taste		Salt
$\frac{1}{2}$ cup	3 ounces, 84 g	Chickpeas, cooked, rinsed, and drained
$\frac{1}{4}$ cup	2 ounces, 56 g	Lentils, red, soaked, and drained
2 tablespoons		Parsley, chopped
I teaspoon		Cilantro, chopped
I cup	6 ounces, 168 g	Tomatoes, peeled, seeded, $\frac{1}{4}$ inch (.6 cm) dice
$\frac{1}{4}$ cup	$\frac{1}{2}$ ounce, 14 g	Vermicelli (broken), orzo, or acini di pepe
2		Beaten egg (optional)
To taste		Lemon

PROCEDURE

1   Heat the ghee over medium heat and sauté the onion until soft, 3 to 4 minutes.

2   Add the lamb; cook 10 minutes or until lightly browned.

3   Add all the dry spices and ginger; cook 3 minutes, stirring constantly.

4   Add white stock, celery, salt, chickpeas, and lentils; simmer 45 minutes.

5   Add parsley, cilantro, and tomatoes; simmer 10 minutes.

6   Bring to a boil and add vermicelli; cook 1 minute or until pasta is just cooked.

7   Beat in egg, correct seasoning with lemon juice and serve.

Fava Bean Salad   SERVES 4

AMOUNT	MEASURE	INGREDIENT
3 cups	18 ounces, 504 g	Fava (or broad) beans, fresh or dried, shelled, or lima beans (lima beans may need to be cooked longer)
1		Onion, cut in half
1 teaspoon		Salt

PROCEDURE

1 Place the beans in water to cover to a depth of 2 inches (5 cm). Add the onion and salt; bring to a boil, reduce to a simmer, and cook 20 to 25 minutes. The beans should be very tender (creamy) but not mushy. Drain and discard the onion.

AMOUNT	MEASURE	INGREDIENT
$\frac{1}{4}$ cup	4 ounces, 120 ml	Olive oil
$\frac{1}{2}$ cup	4 ounces, 120 ml	Fresh lemon juice
$1\frac{1}{2}$ teaspoons		Cumin, ground
1 tablespoon		Garlic, minced
6 tablespoons		Fresh cilantro, leaves only, chopped
6 tablespoons		Flat-leaf parsley, chopped
To taste		Salt and white pepper
$\frac{1}{2}$ cup	2 ounces, 56 g	Green onions, white and green parts, thinly sliced
$\frac{1}{4}$ cup	1 ounce, 28 g	Red radishes, thinly sliced
$\frac{3}{4}$ cup	4 ounces, 112 g	Black olives, pitted

PROCEDURE

1 Combine olive oil, lemon juice, cumin, and garlic; stir to mix. Add cilantro and parsley and correct seasoning.

2 Combine dressing and beans while the beans are still warm; toss.

3 Add green onions and radishes; toss well.

4 Plate and garnish with olives.

Tagine of Chicken, Preserved Lemon, and Olives   SERVES 4

AMOUNT	MEASURE	INGREDIENT
I tablespoon		Garlic, minced
I tablespoon	$\frac{1}{2}$ ounce, 15 ml	Olive oil
$\frac{1}{2}$ teaspoon		Black pepper
I	$2\frac{1}{2}$ pound, 1.12 kg	Chicken, cut into 8 pieces

PROCEDURE

I   Combine the garlic, olive oil, and black pepper. Rub the chicken with the mixture and let set 2 hours.

AMOUNT	MEASURE	INGREDIENT
2 tablespoons	I ounce, 30 ml	Olive oil
$\frac{1}{4}$ teaspoon		Black pepper
$\frac{1}{4}$ teaspoon		Ginger, ground
Pinch		Saffron
I teaspoon		Cumin, ground
I stick		Cinnamon
I teaspoon		Coriander, ground
$1\frac{1}{4}$ cups	5 ounces, 140 g	Onions, $\frac{1}{4}$ inch (.6 cm) dice
2 cups	16 ounces, 480 ml	Chicken stock
I cup	5 ounces, 140 g	Green olives, pitted
$\frac{1}{2}$ cup	3 ounces, 84 g	Preserved lemons, quartered strips (rinse lemons as needed under running water, removing and discarding pulp)
To taste		Salt and pepper
As needed		Couscous (recipe follows)

PROCEDURE

1   Heat oil over medium heat and brown chicken on all sides, 8 to 10 minutes.

2   Add spices; cook 1 minute. Add onions and sauté over medium-high heat, 2 to 3 minutes.

3   Add stock and bring to a boil, reduce to a simmer, and cover, leaving lid ajar to allow steam to escape. Simmer 20 to 30 minutes or until chicken is tender.

4   Add olive and preserved lemons; cook 5 minutes. Remove chicken and reduce to sauce consistency, stirring. Correct seasoning.

5   Serve covered with sauce on couscous.

Couscous   SERVES 4

Real couscous is always steamed, not boiled. Precooked "instant couscous" cooked in this traditional method may result in mushy, overcooked pasta. If real (not "instant") couscous is not available, reduce the cooking time.

AMOUNT	MEASURE	INGREDIENT
1 cup	8 ounces, 240 ml	Warm water, mixed with 1 teaspoon salt
3 cups	18 ounces, 504 g	Couscous (not "instant couscous")
$\frac{1}{4}$ cup	2 ounces, 60 ml	Olive oil
As needed		Chicken stock
2 tablespoons	2 ounces, 60 ml	Butter

PROCEDURE

1   Sprinkle half the salted water over half the couscous. Rub your hands with a little oil and sprinkle the remaining oil over the couscous. Use your hands to evenly distribute the oil and water into the couscous. Let the couscous form small pellets, but break any lumps. Add the remaining couscous and continue to process, adding more water to make the couscous uniformly damp, but not wet.

2   Place the couscous on a clean cloth; cover it with another cloth, and leave to rest 1 hour.

3   If not cooking over the tagine, bring the chicken stock to a gentle boil in the bottom part of a steamer. Place the couscous in the top part of a steamer; cover and steam couscous about 1 hour over the simmering broth.

4   Remove from the steamer and transfer to a bowl. Massage the butter into the couscous (careful not to burn yourself) and let cool 15 minutes.

5   Return the couscous to the steamer for an additional 30 minutes. Test for tenderness. The last two steps can be repeated.

Harissa

YIELD: 8 OUNCES

AMOUNT	MEASURE	INGREDIENT
2 ounces		**Chile peppers, dried mixture of anchos, New Mexican, and guajillos**
2 ounces		**Cumin seeds**
I teaspoon		**Paprika**
$\frac{3}{4}$ cup	4 ounces, 112 g	**Onions, $\frac{1}{4}$ inch (.6 cm) dice**
3 tablespoons		**Flat-leaf parsley, chopped**
I cup	8 ounces, 240 ml	**Olive oil**
To taste		**Fresh lemon juice**
To taste		**Salt**

PROCEDURE

1 Combine chile peppers, cumin seeds, and paprika over low heat, stirring constantly; toast 5 to 7 minutes. Cool.

2 Using a mortar and pestle, pulverize to a fine consistency.

3 Combine all ingredients and blend well.

4 Correct seasoning with lemon juice and salt

Fish Chermoula   YIELD: 1½ CUPS

AMOUNT	MEASURE	INGREDIENT
Chermoula Marinade		
5 tablespoons	½ ounce, 14 g	Cilantro leaves, chopped
5 tablespoons	½ ounce, 14 g	Flat-leaf parsley, chopped
5	10 g	Garlic cloves, minced
1 tablespoon	¼ ounce, 7 g	Paprika, sweet
2 teaspoon		Cumin, ground
¼ teaspoon		Cayenne
4 tablespoons	2 ounces, 60 ml	Fresh lemon juice
1 cup	8 ounces, 240 ml	Olive oil
1 teaspoon		Salt

PROCEDURE

1　Combine all ingredients in a food processor; pulse until thoroughly blended.

AMOUNT	MEASURE	INGREDIENT
4	5 ounce, 140 g each	Sea bass, scrod, flounder, or any firm white fish
2 tablespoons	2 ounces, 60 ml	Olive oil
As needed		All-purpose flour
As needed		Lemon wedges, for garnish

PROCEDURE

1　Marinate the fillets in chermoula, 2 to 4 hours.

2　Heat oil over medium heat. Remove fillets from chermoula and pat dry.

3　Dredge in flour, shaking off any excess.

4　Sauté on both sides, turning only once, until golden brown on both sides, 2 to 3 minutes per side (depending on type of fish).

5　Serve with lemon wedges and flat bread.

Carrots with Black Currants

SERVES 4

AMOUNT	MEASURE	INGREDIENT
$\frac{1}{4}$ cup	1 ounce, 28 g	Black currants
4 tablespoons	2 ounces, 60 ml	Butter
$\frac{1}{2}$ teaspoon		Cinnamon, ground
$\frac{1}{4}$ teaspoon, or to taste		Cayenne pepper
$2\frac{1}{2}$ cups	15 ounces, 420 g	Carrots, peeled, $2\frac{1}{2}$ to 4 inch (6.25 to 7.5 cm) long julienne cut
$\frac{1}{2}$ cup	4 ounces, 120 ml	Fresh orange juice
Garnish		Flat-leaf parsley, chopped

PROCEDURE

1 Soak currants covered in hot water 30 minutes. Drain and reserve $\frac{1}{4}$ cup (2 ounces, 60 ml) soaking liquid.

2 Heat butter over medium heat, add cinnamon, cayenne, and carrots; cook, stirring 2 to 3 minutes.

3 Add orange juice, currants, and reserved soaking liquid; bring to a boil, reduce to a simmer, and cook 3 to 5 minutes or until tender. If necessary, strain carrots, reduce the liquid to syrup consistency, and then recombine with carrots.

4 Correct seasoning; serve sprinkled with parsley.

Mescouta

Date Cookies   YIELD: 24 TO 30 BARS

AMOUNT	MEASURE	INGREDIENT
$\frac{3}{4}$ cup	3 ounces, 84 g	All-purpose flour
$\frac{1}{2}$ teaspoon		Baking powder
6		Eggs, well beaten
$\frac{1}{2}$ cup	4 ounces, 112 g	Granulated sugar
I teaspoon		Vanilla extract
$\frac{1}{2}$ cup	4 ounces, 120 ml	Butter, melted
I cup	4 ounces, 112 g	Dates, pitted, chopped
$\frac{1}{2}$ cup	5 ounces, 140 g	Walnuts or almonds, finely chopped
3 tablespoons		Confectioner's sugar

PROCEDURE

1 Preheat oven to 350°F (176°C).

2 Sift flour with baking powder.

3 Combine eggs, sugar, vanilla, and melted butter, mix on medium or by hand until well-blended (3 minutes).

4 Gradually add flour mixture, a little at a time.

5 Add dates and nuts; mix well.

6 Put into a greased 8- or 9-inch (20 or 22.5 cm) square cake pan.

7 Bake 30 minutes or until a toothpick inserted in the center comes out clean.

8 While still warm, cut into rectangular bars about 1 inch (2.5 cm) wide.

9 Roll bars in confectioner's sugar.

Equsi Soup (Western Africa) SERVES 4

AMOUNT	MEASURE	INGREDIENT
4 tablespoons	2 ounces, 60 ml	Peanut oil or palm oil
I cup	6 ounces, 168 g	Beef stew meat, $\frac{1}{2}$ inch (1.2 cm) cubes
3 cups	24 ounces, 720 ml	Beef or chicken stock
$\frac{1}{2}$ cup	2 ounces, 56 g	Onion, $\frac{1}{4}$ inch (.6 cm) dice
I		Green chile, seeded, chopped
$\frac{1}{4}$ cup	1 ounce, 28 g	Okra, sliced $\frac{1}{4}$ inch (.6 cm) slices
I tablespoon	$\frac{1}{2}$ ounce, 15 ml	Tomato paste
I cup	6 ounces, 168 g	Tomatoes, peeled, seeded $\frac{1}{4}$ inch (.6 cm) dice
$\frac{1}{2}$ cup	1 ounce, 28 g	Dried shrimp
$\frac{1}{2}$ cup	2 ounces, 56 g	Egusi, roasted and ground (or pumpkin seeds or pepitas)
2 cups	16 ounces, 180 ml	Beef or chicken stock
3 cups	8 ounces, 224 g	Spinach, washed and chopped
To taste		Salt and cayenne pepper

PROCEDURE

1 Heat oil over medium high heat. Pat meat dry and sauté until browned on all sides. Remove meat, reserve pan. Combine meat and first amount of beef stock; bring to a boil and reduce to a simmer.

2 Return pan to heat; when hot add onions and cook 3 to 5 minutes. Add chile and okra and cook 2 minutes stirring. Add tomato paste and cook 1 minute Add tomatoes and cook 3 to 5 minutes or until tomatoes are soft.

3 Add dried shrimp and ground seeds. Stir well.

4 Add onion-tomato mixture to the simmering meat and stir to combine. Add second amount of stock and cook until meat is tender.

5 Add spinach and cook until tender, 5 minutes.

6 Correct seasoning with salt and cayenne pepper.

Akoho sy Voanio

Chicken in Coconut Milk (Southern Africa)   SERVES 4

AMOUNT	MEASURE	INGREDIENT
I	2½ pound, 1.12 kg	Chicken, cut into 8 pieces
2 tablespoons	I ounce, 30 ml	Fresh lemon juice
I teaspoon		Lemon zest
I teaspoon		Salt
½ teaspoon		Black pepper
¼ teaspoon		Cayenne pepper
¼ cup	2 ounces, 60 ml	Coconut oil or peanut oil
I½ cups	6 ounces, 168 g	Onions, ¼ inch (.6 cm) dice
I tablespoon		Garlic, minced
I cup	6 ounces, 168 g	Tomatoes, peeled, seeded, ½ inch (1.2 cm) dice
I teaspoon		Ginger, minced
I cup	8 ounces, 240 ml	Coconut milk
As needed		Rice, cooked, hot

PROCEDURE

1   Combine the chicken, lemon juice, zest, salt, black pepper, and cayenne; marinate 1 hour.

2   Heat oil over medium heat and sauté onions and garlic, 3 to 5 minutes. Add chicken and cook until chicken is almost cooked, 12 to 15 minutes.

3   Add tomatoes and ginger; stir well and cook 3 minutes.

4   Add coconut milk and simmer until chicken is completely cooked. Remove chicken pieces as they cook. Reduce sauce to desired consistency and serve over rice.

Akara Black-Eyed Pea Fritters
(Western Africa) SERVES 4

AMOUNT	MEASURE	INGREDIENT
1 cup	8 ounces, 224 g	Dried cowpeas (black-eyed peas)
$\frac{1}{2}$ cup	2 ounces, 56 g	Onions, $\frac{1}{8}$ inch (.3 cm) dice
$\frac{1}{2}$ teaspoon		Salt
$\frac{1}{4}$ cup	1 ounce, 28 g	Green bell pepper, $\frac{1}{8}$ inch (.3 cm) dice
$\frac{1}{4}$ cup	1 ounce, 28 g	Red bell pepper, $\frac{1}{8}$ inch (.3 cm) dice
1 tablespoon		Jalapeño, minced
$\frac{1}{2}$ teaspoon		Ginger, grated
As needed		Peanut oil, for frying
As needed		African hot sauce (see recipe on page 541)

PROCEDURE

1 Clean, pick over, and wash black-eyed peas. Soak, covered, in hot water 30 minutes. Drain and remove the skins by rubbing them between your hands. Rinse and drain well in a colander.

2 Crush or process the peas to a thick paste. Add enough water to form a smooth, thick batter that will cling to a spoon. Add remaining ingredients except oil; mix well and let stand 30 minutes.

3 Heat 2 inches (5 cm) oil over medium heat to 325°F (162°C).

4 Drop batter by the tablespoonful into the hot oil. Fry until golden, 2 to 3 minutes per side. Drain on paper towels. Serve hot with African hot sauce.

Mchuzi wa Biringani
Eggplant Curry (Eastern Africa) SERVES 4

AMOUNT	MEASURE	INGREDIENT
5 cups	16 ounces, 448 g	Eggplant, unpeeled, 1 inch (2.4 cm) cubes
4 tablespoons	2 ounces, 60 ml	Peanut oil
1 cup	4 ounces, 112 g	Onions, $\frac{1}{4}$ inch (.6 cm) dice
2 teaspoons		Garam masala (see recipe on page 567) or curry powder
1 teaspoon		Ginger, grated
1 tablespoon		Garlic, minced
1		Green chile (serrano), seeded, minced
1 cup	6 ounces, 168 g	Tomato, peeled, seeded, $\frac{1}{2}$ inch dice
To taste		Salt, pepper, and cayenne pepper

PROCEDURE

1 Toss eggplant with a little salt; rub well and set aside 1 hour. Rinse and squeeze out as much liquid as possible from the eggplant cubes; pat dry with paper towels.

2 Heat oil over medium-high heat and sauté onions until soft, 3 minutes. Add garam masala, ginger, garlic and green chile. Cook, stirring continuously, 3 minutes.

3 Add eggplant; stir-fry until it begins to brown.

4 Add tomatoes and simmer until sauce is thickened and eggplant is tender.

5 Adjust seasoning.

Boiled Plantains   SERVES 4

In Africa, boiled plantains are more common than fried plantains.

AMOUNT	MEASURE	INGREDIENT
4 cups	20 ounces, 560 g	Plantains, peeled, 2 inch (5 cm) pieces
To taste		Salt and pepper

PROCEDURE

1 Cover plantains with water and boil until tender.

2 Drain and serve in pieces or mash. Adjust seasoning.

Rice, Kaklo – Banana and Chile Fritter, Mchuzi wa Biringani – Eggplant Curry, and Akoho sy Voanio – Chicken in Coconut Milk

Samaki wa Kupaka
Grilled Fish (Eastern Africa) SERVES 4

One of many traditional Swahili fish dishes from Zanzibar, an African island in the Indian Ocean. *Samaki* is the Swahili word for "fish" and *mchuzi* means "curry" (or gravy, sauce, or soup).

AMOUNT	MEASURE	INGREDIENT
2 teaspoons		Ginger, grated
2 tablespoons		Garlic, minced
1		Green chile (jalapeño), seeded, minced
As needed		Salt
1	2½ to 3 pound, 1.12 kg to 1.34 kg	Whole fish (snapper, sea bass, sea perch, or other fresh white fish), gutted, scales and tail removed
2 cups	16 ounces, 480 ml	Coconut milk
1 tablespoon	½ ounce, 15 ml	Tamarind paste
1 teaspoon		Garam masala (see recipe on page 567)
To taste		Cayenne pepper

PROCEDURE

1 Make a paste out of the ginger, garlic, green chile, and salt.

2 Make 4 shallow slashes on each side of the fish. With your fingers, work the paste into the slashes and cavity. Cover and let sit 1 hour.

3 Combine coconut milk, tamarind, garam masala, salt, and cayenne; simmer over low heat.

4 Heat a well-oiled grill or grill pan until very hot, then carefully lay the fish onto it. Cook the fish until a thin crust forms on the skin, which enables you to turn it with a spatula. After the fish has reached the half-cooked mark, begin spooning the sauce over the fish. Spoon more each time you turn it. Allow 3 to 4 minutes per side. The fish may be transferred to a 350°F (176°C) oven to finish cooking.

Akara – Black-Eyed Pea Fritters, Samaki wa Kupaka – Grilled Fish, and Harissa

Kaklo Banana and Chile Fritters (Western Africa) SERVES 4

AMOUNT	MEASURE	INGREDIENT
2 cups	8 ounces, 224 g	Bananas, peeled and mashed
$\frac{1}{2}$ cup	2 ounces, 56 g	Onions, $\frac{1}{8}$ inch (.3 cm) dice
$\frac{1}{2}$ cup	3 ounces, 84 g	Tomato, peeled, seeded, $\frac{1}{8}$ inch (.3 cm) dice
1 tablespoon		Green chile (jalapeño), seeded minced
$1\frac{1}{2}$ teaspoons		Ginger, grated
$\frac{1}{2}$ teaspoon		Salt
1 cup	4 ounces, 112 g	All-purpose flour
2 tablespoons	1 ounce, 30 ml	Water
As needed		Peanut or coconut oil, for frying

PROCEDURE

1 Combine bananas, onion, tomato, and chile; mash together.

2 Add ginger, salt, flour, and water to banana mixture and stir to combine; do not overwork. Let rest 30 minutes.

3 In a deep pan or fryer, heat 3 inches (5 cm) oil over medium heat to 375°F (190°C).

4 Deep-fry teaspoon-size portions; drain on paper towels.

5 Serve hot or cold as a snack or with a meal.

Muamba Nsusu
Congo Chicken Soup   SERVES 4

AMOUNT	MEASURE	INGREDIENT
1	2½ pound, 1.12 kg	Chicken, cut into 8 pieces
1 quart	32 ounces, 960 ml	Chicken stock
2 tablespoons	1 ounce, 30 ml	Palm oil
1 cup	4 ounces, 112 g	Onions, ¼ inch (.6 cm) dice
1½ teaspoons		Garlic, minced
½ teaspoon		Crushed red pepper flakes
1 cup	6 ounces, 168 g	Tomatoes, peeled, seeded, ½ inch dice
¼ cup	2 ounces, 60 ml	Tomato paste
⅓ cup	2½ ounces, 70 g	Peanut butter, containing only peanuts and salt

PROCEDURE

1 Combine chicken and chicken stock; simmer until chicken is tender. Remove chicken from stock and retain stock at a simmer. Skin chicken and shred meat; set aside.

2 Heat oil over medium heat; add onions and garlic and sauté 3 to 5 minutes, until soft.

3 Add red pepper flakes and diced tomatoes; bring to a simmer.

4 Combine 1 cup (8 ounces, 240 ml) chicken broth from step 1 with tomato paste and peanut butter; stir until smooth.

5 Combine chicken meat, tomato mixture, chicken broth, and peanut butter mixture. Stir and continue to simmer unit the soup is thickened, 5 to 10 minutes; do not boil.

6 Serve hot.

Sosaties (South Africa) SERVES 4

AMOUNT	MEASURE	INGREDIENT
1½ cups	8 ounces, 224 g	Dried apricots
½ cup	8 ounces, 240 m	Dry sherry
1 pound	16 ounces, 448 g	Lamb, lean, cut 1 inch (2.4 cm) cubes
	8 ounces, 224 g	Pork, lean, cut ½ inch (1.2 cm) cubes
6		Whole garlic cloves
To taste		Salt and pepper
3 tablespoons	1½ ounces, 45 ml	Oil
½ cup	2 ounces, 56 g	Onions, ¼ inch (.6 cm) dice
2 teaspoons		Garam masala (see recipe on page 567)
1		Garlic clove, minced
1 tablespoon	½ ounce, 14 g	Granulated sugar
1 tablespoon	½ ounce, 15 ml	Tamarind paste
1 cup	8 ounces, 240 ml	White vinegar
1 tablespoon	½ ounce, 15 ml	Apricot jam
1 tablespoon		Cornstarch
1 tablespoon	½ ounce, 15 ml	Red wine

PROCEDURE

1 Combine apricots and sherry over medium heat; simmer until apricots are plump. Remove from heat and cool.

2 Combine the lamb and pork with the whole garlic cloves, season with salt and pepper, and toss.

3 Heat the oil over medium heat; add the onions and sauté 3 to 4 minutes. Add the garam masala and minced garlic. Sauté, stirring, 1 minute.

4 Add sugar, tamarind paste, vinegar, and jam; stir well and bring to a boil.

5 Dissolve the cornstarch in the red wine, add it to the pan, and cook until sauce has thickened, 2 to 3 minutes. Remove from heat and let cool.

6 Toss meat with half the sauce, reserve the other half. Marinate the meat 1 hour at room temperature or 3 hours under refrigeration.

7 Drain meat from marinade. Thread lamb, pork, and apricots on skewers.

8 Grill until browned on all sides, basting with marinade. Serve with heated sauce on the side.

Sosaties and Yellow Rice with Raisins

Yellow Rice with Raisins
(South Africa)   SERVES 4

AMOUNT	MEASURE	INGREDIENT
2½ cups	20 ounces, 600 ml	Water or chicken stock
2 teaspoons	9 g	Granulated sugar
½ teaspoon		Turmeric, ground
2 teaspoons		Salt
1 tablespoon	½ ounce, 15 ml	Butter
1		Cinnamon stick, 2 inches (5 cm)
½ cup	3 ounces, 84 g	Raisins
½ teaspoon		Lemon, zest
1 cup	7 ounces, 196 g	Long-grain rice, washed twice

PROCEDURE

1 Heat water to a boil, add all ingredients except rice, and stir to dissolve.

2 Add rice and return to a simmer; cover, reduce heat, and simmer about 20 minutes.

3 Remove cover and cook 5 minutes longer. Fluff the rice with a fork and serve.

Grilled Tilapia   SERVES 4

Tilapia are native to the lakes and rivers of Africa, where it is called _ngege_. Outside of Africa, tilapia is called St. Peter's fish.

AMOUNT	MEASURE	INGREDIENT
4 5-ounce	4 112–140 g	Boneless, skinless tilapia fillets
½ cup	4 ounces, 120 ml	Vegetable oil
1 cup	4 ounces, 112 g	Onions, ¼ inch (.6 cm) dice
1 cup	4 ounces, 112 g	Green bell pepper, ¼ inch (.6 cm) dice
1 tablespoon	½ ounce, 15 ml	Fresh lemon juice
2 teaspoons	10 ml	White vinegar
1 teaspoon		Cayenne
½ teaspoon		Salt
		African hot sauce (recipe follows)

PROCEDURE

1   Combine all the ingredients except the tilapia. Mix well, add the fish fillets and marinate for 30 minute to 1 hour.

2   Remove from marinade, grill, broil or sauté.

3   Serve with African hot sauce.

African Hot Sauce   SERVES 4

AMOUNT	MEASURE	INGREDIENT
6		Chile peppers; dried mixture of anchos, New Mexican, and guajillos, or any hot red peppers
1 cup	4 ounces, 112 g	Green bell pepper, stemmed, seeded, chopped
1		Garlic clove, chopped
½ cup	2 ounces, 56 g	Onions, chopped
10 tablespoons	6 ounces, 168 g	Tomato paste
2 tablespoons	1 ounce, 30 ml	Water
½ teaspoon		Granulated sugar
½ teaspoon		Salt

PROCEDURE

1   Remove stems and seeds from peppers. Combine all ingredients in a food processor, or process to a paste using a mortar and pestle.

2   Simmer over medium heat 1 hour. Cool and serve.

Irio (Eastern Africa) SERVES 4

AMOUNT	MEASURE	INGREDIENT
2 cups	16 ounces, 480 ml	Water or chicken stock
1 cup	6 ounces, 168 g	Frozen, canned, or dried green peas, cooked and drained
3 cups	16 ounces, 448 g	Russet potatoes, peeled, quartered
1½ cups	9 ounces, 252 g	Corn kernels (3 ears, on the cob)
3 cups	6 ounces, 168 g	Greens or spinach, washed coarsely chopped
To taste		Salt and pepper

PROCEDURE

1 Combine all ingredients and bring to a boil. Cover and simmer until tender, 15 to 20 minutes; longer if greens are used.

2 Mash with a potato masher until smooth and thick.

India

The Land

Set apart from the rest of Asia by the continental wall of the Himalayas, the Indian subcontinent touches three large bodies of water and is immediately recognizable on any world map. Between Africa and Indonesia, this thick, roughly triangular peninsula defines the Bay of Bengal to the east, the Arabian Sea to the west, and the Indian Ocean to the south. India's twenty-six states hold virtually every kind of landscape imaginable. From its northernmost point on the Chinese border, India extends nearly 2000 miles to its southern tip, off of which the island nation of Sri Lanka is located. India's northern border is dominated mostly by Nepal and the Himalayas, the world's highest mountain chain. Following the mountains to the northeast, India's border narrows to a small channel that passes between Nepal, Tibet, Bangladesh, and Bhutan, then spreads out again to meet Burma in an area called the Eastern Triangle. Apart from the Arabian Sea, its western border is defined exclusively by Pakistan.

India can be organized into north, south, east, and west regions. North India is the country's largest region, an area with terrain varying from arid mountains in the far north to lake country and forests. Along the Indus river valley, the north becomes flatter and more hospitable, widening into the fertile plains, the Himalayan foothills, and the Ganges river valley to the east. India's capital city, Delhi, is found in the north. Uttar Pradesh, the most populated state in the country, has beautiful monuments like Taj Mahal.

India reaches its peninsular tip with South India, which begins with the Deccan Plateau in the north and ends with Cape Comorin, where Hindus believe that bathing in the waters of the three oceans will wash away their sins. The southeast coast, mirroring the west, also rests beneath a mountain range, the Eastern Ghats.

East India is home to the sacred Ganges River and the majority of Himalayan foothills. East India also contains the Eastern Triangle, a small piece of land that extends beyond Bangladesh, culminating in the Naga Hills along the Burmese border.

West India includes the Thar Desert and the remarkable "pink city" of Jaipur. The coast is lined with some of India's best beaches. The land along the coast is typically lush, with rain forests reaching southward from Bombay all the way to into Goa. The long Western Ghats mountain chain separates the verdant coast from the Vindya Mountains and the dry Deccan plateau further inland.

Because of India's size, its climate depends not only on the time of year, but also the location. In general, temperatures tend to be cooler in the north, especially between September and March. The south is coolest from November to January. In June, winds and warm surface currents begin to move northward and westward, heading out of the Indian Ocean and into the Arabian Gulf. This creates a phenomenon known as the southwest monsoon, and it brings heavy rains to the west coast. Between October and December, a similar climatic pattern called the northeast monsoon appears in the Bay of Bengal, bringing rains to the east coast. In addition to the two monsoons, there are two other seasons, spring and autumn. Though the word *monsoon* often brings to mind images of torrential floods and landslides, the monsoon seasons are not all bad. Though it rains nearly every day, the downpour tends to come and go quickly, leaving behind a clean, glistening landscape.

History

The history of India can be traced in fragments to as far back as 700,000 years ago. The Indus Valley civilization, one of the oldest in the world, dates back at least 5,000 years. It is thought that the Aryans, a nomadic people possibly from Central Asia or northern Iran, migrated into the northwest regions of the Indian subcontinent between 2000 B.C. and 1500 B.C. Their intermingling with the earlier Dravidian cultures resulted in classical Indian culture that is known today.

The births of Mahavira (Jainism) and Buddhism around 550 B.C. mark the beginning of well-recorded Indian history. For the next 1500 years, India developed its civilization, and is estimated to have had the largest economy of the ancient world between the first and fifteenth centuries A.D., controlling between one-third and one-fourth of the world's wealth. It rapidly declined during European rule in the course of the Mughals Empire.

Incursions by Arab and Central Asian armies in the eighth and twelfth centuries were followed by inroads by traders from Europe, beginning in the late fifteenth century. By 1858,

India

the British Crown had assumed political control over virtually all of India. Indian armed forces in the British army played a vital role in both the World Wars.

Nonviolent resistance to British colonialism, led by Mohandas Gandhi (more commonly known as Mahatma Ghandi), Vallabhbhai Patel, and Jawaharlal Nehru, brought independence in 1947. The subcontinent was divided into the Secular Democratic Republic of India and the smaller Islamic Republic of Pakistan. A war between the two countries in 1971 resulted in East Pakistan becoming the separate nation of Bangladesh.

In the twenty-first century, India has made impressive gains in economic investment and output, and stands as the world's largest democracy with a population exceeding one billion. It is self-sufficient in terms of food, and is a fast-growing, economically strong country.

The People

Birthplace of civilizations, cradle of world religions, India is home to almost a quarter of the world's population. India has dominated the world stage through most of human history, as the home of mighty empires, as a powerful trading nation, and as a hub of culture and civilization. Rumors of its empires and its wealth brought traders and travelers. Alexander the Great marched across Asia to India. Arab and Jewish traders sailed here. At one time Roman soldiers were barracked here. The ancient Greeks had trading colonies. Columbus wasn't looking for America; he hoped to find a new route to India. European history favored nations with an India connection.

India excelled in international trade. Five thousand years ago the thriving cities of the Indus Valley traded with Mesopotamia. Indian traders spread their goods and influence through Southeast Asia. Spices, gems, pearls, and silks flowed out of India into the rest of the world. Crafts, textiles, and exotic birds and animals were also traded. Hannibal's elephants came from India. So did many of the lavish fabrics craved by Roman nobility. At one point, so much gold was leaving Rome for India that the Roman economy was seriously weakened. Ideas and culture spread with trade goods. Philosophy, sciences, and medicine reached unrivaled heights, enriching the great scientific achievements of China and the Arab world. The influences of Indian thought can be found in early European culture, and still today, Indian philosophy influences modern global cultures.

The British colonial era brought new and different challenges to India, resulting in an independence movement that has left an indelible mark on nonviolent struggles for freedom and justice throughout the modern world. During this time in history, society in India wove an intricate web of relationships, rituals, and duties, yet remained astonishingly tolerant and diverse. Great religions developed and spread from India. Hindus, Buddhists, Jains, and Sikhs trace their roots to India.

English is the major language of trade and politics, but there are fourteen official Indian languages in all. There are more than twenty-four languages spoken by a million Indians, and countless other dialects. India has seven major religions and many minor ones, six main ethnic groups, and countless holidays.

The Food

Throughout history India has been invaded and occupied by other cultures and each has left its own mark on Indian cuisine. Some of the predominant influences have been:

- During the Aryan period the cuisine of the great Hindu empires concentrated on the fine aspects of food and on understanding its essence and how it contributed to the development of mind, body, and spirit. After this period the cuisine was influenced by the following conquests from other cultures.
- Mongolians brought their hotpot cooking to India.
- The most notable later culinary influence in India was the influence of Persian rulers who established the Mughal Rule in India. They introduced their fondness for elegant dining and rich food with dry fruit and nuts. Muslims from western Asia brought their rich artistic and gastronomic culture to India. This influence lasted for more than four hundred years and is now part of the fabric of Indian culinary culture. The two cultures resulted in a magnificent cuisine called *Mughlai cuisine*. The lamb kebabs were laced with spices, the rice pilaf (*pilau*) of India was turned into *biryanis* (any number of layered rice, meat/vegetable, spice, and yogurt recipes) and lamb and meat roasts were flavored with Indian herbs, spices, and seasonings. Indian dishes were garnished with almonds, pistachios, cashews, and raisins. The Muslims also introduced leavened breads to India. The royal chefs created the cylindrical clay oven in which food is cooked over a hot charcoal fire known as the *tandoor*. The Indian *rotis* and the leavened breads were merged into *tandoori naans*. Meats were marinated in yogurt and spices and cooked in *tandoors*. Pork and beef were avoided to respect the traditions of both cultures. Since the Persian rulers loved sweets, sweetmeats were introduced.
- The Chinese introduced stir-fries to Indian and added a sweet taste to food. Their influence is mostly felt in western India.
- The tomato, chile, and potato, which are staple components of today's Indian cuisine, were brought to India by the Portuguese. The Indian *vindaloo* dish is a result of Portuguese influence.
- The British made ketchup and tea popular in India, but British food did not become popular in India. Although the British colonists mainly described Indian food as pungent, chile-spiked curries and rice and *rotis* were considered food for uncivilized pagans. Today, however, Indian food forms a staple diet of British food.

The essential ingredient that distinguishes Indian cooking from all other cuisines is the use of spices. Indian spices have an important place in all international markets and are even a commodity traded on the stock market. *Curry* is an all-purpose term devised by the English to cover the whole range of Indian food spicing. Indian cooks have at least twenty-five spices on their regular list and it is from these that they produce curry flavor. The spices are blended in certain combinations to produce specific dishes. *Garam masala,* for example, is a combination of cloves and cinnamon with peppercorns. Popular spices include saffron that is used to give *biryani* that yellow color and delicate fragrance. *Turmeric* also has a coloring property and acts as a preservative. Red and green chiles are ground, dried, or added whole to give a hot taste to curries. Ginger is considered to be good for digestion. Coriander is added to many *masalas* to cool the body. Cardamom is used in many sweet dishes and in meat preparations. Other popular spices are nutmeg, cinnamon, poppy seeds, caraway seeds, cumin seeds, fenugreek, mace, garlic, and cloves.

Indian dishes are cooked in three stages. The first stage is to prepare the base, or the gravy. This requires warming the oil with the spices and salt. The second stage involves adding the vegetables and stirring it into the gravy base. The third stage is to allow the dish to simmer until completely cooked. While this is the basic technique, the difference is in the blend of spices, which are broadly divided into two categories: powdered spices that have been freshly ground using a mortar and pestle, and the whole spices such as clove, cardamom, mustard seeds, nutmeg, and others.

A complete Indian meal would start with appetizers, which are usually fried or baked. This leads into the main course that comprises one or two vegetable dishes, along with pulses or a curry. Indian food has a number of side dishes to go with the main meal. The most popular is probably the *dahi,* or curd of yogurt. It cools the stomach after a very hot meal. Desserts such as *kulfi* (a kind of Indian ice cream), *rasgullas* (sweet little balls of rose-flavored cream cheese), and rice or milk puddings in sweet syrup are popular. An Indian meal finishes with *paan,* the name given to the collection of spices and condiments chewed with *betel* leaves. Found throughout eastern Asia, *betel* is mildly intoxicating and addictive, but after a meal it is taken as a mild digestive in small amounts. *Paan* sellers have a number of little trays and containers in which they mix the ingredients, which may include a part from the betel nut itself, lime paste, and various spices. Then they place it in the leaf, which is folded up and chewed.

To the western mind, India is perceived as a largely vegetarian cuisine, but this is not necessarily true. To a larger extent, religious beliefs (as compared to personal preference) dictate what a person cannot eat. For example, Islam forbids its followers from eating pork, while many Hindus do not eat beef. Followers of the Jain faith are strict vegetarians and take nonviolence to a very strict level, and respect life at any level, including plant life.

India can be very roughly divided into four culinary regions. Each region has several states in it and each state has its own unique food. Here's a brief look at the cuisines of north, west, east, and south India.

NORTH INDIA

North India includes the states of Jammu and Kashmir, Himachal Pradesh, Punjab, Haryana, Delhi, Uttaranchal, Uttar Pradesh, Bihar, Madhya Pradish, Jharkhand, and Chattisgarh.

North India has extreme climates; summers are hot and winters are cold. There is an abundance of fresh seasonal fruit and vegetables. Its geographical position with relation to the rest of the subcontinent means that this region of the country has had strong Central Asian influences both in its culture and its food. *Mughlai* and *Kashmiri* styles of cooking are prevalent.

The food from north India traces its descent from Persian ancestors who started filtering into India from the eleventh century A.D. onward and then more markedly from the sixteenth century A.D., when the Mughals came to power. The Mughals brought with them Persian and Afghan cooks, who introduced rich and fragrant Persian rice dishes, such as *pilafs* and *biryanis*. Garnished with pounded silver (*vark*), these dishes along with spicy *kormas* (braised meat in creamy sauces), *koftas* (grilled spicy meatballs), and kebabs graced the tables of emperors.

A typical north Indian meal would consist of *pilafs*, thick, creamy *dals* (the Indian word for their many types of dried pulses), vegetables seasoned with yogurt or pomegranate powder, greens like spinach and mustard greens cooked with *paneer* (a fresh and delicate cottage cheese made from whole milk), North Indian pickles, fresh tomato, mint, cilantro chutneys, and yogurt *raitas*. North Indian curries usually have thick, moderately spicy and creamy gravies. The use of dried fruits and nuts is common even in everyday foods. Dairy products like milk, cream, cottage cheese, ghee (clarified butter), and yogurt play an important role in the cooking of both savory and sweet dishes. North Indians prefer breads to rice. This region is home to the stuffed *parathas* (flaky Indian bread with different kinds of vegetarian and nonvegetarian fillings), and *kulchas* (bread made from fermented dough). *Chappatis, parantha,* or *pooris* are their unleavened flat breads. Hot, sweet cardamom milk is commonly taken before going to bed. North Indian desserts and sweets are made of milk, *paneer*, lentil flour, and wheat flour combined with dried nuts and garnished with a thin sheet of pure silver. *Nimbu Pani* (lemon drink) and *lassi* (iced buttermilk) are popular drinks of the north.

In Jammu and Kashmir is found the tradition of *wazwan*, the fabulous aromatic celebratory banquet consisting of thirty-six delectable dishes. Most of the dishes are meat based and contain heavy dose of spices, condiments, and curds. *Rista* (meatballs in red gravy), *tabak maaz* (fried lamb ribs), and *rogan josh* (Indian lamb in spicy cream sauce) are just some of the dishes included in the *wazwan*.

Recipes from the hilly regions of Himanchal Pradesh and Uttaranchal are simple and nutritious, based on a huge variety of *dals* cooked slowly over fire. There is a lot of variety in cooking patterns in these areas as taste preference changes from one region to other.

The cuisine of Punjab and Haryana is rich in dairy products, grains, and most notably is the home of the *tandoori* (Indian clay oven) style of cooking. Favorites such as *tandoori chicken* and *naan* breads are all from this style of cooking. Food in Punjab and Haryana is rich in butter and ghee and contains many spices.

The *bawarchis* (cooks) of Awadh in Uttar Pradesh originated the *dum* style of cooking, or the art of slow cooking over a fire. *Dum pukht* refers to a slow method of cooking food. *Dum* means steam and *dum pukht* literally means to "choke off the steam." To do this the food is placed in a pot, usually made of clay, and dough is used to create a tight seal to prevent steam from escaping. The food is slowly cooked in its own juices and steam, allowing herbs and spices to fully infuse the meat or rice, while preserving the nutritional elements at the same time. The final result is rich in taste and aroma. *Korma* is a preparation of meat in gravy that is an essential item of the Awadh table. *Biryani* is cooked in *dum* style, as are *murg mussallam* (whole chicken) and *shami kebabs* (the "national" kebab of Awadh, made from minced meat heavily seasoned with *garam masala*). Mustard oil is a common cooking medium in north India, where the mustard plant grows extensively and is harvested in February and March. In Awadh the mustard oil is heated in large cauldrons till it smokes. Then it is passed through muslin cloth to remove any impurities. This oil is then collected and sealed in large earthenware pots or urns and buried in the earth, preferably under the shade of a tree or a cool place. It is left to mature for a period of nine to ten months, including through the rainy season, so that the oil is further cooled when the rainwater seeps into the ground. The long period of underground storage transforms the oil to a granular texture, which is used for cooking purposes.

In the vast plateau of Madhya Pradesh, the cuisine consists of both sweet and salty dishes. People of this part of the country do not have a distinct cuisine of their own, but they have combined the best of the food cultures from the neighboring states.

WEST INDIA

The Arabian Sea guards the western region of India. West Indian states of Maharastra, Gujarat, Goa, and Rajasthan are regarded as the gateway to the western countries, particularly the Gulf region. The state of Maharashtra (which means "The Great State"), is one of the largest in India in terms of both size and population, and stands mostly on the high Deccan Plateau. It was the main historical center for the Maratha Empire, which defied the Mughals for almost 150 years, and which carved out a large part of central India as its domain. The capital of Maharashtra was once called Bombay, but the name of the city was changed to Mumbai by an act of the parliament in 1997. It acquired the nickname "Bollywood" because of its resemblance to the American film capital, Hollywood. Gujarat is one of India's wealthier states, with a number of important industries, particularly textiles and electronics, and it has the largest petrochemical complex in the country. Gujarat was the birthplace of Mahatma Gandhi, the father of modern India. The former Portuguese enclave of Goa has some of the world's most beautiful beaches. Almost 500 years of Portuguese rule have given Goa a unique culture, quite distinct from the rest of India, and includes a curious blending of cultures, from religion to architecture, cuisine to art. Rajasthan, literally "land of the kings," was once a group of princely kingdoms. The Rajputs, who ruled here for over a thousand years, were legendary for their chivalry.

The state is diagonally divided into the hilly and rugged southeastern region and the barren northwestern Thar Desert, which extends across the border into Pakistan.

Parts of Maharashtra are coastal and parts arid, and the food varies accordingly. Rice is the staple food grain and as in other coastal states, there is an enormous variety of vegetables, fish, and coconuts in the regular diet. Grated coconuts flavor many dishes, but coconut oil is not very widely used as a cooking medium. Rather, peanut oil is the main cooking medium and peanuts and cashew nuts are widely used in vegetable dishes. *Kokum*, a deep purple berry that has the same souring qualities as tamarind, is used to enhance coconut-based curries or vegetable dishes like potatoes, okra, or lentils. *Kokum* is especially used with fish curries, three or four skins being enough to season an average dish. It is also included in chutneys and pickles. The skins are not usually chopped but are added whole to the dish. Vegetables are steamed and lightly seasoned; there is little deep-frying and roasting. *Jaggery* (the traditional unrefined sugar in India) and tamarind are used in most vegetables or lentils dishes so that the food has a sweet-and-sour flavor, while the *kala masala* (special blend of spices) is added to make the food piquant. Powdered coconut is used for cooking in the inland regions. Among seafood, the popular delicacy is *bombil* (a very strong-smelling fish also known as Bombay duck or dak), which is normally served batter fried and crisp or dried and salted to be used in a curry. *Bangda,* or mackerel, is another popular fish in coastal Maharashtra is curried with red chiles and ginger. *Pomfret* is a fish eaten barbecued, stuffed, fried, or curried. *Pamphlet triphal ambat* is a traditional dish in which fish is cooked in creamy coconut gravy. Besides fish, crabs, prawns, shellfish, and lobsters are used.

In the vegetarian fare, the most popular vegetable is eggplant. A favorite style of cooking them is *bharlivangi,* or baby eggplant stuffed with coconut. Another typical dish is the *pachadi,* which is eggplant cooked with green mangoes and flavored with coconut and *jaggery*. All dishes are eaten with boiled rice or with *bhakris*, which are soft *rotis* made of rice flour. Special rice cakes called *vada* and *amboli* (a pancake made of fermented rice, *urad dal,* and semolina) are also eaten as a part of the main meal. Meals are not complete without *papads* (dried lentil chips), which are eaten roasted or fried. A typical feature is the *masala papad,* in which finely chopped onions, green chiles, and *chat masala* are sprinkled over roasted or fried *papads.* The most popular dessert of Maharashtra is the *puran poli,* which is *roti* stuffed with a sweet mixture of *jaggery* and *gram flour* (made from ground chickpeas, or chana dal) and is made at the time of the Maharashtrian New Year. Other popular sweets are the *ukdiche modak* (steamed rice flour dumplings), and the *shreekhand* (a thick yogurt sweet dish flavored with cardamom powder and saffron).

The state of Gujarat excels in the preparation of vegetarian dishes. The recipes are known for the subtle use of spices and rich texture. A selection of different dishes, usually served in small bowls on a round tray, is known as a *thali*. The *thali* consists of *roti, dal*, or *kadhi* (a "soup" made with chickpea flour, yogurt, water, lemon juice, and spices, along with fritters of chickpea flour and chopped vegetables that swell and soften), rice, and *sabzi/shaak* (a dish made up of different combinations of vegetables and spices, which may be stir-fried, currylike, or even dry-boiled). Cuisine varies in taste and heat, depending on a given family. Gujarati food has been influenced by Chinese cuisine and is different from most all Indian cuisines in that the sweets are served with the meal. This is also a reason why there is more sweet and sour taste in their dishes. Other popular items include a vegetable preparation *Undhiu* (mixed winter vegetables), *gujarati kadhi*, a savory curry made of yogurt. Some common dishes include *khaman dhokla*, a salty steamed cake; *doodhpak*, a sweet, thickened milk confectionery; and *shrikhand*, a dessert made of yogurt, flavored with saffron and cardamom.

A particularly important part of the cuisine of the region is the unparalleled variety of snacks called *farsan*. *Farsan* means savory snack and usually refers to anything salty, fried, and crunchy. *Patra*, a famous *farsan*, is made from the long, black-stemmed *colocasia* (taro) leaves and Bengal gram flour. The leaves are spread with a batter of flour into which a pulp of tamarind and *jaggery* is mixed. Green chiles, ginger, sesame seeds, coriander seeds, mustard seeds, and salt are added. The leaves are placed one on top of the other and then folded from both sides. They are rolled tightly, the roll is tied with a thread, and then steamed for an hour. The rolls are then cut into half-inch-thick slices. These are sautéed in oil with mustard seeds and served hot, garnished with chopped coriander leaves and grated coconut.

As mentioned earlier, food in Goa has been influenced by the Portuguese. Local dishes like *vindaloo* (fiery hot and known as the "king of curries") and *xacut* (a curry, usually chicken, with white poppy seeds and red peppers) are evidence that Goa was a Portuguese colony until the 1960s. *Pork vindaloo* is a spicy concoction of red chiles, garlic, cooked with chunks of pork, Goa vinegar, and hard palm sugar served with plain boiled rice. Rice, fish, and coconut are the basic components of the typical Goan platter. The Goans make full use of their proximity to the sea coast by using fish, crabs, lobsters, and tiger prawns, which are cooked in a coconut, garlic hot sauce, or dry spices. An essential ingredient in Goan cooking is coconut milk made by grating the white flesh of a coconut and soaking it in a cup of warm water. Equally important is the *kokum* that gives it a sharp and sour flavor. The famous red Goan chiles are also a must for most dishes, as is tamarind. Goans make their own version of vinegar from toddy, which is distilled from the sap of coconut palm trees. Then there are the innumerable chutneys that are typical of the state.

Though there are two separate traditions in cuisine influenced by the respective religions of Hinduism and Christianity, there are some meeting points that present interesting harmony. While Hindus like lamb and chicken, Christians seem to prefer pork. However, both prefer fish and seafood to any other protein. Grinding spices is always part of the recipe and the nicer the dish the longer it takes to make. Although the styles of the various cultures, past and present, have had their effect on each other, the gravies of each style are at a complete variance. The names used are the same, as are the ingredients used, yet their aroma, flavor, taste, texture, and color can be completely different. The most commonly used spices are cumin, chiles, coriander, garlic, and turmeric. Subtle differences in ingredients or their use make the outcome of these similar recipes so different. The Christians prefer to use vinegar, while the Hindus use *kokum* and tamarind to get the tang in their respective cuisines. Northern

Goans grind their coconuts and masalas individually, while the southern Goans like to grind them together, and then pass it through a fine muslin cloth to retain flavor. Many times people vary the pork to mutton and chicken to make the various curries. The most famous Goan sweet meat is the many-layered *bebinca*. It is prepared by adding extract of coconut milk to flour, sugar, and other flavorings. Each layer is baked before adding the next one and the traditional version has sixteen layers. A soft jaggery-flavored fudge called *dodol* is made from palm-sap jaggery, rice flour, and coconut. *Rose-a-coque* is a flowerlike waffle that can be eaten alone or with cream or honey.

Cuisine from Rajasthan tells the tale of the struggle of its inhabitants who had to combat the harsh climate of the region. Historically food preparation in the royal kitchens was a very serious matter. Hundreds of cooks worked in the stately palaces and kept their recipes very closely guarded. Some recipes were passed on to their sons, while others were lost forever. The climate conditions, the lack of availability of vegetables, and the tradition of royal hunts all shaped the culinary traditions. Game cooking is considered a respected art form, largely because the skills required to clean, cut, and cook game are not easily acquired. With the Pathani invasions the art of barbecuing became highly regarded and some of the most popular dishes include *sula-smoked kebabs,* skewered boneless tender morsels of meat, such as lamb, that can be prepared eleven different ways. Perhaps the best-known Rajasthani food is the combination of *dal*, *bati*, and *churma*—dal is lentils, *bati* is a baked wheat ball, and *churma* is powdered sweetened cereal. Two meat dishes, *lal maans* (red meat), a fiery heavily spiced dish, and *safed maans* (white meat) cooked with almonds, cashew nuts, and coconut, are specialties in the region. In Rajasthan, *besan* is a major ingredient here and is used to make some of the delicacies like *gatte ki sabzi* (a popular curry), and *pakodi* (a curd-based curry with dal and red chiles). Also known as *gram flour* in many recipes, *besan* is a fine, pale yellow flour made from roasted *chana dal*. It is used as a batter for deep frying, such as vegetable fritters (*pakoras*), and in soups as a binding agent. Many Indian sweets are made from *besan*. It is to an Indian kitchen what eggs are to a Western kitchen.

The vegetarian cooking prepared by the Maheshwaris of Jodhpur is considered exceptional. And then there are the Jains, who are not only vegetarians, but who do not eat after sundown, and whose food must be devoid of garlic and onions. The region is also popular for the chutneys that are made out of local spices such as coriander, mint, garlic, and turmeric.

EAST INDIA

The eastern region of India includes the states of Assam, Arunachal Pradesh, Manipur, Meghalaya, Mizoram, Nagaland, Orrisa, Sikkim, Tripura, and West Bengal. This is the least explored region of India for various reasons, including an underdeveloped infrastructure, the necessity of special permits, and the overall instablity of the whole region. The area is dominated by various tribes speaking many different languages and dialects. These states and union territories border with Myanmar, Bhutan, Tibet, and Bangladesh.

Fish and rice are a very important part of the diet of east India as a result of the many rivers and tributaries originating in the Himalayas. Centuries of silt carried from the Himalayan Plains and the shifting of river courses has resulted in uniquely fertile soil capable of producing a wide variety of crops and choice vegetables. The population is a balanced mix of vegetarian and nonvegetarian. The geographical location of this region means its food shows a strong influence of Chinese and Mongolian cuisine.

The eastern state of West Bengal is considered to be the cultural capital of India. Bengali food is coastal cuisine symbolized by rice and fish. The market is busy at all times with all sizes and shapes of carp, salmon, *hilsa, bhekti, rui, magur*, and prawns. Their *Macherjhol* (fish curry) is legendary all over India. Fish are also smoked, grilled, fried, made into *pakoras* (patties), stuffed into green coconuts, and then into burgers. Preparation is not elaborate and neither are most of the ingredients. Steaming and frying are popular methods of cooking. Mustard oil is used for cooking instead of ghee or peanut or coconut oil. The specialty of Bengali cuisine is the use of *panchphoron:* five basic spices of *nigella* (similar to black cumin or black caraway seed), fennel, cumin, mustard, and fenugreek. While sweets of north India are based on *khoya* (milk thickened slowly until it forms a sweet doughlike consistency), which is quite heavy, those of east India are based on *chena* (light cottage cheese) and are lighter on the palate and overall very delicate. The tradition of making cakes, locally known as *pitha*, flourishes. They are usually made from rice or wheat flour mixed with sugar, or grated coconut, then fried or steamed and served with a sweet syrup.

Sikkim has a completely different cuisine as compared to other states of east India. The food shows its apparent influence of food culture of neighboring countries, especially Tibet. *Momos* (steamed meat or vegetable filled wontons) are especially popular.

Rice is the staple diet in Assam and is eaten in various forms throughout the day. The Assamese eat a huge variety of rice-based breakfast cereals with milk, yogurt, or thick *cream akhoi* (puffed rice), *chira* (chura), *muri, komal chaul* (a specially processed rice which doesn't require cooking but just an hour's soak in cold water), and *hurum* to name but a few. Normally *jaggery* or sugar is added but for those who prefer savory items, salt can be added. Also there are the various kinds of *pitha* that are prepared from rice powder. Historically, Assam is the second commercial tea production region after southern China. Assam and southern China are the only two regions in the world with native tea plants. Assam tea revolutionized tea drinking habits in the nineteenth century since the tea, produced from a different variety of the tea plant, yielded a different kind of tea. Sold as "breakfast teas" the black tea is known for its body, briskness, malty flavor, and strong, intense color. Most recently, a home-grown chile pepper called *bhut jolokia*—known as "ghost chile"—became known officially in the Guinness World Records as the world's hottest chile. This thumb-sized red chile has more than 1,000,000 Scoville units (the level of a chile's heat measured by the content of capsaicin, the chemical that "heats" a chile) and is 125 times hotter than a jalapeño. The Meghalayan cuisine is based on meat, particularly pork. *Jadoh*—a spicy dish of rice and pork—is eaten almost any time. The city of Shillong is the source of authentic Chinese food. *Kyat*, the local brew is made from rice.

SOUTH INDIA

The states within South India include Karnataka, Tamil Nadu, Kerala, and Andhra Pradesh. India's Great Divide is the Vindhya Mountains. They run from east to west, separating the fertile river valley of the Ganges River from the Deccan Plateau, which occupies much of the peninsula of India. South India's coastal plains are backed by the mountains rimming the wedge of the Deccan Plateau. On these plains lie the best beaches in South India. On the rimming mountains, the Western and Eastern Ghats, are the tea, coffee, and spice lands. Beyond these mountains are great old cities supported by rich farm lands. The south is gracious, graceful old India.

South India has hot, humid climate and all its states are coastal. Rainfall is abundant and so is the supply of fresh fruit, vegetables, and rice. South Indian cuisine is rice based. Rice are of three basic categories: the white long-grain rice is most commonly used; short-grain rice is used to make sweet dishes; and a round grain rice that is used for worship representing Health, Wealth, and Fertility. Steamed rice dumplings (*idlis*) and roasted rice pancakes (*dosais*) are paired with coconut chutneys for breakfast. The famous *masala dosai* is stuffed with spiced potatoes, vegetables, or even minced lamb.

A formal South Indian meal is divided into three courses of rice. The first is rice with *sambhar*, the everyday food of South India. Made from a handful of lentils or mung beans simmered in a pot of water until they disintegrate into a smooth, creamy mixture, *sambhar* is flavored with turmeric, sour tamarind, *asafetida* (a gum resin used for flavor and digestion), curry leaves, and toasted mustard seeds. The second course is rice served with *rasam*, a tangy, spicy tamarind and tomato-based soup with lentils. A small amount of one or two vegetables, fresh herbs, and spices are added. The third course is a cooling mixture of rice and buttermilk or yogurt. It may be served with nonspicy assorted vegetable dishes, namely the *aviyal* (mixed vegetable stew), *kari* (dry masala vegetables), and *kootu* (coconut and vegetable sauté).

South Indian *dals* and curries are soupier than north Indian *dals* and curries. South Indian chutneys are made of tamarind, coconut, peanuts, *dal,* fenugreek seeds, and cilantro. Coconut, either in a shredded, grated, or blended form, is found in most dishes here and coconut water is drunk for its cooling effect on the system. Meals are followed by coffee.

Before stainless steel became widespread, banana leaves were the plate of choice. There are specific dictates in India to serving food on a banana leaf, especially for celebratory feasts or religious offerings. From alternating dry vegetables with gravies to the exact corner for placing a sweet dessert, the order of up to twenty different foods follows a circular pattern that incorporates health, religion, and regional traditions.

Dishes are seasoned with toasted mustard seeds, red chiles, curry leaves, and oil. Coconut oil is most commonly used for cooking and frying. Vegetable oils like sunflower and canola are also used and ghee is poured over rice during daily meals or in special occasion dishes.

Andhra Pradesh produces fiery Andhra cuisine, which is largely vegetarian yet also includes a wide range of seafood. Fish and prawns are curried in sesame and coconut oils, and flavored with freshly ground pepper. Hyderabad, the capital of Andhra Pradesh, has a cuisine that is a direct result of the kitchens of the Muslim rulers, with the vibrant spices and ingredients of the predominantly local Hindu people. Its tastes range from the sour and the sweet to the hot and the salty, and foods are studded with dry fruits and nuts and exotic, expensive spices like saffron.

Tamil Nadu has *Chettinad* cuisine, which consists of meat and poultry cooked in tamarind and roasted spices and is one of the most fiery of all Indian food. Oil and spices are used liberally and most dishes have generous amounts of peppercorns, cinnamon, bay leaves, cardamom, nutmeg, and green and red chiles. From Kerala comes *Malabari* cooking, with its seafood dishes; it is noted for its variety of pancakes and steamed rice cakes made from pounded rice.

Glossary

Ajwain Seed Carom seed, bishop's weed; resembles a small caraway seed but with the flavor of pungent thyme. Usually sprinkled on breads.

Amchoor Dried green mango powder used as a souring agent or to tenderize meats.

Appam Wafer-thin, round, flat bread, usually made of rice, potato, and/or various lentil flours.

Asafetida Known as *devil's dung* or *food of the gods*, it is a powdered gum resin that imparts a very strong onion-garlic flavor; a little goes a long way.

Baghar, Tadka, or Chounk The technique of adding spices and herbs all at one time to hot oil. This is done as a first step in the cooking process, or as the last, and then pouring the tempered oil over a cooked dish. The oil extracts and retains the sharp flavors of the spices, flavoring the entire dish.

Balti Means "pot" or "bucket." This stir-fried curry takes its name from the heavy, woklike dish in which the food is cooked and served. The dish is also known as a *karhai* or *karahi*.

Barfi A dessert made from milk that has been cooked slowly and reduced to a fudgelike consistency.

Basmati Rice Authentic Indian long-grained white rice with a unique nutty flavor.

Belan Rolling pin, about 12 inches long, with a long taper from the center toward each end.

Biryani A mixture of rice and spicy meat or vegetables arranged in layers, sprinkled with saffron and *ghee*. Traditionally the ingredients are tightly packed and sealed with *naan* dough. This method is also termed the *dum* style.

Black Cumin Seeds (Kala Jeera, Saahjeers) Darker and sweeter than ordinary cumin, used in curries and tandooris.

Black Mustard Seeds Preferred over the larger yellow mustard seeds common in the West.

Bondas or Vadas Round deep-fried savory snack made in different varieties usually from lentils or potatoes and eaten with a chutney.

Chappati The most common unleavened flat-bread in north India made with wheat flour, water, oil, and salt. Usually cooked on a *tava* or thick griddle and brushed with ghee. Similar to those prepared in Greece, the Middle East, and Mexico.

Chutney Fresh relishes made with fruits, vegetables, and herbs.

Curry The term "curry" means gravy or sauce. An authentic Indian curry is a combination of stir-fried wet masala (a mixture of onion, garlic, ginger, and tomato), various spices, and seasoning, to which other items are added and prepared as a stew-type dish.

Dal, Daal Dals are the primary source of protein in a vegetarian diet (especially in southern India). They include dried peas, beans, and lentils, plus split peas and other legumes. Ground powdered dal is used in crackers, unleavened breads, and spice mixtures.

Dosas, Dhosas Lentil flour-based pancakes, traditionally stuffed with mashed potatoes and onions, flavored with mustard seeds and turmeric, much like an Indian crepe or enchilada. A southern Indian delicacy, originally from Madras but now found all over India.

Feni A drink made from cashews or coconut is the perfect beach drink. It was originally a very basic and local drink; recently it has been commercialized.

Fenugreek Adds an earthy flavor to foods; available as seeds or powder.

Ghee, or Desi Ghee Clarified butter.

Halva Indian sweet made from a variety of finely grated vegetables, milk, and sugar, and flavored with cardamom. The consistency is that of a thick pudding.

Jalfrezi A style of cooking mixed vegetables or chicken in a tangy sauce.

Kachumber Indian salad usually made with cucumber, tomatoes, and onions flavored with salt, sugar, and lemon juice.

Kadhai A traditional Indian iron wok, much deeper and narrower than the Chinese wok. Used mainly for frying or braising. In authentic kadhai-style cooking, ingredients are cooked together in a thick, tomato-based sauce and seasoned with a savory garlic-ginger mixture.

Kari Leaf or Curry Leaf (Kadi Patta) Imparts an herbal, concentrated flavor of curry with a slight hint of lemon. Substitute chopped cilantro.

Khoya Also known as "mawa," it is made by reducing milk to a thickened consistency of soft cream cheese. Used widely in the making of many Indian desserts and sweet meats.

Korma, Khorma Indian braising, similar to Western braising. Indian cooks create rich thick braising liquids, as opposed to using a stock. Korma are generally made from yogurts, creams, and purees; spices are delicate and not usually hot or spicy. The meats are marinated in the braising liquid and then slow cooked.

Kofta Balls made of minced meat or mashed vegetables fried and mixed with a sauce or a curry.

Kulchae Flatbread often stuffed with onion or potatoes, seasoned with cilantro.

Masala Spices, herbs, and other seasonings ground or pounded together. When wet ingredients like water, vinegar, yogurt, and so on are added to the spice mixture, it is appropriately called a wet masala. Dry spice mixtures are also called garam masala or commonly known in the world as curry powder. Indian cooks generally don't use preprepared curry powder—originally a British invention to approximate Indian seasoning—but prefer making their own ever-changing blends.

Muglai (Bawarchi) Typical north Indian food named after the Mughal dynasty of Muslim rulers who ruled India for four hundred years.

Naan A traditional leavened bread, baked at very high temperatures against the wall of a tandoor oven.

Pakora Batter made of besan flour (ground chickpeas). Popular Indian crispy and spicy snack, served hot with coriander chutney, sometimes called *bhajias*.

Papadam, Poppadum, or Paapar Thin crisp discs, plain or flavored with spices and seasonings. A seasoned dough made from dried pulses that have been rolled, shaped, and dried in the sun. Papadam can be deep-fried, in which they puff up and turn airy, which also maximizes flavor. They can also be roasted over a flame, although these do not expand and are denser.

Paratha Whole-wheat flatbread, which has butter blended into the dough, and is then shallow-fried.

Pasanda A mild sauce prepared with mint leaves; adds aroma to dishes, in particular with paneer.

Pomegranate Seeds (Anardana) These serve as a souring agent in Indian cuisine.

Pulao or Biryani Indian basmati rice dish.

Puri Deep-fried whole-wheat flatbreads; they puff up when fried.

Rahra Lamb dishes with a partial stuffing of minced lamb.

Raita A traditional Indian side dish where the plain yogurt is combined with assorted items like dry fruits, or vegetables such as tomatoes, onions, or cucumbers.

Roti The word for bread in Hindi. *Tandoori roti* is bread baked in a tandoor; *rumali roti* (literally, "handkerchief bread") is a thin and flaky *paratha* made up of many layers.

Samosa A triangular deep-fried pastry appetizer.

Seekh Kebab The word *seekh* in Hindi means "skewer." Seekh kebab simply means kebabs on a skewer. Kebabs are usually made out of ground lamb mixed with various spices, cooked in a *tandoor* oven.

Tikka Tender pieces of poultry, meat, fish, prawns, and cottage cheese grilled in a tandoor.

Tandoor The traditional Indian oven made of special clay. All tandoori food is grilled on a charcoal at very high temperatures. Practically no fat is used in tandoori preparations.

Tandoori Murgh The bright red world-famous tandoori chicken. Chicken marinated with spices, red color, and yogurt is cooked in a tandoor.

Tava Traditional iron griddle used for making Indian breads and toasting spices.

Tel (Oil) Indian regional cooking is characterized by the use of different oils. Northern and central regions use peanut oil. Mustard oil is preferred in the eastern and some northern parts, while most southern regions prefer sesame and coconut oil. Sesame oil, peanut oil, and ghee are used in the western regions. Indian sesame oil is light and colorless, unlike the dark and aromatic Chinese type, which cannot be substituted.

Varak Fine thin edible silver foil used to decorate or garnish Indian desserts and *paan*. It is considered to be an aid to digestion.

Vindaloo An amalgamation of two Portuguese words: *vinho,* meaning "wine" (or vinegar) and *alho,* which means "garlic." A dish of Portuguese origin prepared with extra garlic, ginger, pepper, coconut (grated or milk), vinegar, and chiles to give a sharp, rich taste.

Menus and Recipes from India

Ananas Sharbat

Pineapple Smoothie   SERVES 4

AMOUNT	MEASURE	INGREDIENT
$\frac{1}{4}$ cup	1 ounce, 28 g	Pistachios, shelled, roasted, salted or unsalted
4 cups	32 ounces, 960 ml	Pineapple juice
$1\frac{1}{3}$ cups	8 ounces, 224 g	Fresh pineapple, peeled, diced
1 cup	8 ounces, 240 ml	Buttermilk
$\frac{1}{4}$ cup	2 ounces, 60 ml	Sour cream or plain yogurt
$\frac{1}{4}$ cup	2 ounces, 56 g	Granulated sugar
1 teaspoon		Salt

PROCEDURE

1 Add pistachios to blender and process until finely powdered.

2 Add remaining ingredients and process until mixed and frothy.

Vegetable Samosas   YIELD: 16

AMOUNT	MEASURE	INGREDIENT
Pastry		
2 cups	8 ounces, 288 g	All-purpose flour
$\frac{1}{2}$ teaspoon		Salt
4 tablespoons	2 ounces, 60 ml	Ghee, melted, or vegetable oil
4 tablespoons	2 ounces, 60 ml	Cold water
Filling		
4 tablespoons	2 ounces, 60 ml	Vegetable oil
$\frac{1}{2}$ cup	2 ounces, 56 g	Onion, $\frac{1}{4}$ inch (.6 cm) dice
I cup	5 ounces, 140 g	Fresh or frozen green peas, cooked
I tablespoon		Ginger root, grated
I		Fresh hot green chile, seeded, minced
2 tablespoons		Cilantro, leaves only, minced
I $\frac{1}{2}$ cups	9 ounces, 252 g	Potatoes, boiled until tender, peeled, cut into $\frac{1}{4}$ inch (.6 cm) cubes.
Seasoning		
$\frac{1}{2}$ teaspoon		Fennel seeds, ground
$\frac{1}{2}$ teaspoon		Cumin seeds, ground
I teaspoon		Turmeric
I teaspoon		Garam masala (recipe follows)
2 tablespoons	I ounce, 30 ml	Fresh lemon juice
As needed		Vegetable oil, for frying
As needed		Mint chutney, for serving

PROCEDURE

Pastry

1   Sift the flour and salt into a bowl.

2   Add the melted ghee and rub it with your hands until the mixture resembles coarse bread crumbs.

3   Gradually add the cold water (more if necessary) and gather the dough into a stiff ball. Knead the dough for about 10 minutes, until smooth; make a ball, oil it, and wrap it up with plastic. Set aside 30 minutes.

Filling

1 Heat the oil over medium heat; add the onions and sauté until brown at the edges, 3 to 4 minutes.

2 Add peas, ginger, chile, cilantro, and 3 tablespoons (1$\frac{1}{2}$ ounces, 45 ml) water. Cover, lower heat to a simmer, and cook 3 minutes. Add more water if pan dries out.

3 Add diced potatoes and seasoning; stir to mix. Cook on low heat 2 to 3 minutes, stirring occasionally. Correct seasoning and balance with lemon juice and salt. Let cool.

Filling the Pastry

1 Divide dough into 8 balls. Roll each out into 6-inch (15 cm) circles and cut the circles in half.

2 Pick up one-half and form a cone, making a $\frac{1}{4}$-inch (.6 cm) wide, overlapping seam. Seal seam with a little water. You should now have a small triangular pocket.

3 Fill the pocket with 2 tablespoons (1 ounce, 30 ml) potato mixture. Close the top by sticking the open edges together with a little water. Press the seams down with the prongs of a fork. Repeat with the remaining dough.

Cooking

1 Fry the samosas until golden brown and hot; drain them on paper towels.

2 Serve hot, warm, or at room temperature, with mint chutney.

Chicken Korma, Kashmiri Style

SERVES 4

AMOUNT	MEASURE	INGREDIENT
1	$2\frac{1}{2}$ pound, 1.12 kg	Chicken
4		Garlic cloves, minced
2 tablespoons		Fresh ginger, grated
2 tablespoons	1 ounce, 30 ml	Vegetable oil
$1\frac{1}{2}$ cups	6 ounces, 168 g	Onions, cut in half lengthwise, then finely sliced
2 tablespoons	1 ounce, 30 ml	Ghee (clarified butter)
2 inch (5 cm)		Cinnamon stick
6		Cardamom pods
6		Cloves
1 teaspoon		Fennel seeds, ground
1 tablespoon		Sweet paprika
1 teaspoon		Coriander, ground
1 teaspoon		Cumin, ground
$\frac{1}{2}$ teaspoon		Cayenne pepper
1 teaspoon		Turmeric
2 teaspoons		Salt
$1\frac{1}{2}$ cups	9 ounces, 252 g	Tomatoes, peeled, seeded, $\frac{1}{4}$ inch (.6 cm) dice
$\frac{1}{4}$ cup	2 ounces, 60 ml	Chicken stock or water
$\frac{1}{4}$ cup	1 ounce, 28 g	Roasted unsalted cashews
1 cup	8 ounces, 240 ml	Plain yogurt, plain
As needed		Cilantro sprigs, for garnish

PROCEDURE

1 Cut chicken into 12 pieces as follows. Quarter chicken, remove skin, then cut each breast into four pieces and each leg into two pieces (between drumstick and thigh). Pat dry and reserve.

2 Using a mortar and pestle with a little water, make a smooth paste with the garlic and ginger.

3 Heat oil over medium heat; add the onion and cook, stirring often, until deep golden, 8 to 10 minutes. Remove from pan and set aside.

Chicken Korma Kashmiri Style, Mango Chutney, Cucumber, Tomato, Onion Katchumber, and Basimati Rice

4 Add ghee to the pan and when hot, add the ginger-garlic paste. Cook, stirring, until the mixture is fragrant and light brown, 2 to 3 minutes. Add cinnamon, cardamom pods, and cloves; stir for a few seconds. Add remaining dry spices and cook, stirring, until the mixture takes on an orange-red color and becomes fragrant, about 30 seconds.

5 Add chicken pieces and sear to light golden, about 3 minutes per side.

6 Add tomatoes with chicken stock and cook, stirring occasionally, unit tomatoes are very soft, 6 to 8 minutes.

7 As the tomatoes are cooking, combine the cashews with 2 tablespoons (1 ounce, 30 ml) water in a blender and process to a smooth paste, or use mortar and pestle. Add to the chicken mixture.

8 Whisk in the yogurt and stir to combine. Add reserved onions, bring to a boil, and reduce to a simmer. Cook, covered, until chicken is tender, approximately 15 to 20 minutes. Remove pieces as they cook completely; breast meat will cook before leg and thigh.

9 Serve chicken pieces covered with sauce and garnished with cilantro.

Cucumber, Tomato, and Onion Katchumber

SERVES 4

AMOUNT	MEASURE	INGREDIENT
$\frac{1}{2}$ cup	2 ounces, 56 g	Red onion, $\frac{1}{4}$ inch (.6 cm) diced
1 cup	6 ounces, 168 g	Tomato, peeled, seeded, $\frac{1}{2}$ inch (1.2 cm) dice
1 cup	6 ounces, 168 g	Cucumber, peeled, seeded, $\frac{1}{2}$ inch (1.2 cm) dice
2 tablespoons		Cilantro, coarsely chopped
1 teaspoon		Green chile (jalapeño), minced
3 tablespoons	$1\frac{1}{2}$ ounces, 45 ml	Fresh lime juice
1 teaspoon		Nigella seeds, toasted
To taste		Salt and freshly ground black pepper

PROCEDURE

1 Combine all ingredients, toss together, and let stand at least 1 hour before serving.

Garam Masala Ground Spice Mixture

SERVES 4

AMOUNT	MEASURE	INGREDIENT
$\frac{1}{2}$		Whole nutmeg
3 tablespoons		Cardamom seeds
2 tablespoons		Whole cloves
2 tablespoons		Whole cumin
I tablespoon		Whole coriander
2 tablespoons		Whole black peppercorns
3 inches		Cinnamon stick
4		Bay leaf

PROCEDURE

1 Dry-roast all ingredients separately in a heated heavy skillet over medium heat until the spices emit a toasty aroma. Let cool.

2 Combine all ingredients except nutmeg in a clean spice grinder and grind them into a very fine powder or use a mortar and pestle. Finely grate nutmeg.

3 Store in a tightly closed jar until needed.

Podina Chatni Green Chutney SERVES 4

AMOUNT	MEASURE	INGREDIENT
I cup (firmly packed)	2 ounces, 56 g	Mint leaves, picked
$\frac{1}{3}$ cup	$\frac{1}{3}$ ounce, 8 g	Cilantro leaves
I		Green chile (jalapeño), seeded
I cup	2 ounces, 56 g	Green onions, I inch (2.4 cm) lengths
$1\frac{1}{4}$ cups	2 ounces, 60 ml	Jalapeño, seeded, minced
		Lemon juice
I teaspoon		Garam masala
2 teaspoons		Granulated sugar
I teaspoon		Salt
$\frac{1}{4}$ cup	2 ounces, 60 ml	Water

PROCEDURE

1 Place all ingredients in a food processor and purée, or pound in mortar and pestle a little at a time, until ground to a paste. If too dry, add a little oil and/or water. Chill.

Palak Paneer Spinach with Curd Cheese

YIELD: 8 OUNCES; SERVES 4

Paneer is a popular Indian soft cheese that is very similar to Ricotta cheese. It is high in protein and is substituted for meat in vegetarian dishes of Indian cuisine.

AMOUNT	MEASURE	INGREDIENT
Curd Cheese		
6 cups	240 ml	Milk, whole or 2% low-fat
I cup	8 ounces, 240 ml	Yogurt, at room temperature
I $\frac{1}{2}$ tablespoons	$\frac{3}{4}$ ounce, 20 ml	Fresh lemon juice
To taste		Salt
As needed		Ghee (clarified butter)
Spinach		
5 cups	12 ounces, 336 g	Spinach, packed leaves, washed
I cup water	8 ounces, 240 ml	Water
2 tablespoons	I ounce, 30 ml	Ghee (clarified butter)
I teaspoon		Cumin seeds
I cup	5 ounces, 140 g	Onions, minced
I		Green chile (jalapeño), slit lengthwise
2 teaspoons		Ginger, grated
2 teaspoons		Garlic, minced
4 tablespoons	2 ounces, 60 ml	Cream
As needed		Salt, black pepper, and lemon juice

PROCEDURE

Curd Cheese

1   Bring milk to a boil; be careful, because as soon as it boils it will start to froth. Remove from the heat; add yogurt and lemon juice. Reduce heat to medium and let mixture return to a boil, stirring gently, until the milk curdles and separates from the whey (the pale yellowish green transparent liquid), 6 to 8 minutes. The longer you cook the mixture, the firmer the final cheese. Turn off the heat and let stand, uncovered, to cool, about 15 minutes.

2   Line a colander with a double thickness of cheesecloth. Gently pour the contents of the pan into the colander. Gather the four corners of the cheesecloth and twist them together

Cascabel chile, on the cutting board clockwise from right: Red Fresno chiles, green chile de arbol, chipotle chile, dried chile de árbol, red chile de árbol, ancho chile, güero chile, serrano chile, santaka chile, jalapeno chile, habanero chile, pasilla chile. In the mortar, clockwise from left: bell pepper, sweet Italian pepper, mulato pepper, yellow wax hot pepper.

Tapas—in the middle, Croquetas de Jamón—Serrano Ham Fritters; clockwise, from bottom: Calamares encebollados—Squid with Caramelized Onions; Tortilla de Patatas—Potato Omelet; Pan Con Tomate—Tomato Toast; Aceitunas Verdes Rellenas de Pimiento y Anchoa—Green Olives Filled with Piquillo Peppers and Anchovy; Gambas Al Ajillo—Sizzling Garlic Shrimp (Spain)

Rape con Romesco—Monkfish with Romesco Sauce; Fabes con Almejas—Asturian Bean Stew with Clams; and Espinacas a la Catalana—Spinach, Catalan-Style (Spain)

Paella Valenciana (Spain)

Clockwise from the bottom: Falafel – Dried Bean Croquettes; Borani Chogondar—Beet and Yogurt Salad; Hummus Bi Tahini—Chickpea and Sesame Dip; Baba Ghannouj/Moutabal—Eggplant Dip; Tabbouleh—Cracked Wheat and Herb Salad; assorted flat breads (Middle East)

Psari Savoro—Fried Fish with Rosemary and Vinegar; Dolmathakia Me Rizi—Stuffed Grape Vine Leaves; and Salata me Portokalia kai Elies—Orange and Olive Salad (Turkey, Greece, Crete)

Tagine of Chicken, Preserved Lemon and Olives (North Africa)

Platter and plate, clockwise from bottom: Roast beef, roasted new potatoes, broccoli, glazed shallots, watercress, Yorkshire pudding, au jus (British Isles)

Tomato Water Ice with Julienne of Smoked Salmon (British Isles)

Poulet Sauté Marengo (France)

Fillet of Fish Belle Mouginoise with Turned Potato (France)

Ossobuco Milanese and Risotto Alla Zafferano – Braised Veal Shanks and Risotto with Saffron (Italy)

**Peperonata –
Stewed Peppers
(Italy)**

**Schweinelendchen im
Schwarzbratmantel—
Pork Tenderloin in a
Dark Bread Crust;
Rotkraut und
Spätzle—Braised Red
Cabbage and
Spaetzle (Germany,
Austria, Switzerland)**

Borshch Moskovsky—Moscow-Style Beet Soup; Blini—Buckwheat Pancakes; Kulebiaka—Salmon in Pastry (Scandinavia and Russia)

Fried Dill-Cured Salmon with Sweet Sour Raisin Sauce, Hasselback Potatoes and Green Beans (Scandinavia and Russia)

to pack the curds into a ball. Squeeze out as much liquid as possible by twisting the cheesecloth. Tie the corners and hang the cheese over a container to drain 2 to 3 hours.

3   When most of the liquid has drained, place the cheese on an upside-down plate. Put another plate or a sheet pan on top and 6 to 8 pounds of additional weight to squeeze the cheese further. Leave for an additional hour before unwrapping and using.

4   Unwrap and cut into 2-inch × $\frac{1}{2}$-inch × $\frac{1}{4}$-inch (2.4 cm × 1.2 cm × .6 cm) pieces.

5   Preheat the broiler. Brush about $\frac{1}{2}$ tablespoon (8 ml) ghee on paneer. Place on a lightly greased pan 4 to 6 inches (9.6 cm x 14.4 cm) from the heat source and broil until speckled with light brown spots, 2 to $2\frac{1}{2}$ minutes; watch closely, as it burns quickly. Brown both sides.

Spinach

1   Blanch the spinach in boiling salted water until wilted, 3 to 4 minutes. Immediately transfer to an ice water bath. Let cool completely; squeeze the spinach gently. Puree in blender or food processor, with $\frac{1}{2}$ cup (4 ounces, 120 ml) water or more if necessary. Process until smooth and velvety.

2   Heat the ghee and add the cumin seeds; let them splutter.

3   Add the onions and green chile; sauté until light brown, 3 to 5 minutes.

4   Add ginger and garlic, cook 2 minutes.

5   Add spinach and cook 2 to 3 minutes. Adjust consistency with additional water.

6   Add the browned paneer and cream; cook covered on low heat 3 minutes.

7   Adjust seasoning with salt, black pepper, and lemon juice.

Rajmah Red Kidney Bean Dal   SERVES 4

AMOUNT	MEASURE	INGREDIENT
1¼ cups	8 ounces, 224 g	Red kidney beans, picked over, washed, and drained
6 cups	48 ounces, 1.4l	Water
3		Ginger slices, ¼ inch (.6 cm) thick
1 tablespoon		Salt
3 tablespoons	1½ ounces, 45 ml	Fresh lemon juice
¼ teaspoon		Garam masala (p. 567)
⅔ cup	5 ounces, 150 ml	Heavy cream
3 tablespoons	1½ ounces, 45 ml	Ghee or vegetable oil
1 teaspoon		Cumin seeds
½ teaspoon		Coriander seeds
1 teaspoon		Ginger, peeled, finely minced
1 teaspoon		Garlic, minced
½ teaspoon		Cloves, ground
2		Dried hot red chiles, split in half

PROCEDURE

1   Bring beans and water to a boil, reduce to a simmer for 2 minutes. Turn off heat and let stand, uncovered, 1 hour.

2   Add 3 slices ginger and return to a boil; boil 10 minutes.

3   Reduce heat and simmer 1 hour with lid slightly ajar. Discard the ginger slices.

4   Mash half the beans or puree half in a blender. Add the salt, lemon juice, garam masala, and cream. Combine puree and whole beans, stir to mix, and adjust seasoning.

5   Heat ghee over medium heat. When hot, add cumin and coriander seeds; sauté two minutes. Add minced ginger and garlic; stir-fry until lightly browned. Add ground cloves and red chiles; stir once. Add spice mixture to beans.

6   Stir to mix.

Mango Chutney   SERVES 4

AMOUNT	MEASURE	INGREDIENT
$\frac{1}{4}$	2 ounces, 60 ml	Cider vinegar
2 tablespoons	1 ounce, 28 g	Granulated sugar
2 tablespoons	1 ounce, 28 g	Brown sugar
1		Bay leaf, whole
2		Whole cloves
$\frac{1}{8}$ teaspoon		Cayenne pepper
$\frac{1}{8}$ teaspoon		Turmeric
$\frac{1}{2}$ cup	4 ounces, 120 ml	Water
1 inch piece	2.4 cm piece	Ginger, peeled, julienned
$\frac{1}{2}$ cup	8 ounces, 224 g	Mango, peeled, cored, sliced

PROCEDURE

1 In a nonreactive pan, bring vinegar, sugar, brown sugar, bay leaf, cloves, cayenne, turmeric, and water to a boil. Cook over medium heat until a light syrup forms, 8 to 10 minutes.

2 Add the ginger and cook another 5 minutes. Remove bay leaves and cloves.

3 Add the mango slices and cook, covered, over low heat until the fruit softens and absorbs the flavors, about 25 to 30 minutes.

4 If the chutney becomes too thick, add no more than 1 ounce of water at a time. The chutney should resemble preserves.

Chapatis Flat Bread SERVES 4

AMOUNT	MEASURE	INGREDIENT
1½ cups	6 ounces, 168 g	Whole wheat flour
½ cup	2 ounces, 56 g	All-purpose flour
1 tablespoon	½ ounce, 15 ml	Oil
½ teaspoon		Salt
¾ cup plus 2 tablespoons	7 ounces, 210 ml	Water
As needed		Ghee

PROCEDURE

1 In a mixer, food processor, or by hand, combine all ingredients except ghee to form a soft dough.

2 Knead the dough 6 to 8 minutes or until smooth. Cover and let rest 30 minutes.

3 Knead and divide into 10 equal parts. It will be somewhat sticky, so use flour to dust. Roll each into a ball on a floured surface. Press the ball into a patty. Roll patty out, dusting frequently, until it is about 3–4 inches (7.2 cm–9.6 cm) in diameter. Keep covered so they do not dry out.

4 Pick up to remove excess flour. Keep covered so they do not dry out.

5 Heat a tava, griddle, or skillet over medium-high heat. Cooking surface is hot enough when a little water sprinkled on bounces off the surface. Rub surface with a little oil.

6 Flatten a piece of dough with your palm, dust with flour, and roll the dough from the center outward into a circle 6–7 inches (14.4 cm–16.8 cm) across, $\frac{1}{16}$ inch (.15 cm) thick (don't be concerned if the finished shape is not perfect).

7 Pick up flatbread, slap it back and forth to shake off any excess flour, and gently slap it on to the pan. Make sure there are no creases, or use a spatula to spread it evenly. Cook until it starts to puff in places, then press the unpuffed portions very gently with the back of a spoon and guide the air to puff the whole chapatis. This process should take about 1 minute.

8 Drizzle 1 teaspoon ghee around the edges of the chapati. Use a spatula to turn over. The flatbread should start to balloon again; press gently and guide the air to parts that have not puffed so they fill with steam, about 30 seconds. Both sides should be lightly speckled brown.

9 Transfer cooked flatbreads to a cloth-lined basket and continue cooking the remaining pieces.

Various flat breads

Khumbi Pullao Mushroom Rice SERVES 4

AMOUNT	MEASURE	INGREDIENT
1 cup	7 ounces, 196 g	Long-grain rice
2 tablespoons	1 ounce, 30 ml	Ghee or vegetable oil
$\frac{1}{2}$ cup	2 ounces, 56 g	Onions, halved lengthwise, then finely sliced
1 teaspoon		Garlic, minced
1 cup	3 ounces, 84 g	Mushrooms, washed, cut $\frac{1}{8}$ inch (.3 cm) slices
$\frac{1}{4}$ teaspoon		Ginger, minced
To taste		Salt and garam masala (p. 567)
2 cups	16 ounces, 480 ml	Water

PROCEDURE

1 Wash the rice in several changes of water and drain. Cover rice with cold water and let stand 30 minutes. Drain.

2 Heat ghee over medium heat; when hot, add onions and garlic and stir-fry 2 minutes or until onions are browning around the edges.

3 Add mushrooms and cook 2 minutes.

4 Add rice, ginger, salt, and garam masala; stir-fry two minutes.

5 Add water and bring to a boil. Cover tightly, turn heat to very low, and cook 25 minutes. Turn off heat and let sit, covered and undisturbed, 5 minutes.

Banana Erccherry   SERVES 4

AMOUNT	MEASURE	INGREDIENT
4 cups	16 ounces, 114 g	Raw bananas, peeled, $1\frac{1}{2}$ inch (3.6 cm) pieces
$\frac{1}{2}$ cup	4 ounces, 120 ml	Water
$\frac{1}{4}$ teaspoon		Turmeric powder
To taste		Salt
1 cup	6 ounces, 168 g	Fresh coconut scrapings or unsweetened flakes
1		Whole red chile
$\frac{1}{2}$ teaspoon		Cumin seeds
$\frac{1}{2}$ teaspoon		Mustard seeds
2		Green chiles, sliced (remove seeds to reduce hotness)
4		Curry leaves
1 tablespoon	$\frac{1}{2}$ ounce, 15 ml	Coconut oil

PROCEDURE

1 Combine banana pieces, water, turmeric, and salt, cook until soft; mash.

2 Make a paste with $\frac{1}{2}$ the coconut, red chile and cumin seeds. Add to mashed bananas and set aside.

3 Heat coconut oil and add mustard seeds, green chiles, curry leaves, and remaining coconut and fry till golden. Mix in the banana mash and serve hot.

Dosal Fermented Lentil Crepes with Potato Masala Stuffing SERVES 4

AMOUNT	MEASURE	INGREDIENT
Batter		
$\frac{3}{4}$ cup	6 ounces, 168 g	Urad dal (black lentils)
$2\frac{1}{2}$ cups	$17\frac{1}{2}$ ounces, 490 g	Raw rice
1 teaspoon	5 gram	Fenugreek
Masala Filling		
2 tablespoons	1 ounce, 30 ml	Ghee or vegetable oil
1 teaspoon	5 gram	Mustard seeds
1 cup	4 ounces, 112 g	Onion, $\frac{1}{4}$ inch (.6 cm) dice
1		Green chile (jalapeño), seeded, minced
4		Curry leaves
$\frac{1}{2}$ teaspoon		Turmeric
2 cups	12 ounces, 336 g	Russet potatoes, cooked in their skins, peeled, and mashed lightly (chunky)
1 tablespoon	$\frac{1}{2}$ ounce, 15 ml	Fresh lime juice
To taste		Salt and white pepper
2 tablespoons		Cilantro, coarsely chopped
As needed		Tamarind sauce (recipe follows)

PROCEDURE

Batter

1 Combine the dal and rice and soak 6 hours.

2 Drain and grind to a paste. Keep the liquid.

3 Let the paste ferment 4 hours.

4 Thin the paste to a crepe-batter consistency, using the retained soaking liquid.

5 Cook like a crepe and fill with masala filling.

Masala Filling

1 Heat ghee over medium heat, add mustard seeds, and sauté 30 seconds. Add the onion, jalapeño, curry leaves, and turmeric. Sauté until onions are transparent, 3 to 5 minutes.

2 Fold in the potatoes, heat the mixture through, and adjust seasoning with lime juice, salt, and white pepper. Finish by folding in the cilantro. Serve with tamarind sauce.

Tamarind Sauce

Frequently used in Indian cuisine, dark brown, crumbly palm sugar—also known as jaggery or _gur_—is made from the reduced sap of either the sugar palm or the palmyra palm. Substitute brown sugar only as a last resort.

SERVES 4

AMOUNT	MEASURE	INGREDIENT
7 tablespoons	$3\frac{1}{2}$ ounces, 105 g	Tamarind paste
10 tablespoons	5 ounces, 150 g	Palm sugar
2 cup	16 ounces, 480 ml	Water
To taste		Cayenne pepper
To taste		Salt

PROCEDURE

1 Combine tamarind, sugar, and water; bring to a boil, reduce to a simmer, and cook to a jamlike consistency.

2 Add salt and cayenne to taste.

Jhinga Kari Shrimp Curry SERVES 4

AMOUNT	MEASURE	INGREDIENT
$\frac{1}{4}$ cup	2 ounces, 60 ml	Ghee
I cup	4 ounces, 112 g	Onions, cut in half lengthwise, then finely sliced
2		Garlic cloves, minced
I teaspoon		Ginger, minced
2 teaspoons		Coriander, ground
I teaspoon		Turmeric
$\frac{1}{2}$ teaspoon		Chile powder
$\frac{1}{2}$ teaspoon		Cumin ground
2 tablespoons	I ounce, 30 ml	White vinegar
I pound	448 g	Shrimp (16 to 20 count), shelled and deveined
$\frac{3}{4}$ cup	6 ounces, 180 ml	Water

PROCEDURE

1 Heat ghee over medium heat and add the onions and garlic. Cook until soft and slightly brown, 10 to 12 minutes. Add ginger and cook 1 minute.

2 Make a paste out of the dry ingredients and vinegar.

3 Add paste to cooked onions and stir fry for 3 minutes, stirring constantly.

4 Add shrimp and toss to coat. Add water and cook until just cooked, 2 to 3 minutes.

5 Serve hot.

Tomato Chutney, Gobhi Pakode – Cauliflower Fritters, Jhinga Kari – Shrimp Curry, and Kheere ka Raita – Yogurt with Cucumber and Mint

Eratchi Ularthiyathu
Kerala-Style Lamb   SERVES 4

AMOUNT	MEASURE	INGREDIENT
I pound	448 g	Boneless lamb shoulder, $\frac{1}{2}$ inch (1.2 cm) cubes
3 tablespoons	$1\frac{1}{2}$ ounces, 45 ml	Vegetable oil
I teaspoon		Mustard seeds
2 cups	8 ounces, 224 g	Onions, cut in half lengthwise, then finely sliced
I	I inch (2.4 cm)	Fresh ginger, peeled and chopped
4		Garlic cloves
3		Dried hot red chiles (cayenne or chiles de arbol), stemmed and softened in $\frac{1}{4}$ cup (2 ounces, 60 ml) water
20		Curry leaves
I tablespoon		Coriander, ground
$\frac{1}{4}$ teaspoon		Black pepper, freshly ground
2 cups	12 ounces, 336 g	Tomato, peeled, seeded, chopped, with juice
2 tablespoons		Unsweetened flaked dried coconut
I teaspoon		Fennel, ground
I teaspoon		Salt
$\frac{1}{2}$ cup	4 ounces, 120 ml	Water

PROCEDURE

1   Rinse the lamb pieces, combine with $1\frac{1}{2}$ cups (12 ounces, 360 ml) water over medium heat, and bring to a boil. Cover partially, reduce to a simmer, and cook until it is just becoming tender but is still chewy, 15 to 20 minutes. Remove from heat. Drain and discard cooking liquid.

2   Heat oil over medium heat; sputter mustard seeds and curry leaves in hot oil. Add onions and cook, stirring, until richly browned, 10 minutes.

3   Make a paste with the ginger and garlic, use a little water if necessary. Can be done in a blender or mortar and pestle.

4   Add paste to browned onions and cook until it begins to brown, 3 to 4 minutes.

5   Puree chiles and soaking water in blender. Add chile puree to onion mixture, add curry leaves, and cook 30 seconds or until fragrant.

6 Add coriander and black pepper and stir for 20 seconds. Add tomatoes with juice and cook, stirring, until very soft and the mixture starts to dry out, 7 to 9 minutes.

7 Add drained lamb cubes, coconut and stir until the meat is well coated with the masala.

8 Add fennel, salt, and water; bring to a boil and reduce to a simmer. Cook, stirring occasionally, until all the liquid is absorbed and lamb is tender, 25 to 35 minutes, adding additional water if necessary.

9 Serve hot.

Vegetable Samosas, Palak Paneer – Spinach with Curd Cheese, and Eratchi Ularthiyathu – Kerala Style Lamb

Gobhi Pakode Cauliflower Fritters   SERVES 4

AMOUNT	MEASURE	INGREDIENT
3 cups	12 ounces, 336 g	Cauliflower florets
1 cup	7 ounces, 196 g	Besan (chickpea flour)
1 tablespoon		Coriander, ground
1 teaspoon		Turmeric
$\frac{1}{4}$ teaspoon		Black pepper, freshly ground
$\frac{1}{8}$ teaspoon		Cayenne pepper
1 teaspoon		Salt
1 tablespoon	$\frac{1}{2}$ ounce, 15 ml	Vegetable oil
$\frac{3}{4}$ cup	6 ounces, 180 ml	Cold water
As needed		Oil for frying

PROCEDURE

1   Parboil cauliflower, keeping firm. Transfer to ice water and drain.

2   Mix remaining dry ingredients; add water until a smooth nape consistency (coats the back of a spoon) is formed.

3   Let batter stand 30 minutes.

4   Heat frying oil to 375°F (190°C)

5   Coat cauliflower florets in batter; fry until golden brown. Drain on paper towels.

6   Serve hot or warm.

Tomato Chutney   YIELD: 2 CUPS

AMOUNT	MEASURE	INGREDIENT
1	1 inch (2.4 cm)	Fresh ginger, peeled
9		Garlic cloves
1 teaspoon		Caraway seeds
1 cup	8 ounces, 240 ml	Cider vinegar
4 cups	24 ounces, 672 g	Tomatoes, peeled, seeded, rough chopped
3		Green chiles (serranos) seeded, chopped
$\frac{3}{4}$ cup	5 ounces, 147 g	Granulated sugar
1 tablespoon		Golden raisins
1 tablespoon		Almonds, slivered, blanched
1	2 inch, 4.8 cm	Cinnamon stick
5		Whole peppercorns
$\frac{1}{4}$ teaspoon		Cayenne pepper
4		Whole cloves

PROCEDURE

1   Grind ginger, garlic, and caraway with $\frac{1}{4}$ cup (2 ounces, 60 ml) vinegar to a paste.

2   Combine all ingredients and bring to a boil; reduce to a simmer. Cook until mixture thickens and turns dark, 1 to $1\frac{1}{2}$ hours.

3   Serve chilled or room temperature.

Basmati Chaaval
Plain Basmati Rice   SERVES 4 TO 6

AMOUNT	MEASURE	INGREDIENT
2 cups	15 ounces, 450 g	Long-grain rice
1 teaspoon		Salt
1 tablespoon	$\frac{1}{2}$ ounce, 15 ml	Butter
2$\frac{2}{3}$ cups	19 ounces, 570 ml	Water

PROCEDURE

1   Wash rice in several changes of water. Drain.

2   Soak rice in 5 cups (40 ounces, 1.2 l) water 30 minutes. Drain thoroughly.

3   Combine rice, salt, butter, and water. Bring to boil. Cover with a tight-fitting lid, turn heat to low, and cook for 20 minutes.

4   Lift lid, mix gently but quickly with a fork, and cover again.

5   Cook additional 5 to 10 minutes or until rice is tender.

Kheere ka Raita
Yogurt with Cucumber and Mint   SERVES 4

AMOUNT	MEASURE	INGREDIENT
1$\frac{1}{2}$ cups	12 ounces, 360 ml	Plain yogurt
$\frac{2}{3}$ cup	4 ounces, 120 ml	Cucumber, peeled, coarsely grated
1$\frac{1}{2}$ tablespoon		Fresh mint, chopped
$\frac{1}{2}$ teaspoon		Cumin seeds, roasted and ground
$\frac{1}{4}$ teaspoon		Cayenne pepper
To taste		Salt and freshly ground black pepper

PROCEDURE

1   Whisk yogurt until smooth and creamy.

2   Combine all ingredients and correct seasoning.

Puris (Poori)
Deep-Fried Puffed Bread   YIELD: 12 POORI; SERVES 4

AMOUNT	MEASURE	INGREDIENT
1 cup	4 ounces, 112 g	Whole wheat flour, sifted
1 cup	4 ounces, 112 g	All-purpose flour
$\frac{1}{2}$ teaspoon		Salt
2 tablespoons	1 ounce, 30 ml	Vegetable oil
$\frac{1}{2}$ cup	4 ounces, 120 ml	Water
As needed		Oil for frying

PROCEDURE

1 Combine flours with salt.

2 Add vegetable oil and work with fingers until the mixture resembles coarse breadcrumbs.

3 Slowly add the water to form a stiff dough. Knead 10 to 12 minutes or until smooth. Rub with a little oil and set aside 30 minutes.

4 Work the dough again and divide into 12 equal pieces; round them into balls.

5 Keep them covered so they do not dry out.

6 Flatten and roll out into a 5-inch (12 cm) disk. Let disks set 5 minutes before frying.

7 Heat 1 inch frying oil to 350°F (176°C).

8 Place poori gently into the pan and use the back of a slotted spoon to push the poori gently into the oil with small swift strokes. Within seconds the poori will puff up.

9 Turn it over and cook an additional 30 seconds or until golden.

10 Remove with slotted spoon; drain on paper towels. Repeat until all are cooked.

11 Serve immediately.

Chai Masala Spiced Tea   SERVES 4

AMOUNT	MEASURE	INGREDIENT
I cup	8 ounces, 240 ml	Milk
2 cups	16 ounces, 480 ml	Water
3		Cardamom pods
2		Cloves
$\frac{1}{2}$ stick		Cinnamon
$\frac{1}{4}$ teaspoon		Fennel seed
To taste		Granulated sugar
4		Orange pekoe teabags

PROCEDURE

1   Combine milk and water and bring to a boil. Stir in the spices and sugar to taste.

2   Turn off the heat, cover and let the spices steep 10 minutes.

3   Add the tea bags. Bring back to a boil, then turn off the heat and steep 3 minutes.

4   Strain and serve piping hot.

Akhrote ka Raita
Yogurt with Walnuts   SERVES 4

AMOUNT	MEASURE	INGREDIENT
I$\frac{1}{2}$ cups	12 ounces, 360 ml	Yogurt
2 tablespoons		Fresh cilantro, chopped
I teaspoon		Green chile, minced
2 tablespoons		Green onions, chopped fine
$\frac{1}{4}$ cup	I ounce, 28 g	Walnuts, chopped $\frac{1}{2}$ inch (1.2 cm) pieces
To taste		Salt and pepper

PROCEDURE

1   Whisk yogurt until smooth and creamy.

2   Fold in remaining ingredients and correct seasoning.

Buttermilk Kadhi Soup SERVES 4

AMOUNT	MEASURE	INGREDIENT
1 1-inch (2.4 cm)		Fresh ginger, peeled
3		Garlic cloves
1		Green chile (serrano) stemmed
$\frac{1}{2}$ teaspoon		Cumin seeds
$2\frac{1}{2}$ tablespoons		Chickpea flour
1 cup	8 ounces, 240 ml	Water
2 cups	16 ounces, 480 ml	Buttermilk
1 teaspoon		Salt
1 teaspoon		Granulated sugar
2 tablespoons	1 ounce, 30 ml	Ghee
$\frac{1}{2}$ teaspoon		Brown mustard seeds
1 teaspoon		Fenugreek seeds
1 teaspoon		Coriander seeds
$\frac{1}{2}$ teaspoon		Turmeric
15		Curry leaves or cilantro
Pinch		Asafetida

PROCEDURE

1   Using a mortar and pestle or a food processor, pulverize the ginger, garlic, chile, and cumin seeds to a coarse-textured paste.

2   Combine the chickpea flour, half the water, the buttermilk, salt, sugar, and ginger-garlic paste. Bring to a low simmer, stirring to dissolve spices; cook uncovered 6 to 8 minutes. Correct seasoning with sugar and salt. Remove from heat.

3   Heat ghee over medium-high heat. Add mustard seeds, fenugreek seeds, and coriander seeds (if available). Cover with a spatter screen; cook until mustard seeds stop popping, about 30 seconds. Add turmeric, curry leaves, and asafetida; stir fry until leaves are crisp, 20 seconds.

4   Pour the seasoned oil over the soup. Serve hot.

Sambhara Gujerati-Style Cabbage with Carrots, Eggplant, and Potato SERVES 4

AMOUNT	MEASURE	INGREDIENT
4 tablespoons	2 ounces, 60 ml	Ghee
I tablespoon		Whole black mustard seeds
I		Red hot chile, whole
3 cups	12 ounces, 336 g	Green cabbage, fine, long shreds
I cup	4 ounces, 112 g	Carrots, peeled, coarsely grated
I		Green chile (jalapeño), seeded, julienned
To taste		Salt
To taste		Granulated sugar
$\frac{1}{4}$ cup		Cilantro leaves and some stems, chopped
I tablespoon	$\frac{1}{2}$ ounce, 15 ml	Fresh lemon juice

PROCEDURE

1   Heat ghee; when hot, add mustard seeds; cook 5 seconds (seeds will start to pop). Add dried red chile and cook 10 seconds; chile should turn dark red.

2   Add cabbage, carrots, and green chile; toss to combine.

3   Reduce heat to medium and stir-fry 1 minute.

4   Add salt, sugar, and cilantro; stir and cook 5 minutes or until vegetables are just done but still crispy.

5   Add lemon juice and adjust seasoning. Remove red chile.

Sambhara—Gujerati Style Cabbage with Carrots, Eggplant, and Potato served with Flat Bread

Eggplant and Potato   SERVES 4

AMOUNT	MEASURE	INGREDIENT
$\frac{1}{4}$ cup	2 ounces, 60 ml	Vegetable oil
$\frac{1}{2}$ teaspoon		Black mustard seeds
I cup	4 ounce, 112 g	Potatoes, cut $\frac{1}{2}$ inch (1.2 cm) dice
I cup	4 ounces, 112 g	Eggplant, cut $\frac{1}{2}$ inch (1.2 cm) dice
$1\frac{1}{2}$ teaspoons		Coriander seeds, ground
I teaspoon		Cumin seeds, ground
$\frac{1}{4}$ teaspoon		Turmeric
$\frac{1}{4}$ teaspoon		Cayenne pepper
$\frac{1}{2}$ teaspoon		Salt

PROCEDURE

1   Heat oil over medium heat; when hot add mustard seeds, and as soon as they start to pop (5 seconds), add potatoes and eggplant.

2   Toss to coat and add coriander, cumin, turmeric, cayenne, and salt. Stir and sauté 2 minutes.

3   Add 3 tablespoons ($1\frac{1}{2}$ ounces, 45 ml) water, cover with tight-fitting lid, reduce heat to low, and simmer 10 minutes or until potatoes are tender. Stir occasionally. If vegetables stick to the pan, add a little more water.

Matira Curry   SERVES 4

AMOUNT	MEASURE	INGREDIENT
1 cup	8 ounces, 240 ml	Watermelon juice; use cutting scrapes for puree
1 teaspoon		Chile powder
1 teaspoon		Turmeric
$\frac{1}{2}$ teaspoon		Coriander seed, toasted
2		Garlic cloves, minced
To taste		Salt
$\frac{1}{4}$ teaspoon		Cumin seeds, toasted
1–2 tablespoons	$\frac{1}{2}$ to 1 ounce, (15 to 30 ml)	Fresh lime juice
To taste		Granulated sugar
4 cups	16 ounces, 448 g	Watermelon, peeled, $1\frac{1}{2}$ inch (3.6 cm) cubes
1 tablespoon		Cilantro leaves, chopped
1 tablespoon		Mint, chopped

PROCEDURE

1   Combine the juice, chile, turmeric, coriander, and garlic with a pinch of salt. Add toasted cumin seeds, bring to a boil, and reduce by $\frac{1}{3}$.

2   Season with lime juice and sugar to taste and continue to reduce to syrup consistency.

3   Add the melon cubes and cook over low heat until melon is heated throughout. Toss gently to coat all melon cubes with syrup.

4   Adjust the seasoning with salt, sugar, and lime juice. The final result should be tart.

5   Serve hot, garnished with cilantro and mint leaves.

Pomfret Caldeen
Fish in Coconut Sauce SERVES 4

AMOUNT	MEASURE	INGREDIENT
2 tablespoons	1 ounce, 30 ml	Fresh lime juice
1 teaspoon		Salt
1 teaspoon		Turmeric
4	5 ounces, 140 g portions	Skinless and boneless pompano fillets, or red snapper, grouper, bass, or cod
3		Hot red chiles, stemmed and softened in $\frac{1}{4}$ cup water
2 teaspoons		Coriander seeds, toasted
1 teaspoon		Cumin seeds, toasted
$\frac{1}{2}$ cup	3 ounces, 84 g	Coconut, freshly grated or unsweetened flakes
$1\frac{1}{2}$ cups	6 ounces, 170 g	Onions, cut in half lengthwise, then finely sliced
2		Garlic cloves
1 teaspoon		Tamarind concentrate, dissolved in $\frac{1}{4}$ cup (2 ounces, 60 ml) water
1 cup	8 ounces, 240 ml	Water
2 tablespoons	1 ounce, 30 ml	Vegetable oil
1 cup	6 ounces, 170 g	Tomato, peeled, seeded, $\frac{1}{4}$ inch (.6 cm) dice

PROCEDURE

1 Combine lime juice, salt, and turmeric to make a marinade. Spread on fillets and let stand 30 minutes at cool room temperature or 1 hour under refrigeration.

2 Puree red chile, coriander seeds, cumin seeds, coconut, 1 cup onions, garlic, tamarind liquid and $\frac{1}{2}$ cup (4 ounces, 120 ml) water. Process until very smooth, adding more water if necessary.

3 Heat oil over medium-high heat; add remaining onions and cook, stirring, until deep golden brown, 6 to 8 minutes.

4 Add puree mix and continue to cook an additional 8 to 10 minutes.

5 Add tomato and remaining water; cook 8 minutes, stirring occasionally, until tomatoes are soft.

6 Correct seasoning and add the fish fillets. Simmer, turning once or twice if necessary, until the fish is just cooked.

7 Transfer fish to serving dish and correct consistency of sauce reducing or adding additional water. Correct seasoning and spoon sauce over fillets.

Chana Dal Yellow Dal SERVES 4

Chana dal is perhaps the "meatiest" tasting, with the slight sweetness of all the dals. Yellow split peas may be substituted; however, they are not the same.

AMOUNT	MEASURE	INGREDIENT
1½ cups	9 ounces, 250 g	Chana dal (Indian yellow split peas)
5 cups	40 ounces, 1 l	Water
1		Dried red chile, soaked and seeded
3		Ginger, unpeeled, sliced $\frac{1}{4}$ inch (.6 cm) thin
¼ teaspoon		Turmeric, ground
¼ teaspoon		Garam masala (p. 567)
To taste		Salt
3 tablespoons	1½ ounces, 45 ml	Ghee
1 teaspoon		Cumin seeds
2		Garlic cloves, chopped
½ teaspoon		Red chile powder

PROCEDURE

1 Pick over dal to remove small stones and discolored seeds. Put in a bowl of water, soak 15 minutes, and remove any that float. Wash well and drain thoroughly.

2 Combine dal and water, bring to a boil, and remove any surface scum.

3 Add red chile, ginger, and turmeric. Cover, leaving lid slightly ajar, and simmer gently 45 to 50 minutes or until the dal is tender. Stir every 5 minutes to prevent sticking. Remove ginger slices and chile. Add garam masala and salt; stir to mix.

4 Heat the ghee over medium heat. When hot, add cumin seeds; 10 seconds later add garlic. Cook until garlic is slightly brown. Add chile powder, stir to mix, and immediately add contents of pan to the dal. Stir to mix.

Tarapori Patio Dried Bombay Duck Patio

SERVES 4

Despite its name, Bombay duck is a lizardfish. Native to the waters between Mumbai (formerly Bombay) and Kutch in the Arabian Sea, they are also found in small numbers in the Bay of Bengal. Great numbers are caught in China Sea, too. The fish is often dried and salted before it is consumed. After drying, the odor of the fish is extremely powerful, and it must consequently be transported in airtight containers. The bones of the fish are soft and easily chewable.

Jaggery is the traditional unrefined sugar used in India.

AMOUNT	MEASURE	INGREDIENT
1$\frac{1}{4}$ tablespoons	14 g	Jaggery, grated
$\frac{1}{4}$ cup	2 ounces, 60 ml	Cider vinegar
6		Dried Bombay ducks
6		Garlic cloves
4		Red chiles, dry
I teaspoon		Cumin seeds
I tablespoon	$\frac{1}{2}$ ounce, 15 ml	Ghee
$\frac{1}{2}$ cup	2 ounces, 56 g	Onions, cut in half lengthwise, then finely sliced
I teaspoon		Salt

PROCEDURE

1 Soak jaggery in $\frac{1}{2}$ the vinegar.

2 Remove head and tail from each Bombay duck and any finlike protrusions near the tail. Cut each Bombay duck into 4 pieces.

3 Grind to a paste garlic, red chiles, and cumin seeds with 1 tablespoon vinegar.

4 Heat ghee in a pan and fry the onion until brown.

5 Add masala paste and cook 5 minutes.

6 Add pieces of Bombay duck and mix well.

7 Add salt and remaining vinegar and cook 3 minutes.

8 Add vinegar and jaggery mixture and $\frac{1}{4}$ cup (2 ounces, 60 ml) water; cover and cook on low heat 10 minutes or till Bombay duck are soft.

Hara Dhania Chatni

Cilantro Chutney with Peanuts   YIELD : 1¼ CUP

AMOUNT	MEASURE	INGREDIENT
3 cups	6 ounces, 168 g	Cilantro leaves and tender stems
2		Green chiles (serrano), seeded
1 teaspoon		Cumin seeds
½ teaspoons		Coriander seeds
1 teaspoon		Salt
¼ cup	1½ ounces, 42 g	Unsalted peanuts, rough chopped
¼ cup	2 ounces, 60 ml	Fresh lime juice
¼ cup	2 ounces, 60 ml	Water
To taste		Granulated sugar

PROCEDURE

1   Combine all ingredients, using a mortar and pestle to make coarse chutney, or purée in a blender or food processor. Let stand 15 minutes.

Pork Vindaloo

SERVES 4

Pork Vindaloo is the benchmark of Goan food. Goa is a tiny state on the west coast of India, famous for its distinctive cuisine.

MARINADE

AMOUNT	MEASURE	INGREDIENT
3 tablespoons	1½ ounces, 120 ml	Malt vinegar
1½ teaspoons		Black peppercorns, crushed
1½ teaspoons		Brown sugar or jaggery
8		Cardamom seeds, green
8		Cloves
3		Green chiles, seeded
To taste		Salt
1½ pounds		Boneless pork shoulder, 1 inch (2.4 cm) cubes

PROCEDURE

| Combine all ingredients except pork and mix well. Add pork, and marinate 1 hour.

VINDALOO SPICE MIXTURE

AMOUNT	MEASURE	INGREDIENT
4		Garlic cloves, chopped
2 tablespoons	½ ounce	Ginger, peeled, chopped
2		Red chiles, seeded
½ teaspoon		Mustard seed
½ teaspoon		Fenugreek seed
1 teaspoon		Cumin seeds
2 teaspoons		Coriander seeds
½ teaspoon		Turmeric
½ teaspoon		Cinnamon, ground
2 tablespoons	1 ounce, 30 ml	Malt vinegar

PROCEDURE

| Using a mortar and pestle or blender, make a paste with the garlic, ginger, spices, and vinegar.

AMOUNT	MEASURE	INGREDIENT
3 tablespoons	1½ ounces, 45 ml	Oil
1½ cups	6 ounces, 168	Onions, ¼ inch (.6 cm) dice

PROCEDURE

1 Heat the oil over medium heat, add onions, and cook until golden brown, 6 to 8 minutes.

2 Add spice paste and cook over medium low heat, 10 minutes, or until the oil separates from the paste. Add up to 2 tablespoons (1 ounce, 30 ml) water, if necessary.

3 Remove pork cubes from marinade and add to pan. Cook 5 minutes over medium-high heat, stirring constantly. Add marinade.

4 Add 1 cup (8 ounces, 240 ml) warm water. Bring to simmer, cover, and lower heat. Cook 45 minutes or until pork is tender. Stir to prevent sticking.

Pork Vindaloo, Basmati Rice, and Cilantro Chutney

Naan   SERVES 4

AMOUNT	MEASURE	INGREDIENT
2 tablespoons	1 ounce, 30 ml	Milk, 110°F (43°C)
1 teaspoon		Granulated sugar
1 teaspoon		Dry yeast
2 cups	8 ounces, 224 g	All-purpose flour
$\frac{1}{2}$ teaspoon		Baking powder
$\frac{1}{4}$ teaspoon		Salt
$\frac{1}{4}$ cup	2 ounces, 60 ml	Yogurt
$\frac{1}{4}$ cup	2 ounces, 60 ml	Milk
1		Egg yolk
2 tablespoons	2 ounces, 60 ml	Ghee

PROCEDURE

1   Combine the milk and sugar; stir to dissolve. Sprinkle yeast over and let stand until the yeast begins to froth, about 10 minutes.

2   Sift together flour, baking powder, and salt.

3   In another container, mix together the yogurt, milk, egg yolk, and ghee.

4   Make a well in the center of the flour and add the liquid mixtures; work to form dough.

5   On a floured surface, knead the dough until it is smooth and elastic, 15 minutes.

6   Shape into a ball, cover, and let stand in warm area 1 hour.

7   Set a heavy baking tray (sheet pan) on the bottom rack of a preheated 500°F (260°C) oven. Preheat broiler.

8   Divide dough into 6 equal pieces and shape into balls. Flatten a piece of dough with your palm, dust with flour, and roll the dough from the center outward into a tear-shaped naan, about 8 inches (19.2 cm) long and 4 inches (9.6 cm) at its widest.

9   Remove the hot baking tray from the oven and slap the naan on to it. Immediately return the tray to the oven for 3 minutes; the naan should puff up.

10   Place the baking tray and naan under the broiler, about 3 to 4 inches (7.2–9.6 cm) away from the heat, for about 30 seconds or until the top of the naan browns slightly.

11   Wrap naan and serve hot.

The British Isles

The Land

The United Kingdom of Great Britain and Northern Ireland is a country in Western Europe and a member of the British Commonwealth and the European Union. Usually known as the United Kingdom, or UK, it is made up of four parts. Three of these parts—England, Wales, and Scotland—are located on the island of Great Britain and are considered nations in their own right. The fourth is Northern Ireland, which is located on the island of Ireland and is a province of the United Kingdom. The UK was formed by a series of Acts of Union, which united the countries of England (Wales already was a part of England), Scotland, and Ireland under a single government housed in London. The greater part of Ireland left the United Kingdom in 1922 to form a separate country when it became the Republic of Ireland, while the northeastern portion of the island, Northern Ireland, remains part of the United Kingdom. The UK is situated off the northwestern coast of continental Europe and is surrounded by the North Sea, the English Channel, the Celtic Sea, the Irish Sea, and the Atlantic Ocean.

England consists of mostly low hills and plains with a coastline cut into by bays, coves, and estuaries. Upland regions include the Pennine Chain, known as the "backbone of England," which splits northern England into western and eastern sectors. The highest point in England is Scafell Pike in the Lake District in the northwest, while the northeast includes the rugged landscape of the Yorkshire moors.

Wales has a varied geography with strong contrasts. In the south, flat coastal plains give way to valleys, then to ranges of hills and mountains in mid and north Wales.

Scotland is located in the north of Great Britain. The Scottish Lowlands and Borders are areas of gentle hills and woodland, contrasting dramatically with the rugged landscape of the Highlands in the north. A striking feature is Glen More, or the Great Glen, which cuts across the central Highlands from Fort William on the west coast northeast to Inverness on the east coast. A string of deep, narrow lochs (lakes) are set between steep mountains that rise past forested foothills to high moors and remote, rocky mountains.

Northern Ireland's northeast coast is separated from Scotland by the North Channel and is bordered by the Republic of Ireland in the west and south. The landscape is mainly low hill country. There are two mountain ranges: the Mournes, extending from South Down to Strangford Lough in the east, and the Sperrins in the northwest. Lough Neagh is the largest freshwater lake in the United Kingdom and one of the largest in Europe.

History

The term *Celtic* is used rather generally to distinguish the early inhabitants of the British Isles from the later Anglo-Saxon invaders. After two expeditions by Julius Caesar in 55 and 54 B.C., contact between Britain and the Roman world grew, culminating in the Roman invasion in A.D. 43. Roman rule lasted until about 409, and its reach extended from southeast England to Wales and, for a time, the lowlands of Scotland.

When the Romans withdrew from the area, the lowland regions were invaded and settled by Angles, Saxons, and Jutes (tribes from what is now northwestern Germany). The last successful invasion of England took place in 1066 when Duke William of Normandy defeated the English at the Battle of Hastings and became King William I, known as William the Conqueror. Many Normans and others from France came to settle and French became the language of the ruling classes for the next three centuries. The legal and social structures of England were influenced by those across the Channel.

Scotland and England have existed as separate unified entities since the tenth century. Wales, under English control since 1284, became part of the Kingdom of England in 1536. In 1707 the separate kingdoms of England and Scotland, having shared the same monarch since 1603, agreed to a permanent union as the Kingdom of Great Britain. This was at a time when Scotland was on the brink of economic ruin and was ruled by a deeply unpopular monarch.

In 1800 the Kingdom of Great Britain united with the Kingdom of Ireland, which had been gradually brought under English control between 1169 and 1691 to form the United Kingdom of Great Britain and Ireland. This was an unpopular decision, taking place just after the unsuccessful United Irishmen Rebellion of 1798. The timing, when further Napoleonic

NORTH
ATLANTIC
OCEAN

North
Sea

GRAMPIAN
Aberdeen
TAYSIDE

Edinburgh

Belfast

IRELAND
Dublin

Dingle
Peninsula

COUNTY
KERRY

Liverpool

UNITED
KINGDOM

Bath COTSWOLDS Oxford

London

English Channel

The United Kingdom

intervention or an invasion was feared, was predominantly due to security concerns. In 1922, after bitter fighting, the Anglo-Irish Treaty partitioned Ireland into the Irish Free State and Northern Ireland, with the latter remaining part of the United Kingdom. As provided for in the treaty, Northern Ireland, which consists of six of the nine counties of the Irish province of Ulster, opted out of the Free State and chose to remain in the UK. The nomenclature of the UK was changed in 1927 to recognize the departure of most of Ireland, and the name *United Kingdom of Great Britain and Northern Ireland* was adopted.

The United Kingdom, the dominant industrial and maritime power of the nineteenth century, played a leading role in developing Western ideas of property, liberty, capitalism, and parliamentary democracy as well as advancing world literature and science. At its zenith, the British Empire stretched over one-quarter of the earth's surface. The first half of the twentieth century saw the UK's strength seriously depleted in the two World Wars. The second half witnessed the dismantling of the empire and the UK rebuilding itself into a modern and prosperous nation.

The People

A group of islands close to continental Europe, the British Isles have been subject to many invasions and migrations. Contemporary Britons are descended mainly from the varied ethnic stocks that settled there before the eleventh century. The pre-Celtic, Celtic, Roman, Anglo-Saxon, and Norse influences were blended in Britain under the Normans and Scandinavian Vikings who had lived in northern France. Although Celtic languages persist in Wales, Scotland, and Northern Ireland, the predominant language is English, which is primarily a blend of Anglo-Saxon and Norman French.

Since World War II the UK has absorbed substantial immigration, with Europe, Africa, and South Asia being the major areas from which people currently emigrate.

The Food

Traditionally, England has been known as a country of "beefeaters," and roast beef and Yorkshire pudding has long been the country's usual Sunday dinner. Steak is also popular as an ingredient in hearty savory dishes such as steak and kidney pie or steak and mushroom pie. Being an island, Britain has always had a fresh supply of fish and seafood, both from the sea and from freshwater rivers. Salmon, Dover sole, turbot, mackerel, herring, oysters, eel, and shrimp are popular. Smoked fish is an English specialty, and smoked herrings, known as kippers, were once a very common breakfast dish. Fish and chips is traditional England takeaway food. Fish (cod, haddock, huss, plaice) is deep-fried in flour batter with chips (fried potatoes) and dressed in malt vinegar. England is renowned for its dairy products, particularly the rich clotted Devon cream from the country's southwest. There are also world-class cheeses produced in many counties, each fine variety bearing the name of its place of origin: Cheddar, Stilton, Cheshire, Derby, Lancashire, and Wensleydale, to name a few.

A traditional English breakfast provides a hearty start to the day. A typical menu may include several of the following: bacon, ham steak, homemade sage sausage, bratwurst, corned beef hash, scrapple, fried smelt, finnin haddie (smoked haddock), fried perch, home fries, baked stuffed tomato, fried green tomatoes, grilled whole mushrooms, roasted fresh garden vegetables, homemade baked beans, oven roasted potatoes, fried butternut or kabocha squash (a variety of winter squash), fried squash blossoms, and broiled baby zucchini. Pubs are popular for lunch and many still enjoy a typical "ploughman's lunch," consisting of bread, cheese, pickles, and sometimes cold meat, all washed down with a good glass of ale. Another simple and popular lunch item is the Cornish pasty, a pastry turnover filled with chopped meat, potatoes, and vegetables. It is said it had its origin in Cornwall, where it served both as a meal and "lunch box" for workers heading off to the mines. The pasty became the miners' meal of choice for many reasons. Not only was it a complete meal, but since arsenic was often found in the tin mines, the thick pastry crimp on the pasty allowed the miners to hold the pasty by this crust, then throw it away to avoid poisoning after they had eaten the body of the pasty.

For supper or "high tea," some favorite traditional English dishes include shepherd's pie, made with minced lamb and vegetables and topped with mashed potatoes; Gammon (ham) steak with egg; and Lancashire hotpot, a casserole of meat and vegetables topped with sliced potatoes. Bubble and squeak is made from cold vegetables and meat that have been leftover from a previous meal. This is fried in a pan together with mashed potatoes until the mixture is well cooked and brown on the sides. The name is a description of the sight and sound the ingredients make during the cooking process.

A sandwich has always been a very popular snack, but the first to eat one was the Earl of Sandwich (1718–1792). He was a dedicated gambler and refused to leave the gaming tables to eat. During one of his marathon gambling sessions he asked a waiter to bring him a piece of ham between two pieces of bread, and so invented the sandwich.

Afternoon tea was introduced in England by Anna, the seventh duchess of Bedford, in 1840. A tray of tea, bread, and butter was brought to her room during the late afternoon. This became a habit of hers and she began inviting friends to join her. This pause for tea became a fashionable social event. During the 1880s upper-class and society women would change into long gowns, gloves, and hats for their afternoon tea, which was usually served in the drawing room between four and five o'clock. Traditional afternoon tea consists of a selection of dainty sandwiches, scones served with clotted cream and preserves, cakes, and pastries. Tea grown in India or Ceylon is poured from silver teapots into delicate bone china cups.

Fruit desserts are popular, from pies and fruit crumbles to trifles and summer puddings made with fresh berries, as well as cakes flavored with spices or dried fruits, or filled with jam and cream. Dense steamed puddings such as plum pudding with brandy sauce are considered English Christmas traditions. French and Italian cooking are extremely popular in England, but it is Indian cuisine, first brought to Britain in the days of the Raj and further popularized with the arrival of Indian immigrants, that has become an important English food. In every city and town throughout the country there are Indian restaurants and "takeaways" serving a range of curries, chutneys, and Indian specialties.

The importance of agriculture to the Welsh economy as well as the availability of local products has created a cuisine and national diet that is based on fresh, natural food. In coastal areas fishing and seafood are important to both the economy and the local cuisine. While the Welsh national specialty is mountain lamb, it was the pig that was the basis of the diet in rural areas. Bacon remains an essential food, used today with the only two vegetables cultivated in Wales—leeks and cabbage. The national dish of Wales is *cawl,* a word for broth or soup that is a classic one-pot meal. Cooked in an iron pot over an open fire, it is made of bacon, lamb, cabbage, new potatoes, and leeks. The recipes vary from region to region and from season to season, based on what is available. Herring and mackerel are fried in bacon fat, roasted on a toasting fork, salted, or preserved. Oysters used to be prolific and one shellfish that remains plentiful is the cockle (a mollusk similar to a clam). Special traditional Welsh dishes include *laverbread* made from an edible seaweed known as laver. Also known as *bara lawr,* the *laverbread* is usually eaten sprinkled with oatmeal, then warmed in hot bacon fat and served with bacon for supper. Local markets and fairs usually offer regional products and baked goods. Wales is particularly known for its cheeses. Welsh rabbit, also called Welsh rarebit, a dish of melted cheese mixed with ale, beer, milk, and spices served over toast, has been popular since the early eighteenth century. Welsh cakes and breads include *bara brith,* the famous "speckled bread" with raisins and orange peel; *teisen lap,* a moist shallow fruitcake; and *teisen caraw,* a caraway seed cake. The type of food available in Wales is similar to that found in the rest of the United Kingdom and includes a variety of foods from other cultures and nations.

Scottish food is simple, with a heavy emphasis on meat. Roast lamb, roast beef, and steaks from Aberdeen-Angus cattle served with potatoes and bread make up the main meals. For many centuries Scottish cuisine centered on making use of every scrap of food available. This frugal attitude is seen in the Scottish national dish, a sausagelike concoction called *haggis.* It is made by chopping up the heart, liver, and lungs of a sheep, putting these ingredients in a bag made of the sheep's stomach, and boiling the bag and its contents. There are several types of breakfast foods and a full breakfast consists of fried eggs, bacon, sausage, tomatoes, and occasionally white or black pudding, which is a kind of blood sausage. Another Scottish breakfast dish is Arbroath smokies, known in England as kippers. They are lightly smoked herring served with butter. Oatcakes, known as *breed,* are made with oatmeal and bacon fat. The ingredients are mixed into a dough with warm water and then cut into rounds that are quickly fried on a griddle and then left to dry out. Traditional Scottish oatmeal is made with pinhead oats, or oats that have not been crushed or rolled. Scotch broth is a thick, wholesome soup made of various ingredients; the most important is barley, which is cooked with either lamb or beef as well as vegetables. This dish takes a lot of preparation and in the old days the Scotch broth pot never left the stove, with the last batch of broth forming the stock for a new pot of broth with a new set of ingredients.

Mince and tattties is similar to the English shepherd's pie. Minced beef, onions, and pinhead oatmeal are first fried and then mixed with vegetables and braised in gravy. The dish is served with boiled potatoes. *Cullen skink* is a thick stewlike soup made from smoked haddock, onions, and potatoes. *Stovies* are made from leftover cooked meat and potatoes, similar to corned beef hash. This is a very old dish with roots in the lives of the working poor. It is usually served with oatcakes and a glass of milk. *Clapshot* is not a main dish but an accompaniment to meat dishes; it is a mixture of mashed potatoes, turnips, and onions. Sweet puddings are popular and include *clootie dumping,* a mixture of fruitcake ingredients combined with spices, molasses, and suet wrapped in cloth and simmered in water for about four hours. *Cranachan* is the traditional harvest dish and is considered a very luxurious dessert. The table is laid with oatmeal, cream, honey, whisky, and raspberries. The family serves themselves with whatever combination of ingredients they choose. The traditional New Year's dessert is called *black bun* and is made from fruitcake baked inside a pastry case. The Scottish are also known for very fine shortbreads made with butter.

It is said when it comes to food there are three major periods in Irish history: before the potato arrived, after the potato arrived, and after the potato failed. Potatoes came to Ireland by way of South America, and by 1688 they were a staple of the Irish diet. The Irish population exploded in the first half of the nineteenth century, reaching about 8.5 million by 1845. The peasants were almost totally dependent on the potato for food—this crop produced more food per acre than wheat and could also be sold as a source of income. Unfortunately, it was particularly susceptible to potato blight, which could wipe out an entire crop very quickly. The crop regularly failed nationwide about every twenty years or so, but during the failure that began in 1845 and continued until 1849, at least a million people starved to death, while more than a million others emigrated to avoid starvation. Many peasants became too weak to work their tiny farms and were evicted from their homes because they could not pay rent. Meanwhile, unaffected crops such as corn sat in grain stores waiting to be shipped to England.

The diet changed dramatically after the famine. Potatoes continued to be important, but increasingly imports of cheap cornmeal, mainly from America, provided an alternative and cheap source of nutrition for the very poor. The fact that this cornmeal could also be fed to pigs and poultry made keeping them cheaper, which led to an increase in the availability of meat and eggs, both for consumption and as a means for farmers to earn cash. But most Irish people believed that pigs were all that this unpopular food was fit for, and by the end of the 1800s cornmeal was no longer eaten and had been replaced by locally grown oatmeal. Bread, potatoes, and oatmeal were staple foods and the people began to include bacon and eggs at breakfast time. The main meal was taken in the middle of the day and was usually meat, potatoes, and vegetables, usually cabbage, carrots, turnips, parsnips, or peas.

Historically the traditional Irish kitchen was the main living room of the house with a hearth built inside the chimney. Built into the wall of the chimney was a crane that could swing out over the fire or be pushed back against the wall when not in use. Whatever food had to be cooked was hung from this crane, usually in a large iron pot. The pot served as a saucepan and oven. When bread was baked it was put inside the pot and the lid placed firmly over it. Stew and potatoes were cooked in this same pot. Fish and mollusks were put into the stews on the coasts, while game, cattle, pig, goat, and sheep were available inland. Irish stew is a classic example, made from mutton, potatoes, onions, and flavored with parsley and thyme. Mutton is the dominant ingredient because the economic importance of sheep lay in their wool and milk produced and only old or economically nonviable animals ended up in the cooking pot, where they needed hours of slow boiling. Traditional foods include soda bread, originally made in the huge, black cooking pot and leavened with baking soda and sour milk. In the old days it served to use up milk left from the previous day. Another traditional food is *brack,* a cake made of dried fruit, eggs, lard, and flour. *Colcannon* is a dish made of potato and wild garlic, cabbage, or curly kale. *Champ* is a combination of mashed potato and egg, into which chopped scallions are mixed. *Carrageen moss* is another Irish delicacy, a seaweed that is collected and dried. The dried material is boiled and strained and the liquid left to cool, forming a jellylike substance said to be a very healthy food. Probably associated with Ireland more than other food or beverage is *stout* (black beer) originally produced by the Guinness brewery. It is an Irish success story of which all Irish people are proud.

During the 1980s and 1990s Ireland transitioned from an agricultural economy to a high-tech economy. The country, which has earned the nickname the Celtic Tiger, has one of the fastest growing economies in Europe. This has resulted in an increasingly sophisticated society. Dublin in particular has been transformed into an international city. By skipping the industrial revolution, it was necessary for everyone to rely on locally produced and home-grown foods from meat and seafood to dairy and vegetables, as there are few roads and factories to work in. Today, Ireland's chefs are taking advantage of international training, and a culinary renaissance is taking place producing dishes that are lighter and more sophisticated. The Irish Tourism Board has capitalized on this trend and coined the phrase "new Irish cuisine." Food today includes river oysters, grass-fed lamb, cows and pigs, and fresh or smoked salmon. Ireland's cheese-making tradition is developing, though Irish farmers have been making butter for hundreds of years. (Kerrygold butter is found around the world.) In the 1980s a group of small farmhouse cheese producers began making cheeses with milk from their own cows, goats, and sheep, and today artisan cheese makers are found all across the country. The farm-to-market movement is developing a great following, with its back-to-basics philosophy and emphasis on the true flavors of home grown, freshly prepared meals.

Glossary

Bangers Sausages are called bangers in England and Ireland. They are traditionally made with pork, although beef bangers are now common. "Bangers and mash," the familiar pub meal, is made from mashed potatoes, good-quality sausages, and onion gravy.

Bara Brith A fruit bread made with raisins and orange peel.

Barmbrack A cross between fruitcake and bread, this round loaf is leavened with yeast, flavored with spices like allspice and nutmeg, and dotted with dried fruit such as raisins, currants, and candied citrus peel (Ireland).

Biscuit British term for a hard-baked product, such as a flat cracker or cookie.

Black Pudding, Blood Pudding, or Blood Sausage Sausage made of pork and seasoned pig's blood.

Boxty Potato cake that comes in three forms. *Pan boxty* consists of grated potatoes mixed with flour and fried in hot fat. *Pancake boxty* is grated raw potato mixed with cooked mashed potato, flour, and baking soda and fried on a griddle pan. Boiled boxty is grated raw and cooked mashed potatoes, but the dough is formed into a ball, boiled in water, allowed to cool, and then sliced and pan-fried (Ireland).

Brawn A coarse terrine, made using parts of a pig's head and sometimes pig's feet, it originated as a way to use every scrap of meat after the traditional village pig slaughter (Ireland).

Bubble and Squeak An old English dish, made from leftovers and named for the sounds the ingredients make while cooking.

Carrageen Pudding This milk and vanilla pudding is thickened with carrageen moss, a sea vegetable that contains natural gelatin. The dish dates back to the era when seaweed played a prominent role in the diets of coastal dwellers (Ireland).

Cawl A traditional Welsh soup made with lamb, chopped potatoes, leeks, carrots, swede (rutabagas), turnip, parsnips, and onions.

Champs, or Poundies Mashed potatoes with green onion, with a well of butter in the center. The mashed potatoes are eaten from around the outer edge of the well and dipped into the butter. To *champ* means to bruise, pound, or smash, hence the term *poundies*.

Cheese

> **Ardrahan** Irish cheese with a semi-soft, smooth texture, a rich buttery flavor with a zesty tang, and an edible full-bodied rind from County Cork in South Ireland.

> **Buxton Blue** A cousin of blue Stilton. It is lightly veined and has a deep russet coloring that hints at the very special tang of its flavor.

> **Caboc** A rich, smooth, buttery cheese with a slight nutty flavor, due to being rolled in toasted pinhead oatmeal. One of Scotland's oldest cheeses, it is generally eaten when young, within five days of making.

> **Caerphilly** The most famous of Welsh cheeses, a fresh, white, mild cheese with a delicate, slightly salty and lightly acidic flavor. Having a moderately firm, creamy, open texture, it was originally made a century and a half ago and eaten by hard-working Welsh miners.

> **Cashel Blue** Soft-textured blue cheese from Wales.

> **Cheddar** A hard cheese, its color can range from pale to deep yellow, depending on maturity. Produced in range of tastes from mild with a mellow flavor to vintage with a rich, strong flavor. Originating from the village of the same name in Somerset, though now produced worldwide, and falsely called Cheddar. It was originally made from ewe's milk, but by Tudor times it was also being produced from cow's milk.

Cheshire Its unique flavor derives from salt deposits in nearby pasturelands. Colored Cheshire does not differ in flavor from white Cheshire. Both have a slightly crumbly and silky texture and both have a wonderfully full-bodied, fresh flavor. The only difference is its color, produced by an ancient vegetable dye called annatto.

Cornish Yarg A semi-hard cheese that is creamy under the rind and slightly crumbly in the core. It has a young, fresh, slightly tangy taste and is made by hand in open round vats. After pressing and brining, the cheese is wrapped in nettle leaves.

Crowdie A Scottish cream cheese; the texture is soft and crumbly, the taste slightly sour.

Derby Has a smooth, mellow texture with a quite mild, buttery flavor. It is similar in taste and texture to Cheddar and ripens between one and six months.

Double Gloucester Pale orange in color, with a smooth, buttery texture and a clean, creamy, mellow flavor. Usually matured for around three or four months.

Dovedale A creamy soft, mild blue cheese. Most British cheeses are dry salted; however, Dovedale is brine-dipped to add the salt, giving it a distinctive appearance and flavor.

Dubliner Tastes like a mature Cheddar with the sweet aftertaste of Reggiano.

Gubbeen, Smoked Has a silky, pliable texture and a light smoked flavor.

Lancashire Creamy open-textured cheese with a mild flavor. Usually matured for two to three months. Creamy white in color.

Laverbread Cow's milk cheese, which is speckled with laverbread, an edible seaweed sometimes called Welsh caviar.

Llanboidy A Welsh cow's milk cheese, firm, smooth and silky in texture with a buttery, herby flavor.

Sage Derby Green-veined, semi-hard cheese with a mild sage flavor.

Shropshire Blue A British blue cheese invented in Scotland, made in a way similar to Stilton. The cheese is a bright red with blue veining, and a sharper taste than Stilton.

Stilton Known as the "King of English Cheeses." Smooth and creamy with complex, slightly acidic flavor. An excellent dessert cheese, it is traditionally served with Port.

Warwickshire Truckle Full-flavored, mature hard Cheddar-like cheese with a firm but creamy texture and nutty taste.

Wensleydale A moist, crumbly, and flaky-textured cheese with a mild buttermilk and slightly sweet flavor.

Chips Thickly cut French fries.

Cockaleekie A thick chicken, leek, and barley soup from Scotland.

Colcannon Typical country winter dish comprising mashed potato and chopped cooked kale or cabbage (Ireland).

Cornish Pasty The word "pasty" comes from "pasta." Originally made with a hard pastry that served as a container rather than something to be eaten, forming a sealed pastry envelope. Although it originally contained almost anything, the Cornish pasty now contains seasoned chopped root vegetables and minced beef. Also known as an *oggie* or *Bedforshire clanger.*

Cruibeens Salted pig's feet. Today, contemporary chefs who enjoy cruibeens' crisp skin and gelatinous meat stuff them with everything from sweetbreads to morel mushrooms (Ireland).

Crumpet A light and spongy small, round, unsweetened bread, cooked on a griddle, similar to an English muffin.

Dingle Pies A simple, filling, one-handed meal, these small meat pies traditionally fed farmers working the fields or fishermen out at sea. They consist of a "hot-water pastry"—a sturdy mixture made by boiling butter and water, then combining them with flour—with a filling of mutton, carrots, and onions.

Double Cream Very rich cream, containing 48 percent butterfat. Whipping cream in the U.S., by contrast, contains between 30 percent and 40 percent butterfat.

Drisheen Spectacularly strong-flavored sheep's-blood pudding, a specialty of Cork city, typically served with tripe (Ireland).

Dublin Coddle Dublin's contribution to the national cuisine, this simple stew of onions, bacon, and sausage was, like *cruibeens,* historically popular after a night of drinking (Ireland).

Fadge Also called potato bread, *fadge* is made from leftover mashed potatoes mixed with flour and butter, pressed into a thin disk, fried on a hot griddle (Ireland).

Fish and Chips Fish (cod, haddock, huss, plaice) deep fried in flour batter with chips dressed in malt vinegar. In northern English they often served with "mushy peas" (mashed processed peas). Not normally home cooked but bought at a fish and chip shop known as a *chippie.*

Guinness Stout A brand of strong dark beer that originated in the British Isles; made with dark-roasted barley and more fragrant of hops than other types of beer.

Haggis A Scottish pudding made of the heart, liver, and other parts of a sheep or lamb, minced with suet, onions, and oatmeal, highly seasoned and boiled in the stomach of the same animal.

Hardtack A large, hard biscuit made with unsalted, unleavened flour and water dough, baked and dried to give a longer shelf life. Hardtack has been used as a staple by sailors at least since the 1800s. Also known as ship biscuit or sea bread.

Kedgeree Originally known as *Khitcheri* in India; consists of boiled rice, fish, and eggs (cumin seeds and lentils are optional).

Kippers Split and smoked herring.

Melba Toast A very thinly sliced crisp toast, served warm.

Mulligatawny Curry-flavored soup, which reflects the British period in India.

Mutton Aged older lamb, with a very strong flavor and tougher texture than younger lamb.

Pastie or Pastry Individual pies filled with meats and vegetables. They should weigh about two pounds or more. The identifying feature of the Cornish pasty is the pastry and its crimping.

Porridge A simple dish of boiled oatmeal. It needs to be boiled slowly and stirred continuously with the traditional spirtle—a wooden stick about 12 inches long—to avoid lumps.

Rarebit (Welsh Rarebit) Cheese melted with ale or beer served over toast.

Sandwiches Said to have been invented by the fourth Earl of Sandwich so that he could eat conveniently at the gaming table. The first printed reference to it is from 1762. The cucumber sandwich is probably regarded as the typically English sandwich, although it is not very common. *Butties* and *sarnies* are slang for sandwiches.

Scones A Scottish quick bread said to have taken its name from the Stone of Destiny (or Scone), the place where Scottish kings were once crowned.

Shepherd's Pie Traditionally, minced lamb or mutton stew topped with mashed potatoes. Cottage pie is the beef version.

Swede The English name for rutabaga, a yellow root vegetable with a slightly sweet flavor. Mashed veggies like swedes, turnips, and potatoes are an important, although often maligned, part of British culinary history.

Treacle Molasses.

Toad in the Hole A large Yorkshire pudding cooked with sausages embedded in it.

Trifle A dessert typically consisting of ladyfingers, plain or sponge cake soaked in sherry, rum, or brandy, and topped with layers of jam or jelly, custard, and whipped cream.

Yorkshire Pudding A batter of egg, flour, and milk cooked in beef drippings. Originally served with gravy before the main course to reduce the appetite, today it is used as an accompaniment to beef roast.

Menus and Recipes from the British Isles

Fennel and Red Onion Salad with Tarragon Dressing

SERVES 4

AMOUNT	MEASURE	INGREDIENT
2 tablespoons	1 ounce, 30 ml	White wine vinegar
1 teaspoon		Tarragon, chopped
$\frac{1}{2}$ cup	4 ounces, 120 ml	Olive oil
To taste		Salt and pepper
1 cup	4 ounces, 112 g	Red onion, sliced into thin rings ($\frac{1}{8}$ inch, .3 cm)
3 cups	12 ounces, 336 g	Fennel, sliced thin ($\frac{1}{8}$ inch, .3 cm)

PROCEDURE

1   Mix vinegar, tarragon, olive oil, salt, and pepper.

2   Add red onions and fennel; toss to combine.

3   Cover and let stand 1 hour.

Fennel and Red Onion Salad with Tarragon Dressing

Langoustine Soufflés

SERVES 4 TO 6

The langoustine, also called **Norway lobster**, is available mainly from **Brittany**. It is a large prawn with a unique silky texture and succulent flavor.

AMOUNT	MEASURE	INGREDIENT
3 tablespoons	$\frac{3}{4}$ ounce, 21 g	Bread crumbs, toasted
I cup	8 ounces, 224 g	Raw shelled langoustine tails (substitute shrimp if langoustine are not available)
I cup	8 ounces, 240 ml	Fish stock
3 tablespoons	$1\frac{1}{2}$ ounces, 45 ml	Butter
I tablespoon		Shallots, minced
3 tablespoons	$\frac{3}{4}$ ounce, 21 g	All-purpose flour
3		Egg yolks, beaten
$\frac{1}{8}$ teaspoon		Cayenne pepper
2 teaspoons		Fresh lemon juice
I teaspoon		Lemon zest
$\frac{1}{8}$ teaspoon		Nutmeg
3		Egg whites
Pinch		Salt

PROCEDURE

1 Preheat oven to 350°F (176°C).

2 Grease 4 to 6 individual 6- to 7-ounce (168 g to 196 g) ramekins and coat the insides with toasted bread crumbs. Chill.

3 Poach the langoustine tails in the fish stock about 2 minutes. Drain and roughly chop. Reserve the fish stock.

4 Melt the butter over medium heat; sauté shallots 2 minutes or until soft. Stir in the flour and cook 2 to 3 minutes.

5 Remove from heat; gradually stir in reserved fish stock. Return to heat and cook, stirring, 3 to 5 minutes, or until thick. Remove from heat and stir in egg yolks and langoustine tails. Season with cayenne, lemon juice, lemon zest, and nutmeg. Let cool slightly.

6 Whisk egg whites with the salt until stiff peaks form; fold into the langoustine mixture.

7 Spoon into prepared ramekins and bake 30 to 35 minutes. Soufflé should be puffed, browned, and fairly firm. Serve immediately.

Glazed Shallots   SERVES 4

AMOUNT	MEASURE	INGREDIENT
4 cups	1 pound, 448 g	Shallots, peeled
4 tablespoons	2 ounces, 60 ml	Butter
2 tablespoons	1 ounce, 28 g	Granulated sugar
To taste		Salt and pepper
1 tablespoon		Parsley, chopped

PROCEDURE

1   Over medium-high heat, cover shallots with cold water. Bring to a boil and simmer 10 minutes. Drain.

2   In a saucepan, melt the butter over medium heat; add sugar and stir to dissolve. Add the shallots; season with salt and pepper. Cover and cook until the shallots are tender and well glazed, 5 to 8 minutes. Stir occasionally to prevent the sugar from burning. Sprinkle with parsley and serve.

Roast Beef and Yorkshire Pudding SERVES 4

Yorkshire pudding was originally cooked under the roast to catch the juices as the meat cooked and was then served as a first course with thick gravy. Mustard and horseradish sauce are the traditional accompaniments for roast beef.

AMOUNT	MEASURE	INGREDIENT
3 pounds	1.34 kg	Standing rib roast, or about a 2-pound (900 g) boneless sirloin-tip roast
Yorkshire Pudding		
$\frac{3}{4}$ cup	3 ounces, 84 g	All-purpose flour
Pinch		Salt
$\frac{1}{2}$ cup	4 ounces, 120 ml	Milk, room-temperature
$\frac{1}{2}$ cup	4 ounces, 120 ml	Water, room-temperature
1		Egg, room temperature
1 tablespoon	$\frac{1}{2}$ ounce, 15 ml	Melted fat from the roasting pan
Gravy		
2 teaspoons		All-purpose flour
$1\frac{1}{4}$ cups	10 ounces, 300 ml	Beef stock
To taste		Salt and pepper

PROCEDURE

1 Sift the flour and salt together. Mix milk, water, and egg together and gradually beat into the flour; continue mixing until batter is smooth and lump free. Let stand 30 to 40 minutes.

2 Preheat oven to 425°F (218°C).

3 Place the beef on a rack in a roasting pan; season with salt and pepper.

4 Cook 15 minutes. Reduce the temperature to 350°F (176°C) and continue to roast until desired temperature is reached. Remove from oven and let rest 20 minutes before carving. Return oven to 425°F (218°C).

5 While the meat is resting, put the fat from the beef into a 9-inch-square (22 cm) 2-inch-deep (4.8 cm) pan. Return pan to oven, until fat is smoking hot. Immediately pour batter

into the hot pan. Bake in the hot oven until puffed and dry, 20 to35 minutes. Do not open the oven for the first 20 minutes. Cut into portions and serve with the roast.

6 To make the gravy, degrease the roasting pan. Sprinkle in the flour and stir well, scraping up the brown sediment. Cook, stirring, over high heat until flour has browned slightly. Add beef stock and stir well; bring to a boil and simmer 5 minutes. Add any juices from the resting meat and correct seasoning.

7 Serve with glazed shallots, steamed broccoli, and roasted new potatoes.

Horseradish Sauce   SERVES 4

AMOUNT	MEASURE	INGREDIENT
3 tablespoons	$1\frac{1}{2}$ ounces, 45 ml	Fresh or prepared horseradish, grated
I teaspoon		White vinegar
2 teaspoons		Fresh lemon juice
$\frac{1}{4}$ cup	2 ounces, 60 ml	Sour cream or double cream
2 tablespoons	I ounce, 30 ml	Heavy cream
$\frac{1}{4}$ teaspoon		Dry mustard powder
To taste		Salt and white pepper

PROCEDURE

I Combine all ingredients and mix well; correct seasoning.

Mustard Sauce   SERVES 4

AMOUNT	MEASURE	INGREDIENT
2 tablespoons	2 ounces, 30 ml	Butter
2 tablespoons	$\frac{1}{2}$ ounce, 14 g	All-purpose flour
1 cup	8 ounces, 240 ml	Milk
$\frac{1}{4}$ cup	2 ounces, 60 ml	Heavy cream
1 tablespoon	$\frac{1}{2}$ ounce, 15 ml	White vinegar
1 tablespoon	$\frac{1}{4}$ ounce, 7 g	Dry mustard
1 tablespoon	$\frac{1}{2}$ ounce, 15 ml	Dijon mustard
1 teaspoon		Salt
$\frac{1}{2}$ teaspoon		White pepper

PROCEDURE

1   Over medium heat, thoroughly combine butter and flour. Cook 2 minutes.

2   Add milk, stirring constantly; bring to a boil. Reduce heat and simmer 3 minutes. Whisk in the cream, vinegar, mustards, salt, and pepper. Serve immediately.

Cheese and Herb Bread   SERVES 4

AMOUNT	MEASURE	INGREDIENT
1 teaspoon		Granulated sugar
$1\frac{1}{4}$ cups	10 ounces, 300 ml	Warm water (105°F, 40.5°C)
$2\frac{1}{4}$ teaspoons	$\frac{1}{4}$ ounce, 7 g	Active dry yeast
As needed		Butter
3 cups	12 ounces, 336 g	All-purpose flour
$\frac{1}{2}$ cup	2 ounces, 56 g	Bread flour
2 teaspoon		Salt
1 teaspoon		Dry mustard
$\frac{1}{2}$ teaspoon		White pepper
1 tablespoon		Chives, minced
2 tablespoons		Parsley, chopped
2 cups	8 ounces, 224 g	Cheddar cheese, grated

PROCEDURE

1 Preheat the oven to 375°F (190°C).

2 Dissolve the sugar in the water, and sprinkle in the yeast. Let stand 10 to 12 minutes, until frothy.

3 Butter $8\frac{1}{2} \times 4\frac{1}{2} \times 3\frac{3}{4}$-inch (20.4 × 10.8 × 6.6 cm) loaf pan.

4 Sift the flours, salt, mustard, and pepper into a bowl. Stir in the chives, parsley and three-quarters of the cheese. Add the yeast liquid to the dry ingredients and mix to a soft, smooth dough, 8 to 12 minutes using the hook attachment. Turn out onto a floured surface and round. Cover and let rise in a warm place about 1 hour, until doubled in size.

5 Turn the dough onto a floured surface and knead 2 to 3 minutes.

6 Fit into prepared loaf pan. Cover and let rise in a warm place 40 to 50 minutes.

7 Sprinkle the top with remaining cheese. Bake 45 minutes, until well risen and golden brown. Turn out and cool on a wire rack.

Strawberry Shortbread   SERVES 4

AMOUNT	MEASURE	INGREDIENT
1½ cups	12 ounces, 360 ml	Strawberry coulis (pureed strawberries)
¾ cup	6 ounces, 168 g	Granulated sugar
As needed		Fresh lemon juice
4 cups	16 ounces, 448 g	Strawberries

PROCEDURE

1 Combine strawberry coulis and sugar; correct flavor with more sugar or a little lemon juice.

2 Wash strawberries, hull, and either half or leave them whole, depending on their size.

3 Toss with two-thirds of the strawberry coulis and set in the refrigerator.

Shortbread Dough

AMOUNT	MEASURE	INGREDIENT
1 cup	8 ounces, 240 ml	Butter
1 cup	3.75 ounces, 105 g	Confectioner's sugar
½ teaspoon		Salt
2		Egg yolks
2¼ cups	9 ounces, 252 g	All-purpose flour, sifted
½ teaspoon		Vanilla extract
		Egg yolk, beaten with 1 tablespoon (½ ounce, 15 ml) milk

PROCEDURE

1 Cut the butter into small pieces. Work the butter with your fingertips until very soft. Sift confectioner's sugar and add to the butter with the salt. Continue to work the mixture with the fingertips until the ingredients are thoroughly blended, then add the egg yolks, mixed with vanilla extract, and mix lightly.

2 Add the flour and mix evenly into the mixture.

3 Rub the pastry gently 2 or 3 times (only) using the palm of the hand. Do not overwork the short dough. Roll into a ball and flatten it out lightly. Wrap and chill 2 to 3 hours, until very firm. (When working with the dough later, it will soften very quickly.)

4 Preheat oven to 400°F (204°C).

5 On a lightly floured work surface, roll out the pastry to the thickness of about $\frac{1}{8}$ inch (.3 cm). Cut out 12 circles with a 4-inch (10 cm) scallop-edged pastry cutter and arrange on a baking sheet.

6 Brush with egg wash, and then draw lines with the back of a small knife or fork on the surface for decoration.

7 Bake 8 minutes; remove from oven, and let cool on baking sheet 1 to 2 minutes to firm. Then use a palette knife to transfer to a wire rack and cool.

8 To serve, place a shortbread disk on each plate. Over each spread a few prepared strawberries, then on top, balance a second layer of shortbread; garnish with more strawberries. Top with a shortbread dredged with confectioner's sugar. Spoon a little of the reserved coulis around and serve.

Scotch Broth   SERVES 4

AMOUNT	MEASURE	INGREDIENT
12 ounces		Mutton
$\frac{1}{4}$ cup	1 ounce, 28 g	Pearl barley, soaked
1 quart	960 ml	Lamb, beef, or chicken stock
2 tablespoons	1 ounce, 30 ml	Butter
$1\frac{1}{2}$ tablespoons		Garlic, minced
$\frac{1}{2}$ cup	2 ounces, 56 g	Onion, $\frac{1}{4}$ inch (.6 cm) dice
$\frac{3}{4}$ cup	3 ounces, 84 g	Leek, white and light green parts, $\frac{1}{4}$ inch (.6 cm) dice
$\frac{1}{2}$ cup	2 ounces, 56 g	Celery, $\frac{1}{4}$ inch (.6 cm) dice
$\frac{1}{2}$ cup	2 ounces, 56 g	Carrots, $\frac{1}{4}$ inch (.6 cm) dice
$\frac{1}{2}$ cup	2 ounces, 56 g	Rutabaga, $\frac{1}{4}$ inch (.6 cm) dice
To taste		Salt and pepper
2 tablespoons		Parsley, chopped
1 tablespoon		Fresh thyme, chopped

PROCEDURE

1   Trim any excess fat from the mutton. Combine mutton, barley, and stock over medium heat and bring to a boil. Reduce to a simmer and cook 1 hour.

2   In a separate pan, heat butter until foamy. Add the garlic and onion and cook 2 minutes. Add the leeks and cook 2 minutes. Transfer to soup and add the celery, carrots, and rutabaga. Simmer 20 to 30 minutes or until vegetables are tender.

3   Remove meat, cut into $\frac{1}{2}$-inch (1.2 cm) cubes, and return to soup.

4   Skim off any fat, correct seasoning, and add parsley and thyme.

Tomato Water-Ice with a Julienne of Smoked Salmon

SERVES 4

AMOUNT	MEASURE	INGREDIENT
1½ pounds	672 g	Ripe tomatoes, peeled, seeded, chopped
2 tablespoons	1 ounce, 30 ml	Fresh lemon juice
1 teaspoon		Worcestershire sauce
Few drops, to taste		Tabasco
To taste		Salt
½ teaspoon		Granulated sugar
¼ pound	4 ounces, 112 g	Smoked salmon, julienned strips
Garnish		Fresh dill sprigs

PROCEDURE

1 Rub tomatoes through a sieve into a bowl. Stir in the lemon juice, Worcestershire sauce, Tabasco sauce, salt, and sugar.

2 Pour the mixture into a shallow container and freeze until frozen around the edges. Turn into a chilled bowl and beat to break up the ice crystals. Return to the container and freeze until hard.

3 To serve, chill serving plates. Scrape water-ice and shape into quenelles; place two onto each plate. Arrange 1 ounce (28 g) of smoked salmon on the plates and garnish with a dill sprig.

Salad of Steamed Skate SERVES 4

AMOUNT	MEASURE	INGREDIENT
I	1¼ pound, 20 ounces, 560 g	Skate wing, outer fins removed, washed
¼ cup	2 ounces, 60 ml	Butter, melted
I tablespoon		Garlic, minced
I tablespoon	½ ounce, 15 ml	Fresh lemon juice
¼ teaspoon		Cayenne pepper
I tablespoon		Tarragon, blanched in boiling water and chopped
1½ cups	6 ounces, 168 g	Carrots, julienned
1½ cups	6 ounces, 168 g	Zucchini, julienned, on seeds

PROCEDURE

1 Combine the butter, garlic, lemon juice, cayenne pepper, and tarragon; correct seasoning. Brush the flavored butter over the skate wing.

2 Sprinkle the julienned vegetables over the perforated part of a steamer. Season the skate, place on top of the vegetables, brush with more butter.

3 Steam in a covered container 5 minutes on each side or until tender.

4 Remove; save the julienne to use in the salad.

5 Remove the skin from both sides and fillet the skate. Keep covered to retain the moisture.

Salad

AMOUNT	MEASURE	INGREDIENT
½ cup	4 ounces, 120 ml	Fish stock
I tablespoon		Shallots, chopped
2 tablespoons		Chives, chopped
I teaspoon		Worcestershire sauce
4 cups	8 ounces, 224 g	Mixed baby greens
To taste		Fresh lemon juice, salt, and black pepper
I cup	6 ounces, 168 g	Tomato, peeled, seeded, ¼ inch (.6 cm) dice

PROCEDURE

1 Warm fish stock.

2 Combine stock with 1 tablespoon ($\frac{1}{2}$ ounce, 15 ml) tarragon dressing, shallots, and chives. Add Worcestershire sauce and correct seasoning.

3 To serve, toss the salad greens with 4 to 6 tablespoons (2 to 3 ounces, 60 to 90 ml) of dressing and arrange in the center of 4 plates. Place the warm skate, cut in slices, around the edge of the greens. Season the fish with lemon juice and sprinkle the reserved julienne of carrot and zucchini over. Toss the diced tomato with a little dressing, and place a tablespoon on top of each serving.

4 Spoon the warm sauce over the skate and serve.

Tarragon Vinaigrette

AMOUNT	MEASURE	INGREDIENT
1 tablespoon		Shallots, chopped
1 tablespoon		Chives, chopped
1 tablespoon	$\frac{1}{2}$ ounce, 15 ml	White wine vinegar
1 tablespoon	$\frac{1}{2}$ ounce, 15 ml	Virgin olive oil
1 tablespoon	$\frac{1}{2}$ ounce, 15 ml	Corn oil
1		Garlic clove, flattened
$\frac{1}{2}$ teaspoon		Granulated sugar
To taste		Salt and black pepper
1 tablespoon		Tarragon, chopped

PROCEDURE

1 Combine all ingredients and mix well.

Roast Belly of Pork with Black Pudding and Apples   SERVES 4

AMOUNT	MEASURE	INGREDIENT
1 cup	4 ounces, 112 g	Onions, $\frac{1}{4}$ inch (.6 cm) slices
2 tablespoons		Garlic, chopped
1 tablespoon		Fresh sage, minced
3 pounds	1.34 kg	Pork belly, rind removed
2 cups	16 ounces, 480 ml	Chicken stock
$\frac{1}{4}$ cup	2 ounces, 60 ml	Cider
$\frac{1}{8}$ teaspoon		Allspice
$\frac{1}{8}$ teaspoon		Cinnamon
To taste		Salt and pepper
$\frac{1}{4}$ cup	2 ounces, 56 g	Brown sugar

PROCEDURE

1   Preheat the oven to 325°F (163°C). In a roasting pan, place the onions in a single layer; sprinkle the chopped garlic and half the sage over the onions. Place the pork on top of the onions. Add the stock and pour the cider over the pork. Sprinkle the pork with the allspice, cinnamon, and remaining sage. Cover with aluminum foil and cook, basting every 20 minutes, for 3 hours or until the pork is tender.

2   Uncover and sprinkle with the brown sugar. Increase oven temperature to 400°F (204°C); return to the oven and cook, uncovered, 20 minutes or until glazed and golden brown. Correct seasoning and transfer to a platter and keep warm.

Sauce

AMOUNT	MEASURE	INGREDIENT
2 cups	16 ounces, 480 ml	Beef stock
1 tablespoon		Sage, chopped

PROCEDURE

1   Combine stock and sage and reduce by half. Strain and keep warm.

Roast Belly of Pork with Black Pudding and Apples

Garnish

AMOUNT	MEASURE	INGREDIENT
I tablespoon	$\frac{1}{2}$ ounce, 15 ml	Vegetable oil
4	2 ounces, 56 g	Black pudding slices, cooked crisp on each side
I		Granny Smith apple, cut into 8 wedges, cooked in the same pan as the black pudding, until soft. Add I tablespoon of oil if necessary
4 each	I ounce, 28 g	Bacon, cooked crisp, crumbled

TO SERVE

1 Slice pork thin; add any meat juices to the sauce.

2 Serve pork on a plate with sliced black pudding and apple. Spoon the sauce over and top with crumbled bacon.

Colcannon **SERVES 4**

AMOUNT	MEASURE	INGREDIENT
2 cups	8 ounces, 224 g	Cabbage, cored and shredded
4 cups	20 ounces, 560 g	Russet potatoes, peeled and cut into 2 inch (5 cm) pieces
1 cup	4 ounces, 112 g	Leeks, white and light green parts, washed and sliced
$\frac{1}{2}$ cup	4 ounces, 120 ml	Milk
To taste		Salt and pepper
$\frac{1}{4}$ teaspoon		Mace
5 tablespoons	$2\frac{1}{2}$ ounces, 75 ml	Butter, cut into small pieces

PROCEDURE

1 Cook cabbage and potatoes separately in boiling salted water until tender, 10–12 minutes. Drain the cabbage and chop. Drain the potatoes and mash.

2 Combine the leeks and milk over medium heat. Bring to a simmer and cook 8 to 10 minutes or until tender. Add the potatoes, salt, pepper, and mace; stir to blend. Add the cabbage and butter; mix well until butter has melted and blended in. Correct seasoning and serve hot.

Irish Soda Bread   SERVES 4

AMOUNT	MEASURE	INGREDIENT
1½ cups	6 ounces, 168 g	Whole wheat flour
1 cup	4 ounces, 112 g	All-purpose flour
1 cup	4 ounces, 112 g	Bread flour
1½ teaspoons		Baking powder
1 teaspoon		Salt
1½ cups	12 ounces, 360 ml	Buttermilk or plain yogurt

PROCEDURE

1   Preheat oven to 450°F (232°C).

2   Sift together the flours, baking soda, and salt. Make sure to include any bran in the sieve. Stir to mix well.

3   Add the buttermilk, all at once, and mix to form a soft but not sticky dough.

4   Knead 2 minutes on a lightly floured surface, shape the dough into two small balls, and flatten slightly. Cut a deep cross in the dough with a sharp knife. Dust with flour and place on a floured cookie sheet.

5   Bake 10 minutes, then reduce the heat to 400°F (204°C). Bake an additional 25 to 30 minutes. When cooked, the loaf will be well browned and sound hollow when tapped on the bottom. Cool on a wire rack and serve the same day; it becomes stale quickly.

Dundee Cake   SERVES 4

AMOUNT	MEASURE	INGREDIENT
$\frac{3}{4}$ cup	6 ounces, 168 g	Butter
$\frac{2}{3}$ cup	5 ounces, 140 g	Granulated sugar
4		Eggs
2 cups	8 ounces, 224 g	All-purpose flour
$\frac{1}{4}$ cup	1 ounce, 28 g	Sliced blanched almonds
$\frac{1}{4}$ cup	$1\frac{1}{2}$ ounces, 42 g	Mixed candied citrus peel
$\frac{1}{2}$ cup	3 ounces, 84 g	Currants
$\frac{1}{2}$ cup	3 ounces, 84 g	Raisins
$\frac{1}{2}$ cup	3 ounces, 84 g	Sultanas (seedless white raisins)
2 tablespoons	1 ounce, 30 ml	Fresh lemon juice
To taste		Lemon zest
1 teaspoon		Baking powder
2 tablespoons	1 ounce, 30 ml	Irish whisky (optional) or milk
2 tablespoons	1 ounce, 30 ml	Hot milk
1 tablespoon	$\frac{1}{2}$ ounce, 14 g	Granulated sugar

PROCEDURE

1 Preheat the oven to 325°F (163°C).

2 Cream the butter and sugar until white and creamy.

3 Add the eggs, one at a time, with one tablespoon of flour with each addition; mix well after each.

4 Stir in the almonds, dried fruit, lemon juice, and lemon zest. Sift flour with baking powder and add. Mix well. Add the whisky or milk. If it is too stiff, add a little milk.

5 Place in an 8-inch (20 cm) greased and lined cake tin. Wet your hands and flatten the top. Cover with foil or parchment paper and bake at 325°F (163°C) 2 hours.

6 After 1 hour, remove the cover. Check the cake with a skewer toward the end of cooking; if it is still wet in the middle, return to the oven for an additional 5 to 10 minutes.

7 Combine the hot milk and sugar and brush top to create a dry glaze.

8 Keep in the pan 15 minutes, then turn out on a wire rack to cool.

Baked Oysters with Bacon, Cabbage, and Guinness Sabayon   SERVES 4

AMOUNT	MEASURE	INGREDIENT
12		Oysters
I cup	4 ounces, 224 g	Green cabbage, finely shredded
$\frac{1}{2}$ cup	2 ounces, 56 g	Celery, peeled, finely julienned
I teaspoon		Vegetable oil
4 slices	I ounce, 28 g	Traditional Irish bacon or Canadian bacon, $\frac{1}{4}$ inch (.6 cm) dice
As needed		Sabayon (recipe follows)

PROCEDURE

1 Preheat oven to 450°F (232°C).

2 Open the oysters, saving the juice and reserving the deeper half of each shell.

3 Rinse the oysters and drain on a paper towel.

4 Rinse and dry the shells, then place on a bed of rock salt.

5 Strain oyster juice through a fine sieve.

6 Blanch cabbage and celery separately in salted boiling water 1 to 2 minutes, or until slightly wilted. Drain and immerse in ice water; drain well again.

7 Heat the oil over medium heat and cook the bacon until crisp. Remove and drain on paper towels. Remove most of the bacon fat from pan.

8 Add the cabbage and celery to pan and sauté just until warm.

9 Combine the oysters and their liquor and poach at a bare simmer until their edges begin to curl, about $1\frac{1}{2}$ minutes.

10 Divide the cabbage and celery mixture among the shells, put an oyster on top of each, and sprinkle the bacon over the oysters.

11 Spoon sabayon over each. Bake 5 minutes, or until the sabayon is just beginning to brown.

12 Grind pepper over the oysters and serve at once.

Sabayon

AMOUNT	MEASURE	INGREDIENT
4		Egg yolks
$\frac{1}{2}$ cup		Guinness stout
$\frac{1}{2}$ teaspoon		Kosher salt
To taste		Black pepper

PROCEDURE

1. Combine the egg yolks, Guinness, salt, and pepper over simmering water and beat with a wire whisk until light, fluffy, and just beginning to set, 3 to 5 minutes. The sabayon must not get too hot during the cooking or it will become grainy; if it begins to feel warmer than body temperature, remove the pan briefly from the heat and beat continuously, until the mixture cools. Then return to the heat and continue cooking. When the sabayon has thickened into stable foam, remove from the heat and keep warm.

Crab and Champ Bake   SERVES 4

Tomato-Watercress Dressing

AMOUNT	MEASURE	INGREDIENT
$\frac{1}{2}$ cup	3 ounces, 84 g	Tomato, peeled, seeded, $\frac{1}{4}$ inch (.6 cm) dice
I cup	4 ounces, 112 g	Watercress, rinsed, stemmed, and coarsely chopped
$\frac{1}{4}$ cup	2 ounces, 60 ml	Olive oil
I teaspoon		Whole grain mustard
I teaspoon		Granulated sugar
$\frac{1}{4}$ cup	2 ounces, 60 ml	Cider vinegar
To taste		Salt and fresh black pepper

PROCEDURE

1   Combine all ingredients and stir to mix. Correct seasoning and chill.

Champ

AMOUNT	MEASURE	INGREDIENT
5 cups	$1\frac{1}{2}$ pounds, 672 g	Russet potatoes, peeled, quartered
$\frac{1}{2}$ teaspoon		Salt
$\frac{1}{4}$ cup	2 ounces, 60 ml	Butter
2 tablespoons		Green onion, white part only, minced
Pinch		Nutmeg
To taste		Salt and pepper

PROCEDURE

1   Cover the potatoes with cold water, add salt, bring to a boil, and simmer until tender, about 20 minutes.

2   Drain the potatoes and return to the pot. Cook over low heat about 3 minutes to allow them to dry.

3   Mash, grind, or rice the potatoes.

4   Heat the butter over medium heat; sauté the onion 1 minute, then mix into the potatoes. Season with nutmeg, salt, and pepper.

Crab Filling

AMOUNT	MEASURE	INGREDIENT
1½ tablespoons	⅓ ounce, 10 g	All-purpose flour
½ cup	4 ounces, 120 ml	Fish stock
1 cup plus 2 tablespoons	9 ounces, 300 ml	Heavy cream
¼ teaspoon		Lemon zest
1 cup	8 ounces, 224 g	Crabmeat, picked over for shells
To taste		Salt, pepper, and Tabasco sauce
¼ cup	1 ounces, 56 g	Smoked Cheshire cheese or other smoked cheese, grated

PROCEDURE

1 Preheat oven to 400°F (204°C).

2 Combine the flour with ½ the fish stock; mix until smooth.

3 Over medium heat, combine cream, remaining fish stock, and lemon zest; reduce by ⅓. Mix in fish stock and flour slurry, and cook until thick, 3 to 5 minutes. Remove from heat, stir in the crabmeat, and season with salt, pepper, and Tabasco.

4 Butter four 6-ounce (180 ml) ramekins and place on a baking sheet. Fill halfway with mashed potatoes, fill the top half with crab filling.

5 Bake 15 minutes or until the filling is set. Sprinkle with cheese and brown under the broiler until tops are brown and the cheese bubbles.

6 Serve with a small amount of dressing drizzled around the ramekin and the remaining dressing on the side.

Stuffed Shoulder of Lamb   SERVES 4

AMOUNT	MEASURE	INGREDIENT
4 cups	8 ounces, 224 g	Spinach, fresh
$\frac{1}{4}$ cup	2 ounces, 60 ml	Butter
2 tablespoons		Shallots, minced
1 tablespoon		Garlic, minced
$\frac{1}{4}$ cup	$\frac{1}{2}$ ounce, 14 g	Sun-dried tomatoes, chopped
$\frac{1}{4}$ cup	1 ounce, 28 g	Dried apricots, soaked 15 minutes in warm water, chopped
To taste		Salt and black pepper
3 pounds	1.36 kg	Lamb shoulder, boned
Two 6 x 3 inch strips	Two 15 x 7.5 cm strips	Pork fat
$\frac{1}{2}$ cup	4 ounces, 120 ml	Port or good red wine
1 cup	8 ounces, 240 ml	Beef stock
2 tablespoons	1 ounce, 30 ml	Water
1 tablespoon		Cornstarch

PROCEDURE

1   Blanch the spinach in boiling salted water 1 minute. Drain. Run under cold water and press to remove as much water as possible.

2   Heat the butter over medium heat; sauté the shallots and garlic 3 minutes. Add sun-dried tomatoes and apricots; cook 1 minute.

3   Add spinach and mix well; correct seasoning, remove from heat, and let cool.

4   Lay the lamb skin-side down on a flat surface. Score a cross, about 3 inches (7.5 cm) wide, in the center of the meat. Place stuffing in the center of the meat. Pull the edges of meat up and around the filling to make a neat roll.

5   Wrap the pork fat around the meat and tie tightly with string.

6   Roast at 350°F (176°C) 30 minutes per pound, basting occasionally or until desired doneness is achieved.

7   About 20 minutes before the end of the cooking time, remove the fat.

8   When cooked, remove lamb to a holding platter and let rest 15 minutes.

9   Pour off fat from the roasting pan. Add port and stir to dissolve pan juices. Add stock and reduce by half. Combine water and cornstarch and thicken the sauce if desired.

10   Adjust seasoning and serve sauce with meat.

Blue Cheese Potato Cakes SERVES 4

AMOUNT	MEASURE	INGREDIENT
2 cups	10 ounces, 300 g	Russet potatoes, peeled and cut into 2 inch (5 cm) pieces
2 tablespoons	1 ounce, 30 ml	Butter
1 tablespoon		Chives, minced
1 tablespoon		Garlic, minced
$\frac{1}{4}$ teaspoon		Nutmeg
To taste		Salt and fresh black pepper
1 tablespoon		Fresh dill, minced
1 tablespoon		Flat-leaf parsley, minced
$\frac{1}{2}$ cup	2 ounces, 56 g	Cashel blue cheese or other blue cheese, crumbled
1		Egg yolk
1		Egg, beaten
$\frac{1}{4}$ cup	2 ounces, 60 ml	Milk
$\frac{1}{2}$ cup	2 ounces, 56 g	All-purpose flour (breading station)
1 cup	4 ounces, 112 g	Fresh bread crumbs (breading station)
1 cup	8 ounces, 240 ml	Oil for pan frying
$\frac{1}{2}$ cup	4 ounces, 120 ml	Sour cream for topping (optional)

PROCEDURE

1 Cook potatoes in salted boiling water until tender, 12 to 15 minutes. Drain and mash.

2 Melt butter over low heat; add chives and garlic and cook until soft, 1 to 2 minutes.

3 Add mashed potatoes, continue to stir; add nutmeg, salt, pepper, dill, and parsley. Remove from heat and cool.

4 When potato mixture is cool, add cheese and egg yolk. The cheese should remain in lumps; do not blend smooth. Shape the mixture into 8 cakes and refrigerate 30 minutes.

5 Combine egg and milk and set up a standard breading station (flour, egg wash, bread crumbs). Process potato cakes through the breading station.

6 Over medium-high heat, bring the oil to 350°F (176°C). Add the cakes and cook 3 to 5 minutes on each side, or until well browned on both sides. Serve hot with sour cream.

Whole Wheat Scones   SERVES 4

AMOUNT	MEASURE	INGREDIENT
1½ cup	6 ounces, 168 g	Whole wheat flour
1½ cup	6 ounces, 168 g	All-purpose flour
2 teaspoons		Baking powder
¼ cup	2 ounces, 60 ml	Butter
2 teaspoons		Warm corn syrup
½ cup plus 2 tablespoons	5 ounces, 150 ml	Milk
Pinch		Salt

PROCEDURE

1 Preheat the oven to 375°F (190°C).

2 Mix dry ingredients.

3 Add butter and mix until it resembles coarse bread crumbs.

4 Stir in corn syrup and add enough milk to make a soft dough.

5 Turn out on a floured surface and roll out to about ½ inch (1.2 cm) thick. Cut into small rounds with a cutter about 1½ inch (3.8 cm) in diameter. Place the rounds on a floured baking sheet and cook in a preheated oven 10 to 15 minutes. Serve hot, spread with butter.

Caledonian Cream

Marmalade was developed in Dundee, Scotland, in 1797.

SERVES 4

AMOUNT	MEASURE	INGREDIENT
$\frac{1}{2}$ cup	4 ounces, 112 g	Cream cheese
$\frac{1}{2}$ cup	4 ounces, 120 ml	Double cream
1 tablespoon	$\frac{1}{2}$ ounce, 15 ml	Bitter orange marmalade
2 tablespoons	1 ounce, 30 ml	Brandy or rum
2 teaspoons		Fresh lemon juice
To taste		Granulated sugar
4		Oranges, segmented, pith removed
2 tablespoons		Orange zest, blanched 30 seconds in boiling water and cooled

PROCEDURE

1 In a blender, combine all ingredients except orange segments. Blend smooth; adjust sweetness with sugar.

2 Toss orange segments with additional brandy or rum, if desired.

3 Serve chilled, with cream on top of oranges. Garnish with orange zest.

France

The Land

France is located in western Europe. It borders the English Channel and the Bay of Biscay to the west; the Mediterranean Sea to the south; Italy, Germany, Switzerland, and Belgium to the east; and Spain and Andorra to the southwest. The unique geography of France allows it to connect to all major western European nations by the land or the sea. France is connected to the UK by the English Channel Tunnel, and by land to Spain, Italy, Switzerland, Germany, and Belgium. The French coastline provides access by sea to northern Europe, America, and Africa via the North Sea, the Atlantic Ocean, and the Mediterranean.

France is the largest country in western Europe and the second largest country in Europe, with the fifth largest population in Europe. Over two-thirds of France is covered with mountains and hills, with the Alps, Pyrenees, and Vosges mountains the primary ranges. The Vosges mountains lie in northeast France, while the Pyrenees are sprawled along the Spanish border. Europe's highest peak, Mont Blanc, lies in the French Alps near the Italian and Swiss borders. Major rivers include the west-flowing Seine, the Loire, and the Garonne; the south-flowing Rhone that drains into the Mediterranean; and the Rhine River that forms the border with Germany. The topography chiefly comprises flat plains or gently rolling hills in the north and west, while the rest of the country is mountainous. It lies midway between the equator and the North Pole and enjoys a temperate climate. France generally has cool winters and mild summers, but the warm Gulf Stream current along the Mediterranean coast provides for mild winters and hot summers in the coastal region.

History

The history of France is filled with tales of aristocrats, wars, and revolutions that have played a major role in its emergence as one of the most developed nations of the world.

In ancient times, France was a part of Celtic territory called Gaul. The Romans, led by Julius Caesar, captured Gaul in the first century B.C. During the second century A.D. Christianity gained a strong foothold in this region and thus became the major religion.

During the fourth century A.D., a German tribe called the Franks captured the eastern side of Gaul, along the banks of the River Rhine. By the seventh century, the entire region was taken over by the Franks. The Treaty of Verdun and the division of Charlemagne's Carolingian Empire into three parts (East Francia, Middle Francia, and West Francia) in 843 A.D. actually led to the emergence of France as a separate country. Over the years the country was ruled by the monarchy and royal dynasties like the Capetians, Valois, and finally the Bourbons.

The French monarchy reached its height in the seventeenth century during the reign of King Louis XIV. During his rule, the country became extremely powerful. Trade flourished and the country became a center for art and culture. The rule of the French monarchy, however, came to an end after the French Revolution of 1789, and the execution of the King Louis XVI and his wife, Queen Marie Antoinette. The French Revolution was a major event in the history of France and to the rest of the world. In 1799, Napoleon Bonaparte took control of France; he ruled from 1804 to 1814. After his defeat in the Battle of Waterloo in 1815, the monarchy was reestablished.

France had numerous colonial territories and it had the second largest holdings after those of the British Empire. France's ultimate victory in World War I and World War II after initially being invaded and partly occupied by German forces did not prevent the loss of the colonial empire, the comparative economic status, population, and status as a dominant nation state. Over the years the country has fought many wars, including the French Indochina War and a war with Algeria. France signed a peace declaration with Algeria in 1962 to bring an end to its colonial rule in that country.

In recent decades, France's reconciliation and cooperation with Germany have proved central to the political and economic integration of the evolving European Union, including the introduction of the euro in January 1999. France has been at the forefront of European Union member states seeking to exploit the momentum of the monetary union to create a more unified and capable European Union based on political, defense, and security apparatus. However, the French electorate voted against ratification of the European Constitutional Treaty in May 2005.

France

The People

Until recently French culture has been characterized by tradition and continuity. Although much of the French identity comes from past glories and long-standing customs, the country has been faced in the last few decades with the realization that neither its history nor its traditional ways will be enough to keep the country peaceful and productive or a vital force on the international stage.

The twentieth century was a difficult one for France. The country that produced Charlemagne and Napoleon was occupied by Germany in two world wars, requiring rescue by nations it had seen as its cultural inferior. The country that had produced great humanitarians such as Voltaire and Rousseau was the only European nation to collaborate actively and officially with the Nazis. Its status after the war was questioned.

Though Charles de Gaulle was able to rekindle a sense of French pride, the post-WWII era was again a struggle. The student protests of 1968, which quickly grew to involve a wider range of people than had ever participated in protests before, raised issues that have not been fully resolved even today. Likewise, the dark side of French pride, the tolerance of intolerance, still has a negative impact on millions of French citizens. Yet France, according to historians and social scientists, seems more ready than ever to tackle its social issues, rather than assuming that the nation can continue as it always has.

The Food

Since the sixteenth century, French cooking has been celebrated as the Western world's finest. Recipes prepared in the traditional style of haute cuisine, as developed by such renowned chefs as Jean-Anthelme Brillat-Savarin (1755–1826) or Georges Auguste Escoffier (1847–1935) are still featured in distinguished restaurants. This style features meats and fish prepared with sauces containing cream, egg yolks, sugar, brandy, flour, and other starches. Today's concern with dieting and health has produced a new style of cooking. Nouvelle cuisine, said to have been introduced by Paul Bocuse, emphasizes lighter, subtler tastes, requiring the best and the freshest raw ingredients. The term itself was created by two well-known food critics, Henri Gault and Christian Millau.

The diversity of French cuisine is due to the cultural influences and ingredients available in France's different regions. The French landscape is so varied that an accurate description requires breaking it down into nine separate geographic categories: the Paris Basin, northeastern France, the Rhone-Saone Valley, the Alps-Jura region, the Central Plateau, northwestern France, the Riviera, the Acquitaine Basin, and the Pyrenees Mountains.

THE PARIS BASIN

The Paris Basin occupies north central France. This vast fertile plain is one of the world's richest farming areas. The city of Paris has played a unique role in French life. Ever since the Middle Ages, it has been not only the nation's capital, but also the leading center of culture, learning, the arts, fashion, commerce, and industry. Though there is no single culinary style, the area is referred to as "the garden of France." Numerous types of fruit and vegetables are grown, and fruit tarts are common—tarte tatin originated in the Loire River Valley in the south of the Basin. Game, from the Sologne forests in the east of the region, is a common ingredient in the region's excellent charcuterie.

Freshwater fish, particularly pike, shad, and eels, caught from the Loire and its tributaries are featured widely on menus. These are often accompanied by beurre blanc, an emulsified sauce made with a reduction of acid (which may be vinegar, wine, or citrus juice) and shallots into which cold, whole butter is blended.

Even better known as one of the world's premier wine-growing areas is the nearby province of Burgundy, east of the Loire valley. Few red wines produced anywhere are more cherished than Burgundirs. People eat well in Burgundy and the region boasts some of the best produce and meats. The cuisine is delicate without being overly fussy. Common components are pork, beef, chicken, onions, mushrooms, garlic, snails, and cream. Many of the traditional dishes are well known outside France, such as *coq au vin* (chicken in a red wine, mushroom, and onion sauce) and *bœuf à la bourguignonne* (beef stewed in red wine with mushrooms and onions). Other regional specialities include *marcassin farci au saucisson* (young wild boar with a sausage stuffing), *escargots à la bourguignonne* (snails raised on grape leaves, sautéed and served with parsley and garlic butter) and meat or fish dishes *en meurette* (in a red wine sauce). This region is also known for its wide variety of mustards; the city of Dijon is located in this region. Kir—blackcurrant liqueur mixed with white wine—is an aperitif from Burgundy.

Champagne is another province along Paris Basin's easternmost sections renowned for its vineyards. Its gently rolling terrain and chalky soil are ideal for cultivation of the grapes from which the celebrated sparkling wine is produced. The *méthode champenoise* for making champagne was invented by Dom Pérignon, a monk. Once the wine has been fermented and blended, a mix of cane sugar and yeast is added into the bottle to induce a second fermentation and produce the sparkle. It is left to mature for between one and five years, then the cork and any sediment is removed and the sweetness adjusted before being recorked and sold.

The Paris Basin's western region is along the Belgian border so there are also rich dishes of Flemish influence. The cooler climate lends itself to growing potatoes, cabbages, beets, watercress, endive, and leeks. *Flamiche* is a simple dish of leeks cooked with cream and eggs in a pastry crust. *Endive flamande* is made by wrapping endives in ham and serving them with a white sauce. *Carbonnade de boeuf* is another classic dish, where the beef is slowly braised in onions and beer. A stew called *chaudrée* (hence the word chowder) makes good use of the region's fish. The city of Lille is an important producer of charcuterie and beer. Pastries are quite basic, with *gaufres* (waffles eaten with sugar and fresh cream) being among the best known. In Champagne, *biscuits de Reims* are sweet, paper-thin macaroons.

NORTHEASTERN FRANCE

Northeastern France consists mainly of the provinces of Alsace and Lorraine. Control of Alsace and Lorraine has gone back and forth between France and Germany over the centuries and this influence is evident in many of the local dishes. Pickled cabbage and pork are common. *Baeckeoffe* is a stew of marinated beef, pork, and mutton stewed with onions and potatoes in wine. *Choucroute alsacienne* is pickled cabbage flavored with juniper berries and served with sausages, bacon, or pork knuckle. The locals also enjoy all kinds of savory pies and tarts, the best-known being *tarte flambée* or *flammekuche,* which is a thin layer of pastry topped with cream, onion, and bacon and cooked in a wood-fired oven. The region is ideal for growing grains, which give Alsace a well-known reputation for the excellence and variety of its breads. Hops are also grown here and Alsace is the only region in France that brews beer. The fruit orchards, besides giving wonderful fruits, also foster the production of a variety of fruit-flavored brandies, known as *eaux-de-vie.*

From Lorraine comes the most famous of all, *quiche Lorraine.* Originally, this dish was made without cheese, but most recipes now include it and also add vegetables, seafood, or ham to the basic mix of eggs and cream.

THE RHONE-SAONE VALLEY

Located in east central France, Lyons is this region's most important city. It dates back to the time of the ancient Gauls and today it ranks as France's second city. The Lyonnaise take pride in their city's reputation as a world capital of good eating and it is said that gastronomy is to Lyon what haute couture fashion is to Paris. The most obvious reason for Lyon's reputation as a leading gastronomic center of the world is that it is so well situated: it has access to the very best food supplies. It is near the Dauphine, one of the first regions of France where potatoes were successfully cultivated (in the seventeenth century). It is near the Charolais for beef, the farms of Bresse for poultry, the Auvergne for lamb, the lakes of the Dombes and Bourget for carp and frogs, Savoy for mushrooms, and innumerable rivers for fish.

It was a native of Lyons, the renowned chef Anthelme Brillat-Savarin, who said, "Tell me what you eat and I'll tell you who you are." Lyon's culinary fame is based on two main styles of cooking: hearty home cooking that uses seasonal vegetables and organ meats (offal, tripe, chicken gizzards, liver, and hearts), and the loftier traditional cuisine.

Classic bistros known as bouchons are an integral part of the gastronomic heritage of Lyon. *Bouchons* do not have the reputation of being fancy restaurants, though they offer a wide variety of meals, among which are the famous *pâté aux foies de volailles* (chicken liver pate), *quenelles* (light dumplings made of meat, fish, or cheese), *sauce nantua* (a crayfish butter béchamel), and *cervelle de canut* (traditionally, a farmhouse-style cheese would be used for this cream cheese spread/dip; the rather derogatory name translates as "silk weaver's brains," and is thought to reflect the poor regard in which the richer community held weavers). Bouchons offer a warm, convivial atmosphere, where customers sit elbow to elbow with a glass pot, the quintessential Lyon container filled with local wine.

THE ALPS-JURA REGION

The mountainous Alps-Jura region is directly east of the Rhone valley. It borders on Switzerland and Italy. Rising to the south are the lofty French Alps. The Ognon and Doubs rivers, as well as the mountain lakes, provide a plentiful supply of fish, particularly salmon, and the forests are a good source of game. Fondue, and cheese in general, is common. For example, *brochette jurassienne* (pieces of cheese wrapped in ham and fried on a skewer) or *escalope de veau belle comtoise* (veal escalopes covered in breadcrumbs and baked with slices of ham and cheese) are classic dishes. Other specialities include *brési* (cured beef in thin slices) and *poulet au vin jaune* (chicken and morels in a creamy sauce flavored with the local wine).

THE CENTRAL PLATEAU

Largest of the geographic regions, sprawling across south central France, is the forbidding, thinly populated Massif Central, or Central Plateau. It takes up one-sixth of the entire country. The province of Auvergne is a remote and rural region; its traditional cuisine is simple and filling. Dishes often feature a combination of pork, cabbage, potatoes, and cheese, such as *potée auvergnate,* a souplike stew of pork and cabbage with potatoes, onions, turnips, leeks, and garlic. A common accompaniment to meat is *truffade,* mashed potatoes made with cheese and then fried with bacon and garlic. A well-known local specialty is Roquefort cheese, made from sheep's milk. Roquefort-sur-Soulzon, the village where the cheese is produced, sits on top of a cliff. The cheese is aged in deep caves, noted for their high humidity and cool, even temperatures all year—46°F. A penicillin fungus that grows naturally in the caves is added to the cheese to produce its unique flavor. The process dates back to Roman times.

NORTHWESTERN FRANCE

Northwestern France is dominated by the rocky Amorican Plateau. The area is largely taken up by the provinces of Normandy and Brittany. Each forms a peninsula protruding into the Atlantic Ocean.

Normandy is famous for raising fine brindled cattle. The milk of Norman cattle is unusually creamy, with a high fat content that is perfect for fatty cheese such as Camembert, as well as the rich, slightly salty Normandy butter. Normandy boasts extensive apple orchards. They produce a special variety of apple too small and bitter tasting for eating; instead, they are used for cider and calvados. Traditional dishes invariably feature creamy sauces laced with apples, cider, or calvados, such as *filet mignon de porc normande* (pork tenderloin cooked with apples and onions in cider and served with caramelized apple rings). The proximity of the sea means that fish and seafood feature commonly on menus. Favorites include *moules à la normande* (mussels in a cream and white wine sauce) and *sole normande* (Dover sole poached in cider and cream with shrimp). There are also some good meats. The lamb and mutton from the Cherbourg peninsula are rated very highly, as are the *andouilles from Vire* (smoked and cooked pork and tripe sausage, usually served cold as a starter). Rouen is known as the gastronomic capital of Normandy, famous for its duck dishes such as duck with cherries and *canard à la Rouennaise*, duck stuffed with its liver and cooked in red wine.

Brittany presents a bleaker landscape. Large areas are too rocky and barren for cultivation, though they do supply sparse grazing for cattle. Brittany tends to set itself apart from the rest of France, so it is surprising that it does not have its own distinctive style of cooking. Generally, Breton cuisine is simple, with little use of sauces, and features much fish and seafood. The only true Breton specialty is the pancake. *Crêperies* are a common sight, offering a range of savory and sweet pancakes (*galettes* and *crêpes,* respectively). The other regional dish is *cotriade,* a fish stew traditionally made from conger eel and the remains of the day's catch. Other specialties include *palourdes farcies* (baked clams stuffed with garlic, herbs, and shallots) or *pot au feu d'homard* (lobster, shrimp, scallop, mussel, and oyster stew). Brittany's young lambs, raised on the salt meadows, are also very good. Cider is the main drink associated with Brittany.

THE RIVIERA

The best-known area within the Mediterranean region is the spectacularly scenic Riviera, with its mountains loping abruptly down to the coastal plain and the popular beaches. Nice and Cannes are the largest resort cities. Not far from the Italian border is glamorous Monte Carlo, capital of the tiny independent principality of Monaco.

France's busiest seaport, Marseilles, stands between the Riviera and the Rhone River. Marseilles is the main point of focus for trade between France, the Mediterranean region, and the vast world to the south and east. The mild Mediterranean climate ensures farmers a longer growing season than elsewhere in France. The lower valley of the Rhone is France's richest garden area, producing peaches, melons, strawberries, and asparagus. Olive and almond groves that are hundreds of years old are scattered across the region. West of the Rhone is an area devoted mostly to vineyards. They produce grapes suitable only for vin ordinaire, a good but inexpensive type of wine that is rarely exported.

Inland lies Provence, a region rich in history and tradition. Provençal cuisine is known for its use of herbs, olive oil, tomatoes, garlic, onions, artichokes, olives, and sweet and hot peppers. Dishes prepared *à la provençale* are made with tomatoes, garlic, olive oil, onions, herbs, and sometimes eggplant, while dishes made *à la niçoise* are similar but also include olives, capers, anchovies, and tarragon. It's not an area famous for its meat dishes, but a winter staple is *boeuf en daube* (beef stewed with red wine, onions, garlic, vegetables, and herbs). Fish and shellfish—sardines, red mullet, tuna, monkfish, sea bass, and anchovies—are commonly found on menus, even inland, and are often accompanied by *raï to* or *rayte* (red wine, tomato, garlic, and ground walnut sauce). Other fish dishes include *bouillabaisse* (stewlike soup with conger eel, scorpion fish, gurnet, and other fish; saffron, fennel, garlic, and bitter orange peel, served with garlic mayonnaise) and *soupe aux poissons* (smooth soup made from white fish and a chile and garlic mayonnaise). Slowly cooked stews such as *estouffade* and *daube* are based on beef or mutton. On the Côte d'Azur, Italian influences are noticeable, with wide use of pasta, especially ravioli and cannelloni, gnocchi, and *pistou* (similar to pesto).

Sharing the Mediterranean climate is the French island of Corsica about 120 miles to the southeast. This mountainous, heavily forested locale permits little farming. Its people fish and raise livestock.

THE AQUITAINE BASIN

The gently rolling Aquitaine Basin occupies the area of southwestern France between the Central Plateau and the Atlantic. Fruit orchards and vineyards fill the river valleys. The region's primary river, the Garrone, flows in a northwesterly direction to the famous harbor of Bordeaux. It has given its name to the famous Bordeaux wines produced from the nearby vineyards. Grapes grown in the Cognac district to the north and the Armagnac district to the south are the raw material for well-known brandies. Bordeaux is known for its meat and its most celebrated dish is *entrecôte marchand de vin* (rib steak cooked in a rich gravy made from Bordeaux wine, butter, shallots, herbs, and bone marrow). Sweet treats include *cannelés* (caramelised brioche-style pastries) and the famous *marrons glacés* (candied chestnuts).

East of Bordeaux is a small agricultural district known as the Périgord. For such a rural region, the cuisine is surprisingly sophisticated. Two common ingredients are truffles (used in soups, sauces, pâtés, stuffing, and in meat preparations) and *foie gras* (enlarged liver of goose or duck that has been force-fed maize). Items on menus that are served *à la périgourdine* are stuffed with, accompanied by, or have a sauce of *foie gras* and truffles. *Ballottine de lièvre á la périgourdine* is hare stuffed with veal, rabbit, or pork, foie gras, and truffles, and flavored with brandy. *Cassoulet périgourdin* is a stew of mutton, haricot beans, garlic sausage, and goose neck stuffed with truffles and *foie gras*. Food is often cooked in goose fat, giving the cuisine its own distinctive taste. Walnut oil is a common salad dressing.

In the southernmost section of the Aquitaine, on the Atlantic coast and in the foothills of the Pyrenees, lives a unique culture, the Basques. They are a people apart from any in France or indeed any in Europe. Their place of origin is unknown. There are about a million Basques, but 90 percent of them live across the border in Spain. Languedoc-Roussillon, Gascony, and Basque country cooking use an abundance of olive oil, tomatoes, peppers, and spicy sausage; their food shares many similarities with that of Spain. *Cassoulet* (a casserole with meat and beans) is Languedoc's signature dish; Roussillon has a similar dish called *ouillade*. There are strong Spanish and Catalan influences in Roussillon too, with tapas-style dishes served in many wine bars. Gascon dishes are kept simple but hearty with lots of meat, fat, and salt. *Garbure* is a thick stew made with vegetables, herbs, spices, and preserved meats. *Poulet Basque* is a chicken stew with tomatoes, onions, peppers, and white wine; piperade is Basque comfort cooking (peppers, onions, and tomatoes cooked with ham and eggs). *Chipirones* (squid cooked in its own ink) is featured widely on menus along the coast. A common sweet is *gâteau basque* (black cherry pie). The locally prepared Bayonne ham is usually eaten sliced with bread but is also the basis of *jambon á la Bayonnaise* (ham braised in Madeira).

THE PYRENEES MOUNTAINS

The Pyrenees Mountains loom south of the Aquitaine Basin. They form a range running nearly 280 miles in an east-west direction. With many peaks rising above 10,000 feet, the Pyrenees make a formidable barrier between France and Spain. Cattle and sheep graze along these hillsides. The cuisine, drawing on the wealth of local produce, has strong flavors. Particularly in the Pyrenees, Catalan dishes such as *boles de picoulat* (meatballs made with onions and olives in a sauce of tomatoes and herbs) and *saucisse à la catalane* (sausage fried with garlic, orange peel, and herbs) feature widely on menus. Game such as guinea fowl and partridge is common, as is trout from the mountain streams. Along the coast in the Mediterranean seacoast town of Collioure, dishes are served in a sauce of anchovy-and-garlic-flavored mayonnaise.

Glossary

Aiguillettes Long, thin strips of duck breast.

Aioli A sauce from Provence, similar to mayonnaise but heavily flavored with garlic; the Spanish version is called ali-oil (garlic oil).

Allspice A berry from the allspice tree. Pungent and aromatic, primarily used in pickling liquids, marinades, and spice cakes and fruitcakes.

Americaine Refers to a garnish of tomatoes and garlic, originally created for a lobster dish.

Amoricaine Refers to dishes that originated in Amorica, the Roman name for Brittany.

Ancienne Usually refers to dishes with a long history; often two or more garnishes are combined.

Andalouse Usually refers to a dish characterized by tomato paste, sweet peppers, and chipolata sausages.

Anise Sweet-smelling herb with feathery leaves producing aniseed; anise is the true taste of licorice.

AOC Appelation d'Origine Controlee, which roughly translates to "term of origin," is a certification granted to certain French wines, cheeses, butters, and other agricultural products by a government bureau known as the *Institut National des Appellations d'Origine* (INAO). Under French law, it is illegal to manufacture and sell a product under one of the AOC-controlled names if it does not comply with the criteria established by the AOC.

Argenteuil Refers to a dish that includes asparagus. The Argenteuil region (a suburb of Paris) has sandy soil in which the best asparagus used to grow.

Aspic Clear jelly used to coat cold foods.

Attelets Small skewers with ornamental heads used to decorate very elaborate dishes.

Aurore (Sunrise) A sauce or dish flavored with tomato paste or tomatoes.

Babas Small raisin-filled yeast cakes that are soaked in rum-flavored sugar syrup after baking.

Batterie de Cuisine French term for cooking equipment.

Bavarian Cream (Bavarois) A rich egg custard stiffened or set with gelatin and whipped cream added.

Béchamel A white sauce made from milk infused with flavoring and thickened with a roux.

Beignets Light French fritters made from choux pastry, or dipped in batter and deep-fat-fried.

Bigarade Means bitter.

Bisque A highly seasoned thick, creamy soup, classically of pureed crustaceans, thickened with rice.

Blanquette A stew of lamb, veal, chicken, or rabbit with a rich sauce made from the cooking liquid, often garnished with small onions and mushrooms.

Bleu A method of cooking trout in a vinegar-flavored court bouillon. Fresh-killed trout take on a bluish tinge.

Bombe A molded ice cream that is made in a traditional bomb-shaped mold, almost spherical with a flat bottom.

Bonne Femme Literally "good woman"; refers to traditional garnish of onion, bacon, and potato.

Bordelaise A dish containing red or white Bordeaux wine and beef marrow.

Bouillabaisse A Mediterranean fish stew that originated in Marseilles. Traditionally served in two dishes, one for the pieces of fish and the other containing slices of French bread with the broth poured on top.

Boulangere French for "baker"; refers to meat or poultry cooked on a bed of sliced potatoes. At one time, small houses in country districts of France had no ovens, so the Sunday lunch of leg of lamb was set in a dish with sliced potatoes and onions, which was left with the local baker to cook while the family was at church.

Bourgeoise Garnish of diced bacon, baby onions, and carrots cut to a consistent size.

Bourguignonne Cooked in the style of Burgundy, with mushrooms, onions, and red Burgundy wine.

Braisiére The traditional pan for braising, designed for kitchens that did not have an oven. The pan has an indented lid, in which live coals were placed so that the pan was heated from the top as well as from the bottom.

Brandade A mousse of salt cod (morue). *Brandade de morue* originally comes from Nimes in the Languedoc region of southern France.

Bretonne Cooked in the style of Brittany, on the northwest coast of France; beans are usually included in the dish.

Brioche Rich yeast dough; high egg and butter content give it a rich and tender crumb.

Broche To cook on a spit.

Brochette (en) Term for small pieces threaded on a skewer and broiled.

Butter

> **Beurre Blanc** White butter sauce.
>
> **Beurre Manie (Kneaded Butter)** A liaison of twice as much butter as flour worked together into an uncooked paste, added in small pieces to thicken a liquid at the end of cooking.
>
> **Beurre Noir** Also called black butter, it is heated until the solids turn a darker brown, then a few drops of vinegar are added.
>
> **Beurre Noisette** Literally, "hazelnut butter," this is melted butter that's cooked until the milk solids turn a very light brown, and the butter gives off a nutty aroma. When clarified at this point, this butter is called *ghee* in Indian cooking.

Calvados Apple brandy.

Canape Small open-faced, garnished pieces of bread or toast, they are always small (one or two bites) and served as an appetizer or with cocktails.

Carbonade Originally a dish that was simmered over coals (charbon), now it refers to a rich beef stew made with ale or beer.

Cardinal A dish characterized by a sauce with a red color; for savory dishes the sauce usually contains lobster coral (roe), tomato paste, or pimiento; and for sweet dishes a strawberry or raspberry sauce.

Cassolettes Containers made from pastry or vegetables such as cucumber.

Cassoulet A rich, slow-cooked bean stew or casserole originating in the southwest of France, typically containing pork sausages, pork, goose, duck, and sometimes mutton; pork skin (*couennes*); and white haricot beans.

Celeriac (Celery Root) Large knobby root resembling a turnip or rutabaga with a taste of celery.

Cepes Wild mushrooms; known as porcini mushrooms in Italy and *Steinpilzen* in Germany.

Chasseur Means "hunter-style"; refers to a mushroom garnish flavored with shallots and white wine.

Chaudfroid Means "hot-cold"; typically refers to a cold dish that is first coated with a cold velouté or béchamel-based sauce, then coated with a layer of aspic.

Cheese

Abondance Cow's milk cheese with both a fruity and nutty flavor and a unique aroma.

Banon Goat's milk cheese, a mild soft cheese with a nutty flavor and a firm supple texture. As it ripens, the surface of the cheese takes on the color of a leaf, and the odor of wet earth.

Beaufort Cow's milk cheese, aromatic, fruity, and vegetable-like.

Bleu d'Auvergne Cow's milk blue cheese with a spicy, nutty strong flavor.

Bleu de Gex, Bleu du Haut-Jura Cow's milk, blue cheese, soft and creamy, sometimes a bit crumbly; it is mild with a hint of hazelnut.

Bleu des Causses Cow's milk blue cheese; the flavor is spicy, nutty, and strong.

Brie The name is applied to big, round, soft cheeses with white mold. On average they have a diameter of 28 cm. The taste is aromatic, with mushroom and hazelnut overtones.

Brie de Meaux Cow's milk soft cheese with a hazelnut, herb, lightly acidic and fruity taste, known as "the cheese of kings."

Brie de Melun Known as the "little brother" of Brie de Meaux, it is small in size. Its aroma is much stronger, more robust, and saltier. It has a slightly bitter taste that, if left to unfold, develops into a completely soft, hazelnut and fruit flavor.

Brillat-Savarin Soft, bloomy-rind cow's milk cheese; it has a finely acidic taste with tender or creamy consistency.

Brocciu Ewe's and goat's milk cheese, with a very creamy and fresh taste.

Cabecou du Perigourda Raw goat's milk cheese; the taste is goaty and soft on the palate.

Camembert de Normandie Cow's milk soft cheese, fresh, lightly acidic, ripe, fruity, mushroom flavored. Camembert is perfectly ripe when the body is the same supple, butter-smooth texture throughout.

Cantal Firm cow's milk cheese with a taste of hazelnut and fresh milk.

Chabichou A whole-milk goat cheese and one of the best French goat cheeses. It has a light and goaty aroma. It is very creamy and soft.

Comté The very first cheese to gain French AOC status, protecting its manufacturing and maturing methods. It is a cow's milk, pressed, and cooked cheese, with a nutty and rich but clean flavor, with a fruity aftertaste.

Crottin de Chavigol Small cylindrical shaped cheese, the flavor is subtle and slightly nutty. Young cheese is solid and compact, as it ages it becomes crumbly and the mold on the rind matures into a bluish color.

Emmental Has been produced since at least the thirteenth century in the Rhône-Alpes region. It is a hard cheese made from cow's milk, cooked and pressed. There are many holes (also called eyes) inside it. A good Emmental must have at least three holes every 6 inches. Its taste is fruity with a subtle nutty core, and its aroma is very delicate.

Fourme d'Ambert A tangy representative of the French variety of blue mold cheeses. It has quite strong mold veins and a yellowish-gray rind. Its flavor is mild, with light nut and mushroom overtones.

Laguiole Pressed, uncooked cow's milk cheese with an aromatic, lightly acidic, herbal, strong, tangy-sour taste.

Langres Soft cheese, with red culture; the rind has an intense smell. The flavor is full but quite salty.

Maconnais Goat cheese, which becomes harder, saltier, and tangy with ripening. It has an ivory-colored rind which becomes brown with age. Soft cheese with a fresh milky flavor when young, becoming dry and crumbly with maturity.

Morbier Cow's milk cheese; melting, lightly fruity and aromatic are all characteristics of this sliced cheese with a beige-colored rind and ivory-colored dough.

Neufchâtel The slight tangy and sour soft cheese with white mold is available in six different shapes and sizes. Especially characteristic of Neufchâtel is the shape of a heart.

Ossau Iraty A ewe's milk cheese from the Basque region. Nutty, aromatic, vegetable-like taste.

Pasteurized Camembert Less strong and more neutral than Camembert de Normandie.

Pélardon Pélardon of the Cévennes is one of the oldest goat's milk cheeses in Europe; it has a goat's milk flavor, light and nutty.

Pont-l'Eveque This soft, washed-rind cow's milk cheese may be the oldest cheese variety from Normandy that is still produced today. It is a very flavorful cheese, with a lightly herbal taste.

Pouligny Saint-Pierre With a characteristic cone shape, this goat cheese has the nickname pyramid or Eiffel tower. It has a smooth goat's milk taste, a bit sour, and a nutty aroma.

Reblochon Cow's milk cheese, full-flavored, buttery, and creamy.

Rocamadour Goat's milk cheese, with a fresh, lightly acidic, heavy, ripe, and nutty taste.

Roquefort Ewe's milk cheese, from the south of France, characterized by its very white body pierced by blue-green mold veins. It is exceptionally smooth and rich on the palate. It has a ewe's milk flavor, tangy, salty, and strong. Even today, this cheese can only be ripened in the natural stone caves of Mont Combalou in the community of Roquefort-sur-Sulzon.

Saint-Maure de Touraine The most obvious way to identify this cheese is by the straw through its center. The straw is there to keep the roll-formed cheese together and to allow air through to the core. This goat's milk cheese has a subtle flavor with a slight hint of mushroom.

Saint-Nectaire The supple, white center melts in the mouth and unfolds a fine, bitter flavor with a touch of salt, walnuts, and spices.

Salers Cow's milk, pressed, uncooked cheese that is firm, very aromatic, and fruity.

Tome des Bauges (or Tome de Savoie) Cow's milk cheese, with a semisoft texture and a mild, creamy taste.

Valencay Goat's milk cheese, with a mild, lightly nutty taste.

Chervil Herb that is a member of the parsley family. It is sweeter and more aromatic than parsley.

Clamart A dish garnished with peas, often piled onto artichoke bottoms. Clamart is a suburb of Paris where peas used to be grown.

Compote Term for fresh or dried fruit poached in a thick simple syrup to which flavorings may be added.

Coulis French for a puree of any liquid pulp.

Cream of Tartar Juice from grapes that is pressed out after fermentation, then refined to powder. It is used as a leavening agent, to keep egg whites firm and to cut the grain of sugar syrup and prevent it from crystallizing.

Crecy A dish characterized by carrots.

Crepe A very thin French pancake that can be sweet or savory.

Cressonniere Refers to a dish garnished or made with watercress.

Croissants French pastries that are made into the shape of crescents.

Croustade A case made from pastry or bread that is filled with a savory mixture.

Crudites Raw vegetables that are arranged and served as an appetizer.

Darne "Slice" or "slab" in French; refers to the center cut of a large fish, usually salmon, cod, or haddock.

Degorger To remove impurities and strong flavors before cooking.

Diable (à la) Means "deviled"; refers to dishes flavored with spices and prepared hot sauces.

Dieppose (à la) Food prepared in the style of Dieppe, a French port on the northern coast, known for its shrimp and mussels, usually combined with mushrooms and white wine.

Dijonnaise (à la) A dish that includes Dijon-style mustard.

Doria (à la) A dish garnished with cucumber.

Dubarry (à la) Refers to cauliflower.

Duglere A dish that includes a velouté sauce with tomatoes and parsley.

Duxelles Finely chopped mixture of mushrooms, shallots, and herbs, cooked in butter and used to flavor soups, sauces, and stuffings.

Entremet Means "between dishes"; used to refer to all vegetables and salads served as the second course, except for the meat. Now *entremets* is used to refer to any dessert (served after the cheese in France).

Espagnole Basic brown sauce on which all other brown sauces are based.

Financiere (à la) Literally, "banker's style," referring to a rich garnish of kidneys, sweetbreads, mushrooms, and quenelles.

Fines Herbes A classic blend of chopped herbs that includes chervil, tarragon, and chives. Note that parsley is not considered a fine herb.

Flamande (à la) In the Flemish style, normally a garnish of braised root vegetables.

Fleuron Small crescents of cooked puff pastry used as a garnish.

Florentine (à la) A dish with spinach.

Foie Gras The liver of a goose that has been specially fattened.

Frangipane An almond, sugar, and butter mixture used in cakes and pastries.

Frappe Iced dessert.

Fricassee A stew of white meat, poultry, fish, or vegetables with a white or velouté sauce.

Galantine Boned chicken, turkey, duck, or game bird or a boned breast of veal, stuffed, rolled, tied, and poached. Served cold.

Galette Any sweet or savory mixture that is shaped in a flat round.

Gateau French for "cake"; refers to the classic French cakes with genoise base.

Genoise A sponge cake, richer and with a closer textured than regular sponge cake; made in the same manner but without fat.

Georgette Dishes with baked potato.

Gougere Savory choux pastry mixed with cheese, then baked plain or filled with a savory mixture.

Grand'mere Home-style dishes made with potatoes, onions, and bacon.

Gratin (au) To cook food covered in crumbs, butter, sauce, or grated cheese in the oven. *Gratiner* means to brown cooked food under the broiler.

Grenadin A small piece of veal resembling a tournedos steak, usually taken from the round.

Hongrois Dish using Hungarian paprika in a sour cream sauce.

Jardiniere French for "garden-style"; a garnish of small carrots, peas, string beans, button onions, and small potatoes.

Jus (au) The term used for meat served in its own natural cooked juices.

Lyonnaise (à la) Dishes made with onion and potato garnish.

Macedoine Either a mixture of diced or sliced cooked vegetables served in a dressing, or uncooked fruits in a syrup or liqueur.

Madeleine Shell-shaped light sponge cakes, made in special Madeleine pans that give the characteristic shape.

Marmite Stockpot; originally the name of the French pot used for making pot-au-feu. Petite marmite is a clear soup made in a marmite pot.

Matelote French name (meaning "sailor style") for a fish stew made with wine, the dish may be made with veal or poultry.

Menagere (à la) Means "housewife" and refers to simply prepared dishes like mashed potatoes or meat garnished with carrots, turnips, and potatoes.

Meunière The term used to describe sautéing fish in butter and completing the dish with meunière butter—butter cooked to a nut-brown color, flavored with fresh chopped herbs and lemon juice.

Milanaise (à la) In the style of Milan; dishes with macaroni, cheese, tomato, and ham.

Morels (Morilles) Wild mushrooms with a rich aromatic flavor.

Mousse A sweet smooth mixture, airy and rich. Savory mousses set with gelatin are always served chilled.

Nantua (à la) Name given to dishes that include a shrimp or crayfish puree or garnish.

Navarin A lamb stew cooked with root vegetables.

Niçoise (à la) A dish characterized by tomatoes, anchovies, tuna fish, garlic, and black olives.

Nivernaise (à la) Dish that includes carrots as a major ingredient.

Normande (à la) Refers to braised fish dishes with a cream (Normande) sauce. With meat or chicken it includes apple cider and Calvados (apple brandy).

Orloff A presentation for veal where the roasted meat is carved and each slice is coated with mornay or soubise sauce, and then reassembled.

Orly Fish or meat coated with a rich batter and fried crisp.

Panada A binding agent of choux pastry, thick béchamel sauce or bread crumbs used to thicken.

Papillote (en) French for "cocoon," it means to wrap in a buttered paper case, then cook and serve in the case.

Parfaits Rich iced dessert, with an egg mousse base and lightly flavored whipped cream. May be layered with meringues or ladyfingers.

Parmentier Dishes garnished with potatoes.

Pâté A savory mixture usually made from ground meat.

Patisserie A small pastry or pastry shop.

Paupiette A piece of meat, fish, or poultry that is filled with a stuffing, then rolled into a small cylinder and cooked.

Paysanne Peasant fashion or homey cooking style.

Perigourdine (à la) Dishes prepared with truffles.

Petits Fours Small pastries that are easy to eat, in one or two bites.

Pilaf Rice dish made from long-grain rice sautéed with onions in fat, and then cooked in stock.

Piquante A brown sauce flavored with capers and gherkins; also means a sharp or stimulating flavor.

Poeler Literally, "to cook in a frying pan."

Princesse (à la) Dishes garnished with asparagus tips.

Printanier (à la) Garnish of fresh spring vegetables.

Provencale (à la) Dishes using tomatoes, peppers, eggplants, garlic, olives, and other specialties of the Provence region of southern France.

Quatre Epices (Four Spices) A French spice mixture consisting of white pepper, ginger, nutmeg, and cloves.

Quenelles Oval dumplings made from fish, chicken, rabbit, or veal. A mousseline mixture with the addition of egg whites, seasoning, and cream, poached and served with sauce.

Quiche A savory egg custard. The most famous version is quiche Lorraine made with cheese, ham, or bacon and sometimes onions.

Ragout A slow-cooked stew that is not thickened.

Reine (à la) Sauce suprême with a puree of white meat chicken.

Remoulade Mayonnaise-based sauce.

Ravenir To fry lightly without really cooking.

Rillette Type of pork pâté made from unsmoked pork belly and goose, rabbit, chicken, or turkey.

Rissoler To brown slowly in fat.

Rossini A dish made with small cuts of meat, foie gras, and truffles served with a Madeira sauce.

Salmis A form of ragout (stew) made from feathered game or poultry that is lightly roasted, cut up, and gently simmered.

Salpicon Mixture of ingredients that have been cut into shreds or strips, often bound with a rich white or brown sauce.

Shallot A member of the lily family, closely related to the onion. Their small bulbs usually sport a papery, reddish-brown skin and a white interior flesh that has a sweeter flavor than even mild onions.

Socle Means "base" in French, name given to edible food that forms a platform on a serving dish.

Sorrel Dark green long, narrow, tender, succulent leaves with a slightly acid tang or lemony flavor.

Soubise Garnish or flavoring of pureed or finely sliced onions, normally mixed with rice.

Souse Food covered in wine vinegar or wine and spices, and cooked slowly; it is cooled in the same liquid. Sousing gives the food a pickled flavor.

Supreme All the white meat on the chicken from the breast down to the wing bone, removed from the bone in one piece.

Tournedos Steak cut from the filet. It can be as thick as 2 inches (5 cm), but should be completely trimmed of fat. Typically tied to keep their shape during cooking.

Velouté Basic French sauce made with a roux and white stock; enriched with an egg yolk and cream liaison.

Veronique Refers to a dish containing green grapes.

Vol-au-vent Round case of puff pastry.

Menus and Recipes from France

Endives au Lait d'Amandes Douces

Braised Endive with Almond Cream SERVES 4

AMOUNT	MEASURE	INGREDIENT
8		Small to medium Belgian endives
2 tablespoons	1 ounce, 30 ml	Vegetable oil or peanut oil
1 teaspoon		Granulated sugar
1 tablespoon	$\frac{1}{2}$ ounce, 15 ml	Fresh lemon juice
To taste		Salt
$\frac{1}{2}$ cup	$2\frac{1}{2}$ ounces, 70 g	Blanched slivered almonds
$1\frac{1}{4}$ cups	10 ounces, 300 ml	Heavy cream
$1\frac{1}{2}$ tablespoons	$\frac{3}{4}$ ounce, 22 ml	Butter

PROCEDURE

1 Preheat the oven at 350°F (175°C).

2 Trim the endives; discard any brown outside leaves. Trim $\frac{1}{8}$ inch (.3 cm) from the pointed end. Wash in cold water and drain well. Arrange them tightly in a oiled flameproof pan with oil, sugar, lemon juice, and salt. Add cold water to cover.

3 Place something on top to weight them; cover and bake 30 to 40 minutes or until tender. Check for doneness by piercing the base with a paring knife; the blade should go in easily. When cooked, raise the oven temperature to 400°F (205°C).

4 Drain the endives and pat dry.

5 Combine the almonds and cream and bring slowly to a boil. Simmer 6 to 8 minutes over low heat, making sure the cream does not boil over.

6 Puree the almonds and cream in a blender; strain through a fine sieve, stirring and pressing with a wooden spoon so that as much mixture as possible passes. Correct seasoning and keep warm.

7 Heat the butter over medium heat until it just begins to color. Add endive and sauté until golden-brown on both sides, 6 to 8 minutes.

8 Arrange in a gratin or baking dish, cover with almond cream, and bake 15 minutes or until the cream has thickened.

Consommé Brunoise
Beef Consommé with Vegetables   YIELD: ½ GALLON

AMOUNT	MEASURE	INGREDIENT
I pound		Fresh beef shank meat (coarsely ground)
1½ cups	8 ounces, 224 g	Mirepoix, coarsely ground (½ onion, ¼ carrot. ¼ celery)
I cup	8 ounces, 240 ml	Egg whites, beaten
¾ cup	4 ounces, 112 g	Tomatoes, coarsely chopped
I cup	4 ounces, 112 g	Leeks, chopped
½ cup	4 ounces, 120 ml	Crushed ice
½ teaspoon		Dried thyme leaves
I		Bay leaf
3		Parsley stems
I		Garlic clove
I tablespoon		Whole peppercorns
I		Clove
2½ quarts	80 ounces, 2.4 l	Beef stock, cold
½ cup	2 ounces, 56 g	Onion brulé, chopped
To taste		Salt
Garnish		
⅓ cup each		Brunoise carrot, turnip, celery, and leek

PROCEDURE

1 Combine ground meat, mirepoix, egg whites, tomatoes, leeks, ice, and spices. Mix well, keep chilled.

2 Mix stock into above mixture. Agitate well to distribute ingredients evenly throughout stock to insure better clarification.

3 Place mixture in a heavy-bottomed stockpot.

4 Bring gently to a simmer; stir occasionally until raft forms. Do not stir after the raft has formed.

5 Vent the raft.

6 Simmer carefully for 1½ hours.

7 In the last half hour, make a small hole in the raft and place the onion brulé in the consommé.

8 Strain carefully through several layers of cheesecloth.

9 Degrease, adjust salt.

10 Blanch garnish ingredients in boiling salt water until just cooked, then shock in an ice water bath. Heat in a little consommé and add to soup when serving; each portion requires 2 tablespoons garnish.

11 Add garnish just before serving, and serve hot.

Tomato Clamart   SERVES 4

AMOUNT	MEASURE	INGREDIENT
4	5 × 6 (12.5 cm × 15 cm)	Tomatoes
To taste		Salt and pepper
$\frac{1}{4}$ cup	2 ounces, 60 ml	Butter
$1\frac{1}{4}$ cups	8 ounces, 224 g	Peas, cooked

PROCEDURE

1 Peel the tomatoes, cut off $\frac{1}{4}$ of the top, remove the seeds and juice, and season the inside with salt and pepper. Place in a 350°F (175°C) oven until half cooked.

2 Heat the butter, add the peas, season, and fill tomatoes with the peas.

3 Return to the oven and reheat.

Huîlres Chaudes aux Courgettes
Warm Oysters with Zucchini SERVES 4

AMOUNT	MEASURE	INGREDIENT
12		Large oysters
		If needed, additional oyster liquor
4		Nori sheets, for presentation
1½ cups	9 ounces, 252 g	Zucchini, sliced into very thin rounds ($\frac{1}{8}$ inch, .3 cm), about 10 slices per oyster
½ cup	4 ounces, 120 ml	Heavy cream
1 cup	8 ounces, 240 ml	Butter
4 teaspoons	40 ml	Fresh lemon juice
To taste		Salt, pepper, and cayenne

PROCEDURE

1 Open the oysters, pour their liquor through a cheesecloth-lined strainer into a small heavy saucepan, and reduce over high heat to $\frac{1}{4}$ cup (2 ounces, 60 ml). Set oysters aside until ready to serve.

2 Arrange a sheet of nori on each of the four plates and put the deep halves of the oyster shell on the seaweed, 3 per order.

3 Blanch the zucchini in salted boiling water for 2 minutes and then drain.

FINISHING AND SERVING

1 Bring reduced oyster liquor to a boil and add the cream. Reduce on high heat 1 minute, then whisk in 12 tablespoons (6 ounces, 180 ml) butter, bit by bit, still at a boil. When all the butter is absorbed, add the lemon juice, remove from the heat, and check seasoning.

2 Whisk the sauce 1 minute off the heat. This step is essential so the temperature is reduced or the sauce may separate.

3 Melt remaining butter over medium heat and add the zucchini. Season with salt, pepper, and cayenne to taste. Cook until the zucchini is just warm, then remove from heat.

4   Add the oysters to the butter sauce and heat over very low heat for 30 seconds, shaking the pan in a circular motion while heating the oysters.

5   Place one oyster in each shell.

6   Arrange the zucchini rounds on top of each oyster, overlapping them.

7   Lightly coat with sauce and serve.

Potatoes Parmentier   SERVES 4

AMOUNT	MEASURE	INGREDIENT
2 tablespoons	1 ounce, 30 ml	Vegetable oil
4 tablespoons	2 ounce, 60 ml	Butter
3 cups	16 ounces, 448 g	Russet potatoes, peeled, $\frac{1}{2}$ inch (1.2 cm) cubes
To taste		Salt and pepper
1 tablespoon	4 g	Parsley, chopped

PROCEDURE

1   Over medium heat, combine the oil and butter.

2   Add the potatoes and sauté 10 to 12 minutes, or until an even golden color and completely cooked.

3   When ready to serve, correct seasoning and toss with parsley.

Poulet Sauté Marengo
Chicken Sauté Marengo   SERVES 4

AMOUNT	MEASURE	INGREDIENT
2 tablespoons	1 ounce, 30 ml	Vegetable oil
2 tablespoons	1 ounce, 30 ml	Butter
1 2½ to 3 pound	1.12 kg to 1.34 kg	Chicken, disjointed, (drumstick cut at knuckle, thigh boneless, wing center, wing thick end, breast cut in half)
1 tablespoon		Shallot, minced
1 tablespoon		Garlic, minced
1 tablespoon	½ ounce, 15 ml	Tomato paste
1 cup	6 ounces, 168 g	Tomato, peeled, seeded ¼ inch (.6 cm) dice
½ cup	4 ounces, 120 ml	White wine
1½ cups	12 ounces, 360 ml	Espagnole, demi-glaze or jus lié
1 cup	4 ounces, 112 g	Button mushrooms, washed and trimmed
As needed		Salt and pepper
Garnish		
4		Crayfish tails or 4 large shrimp
2 tablespoons	1 ounce, 30 ml	Stock
4		Eggs
1 tablespoon		Parsley, chopped
4		Bread slices, cut into heart shapes
4 tablespoons	2 ounces, 60 ml	Butter

PROCEDURE

1 Heat oil and butter over medium high heat and brown the chicken pieces on all sides. Remove chicken from the pan; drain and reserve the fat.

2 In the same pan, return 2 tablespoons (1 ounce, 30 ml) reserved fat; add the shallot and garlic; cook 2 minutes or until soft.

3 Add tomato paste, cook 1 to 2 minutes. Add chopped tomato; cook gently, stirring 3 to 4 minutes.

4 Add wine and reduce by half. Add espagnole sauce, return chicken pieces, add mushrooms, and bring to a simmer. Cover and cook slowly 25 to 30 minutes or until the chicken is tender. Remove pieces as they cook.

5   To prepare the garnish, simmer the crayfish tails or shrimp in the stock until just cooked, 2 to 3 minutes; drain and keep warm.

6   Heat the reserved fat and French fry the eggs (cook egg in fat at 160 degrees, very slowly until the whites are creamy and the yolk is hot but still liquid.)

7   Heat the remaining butter and fry the heart-shaped bread slices.

8   Arrange the chicken on a platter, spoon the sauce over.

9   Dip the point of each crouton in the sauce, then into the chopped parsley, and arrange around the edge with the crayfish tails. Place a fried egg on each crouton and serve at once.

Salade Bigouden Lettuce Salad   SERVES 4

AMOUNT	MEASURE	INGREDIENT
2		Boston lettuce heads, washed and dried
6 tablespoons	3 ounces, 90 ml	Cider vinegar
2 tablespoons	1 ounce, 28 g	Granulated sugar

PROCEDURE

1   When ready to serve, tear up the lettuce and toss with the vinegar.

2   Sprinkle the sugar over the lettuce and toss lightly again.

3   Serve as salad course.

Crème Brulée   SERVES 4

AMOUNT	MEASURE	INGREDIENT
2 cups	16 ounces, 480 ml	Heavy cream
6		Egg yolks
$\frac{1}{2}$ cup	4 ounces, 112 g	Granulated sugar
1 teaspoon, or to taste		Vanilla
Pinch		Salt
4 tablespoons	2 ounce, 56 g	Brown sugar

PROCEDURE

1   Place cream in a nonreactive pan and heat to the scalding point; remove from heat.

2   Mix—do not whip—the egg yolks and sugar until combined. Gradually pour in a little of the hot cream to temper the eggs. Add remaining cream, stirring constantly; add vanilla and a pinch of salt; strain.

3   Pour the custard into 4 (5-ounce) ramekins; be sure to fill the forms to the top because, like any custard, it will settle slightly once it is cooked. Place forms in a hotel pan, or other suitable container, and add hot water around the forms to reach halfway up the sides.

4   Bake at 350°F (175°C) for about 30 minutes, or until the custards are set. Do not overcook or you will have a broken and unpleasant finished product.

5   Remove from the water bath and let cool slightly at room temperature, then refrigerate until thoroughly chilled.

6   Spread brown sugar over a sheet pan lined with paper, and dry in the oven for a few minutes. Let cool. Use a rolling pin or dowel to crush the sugar and separate the grains. Reserve.

7   For the presentation, sift or sprinkle just enough of the dry brown sugar on top of the custard to cover. Whip away any sugar that is on the edge of the form. Caramelize the sugar in a salamander or under a broiler or use a torch.

8   Serve plain or garnished with fresh fruit or berries.

Soupe à l'Oignon
French Onion Soup   SERVES 4

AMOUNT	MEASURE	INGREDIENT
$\frac{1}{4}$ cup	2 ounces, 60 ml	Butter
5 cups	16 ounces, 448 g	Onions, peeled, thinly sliced
2 tablespoons	$\frac{1}{2}$ ounce, 14 g	All-purpose flour
$\frac{3}{4}$ cup	6 ounces, 180 ml	White wine
$1\frac{1}{4}$ quarts	40 ounces, 1.2 l	Beef stock
1		Bouquet garni (recipe follows)
8		Slices French baguette
$\frac{1}{2}$ cup	2 ounces, 56 g	Gruyère cheese, grated
Bouquet Garni		
2		Leek, green parts only, 4-inch (10 cm) pieces
1		Bay leaf
3		Fresh sprigs thyme
4		Large fresh sprigs parsley
1		Celery stalk

PROCEDURE

1 To prepare bouquet garni, lay herbs on one piece of leek green and cover with remaining piece of leek. Tie securely with kitchen string, leaving a length of string attached so the bouquet garni can be easily retrieved.

2 Heat butter over medium heat. Add onions and cook until tender and golden brown, 15 to 20 minutes.

3 Add the flour and cook 2 minutes, stirring.

4 Add wine, bring to a boil, reduce heat, and simmer 2 minutes. Gradually add the stock. Add bouquet garni and bring to a boil. Reduce to a simmer; cover and cook 30 minutes.

5 To serve, add two slices of bread to each soup bowl and sprinkle with cheese. Pour the boiling soup over the bread and cheese. Or toast the bread slices and float on top of the soup and sprinkle with cheese. Broil unit the cheese melts.

Émincés de Rognons de Veau
Sliced Veal Kidneys SERVES 4

Veal kidneys have nothing in common with the taste of lamb, pork, or beef kidneys. Kidneys should be cooked a few minutes only at the highest possible heat. They should be pink in the middle. Drain the kidney in a sieve for a few minutes (pink liquid will run out of the kidneys and should be discarded). Veal kidneys must be served pink; if overcooked they become chewy and lose their delicate flavor.

AMOUNT	MEASURE	INGREDIENT
2 each	10 ounces, 280 g	Veal kidneys (total 20 ounces, 560 g), as clean as possible, in their own suet, which should be white and crumbly
To taste		Salt and pepper
10 tablespoons	5 ounces, 150 ml	Butter
20 each		Shallots, peeled whole
4 tablespoons	2 ounces, 60 ml	Madeira wine
$\frac{3}{4}$ cup	6 ounces, 180 ml	Beef stock
$\frac{1}{2}$ cup	1 ounce, 28 g	Flat-leaved parsley
2 each		Garlic cloves, mashed whole

PROCEDURE

1. Remove the outer membrane from the kidneys with the point of a paring knife. Butterfly the kidney into lengthwise halves and remove most of the strip of fat and gristle that runs through the middle. Season with salt and pepper.

2. Use a small cast-iron pan (if possible), heat over high heat 2 tablespoons (1 ounce 30 ml) butter to brown the kidneys. Brown on all sides and move to a 450°F (230°C) oven. Cook 10 to 15 minutes, turning frequently.

3. Remove from oven, set kidneys aside, and cover to keep warm. Pour out all the fat and replace with 4 tablespoons (2 ounces, 60 ml) butter, and then add the shallots.

4. Cook shallots in oven until soft. Crush to a puree using a fork. The sugar they contain will bind the kidney juices and caramelize slightly.

5   Stir in the Madeira and then add the stock, a little at a time. Reduce to sauce consistency, then strain. Whisk in 1 ounce (30 ml) butter and correct seasoning.

6   Discard any juices that have accumulated around the kidneys. Slice into medium to thin slices. Arrange on a plate and brush with a little melted butter.

7   Blanch the parsley in boiling salted water, then dry on a cloth. Melt 1 ounce (30 ml) of butter, sauté mashed garlic cloves for 30 seconds, and remove them. Add parsley, stirring continuously until just crisp.

8   Serve kidneys with sauce spooned over and parsley garnish.

Navarin d'Agneau Lamb Stew   SERVES 4

AMOUNT	MEASURE	INGREDIENT
2 pounds	896 g	Lamb stew meat, 1 inch (2.4 cm) cubes
2 tablespoons	1 ounce, 30 ml	Olive oil
2 tablespoons	1 ounce, 30 ml	Butter
As needed		All-purpose flour
1 cup	4 ounces, 112 g	Onions, $\frac{1}{4}$ inch (.6 cm) dice
2 tablespoons		Garlic, minced
2 tablespoons	1 ounce, 30 ml	Tomato paste
1 cup	6 ounces, 168 g	Tomatoes, peeled, seeded, $\frac{1}{4}$ inch (.6 cm) dice
$\frac{3}{4}$ cup	6 ounces, 180 ml	White wine, dry
2 cups	16 ounces, 480 ml	White stock
1 each		Bouquet garni (see page 669)
$1\frac{1}{2}$ cups	6 ounces, 168 g	Russet potatoes, peeled, $\frac{1}{2}$ inch (1.2 cm) dice
1 cup	4 ounces, 112 g	Carrots, peeled, $\frac{1}{2}$ inch (1.2 cm) dice
1 cup	4 ounces, 112 g	Turnips, peeled, $\frac{1}{2}$ inch (1.2 cm) dice
1 cup	4 ounces, 112 g	Pearl onions, peeled
$\frac{1}{2}$ cup	2 ounces, 56 g	Green peas
To taste		Salt and white pepper
1 tablespoon		Chervil, chopped
1 tablespoon		Parsley, chopped

PROCEDURE

1   Trim the meat, removing any excess fat. Dry lamb cubes.

2   Heat the oil and butter over medium-high heat.

3   Dredge lamb in flour and shake to remove any excess; add to hot fat and sear on all sides; remove and set aside.

4   Add onions to pan and sauté onions 3 to 4 minutes or until soft. Add garlic and cook 1 minute.

5   Add tomato paste and cook 2 minutes or until fragrant. Add diced tomato and cook three minutes.

6   Add white wine and cook 2 minutes; scrape bottom of pan to get all the drippings.

7   Add stock and bouquet garni, and return meat to pan. Bring to a boil, reduce to a simmer, and cook 40 minutes or until meat is almost tender.

8   Remove meat and strain sauce; discard bouquet garni.

9   Add potatoes, carrots, turnips, and pearl onions to sauce and return meat; simmer until vegetables and meat are tender, 15 to 20 minutes.

10   Add green peas; simmer 3 minutes or until hot.

11   Adjust seasoning, stir in chervil, and sprinkle with chopped parsley when serving.

Farcis de Blettes Stuffed Swiss Chard
SERVES 4

Broad-stemmed Swiss chard tends to oxidize, so it should be cooked in a *blanc*.

AMOUNT	MEASURE	INGREDIENT
I tablespoon	$\frac{1}{4}$ ounce, 10 ml	Dried currants
4 teaspoons		Rice
I cup	4 ounces, 112 g	Onions, $\frac{1}{4}$ inch (.6 cm) dice
$\frac{1}{2}$ cup	4 ounces, 120 ml	Olive oil
12 each		Large Swiss chard leaves
4 tablespoons		All-purpose flour
I tablespoon	$\frac{1}{2}$ ounce, 14 g	Pine nuts
To taste		Salt and pepper

PROCEDURE

1 Preheat oven to 275°C (135°C).

2 Soak currants in warm water to cover for 10 minutes.

3 Parboil rice in salted water for 12 minutes; drain and cool under cold running water.

4 Over medium heat, sauté onions in 2 tablespoons (1 ounce, 30 ml) oil for 1 minute.

5 Prepare a *blanc*.

6 Wash and dry the chard, making sure not to damage the leaves. Run a knife along the stalk; separate the green from the white. Cut stalks into 2-inch (5 cm) lengths. Blanch leaves in a blanc for 1 minute, run under cold water and dry.

7 Cook chard stalks in a blanc until just tender, 10 to 15 minutes

8 Heat 4 tablespoons (2 ounces, 60 ml) olive oil over medium heat. Add the cooked chard stalks and sauté, stirring often, 5 minutes.

9 Combine sautéed stalks, currants, pine nuts, rice, and onions; correct seasoning.

10 Form stuffing into balls, 1 tablespoon each. Wrap each ball neatly in a Swiss chard leaf.

11 Arrange the balls tightly in a baking dish, smooth side up. Sprinkle with the remaining olive oil, add about $\frac{1}{4}$ inch (.6 cm) water, and bake 30 to 35 minutes.

12 Serve hot, in the baking dish.

Blanc

AMOUNT	MEASURE	INGREDIENT
4 tablespoons	1 ounce, 28 g	Flour
3 quarts	96 ounces, 2.8l	Cold water
1 tablespoon	$\frac{1}{2}$ ounce, 15 ml	White vinegar
$\frac{1}{2}$ cup	$3\frac{1}{2}$ ounces, 98 g	Coarse salt

PROCEDURE

1   Hold a fine-mesh strainer over a deep pot and place the flour in the strainer.

2   Pour cold water in a slow stream through the flour, stirring with a whisk to make the flour disperse and pass through the strainer.

3   Add white vinegar and coarse salt.

4   Bring to a boil and add the chard stalks.

5   Cook 10 or 15 minutes or until just tender.

6   Drain stalks and chop coarsely.

Watercress Salad with Endive and Cucumbers   SERVES 4

AMOUNT	MEASURE	INGREDIENT
2 cups	6 ounces, 168 g	Watercress (two bunches)
I cup	6 ounces, 168 g	Cucumbers, peeled, seeded, thinly sliced
2		Belgian endive
I teaspoon		Dijon-type prepared mustard
I tablespoon	$\frac{1}{2}$ ounce, 15 ml	Fresh lemon juice
4 tablespoons	2 ounces, 60 ml	Olive oil
To taste		Salt and pepper
8 each		Cherry tomatoes, for garnish

PROCEDURE

1   Trim off tough stem from watercress; wash, spin dry, and refrigerate until needed.

2   Soak cucumbers in ice cold salt water until needed. When ready to make the salad, drain cucumbers and dry before serving.

3   Separate the leaves from the central stems of the endive and refrigerate.

4   Combine the mustard, lemon juice, and oil; whisk and correct seasoning.

5   At serving time, toss each ingredient separately in a little of the dressing; correct the seasoning for each.

6   Arrange on plates, endives first, like the spokes of a wheel, then make a bed of cress, and a topping of cucumber slices. Add a few halved cherry tomatoes.

Watercress Salad with Endive and Cucumbers

Pannequets au Citron
Crêpes Stuffed with Lemon Soufflé SERVES 4

AMOUNT	MEASURE	INGREDIENT
Crepe Batter		
2 each		Eggs
$\frac{1}{2}$ cup	4 ounces, 120 ml	Milk
2 tablespoons	1 ounce, 30 ml	Butter, melted
$\frac{1}{2}$ cup	2 ounces, 56 g	All-purpose flour
2 tablespoons	1 ounce, 28 g	Granulated sugar
Pinch		Salt
1 teaspoon		Vanilla extract
Raspberry Sauce		
1 cup	6 ounces, 168 g	Raspberries, fresh or frozen, pureed and strained
$\frac{1}{4}$ cup	2 ounces, 56 g	Granulated sugar
Soufflé Batter		
1 cup	7 ounces, 210 ml	Pastry cream (recipe follows)
2 tablespoons	1 ounce, 30 ml	Lemon juice
1 teaspoon		Lemon zest
4 each		Eggs whites
As needed		Confectioner's sugar

PROCEDURE

1 Combine all ingredients for the crepe batter into a smooth paste; adjust the thickness to the consistency of heavy cream. Refrigerate 30 minutes before making crepes.

2 Over medium heat, preheat a crepe pan and brush with a little melted butter.

3 Place an enough batter to just coat the bottom of the pan with a thin layer.

4 Cook the crepes until almost dry; turn over and cook the other side. Make two per serving.

5 For the raspberry sauce, combine raspberry puree with the sugar and bring to a boil. If sauce is not thick enough, thicken with a little cornstarch slurry. Remove from heat; set aside to cool.

6 For the soufflé, combine pastry cream, lemon juice, and zest.

Pannequets au Citron – Crêpes Stuffed with Lemon Soufflé

7 Whip egg whites to a firm peak and gently fold into pastry cream.

8 Place 3 to 4 tablespoons of lemon soufflé mixture on one half of each crepe; fold the second half lightly over the soufflé mixture.

9 Bake at 375°F (190°C) on a well-buttered baking tray for 12 minutes.

10 Dust well with sugar and serve immediately, with raspberry sauce.

Pastry Cream   YIELD: ABOUT 3 CUPS

AMOUNT	MEASURE	INGREDIENT
2 cups	16 ounces, 480 ml	Milk
2/3 cup	5 ounces, 140 g	Granulated sugar
$\frac{1}{4}$ cup	1 ounce, 28 g	Cornstarch
6		Egg yolks
2 tablespoons	1 ounce, 30 ml	Butter, soft
2 teaspoons		Vanilla extract

PROCEDURE

1 Combine $1\frac{1}{2}$ cups (12 ounces, 360 ml) of the milk and all the sugar in a saucepan. Stir to dissolve the sugar, then place over medium heat and bring to a boil.

2 Combine the remaining milk and the cornstarch, then the egg yolks.

3 Whisk about $\frac{1}{2}$ cup (4 ounces, 120 ml) boiling mixture into the yolk mixture. If there are any apparent lumps, strain the yolk mixture into another container.

4 Return the remaining milk to medium heat and bring to a boil. Begin whisking the milk and pour the yolk mixture into the boiling milk in a steady stream.

5 The pastry cream will begin to thicken immediately. Whisk until it comes to a boil; make sure you get all the corners and sides to prevent scorching. Continue to cook 1 minute. Immediately remove the pan from the heat.

6 Add the butter and vanilla; whisk until smooth.

7 Pour the pastry cream into a container and cover the surface directly with plastic wrap. Chill immediately until cold.

Ratatouille   SERVES 4

AMOUNT	MEASURE	INGREDIENT
1 cup	8 ounces, 240 ml	Olive oil
1 cup	4 ounces, 112 g	Onions, $\frac{1}{2}$ inch (.6 cm) dice
1 cup	4 ounces, 112 g	Green bell peppers, $\frac{1}{2}$ inch (.6 cm) dice
1 cup	4 ounces, 112 g	Zucchini, $\frac{1}{2}$ inch (.6 cm) dice
2 cups	8 ounces, 224 g	Eggplant, $\frac{1}{2}$ inch (.6 cm) dice
2 cups	12 ounces, 336 g	Tomatoes, peeled, seeded, $\frac{1}{2}$ inches (.6 cm) dice
2		Garlic cloves, minced
To taste		Salt and pepper
2 tablespoons		Fresh thyme
2		Bay leaves

PROCEDURE

1   Over medium heat, heat $\frac{1}{2}$ the oil and sauté the onions and green peppers, 4 to 5 minutes.

2   In a second sauté pan, heat the remaining oil and sauté the zucchini and eggplant, 10 to 15 minutes or until tender. Combine the onion mixture with the eggplant mixture.

3   Add the tomatoes, garlic, salt, pepper, thyme, and bay leaves. Cook, covered, on top of the stove, 30 to 40 minutes. Remove bay leaves. Serve warm or at room temperature.

Ratatouille

Soupe de Legumes aux Petits Coquillages Vegetable Soup with Shellfish

SERVES 4

Paysanne cut: A flat, square, round or triangular cut with dimensions of $\frac{1}{2}$ inch x $\frac{1}{2}$ inch x $\frac{1}{8}$ inch (1.2 cm x 1.2 cm x .3 mm).

AMOUNT	MEASURE	INGREDIENT
2 cups	10 to 12	Small mussels
2 cups	10 to 12	Small clams
4		Sea scallops
3 tablespoons	$1\frac{1}{2}$ ounces, 45 ml	Olive oil
1 cup	8 ounces, 240 ml	Vegetable stock
$\frac{1}{4}$ cup	2 ounces, 60 ml	White wine
$\frac{1}{4}$ cup	1 ounce, 28 g	Green onion, minced
1 each		Garlic clove, minced
$\frac{1}{2}$ cup	2 ounces, 56 g	Tender green part of leek, paysanne cut
$\frac{1}{2}$ cup	2 ounces, 56 g	Turnip, paysanne cut
$\frac{1}{2}$ cup	2 ounces, 56 g	Carrots, paysanne cut
$\frac{1}{2}$ cup	2 ounces, 56 g	Zucchini, paysanne cut
$\frac{1}{2}$ cup	2 ounces, 56 g	Savory cabbage, paysanne cut
$\frac{1}{2}$ cup	3 ounces, 84 g	Tomato, peeled, seeded, $\frac{1}{4}$ inch (.6 cm) dice
$\frac{1}{4}$ cup	2 ounces, 60 ml	Butter
To taste		Salt and pepper

PROCEDURE

1 Wash the mussels and clams; remove the beards from the mussels.

2 Cut the scallops into 3 slices and cut each slice into 3 sticks.

3 Heat 1 tablespoon ($\frac{1}{2}$ ounce, 15 ml) olive oil and add the clams and $\frac{1}{2}$ cup vegetable stock. Simmer the clams only until they open; remove from the heat immediately as they open or they will become tough. Set aside and strain the cooking liquid through a cheesecloth-lined sieve into a saucepan. Save the cheesecloth; it will be used again.

4 Combine the remaining vegetable stock and white wine over low heat and add the mussels. Check the mussels and remove as they open. When all are open, strain the cooking liquid

and combine with the clam liquid. Reduce the mussel and clam liquid by half. Shell mussels and clams; reserve meat.

5   Heat the remaining olive oil over medium heat and add the onions and garlic; cook 1 minute; add to the shellfish cooking liquid and bring to a boil over high heat.

6   Add vegetables and cook 2 minutes. Remove from heat and stir in the butter.

7   Add the tomato dice and mussels and return to a boil; immediately remove from the heat and add the clams and scallops. Check seasoning and serve.

Soupe de Legumes aux Petits Coquillages – Vegetable Soup with Shellfish

Le Blanc de Poisson Belle Mouginoise Fillet of Fish Mouginoise

SERVES 4

Roger Verges' Moulin de Mougins restaurant is the inspiration for this recipe.

AMOUNT	MEASURE	INGREDIENT
2	5 × 6 in (12.5 cm × 15 cm)	Firm red tomatoes, peeled
1 each		English seedless cucumber, unpeeled
4 each		Very large mushrooms, white as possible, more if large are not available
4 each	5 ounces, 140 g	Skinless and boneless fish fillet, $\frac{1}{2}$ inch (1.2 cm) thick (sea bass, red snapper, ling, turbot, orange roughie, or any firm white fish)
To taste		Salt and pepper
Enough to grease pan		Butter
3 tablespoons		Shallots, minced
3 tablespoons	$1\frac{1}{2}$ ounces, 45 ml	Vermouth
6 tablespoons	3 ounces, 90 ml	White wine
2 tablespoons	1 ounces, 30 ml	Chicken or fish stock, jelled
$\frac{1}{2}$ cup	4 ounces, 120 ml	Heavy cream
4 tablespoons	2 ounces, 60 ml	Butter
2 tablespoons		Chives, minced

PROCEDURE

1　Finely slice ($\frac{1}{8}$ inch, .3 cm) tomatoes, cucumbers, and mushrooms.

2　Arrange the vegetables in 3 separate neat rows along the length of the fish fillets, with slices overlapping: mushrooms overlapped by tomatoes and cucumbers overlapping the tomatoes. Season with salt and pepper.

3　Butter a pan large enough to hold the fish. Spread the shallots on the bottom of the pan and the place the fish on top.

4　Add the vermouth and wine, place in a preheated 400°F (205°C) oven, and cook 4 to 6 minutes or until fish is just cooked; do not overcook.

5 Remove the fish from the cooking liquid; set aside and keep moist and warm.

6 Add fish stock and cream; reduce liquids to sauce consistency (coats the back of a spoon), 1 to 2 minutes. Whisking vigorously, add the butter, then the chives. Correct seasoning and remove from heat.

7 Sauce the base of each plate. With a pastry, brush the vegetables with a little melted butter to give them sheen.

8 Place fish on the sauced plate and serve hot.

Filet de Porc Farci Lyonnaise
Stuffed Pork Tenderloin SERVES 4

AMOUNT	MEASURE	INGREDIENT
Stuffing		
$\frac{1}{2}$ cup	2 ounces, 56 g	Onions, $\frac{1}{4}$ inch (.6 cm) dice
I tablespoon	$\frac{1}{2}$ ounce, 15 ml	Butter
$\frac{1}{2}$ cup	2 ounces, 56 g	Ground pork
$\frac{1}{2}$ cup	2 ounces, 56 g	Fresh white bread crumbs
2 teaspoons		Sage, chopped
I tablespoon		Chervil, chopped
To taste		Salt and pepper
I each		Egg yolk
Pork		
I pound	448 g	Pork tenderloin (I large)
2 tablespoons	I ounce, 30 ml	Butter
I cup	4 ounces, 112 g	Red onions, thinly sliced
$\frac{1}{2}$ cup	2 ounces, 56 g	Celery, peeled, $\frac{1}{4}$ inch (.6 cm)
$\frac{1}{2}$ cup	4 ounces, 120 ml	Brown stock
$\frac{1}{4}$ cup	2 ounces, 60 ml	Heavy cream
I teaspoon		Arrowroot, mixed to a paste with I tablespoon ($\frac{1}{2}$ ounce, 15 ml) water

PROCEDURE

1 Make the stuffing: sauté the onions in the butter over medium heat unit soft but not brown.

2 Off the heat, combine the onions, ground pork, bread crumbs, herbs, salt, pepper, and egg yolk. Mix well.

3 Make a slit down the length of the pork tenderloin and open the meat so it is flat. Tap to even out the thickness and flatten slightly.

4 Spread the stuffing, arranging neatly head to tail. Roll to shape and truss with string.

5 Preheat oven to 350°F (176°C).

6   Over medium heat, brown the pork in 2 tablespoons (1 ounce, 30 ml) butter on all sides; remove.

7   Add the sliced onions and celery; cook 7 to 8 minutes, stirring frequently. Place pork on top of onion mixture, add stock, cover pan, and braise in the oven 30 to 40 minutes, or until pork stuffing is cooked.

8   Remove pork; arrange onions and celery on a platter or plates.

9   Add the cream to the cooking pan, bring to a boil, and cook 2 minutes. Use slurry to adjust consistency. Correct seasoning.

10   Remove string and slice pork; arrange on top of onion/celery mixture. Spoon sauce over pork.

11   Serve with mashed potatoes.

Salade de Poire Pear Salad SERVES 4

AMOUNT	MEASURE	INGREDIENT
I cup	4 ounces, 112 g	Carrots, peeled, julienned
I cup	4 ounces, 112 g	Turnips, peeled, julienned
2 tablespoons	I ounce, 30 ml	Sherry vinegar
6 tablespoons	3 ounces, 90 ml	Olive oil
2 each	Medium size	Pears, peeled, cored, cut into 4 slices
I cup	4 ounces, 112 g	Celery, peeled, $\frac{1}{4}$ inch (.6 cm) dice
I cup	4 ounces, 112 g	Leeks, white part only, $\frac{1}{4}$ inch (.6 cm) dice
To taste		Salt and pepper
Garnish		Pomegranate seeds (optional)

PROCEDURE

1 Separately blanch carrots and turnips in salted water until crispy tender, 3 to 4 minutes. Drain, cool, and set aside.

2 Combine sherry vinegar and olive oil to make vinaigrette; correct seasoning.

3 Toss pears in vinaigrette as soon as they are peeled.

4 Moisten each vegetable with a little of the vinaigrette.

5 Arrange pears on 4 plates, surround with small heaps of each vegetable, and garnish with pomegranate seeds, if desired.

Mousse au Chocolat

Chocolate Mousse   YIELD: 1½ QUARTS

AMOUNT	MEASURE	INGREDIENT
12 ounces	336 g	Bittersweet or semisweet chocolate, finely chopped
6 tablespoons	3 ounces, 90 ml	Butter, softened
½ cup	3¾ ounces, 105 g	Granulated sugar
6 each		Egg yolks
½ cup	4 ounces, 120 ml	Coffee
1¼ cup	10 ounces, 300 ml	Heavy cream

PROCEDURE

1   Place chocolate over a hot water bath. After the chocolate begins to melt, stir with a rubber spatula. Continue stirring until the chocolate is ¾ melted. Remove the bowl from over the water and stir continuously to complete the melting.

2   To be sure that the butter is very soft, but not melted, divide the butter into 4 or 5 parts and whisk into the chocolate, until the butter has been completely absorbed. Set aside to cool to room temperature. If the butter is too cool it will set the chocolate. If the butter is too soft, the whey will release and cause the chocolate to seize.

3   Slowly whisk the sugar into the egg yolks in a stream. Whisk in the coffee and place the egg yolk mixture over the simmering hot water bath, whisking constantly until very thick. Transfer to a mixing bowl and whip by machine on medium speed until cool.

4   When mixture is cool, fold in the chocolate-butter mixture.

5   Whip cream to soft peaks; fold into the chocolate mixture.

6   Serve in small portions. Recommended accompaniments are Crème Chantilly, Crème Anglaise, or a flavored Crème Anglaise.

Italy

The Land

Italy is a long, thin peninsula that extends from the southern coast of Europe. Its immediate neighbors—France, Switzerland, Austria, and Slovenia—are in the north, where the Alps form a broad arc around the northern part of the country. Except in the north, Italy is surrounded by water. The country has a coastline of about 4,700 miles, bordered by the Adriatic Sea to the east, the Ionian Sea to the south, the Tyrrhenian Sea to the west, and the Ligurian Sea to the northwest. On a map, the Italian peninsula resembles a tall boot extending into the Mediterranean Sea toward the northern coast of the African continent, which at its closest point is only about 90 miles away. Italy includes a number of islands; the largest two are Sicily and Sardinia. And it has two small independent states within its borders: the Republic of San Marino (just 25 square miles in the Italy's northeast) and Vatican City (only 0.17 square miles within the city of Rome).

Italy's boot shape is formed around two ranges of mountains that form a T. The top crossbar is the Alps mountain range, which stretches from France to Slovenia. The north-south range is the Apennines, which twist along the length of the boot, leaving very little low coastal land.

Italy's northern region consists of the Alps and the Po valley. The largest city in the region is Genoa, the center of Italy's shipbuilding industry and the birthplace of Christopher Columbus. The Po valley contains Italy's most productive farmland, much of which is devoted to growing grain, especially rice, corn, and wheat.

The central southern region contains the nation's capital, Rome, and Tuscany's capital, Florence, historically two of the most influential cities in Europe. Much of the land to the south is dry and yields few agricultural products.

Southern Italy is characterized by the rugged terrain of the Apennine Mountains. Land in the central part of this region is not as fertile or as well-irrigated as in the north; however, the area has many small farms that grow beans, wheat, olives, and the grapes used to produce Chianti wines.

Sicily is the largest of all the Mediterranean islands. Most of its hilly terrain is used to grow wheat and beans and as grazing land for sheep. In the shadow of the active volcano Etna, tropical fruit trees thrive.

Sardinia has few good roads and a harsh, mountainous terrain that is mainly used for raising sheep and, where irrigation is possible, growing wheat, olive trees, and grapevines.

History

Italy has been ruled by emperors, popes, monarchs, democratically elected presidents, and prime ministers. The country has experienced periods of astonishing development, from the grandeur of the Roman Empire and the beauty of the Renaissance to devastating wars in the nineteenth and twentieth centuries and an economic boom in the 1960s.

The migrations of Indo-European peoples into Italy probably began about 2000 B.C. and continued to 1000 B.C. Know as the Etruscans, this founding civilization ruled from about the ninth century B.C. until they were overthrown by the Romans in the third century B.C. By 264 B.C., much of Italy was under the leadership of Rome. For the next seven centuries, until the barbarian invasions destroyed the western Roman Empire in the fourth and fifth centuries A.D., the history of Italy is largely the history of Rome. From A.D. 800 on, the Holy Roman Emperors, Roman Catholic popes, Normans, and Saracens all fought for control over various segments of the Italian peninsula. Numerous city-states, such as Venice and Genoa, whose political and commercial rivalries were intense, as well as many small principalities, flourished in the late Middle Ages. The commercial prosperity of northern and central Italian cities, beginning in the eleventh century, combined with the influence of the Renaissance starting in the fourteenth century, reduced the effects of these medieval political rivalries. Although Italy's influence declined after the sixteenth century, the cultural Renaissance had strengthened the idea of a single Italian nationality. By the early nineteenth century, a nationalist movement developed and led to the reunification of Italy in the 1860s, except for Rome, which joined a unified Italy in 1870.

Followed by a monarchy, a dictatorship, and a new Italian government after World War II, Italy has maintained its unity. Today, Italy is officially the Italian Republic, with twenty regions that are based primarily on history and culture.

The People

Italians trace their culinary heritage to Romans, Greeks, Etruscans, and other Mediterranean peoples who developed the methods of raising, refining, and preserving foods. Dining customs acquired local accents influenced both by culture and a land divided by mountains and seas. Additionally, independent-minded spirits developed among the regions during the repeated shifts of ruling powers that fragmented Italy throughout history.

Because of its geographical position, Italy has direct contact with and the influence of the main ethnic and cultural areas of old Europe (neo-Latin, Germanic, and Slavic-Balkan areas) as well as through North African countries, along with the world of Arab-Islamic civilizations. Consequently, while still anchored in the European and Western civilization, Italy can be considered a natural link to those African and western Asian countries that, bordering as they do on the same Mediterranean Sea, have shared historical events and cultural influences over many centuries.

The Food

Italians are very proud of their cuisine since their food is renowned throughout the world. Italian cooking is still, however, very regional, with different towns and regions having their own traditions and specialties. The tomato, one of the signature ingredients of Italian cuisine, did not exist in Italy until Columbus brought some back from the New World. Olive oil is the principal cooking oil in the south. Butter is preferred in most of the north. Pasta in the south is normally tubular-shaped and made from eggless dough, while in the north it is usually flat, ribbon-shaped, and egg-enriched. Southern cooks season more assertively than northern ones, using garlic and lots of strong herbs. Northern cooks strive more for subtleties. Antipasto means "before the meal" and is the traditional first course of a formal Italian meal and may consist of many things. The most traditional offerings are cured meats, marinated vegetables, olives, peperoncini (marinated small peppers) and various cheeses. Other additions may be anchovies, bruschetta (toasted bread) upon which one may stack the meats or cheeses. The antipasto is usually topped off with some olive oil. Italians vie with the French for the title

Monte
Rosa
Matterhorn
Como
Milan
Bergamo
Treviso
Trieste
Turin
Verona
Venice
Gulf
of Venice
Piacenza
Reggio
Genoa
Bologna
SAN MARINO
Florence
Pisa
Siena
San Benedetto
Ligurian Sea
Adriatic
Sea
I. d'Elba
Grosseto
Orvieto
Pescara
CORSICA
Civitavecchia
Termoli
Vieste
Gulf
of Manfredonia
VATICAN CITY
ROME
Bari
Gulf of Gaeta
Vesuvius
Brindisi
Naples
Potenza
Taranto
I. d'Ischia
Gulf
of Naples
Salerno
Gallipoli
Tyrrhenian
Sea
Gulf of
Taranto
Tricase
Nuoro
Scalea
Rossano
SARDINIA
Cosenza
Amantea
Catanzaro
Lipari Islands
Nicotera
Mediterranean
Sea
Palmi
Palermo
Messina
Trapani
Reggio
Alcamo
Mt. Etna
Ionian Sea
SICILY
Sicilian Channel
Agrigento
Ragusa
Siracuse

Malta Channel

MALTA

Italy

of the world's foremost wine drinkers. Italy, with a population of about 57 million, consists of twenty regions subdivided into ten provinces that take the names of prominent towns. Each province has its own distinctive foods and wines.

NORTHERN ITALY

Northern Italy encompasses eight of the country's twenty regions:

- Emilia-Romagna
- Fruili-Venezia Giulia
- Liguria
- Lombardy
- Piedmont
- Trentino-South Tyrol
- Asota Valley
- Veneto

These eight regions boast the nation's highest standard of living and its richest diet in terms of both abundance and variety. The plains that extend along the Po and lesser rivers from Piedmont to the northern rim of the Adriatic proliferate with grain, corn, rice, fruit, livestock, and dairy products. Vineyards on slopes along the great arc formed by the Alps and Apennines mountains are Italy's prime sources of premium wine. Northern Italy also has a flourishing tourist trade on the Italian Riviera, in the Alps, and on the shores of its lakes.

The cuisine here is characterized by the use of butter (or lard), rice, corn (for polenta), and cheeses for cream sauces. An exception would be the olive oils of the Liguria and the Lakes regions. Pasta in the north is less popular than risotto and polenta. Seafood and shellfish are very popular on the coasts, and rivers and streams provide carp and trout. The eight northern regions produce about a third of Italian wine, though they account for more than half of the DOC/DOCG total.

Emilia Romagna Known as "Italy's Food Basket," this area produces some of the country's most famous foods, including Prosciutto de Parma, Mortadella, Parmigian-Reggiano, and balsamic vinegar. Cooks here are especially skilled at making stuffed pasta by hand, including the tortellini of Emilia and the cappelletti of Romagna, served with the famous Bolognese meat sauce (*Ragu*). Parmigiano-Reggiano is available around the world but its production is strictly enforced to ensure a continued tradition of quality. It takes about eight quarts of milk to make one pound of this delicacy, the so-called "king of cheeses." Aged for a minimum of twelve months and for as long as twenty-four months, Parmigiano-Reggiano is made according to the age-old traditions passed down from generation to generation. Pork products include Parma's famous *prosciutto* made from the meat of carefully raised local pigs, which is salted, cured with air descended from the Apennine mountains, then aged in special underground caves and closely tended to by Parma's *salumieri*.

Romagna is home to fish and seafood dishes, with eels being a favorite of Comacchio. Aceto balsamico, or balsamic vinegar, is produced exclusively in the province of Modena by the same time-honored method used for centuries. It is made from the must, or fresh juice, of wine grapes, most commonly from the Trebbiano grape. The grapes are left on the vine for the longest possible time to achieve maximum sweetness. The must is then cooked until it has reduced to a thick, sweet syrup. It then undergoes a fermentation process, poured into barrels made of ancient woods that impart their own distinctive flavor to the developing vinegar. When the vinegar is transferred to a smaller barrel, a bit of the old vinegar is left so the new vinegar comes into contact with the old. Time allows the vinegar to evaporate and become more deeply flavored, more richly colored, and more concentrated. It may be aged for years, decades, even centuries. By the time it is ready to bottle it is dark brown, slightly sweet, and highly concentrated. There is a panel of experts that approves a balsamic vinegar to be labeled as special after aging for twelve years and extra special after aging twenty-five years to ensure that the quality of these prized vinegars from Modena are maintained.

Friuli-Venezia Giulia Slavic, Austrian, and Hungarian influences make the cuisine of Friuli-Venezia Giulia unique. Trieste, the region's capital, straddles the Adriatic Sea and has long been the gateway to the East; the city's Viennese sausage, goulash, cabbage soups, and strudel pastries come from years under Austro-Hungarian rule. Particular to the cooking of the Friuli-Venezia Giulia is a pungent fermented turnip preparation known as *brovada,* served alongside spiced pork dishes. *San Daniele prosciutto* is considered one of the world's best hams, made only by twenty-seven small producers in the town of San Daniele. Free of additives and seasoned only with sea salt, San Daniele prosciutto has no more than 3 to 4 percent fat, and this is found only on the edges of the meat. The region is known for its vast cornfields, which feed the area's demand for *polenta.* For centuries, polenta, more than bread, was the staff of life for the frugal mountaineers of this region. Depending on the region and the texture desired, polenta is made with either coarsely, medium, or finely ground dried yellow or white cornmeal. Polenta derives from earlier forms of grain mush (known as *puls* or *pulmentum* in Latin, or more commonly as gruel or porridge) commonly eaten in Roman times and after. Early forms of polenta were made with such starches as the grain farro or chestnut flour, both of which are still used in small quantity today. When boiled, polenta has a smooth creamy texture, caused by the presence of starch molecules dissolved into the water.

Liguria Ligurian cuisine is called *cucina del ritorno,* or "homecoming" cooking, as a tribute to the sailors who would return home after months at sea. Fish dominates the menu, found in soups, stews, and salads. Liguria's best-known seafood specialty is *burida,* a seafood stew made with various fishes. The most famous of all culinary works from Liguria is its basil pesto sauce. Traditionally basil, olive oil, garlic, pine nuts, and Parmesan cheese are put in a mortar and pounded with a pestle to achieve a smooth sauce. The olive oil of the region is an exception to most of northern Italian cooking and plays an everyday role along this region's rocky coast. Because the salty air and humidity makes it difficult to bake good bread and keep it from spoiling quickly, *focaccia* was devised as a bread alternative that could be eaten hot out of the oven. This unleavened, thin, flat bread is usually topped with olive oil and salt, or with sage, cheese, or onions.

All cuisines have some type of dumpling and in Italy gnocchi recipes are recorded as far back as cookbooks of the thirteenth century. In some places gnocchi made of flour and water are considered "pasta" while dumplings made of different ingredients are called gnocchi. Gnocchi can be made with the most varied ingredients such as squash, bread, and semolina flour; and they can be flavored mixing the dough with spinach, saffron, and even truffles. They are boiled in water or broth, and like pasta, they can be dressed with many sauces such as pesto, tomato, butter and cheese. Today, gnocchi are primarily made with potatoes.

Lombardy   The region's capital city of Milan is the most modern and cosmopolitan of cities and the cutting-edge fashion center of Italy. Lombardy occupies the central part of the Po Valley. It is known for its rice dishes including *minestrone alla Milanese,* made with vegetables, rice, and bacon. *Risotto alla Milanese* is a creamy dish of braised short-grain rice blended with meat stock, saffron, and cheese. Generous use of butter is a hallmark of Milanese/Lombard cooking. So is the preference for rice or polenta over pasta. Cream sauces are more popular here than in other regions. Being landlocked, Lombardy has few notable seafood specialties. Meat (especially veal) is most popular. The internationally renowned dish *osso buco* is veal shank braised with tomato, onion, stock, and wine, then topped with *gremolata,* a garnish made with parsley, garlic, and lemon rind. The choicest morsel in *osso buco* ("hole in bone") is the cooked marrow clinging to the hollow of the bone.

Regional Lombard cheeses include the blue-veined Gorgonzola, the creamy and mild Bel Paese, mascarpone, and the surface-ripened Taleggio. *Panettone* is the cherished Italian holiday bread. Jeweled with candied fruits (particularly citrus) and raisins, it first appeared in Milan about 1490 and was quickly adopted throughout Italy, from the Alps to Sicily. The traditional recipe calls for using nothing but white wheat flour, sugar, top-quality butter, eggs, and sultana raisins. In order to safeguard tradition and ensure that *panettone* is made in the time-honored, nonindustrial manner, efforts are currently underway to establish guidelines for ingredients and procedures that will serve as the basis for obtaining a special DOP (Protected Designation of Origin) certification from the European Union.

Piedmont   Piedmont means "the foot of the mountains" in Italian. Although culinary influences from neighboring France can be seen in the regional cuisine, Piedmontese cookery is nonetheless distinct unto itself. The white Alba truffle is considered the most delicious and sought-after truffle in the world. An uncultivable mushroom, the valuable fungus can only be found between the months of November and February, in a few spots in France and Italy, including the Piedmont region. Gathering white truffles is a difficult process requiring a *trifulau,* or professional truffle hunter, and his trained dog or pig. The white truffle is found in five different varieties, determined by the species of tree on whose roots it originates. So depending on whether it is associated with the weeping willow, oak, poplar, linden, or vine plant, its color can range from white, sometimes veined with pink, to gray verging on brown. Italians eat them raw, shaved paper-thin over egg dishes, in plain pastas (dressed only with butter and cheese), fonduta (fondue), risotto, and other light foods. *Bagna cauda* is dipping sauce made with olive oil, chopped garlic, anchovies, butter, and sometimes sliced white truffles. Into this heated sauce the diner dips a wide choice of cold raw vegetables. Red wine is the traditional accompaniment. *Grissini* are thin and crispy breadsticks that have become popular throughout the country. Piedmonte produces about half of Italy's rice, and rice-based dishes like *panicia de Novara* (a vegetable soup with rice) and *risotto all Piedmontese* (risotto with meat stock, Parmesan, nutmeg, and truffle) are regional specialties. *Ribiola di Roccaverano* is a fresh cheese that is neither aged nor matured. Cylindrical in shape and high in fat, it is made from a combination of cow's, goat's, and sheep's milk, derived from two daily milkings. The texture is grainy and the color milky white. It has a delicate aroma and acidic flavor. The famous *Barolo* and *Barbaresco* wines are produced in this region. In addition to hunting truffles, fall is the time for hunting wild game, gathering nuts, and harvesting grapes.

Trentino–South Tyrol   This region shares culinary traditions from both the Italian and German sides of the border. The cuisine combines Germanic, Hungarian, and Italian touches, and includes sauerkraut, beef goulash, and fruit-stuffed gnocchi with browned butter and breadcrumbs. Rather than pasta or risotto, cooks in this region prefer to prepare polentas made of cornmeal or buckwheat, or hearty soups garnished with bread dumplings. *Speck,* the region's prized smoked ham, flavors numerous dishes, from braised cabbage in red wine to long-simmered pork stews. *Speck* shares its name with a German pork product, but while German *speck* is basically lard, Italian *speck* has some similar characteristics to smoked bacon. Unlike American bacon that comes from the belly portion of the hog (same as *pancetta*), *speck* is made from hog legs. Speck originates from the Alto Adige region, where it is still a homemade process protected by a PGI designation. The meat is seasoned with salt and spices that include pepper, laurel, and juniper berries before being allowed to rest for about a month. *Speck* is then smoked using flavorful beech, ash, or juniper wood for ten days. Following that, the meat is aged for months to produce a smoky and slightly spicy product with a distinct pink/red interior with a small amount of fat. It is then used in pasta sauces, or with meat or eggs. Genuine *speck* must have a rind that is well marked, and should be slightly firm to the touch. *Canderlt,* made with bread and flour and served in a broth, is just one of several types of gnocchi (dumplings) popular in the region. The most popular cheeses include the fresh *Tosela, Spressa delle Giudicarie (DOP),* and *Puzzone di Moena.*

Valle d'Osta (Asota Valley)   The traditional cooking of this region incorporates both French and Swiss influences. Stone-ground cornmeal is transformed into polentas. Traditionally polenta is prepared by constantly stirring cornmeal, water, and salt over heat for 40 to 45 minutes with a wooden stirring stick called a *mescola.* The resulting "mush" is then poured onto a wooden board to cool slightly and is cut with kitchen string while still hot. At one time, families would take "shifts" as stirrers; today, automatic stirring machines make the job easier. Fontina cheese, a semi-cooked, straw-yellow cheese with tiny holes and a soft texture, is used to make fonduta, or fondue, one of the region's famous dishes. Local bread is made of cold-hardy northern grains like rye or buckwheat. *Pane nero* (black bread) is a staple food made with rye and wheat flours that was once baked in the communal oven just once a year and dried to preserve it. Beef is the staple meat. *Carbonade* is a classic stew made with salt-cured or fresh beef, onions, red wine, butter, and nutmeg, often served with polenta.

Veneto   In general, the cooking in this region is based on four basic foods: polenta, rice, beans, and vegetables along with wild fowl, mushrooms, or seafood. Traditional courses include *risi e bisi* (rice and peas), and *fegato alla Veneziana* (calf's liver fried with onions). *Radicchio di Treviso* is a bitter red chicory served as a salad but more often grilled and served with salt and olive oil. *Sopressa* is a finely ground pure pork sausage, traditionally made from pigs fed on chestnuts and potatoes. Veneto's contribution to Italy's pasta culture is a style of fresh pasta called *bigoli,* which gets its name from the traditional kitchen implement, a four-inch-wide bronze tube called a *bigolaro. Bigoli,* a long, spaghetti-style pasta with a hole in its middle, is made on a hand-operated press by forcing pasta dough through the bigolaro, then cutting the strands to the desired length. A typical preparation is *bigoli in salsa,* in which the pasta is tossed with a sauce of anchovies, olive oil, and cooked onions. This region is home to the city of Venice, known for its romantic canals and bridges. The main difference between the cuisines of Venice and other parts of Veneto is the availability of fresh seafood, ranging from prawns, shrimp, and clams to fresh fish and eels. *Baccala,* dried, salted codfish, is served throughout the area, often mixed with polenta into a "cream" that is served as an appetizer or first course.

CENTRAL ITALY

Central Italy encompasses six of the country's regions:

- Abruzzo
- Latium
- Marches
- Molise
- Tuscany
- Umbria

The summers are hotter and longer than those in the north, and consequently tomato-based dishes are more common than they are further north. Braised meats and stews, grilled or roasted beef, lamb, poultry, pork, and game are popular. Central Italy has a rich farming tradition and cultivates many crops that are difficult to find elsewhere, including farro, an ancient grain domesticated by the Romans, and saffron. Miles of olive groves and vineyards dominate parts of the landscape. The cuisine is simple and rustic dishes are served with light sauces and seasonings.

Abruzzo   This region is sparsely populated and geographically diverse. It is known for its livestock production and farming, the growing and production of the highly prized herb saffron, and an abundance of seafood specialties. Pasta, vegetables, and meat (especially lamb and pork) are the staples of this region. The pasta most often associated with Abruzzo is *maccheroni alla chitarra,* a square spaghetti so named because the device used in its production, made of a wooden box strung with steel wire, resembles a guitar. This is traditionally served with a lamb, tomato, and peperoncino sauce, sprinkled with local pecorino (sheep's milk) cheese. The red chile pepper peperoncino is known as *diavolino,* or little devil, and is a key ingredient in the cuisine of this area. The town of Sulmona is Italy's confectionary capital and is where the sugared almond was created 250 years ago. A blend of the best almonds and extra-fine sugar produce this traditional wedding candy *(confetti)*, which signifies the union of life through the bitterness of the almond and the sweetness of the candy of what matrimony and life may offer. The tradition is to give confetti candy to the guests at weddings; it is usually done in a group of five candies, each of which signifies Health, Wealth, Happiness, Longevity, and Fertility. The region's cheeses include a vast assortment of pecorino, and scamorza, a close relative of mozzarella. Three types of wine are predominant: *Montepulciano,* a robust red; *Cerasuolo,* a rosé; and *Trebbiano d'Abruzzo,* a crisp white.

Latium   This rustic region is home to Rome, the capital of Italy, and much of its countryside remains as it must have been in the days of the Empire: quiet, dotted with sheep, the domain of farmers and shepherds who make a living in its hills and valleys. In Latium, milk-fed lamb is a favorite dish, usually baked and served with seasonal vegetables, and sheep's milk cheese is produced abundantly in small dairies and large cooperatives. Simple pastas made of flour and water are the basis of many famous pasta dishes that include *bucatini all'amatriciana,* with tomato, onion, bacon, and a dash of cognac; *spaghetti alla carbonara,* with bacon, eggs, butter, and cheese sauce dusted with black pepper "coal flakes"; and *spaghetti alla puttansesca,* which includes garlic, tomatoes, capers, olives, herbs, and anchovies. Over 90 varieties of artichokes are grown in Italy and are very popular in Rome where they are flattened and fried twice for *carcioif alla guidia* (Jewish style) or prepared *alla Romana,* stuffed with bread crumbs, parsley, anchovies, salt, and pepper. Meat dishes include *abbacchio al forno* (roast lamb) or *alla cacciatora* (lamb with an anchovy and rosemary sauce) and *saltimbocca* (a fillet of veal rolled in ham and flavored and served in a Marsala sauce).

Marches   The food of Marches is a mix of rustic fare and seafood. *Brodetto* is a fish stew found along the Adriatic coast and varies in form from each coastal town. This regions' *brodetto* includes red and gray mullet, cuttlefish or squid (or both), oil, garlic, and saffron, served on either fried or toasted bread. Dried cod is used in a dish called *stoccafisso,* while sea snails cooked in fennel are a delicacy. The Marches signature dish is *porchetta,* where a roast suckling pig is either served whole, or is sliced into crispy bread rolls. Classic pastas include *papardelle alla papara,* a flat pasta with duck sauce, and *vincigrassi,* a lasagna containing cream, truffles, ragu, butter, Parmigiano-Reggiano, mozzarella, and various other ingredients. Other specialties include Ascolana olives stuffed with meat and lightly fried, pasta served with clams and mussels, risotto with farro grain, smoked trout from mountain streams, rabbit with fennel and sausage, and fava beans with fresh pecorino cheese. *Ciauscolo* salami is a specialty made by kneading very finely ground pork from the belly and shoulder of the pig with a good quantity of fat until the mixture is very soft. The meat is flavored simply with garlic, salt, and pepper, and it is often smoked. Given its soft consistency, much like a pâté, *ciauscolo* is meant to be spread onto bread rather than sliced. Casciotta d'Urbino cheese is pale yellow and is lightly perforated by characteristic little holes. Made from sheep's and cow's milk, it is eaten after maturing for twenty to thirty days.

Molise   Because of their joint history, Molise shares many of the culinary traditions of the Abruzzo region, but there are also a few dishes unique to the region. One is *p'lenta d'iragn,* a white polenta made with potatoes and wheat and served with a tomato sauce. Another is *calconi di ricotta rustica*, ravioli stuffed with ricotta, provolone, and prosciutto, then fried in oil.

Traditionally, townspeople migrated to the area each year, bringing their sheep to Puglia. Because the animals were meant to be sold, not used for personal needs, meat was considered a luxury. As a result, very little meat is eaten. Vegetables, cheese, pasta, grains, and fresh fruit still dominate the diet today. Chile and garlic lace nearly every dish, as does Molise's golden olive oil. The cheeses of Molise include *scamorza, mateca,* and *burrino.* The interior of Molise is dotted with apple orchards of a very old type of tree that produces very aromatic fruit known as *mela limoncella.* Many families used to display these apples around their kitchen and living room doorframes because of their special scent. They have a green-yellow peel, a very strong scent, and a slightly acidic yet sweet flavor.

Tuscany   The Etruscans, who likely hailed originally from Asia Minor, settled primarily in Tuscany around 1000 B.C., planting vines and olive groves and spreading their cultural and culinary influence as far as the islands of Corsica and Elba. It has been said that this is where Italian cooking was born—at the court of the Medici. The region is home to the extra-virgin Tuscan olive oil, an intense oil with a green to golden color. The white-hided cattle found in Tuscany's Chianna valley produce large cuts of meat that is low in fat. Florence offers its famous *alla fiorentina* steak and specialties that include *ribollita* (a thick vegetable soup), *fagioli all'uccelletto* (beans sautéed in garlic and sage with tomatoes), and *fagioli al fiasco* (beans with oil, onions, and herbs cooked in a round bottle—a *fiasco*—over a coal fire. Seafood dishes include *triglie* (red mullet) and a delicious fish soup known as *Cacciucco alla Livornese.* Known as "strong bread" and once considered an aphrodisiac, *panforte* is a cake containing almonds, honey, candied lemon and orange peel, flour, sugar, and spices. Tuscan wines are known worldwide, including *Chianti,* which comes in both red and white varieties.

Umbria   Nicknamed "The Green Heart of Italy," Umbria is just southeast of Tuscany. Landlocked, it relies on pork for most of its classic preparations, and its pork butchers are said to be the best in Italy: every scrap of the pig is put to good use. Specialties like *guanciale* (the salted and cured meat from the pig's cheek) are added to pasta sauces and pots of fava beans or peas. Norcia in the Apennine foothills is the home of Italy's best black truffles (*tartufo nero*). Covered by a black skin with small wartlike bumps, the truffle has a purple-black flesh with distinctive white veins and a delicate scent. Unlike white truffles, which can only be eaten raw, black truffles can be heated and added to sauces and pastas without losing their flavor. Many types of handmade pasta like *strozzapreti* (priest stranglers) are not typically found outside Umbria. Besides homemade fresh egg pastas, the production of much of the dried pasta consumed throughout Italy occurs in Umbria. The wines of Umbria rank among Italy's finest. They include *Orvieto, Rosso di Montefalco, Sagrantino di Montefalco,* and vin santo, a sweet dessert wine often consumed with biscotti. Umbria is home to Perugina (now owned by Nestle), one of the major chocolate producers in Italy.

SOUTHERN ITALY

Southern Italy, often referred to as the Mezzogiorno, encompasses four of the country's regions:

- Basilicata
- Campania
- Calabria
- Apulia (Puglia)

and the islands of:
- Sicily
- Sardinia

The symbol of southern Italian cooking is the tomato, although it arrived with peppers, beans, and potatoes from America in the 1500s. The eggplant was originally cultivated in Asia, although it now distinguishes the *parmigiana* classics of the Campania region and many other classic Italian dishes. The piquancy of southern cooking comes from herbs and spices, especially garlic and chile peppers. Italy's first pasta was produced in the south, though noodles were preceded by flatbreads called *focacce,* forerunners of pizza, which originated in Naples. Baked goods, including pastries, biscuits, and cakes, abound in the Mezzogiorno, though nowhere as evident as in Sardinia, where each village has its own style of bread making. Arab settlers in Sicily established a pasta industry during the Middle Ages, using durum wheat for the dried pasta types that still prevail in the south. Tubes and other forms of "short" pasta may be referred to generically as *maccheroni,* distinguished from "long" types such as spaghetti and vermicelli. Also popular are spiral-shaped fusilli, oblique tubes called penne, and larger tubes called ziti, or zite. Fresh pasta is also prized, sometimes, but not usually, made with eggs, in such familiar dishes as lasagna, fettuccine, and ravioli, with no shortage of local versions.

Basilicata Historically one of Italy's poorest regions, Basilicata is also one of its least popu-lated. Today, the economic situation is much improved, but the cuisine remains anchored in peasant traditions. Along the region's coastline, seafood plays a major role in the diet, with fa-vorites including mussels, oysters, octopus, red mullet, and swordfish. Vegetables include fava beans, artichokes, chicory, and various greens including *rucola* (rocket). Eggplants, peppers, *lampasciuoli* (a bitter type of onion), cauliflower, olives, and olive oil are all regional staples. Regional pastas include *orecchiette* and *bucatini,* both typically served with tomato sauce or with olive oil, garlic, and cauliflower.

Campania Best known around the world for its pizza, Campania's cuisine relies on vegeta-bles and herbs, capers, dried pasta, and fresh farmhouse cheeses. In the nineteenth century, people living in the capital city of Naples were nicknamed *mangia maccheroni* (maccheroni eaters) and to this day, Neapolitans remain devoted pasta eaters. Their pasta is considered among the best and the most varied in all of Italy. Italian food would not be the same without spaghetti with *pommarola,* the famous tomato sauce. The volcanic soils of Campania grow some of the best produce in Italy, including San Marzano tomatoes, peaches, grapes, apricots, figs, oranges, and lemons. Campania's most famous cheese is *mozzarella di bufalo campania,* made from the milk of local water buffalos. Other popular cheeses include sheep's milk Pecorino, scamorza, ricotta (both cow and buffalo versions), and mascarpone. Parmigiano-Reggiano is popular in recipes of Campania, with meat and vegetable dishes served *alla Parmigiana.*

The region is also renowned for its fish and seafood specialties. Octopus is tenderized by stewing it in a sealed clay pot with olive oil, garlic, capers, olives, and parsley or with chiles and tomatoes. Squid and cuttlefish are boiled and served in salads, stuffed and baked, or fried into rings, while mussels and clams are cooked and tossed with handmade pasta or added to seafood salads. Salt cod, fresh sardines, and anchovies too are staples. Christmas is celebrated with a dish of eel marinated with vinegar and herbs or cooked with tomatoes and white wine.

Originating in Naples more than three hundred years ago, pizza is often thought of as "genuine" Italian food by non-Italians; but pizza was little known in Italy (outside of Naples) until the 1970s. Pizza came to the United States early in the twentieth century during the great migration of Italians from southern Italy. In 2004, Italy drew up a series of rules that must be followed to make a true Neapolitan pizza: the dough must rise for at least six hours and must be kneaded and shaped by hand; the pizza must be round and no more than 13.7 inches in diameter; and it may only be cooked in a wood-fired oven. And only three variations of pizza are permitted: *marinara* with garlic and oregano; *Margherita* with basil, tomatoes, and cheese from the southern Apennine Mountains; and the "extra" *Margherita,* which includes buffalo mozzarella from the Campania region.

Calabria Surrounded by the Tyrrhenian and the Ionian Seas, Calabria has 500 miles of coastline (the longest of any Italian region). Over the centuries, Greek, Arab, and Albanian influences have shaped the cuisine, where characteristic dishes are flavored with chile pepper;

sweet-and-sour preparations are popular; and desserts are often deep-fried and soaked in honey. *Melanzane alla parmigiana,* or eggplant Parmesan (eggplant that is fried, then baked in the oven with tomato and cheese), was created in Calabria, where the eggplant crop thrives. The dry climate, high temperature, and nearly calcium-free soil are ideal for growing eggplants because they prevent a buildup of the fruit's bitter juices and concentrate its sweet flavor. A popular breakfast in this region is called *murseddu.* It consists of a ragu made from pig and calf's liver that is cooked slowly in tomatoes, herbs, and hot red pepper, and then stuffed in the local *pitta bread.* Despite numerous attempts to export production to other areas in Italy and the world, *bergametto,* or bergamot oranges, thrive only in Calabria. Bergamot oranges have a smooth, thin peel, an acidic flavor, and an intense scent. They look like an orange, but their color ranges from green to yellow, depending on how ripe they are. Their essential oil is used to flavor liqueurs, tea (such as Earl Grey), sweets, and drinks.

Apulia Three staples are essential to the Apulian kitchen: wheat, vegetables, and olive oil. Semolina flour is turned into a variety of handmade pastas (some shaped like little ears, others like concave shells, others still like thick ropes), which are boiled with wild or cultivated greens, tossed with hearty meat ragus, or cooked into soups. Wheels of rustic bread are baked to be enjoyed as companions to daily meals and serve as the starting point for numerous appetizers, salads, soups, and simple desserts. The most interesting offering is *frisedda,* a twice-baked ring-shaped bread. And almost every dish is topped with olive oil—after all, Apulia is Italy's largest producer of olive oil. Fava beans are used to prepare thick soups, salads, and side dishes, and rice is baked with potatoes and seafood or vegetables to make an unusual main course called *tiella* (named after the pot in which it is cooked). The Apulians, shepherds by trade since ancient times, tend to prefer lamb, mutton, kid, and goat meat, which they cook simply with fragrant herbs, olive oil, and tomatoes or potatoes. Offal is popular in the area and lamb's hearts and intestines are skewered and cooked on a grill, then eaten with raw celery and sharp sheep's milk cheese. Pastries, cakes, and fritters are based on honey, nuts, and dried fruit, their origins in ancient Greece and echoes of the Orient. Apulians use a wide variety of wild and cultivated greens in the kitchen. Some, like sorrel, are relatively mild and astringent; others, like broccoli rabe and dandelions, can be bitter. Apulians tame the bitterness of these potent greens by lengthy cooking. They don't believe in undercooking vegetables; they prefer vegetables slippery soft, never crunchy. Bitter greens are typically boiled first in ample water, then sautéed slowly in olive oil.

Sicily The cuisine reflects the many invaders in this island's history and focuses on seafood (swordfish, tuna, mussels, prawns, sea bass, red mullet, anchovies, and more), eggplant, tomatoes, potatoes, beans and other vegetables, pecorino and many other cheeses, figs, capers, olives, almonds, pine nuts, fennel, raisins, lemons, and oranges. In parts of Sicily there are sweet-and-sour combinations like capers with sugar in *caponata,* a mix of eggplant, tomatoes, celery, olives, and capers cooked with vinegar and sugar. The *ceci,* or chickpea, has played an important role in Sicilian history and is well represented in the diet. *Panella* is a thin paste made of crushed *ceci* and served fried. *Maccu* is a creamy soup made from the same bean. Pasta is often served with a rich, spicy tomato sauce. Popular seafood dishes include grilled swordfish or snapper, *finocchio con le sarde* (fennel with sardines), and *sepia* (cuttlefish) served in its own black sauce with pasta. The best known Sicilian meat dish is *vitello al Marsala* (veal marsala) and is just one of many regional meat specialties that can also be made with lamb, kid, or rabbit. No other part of Italy has as many sweets and ices. Many desserts are derived from Arab and Greek influences and are made with almond pastes, candied fruits, ricotta, honey, raisins, and nuts. The best-known wine is Marsala, which is dark and strong.

Sardinia   The island of Sardinia has been inhabited since the Neolithic age. Phoenician, Greek, Arab, Spanish, and French invaders have come and gone, marking the local language, customs, and cuisine. The mountainous inland terrain is home to wild animals (boar, mountain goat, and hare), which are transformed into pasta sauces, stews, and roasts. Lamb, the island's favorite meat, is often cooked with wild fennel, and sheep's milk cheese appears at nearly every meal. Spicy fish soups called *burrida* and *cassola,* along with lobsters, crabs, anchovies, squid, clams, and fresh sardines are all very popular along the Sardinian coast. Favorite Sardinian pasta dishes include *spaghetti con bottarga,* with dried gray mullet roe shaved on top, and *malloreddus,* gnocchi flavored with saffron and served with tomato sauce. *Culingiones* are round ravioli stuffed with spinach and cheese. Sardinia is known for its rustic sheep and goat cheeses like Pecorino Sardo and Fiore Sardo, which can be served either fresh or aged. The Sardinian interior produces some of the best lamb in all of Italy, known for being very lean. Sardinians enjoy their meats roasted and *porceddu* (the Sardinian version of porchetta), suckling pig, or kid (suckling goat) is roasted outdoors over aromatic woods.

Glossary

Agro Foods may be referred to *agro/dolce. Agro* refers to the sour, often achieved through the use of vinegar. *Dolce* means sweet. Commonly found in some dishes from Sicily.

Al dente Literally "to the tooth," meaning cooked to the "point" or until just done but still crisp.

Amaretti Crisp almond macaroons sprinkled with coarse sugar.

Amaretto Almond liquor.

Antipasto Hors d'oeuvre; literally, "before the pasta."

Apertivo A beverage intended to awaken the palate and stimulate the appetite.

Arborio Rice Stubby, short-grain polished rice grown in Italy's Po valley. Its particular starch composition makes it the preferred rice for Italian risotto. It is perfect for dishes that are expected to absorb the flavor of the liquid in the recipe. *Carnaroli superfino* is the risotto rice most preferred by chefs due to its exceptional quality and structure, owing to high amylose starch content, which improves consistency, resistance to overcooking, and capacity for absorbing condiments and flavoring agents. The ideal rice for long-simmer, nonsticky risottos.

Vialone nano is another preferred risotto rice, with small, rounded grains, rich in amylose and very compact, allowing them to expand greatly during cooking. An ideal rice for no-stir risottos and rice salads, it is prized for its soft, light body.

Arugula Also known as rocket, garden rocket, rocket salad, rugola, or rucola; a type of leaf lettuce and a member of the mustard family. It is often served with air-dried beef Bresaola.

Baccala Cod that has been preserved with salt. In the Italian markets it's sold in slabs. It takes several soakings to remove the salt. Dry salt cod will keep indefinitely.

Balsamic Vinegar (Aceto Balsamico) An aged reduction of white sweet grapes (Trebbiano for red and Spergola for white sauvignon) that are boiled to a syrup. The grapes are cooked very slowly in copper cauldrons over an open flame until the water content is reduced by over 50 percent. The resulting "must" is placed into wooden barrels and older balsamic vinegar is added to assist in the acidification. Each year the aging vinegar is transferred to different wood barrels so that the vinegar can incorporate some of the flavors of the different woods. The only approved woods are oak, cherry, chestnut, mulberry, acacia, juniper, and ash. The age of the vinegar is divided into young (from 3 to 5 years maturation), middle (aged 6 to 12 years), and the highly prized very old (at least 12 years and up to 150 years old).

Bianco White, as in white sauce or white wine.

Bollito Misto alla Piemontese A rich and flavorful boiled dinner containing seven kinds of meat, seven vegetables, and seven condiments. The variety is important because each complements the others, producing a whole that is greater than the sum of the parts. Includes beef, veal, pork, chicken, tongue, *zampone,* or *cotechino* served with bagnet verde (green salsa made with parsley), bagnet ross (red salsa with tomatoes), mustard, horseradish, and salt.

Bottarga Sometimes called the poor man's caviar, bottarga is the roe pouch of tuna, grey mullet, or swordfish. It is massaged by hand to eliminate air pockets, then dried and cured in sea salt for a few weeks. The result is a dry hard slab, which is coated in beeswax for keeping. It is usually used sliced thin or grated. In Italy, it is best known in Sicilian and Sardinian cuisine; its culinary properties can be compared to those of dry anchovies, though it is much more expensive. Bottarga is often served with lemon juice as an appetizer or used in pasta dishes.

Bresaola Air-dried salted beef eye of round that has been aged about two to three months until it becomes hard and a dark red, almost purple color. It originated in the Valtellina valley in northern Italy's Lombardy region, with pieces of beef being strung up to cure in the cool Alpine air.

Brodetto Fish soup similar to the French bouillabaisse.

Brodo Broth, or stock, is a staple element in making good soups. In the Emilia Romagna region, stuffed pasta is often served in *brodo.*

Bruschetta A food originating in central Italy, typically made of grilled bread rubbed with garlic and topped with extra-virgin olive oil, salt, and pepper. It is usually served as a snack or appetizer. In Tuscany, bruschetta is called *fettunta,* meaning "oiled slice."

Cacciatore Chicken braised *alla cacciatora,* meaning "hunter's style," is a northern Italian preparation that usually includes onions, tomatoes, pancetta or lardo, and often mushrooms. In central Italy, garlic, rosemary, olives, and a touch of vinegar may be used.

Caffe Latte Espresso made with more milk than a cappuccino but only a small amount of foam. In Italy it is usually a breakfast drink.

Cannoli Italian pastry desserts. The singular is *cannolo,* meaning "little tube," with the etymology stemming from the Latin *canna,* or reed. Cannoli originated in Sicily and are an essential part of Sicilian cuisine.

Capicola Italian cold cut or salami.

Cappuccino Espresso with foamed milk and containing equal parts espresso, steamed milk, and foamed milk.

Carpaccio A dish of raw beef, veal, or tuna traditionally cubed and pounded thin, served as an appetizer. The name comes from the painter Vittore Carpaccio, who favored red colors reminiscent of raw beef. The dish was supposedly invented during 1950 in Venice when a famous actress of the day informed the owner of Harry's Bar that her doctor had recommended she eat only raw meat. Typically the thin slices are served with a dressing of olive oil and lemon juice plus seasoning, often with green salad leaves such as arugula or radicchio and thinly sliced Parmesan cheese.

Cassata, Cassata Siciliana A traditional sweet from the province of Palermo, Sicily, similar to the French gateau. It consists of pound cake moistened with kirshwasser or an orange liqueur and layered with a ricotta, candied peel, and chocolate filling, similar to cannoli cream. Most variants are also covered with a shell of marzipan or chocolate frosting.

Coppa A type of salami made from pork, salted, naturally aged, and stored raw. The finished product is cylindrical in shape and when sliced open it displays a homogenous interior of red meat flecked with pinkish-white spots.

Fagato Calf liver.

Farro *Grano farro* has a long and glorious history: it is the original grain from which all others derive, and fed the Mediterranean and Near Eastern populations for thousands of years; somewhat more recently it was the standard ration of the Roman legions that expanded throughout the Western world. Ground into a paste and cooked, it was also the primary ingredient in *plus,* the polenta eaten for centuries by the Roman poor. Important as it was, however, it was difficult to work and produced low yields. In the centuries following the fall of the Empire, higher-yielding grains were developed and farro's cultivation dwindled. By the turn of the century in Italy there were a few hundreds of acres of fields scattered over the regions of Lazio, Umbria, the Marches, and Tuscany. Often used in soups and salads.

Frito Misto di Mare Assorted deep-fried fish and seafood.

Formaggi (Cheese)

Asiago d'allevo A pressed, cooked cheese made from ewe's or cow's milk. It is a firm, strong table cheese after two to six months. Cheese ripened for longer periods of time are used for grating.

Dolcelatte A smooth, creamy blue cheese, milder than gorgonzola. Its name is officially registered and means "sweet milk."

Fontina A medium-hard cheese that melts easily. Made from full cream milk, it is ripened for about three months.

Gorgonzola A compact, creamy textured cheese with a strong flavor. A protected cheese, it is produced year round and is Italy's major blue-veined variety.

Grana Padano A cheese similar to Parmigiano-Reggiano but it ripens more quickly and is left to mature for one to two years

Gruviera A cheese with a sweet, nutlike flavor that is similar to Swiss Gruyère.

Mascarpone A cow's milk cheese that must be eaten very fresh. Its texture is like whipped butter or stiffly whipped cream. It is a delicious creamy dessert cheese.

Montasio A cow's milk cheese that is sold in one of three ways based on aging time of sixty days to up to ten months: fresh, middle, and aged. The fresh cheese is characterized as sweet. As it ages, the cheese takes on a certain piquancy.

Mozzarella A mild, white fresh cheese made by the special *pasta filata* process, whereby the curd is dipped into hot whey, then stretched and kneaded to the desired consistency. Fresh mozzarella, called *mozzarella di bufala* (buffalo mozzarella), has a soft texture and sweet, delicate flavor.

Parmigiano-Reggiano A finely grained hard cheese.

Pecorino Romano Made from sheep's milk, generally aged and classified as *grana* (hard, granular, and sharply flavored). A young, unaged ricotta pecorino is soft, white, and mild in flavor. The hard, dry cheeses are good for grating and may be used in recipes calling for Parmesan cheese, especially if a sharper flavor is desired.

Provolone Southern Italian cow's milk cheese with a firm texture and a mild, smoky flavor.

Ricotta Rich fresh cheese, slightly grainy but smoother than cottage cheese. It is white and moist and has a slightly sweet flavor.

Stracchino A fresh cow's milk cheese that contains about 50 percent milk fat. Its flavor is mild and delicate, similar to but slightly more acidic than cream cheese.

Espresso *Caffe* in Italy, strong in taste with a rich bronze froth known as a cream on top.

Gelati Italian ice creams.

Grappa Strong, clear Italian brandy made from the distilled remains of pressed grapes.

Lardo A type of *salumi*. It is made from the layer of fat directly under the skin of a pig, cured with salt and other spices, often pepper and garlic. This Italian specialty is often eaten raw in Italy as part of an antipasto. It is made from the back of the pig and is prepared by first cutting the meat and treating the individual pieces with salt and spices such as cinnamon. They are then immersed in brine and placed inside a vessel excavated from marble. So starts a slow process of seasoning in a unique microclimate at the end of which the meat achieves a distinctive smell and smooth consistency. Cut into slices at least 2 inches (5 cm) wide, the lardo can be white or slightly red. To serve, the meat is laid on hot toast. If it is produced well, the whole combination should just melt in the mouth.

Limoncello A lemon liqueur produced in southern Italy, mainly in the region around the Gulf of Naples and the coast of Amalfi and islands of Ischia and Capri, but also in Sicily, Sardinia, and the Maltese island of Gozo. It is made from lemon rinds, alcohol, water, and sugar. Bright yellow in color, sweet and lemony, but not sour since it contains no lemon juice.

Marinara Meatless tomato-based sauce.

Minestrone Italian vegetable soup.

Mortadella Bologna's most famous pork product, a softly flavored cooked sausage made from lean pork studded with small cubes of flavorful fat.

Osso Buco Braised veal shanks.

Panettone A typical cake of Milan, usually prepared and enjoyed for Christmas and New Year around Italy, and one of the symbols of the city. It is a delicate sweet yeast dough studded with golden raisins and jewel-toned glacéed citron.

Panforte A traditional Italian dessert containing fruits and nuts, and resembling fruitcake or *lebkuchen*. It may date back to thirteenth-century Siena, in Italy's Tuscany region.

Pasta In Italian the word *pasta* means "paste," and refers to the dough made by combining a durum wheat flour called semolina with a liquid, usually water or milk. The term *pasta* is used broadly and generically to describe a wide variety of noodles made from this type of dough.

> **Agnolotti** Piemontese stuffed pasta; comes in a great many different varieties, some filled with cheese, others meat, and others still meatless. They are square and small, about an inch on a side, and are made using very thin sheets of pasta. They also are often made from cooked meat or leftovers.
>
> **Angel Hair** "Fine hair" pasta, thinner and finer than spaghetti.
>
> **Farfalle** Bow ties or butterfly-shaped pasta.
>
> **Fettuccine** "Small ribbons" of pasta similar to spaghetti, but wider and slender, just like a ribbon.
>
> **Fusilli** Pasta shaped like screws or springs.
>
> **Lasagna** Thin, flat pasta with straight or rippled edges.
>
> **Lumache** Large, conch shell–shaped pasta suitable for stuffing.
>
> **Macaroni** A kind of moderately extended, machine-made dry pasta. Much shorter than spaghetti, and hollow, macaroni does not contain eggs.
>
> **Manicotti** Long, plain tube-shaped pasta suitable for stuffing.
>
> **Orecchiette** "Little ears" pasta shaped like tiny ears or bowls.
>
> **Penne** Tubular pasta cut on the diagonal into pieces about an inch long.
>
> **Ravioli** Square pasta dough that is stuffed.
>
> **Spaghetti** A long, thin, slender pasta.
>
> **Tortellini** A ring-shaped pasta typically stuffed with (but not limited to) a mix of meat (such as pork loin, prosciutto crudo, or mortadella) or cheese (such as Cheddar or Parmesan). Originally from the Italian region of Emilia (in particular Bologna and Modena), they are usually served in broth, with cream, ragu, or similar sauce.
>
> **Tortelloni** A larger version of tortellini, usually stuffed with ricotta cheese and leaf vegetables, such as spinach

Pesto A puree of fresh herbs garlic, oil, and pine nuts.

Polenta Originating in Venice when maize was imported from America, polenta is made from coarsely ground cornmeal and is used in a variety of northern Italian dishes.

Porcini The same wild mushrooms known as *cepes* in French and *Boletus edulis* in Latin. Fresh porcini are fleshy, velvety, and earthy in flavor; dried porcini are highly aromatic, with an intense woodsy flavor.

Primo Piatto Literally, "first course."

Prosciutto Italian word for ham, usually referring to the raw cured hams of the Parma region. Prosciutto is seasoned, salt cured, and air dried. *Prosciutto cotto* means cooked and *prosciutto crudo* means raw.

Risotto Rice that has been toasted briefly in a *soffritto* and then cooked by gradually adding boiling stock or water and *mantecato* (adding butter and parmigiano). Rice suitable for risotto absorbs three times its weight in liquid. Risotto rice should be cooked al dente. The rice should be slightly moist but never sticky; each grain should be separate.

Salumi Italian meat products usually cured and predominantly made from pork. The term also encompasses bresaola, which is made from beef, and also cooked products such as mortadella and prosciutto cotto. It is equivalent to the French *charcuterie*.

Sambuca Clear, anise-flavored liqueur.

Semolina A yellow flour ground from high-protein durum wheat. Semolina is used in many brands of dried pasta because of its ability to stand up to kneading and molding. Semolina is also used to make gnocchi.

Sformato Derives from *sformare,* which means to unmold. The batter used to make a sformato typically contains beaten eggs (or white sauce), though what else goes into the preparation is up to the cook. Savory sformati can be made with vegetables, which are generally served as side dishes or light entrees, or they can be made with pasta, potatoes, or rice, set in ring molds and used to accompany stews. Sformati can also be sweet. In almost all cases they are served with sauces of one sort or another.

Sopressate Dry-cured salami, hung to dry for six to eight weeks. It loses 40 percent of its original weight.

Zabaglione Italian warm custard made with Marsala wine.

Zampone Stuffed pig's trotter. The foot and shin are boned and stuffed with ground pork snout and other ingredients. Zampone is traditionally eaten in Modena on New Year's Eve.

Menus and Recipes from Italy

Zuppa alla Pavese Pavia-Style Bread Soup with Cheese and Raw Egg SERVES 4

AMOUNT	MEASURE	INGREDIENTS
1		Garlic clove, slit in half
4		Bread slices, cut into 3 inch (7.6 cm) rounds
$\frac{1}{4}$ cup	2 ounces, 60 ml	Butter
4		Eggs
$\frac{1}{4}$ cup	1 ounce, 28 g	Parmesan cheese, grated
1 quart	32 ounces, 960 ml	Clear chicken broth, boiling

PROCEDURE

1 Rub garlic on both sides of bread slices.

2 Heat butter over medium heat until hot, but do not brown.

3 Add bread slices and cook until golden brown; remove from fat. If the bread soaks up all the butter, add more so the bread does not burn.

4 Place one crouton in each bowl.

5 Top each crouton with a raw egg and Parmesan cheese.

6 Add boiling chicken stock around egg, to poach the egg. Serve.

Gnocchi Di Patate in Salsa Di Parmesan Reggiano E Porie

Potato Gnocchi in Parmesan Cheese and Leeks

SERVES 4

AMOUNT	MEASURE	INGREDIENTS
4 cups	1 $\frac{1}{5}$ pounds, 538 g	Russet potatoes, washed and dried
$\frac{3}{4}$ cup	3 ounces, 84 g	All-purpose flour
2		Egg
4 tablespoons	2 ounces, 60 ml	Butter, melted
$\frac{1}{2}$ cup	2 ounces, 56 g	Parmesan cheese, grated
To taste		Salt and white pepper
Sauce		
1 cup	4 ounces, 112 g	Asiago, or Gorgonzola, or fontina cheese, grated
$\frac{1}{2}$ cup	2 ounces 56 g	Parmesan cheese, grated
$\frac{1}{2}$ cup	4 ounces, 120 ml	Heavy cream
1 tablespoon	$\frac{1}{2}$ ounce, 15 ml	Olive oil
1 cup	4 ounces, 112 g	Leek, white part only, julienned

PROCEDURE

1 With a fork make a few vent holes in the potatoes to allow the steam to escape. Bake in a 400°F (205°C) oven until tender, 45 minutes. While potatoes are still warm, peel and pass through a food mill or rices.

2 While still warm, mix in flour, egg, butter, Parmesan cheese, and a pinch of salt until dough is formed.

3 Roll the mixture into two rolls about 1 inch (2.4 cm) thick on a lightly floured surface; cut them into $\frac{3}{4}$ inch (1.8 cm) pieces. Roll the back of a fork across each piece. Place pieces on cheesecloth, dusted with flour.

4 To make sauce, melt Asiago and Parmesan cheese together with cream. Heat olive oil and sauté leeks until translucent; add to cheese sauce.

5 When ready to serve, place gnocchi in boiling salted water; cook until they rise to the surface. Drain well and serve with the sauce; grate additional cheese on top if desired.

Vitello Tonnato Chilled Veal in Tuna Sauce

SERVES 4

AMOUNT	MEASURE	INGREDIENT
10 ounces	280 g	Veal, eye round or top round
To taste		Salt and pepper
1 quart	32 ounces	Veal stock
1 cup	8 ounces, 240 ml	Dry white wine
1		Bouquet garni, with parsley, bay leaf, and oregano
Sauce		
$\frac{1}{2}$ cup	4 ounces, 112 g	Tuna fish, canned in oil, drained
2		Anchovy fillets, in oil, drained
1 tablespoon	$\frac{1}{2}$ ounce, 14 g	Capers in wine vinegar, drained
2 tablespoons	1 ounce, 30 ml	Olive oil
To taste		Salt, pepper, and fresh lemon juice
Garnish		
1		Lemon, sliced thin
1 tablespoon	$\frac{1}{2}$ ounce, 14 g	Capers, rinsed
8		Cetriolini (small pickled cucumbers), like cornichons

PROCEDURE

1 Trim veal of all fat and silver skin, season with salt and pepper, wrap in cheesecloth, and tie like a salami.

2 Combine the stock, wine, and bouquet garni. Bring to a boil, add veal.

3 Reduce to a simmer and cover.

4 Poach 15 to 20 minutes; keep meat medium rare. Remove from heat and place pot in an ice bath. Let meat cool in liquid. Remove meat and discard bouquet garni.

5 Puree the tuna, anchovy, and capers in blender or food processor; drizzle in the olive oil. If too thick, thin with some poaching liquid. Season with lemon juice, salt, and pepper.

6 Remove string and cheesecloth from veal; cut into 12 thin slices.

7 Arrange veal on platter with a thin lemon slice between each slice of meat. Pour sauce over meat. Garnish with remaining lemon slices, capers, and cetriolini. Serve cold.

Osso Buco Milanese SERVES 4

AMOUNT	MEASURE	INGREDIENT
4 ($\frac{1}{2}$ inch thick)	10 ounce, 280 g each	Veal shanks, bone and marrow in center
As needed		All-purpose flour
3 tablespoons	$\frac{1}{2}$ ounce, 45 ml	Olive oil
3 tablespoons	$\frac{1}{2}$ ounce, 45 ml	Butter
2 cups	8 ounces, 224 g	Onions, $\frac{1}{4}$ inch (.6 cm) dice
1 cup	4 ounces, 112 g	Carrots, peeled, $\frac{1}{4}$ inch (.6 cm) dice
1 cup	4 ounces, 112 g	Celery, $\frac{1}{4}$ inch (.6 cm) dice
2		Garlic cloves, minced
$\frac{1}{2}$ teaspoon		Dried marjoram
$\frac{1}{2}$ cup	4 ounces, 120 ml	Dry white wine
2 cups	12 ounces, 340 g	Tomatoes, peeled, seeded, $\frac{1}{4}$ inch (.6 cm) dice
$\frac{3}{4}$ cup	6 ounces, 180 ml	Veal stock
To taste		Salt and pepper
1		Lemon peel, grated
Gremolata		
3 teaspoons		Fresh parsley, chopped
1 teaspoon		Lemon zest
2		Garlic cloves, minced

PROCEDURE

1 Tie each piece of veal around the perimeter so that the meat does not separate from the bone during cooking. Lightly dust veal with flour.

2 Preheat an appropriate-sized cooking vessel in a 350°F (176°C) oven.

3 Add oil and butter to preheated cooking pan. Brown veal, remove from pan, and reserve in a warm place.

4 To the same pan, add onions, carrots, celery, garlic, and marjoram; cook over medium heat until soft.

5 Add wine, deglaze pan, and reduce by half. Add tomatoes and stock; simmer 10 minutes. Season with salt and pepper.

6 Return browned veal shanks to the mixture, add lemon peel, and braise in a 350°F (176°C) oven 1 hour or until tender.

7 When done, remove meat and degrease sauce. Adjust seasoning and return meat to sauce.

GREMOLATA

1   Combine parsley, lemon zest, and garlic; mix well.

2   Five minutes before serving, add the gremolata to the veal shanks and sauce, turning them gently from time to time so that they will take on the flavors.

3   Remove the string before serving. Place 1 shank on each place and serve with sauce.

Cicorietta Saltata con Pancetta
Chicory Sautéed with Pancetta   SERVES 4

AMOUNT	MEASURE	INGREDIENT
8 cups	1 pound, 448 g	Chicory
2 tablespoons	1 ounce, 30 ml	Olive oil
$\frac{1}{4}$ cup	2 ounces, 56 g	Pancetta, $\frac{1}{4}$ inch (.6 cm) dice
2	1 tablespoon	Garlic cloves, minced
$\frac{1}{4}$ cup	$\frac{1}{2}$ ounce, 15 g	Parsley, chopped
$\frac{1}{2}$ cup	4 ounces, 120 ml	Dry white wine
To taste		Salt and pepper

PROCEDURE

1   Clean and wash chicory at least 2 times. Blanch in boiling salt water, shock in ice water. Drain, removing as much moisture as possible.

2   Heat oil over medium heat, add pancetta, and cook until brown and crisp.

3   Add garlic; lightly brown. Add chicory; sauté until hot. Add parsley. Add wine and reduce until almost dry.

4   Correct seasoning and serve.

Risotto allo Zafferano
Risotto with Saffron   SERVES 4

Use a large-bottom pan so the flame can spread underneath.

AMOUNT	MEASURE	INGREDIENT
I tablespoon	$\frac{1}{2}$ ounce, 15 ml	Olive oil
I tablespoon	$\frac{1}{2}$ ounce, 15 ml	Butter
$\frac{1}{2}$ cup	2 ounces, 56 g	Onions, $\frac{1}{8}$ inch (.3cm), dice
I cup	$6\frac{1}{2}$ ounces, 184 g	Medium-grain arborio rice
$\frac{1}{2}$ cup	4 ounces, 120 ml	Dry white wine
3 cups	24 ounces, 720 ml	Chicken stock, hot
I pinch		Saffron threads
$\frac{1}{4}$ cup	I ounce, 28 g	Parmesan cheese, grated
2 tablespoons	I ounce, 28 g	Butter
To taste		Salt and pepper

PROCEDURE

1 Heat first butter and olive oil over medium heat until it melts; cook onions until translucent.

2 Add the rice and cook until lightly toasted and fat has been absorbed, 1 to 2 minutes.

3 Add the white wine; stir until fully absorbed.

4 Add the chicken stock, $\frac{1}{4}$ at a time, stirring often. Allow stock to be completely absorbed before adding more stock.

5 Halfway through cooking (after 6 to 8 minutes), dissolve saffron in a little hot broth, let soak 3 minutes and add to the rice. Do not add at the beginning.

6 Stir the rice frequently, so it does not stick to the bottom of the pan. From start to finish, this dish should take 18 to 20 minutes.

7 When the rice is cooked al dente, turn off the heat. Vigorously beat in Parmesan cheese and butter off the heat. Correct seasoning and let stand, covered, for a few minutes, so the rice finishes cooking. Serve immediately.

Panna Cotta with Fresh Berries

SERVES 4

AMOUNT	MEASURE	INGREDIENT
I tablespoon	$\frac{1}{2}$ ounce, 14 g	Butter
$\frac{3}{4}$ tablespoon		Unflavored gelatin
$\frac{1}{2}$ cup	4 ounces, 120 ml	Milk
$\frac{1}{2}$ cup	12 ounces, 360 ml	Heavy cream
$\frac{1}{4}$ cup	2 ounces, 56 g	Granulated sugar
$\frac{1}{2}$		Vanilla bean, split, or 2 teaspoons vanilla extract
I cup	3 ounces, 84 g	Assorted fresh berries
2 tablespoons		Spearmint, chiffonade

PROCEDURE

1 Lightly butter the inside of four 6-ounce ramekins.

2 Sprinkle gelatin over $\frac{1}{4}$ cups (2 ounces, 60 ml) of milk. Let stand 3 to 4 minutes until soft.

3 Heat remaining milk, cream, sugar, and vanilla bean over medium heat, stirring occasionally, until simmering, about 5 minutes; remove from heat.

4 Combine softened gelatin with hot milk mixture; stir to completely dissolve, 1 minute. Strain through fine china cap; save vanilla bean.

5 Fill ramekins, cover with plastic wrap, and chill until set.

6 To unmold, fill a shallow pan with $\frac{1}{2}$ inch (1.25 cm) very hot water. One at a time, place ramekins in the hot water 15 seconds. Remove from water and dry the outside of the ramekins. Press the panna cotta around the edges to loosen and invert onto the center of 4 dessert plates.

7 Scatter berries and spearmint around the panna cotta and serve.

Tagliatelle al Peperoncino
Red Pepper Tagliatelle   SERVES 4

AMOUNT	MEASURE	INGREDIENT
2 teaspoons		Red pepper flakes
1¼ cups	6 ounces, 168 g	All-purpose flour
½ cup	2½ ounces, 70 g	Semolina flour
3		Extra large eggs
2 teaspoons		Olive oil
Pinch		Salt
Sauce		
1 cup	2 ounces, 56 g	Italian parsley, leaves only
To taste		Coarse salt
½ cup	4 ounces, 120 ml	Olive oil

PROCEDURE

1 Coarsely grind the red pepper flakes with a mortar and pestle.

2 Prepare pasta: place flours in a mixing bowl with dough hook, add red pepper flakes. Combine eggs, oil, and salt, and beat together. Add egg mixture to dry ingredients while mixing on low; mix until well incorporated. Wrap dough and refrigerate 30 minutes.

3 Roll the dough through the pasta machine several times. Start at a thick setting and work down to almost the thinnest setting, a little more than $\frac{1}{16}$ inch (.2 cm). The red pepper specks should not break through.

4 Cut into tagliatelle (about $\frac{3}{8}$ inch wide); let stand until needed.

5 Chop parsley coarsely and set aside until needed.

6 Bring a large pot of salted water to a boil. Add coarse salt to taste.

7 Add pasta to boiling water and cook a maximum of 1 minute after the water has returned to a boil.

8 Drain and put in serving bowl.

9 Add oil and parsley; toss well. Serve immediately. No cheese should be added.

Melanzane Involtino

Eggplant Roll   SERVES 4

AMOUNT	MEASURE	INGREDIENT
1	16 ounces, 448 g	Large eggplant, in 8 thin slices
As needed		Coarse salt
$\frac{1}{2}$ cup	4 ounces, 120 ml	Olive oil
8	4 ounces, 112 g	Ham, in 8 thin slices
8	4 ounces, 112 g	Mozzarella cheese, 8 thin slices
1 quart	32 ounces, 960 ml	Fresh tomato sauce (see recipe on page 731)
$\frac{1}{4}$ cup	$\frac{1}{2}$ ounce, 42 g	Ricotta salata, crumbled
1 tablespoon		Fresh basil, chiffonade

PROCEDURE

1   Salt sliced eggplant and let sit 30 minutes. Rinse and pat dry.

2   Heat oil over medium-high heat and fry eggplant slices until nicely browned; add more oil if needed. Drain and blot excess oil.

3   Lay out eggplant, top with slices of ham and cheese, and roll up.

4   Place in hot oven to melt cheese.

5   Serve hot, topped with warm tomato sauce, ricotta salata, and basil.

Tomato Bruschetta   SERVES 4

AMOUNT	MEASURE	INGREDIENT
$\frac{1}{3}$ cup	2 ounces, 56 g	Red onions, shaved very thin
$\frac{1}{2}$ cup	3 ounces, 84 g	Tomatoes, peeled, seeded, $\frac{1}{8}$ inch (.3 cm) dice
$\frac{1}{2}$ cup	3 ounces, 84 g	Yellow tomato, peeled, seeded, $\frac{1}{8}$ inch (.3 cm) dice
$\frac{1}{4}$ cup	1 ounce, 28 g	Shallot, finely diced
1		Garlic clove, minced
8		Basil sprigs
$\frac{1}{4}$ cup	2 ounces, 60 ml	Olive oil
$\frac{1}{2}$ teaspoon	8 ml	Red wine vinegar
1 teaspoon	5 ml	Balsamic vinegar
To taste		Course salt and freshly ground pepper
8 $\frac{1}{2}$-inch slices	1.25 cm	Country bread
$\frac{1}{4}$ cup	2 ounces, 60 ml	Roasted garlic aioli (recipe follows)
$\frac{1}{2}$ cup	3 ounces, 84 g	Ricotta salata, crumbled

PROCEDURE

1   Soak red onions in ice water 1 hour; drain and dry.

2   Combine tomatoes, shallots, and garlic; toss.

3   Remove 8 nice basil leaves for garnish. Finely chop remaining leaves and combine with tomato mixture.

4   Add the oil and vinegars; correct seasoning with salt and pepper. Let marinate at room temperature at least 30 minutes.

5   Lightly grill or toast the bread slices. Cool and spread with aioli.

6   Add red onions to tomato mixture and correct seasoning.

7   Set bread slices on plate and top with tomato mixture.

8   Garnish bruschettas with crumbled cheese and reserved basil leaves.

Roasted Garlic Aioli   SERVES 4

AMOUNT	MEASURE	INGREDIENT
1	1 ounce, 28 g	Green onion, white part only
1		Large egg yolk, at room temperature
3		Garlic cloves, roasted and mashed to paste
$\frac{1}{4}$ teaspoon		Dijon mustard
To taste		Salt and pepper
$\frac{1}{2}$ cup	4 ounces, 120 ml	Vegetable oil
$\frac{1}{4}$ cup	2 ounces, 60 ml	Olive oil
$\frac{1}{2}$ teaspoon		Fresh lemon juice

PROCEDURE

1   Blanch green onion in boiling salted water 10 seconds. Transfer to a bowl of ice water. Drain and gently squeeze out excess water.

2   Chop onion.

3   Combine onion, egg yolk, garlic, mustard, and seasoning in a blender or small food processor fitted with metal blade. Process about 30 seconds until smooth and well combined.

4   With blender or processor running, slowly add the oils in a steady steam. Scrape down sides of bowl several times during blending. When the emulsion is thick and fluffy, season with lemon juice and correct seasoning. Refrigerate until needed.

Pollo alla Toscana
Chicken Sautéed with Mushrooms   SERVES 4

AMOUNT	MEASURE	INGREDIENT
1 ounce	1 ounce, 28 g	Porcini mushrooms, dried
1 cup	8 ounces, 240 ml	Chicken stock, warm
1 3 to 3$\frac{1}{2}$ pound	1 1.36 kg to 1.58 kg	Chicken, cut into 8 pieces
$\frac{1}{4}$ cup	1 ounce, 28 g	All-purpose flour
4 tablespoons	2 ounces, 56 g	Butter
$\frac{1}{4}$ cup	2 ounces, 60 ml	Olive oil
4		Fresh sage leaves
$\frac{1}{2}$ cup	4 ounces, 120 ml	Dry red wine
1 cup	6 ounces, 180 ml	Tomatoes, peeled, seeded, passed through a food mill
To taste		Salt and freshly ground black pepper

PROCEDURE

1　Soak mushrooms in warm chicken stock 30 minutes; remove and reserve both. Check to make sure mushrooms are free of sand and strain stock through cheesecloth.

2　Lightly flour chicken and remove excess flour.

3　Heat butter and olive oil over medium heat.

4　Sauté chicken until light golden brown, about 10 minutes.

5　Add sage leaves and wine; reduce to almost dry over low heat.

6　Add mushrooms and chicken stock; reduce by half.

7　Add tomatoes; simmer 10 minutes. Check chicken to ensure it is cooked.

8　Correct seasoning, cook 1 minute, and serve.

Basic Polenta   SERVES 4

This ratio applies to soft polenta. For polenta that is to be baked, grilled, or used as a substitute for bread, use a 3:1 ratio of water to polenta, and the same amount of salt.

AMOUNT	MEASURE	INGREDIENT
1 quart	32 ounces, 960 ml	Water
$\frac{1}{2}$ teaspoon	3 g	Salt
1 $\frac{1}{3}$ cup	8 ounces, 224 g	Yellow polenta, coarsely ground

PROCEDURE

1   Bring water to a boil and add salt.

2   Reduce heat to low.

3   Add cornmeal, little by little, stirring constantly. Do not pour directly from the container, but use your hands, pouring a handful at time.

4   After all cornmeal has been added and incorporated, turn up heat to medium-high.

5   Cook 40 to 45 minutes, stirring constantly. The heat should be high enough to cause bubbles to rise and burst on the surface.

6   While stirring, pull the cornmeal off the sides and from the bottom up. Serve hot.

Asparagi al Parmigiano-Reggiano Asparagus with Parmigiano-Reggiano SERVES 4

AMOUNT	MEASURE	INGREDIENT
I pound	448 g	Asparagus
As needed		Salt
2 tablespoons	I ounce, 28 g	Butter
½ cup	2 ounces, 56 g	Parmigiano-Reggiano, grated

PROCEDURE

1 Trim, peel, and blanch asparagus in salted boiling water until tender but not limp.

2 Preheat oven to 400°F (205°C).

3 Place asparagus lengthwise in buttered baking dish, staggering so the tips protrude.

4 Dot with remaining butter, sprinkle cheese on top, and bake until top forms a light brown crust.

Tiramisu   SERVES 4

Tiramisu may be made with sponge cake instead of ladyfingers. Ladyfingers can also line the side of a mold instead of being placed in layers.

AMOUNT	MEASURE	INGREDIENT
4		Eggs, separated
1¾ cups	12 ounces, 336 g	Granulated sugar
2 cups	15 ounces, 420 g	Mascarpone cheese
3 tablespoons	½ ounce, 45 ml	Brandy
18		Ladyfingers
2 tablespoons	½ ounce, 14 g	Cocoa power
½ cup	4 ounces, 120 ml	Strong espresso
5 tablespoons	1¼ ounces, 42 g	Pistachios, chopped fine

PROCEDURE

1 Using the whisk attachment, beat on medium high speed the yolks with half the sugar until pale yellow and thick.

2 With mixer on medium speed, add cheese and whip until smooth.

3 Beat egg whites with half of the remaining sugar, and a pinch of salt to firm peaks.

4 Fold the egg whites into the egg yolk mixture.

5 Make a simple syrup with the remaining sugar and ½ cup (4 ounces, 120 ml) water.

6 Add the espresso and brandy to simple syrup; mix well.

7 Moisten the ladyfingers or sponge cake with espresso mixture and make a layer in a deep serving dish.

8 Cover ladyfinger layer with a layer of mascarpone mixture, continue alternating layers of ladyfingers and the mascarpone mixture.

9 The last layer should be mascarpone, not ladyfingers.

10 Refrigerate 2 hours or more.

11 Just before serving, dust top with cocoa powder and sprinkle with chopped pistachios.

Peperonata
Peppers Sautéed with Olive Oil and Capers   SERVES 4

AMOUNT	MEASURE	INGREDIENT
1 cup	4 ounces, 112 g	Red bell peppers, seeded, 1 inch (2.5 cm) wide strips
1 cup	4 ounces, 112 g	Green bell peppers, seeded, 1 inch (2.5 cm) wide strips
1 cup	4 ounces, 112 g	Yellow bell peppers, seeded, 1 inch (2.5 cm) wide strips
$\frac{1}{4}$ cup	2 ounces, 60 ml	Olive oil
1 cup	4 ounces, 112 g	White onion, $\frac{1}{4}$ inch (.6 cm) dice
1		Garlic clove, minced
$\frac{3}{4}$ cup	4 ounces, 112 g	Tomatoes, peeled, seeded, $\frac{1}{4}$ inch (.6 cm) dice
2 tablespoons		Fresh basil, chopped
1 tablespoon		Capers, rinsed

PROCEDURE

1 Seed, rib, and cut the peppers.

2 Heat half the oil over medium heat and sauté onions and garlic (*soffritto*) until golden brown.

3 Add tomatoes and basil, cook 10 minutes over low heat, and set aside.

4 Heat remaining oil and the add peppers. When peppers are just beginning to soften, add *soffritto* and capers.

5 Cook peppers until tender but still crisp. (If the skin begins to fall off, the peppers are overcooked.)

6 Remove from heat, correct seasoning, and serve.

Braciole Calabresi Stuffed Pork Bundles

SERVES 4

AMOUNT	MEASURE	INGREDIENT
2		Eggs, beaten
$\frac{1}{2}$ cup	2 ounces, 56 g	Pecorino cheese, thinly sliced or slivered
2		Garlic cloves, minced
2 tablespoons	10 g	Italian parsley leaves, chopped fine
$\frac{1}{2}$ cup	$\frac{1}{2}$ ounce, 42 g	Italian dried bread crumbs
As needed		Salt and freshly ground pepper
	16 ounces, 448 g	Pork loin, boned, cleaned of fat and silver skin, cut into 8 pieces
$\frac{1}{2}$ cup	4 ounces, 120 ml	Olive oil
$\frac{1}{2}$ cup	4 ounces, 120 ml	Fresh tomato sauce (recipe follows)
$\frac{1}{2}$ cup	4 ounces, 120 ml	Chicken stock
$\frac{1}{4}$ cup	2 ounces, 60 ml	Dry red wine
2		Fresh rosemary sprigs

PROCEDURE

1   Combine egg, cheese, garlic, and chopped parsley.

2   Slowly drizzle in the seasoned bread crumbs while mixing constantly. Use only enough bread crumbs to bring the mixture to a soft, spreadable paste. Correct seasoning. Be careful with the salt; consider the flavor of the cheese.

3   Tap the pork until the slices are about $\frac{1}{8}$ inch (.3 cm) thick and a rectangular shape.

4   Lightly brush the meat with olive oil. Season with salt and pepper.

5   Divided stuffing into 8 portions and spread each piece of pounded pork with stuffing, leaving $\frac{1}{4}$ inch (.6 cm) space around the edge of each piece.

6   Roll up and tie on each end and once in the middle.

7   Heat remaining oil over medium heat, brown braci:oles on all sides. Place in an appropriate-sized ovenproof pan.

8   Combine tomato sauce, stock, red wine, and rosemary; mix well.

9   Pour liquid over the pork, bring to simmer, cover tightly, and cook for about 20 minutes just until tender. (Because the dish is made with loin it does not need to cook for a long period of time. Overcooking will dry and toughen the pork.)

10   When meat is tender, remove and reduce sauce. Serve 1 or 2 pieces, with braising liquid.

Melanzane Involtino – Eggplant Roll and Braciole Calabresi – Stuffed Pork Bundles

Caponata SERVES 4

AMOUNT	MEASURE	INGREDIENT
I pound	16 ounces, 448 g	Japanese eggplant (small, long eggplants), stems removed
I tablespoon	$\frac{1}{2}$ ounce, 15 g	Coarse salt
$\frac{1}{2}$ cup	4 ounces, 120 ml	Olive oil
$\frac{1}{2}$ cup	2 ounces, 56 g	Celery, $\frac{1}{4}$ inch (.6 cm), dice
$\frac{1}{2}$ cup	2 ounces, 56 g	Red onion, $\frac{1}{4}$ inch (.6 cm) dice
I tablespoon	$\frac{1}{2}$ ounce, 28 g	Tomato paste
2 teaspoons	10 g	Granulated sugar
$\frac{1}{4}$ cup	2 ounces, 60 ml	Red wine vinegar
$\frac{1}{4}$ cup	2 ounces, 60 ml	Cold water
$\frac{1}{2}$ cup	4 ounces, 112 g	Black Greek olives in brine, drained, pitted $\frac{1}{4}$ inch (.6 cm) dice
3 tablespoons	I ounce, 28 g	Capers, rinsed
To taste		Salt and pepper

PROCEDURE

1. Wash eggplants and cut into 1 inch (2.5 cm) square cubes. (Do not peel the eggplant).

2. Place eggplant in a colander and sprinkle with coarse salt; toss well to coat eggplant evenly. Set colander in the sink and place dish inside the colander so it is in direct contact with the eggplant. Place a weight on top of the plate and let stand 1 hour.

3. Wipe off the eggplant to remove as much of the salt and clinging juices.

4. Heat oil over medium heat; add eggplant, and sauté 10 to 12 minutes or until completely cooked, stirring often.

5. Remove cooked eggplant from oil and reserve.

6. Over medium heat, sauté celery and onions in the same oil until soft, 5 to 10 minutes, stirring often.

7. In a bowl combine tomato paste, sugar, red wine vinegar, and cold water; blend well.

8. Remove cooked celery and onion mixture and combine with eggplant.

9. Add vinegar mixture to sauté pan, cook 5 minutes or until reduced by $\frac{2}{3}$.

10. Add olives to vinegar mixture; simmer 10 minutes.

11. Add vegetables and capers back to olive mixture and simmer together 10 minutes.

12. Correct seasoning and transfer to serving dish. This may be served warm, but it is better to let it marinate 1 hour in the refrigerator. Serve at room temperature or reheat.

Fresh Tomato Sauce   SERVES 4

AMOUNT	MEASURE	INGREDIENT
2 tablespoons	1 ounce, 30 ml	Olive oil
$\frac{1}{4}$ cup	1 ounce, 28 g	Onions, minced
1		Garlic clove, minced
2 tablespoons	1 ounce, 28 g	Tomato paste
2 cups	12 ounces, 336 g	Tomatoes, peeled, seeded, $\frac{1}{4}$ inch (.6 cm) dice
To taste		Salt and white pepper

PROCEDURE

1 Heat oil over medium heat and sauté onion and garlic until onions are translucent, 3 minutes.

2 Add tomato paste and stir well.

3 Add tomatoes; simmer 10 to 15 minutes, until correct consistency is reached. Do not overcook or you will loose the fresh tomato flavor.

4 Correct seasoning.

Orechietti con Carciofi
Orechietti Pasta with Artichokes   SERVES 4

AMOUNT	MEASURE	INGREDIENT
4		Artichokes
1		Lemon
$\frac{1}{4}$ cup	2 ounces, 60 ml	Olive oil
$\frac{1}{2}$ cup	3 ounces, 84 g	Pancetta, diced
$\frac{1}{4}$ cup	1 ounce, 28 g	Onion, minced
$\frac{1}{4}$ cup	2 ounces, 60 ml	Water or chicken stock
$\frac{1}{4}$ teaspoon		Red pepper flakes
	16 ounces, 448 g	Orechietti pasta, dried
To taste		Salt and pepper
2 tablespoons		Parsley, chopped
1 cup	$4\frac{1}{2}$ ounces, 126 g	Romano cheese, grated

PROCEDURE

1   Clean the artichokes, leaving on the tender parts of the heart; cut into very thin slices.

2   Squeeze the juice of the lemon over them.

3   Heat olive oil over medium heat and add pancetta. Sauté until crisp; add onions and cook 2 minutes.

4   Add sliced artichokes, water or chicken stock, and red pepper flakes. Cook until the artichokes are tender. Correct seasoning.

5   Cook pasta in boiling salt water; drain.

6   Toss pasta with artichoke sauce, herbs, and cheese. Serve.

Orechietti con Carciofi – Orechietti Pasta with Artichokes

Insalata di Seppie, Calamari, e Gamberi
Salad of Cuttlefish, Squid, and Shrimp   SERVES 4

AMOUNT	MEASURE	INGREDIENT
12 ounces	12 ounces, 336 g	Cuttlefish, cleaned, cut into $\frac{1}{4}$ inch (.6 cm) strips
12 ounces	12 ounces, 336 g	Squid, cleaned, cut into $\frac{1}{4}$ inch (.6 cm) strips
8 ounces	8 ounces, 224 g	Shrimp, 31–35 count, peeled, cleaned, whole
		Coarse salt
1 cup	8 ounces, 240 ml	Red wine vinegar
3 cups	15 ounces, 420 g	Boiling potatoes (but not new potatoes), 1 inch (2.5 cm) cubes
Sauce		
1		Garlic clove, minced
$\frac{1}{2}$ cup	1 ounce, 28 g	Italian parsley, leaves only, coarsely chopped
1 cup	8 ounces, 240 ml	Olive oil
		Salt and freshly ground black pepper
$\frac{1}{4}$ cup	$\frac{1}{2}$ ounce, 14 g	Basil leaves, coarsely chopped
$\frac{1}{4}$ cup	$\frac{1}{2}$ ounce, 14 g	Mint leaves, coarsely chopped
2 tablespoons	1 ounces, 30 ml	Fresh lemon juice
1 tablespoon	$\frac{1}{2}$ ounce, 15 ml	Red wine vinegar

PROCEDURE

1   Combine cuttlefish and squid, cover with salted cold water; let stand 30 minutes. Drain.

2   Soak clean shrimp in salted cold water 30 minutes. Drain.

3   Bring a large pot of salted water to a boil with 1 tablespoon of red wine vinegar; add cuttlefish and squid, reduce to simmer, cover, and cook 20 minutes. Drain and cool.

4   Drain the shrimp and cook in boiling salted water, do not overcook. Drain and cool.

5   Cover potatoes with salted cold water and the remaining red wine vinegar; bring to a simmer. Simmer until tender. Drain and let cool at least 1 hour.

6   Combine all the ingredients for the sauce and mix well.

7   Combine cooked seafood and potatoes and toss with sauce.

8   Cool at least 1 hour before serving, for flavors to blend.

Insalata di Seppie, Calamari e Gamberi – Salad of Cuttlefish, Squid, and Shrimp

Focaccia Bread   SERVES 4 TO 6

AMOUNT	MEASURE	INGREDIENT
Sponge		
I cup	8 ounces, 240 ml	**Warm water, 100°F (38°C)**
I teaspoon		**Active dry yeast**
I cup	4 ounces, 112 g	**All-purpose flour**
Focaccia		
$\frac{1}{2}$ cup	4 ounces, 120 ml	**Water**
$\frac{1}{3}$ cup	2.4 ounces, 72 ml	**Dry white wine**
$\frac{1}{3}$ cup	2.4 ounces, 72 ml	**Olive oil**
2 tablespoons		**Fine yellow cornmeal**
$\frac{1}{2}$ teaspoon		**Kosher salt**
$2\frac{3}{4}$ cups	12 ounces, 336 g	**All-purpose flour**
5 teaspoons		**Extra-virgin olive oil**
I		**Garlic clove, minced**
To taste		**Black pepper**
$\frac{1}{2}$ teaspoon		**Rosemary, minced**
To taste		**Kosher salt**

SPONGE

1 Combine warm water and yeast and let stand 2 minutes; stir to dissolve.

2 Stir in flour until the mixture is smooth.

3 Cover and let stand at room temperature 24 hours.

FOCACCIA

1 Preheat oven to 450°F (225°C).

2 Using a small mixer with dough hook attachment, mix sponge.

3 Slowly add the water, white wine, $\frac{1}{3}$ cup olive oil, cornmeal, and $\frac{1}{2}$ teaspoon salt. Mix until thoroughly incorporated.

4 Gradually add the $2\frac{3}{4}$ cups flour, mixing on low speed until the dough is formed.

5 Increase mixer to medium speed and work dough 5 minutes.

6 Remove from mixer to a greased bowl. Cover and let rise at room temperature about $\frac{1}{2}$ hours or until it doubles in size.

7   Grease a sheet pan with olive oil.

8   Transfer the dough to baking sheet and stretch it, using oiled fingers, until the dough completely fills the pan. Let the dough rest 5 minutes; the dough will shrink.

9   Restretch the dough to cover the pan completely. If it is still too elastic, let the dough rest longer and try again.

10 Let the dough rise in the pan at room temperature 1 hour.

11 Brush the focaccia with olive oil and sprinkle with rosemary and kosher salt to taste.

12 Bake for about 15 to 20 minutes or until nicely browned.

Tunnu a Palirmitana
Tuna Fish, Palermo Style   SERVES 4

AMOUNT	MEASURE	INGREDIENT
I cup	8 ounces, 240 ml	Dry white wine
2 tablespoons	I ounce, 30 ml	Fresh lemon juice
I		Sprig rosemary, fresh
2		Garlic cloves, minced
4	6 ounce (168 g) servings	Tuna loin
Basting		
$\frac{1}{2}$ cup	4 ounces, 120 ml	Olive oil
3		Sardine fillets, oil packed
Garnish		
2 cups	4 ounces, 112 g	Fresh arugula
$\frac{1}{2}$ cup	4 ounces, 112 g	Lemon segments
$\frac{1}{2}$ cup	2 ounces, 56 g	Red radish, julienned
$\frac{1}{4}$ cup	2 ounces, 60 ml	Olive oil
To taste		Freshly ground black pepper

PROCEDURE

1   Combine wine, lemon juice, rosemary, and garlic; mix well.

2   Marinate tuna fillets in mixture 1 hour, turning at least once.

3   Heat $\frac{1}{2}$ cup olive oil in a pan until hot; remove from heat, add sardine fillets, and blend or mash together.

4   Remove tuna from marinade. Season with salt and pepper.

5   Grill until nicely marked and medium rare. Baste several times during process with sardine mixture; baste again when cooked.

6   Toss together arugula, lemon segments, radish, and olive oil; season.

7   Serve tuna fillet topped with arugula salad and fresh cracked black pepper.

Torta Caprese
Chocolate Almond Cake   SERVES 6 TO 8

AMOUNT	MEASURE	INGREDIENT
2 cups	8 ounces, 224 g	Semisweet or bittersweet chocolate, chopped
I cup	8 ounces, 224 g	Butter, at room temperature
I cup	7 ounces, 196 g	Granulated sugar
6		Eggs, separated, at room temperature
$\frac{1}{2}$ cup	6 ounces, 168 g	Almonds, very finely ground
Pinch		Salt
		Unsweetend cocoa powder

PROCEDURE

1   Melt chocolate over hot water bath; stir until smooth. Let cool slightly.

2   Preheat oven to 350°F (176°C).

3   Grease and flour a 9-inch (22.5 cm) round cake pan. Tap out excess flour.

4   Using a paddle attachment, on medium speed beat $\frac{3}{4}$ cup (6 ounces, 128 g) of butter and sugar together until light and fluffy, about 3–5 minutes.

5   Add egg yolks, one at a time, beating well after each addition. With a rubber spatula, stir in the chocolate and the almonds; set aside.

6   Using beater attachment, whip egg whites and a pinch of salt until foamy.

7   Increase speed to high and beat in remaining sugar. Beat until egg whites are glossy and hold soft peaks when the beaters are lifted, about 5 minutes.

8   Fold $\frac{1}{4}$ meringue into chocolate mixture to lighten. Gradually fold in the remaining whites.

9   Scrape batter into the prepared pan.

10 Bake 45 minutes or until cake is set around the edges but soft and moist in the center and a toothpick inserted in the center comes out covered with chocolate.

11 Cool on rack 10 minutes.

12 Run thin metal spatula around the inside of pan, invert onto serving plate.

13 Let cool to room temperature, dust with cocoa powder, and serve.

Tagliatelle con Ragu Bolognese

SERVES 4

In and around Bologna each family may have their own particular recipe for ragu. Each feels theirs is the best, much like chili recipes in Texas, or gumbo in Louisiana. They are all based on a similar technique and similar ingredients, but the outcome of the dish has subtle yet distinct differences. Ragu Bolognese is usually composed of three meats: veal, pork fat back, and beef. The modern version presented here was given to Chef Joseph Bonaparte MHM, CCE, CCC, to cook for the Premio Internazionale Della Cucina Bolognese, a cooking contest conducted by the city of Bologna to promote its gastronomic heritage and the products produced in the region of Emilia-Romagna.

AMOUNT	MEASURE	INGREDIENT
2 tablespoons	1 ounce, 30 ml	Olive oil
1 cup	6 ounces, 168 g	Pancetta, $\frac{1}{4}$ inch (.6 cm) dice
1 cup	4 ounces, 112 g	Onions, $\frac{1}{4}$ inch (.6 cm) dice
$\frac{1}{2}$ cup	2 ounces, 56 g	Carrots, $\frac{1}{4}$ inch (.6 cm) dice
$\frac{1}{2}$ cup	2 ounces, 56 g	Celery, $\frac{1}{4}$ inch (.6 cm) dice
$1\frac{1}{4}$ cups	10 ounces, 280 g	Lean ground beef
$\frac{1}{2}$ cup	4 ounces, 120 ml	Italian white wine
2 tablespoons	1 ounce, 30 ml	Tomato paste
$\frac{1}{2}$ cup	12 ounces, 360 ml	Beef stock
$\frac{1}{2}$ cup	4 ounces, 120 ml	Milk
To taste		Salt and pepper
12 ounces		Fresh tagliatelle
$\frac{1}{2}$ cup	2 ounces, 56 g	Grana Pandano or Parmigiano-Reggiano

PROCEDURE

1   Over low heat, combine the olive oil and pancetta. Cook until most of the fat has been rendered, 3 to 5 minutes; do not brown the pancetta.

2   Add the onion and cook 3 minutes. Add remaining vegetables and cook until evenly browned (caramelized), 5 to 7 minutes.

3   Add the ground beef and increase heat to medium. Cook, stirring frequently, until browned but not dried out; be sure to scrape the bits off the bottom of the pan.

4   Add the wine and cook 2 minutes.

5   Mix tomato paste and beef stock. Add to beef mixture and stir well. Bring to a low simmer.

6   Simmer sauce 1 to $1\frac{1}{2}$ hours. During the cooking process (15 mintues into the process), add the milk 2 tablespoons (1 ounce, 30 ml) at a time. After each addition stir well and let cook 5 to 10 minutes before the next addition of milk. The finished sauce should be rich and thick. Correct seasoning.

TO SERVE

1   Cook fresh taliatelle until al dente. Remove from the pasta cooking water directly into the hot ragu. The sauce is a condiment; it should accent the pasta, not overwhelm it.

2   Garnish with freshly grated Grana Pandano or Parmigiano-Reggiano.

Germany, Austria, and Switzerland

The Land

Germany is surrounded by nine countries. To the north along the peninsula called Jutland, which lies between the North Sea and the Baltic Sea, is Denmark. To the west are France, the Netherlands, Belgium, and Luxembourg. Switzerland and Austria lie to the south. The Czech Republic and Poland lie to the east. With its irregular, elongated shape, Germany provides an excellent example of a recurring sequence of landforms found the world over.

From the north, a plain dotted with lakes, moors, marshes, and heaths retreats from the sea and reaches inland, where it becomes a landscape of hills crisscrossed by streams, rivers, and valleys. These hills lead upward, gradually forming high plateaus and woodlands and eventually climaxing in spectacular mountain ranges to the south.

While the Alps along the southern border of Germany are the largest of the European Alps, little Alpine terrain actually lies within Germany compared with Switzerland and Austria. The Black Forest, on the southwestern border with France, separates the Rhine River from the headwaters of the Danube River on its eastern slopes. The Danube cuts across the relatively flat land of central Bavaria, Germany's largest and oldest state, before curving to the southeast around the southern tip of the Bavarian Forest, another range on the border between Bavaria and the Czech Republic.

Austria borders eight countries. To the west are Switzerland and the tiny nation of Liechtenstein. Germany is to the northwest, the Czech Republic is to the north, Slovakia and Hungary are on the east, and Italy and Slovenia lie to the south. Mountains cover more than three-fourths of the Austrian landscape. The Alps, the great spine of Europe, rise in the western and southern half of the country. To the north is the Alpine Forelands, a sprawling valley studded by hills and low mountains. North of the Alpine Forelands is a separate mountainous area called the Granite Plate, made up of granite mountains and rich forests.

The Danube is Austria's major river and runs across the country from West to East. It is the only major river in Europe that follows this direction. The Alps act as a watershed and all major rivers north of the central mountains contribute to the Danube.

Austria is the most densely forested nation in central Europe. Woodlands and meadows cover more than two-thirds of the country. Huge wilderness areas are left undisturbed in Austria because the government has set them aside as national parks and nature areas. The law forbids building roads, houses, and factories in these preserves.

Switzerland is a landlocked country that shares its boundary with Austria and Liechtenstein in the east, France in the west, Italy in the south, and Germany in the north. The topography of Switzerland is mostly mountainous with the Alps in south and the Jura Mountains in the northwest. The central plateau consists of rolling hills, plains, and large lakes. Due to its steep hilly topography, Switzerland is the origin of many great European rivers, including the Rhine and the Rhone. Other rivers, such as the Po and the Danube, are fed by rivers originating here. Glaciers and high waterfalls are a common sight.

History

Germany lies at the center of the continent and at the crossroads of Europe's business and cultural worlds. It also serves as the connection between western Europe and eastern Europe, as well as between Scandinavia and the Mediterranean world.

Germany was originally settled by numerous tribes, including the Ostrogoths, Visigoths, and Vandals, and later occupied by the Roman legions as far north as the Danube River. The country's history, however, really begins in A.D. 800, when various Germanic peoples came together under the rule of Holy Roman Emperor Charlemagne. After the division of Charlemagne's lands among his descendants, the easternmost German portion eventually gained the imperial title, and in ensuing centuries, German territory expanded eastward. Over time central authority weakened and local princes held most real power on the ground.

Growing conflicts between Catholics and Protestants resulted in the Thirty Years' War (1618–1648). The campaigns were fought for the most part in Germany; the countryside was laid waste, major towns were besieged and sacked, and the economy was ruined.

In the early nineteenth century the German states, as well as most of Europe, became part of Napoleon's French Empire. The Congress of Vienna, convened in 1814 after Napoleon's first defeat, instituted a German Confederation of thirty-five autonomous states and free towns. Germany became a unified nation in 1871 following the Franco-Prussian War.

Germany

Twice during the twentieth century, Germany tried to expand outward from its central location to take control of its neighbors by force. World War I and World War II were the greatest conflicts of the century. On both occasions the scales were ultimately tipped against Germany and on both cases some of its original territory was lost.

After World War II, in addition to losing territory, the remainder of the country was occupied by foreign troops and divided into two countries, the democratic West Germany, occupied by the United States, England, and France, and Soviet-dominated communist East Germany. The line dividing Germany bristled with Cold War tension until 1989, when the

Austria

Berlin Wall fell. Reunification came late in 1990, when the two territories joined under West Germany's constitution became the united Federal Republic of Germany. Today Germany has risen to the status of a leading economic power and plays a fundamental role in the continuing development of the European Union.

The history of Austria begins amidst the reign of the Holy Roman Empire. The area that is now Austria was known as Noricum, a Celtic kingdom occupied by Rome. It went through a series of conquerors until it finally ended up back in the hands of the Roman Empire and stayed there until the end of the Empire in 476.

Under the Hapsburg dynasty Austria was one of Europe's dominating powers in the seventeenth and eighteenth centuries. The Empire of Austria was officially founded in 1805, and became Austria-Hungary in 1867. It split from Hungary following the end of World War I in 1918. At that time it was officially referred to as the Republic of German Austria; however, the name was changed in 1919 to the Republic of Austria. In 1938, Austria was annexed by Hitler's Germany and remained in that state until 1945 at the end of World War II. Following the war, the Allies occupied Austria until 1955, at which time the country signed the Austrian State Treaty, became a neutral independent republic, and joined the United Nations. In 1995, Austria joined the European Union, of which it is still a part.

Switzerland is situated in the heart of Central Europe and shares much of its history and culture with its neighbors Germany, France, Italy and Austria. By hard work, compromise,

Switzerland

and a strong will to succeed, this small country has grown from a group of widely scattered settlements to one of the world's most prosperous nations.

Originally inhabited by the Helvetians, or Helvetic Celts, the territory comprising modern Switzerland came under Roman rule during the Gallic wars in the first century B.C. and remained a Roman province until the fourth century A.D. Under Roman influence, the population achieved a high level of civilization and enjoyed a flourishing commerce. Important cities, such as Geneva, Basel, and Zurich, were linked by military roads that also served as trade arteries between Rome and the northern tribes.

In spite of its location between nations that were frequently at war, Switzerland has stayed out of most of Europe's wars by using their diplomatic skills to keep neutral. Switzerland's mountainous terrain has been a natural barrier in times of conflict. Nowhere else do people speaking four different languages (German, French, Italian, and Romansh—closely related to Latin) and three major ethnic groups live in such harmony in so small a place (think of a circle with a radius of less than 71 miles). With a dedication to perfection and service, Switzerland is one of the wealthiest countries in the world, with a solid economic base.

The People

Over the centuries, Germany has been a cradle of European music, literature, theater, and fine arts. From Beethoven and Bach to Goethe, Heine, and Schiller, Germany has produced some of the finest musicians and writers in the history of the civilized world. A strong cultural tradition remains in present-day Germany.

Germany does not celebrate any national festivals, not even a national day. They do, however, celebrate the country's reunification on October 3. What it lacks in national festivals, it makes up for in regional festivals. Each city and state in Germany celebrates colorful festivals that date back hundreds of years. Many of these festivals have been revived to preserve the local heritage. Every year since October 12, 1810, there has been a beer drinking festival in Munich. The Oktoberfest began as a horserace held in honor of the marriage of Bavarian Crown Prince Ludwig I and Princess Therese von Sachsen-Hildburghasen of Saxony. In the following years, the race was combined with the state agricultural fair, and booths serving food and drinks appeared. By the twentieth century these booths had developed into large beer halls. Today, the Oktoberfest lasts sixteen days. The festival is internationally famous and attracts tourists from every corner of the world.

Long ago, Austria was continental Europe's largest and richest empire. Over the ages, artists and architects from every corner of that empire traveled to its central cities to work their crafts. As a result, the towns of modern Austria are considered to be living museums, filled with art treasures and alive with history. The nation today is composed of dozens of ethnic groups, many a mixture of Germanic people from the north, Slavic people from the east, and Mediterranean people from the south. They are united primarily by the German language and the Roman Catholic faith. Austria is known as a storybook place of castles and kingdoms.

Switzerland has been described as a nation with no unity of ethnic heritage, language, or religion, but which is nonetheless united and prosperous. Although the culture could be described as a blend of German, French, and Italian influences, the distinct ethnic strands represent a considerable obstacle to the emergence of any homogeneous cultural identity.

The Food

GERMANY

German cuisine is famous the world over for its wurst, or sausages. There are over two hundred types of wurst. The most ordinary German sausage is bockwurst, made of fine ground meat and fat. Other original German sausages include the Bavarian white sausage *Weisswurst* (boiled and served with sweet mustard), *Bratwurst* (for frying), and *Blut* und *Leberwurste* (blood and liver). Germany is also well known for their hams. Great attention is paid to selecting top breeds of pigs that provide fine-flavored and succulent meat. All hams are first cured then either air-dried or cooked and often smoked. Brines and smoking bring individuality to each style, adding to the variety. The most famous German ham is the *Black Forest ham,* which has no bones and comes from the pig's back. Traditionally, this ham is cured with salt. Afterward, the ham is hung to dry and then smoked with cold smoke from fir wood. This gives the ham its distinguished taste. During this process, the ham will lose 30 to 40 percent of its original weight. *Westphalian ham* is produced from pigs raised on acorns in Germany's Westphalia forest. *Westphalian ham* is cured before being slowly smoked over a mix of beechwood and juniper branches. This results in a dark brown, very dense ham with a distinctive, light smoky flavor.

The heartiest German cuisine is from the state of Bavaria and is the cuisine most foreigners recognize as typically German. Pork remains the most popular meat, as exemplified by such dishes as *Jagerschnitzel,* grilled pork sausage topped with Swiss cheese and mushroom sauce, *Schweinebraten,* pork pot roast, and a Bavarian specialty known as *Beirbratl,* pork roasted in beer. Other meat favorites include *Rheinishcher Sauerbraten* (wine-stewed beef roast), roast knuckle of pork, and a host of recipes for goose, duck, and chicken. Bavarian flour dumplings are called *knoedel. Spaetzle* resembles Italian flat noodles, and both are typically served with meat or vegetables. Pickled radish is a popular accompaniment. Pickled cabbage, or sauerkraut, is found thought the country, prepared in different ways and used as both a vegetable and a garnish. White asparagus is one of those items that has cultural significance. It is a symbol of springtime with many local festivals dedicated to it. The official asparagus season in Germany, known as *Spargelzeit,* begins with the harvesting of the first crop in mid-April until June 24, the feast of St. John the Baptist. Sixty percent of asparagus produced in Germany is harvested during the month of May, the rest in April and June. During Spargelzeit, Germans eat asparagus at least once a day and, overall, consume on average a total of 72,000 tons per year.

The Rhineland, the land along the Rhine River, is known for potato-based dishes. Potato pancakes are a traditional Rheinland staple and go by many names, including Reibekuchen and Kartoffelpuffer. They are sometimes served with applesauce. *Kartoffelsalat* is a potato salad that is served warm. It is very similar to another German salad, *Kartoffel mit speck,* potatoes with bacon. The most famous dish of the region is *Sauerbraten,* which has become one of Germany's national dishes. *Sauerbraten* was originally made from horsemeat, but today beef is more commonly used. The meat is marinated in vinegar, a sweetening agent such as sugar beet syrup, apple syrup, or sugar, and seasonings containing juniper cones and cloves, and then braised. The sauce contains raisins and often a kind of gingerbread.

In northern Germany, seafood replaces pork as the popular protein due to the proximity to the North and Baltic seas. Particularly popular are *rollmopse,* rolled, pickled herring filets. Eel is often served smoked or as the principal ingredient of an eel soup-stew called *Aalsuppe.*

Many German cakes and cookies have their origins in a rich and colorful history going back many centuries. Cookies, cakes, and sweet rich yeast breads are crafted into complex patterns and shapes, often associated with ancient symbolic meanings. Two of the most famous are *Stollen* and *Lebkuchen. Stollen* is a breadlike cake with dried citrus peel, dried fruit, nuts, and spices such as cardamom and cinnamon, and is usually eaten during the Christmas season. The best-known *Stollen* is from Dresden. *Lebkuchen,* the most famous German gingerbread, is from Nuremberg. Known as the "king of cakes," the *Baumkuchen,* or "tree cake," is a kind of layered cake. When cut, the cake reveals the characteristic golden rings that give it its name. To get the ring effect, a thin layer of batter is brushed evenly onto a spit and allowed to bake until golden. The most skilled baker will repeat this process numerous times. Some bakers have been known to create three-foot-long Baumkuchens consisting of twenty-five layers and weighing over a hundred pounds. These layers are then covered with sugar or chocolate glaze.

The German beer industry has been heavily regulated since the sixteenth century. In most countries, a percentage of rice or corn is used in the fermentation process but Germany forbids this practice. The only ingredients allowed in German beers are barley, malt, hops, yeast, and water. Germany has over 1,500 breweries and offers more than 5,000 varieties of beer. Most beers in Germany are of the bitter variety and in the Alpine region malty lagers are dominant. *Weizen,* or "white beer," is a cloudy, effervescent, top-fermented beer.

AUSTRIA

Austrian food is similar to German food, but with Hungarian and Slavic elements lingering from the days of the Austro-Hungarian Empire. The Eastern European influence is mainly Hungarian, and the cooking is characterized by the use of much paprika and the use of more beef than pork. Originally from Turkey, paprika was adopted into Austro-Hungarian cooking in dishes like *goulash* and creamy red chicken *paprikash.* The Turkish influence was also expanded by introducing coffee to Europe via Austria, and still today Austria has the best-developed coffee culture in all of Europe. Its extensive border with Italy made Austria a gateway for the migration of Mediterranean cuisines into northern Europe.

Vienna has a diverse yet harmonious range of dishes reflecting the city's mix of nationalities and food cultures through the centuries. One of the most famous culinary dishes is *Wiener Schnitzel.* A close relative of Italian *veal Milanese, Wiener Schnitzel* probably originated in Italy and then migrated to Austria. In Viennese restaurants, the dish is made with milk-fed veal cutlets that are pounded thin, coated with egg and bread crumbs, and then fried. Many Austrian home cooks prefer pork cutlets for their schnitzel.

Another more traditional Austrian meal is *Tafelspitz* (boiled beef). This national dish is both a general term for the dish and the most common cut of meat used, from the upper leg of the cow. Restaurant menus often offer this with more than 20 other cuts, including the *Kavalierspitz* ("gentleman's portion," from the shoulder) and the *mageres Meisel* ("part without fat," from the front shoulder). The meal begins with the cooking broth as a soup course, and then slices of the meat, accompanied by a chive sauce, horseradish, and sides like creamed spinach and potatoes. Other favorites include *Lungenbraten* (beef tenderloin stuffed with goose liver, served with cream sauce and dumplings), *Backhendl* (chicken dipped in a mixture of flour, breadcrumbs, and beaten egg, and then deep-fried and served with lemon wedges) was considered a symbol of prosperity in Vienna during the reign of Emperor Franz Joseph in the 1800s. *Schlutzkrapfen* are Austrian ravioli filled with cheese, potatoes, herbs, vegetables, or meats and then fried or boiled. Noodles are an integral part of Austrian cooking. Egg pastas, an import from Italy, are popular in the southern provinces of Carinthia and Tyrol, where they are served savory with cheese or pork, or sweet with fruit, nuts, or poppy seeds, butter, and sugar. Pumpkin seed oil is a specialty of the south central province of Styria. This striking dark green oil is pressed from the roasted seeds of squat pumpkins and has an intense, nutty flavor. Traditional in potato salad and drizzled over noodle, fish, egg, and meat dishes, it's also used in a cheese spread for bread.

Austria is famous for their pastries, including the *Linzer Torte,* a jam tart with a lattice of nut pastry, and *Sacher Torte,* a rich chocolate sponge cake glazed with apricot jam and iced in bittersweet chocolate. The Viennese usually serve *Sacher Torte* with unsweetened whipped cream, which complements the chocolate cake and reduces the sweetness. A third pastry, *strudel,* illustrates the diverse origins of Austrian food. Supposedly created by a Hungarian but inspired by Turkish baklava, *strudel* is a wafer-thin pastry rolled around either a sweet or savory filling. Pastry or cakes and coffee are nearly inseparable and are sold in establishments called *Konditorei.* Another sweet specialty is the *Salzburger Nockerl,* a soufflé known to be "as sweet as cream and as tender as a kiss." It is said that the *Nockerl* was invented for a well-known bishop in the early seventeenth century and is supposed to resemble three mountains of Salzburg: Kapuzinerberg, Monchsberg, and Gaisberg.

SWITZERLAND

Though cuisine in Switzerland is influenced by the German, Italian, French, and Austrian cultures, Swiss food has traditionally been marked by important cultural and regional variations. Cheese dishes are typical of the Alpine regions. Switzerland produces a great variety of cheeses, particularly hard cheeses; among them are *Appenzeller* and *Emmenthaler. Emmenthaler* is so typically Swiss that in Germany it is simply called *Schweizerkase* (Swiss cheese). It is world-famous for the large holes that are a result of gases from the fermenting process. The national dish, *fondue neuchateloise,* is a mixture of melted *Emmenthaler* and *Gruyère* cheeses and wine into which bread cubes are dipped. The origins of fondue are thought to be the high valleys where, cut off during the long winter months, the foods that kept the longest were stale bread, cheese, and pickles. Fondues in different regions of Switzerland use the local cheeses, and meat fondues are a popular modern dish where chunks of meat (instead of bread) are dipped into hot oil (instead of cheese) and "deep fried," then dipped in various sauces. Another specialty is *raclette,* which refers to both a famous cheese as well as a meal. Raclette cheeses are typically round, weighing 13 to 17 pounds and are about 11 inches in diameter and 3 inches thick. The cheeses are made from cow's milk and have a creamy consistency, which easily melts but does not get too runny. The semi-firm cheese is normally aged about three or four months. In the Swiss tradition, raclette cheese is melted over an open fire very slowly. As the cheese melts it is scraped off the wheel and served with boiled potatoes, bread, cornichons, and other pickled vegetables. The name comes from the French verb *racler,* meaning to scrape, because of the way the melted cheese is scraped off the block.

The Swiss chocolate industry, which originally grew out of the need to utilize the abundant milk produced in the pre-Alpine dairying regions, is world famous. One of many chocolate making pioneers Rodolphe Lindt (1855–1909) opened a chocolate factory powered by a water-wheel. A born manufacturer, his inventions led him to a new process by which he produced the first melting, or fondant, chocolate. The refining effect, which is known today as "conching," was first noticed by Lindt while processing chocolate over several days in a narrow mixing trough. He incorporated this into his production methods and, at the same time, developed equipment on principles still in use today. The addition of cocoa butter to the chocolate, to give it the necessary melting quality, was another important discovery. These discoveries, and the invention of milk chocolate by Daniel Peter, were essential to the manufacture and success of the fine Swiss chocolate industry.

In Germanic Switzerland, *rosti* comes close to a national dish. Although *rosti* is made with few ingredients—potatoes, salt, cooking oil, and a little milk—it takes skill to make the potatoes brown and crisp in a golden circle without burning them. Sausages and sauerkraut are also popular dishes. Around the lakes of eastern Switzerland freshwater fish like the delicate zander (pike perch), saibling (lake trout), and felchen (whitefish) can be found on menus. Western Switzerland is influenced by French cuisine and culture, and in Ticono, pasta, polenta, and risotto are signs of a common culture with Italy.

Health foods, whole grains, and fresh vegetables were popular in Switzerland long before they caught on elsewhere. This health food movement started at the clinic of Dr. Max Bircher-Benner (1867–1939), which was founded in Zurich in 1897. Nearly a century later, many Swiss people still follow his advice and begin each meal with an uncooked food, limit meats in their diet, and preserve vitamins by cooking vegetables for just a short time. The most famous dish served at Dr. Bircher-Benner's clinic was a breakfast cereal called *Bircher Muesli.* This original muesli used oatmeal, water, lemon juice, milk, apples, and almonds.

Glossary

Auflauf Casserole.

Beilagen Side dishes.

Bier There are over 5,000 varieties of beer brewed in 1,500 breweries in Germany.

    Pils A good all-around lager-style, bottom-fermented light beer, it has a strong hoppy aroma and flavor, with a long, dry finish.

Altbier and Kölsch Aromatic, hoppy, bitter beers. *Altbieris* is darker and *Kölsch* is lighter. Both are considered everyday drinking beer.

Wheat Beers Brewed from malted wheat and malted barley, there are three styles: Hefe (cloudy), for which the yeast is retained; Kristall (clear), when the yeast is removed; and dark wheat beer.

Bockbier "Big" flavor beers with a malty, aromatic, and lightly hoppy bitterness. Color ranges from light golden to dark.

Black Forest Ham (Schwarzwälder Schinken) A smoked and cured ham sold in wafer-thin slices. Made from a single boneless joint with a pronounced smoky flavor. Ideal for appetizers.

Cheeses

Allgäuer Emmentaler German hard cheese with a nutty flavor, similar in taste to Swiss cheese.

Appenzeller Product of northeast Switzerland, a hard cow's milk straw-colored cheese. It has a strong smell and a nutty or fruity flavor, which can range from mild to tangy; depending on how long it is aged.

Bergader German soft, smooth-textured cheese with large blue veins and a strong, piquant taste.

Bergkäse Austrian traditional hard cheese made from raw cow's milk and matured for six months. It is quite mild and creamy but melts well and is used in fondue.

Blauschmimmelbrie (Bavarian Blue Brie) Delicate blue-veined cheese with a creamy center and velvety-ripened skin.

Bruder Basil Bavarian semi-soft cow's milk cheese with a rich, creamy texture and smoky flavor.

Butter Käse (Butter Cheese) Fresh, creamy, flavor reminiscent of better cheddars similar to Parmesan.

Cambazola Creamy, blue cheese made from cow's milk. Texture is smooth and rich, with a spicy and slightly sweet-sour flavor.

Doppelrhamstufel Soft German cheese made with "double cream." It has a mildly lactic aroma and a slightly salty taste.

Emmenthaler Generally known in the U.S. as Swiss cheese, this is a yellow, medium-hard cheese, with characteristic large holes. It has a piquant but not too sharp taste.

Esrom A mild cheese when young, but becomes very robust as it ages, developing a stronger flavor similar to Limburger but with a sweeter edge and the consistency similar to Port Salut.

Gruyère A hard yellow cheese made from cow's milk, it is named after the town of Gruyères in Switzerland. The cheese is sweet but slightly salty, with a flavor that varies widely with age. It is often described as creamy and nutty when young, becoming more assertive, earthy, and complex with age.

Kugelkase An Austrian cheese made from cow's milk. It is a creamy, ball-shaped cheese with pepper, caraway seeds, and paprika added so that the curd becomes infused with their aroma.

Limburger A very strong-smelling German cheese. Made with cow's milk, it has a tangy, creamy, Brie-like flavor and pungent aroma. Most of the strong taste is found in the rind.

Mondseer Austrian cheese also known as Schachtelkase, close to Munster or Limburger despite its relative hardness. It has a slightly spicy aroma and sweet-sour taste.

Sbrinz Originated in Switzerland, it is a whole cow's milk cheese, aged two to three years. Sometimes this hard grating cheese is aged less and then it is called *Spalen*.

Schloss A milder form of Limburger, but with a stronger flavor. It has a white and golden color; the flavor is tangy, mild, and pungent, depending on how ripe it is. Schloss has a semi-firm and creamy texture.

Steppenkäse A mild cheese similar in taste to Tilsit, but lower in fat.

Tilsit A light yellow German and Swiss semi-soft cheese with a hearty flavor that becomes robust with age. It is often flavored with caraway seed and peppercorns.

Cornichons Pickled baby gherkins.

Fondue Probably the most famous Swiss dish. Traditional fondue is made out of melted cheese.

Goulash A type of beef stew from Hungary that always contains paprika.

Gabelfruhstuck Literally a "fork meal," referring to the traditional 10:00 A.M. snack in Austria, usually a small meat dish or sausage.

Jause Literally "gossip time;" refers to pastry and coffee taken in the late afternoon. May occasionally be an elaborate spread of small sandwiches, pastries, and tea (Austria).

Katenspeck *Katen* is the German word for "barn," meaning that this ham is made farmhouse style: cured, smoked, and cooked.

Kartoffel, Kartoffelsalat Potato, potato salad (served warm).

Knödel Dumplings.

Kochwurst Boiled sausages such as leberwurst (liverwurst), ready to eat without heating.

Kuchen Cake, either sweet or savory.

Landbrot Germany's daily bread, made from wheat with a little light rye flour for a moist texture. The name translates to "farm bread."

Leberkäse A high-quality meatloaf made from minced pork and beef that can be eaten hot or cold. Served on a bun, it is the Bavarian's answer to the burger.

Lebkuchen Honey-sweet, richly spiced ginger cake.

Linzer Torte Named for the Austrian town of Linz, this is more a flan than a torte; a rich nut pastry filled with fine raspberry preserves, crisscrossed with more nut pastry, baked, then served with whipped cream.

Marzipan Marzipan is an almond and sugar paste used to ice cakes and other pastries or sculpted into a variety of shapes to be eaten as candy or used as cake decorations. It is governed by strict food laws ensuring a blend of two parts ground almonds to one part sugar, with rose water the only flavoring permitted. After the ingredients are mixed, marzipan reaches a consistency of dough or soft rubber and can be rolled, shaped, cut, or molded.

Muesli A healthy, tasty mixture of raw or toasted grains (such as oats, wheat, millet, barley, and wheat germ), dried fruits, nuts, and seeds.

Palatschinken Thin, small pancakes, similar to crepes, usually served filled and rolled with preserves, sprinkled with nuts or crumbs, and topped with whipped cream (Austria).

Paprika Vivid red powder, ground from dried chile peppers, available in sweet and hot varieties. Originally from Turkey, paprika was adopted by Austro-Hungarians in dishes like goulash.

Pumpernickel Rich, dark 100 percent rye bread made by a unique method involving time, skill, and care.

Pumpkin Seed Oil A specialty of Austria's south central province of Styria, it is a striking dark green oil, pressed from the roasted seeds of pumpkins. It has an intense, nutty flavor.

Quark A thick, cultured dairy product similar to ricotta, but creamier with a tarter flavor.

Raclette A Swiss dish consisting of cheese melted and served on boiled potatoes or bread.

Rathskellar Generally, a restaurant in the basement of a city hall, serving classic dishes.

Reibekuchen/Kartoffelpuffer Potato pancakes.

Roggenbrot Rye bread.

Rohwurst Hard, dry sausages, such as salami, which don't require cooking.

Rosti May be considered Switzerland's national dish. It is made with potatoes, salt, cooking oil, and a little milk.

Rotkohl German pickled red cabbage.

Sacher Torte Two layers of a slightly bitter chocolate cake sandwiched together with apricot jam, glazed with chocolate, and served with of whipped cream on the side. The actual recipe is a closely guarded secret involving as many as thirty two steps. It was created by Franz Sacher in 1832 and continues to be served in the Hotel Sacher, opened in 1832 by Franz's son, Eduard.

Sauerkraut Thinly shredded white cabbage salted and left to ferment for weeks to develop a unique piquant flavor.

Schlutzkrapfen Austrian ravioli filled with cheese, potatoes, herbs, vegetables, or meats, and fried or boiled.

Schnaps Means "gulp" in old German, which is how it should be drunk. There are two main types: The first is *Korn,* a clear grain spirit, neutral liquor similar to vodka. The second is made from distilled spirits known collectively as *Obstwasser*, produced from fruit juices, fermented naturally without the addition of sugar or alcohol. The most important is *Kirschwasser,* made from late-ripening black cherries.

Senf A mustard mixed with vinegar, salt, spices, and sugar. German mustards are very aromatic.

Spätzle (Knodel, Nocker, Spaetzle) Literally, "little sparrows," these are small noodles or dumplings made of flour, eggs, and water or milk.

Stollen A yeast loaf rich with candied fruits, raisins, and other flavorings.

Strudel Layers of flaky pastry wrapped around a fruit filling, often of apples and raisins.

Süsser Senf Unique to Germany, a gentle, piquant, sweet mustard dressing.

Tafelspitz This boiled beef dish is Austria's national dish.

Wacholder Dark blue juniper berries with a clean flavor, at first slightly bitter, then almost sweet. They are often substituted for bay leaf in the typical German "bouquet garni."

Weinstube A small local restaurant where the main beverage is wine.

Weisser Spargel Throughout Germany, white asparagus has a special stature; it symbolizes the beginning of spring, and many local festivals are dedicated to it.

Westphalian ham This ham is produced from pigs raised on acorns in Germany's Westphalia forest. It is cured before being slowly smoked over a mix of beechwood and juniper branches, resulting in a dark brown, very dense ham with a distinctive, light smoky flavor.

Wiener Backhendle A Viennese specialty of egg-dipped, crumbed fried chicken pieces that are then finished by oven baking.

Wienerbrot A Scandinavian term literally meaning Viennese bread, but which actually refers to pastries made from puff pastry; known elsewhere as Danish pastry.

Wiener Schnitzel Perhaps the most famous Viennese specialty; large thin (pounded) scallops of veal, egged and crumbed and crisply fried.

Wurst The term for any sausage. All types of German sausage are required by law to be 100 percent meat with no fillers.

Zopf Special bread, typically served on Sunday for breakfast in Switzerland.

Menus and Recipes from Germany, Austria, and Switzerland

Rahmilinsen mit Salat

Lentil Ragout with Greens   SERVES 4

AMOUNT	MEASURE	INGREDIENT
1 cup	7 ounces, 196 g	Green lentils
2 tablespoons	1 ounce, 30 ml	Olive oil
2 tablespoons	$\frac{1}{2}$ ounce, 14 g	Bacon, minced
$\frac{1}{3}$ cup	2 ounces, 56 g	Carrots, $\frac{1}{8}$ inch (.3 cm) dice
$\frac{1}{3}$ cup	2 ounces, 56 g	Celery, $\frac{1}{8}$ inch (.3 cm) dice
$\frac{1}{3}$ cup	2 ounces, 56 g	Onions, $\frac{1}{8}$ inch (.3 cm) dice
$\frac{1}{3}$ cup	2 ounces, 56 g	Leeks, $\frac{1}{8}$ inch (.3 cm) dice
2		Garlic cloves, minced
$\frac{3}{4}$ cup	4 ounces, 112 g	Potatoes, $\frac{1}{4}$ inch (.6 cm) dice
$1\frac{1}{4}$ cups	10 ounces, 300 ml	Chicken stock
$\frac{1}{2}$ cup	4 ounces, 120 ml	Heavy cream
3		Whole cloves
2		Bay leaves
To taste		Salt and pepper
2 tablespoons	1 ounce, 30 ml	Honey
2 tablespoons	1 ounce, 30 ml	Red wine vinegar
3 cups	6 ounces, 168 g	Mixed baby greens
8		Tomato wedges, peeled, seeded

PROCEDURE

1 Pick over lentils to remove small stones and discolored seeds. Put in a bowl of water and remove any that float. Wash lentils well and drain thoroughly.

2 Heat olive oil over medium heat, add bacon, and cook until slightly brown, 2–3 minutes. Add drained lentils, and stir to coat with oil.

3 Add carrots, celery, onion, leeks, garlic, and potatoes; sauté 3 to 4 minutes.

4 Add stock, cream, herbs, and spices. Simmer on low heat until lentils are soft, 30 to 45 minutes. Remove bay leaves and cloves.

5 Season with salt and pepper.

6 Just before serving, add honey and vinegar to warm ragout.

7 Plate the mixed baby greens with two tomato wedges, spoon the lentils over half the greens, and serve.

Rahmilinsen mit Salat – Lentil Ragout with Greens

Kartoffelsuppe mit Miesmuscheln und Lauch

Potato Soup with Mussels and Leeks   SERVES 4

AMOUNT	MEASURE	INGREDIENT
3 tablespoons	1½ ounces, 45 ml	Butter
2 tablespoons		Shallots, minced
¾ cup	6 ounces, 180 ml	White wine
1 quart		Mussels, washed, beards removed
¼ cup	2 ounces, 60 ml	Cold water
½ cup	2 ounces, 56 g	Leek, white and light-green parts, minced
	8 ounces 224 g	Potato, cooked, peeled, and pureed
To taste		Salt, white pepper, and cayenne pepper

PROCEDURE

1 In a pan large enough to just hold the mussels, melt the butter over medium-low heat. Add shallot and soften for a minute without browning; add white wine and mussels.

2 Cover and raise the heat to medium-high; cook, shaking the pan from time to time, until the mussels open, 3 to 4 minutes. Do not overcook the mussels or they will become tough.

3 Strain the mussels and cooking liquid into another pan through a cheesecloth-lined strainer.

4 Remove mussels from the shells, set the meat aside, discard the shells, and reserve cooking liquid.

5 Combine cold water and cooking liquid, add leeks, and cook over medium heat, 3 to 4 minutes.

6 Add the potato puree to the soup ⅓ at a time, whisking to mix well after each addition. If it is too thick after adding all the potato, thin with a little water.

7 Add mussels, bring back to a boil, remove from heat, and season with salt, pepper, and cayenne.

8 To serve, divide the mussels equally among 4 warm shallow bowls and pour a portion of the soup over.

Kalbslebersteak mit Roter Zwiebelmarmelade und Senfesauce Calf's Liver with Red Onion Marmalade and Mustard Sauce SERVES 4

AMOUNT	MEASURE	INGREDIENT
1 pound	16 ounces, 448 g	Calf's liver, trimmed
1 tablespoon	$\frac{1}{2}$ ounce, 15 ml	Butter
$\frac{1}{4}$ cup per serving		Cooked egg noodles, hot
As needed		Red onion marmalade (recipe follows)
As needed		Mustard sauce (recipe follows)
Garnish		Chopped parsley

PROCEDURE

1 Heat the butter over low heat, add liver, and cook about 1 minute on each side.

2 Turn off the heat and leave the liver to continue cooking in the pan 5 minutes. The liver should be pale pink all the way through.

3 Slice the liver thinly and arrange in overlapping slices on warm plates. Serve with red onion marmalade and mustard sauce, accompanied by noodles and topped with parsley.

Red Onion Marmalade

AMOUNT	MEASURE	INGREDIENT
2 tablespoons	I ounce, 30 ml	Butter
3 cups	18 ounces, 504 g	Red onions, finely sliced
To taste		Salt and pepper
I tablespoon	$\frac{1}{2}$ ounce, 15 ml	Wild-flower honey
1$\frac{1}{2}$ cups	12 ounces, 360 ml	Red wine (Lemberger, Cabernet, or Merlot)
To taste		Fresh lemon juice

PROCEDURE

1   Over medium heat, melt butter, add onions, and cook until transparent. Do not let them color. Season to taste with salt and pepper; stir in honey and wine.

2   Cover and transfer to a 300°F (150°C) oven. Cook 45 minutes, until the sauce has the consistency of marmalade. Check occasionally so it does not burn. Season to taste with lemon juice.

Mustard Sauce

AMOUNT	MEASURE	INGREDIENT
1$\frac{1}{4}$ cups	10 ounces, 300 ml	Brown stock or flavorful chicken stock
1$\frac{1}{4}$ cups	10 ounces, 300 ml	Heavy cream
$\frac{1}{2}$ cup	4 ounces, 120 ml	White wine
I tablespoon	$\frac{1}{2}$ ounce, 15 ml	Medium-hot mustard
$\frac{1}{2}$ teaspoon		Hot mustard
2 tablespoons	I ounce, 30 ml	Cold butter, small cubes

PROCEDURE

1   Combine all ingredients except butter and reduce until the mixture coats the back of a spoon.

2   Just before serving, whisk in the cold butter.

Schweinelendchen im Schwarzbratmantel

Pork Tenderloin in a Dark Bread Crust   SERVES 4

AMOUNT	MEASURE	INGREDIENT
2 tablespoons	I ounce, 30 ml	Vegetable oil
I pound	16 ounces, 448 g	Pork tenderloin, cleaned
12 ounces		Lean ground pork
2		Eggs
$\frac{3}{4}$ cup	6 ounces, 180 ml	Heavy cream
To taste		Salt and pepper
$\frac{1}{2}$ cup	2 ounces, 56 g	Dark rye bread crumbs, dry
I cup	8 ounces, 240 ml	Pork or beef demi-glace

PROCEDURE

1   Heat the oil over medium high heat, sear the pork tenderloin, and set aside to cool.

2   In a food processor, process ground pork. Add eggs one at time, pulsing to incorporate. Scrape down sides and with machine running, add the cream in a steady stream. Scrape down sides; do not overprocess.

3   Remove mixture to a bowl over an ice bath. Poach or sauté a sample and adjust seasoning; add more cream if mixture is too stiff. Fold in bread crumbs.

4   Lay out a piece of plastic wrap large enough to wrap around the pork tenderloin two or three times. Spread the bread crumb mixture in an even layer just large enough to surround the pork tenderloin. Place the tenderloin in the middle of the bread crumb mixture; surround the tenderloin with the mixture. Wrap plastic around and tie ends so it is watertight. Poach in a 160°F (71.1°C) water bath 30 to 40 minutes or until an internal temperature of 155°F (68°C) is reached. Remove from water bath.

5   Let set 5 to 10 minutes, remove wrap, slice, and serve with demi-glace.

Rotkraut und Spätzle
Braised Red Cabbage and Spaetzle   SERVES 4

AMOUNT	MEASURE	INGREDIENT
I pound	16 ounces, 448 g	Red cabbage
2 tablespoons	I ounce, 30 ml	Butter
$\frac{3}{4}$ cup	4 ounces, 112 g	Onions, $\frac{1}{4}$ inch (.6 cm) dice
5		Juniper berries
4		Cloves
$\frac{1}{2}$ tablespoon		Granulated sugar
I cup	6 ounces, 168 g	Tart green apples, peeled, cored, $\frac{1}{4}$ inch (.6 cm) dice
$\frac{1}{4}$ cup	2 ounces, 60 ml	Red wine vinegar
$\frac{1}{2}$ teaspoon		Salt
I		Bay leaf
I tablespoon		Cornstarch
$\frac{1}{2}$ cup	4 ounces, 120 ml	Dry red wine
As needed		Spätzle (recipe follows)

PROCEDURE

1   Trim the coarse outer leaves from the cabbage and discard; quarter the cabbage, remove the hard white core at the point of each quarter and discard, then slice each quarter very thinly.

2   Melt butter over medium high heat; add onions, juniper berries, cloves and sprinkle in the sugar, and cook to dissolve, 2 minutes.

3   Add apples, sauté 5 minutes or until soft and golden.

4   Add cabbage and sauté 5 minutes, until nicely glazed.

5   Add red wine vinegar and bring to a simmer. Add salt and bay leaf; toss to combine, push bay leaf down into the cabbage.

6   Cover and simmer 20 to 25 minutes, until cabbage is crisp-tender.

7   Sprinkle cornstarch over the cabbage and toss well to mix. Add the red wine. Heat to a strong simmer and cook, stirring, 3 to 5 minutes, until liquids are thickened. Remove from heat.

8   Discard bay leaf.

9   Simmer 5 minutes longer, uncovered. Serve with spaetzle.

Spätzle

YIELD: 4 CUPS

AMOUNT	MEASURE	INGREDIENT
2 cups	8 ounces, 224 g	All-purpose flour
$\frac{1}{8}$ teaspoon		Freshly grated nutmeg
$\frac{1}{2}$ teaspoon		Salt
2		Eggs
$\frac{3}{4}$ cup	6 ounces, 180 ml	Milk
3 tablespoons	$1\frac{1}{2}$ ounces, 45 ml	Butter, melted
To taste		Salt and pepper

PROCEDURE

1 Sift together flour, nutmeg, and salt. Make a well in the center.

2 Whisk the eggs with the milk and pour into the well of dry ingredients.

3 Mix with a wooden spoon, then use a mixer or food processor to beat the mixture until it is bubbly and elastic.

4 Pour batter into a spätzle hex or use a colander with medium to large holes. Force the batter through the holes into boiling salted water. Let the dough fall into the slightly bubbling water; cook about 2 to 3 minutes. Generally, the dumplings will float on the surface when sufficiently cooked.

5 Remove from the top with a slotted spoon or skimmer, wash under cold running water to remove excess starch, and let drain.

6 Heat butter over medium heat, add drained spaetzle, and toss to heat, or sautée in butter until golden and crispy. Correct seasoning.

Mohncreme mit Rotweinbrinen

Poppy Seed Cream with Pears in Red Wine   SERVES 4

AMOUNT	MEASURE	INGREDIENT
I cup	8 ounces, 240 ml	Red wine
$\frac{1}{4}$ cup	2 ounces, 56 g	Granulated sugar
I stick		Cinnamon
		Zest from I orange
I		Vanilla pod or I teaspoon vanilla extract
2 tablespoons	I ounce, 30 ml	Pear schnapps, such as Poire William (optional)
2		Pears, peeled, cored, and thinly sliced
As needed		Poppy seed cream (recipe follows)
3 tablespoons		Toasted almonds, sliced
$\frac{1}{2}$ cup	4 ounces, 120 ml	Heavy cream, whipped

PROCEDURE

1   Heat red wine, sugar, cinnamon stick, orange zest, vanilla pod, and schnapps; stir to dissolve. Bring to a boil.

2   Pour hot syrup over pears and macerate 2 to 3 hours, so they take on color.

PRESENTATION

1   Place two quenelles of poppy seed cream on dessert plates. Arrange pear slices attractively on the side, pour a little syrup around, and garnish with almonds and whipped cream.

Poppy Seed Cream

AMOUNT	MEASURE	INGREDIENT
$\frac{1}{4}$ cup	1 ounce, 28 g	Poppy seeds
2 tablespoons	1 ounce, 30 ml	Red wine
1		Egg
1		Egg yolk
2		Gelatin leaves, soaked in 4 tablespoons (2 ounces, 60 ml) water
	$3\frac{1}{2}$ ounces, 98 g	White couverture chocolate
1 tablespoon	$\frac{1}{2}$ ounce, 15 ml	Honey
1 cup	8 ounces, 240 ml	Heavy cream, whipped to soft peaks

PROCEDURE

1 Grind the poppy seeds with a spice grounder or mortar and pestle. Combine the poppy seed paste and red wine; bring to boil for 1 minute. (This tempers their harsh taste.) Strain and reserve the poppy seeds.

2 Combine whole egg and egg yolk.

3 Stir gelatin and soaking water over hot water to dissolve.

4 Melt white chocolate over simmering water.

5 Whisk eggs over hot water until they start to thicken. Add the softened gelatin, the melted chocolate, and honey. Stir in the poppy seeds (but not the red wine) and remove from heat.

6 When mixture has cooled down (do not wait for it to get cold and set), fold in whipped cream. Refrigerate until set.

Chindbettisuppe Childbed Soup   SERVES 4

AMOUNT	MEASURE	INGREDIENT
1 cup	6 ounces, 168 g	Carrots, peeled, coarsely chopped
1 cup	6 ounces, 168 g	Celery, coarsely chopped
1	2½ pound, 1.12 kg	Whole chicken
2 quarts	64 ounces, 1.92 l	Chicken stock
1		Bunch parsley
3		Peppercorns, crushed
1		Bay leaf
½ cup	4 ounces, 120 ml	Milk
½ cup	4 ounces, 120 ml	Heavy cream
To taste		Salt and pepper
¼ cup	1½ ounces, 42 g	Corn kernels
½ cup	2 ounces, 56 g	Leek, trimmed, cut into thin slices
3		Eggs
¼ cup	½ ounce, 14 g	Chives, minced

PROCEDURE

1 Combine carrots, celery, chicken, chicken stock, parsley, peppercorns, and bay leaf; bring to a boil. Reduce to simmer and cook 50 minutes.

2 Remove chicken, bone breast, cut into thin strips, and set aside.

3 Strain stock and reserve.

4 Add 3 cups (24 ounces, 720 ml) stock to a saucepan and reduce by two thirds over medium-high heat.

5 Add milk and cream to reduced broth, correct seasoning, and set aside.

6 Cook corn in boiling salted water until tender. Drain and reserve.

7 Steam leeks until tender.

8 Beat eggs together with a pinch of salt. Bring soup to a boil. Stir in eggs and remove from heat.

9 Arrange chicken meat, corn, and leeks in warm soup plates and cover with soup.

10 Sprinkle with chives and serve.

Filets de Rouget aux Herbettes

Red Mullet Fillets with Herbs   SERVES 4

Rouget is a red-skinned fish with delicate meat, similar to the goatfish found around the **Bahamas** and the Florida Keys. When available, the Hawaiian moano or kumo goatfish can be substituted, or use red snapper.

AMOUNT	MEASURE	INGREDIENT
3 tablespoons	1½ ounces, 45 ml	Olive oil
1½ tablespoons	¾ ounce, 20 ml	Butter
4	3 ounces, 84 g each	Boneless, skinless fillets of fish
To taste		Salt, pepper, and cayenne
3 tablespoons	½ ounce, 14 g	Shallot, minced
2 teaspoons		Garlic, minced
½ cup	4 ounces, 120 ml	White wine
¼ cup	1 ounce, 28 g	Herbs, minced (chervil, parsley, tarragon, chives)
½ cup	3 ounces, 84 g	Tomato, peeled, seeded ⅛ inch (.3 cm) dice

PROCEDURE

1 Preheat oven to 525°F (274°C).

2 Put the oil in an ovenproof dish or sauté pan large enough to hold the fillets in one layer. Add the butter and melt over low heat.

3 Season fish with salt, pepper, and cayenne.

4 Arrange fillets in a single layer, not overlapping. Sprinkle the garlic and shallot over the fish and add the wine.

5 Cook in the preheated oven 2 minutes, turn the fillets, and continue cooking 1 minute more (depending on thickness). Remove fillets to warm plates.

6 Over medium heat, add herbs and diced tomatoes to cooking pan. Bring to a boil; check seasoning.

7 Pour the tomato-herb sauce around the fillets and serve.

Luzerner Chûgelipastete
Puff Pastry with Meat Filling   SERVES 4

Puff Pastry

AMOUNT	MEASURE	INGREDIENT
As needed		All-purpose flour
	8 ounces, 224 g	Puff pastry
I		Egg
Pinch		Salt

PROCEDURE

1 Preheat oven to 375°F (190°C).

2 Lightly flour a work surface and the dough. Press the dough in successive firm strokes in both directions with a rolling pin. Move the dough frequently to renew the flour under and on it. Roll out to $\frac{3}{13}$ inch (.5 cm) thick and place on a paper-lined pan. Allow dough to rest in refrigerator about 1 hour.

3 Remove dough from refrigerator, dock well, and cut into 8 heart shapes, using a cutter or knife. Place 4 of the shapes on a paper-lined pan.

4 Cut out the center of the other 4 hearts and discard them, leaving 4 heart shaped rings.

5 Whisk together the egg and salt and paint the hearts on the pan with the egg wash.

6 Center the heart-shaped rings on the heart bases and firmly press them into place.

7 Dock the rings with the point of a paring knife at $\frac{1}{2}$ inch (1.2 cm) intervals.

8 Bake in preheated oven about 25 minutes, until well risen and deep golden. Cool on rack.

Luzerner Chûgelipastete – Puff Pastry with Meat Filling

Filling

AMOUNT	MEASURE	INGREDIENT
$1\frac{1}{2}$ tablespoons	$1\frac{1}{2}$ ounces, 40 ml	Butter
$\frac{1}{2}$ cup	2 ounces, 56 g	Onion, cut $\frac{1}{4}$ inch (.6 cm) dice
1		Garlic clove, minced
1 cup	6 ounces, 168 g	Veal loin, cut $\frac{1}{2}$ inch (1.2 cm) dice
1 cup	6 ounces, 168 g	Pork loin, cut $\frac{1}{2}$ inch (1.2 cm) dice
$\frac{3}{4}$ cup	6 ounces, 180 ml	White wine
$\frac{1}{3}$ cup	2 ounces, 56 g	Raisins
4 cups	32 ounces, 960 ml	Beef stock
1 cup	6 ounces, 168 g	Uncooked veal sausage meat
1 cup	6 ounces, 168 g	Sweetbreads
$1\frac{1}{2}$ tablespoons	$\frac{3}{4}$ ounce, 20 g	Butter
1 cup	3 ounces, 84 g	White mushrooms, cleaned, trimmed, and thinly sliced
1 tablespoon		Flour
1 cup	8 ounces, 240 ml	Heavy cream
To taste		Salt, pepper, and nutmeg

PROCEDURE

1 Heat first quantity of butter over medium-high heat; sauté onions and garlic until translucent, 2 to 3 minutes.

2 Add veal and pork and brown well. Add white wine and raisins and cook over low heat 10 minutes. Set aside.

3 Bring stock to a boil. Fill a pastry bag with sausage meat and press small balls into simmering stock. Remove pan from heat and allow sausage to cool in stock. Remove from pan and set aside.

4 Reheat stock, add sweetbreads, and poach 20 minutes. Let cool in stock. Trim sweetbreads and remove any filaments of fat, gristle, or tubes. Set aside; retain poaching stock.

5 Heat second quantity of butter over medium-high heat and sauté mushrooms, 3 minutes.

6 Dust with flour and stir well.

7 Add beef stock used to cook sausage and sweetbreads and bring to a boil. Remove mushrooms and set aside.

8 Add cream to stock and cook until it is reduced to sauce consistency (coats the back of a spoon).

9 Return meat, sausage balls, sweetbreads, and mushrooms to sauce; bring back to heat. Season to taste with salt pepper, and nutmeg.

10 Carefully reheat puff pastry to warm. Remove center and use as a lid if desired.

11 Divide 1 cup filling and sauce among the four puff pastry containers; serve remaining filling separately.

Carnard Röti aux Endives
Roast Duck with Chicory   SERVES 4

AMOUNT	MEASURE	INGREDIENT
I	$3\frac{1}{2}$ to 4 pound, (1.58 to 1.81 kg)	Whole duck
To taste		Salt and pepper
I tablespoon	$\frac{1}{2}$ ounce, 15 ml	Vegetable oil
2 tablespoons	$\frac{1}{2}$ ounce, 14 g	Shallots minced
I		Garlic clove, minced
2 tablespoons	I ounce, 30 ml	Red wine vinegar
2 tablespoons	I ounce, 30 ml	Port
$\frac{1}{2}$ cup	4 ounces, 120 ml	Water
3 tablespoons	$1\frac{1}{2}$ ounce, 45 ml	Cold butter, cut in small pieces
$\frac{1}{4}$ cup	2 ounces, 60 ml	Butter, clarified
8		Endive heads, small and dense
Pinch		Granulated sugar
$\frac{1}{2}$		Lemon
To taste		Orange zest
I tablespoon	($\frac{1}{2}$ ounce, 15 ml)	Butter

PROCEDURE

1   Cut off the solid section at the base of each endive and separate the leaves, discarding any that are damaged.

2   Preheat oven to 450°F (232°C).

3   Cut wings off at the second joint. Reserve the heart and liver and chop into small pieces. Remove any excess fat and season inside and out with salt and pepper. Truss.

4   Heat oil in a roasting pan over high heat. Place duck on its side in the pan; sear 2 minutes. Turn to other side and sear 2 minutes. Leave on its side and put in preheated oven. Cook 20 minutes total (8 minutes on one side, 8 minutes on the other side, then 4 minutes on its back), or until desired doneness. Duck should be rare to medium rare. Remove from oven, untruss, and pour the cavity juices into a saucepan. Keep duck warm.

5   Pour off excess fat from the roasting pan. Place pan over low heat; add shallots and garlic, cook 2 minutes. Add vinegar and port, reduce by half, then add water. Stir to deglaze and bring to a boil. Add liquid from duck and return to a boil. Remove pan from the heat, then return it to the heat, so it reboils several times and reduces to 4 tablespoons. Strain into a new pan, correct seasoning, and whisk in cold butter to thicken. Strain and reserve.

6   Heat clarified butter in large frying pan; add endive leaves and fry about 1 minute until they begin to brown. Season with salt, pepper, and sugar and a squeeze of lemon juice. Grate the zest from the orange over endive, using a nutmeg grater.

7   Sauté duck liver and heart in remaining butter.

8   Cut duck into 4 servings. Arrange endive leaves in a circle around the edge of 4 heated plates. Place a quarter of the duck in the center, spoon sauce over duck, and sprinkle with the chopped liver and hearts. Serve remaining sauce on the side.

Carnard Röti aux Endives – Roast Duck with Chicory

Rosti Potato Cake   SERVES 4

AMOUNT	MEASURE	INGREDIENT
11 ounces, 308 g		Idaho potatoes
2 tablespoons	1 ounce, 30 ml	Butter, clarified
To taste		Salt

PROCEDURE

1   Peel the potatoes and cut into thin sticks. Rinse off the starch, drain, and dry well.

2   Heat seasoned pan (so they will not stick) with half the butter and fry half the potatoes without stirring, pressing them down occasionally to form a cake. Season with salt.

3   When the bottom is cooked, about 10 minutes, turn over and fry the other side. The rosti should be cooked through with a golden-brown crust.

4   Keep warm and cook the other half of the potatoes.

Zûrcher Öpfelbachis
Shredded Dough Cakes with Apples   SERVES 4

AMOUNT	MEASURE	INGREDIENT
$\frac{2}{3}$ cup	2.75 ounces, 77 g	All-purpose flour, sifted
$\frac{2}{3}$ cup	5.25 ounces, 158 ml	Milk
$\frac{1}{2}$ cup	4 ounces, 120 ml	Heavy cream
3 tablespoons	1.5 ounces, 42 g	Granulated sugar
$\frac{1}{2}$		Vanilla bean, seeds scraped
$\frac{1}{2}$		Grated lemon zest
Pinch		Salt
1 tablespoon	$\frac{1}{2}$ ounce, 15 ml	Kirsch
3		Eggs
2 tablespoons	1 ounce, 28 g	Granulated sugar
3 cups	12 ounces, 336 g	Apples, tart, peeled, cored, $\frac{1}{4}$ inch (.6 cm) slice
$1\frac{1}{2}$ tablespoons	$\frac{3}{4}$ ounce, 20 ml	Butter
3 tablespoons	1 ounce, 28 g	Dried currants
$\frac{1}{4}$ cup	1 ounce, 28 g	Walnuts, toasted
3 tablespoons		Confection's sugar
1 teaspoon		Cinnamon

PROCEDURE

1 Combine the flour, milk, cream, first quantity of sugar, vanilla seeds, lemon zest, salt, and kirsch. Mix to a smooth batter. Add eggs and mix well.

2 Over medium heat, caramelize second quantity of sugar until a light brown. Add apples and toss to coat; cook 1 minute.

3 Heat the butter in a well-seasoned pan (so it will not stick). Add batter and place pan in an oven preheated to 425°F (220°C), until it has turned golden-brown and the surface has dried, about 5 minutes. Shred the dough into small pieces.

4 Combine currants, walnuts, dough, and apple mixture; toss.

5 Sift together confectioner's sugar and cinnamon.

6 Place dough and apple mixture on 4 warm plates and dust with cinnamon-sugar to serve.

Bodenseefischsuppe mit Safran
Fish Soup from the Bodensee with Saffron   SERVES 4

AMOUNT	MEASURE	INGREDIENT
$\frac{1}{4}$ cup	1 ounce, 28 g	Carrots, $\frac{1}{4}$ inch (.6 cm) dice
$\frac{1}{4}$ cup	1 ounce, 28 g	Onion, $\frac{1}{4}$ inch (.6 cm) dice
$\frac{1}{4}$ cup	1 ounce, 28 g	Celeriac, $\frac{1}{4}$ inch (.6 cm) dice
$\frac{1}{4}$ cup	1 ounce, 28 g	Fennel, $\frac{1}{4}$ inch (.6 cm) dice
6 cups	48 ounces, 1.44 l	Fish stock
5		Peppercorns, crushed
$\frac{1}{2}$ teaspoon		Mustard seeds
1		Bay leaf
1 tablespoon		Fresh dill, chopped
1 tablespoon		Fresh chervil, chopped
1 tablespoon		Fresh parsley, chopped
$\frac{1}{4}$ teaspoon		Pernod
2 teaspoons		Fresh lemon juice
To taste		Salt, white pepper, cayenne pepper
	5 ounces, 140 g	Lake trout fillets, or any mild fish
	5 ounces, 140 g	Lake perch fillets
8		Saffron strands, for garnish
1 teaspoon each		Fresh dill, chervil, and parsley, for garnish

PROCEDURE

1 Combine all vegetables, stock, peppercorns, mustard seeds, and herbs.

2 Simmer, uncovered, 25 minutes. Strain, add Pernod and lemon juice, and correct seasoning.

3 Cut fish fillets into approximately $\frac{1}{2}$ ounce (14 g) spoon-size pieces.

4 Poach in salted water until just done, 3 to 4 minutes; remove to 4 warm soup plates.

5 Pour soup over fish. Garnish each with saffron, dill, chervil, and parsley.

Szegediner Gulasch
Szeged Goulash   SERVES 4

AMOUNT	MEASURE	INGREDIENT
$\frac{1}{4}$ cup	1 ounce, 28 g	Bacon, diced
$1\frac{1}{2}$ pounds	680 g	Boneless pork, trimmed, 1 inch (2.4 cm) cubes
$1\frac{1}{2}$ cups	8 ounces, 224 g	Onions, $\frac{1}{4}$ inch (.6 cm) dice
2		Garlic cloves, minced
1 tablespoon		All-purpose flour
2 tablespoons		Sweet Hungarian paprika
2 teaspoons		Caraway seeds
1		Bay leaf
1 tablespoon		Fresh sage, chopped
1 tablespoon		Fresh oregano, chopped
To taste		Salt and pepper
1 cups	8 ounces, 240 ml	Apple juice or cider
4 cups	32 ounces, 960 ml	Chicken stock
2 cups	16 ounces, 480 ml	Sauerkraut, drained and rinsed
4 cups		Spätzle or egg noodles
$\frac{1}{2}$ cup	4 ounces, 240 ml	Sour cream

PROCEDURE

1 Render the bacon until crisp. Remove and set aside, leaving 1 to 2 tablespoons ($\frac{1}{2}$ to 1 ounce, 15 to 30 ml) fat in pan.

2 Over medium-high heat, add pork and brown the meat. (This step may be done in small batches.) Remove meat and set aside.

3 Add onions and cook 2 to 3 minutes. Add garlic and cook until onions are soft, 2 minutes longer.

4 Sprinkle flour, paprika, and all seasonings, stir to combine, and cook 1 minute (do not fry the paprika). Return the meat to the pan.

5 Add cider and stock, bring to a boil, and reduce to a simmer. Simmer 35 to 45 minutes or until meat is tender.

6 Add well-drained sauerkraut and mix well. Heat and serve with egg noodles. Garnish with sour cream and reserved bacon.

Gemischter Salat Mixed Salad   SERVES 4

Serve the cucumber, cabbage, and tomato salads as separate parts of an assorted salad.

Cucumber Salad

AMOUNT	MEASURE	INGREDIENT
I cup	6 ounces, 168 g	Cucumber, peeled, seeded, thinly sliced
I teaspoon		Salt
I		Garlic clove, minced
I $\frac{1}{2}$ tablespoons	$\frac{3}{4}$ ounce, 20 ml	Cider vinegar
3 tablespoons	I $\frac{1}{2}$ ounces, 45 ml	Salad oil
I teaspoon		Chopped dill
To taste		Salt and pepper

PROCEDURE

1   Toss cucumbers with salt. Let sit 5 minutes, then rinse and drain cucumbers.

2   Add garlic, vinegar, oil, and dill, and correct seasoning.

Krautsalat: Cabbage Salad

AMOUNT	MEASURE	INGREDIENT
3 cups	12 ounces, 336 g	Green cabbage, shredded
I $\frac{1}{2}$ teaspoons		Salt
I teaspoon		Caraway seeds
I $\frac{1}{2}$ teaspoons		Granulated sugar
$\frac{1}{4}$ cup	2 ounces, 60 ml	Cider vinegar
$\frac{1}{2}$ cup	4 ounces, 120 ml	Vegetable oil

PROCEDURE

1   Trim the coarse outer leaves from the cabbage and discard; quarter the cabbage, remove the hard white core at the point of each quarter and discard, then slice each quarter very thin.

2 Toss shredded cabbage with salt and let stand 15 minutes. Squeeze the cabbage, mix again. Let stand 15 minutes, and squeeze again.

3 Combine remaining ingredients and mix well. Toss with cabbage and let stand 30 minutes before serving.

Tomato Salad

AMOUNT	MEASURE	INGREDIENT
1 tablespoon		Fresh oregano, chopped
$\frac{1}{2}$ cup	4 ounces, 120 ml	Vegetable oil
3 tablespoons	$1\frac{1}{2}$ ounces, 45 ml	Red wine vinegar
2 cups	6 ounces, 168 g	Tomatoes, peeled, seeded, cut into wedges
1 cup	4 ounces, 112 g	Onions, very thinly sliced
To taste		Salt and pepper

PROCEDURE

1 Combine oregano, oil, and vinegar; toss with tomatoes and onions. Correct seasoning.

Wiener Schnitzel   SERVES 4

For traditional **Wiener Schnitzel**, the veal is fried in lard. Pork, chicken, or turkey can be substituted and oil can be used for frying.

AMOUNT	MEASURE	INGREDIENT
4	4–5 ounces, 112–140 g	Scallops of veal, pork, or turkey, tapped thin
As needed		All-purpose flour
2		Eggs whisked with a little water and pinch of salt
As needed		Bread crumbs, dry or fresh (not panko)
As needed		Vegetable oil, for frying
4		Lemon slices
To taste		Salt and pepper

PROCEDURE

1 Season and dredge the meat in flour, egg wash, and bread crumbs, coating each scallop.

2 Heat oil and pan-fry over medium-high heat until golden brown on both sides. Remove and drain on paper towels. Correct seasoning.

3 Serve topped with one lemon slice, pressing it down with a fork to season the schnitzel. Serve with Erdäpfelschmarrn and vegetable of choice.

Erdäpfelschmarrn Fried Potatoes   SERVES 4

AMOUNT	MEASURE	INGREDIENT
1 pound	16 ounces, 448 g	All-purpose potatoes
1 teaspoon		Salt
$\frac{1}{2}$ teaspoon		Caraway seeds, crushed
$\frac{1}{4}$ cup	2 ounces, 60 ml	Butter
$\frac{1}{2}$ cup	2 ounces, 56 g	Onions, $\frac{1}{4}$ inch (.6 cm) dice

PROCEDURE

1 Boil potatoes until just cooked; drain. While still hot, slice $\frac{1}{4}$ inch (.6 cm) thick. Sprinkle with salt and crushed caraway seeds.

2 Heat butter over medium-high heat and sauté onions until light brown. Add potatoes and fry until light brown, turning often.

Wiener Schnitzel with Erdäpfelschmarrn – Fried Potatoes

Salzburger Nockerl   SERVES 4

AMOUNT	MEASURE	INGREDIENT
$\frac{1}{4}$ cup	2 ounces, 60 ml	Butter, softened
5 tablespoons	$2\frac{1}{2}$ ounces, 70 g	Granulated sugar
5		Egg yolks
$\frac{1}{4}$ cup	1 ounce, 28 g	All-purpose flour
5		Egg whites, beaten to stiff peaks
$\frac{1}{2}$ cup	4 ounces, 120 ml	Milk
As needed		Vanilla-flavored powdered sugar

PROCEDURE

1   Preheat oven 450°F (232°C).

2   Cream together butter and sugar until light. Add egg yolks in two additions, beating well after each addition until light and fluffy.

3   Fold in flour.

4   Fold in egg whites.

5   Bring milk to a boil in a 10-inch (25 cm) skillet and immediately pour batter into the hot milk.

6   Place pan in preheated oven, reduce heat to 400°F (204°C) and bake for 6 to 8 minutes until golden. Nockerl should be firm on the outside, but light and fluffy on the inside.

7   Cut into portions and place on warm plates dusted with vanilla powdered sugar. Serve immediately. Nockerl will not tolerate waiting; it will collapse.

Scandinavia and Russia

The Land

Scandinavia is located in northern Europe and includes Denmark, Norway, and Sweden. Finland, Iceland, and the Faroe Islands are considered by some to be part of Scandinavia as well. Denmark borders the Baltic and North Seas, on a peninsula north of Germany. It is the smallest of the Scandinavian countries, even including the over four hundred islands, some of which are inhabited and linked to the mainland by ferry or bridge. The landscape consists mainly of low-lying, fertile countryside broken by beech woods, small lakes, and fjords. Greenland and the Faroe Islands are also under the sovereignty of the Kingdom of Denmark, although both have home rule. The Faroe Islands are a group of eighteen islands in the North Atlantic with a population of nearly fifty thousand, whose history dates from the Viking period. Fishing and sheep farming remain the two most important occupations on these islands.

Norway borders the North Sea and the North Atlantic Ocean, west of Sweden. The name Norway comes from *Nordweg,* meaning "way to the north." This country is well named, as almost half of it lies north of the Arctic Circle. Nearly two-thirds of it is mountainous and its mountain ranges extend almost the entire length of the country. From the inland mountains and mountain plateaus, the landscape falls sharply toward a coastline dotted with innumerable islands. The country has traditionally been divided into five principal regions: Nord Norge (North Norway), Trøndelag/Midt-Norge (Trondheim Region/Mid-Norway), Vestlandet (West Country), Østlandet (East Country), and Sørlandet (South Country).

Sweden borders the Baltic Sea and the gulfs of Bothnia, Kattegat, and Skagerrak, and is sandwiched between Finland and Norway. The terrain of Sweden is mostly flat or gently rolling lowlands, with mountains in the west.

Finland is the northernmost country on the European continent. Although other countries have points extending farther north, nearly one quarter of its total landmass lies north of the Arctic Circle. It is the fifth largest country in Europe, yet it is also one of the least populous, with five million people. It is heavily forested and contains thousands of lakes, numerous rivers, and extensive areas of marshland. Only 8 percent is cultivated land, and the rest is wasteland made up of swamps, arctic fells, and sand. Except for a small highland region in the extreme northwest, the country is a lowland that is less than 600 feet above sea level. An archipelago of 17,000 tree-covered islands and smaller rocky islands are scattered off its coast.

Iceland is an island that lies in the North Atlantic Ocean, east of Greenland, and just touches the Arctic Circle. It is one of the most volcanic regions in the world. More than 13 percent is covered by snowfields and glaciers, and most of the people live along the 7 percent of the island that is made up of fertile coastland.

Russia borders the Arctic Ocean, between Europe and the North Pacific Ocean. Due to Russia's immense size, its terrain varies greatly. The most pronounced characteristics are broad plains with low hills west of the Urals; vast coniferous forest and tundra in Siberia; and uplands and mountains (the Caucasus range) along the southern borders.

History

From the Viking age (approximately 800–1066) onward, the Nordics have fought each other, formed unions with each other, and ruled over each other. Sweden ruled over Finland for over six hundred years, Denmark ruled over southern Sweden for over six hundred years (or, alternatively, Sweden has ruled over eastern Denmark for the past three hundred years), and over Norway for nearly five hundred years, while Iceland was ruled from Norway for some two hundred years and then from Denmark yet another five hundred years, and the list goes on. Finland is the only country not to have ruled over any of the others. Unavoidably, this has caused some antipathies, but it has also made the Nordic cultures more uniform.

Denmark, Norway, Sweden, and Iceland shared a more or less homogenous "Viking" culture in the Viking age, and Finland, while not strictly speaking a "Viking" country, did have a Viking age and a culture very close to its western neighbors, and at the close of this era was absorbed into the Swedish kingdom.

Scandinavian culture today could be described as a potpourri of this "original" culture, medieval German influence, French influence in the centuries that followed, and several other smaller sources, not forgetting local development and national romantic inventiveness. A

Scandinavia

significant factor is also the fact that the Nordic countries never had an era of feudalism to speak of; personal freedom has always been highly valued. One of the expressions of this freedom is the "everyman's right" in Norway, Sweden, and Finland, giving all residents free access to the forests, seas, and uncultivated land.

Russia's history extends back over a thousand years with the establishment by Vikings of a territory they named Rus. The Viking presence diminished through gradual absorption by the native Slavic peoples. Several hundred years later, the Mongols swept over Russia, remaining through the fourteenth century. A new ruler, Ivan the Great, brought Moscow to the fore and developed an empire based on his marriage to a Byzantine princess, Sophia, niece of the last Byzantine emperor Constantine XI. The expansion only continued over the next several hundred years and by the end of the seventeenth century, Tsar Peter the Great had made great strides toward transforming Russia into a true power. He devised a new capital called St. Petersburg, which became a glittering European center. But it was Catherine the Great, at the beginning of the eighteenth century, who entered into treaties and alliances with Prussia and Austria that solidified Russia's position as a true power in Europe. Alexander I, part of the group that successfully defeated Napoleon, held the title not only of tsar, but grand duke of Finland and king of Poland. The nineteenth century saw Russia begin to industrialize with development extending to the far reaches of the tsar's realm. In 1917, the tsarist regime fell to revolution led by socialists who intended to create a republican government. This first revolution failed and was supplanted by Bolshevik forces later that year, with Vladimir Lenin as chairman. Communism helped develop the country but it brought with it one of the most repressive governments in world history. Along with some not insignificant successes—modernization, becoming one of the true superpowers on the planet, the space race, athletics—the twentieth century for Russia and its people was marked by brutal wars (at least twenty million citizens died during World War II alone), disastrous participation in Afghanistan's civil war that was compared to the U.S. quagmire in Vietnam, and, for most of the population of the USSR, economic deprivation. Communism fell in 1992, following the collapse of communist governments throughout Eastern Europe. Russia continues to struggle with democracy but seems unlikely to ever return to communism.

The People

People living north of the Arctic Circle are treated to two of the most amazing phenomena on earth. The Northern Lights, or aurora borealis, can be viewed there between November and February. These lights are caused when solar particles collide with the atmosphere of the Earth. And from mid-May through June in this region the sun does not set, while between mid-November and January, the sun does not rise.

The Sami people live in the far north of the Scandinavian peninsula. They are Europe's only indigenous people, and their origins are unknown. With one of the smallest populations in the world, these people, until the early decades of this century, were nomadic, following the reindeer up into the mountains, where they lived together during the summer months. The Sami people of today number about forty thousand in all, divided between Finland, Norway, Russia, and Sweden. In earlier times the Sami were called *Lapps* (as in Lapland and Lappmarken) and *Finns* (as in Finnmark and Finland).

Ethnically, the majority of Danes are of Scandinavian descent, a Germanic people who have occupied Norway, Sweden, and Denmark since pre-Viking times. The languages of the three countries are closely related. A small German-speaking minority lives in southern Jutland

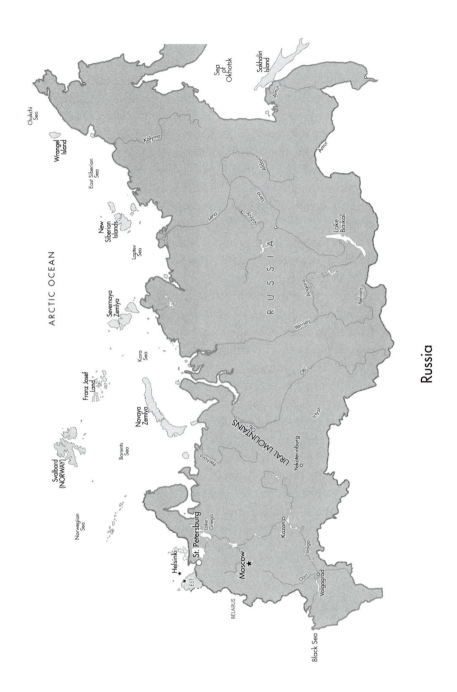

Russia

near the German border. An Inuit population inhabits the Danish territory of Greenland, and the Faroe Islands have a Nordic population, descendents of Viking colonizers.

The Norwegians are a remarkably homogenous people of Germanic origin. Apart from several thousand Sami and people of Finnish origin in the northern part of Norway, the country has no large minority groups. Norway is home to small numbers of Americans, Britons, Chileans, Danes, Iranians, Pakistanis, Swedes, and Vietnamese, among other groups.

Sweden's population consists mainly of Scandinavians of Germanic descent. Sweden's immigrant population and ethnic diversity have increased rapidly in recent decades. For many years, Sweden was a nation of emigrants. From 1860 to World War I, more than one million Swedes left the nation, mainly for the United States. Emigration declined significantly after 1930, as the nation industrialized and grew more prosperous. Sweden welcomed many refugees and displaced people after World War II. Since that time, immigration has accounted for nearly half of Sweden's population growth. Many immigrants have come to Sweden as guest workers or as political refugees. Today, approximately one-fifth of the people are immigrants or have at least one foreign-born parent.

The Finns are a people of unknown geographic origin. They have lived in Finland and in neighboring parts of Russia, Estonia, and Latvia for several thousand years.

Icelanders are one of the most homogenous peoples. They are predominantly of Nordic origin, descendants of hardy people who emigrated from Norway in the Middle Ages. There are also some Celtic influences from immigrants from the British Isles. Often in its history, Iceland has suffered major population losses from epidemics, volcanic eruptions, and earthquakes. From the mid-twentieth century, many rural Icelanders began moving to coastal towns and villages. Today, some 93 percent of the people now live in cities and towns. About 60 percent of Iceland's total population lives in Reykjavík. The overall population density is three people per square kilometer (7.8 per square mile).

Most of the roughly 150 million Russians derive from Eastern Slavic peoples, whose original homeland was likely present-day Poland. Russian is the official language and an official language in the United Nations. The language of writers such as Tolstoy, Dostoevsky, Chekov, Pushkin, and Solzhenitsyn has great importance in world literature.

The Food

DENMARK

The first half of the twentieth century was not a good period for Danish cooking. Though the cuisine was well developed, there was greater emphasis on nutrition, hygiene, and cost than on culinary art. At the same time, the food industry offered cheap substitutes such as margarine, stock cubes, flavor additives, and essences, and the result was an overstretched and heavy cuisine. The change started in the 1960s and the Danish cuisine of potatoes and gravy was rejected. The Danes turned to other countries for innovation, first the French bourgeois cuisine, and later Italy and other Mediterranean countries. The cuisine is now based on white bread and wine and therefore very different from the traditional Danish cuisine with its rye bread and beer. In the late twentieth century, the tendency to regard food as a means of expression and cooking as a lifestyle broke through. Being a chef became prestigious and chefs began to have their own television programs and restaurants at an ever younger age. International cuisines were explored, international trends came and went. After experimenting with fusion cuisine, most people returned to the idea that the best food came from the shortest and simplest trip from soil to table. This brought a focus on the primary produce that thrives best in the Danish climate, including apples, wild berries and fungi, vegetables such as cabbage and root vegetables, and fish, such as gurnard, hake, weever, lemon sole, and turbot, as well as shellfish from the Danish coast.

Danish cuisine still contains elements from the late 1800s, before industrialization. This was the age of what is called storage housekeeping, with a cuisine based on beer and rye bread, salted pork, and salted herring. Among the dishes from those days that are still eaten today are *øllebrød* (a dish made of rye bread, sugar, and nonalcoholic beer), *vandgrød* (porridge, usually barley porridge, made with water), *gule ærter* (split-pea soup), *æbleflæsk* (slices of pork with apples fried in fat), *klipfisk* (dried cod), *blodpølse* (black pudding), *finker* (similar to Scotland's haggis), and *grønlangkål* (thickened stewed kale). In the second half of the nineteenth century, the cooperative movement age, milk and potatoes played a prominent part and dishes such as roast pork and gravy, boiled cod with mustard sauce, consommé with meat, bread or flour dumplings, rissoles (also known as frikadellers, or any variation of meatball), minced beef patties, and other dishes based on minced meat. The same period saw the emergence of many fruit dishes such as *rødgrød* (thickened stewed fruit), *sødsuppe* (fruit soup), and stewed fruits. The range of vegetable dishes was expanded with boiled cabbage in white sauce, red cabbage, pickled beetroot, cucumber salad, and peas and carrots in white sauce.

NORWAY

On the northernmost coast of Norway, cod is hung on poles and dried in the wind without salt. For more than a thousand years this product was sold to other European countries to acquire such rare commodities as wine, wheat, and honey. They called this fish "stockfish," or *stoccafisso* or *estocafix*. A French cookbook manuscript from 1393 explains how boiled *stofix* should be eaten with mustard or dipped in butter. However, the fish must first be pounded with a wooden hammer and then soaked in water for many hours. Adding wood ash lye to the water makes the fish particularly soft and flavorful. The result of this process is the celebrated lye fish (lutefisk), today a Norwegian and Swedish specialty, and as in certain areas of the United States, closely identified with Norwegian and Swedish immigrants. Salmon (fresh and cured), herring (pickled or marinated), trout, codfish, and other seafood balanced by cheeses, dairy products, and excellent breads (predominantly dark/darker) show the influence of long seafaring and farming traditions. *Lefse* is a common Norwegian potato flatbread, especially at Christmas. Game has always been a central ingredient in Norwegian cooking. Elk dominates in most inland areas, with venison served more in western regions. Reindeer is the specialty in the north, even though it is available throughout the country.

SWEDEN

The Swedish culinary tradition is also one of food storage. During the brief harvest period, people gathered what they needed and saved it for future use. During the long, dark period of the year people would have to survive on the preserved foods. Fresh berries were a luxury, since most were cooked into jam for winter. Eating fresh vegetables was almost wasteful, since vegetables needed to be preserved or pickled. The same was true of potatoes and other root vegetables, which were stored in an earth cellar. The fruits that were available in winter were considered more precious than summer apples and August pears. Swedish bread was traditionally also baked with a long shelf life in mind. Rye bread was baked slowly into durable dark *kavring* loaves or dried into crispbread (*knäckebröd*) or rusks (*skorpor*) that could be stored for long periods. Similarly, drinking fresh milk or eating fresh butter and eggs was a pleasure when it occurred. Milk was fermented or otherwise preserved with the aid of bacterial cultures, becoming various yogurt-like soured milks (including *filmjölk* and stringy *léngfil*), curdled milk (*filbunke*), or sour cream (*gräddfil*), or else it was made into cheese.

Surströmming, or fermented Baltic herring, is sold in cans, and when opened a strong, foul smell is released, the result of a fermentation process. This method of preservation was invented long ago, when brining food was quite expensive due to the costs of salt. When fermentation was used, on the other hand, just enough salt was required to keep the fish from rotting. *Surströmming* is served with boiled potatoes and onions and often rolled into a slice of *tunnbröd,* a type of thin, flat unleavened bread.

Today a wider variety of fresh Swedish ingredients are available, including seafood, poultry, lamb, beef, veal, and wild game. On the coast the specialties are shellfish, fresh mackerel, and cod. Modern chefs use lingonberries, cloudberries, root vegetables, Baltic herring, wild game, and Västerbotten cheese in new ways but traditional methods of smoking, fermenting, salting, drying, marinating, and poaching continue. The Swedish word *smorgasbord* has found its way into many other languages. *Smor* means butter, or spread, and *smorgas* has come to stand for bread that has been spread with something—an open-faced sandwich. *Bord* means table, or board, as in room and board. But it has come to mean much more, bringing thoughts of a large display of many foods set out on long tables. Fish dishes are grouped together—pickled herring, herring in cream, salmon with dill, marinated salmon, and oysters with mustard sauce. The cold dishes come next—a variety of cheeses, cottage cheese, a raw vegetable tray, pickled beets, and salads of fresh fruits. In the hot section, choices include stuffed pork loin, meatballs, sliced ham and turkey, rice and potatoes fixed several ways, brown beans, and vegetable casseroles. Several kinds of bread, plus butter are offered. The dessert table is filled with cookies, fruit bread, rice pudding, custard, cheesecake, and fruit tarts.

FINLAND

The Finnish diet has been particularly functional throughout the ages. Their forefathers cultivated rye, oats, and barley and dried the crops for the long winter ahead, when they were used to make porridge or fermented bread. They picked berries in the woods in the summer, preserved lingonberries for the winter, and looked for cranberries under the melting snow in early spring. If the crops failed, pine bark was added to the bread or fresh new spruce shoots eaten in the spring. In the summer, milk was preserved by fermenting it.

ICELAND

Icelanders faced a thousand years of tough times and general famine. Nothing would grow on the island (until they discovered that they could build greenhouses on volcanoes for warmth), and nothing would live there (except Arctic foxes and sheep). They had to subsist on whatever food they could find. As a result of this deprivation, Icelanders have an obsession with preserving food any way they can, and with eating almost anything. *Hákarl* is shark meat that has been buried for three to six months to allow it to putrefy; it is then eaten in small chunks. Icelandic lamb has a distinctively "wild" flavor, reportedly due to roaming the countryside and eating untainted herbs. Some of the most traditional dishes involve making full use of every part of the slaughtered sheep. Offal from a sheep is minced together with its blood and served in the sheep's stomach to make *slatur*. Another delicacy is pickled ram's testicles. Or *svið,* a sheep's head that's been burned to remove the wool, cut in two, boiled, and either eaten fresh or pressed into jelly. Salted, smoked, or slathered in curry sauce, Iceland's national bird, the puffin, is a popular dish. Today, fish pulled from unpolluted waters and lamb that feed on unfertilized fields make up the staples of Iceland's entirely organic cuisine. Lobster, ocean perch, cod, salmon, and trout are other basic elements of the cuisine. Fish is traditionally baked, salted, or combined with garlic and onion in a stew. Smoked salmon is a favorite, along with fish pâtés and pickled herring. For dessert, there's *skyr,* a rich curd best mixed with cream or topped with wild berries. Another national favorite is *randalín,* a cake layered with blueberry jam.

RUSSIA

Peasant food is the foundation of traditional Russian cuisine. The long cold winters meant that the food consumed needed to provide warmth and energy to ensure survival during the very cold winter. Bread made from rye and kasha and various grains including barley, wheat, and millet became staples in the Russian diet. Rye was the ideal grain for planting during the short unpredictable growing season. Domestically produced meat included beef, pork, and mutton. Chickens, geese, and ducks made up domestic fowl. Game comprised just about every kind of available animal, from hares and squirrels, to deer and wild boar. Fish was a major staple, both because of its abundance and because of the numerous fast days in the Eastern Orthodox calendar in which all animal products were prohibited, including butter, milk, and cheese. The varieties of vegetables was limited and included cabbage, onions, garlic, and turnips and they were pickled, salted, boiled, stewed, baked, fried, braised, roasted, and broiled. The forests provided hazelnuts, mushrooms, and berries. Spices and seasonings used in Russian cooking were often imported from Byzantium and the East, including vinegar, cinnamon, mint, anise, pepper, linseed oil, salt, dill, and poppy seed. The principal sweetener was honey. Food preparation was determined by the peculiarities of the Russian oven: it had to be baked, simmered, stewed, or boiled; in other words, it must have consisted of stews, casseroles, pies, soups, but not (or very little) of poached, fried, sautéed foods—those that require an open flame.

Mongol and Tartar invasions in the thirteenth century brought new techniques, such as making sour milk, grilling meat, and the use of spices. Clotted sour milk became a staple diet to most Russians, and lasted well into the twentieth century. Due to Russia's close proximity to Persia and the Ottoman Empire, smoked meat, pastry cooking, green vegetables, salads, wines, and chocolate were introduced in the sixteenth to eighteenth centuries.

An important part of Russian cuisine is the *zakuski* (hors d'oeuvre) ceremony. *Zakuski* are the equivalent of a Scandinavian smorgasbord. By the early nineteenth century, it became fashionable in sophisticated homes to serve *zakuski* on a separate table in the dining room or in an adjacent room. Depending upon the occasion the *zakuski* menu included one or more fish dish, one or more meat dish, one or more salad and vegetable dish, one or more egg dish, marinated and/or salt-pickled vegetables and mushrooms, and marinated fruits (plums, apples, and others), condiments, including mustard, horseradish, and freshly ground pepper, and homemade dark breads.

Soup has always been vital to the Russian cuisine and can be divided into several different groups. Traditional soups ranged from *borsch, ukha, teur,* and *shchi.* Cold soups are based on *kvass,* light soups and stews feature water and vegetables, while noodle soups incorporate meat, milk, and mushrooms. Soups that are based on cabbage are called *shchi,* with thick soups such as *rassolnick* and *solynaka* being based on meat broth. Grain- and vegetable-based soups, as well as fish soups complete the traditional soup list.

One of the traditional meat dishes in Russian cuisine is *Studen,* or *Kholodets,* a dish that is made from jellied pork meat or veal. Spices and vegetables are added, and it is usually served with mustard or ground garlic, together with horseradish and *smetana* (a variety of sour cream similar to crème fraîche). *Pelmeni* are small stuffed dumplings traditional to Siberia, although they may have originated in northern China. Tribal groups in Siberia used these dumplings as portable food as they could be frozen and stored in quantity. Traditionally *pelmeni* are stuffed with a meat or meat mixture, potatoes with onions, *tvorog* cheese (farmer's cheese), or even bits of fish, shrimp, or crab. *Shashlik* is a form of shish kebab made of beef, pork, or lamb. These skewers are either all meat, all fat, or alternating pieces of meat and fat. Meats for *shashlik* (as opposed to other forms of shish kebab) are usually marinated overnight in a high-acidity marinade like vinegar, dry wine, or sour fruit/vegetable juice with the addition of herbs and spices. *Pejmen* is made from finely chopped meat in a thin dough made of flour and eggs, and possibly milk or water. According to the traditional Uralian recipe, the filling is made of 45 percent beef, 35 percent lamb, and 20 percent pork. Pepper, garlic, and onions are added to the meat. Beef Stroganoff is a combination of beef, mushrooms, and sour cream. Beef Stroganoff was the prize-winning recipe created for a cooking competition held in the 1890s in St. Petersburg, Russia. The chef who devised the recipe worked for the Russian diplomat Count Pavel Alexandrovich Stroganov, a member of one of Russia's grandest noble families. Russian blini are descended from one the most common prepared foods, fried flat bread. Russians, in fact, translate "blini" as "pancakes" when speaking English, although the ultra-thin, slightly tart Russian blini is more like the French crepe and German blintz.

Tea is the most popular drink in Russia. The Russian tea party is a social event where tea and biscuits are served. This tradition started back in 1638. The Russian samovar (teapot) is a cultural symbol of the Russian past. *Kvas* is a Russian national drink, a simple fermented drink with a low level of alcohol made from bread, apples, pears or other fruits.

Glossary

Aebleskiver A waffle or a pancake dough formed like a tennis ball, with various fillings. Cooked in an *aebleskive*r pan, typically served sprinkled with powered sugar and raspberry jam. A Danish delicacy.

Almond Potatoes A special variety of potatoes grown in the Nordic countries. The Finnish variety, called *lapin puikula*, has been granted the Protected Designation of Origin label, the PDO, which is given by the European Union to regional foods in order to protect them from any usurpation or imitation. This potato variety is floury. Its tubers are small, long-oval, curved, and pointed, with a yellow-colored flesh and a buttery taste. Outside Scandinavia, the *lapin puikula* may be available under the name yellow Finn. Yukon gold potatoes or other similar varieties may be substituted.

Anise Seeds These tiny seeds, which smell and taste like licorice, are used to flavor breads, rusks, cookies, candies, and beverages. In some dishes, a little anise seed may be used to replace fennel seed.

Aquavit (Akvavit) Flavored distilled liquor, ranging in alcohol content from 42 to 45 percent. It is clear to pale yellow in color, distilled from a fermented potato or grain mash, and flavored with caraway or cumin seeds. Other preparations use lemon or orange peel, cardamom, aniseed, and fennel.

Blini A thin pancake often served in connection with a religious rite or festival in several Slavic cultures.

Borscht (Borsch, Borsht, or Bortsch) Vegetable soup, usually including beet roots.

Caraway Seeds A pungent aroma and a distinctly sweet but tangy flavor, besides the Arab countries and India, the strongly scented and highly aromatic caraway seeds are also widely used in Germany and Russia and in Scandinavian countries like Denmark and Finland.

Caviar Sturgeon eggs that have been salted and allowed to mature. Sold fresh or pasteurized, there are three types of Russian caviar, differentiated by size, color, and species of sturgeon. Caviars have specific grades: they refer to colors, not flavor or size. Grade 1 (000) is the lightest color, also called "royal caviar." Grade 2 (00) is medium dark with a gray tone. The darkest caviar is 0. The three different types of caviar come from three different species of sturgeon: beluga, osetra, and sevruga.

> **Beluga** is the largest sturgeon; the female takes twenty years to mature, weighing up to a ton, and measuring up to fifteen feet long. It produces the largest and most fragile eggs and most expensive caviar. Beluga caviar ranges from light to dark pearl gray, smooth, with a mildly sweet flavor of delicate hazelnut.

> **Osetra** are native to the Caspian Sea, and osetra caviar is usually the best quality available. The female osetra takes up to fifteen years to mature, weighs up to 500 pounds, and measures as much as six feet in length. Osetra produces an even roe, which has a golden hue, strong nutty flavor, and a mild taste.

> **Sevruga** are native to the cold depths of the Caspian Sea. Sevruga is the smallest and most prolific of the caviar sturgeons. The female sevruga takes seven years to mature, and weighs no more than 200 pounds. Sevruga produces caviar that is dark gray or black in color and with a strong taste of mildly fruity flavor.

Cheeses

From Denmark

Blue Castello Soft-ripened, creamy blue Brie from Denmark. A good dessert cheese.

Danablu (Danish Blue) Flavorful blue cheese, slightly spicy with a moist marbled texture.

Danbo The cheese has a pale, elastic interior with a few small holes.

Esrom Creamy, semi-soft cheese made from cow's milk. Esrom has a greasy, yellow-brown rind and is buttery in texture. It has a mild, pleasant taste.

Havarti Has a buttery aroma and can be somewhat sharp in the stronger varieties, much like Swiss cheese. The taste is buttery, and from slightly sweet to very sweet, and it is slightly acidic. The texture, depending on type, can be supple and flexible.

Mycella A Danish version of Gorgonzola with a blue-green mold and mild aromatic taste. It is a traditional, creamy blue cheese made from cow's milk. The veins in the cheese provide an attractive contrast to the very pale, creamy, almost buttery interior.

Saga Original Saga is a cross between blue cheese and Brie, a creamy, blue-veined cheese with a white-mold rind. It is very mild for a blue-veined cheese. Saga is an excellent dessert cheese best served with fruit and wine.

From Sweden

Adelost Creamy blue cheese made from cow's milk. Ripens in two to three months and has a fat content of 50 percent.

Graddost Similar to Gruyère, graddost has a mild nuttiness, somewhat tangy flavor. This cheese melts easily and keeps well.

Hushallsost Creamy, semi-soft cheese made from cow's milk. The flavor is mild and creamy, with a lemon-fresh finish. It is made with whole milk, rather than skimmed.

Mesost A caramelized cheese that looks like fudge and has a caramel flavor with a bitter aftertaste.

Swedish Fontina Milder and firmer than its Italian counterpart. Nutty and mild, it is made from partially skimmed cow's milk.

Vasterbottenost A slow-maturing cheese that ripens for eighteenth months, resulting in a pungent, bitter taste. This cheese is excellent for grilling and grating.

From Norway and Finland

Aura Finnish blue cheese, made with cow's milk, it has a strong and piquant, fruity flavor and a creamy crumbly consistency.

Gjetost Cow's or goat's milk cooked to achieve a cheese with a slightly sour but sweet caramel taste with a smooth texture similar to fudge. Ekte or genuine Gjetost is made with goat's milk alone.

Jarlsberg Cow's milk cheese with large holes, a rich buttery texture and mild, sweet nutty flavor. Similar to Emmentaler with a slightly lower fat content and melts easily.

Juustoleipa A specialty cheese native to Finland and Lapland, the baking process produces a creamy and smooth texture under a browned, crusty surface. It is best served warm.

Nokkelost A spiced semi-soft cheese with caraway, cumin, and cloves.

Turunmaa This Finnish Havarti-type cheese has a smooth and lacy, creamy texture and a mild but full, slightly tangy flavor.

From Russia

Arakadz Made of sheep's milk, it is semi-hard with a nutty flavor.

Brindza Similar to feta cheese, its soft, milky flavor is made from sheep's or goat's milk.

Chanakh or **Klukh Panir** Salty soft cheese.

Chilichil A hard, sour, saltwater cheese that must be rinsed before eating.

Yeghegnatzor Soft cheese made with a mixture of sheep and goat milk, with leavening, herbs, seeds, and roots added.

Cloudberries Relative to the raspberry and blackberry, the cloudberry is the smallest of this group. The fruit is red when unripe, turning soft and orange at maturity.

Coriander Seeds Dried coriander seeds have a pleasant scent and a lemony flavor.

Fċrikċl Called the Norwegian national dish, it is lamb and cabbage stew using the neck, shank, and breast, together with the bones of the lamb. The fat and bones of the parts used for fċrikċl are the key to the flavor of this dish.

Fruit soup Dessert soup popular in Scandinavia, often made with dried fruits.

Golubtsi Cabbage rolls filled with millet.

Gravlax (Gravlaks, Graavilohi, Graflax) Salmon cured with salt, sugar, and dill.

Herring Small saltwater fish found mainly in the North Atlantic and the North Sea. Herring is an oily fish, containing many essential nutrients and healthy fatty acids. Herring is most commonly eaten salted or preserved. Herring preparations include:

Bismarck Fresh, marinated in white wine/vinegar brine with carrots, onions, and spices.

Bloater Ungutted, lightly salted, and mildly hot- or cold-smoked, similar to kipper.

Buckling Briefly pickled in brine and hot-smoked.

Kipper Deboned, split, and flattened, lightly salted, dried, and mildly cold-smoked.

Matjes Fresh or lightly salted herring, or cured in spiced sugar-vinegar brine; also called soused herring.

Schmaltz Mature, fatty herring, filleted and preserved in brine. (*Schmaltz* is Yiddish for rendered chicken or goose fat, whereas in German it means melted animal fat, usually pork or goose fat.)

Kasha In Russian, the word *kasha* is used in a broad sense for various cooked grains such as buckwheat, millet, and oats. In America, the term refers to roasted buckwheat groats, which have a toasty nutty flavor.

Kissel Common dessert, sweetened with juice or milk, thickened with corn or potato starch; red wine or dried fruits may be added. Served hot or cold, often considered a soup.

Knedliky Czech bread dumplings.

Kringle Oval, butter-layered Danish pastries; originally pretzel-shaped, almond filled coffee cakes.

Kulebiaka, Koulibiaka, Koulibiac Large, narrow pie filled with salmon or sturgeon, mushrooms, rice, and hard-boiled eggs.

Kulich Russian traditional yeast-leavened Easter bread containing candied and dried fruits, nuts, and liqueur.

Kvas Russian meaning "sour beverage," a low-fermented drink made from bread and fruit.

Lapskaus Traditional Norwegian dish of leftovers mixed together, cooked as a soup or stew.

Lefse (Lef-suh) A traditional Scandinavian flatbread made from potatoes and flour, similar to the tortilla.

Lingonberries Small, red, pea-sized berries with a delicious flavor combining sweetness and tartness, the taste resembling that of wild cranberry.

Lutefisk Scandinavian delicacy, made from air-dried whitefish (cod), prepared with lye, in a sequence of particular treatments.

Malossol A Russian term used to describe the amount of salt used in the initial curing process. Malossol means "lightly salted" in Russian; today the term has come to mean any high-quality caviar.

Mämmi A traditional Finnish Easter dessert, a baked malt porridge.

Okroshka A cold soup based on kvas; the main ingredients are vegetables that may be mixed with cold boiled meat or fish.

Pelmeni Russian-type ravioli filled with various fillings.

Pirogi, *pierogi* Slavic dumplings that are boiled and then fried.

Piroshki Small meat filled pastry.

Rasstegai Small open-topped pies.

Rissoles A shallow or deep-fried minced meat dish.

Rømmegrøt Norwegian Christmas pudding.

Samovar A classic Russian tea urn.

Sharlotka Charlotte Russe.

Shashlyk Russian version of shish kebabs, marinated meat grilled on a skewer.

Sireniki Cheese fritters.

Smetana Russian in origin, this thick, yellowish-white and slightly sour-tasting cream contains about 40 percent milk fat. It is made by curdling pasteurized cream. Smetana can be replaced with crème fraîche with a similar fat content, but smetana is usually more sour in taste.

Smörgásbord (Smorgasbord) Swedish term meaning an abundant buffet meal set with several hot and cold dishes, from appetizers to desserts, laid out together on the table. The word *smörgásbord* literally means "sandwich table" or "bread and butter table." It is known and served throughout the Nordic countries, enriched with local delicacies in each country. Known as *kolde bord* in Denmark, and as *seisova pöytä, noutopöytä*, or *voileipäpöytä* in Finland. The famous Russian appetizer buffet, zakuska table, has several characteristics similar to smorgasbord.

Smørrebrød Danish word for open sandwiches, a major part of the Scandinavian diet.

Solyanka Thick, spicy, and sour Russian soup.

Surströmming Literally "sour herring," an old, traditional Swedish preparation of fermented Baltic herring cured with dill, sugar, salt, and coarse peppercorns. The process produces lactic acid preserving the fish, similar to the development of sauerkraut.

Syrniki Fried curd fritters, garnished with sour cream, jam, honey, and/or applesauce.

Vodka A distilled drink, the name stemming from the Russian word *voda,* meaning water.

Wallenberg Steak Classic Swedish veal hamburger steak usually served with potato puree, boiled green peas, and sugared lingonberries or lingonberry jam.

Zakouski (Zakuska, Zakuski) Russian hors d'oeuvre presentation.

Menus and Recipes from Scandinavia and Russia

Sillsallad
Herring and Beet Salad (Sweden)   SERVES 4

AMOUNT	MEASURE	INGREDIENT
$\frac{1}{2}$ cup	3 ounces, 84 g	Herring, pickled, $\frac{1}{4}$ inch (.6 cm) dice
$\frac{1}{2}$ cup	3 ounces, 84 g	Red beets, boiled in skin, peeled, $\frac{1}{4}$ inch (.6 cm) dice
3 tablespoons	$1\frac{1}{2}$ ounces, 45 ml	Mayonnaise
6 tablespoons	3 ounces, 90 ml	Sour cream
1 tablespoon, or to taste	$\frac{1}{2}$ ounce, 15 ml	Malt vinegar
1 teaspoon		Pickling brine from herring
$\frac{1}{2}$ cup	2 ounces, 56 g	Golden Delicious apple, peeled, cored, $\frac{1}{4}$ inch (.6 cm) dice
$\frac{1}{2}$ cup	3 ounces, 84 g	Red bliss potato, boiled in skin, peeled, $\frac{1}{4}$ inch (.6 cm) dice
$\frac{1}{4}$ cup	$1\frac{1}{2}$ ounces, 42 g	Red onion, $\frac{1}{4}$ inch (.6 cm) dice
$\frac{1}{4}$ cup	$1\frac{1}{2}$ ounces, 42 g	Sweet pickle, $\frac{1}{4}$ inch (.6 cm) dice
To taste		Salt and pepper
4		Green leaf lettuce
1 tablespoon		Capers, rinsed
12		Thin red onion rings, soaked in ice cold water.

PROCEDURE

1 Set aside 1 tablespoon diced herring and 1 tablespoon diced beets for garnish.

2 Combine mayonnaise and sour cream and season with malt vinegar and pickling brine.

3 Combine apple, herring, potato, beets, onion, and pickle, fold into sour cream dressing, and let set 1 hour before serving.

4 Correct seasoning with salt, pepper, and additional vinegar.

5 Line plates with lettuce leaves and mound salad in center. Garnish with reserved diced herring and beets, capers, and red onion rings.

Grønkćlsuppe
Kale Soup with Poached Egg (Denmark)   SERVES 4

AMOUNT	MEASURE	INGREDIENT
1 pound	448 g	Kale
2 tablespoons	1 ounce, 28 g	Butter
$\frac{1}{2}$ cup	4 ounces, 112 g	Bacon, $\frac{1}{4}$ inch (.6 cm) dice
1 cup	4 ounces, 112 g	Onion, $\frac{1}{4}$ inch (.6 cm) dice
$\frac{3}{4}$ cup	3 ounces, 84 g	Carrots, $\frac{1}{4}$ inch (.6 cm) dice
2 cups	8 ounces, 224 g	Leek, white and light green parts, $\frac{1}{4}$ inch (.6 cm) dice
2 tablespoons, more if necessary		Flour
$4\frac{1}{4}$ cups	34 ounces, 1 liter	Chicken stock
To taste		Salt and white pepper
4		Eggs, poached

PROCEDURE

1 Remove center ribs from kale leaves, wash carefully, blanch, drain well, and chop coarsely.

2 Heat butter over medium-low heat, add bacon, and cook until fat has been rendered; do not brown.

3 Add vegetables; sauté without coloring until soft, 5 to 8 minutes.

4 Add flour to make a roux; cook 3 minutes.

5 Add stock and cook 10 minutes.

6 Add kale; cook until kale is tender, 15 minutes or longer.

7 Adjust seasoning, and place a hot poached egg in the middle of each serving.

Stekt Rimmad Lax med Korintscs Fried Dill-Cured Salmon with Sweet-and-Sour Raisin Sauce (Sweden) SERVES 4

AMOUNT	MEASURE	INGREDIENT
3 tablespoons		Coarse salt
2 tablespoons		Granulated sugar
1 teaspoon		White peppercorns, cracked
4 tablespoons		Fresh dill, chopped
8	$2\frac{1}{2}$ ounce, 70 g	Skinless, boneless salmon, bias cut
3 tablespoons		Raisins
$1\frac{1}{2}$ cups	12 ounces, 360 ml	Brown veal stock
2 tablespoons	1 ounce, 30 ml	Butter
2 tablespoons		Flour
2 tablespoons	1 ounce, 30 ml	Simple syrup
2 tablespoons	1 ounce, 30 ml	Malt vinegar
As needed		Flour, for dredging
$\frac{1}{2}$ cup	4 ounces, 120 ml	Clarified butter

PROCEDURE

1   Combine coarse salt, sugar, peppercorns, and dill, sprinkle on both sides of salmon. Let cure 30 minutes. Rinse under cold water and dry well.

2   To make sauce, simmer raisins and veal stock until raisins are soft but not mushy, 10 minutes. Drain raisins; reserve stock and raisins.

3   Melt butter over medium heat and add flour to make roux; cook 2 minutes. Add stock and cook 15 minutes. Add simple syrup and vinegar, and correct with more of either to create a well-balanced sweet-sour taste. Add raisins and keep hot.

4   Season salmon with salt and white pepper, dredge in flour. Heat clarified butter over medium-high heat and pan-fry salmon pieces until crisp, about 1 minute on each side.

5   Serve with sauce, buttered green beans, and Hasselback potatoes.

Hasselback Potatis

Hasselback Potatoes YIELD: 4

AMOUNT	MEASURE	INGREDIENT
12		Red bliss potatoes, about 2 ounces (56 g) each
4 tablespoons	2 ounces, 60 ml	Butter, melted
$\frac{1}{4}$ cup		Fresh bread crumbs
To taste		Salt and white pepper

PROCEDURE

1   Preheat oven to 400°F (204°C).

2   Put each potato in the bowl of a wooden spoon, like you would carry an egg in an egg-spoon race, and cut across at about $\frac{1}{4}$-inch (.6 cm) intervals. Cut each potato not quite through so they are still joined together at the bottom.

3   Heat butter over medium high heat and add cut potatoes; heat until sizzling.

4   Season with salt and pepper; roast 15 to 20 minutes, basting every 5 minutes.

5   Sprinkle with bread crumbs, baste with butter, and cook until bread crumbs are golden and potatoes are soft, 10 to 15 minutes.

Lefse Potato Flatbreads (Norway)   YIELD: 4

Lefse are also tasty sprinkled with sugar and cinnamon.

AMOUNT	MEASURE	INGREDIENT
$\frac{1}{2}$ cup	4 ounces, 120 ml	Butter, melted
$\frac{1}{4}$ cup	2 ounces, 60 ml	Milk, hot
$\frac{1}{2}$ teaspoon		Granulated sugar
2 cups	12 ounces, 336 g	Russet potatoes, boiled in the skin, peeled and riced while hot
1 cup, plus more for dusting	4.4 ounces, 124 g	All-purpose flour
As needed		Salt
As needed		Butter

PROCEDURE

1   Combine butter, milk, and sugar bring to a simmer.

2   Combine hot milk mixture with potatoes and mix.

3   Add flour and salt; stir to create soft, slightly sticky dough. Do not work the dough; handle as you would "short dough." Chill.

4   Roll out into a rope and cut 8 equal pieces, roll out (thin) to approximately 5-inch (12.5 cm) diameter rounds, like tortillas, dusting rolling surface with flour as needed.

5   Heat a heavy frying pan or flat griddle. Cooking surface is hot enough when a little water sprinkled on bounces off the surface. Lefse are cooked on a dry surface; do not add any fat to griddle.

6   Roll lefse onto the rolling pin, transfer lefse to hot griddle, and cook until brown "freckles" appear on the heated surface, 1 minute.

7   Flip and cook second side until freckled, 1 minute or until lefse looks cooked.

8   Stack between towels and cook remaining lefse. It is important to cool the lefses between towels so they do not dry out.

9   Restack lefses once or twice to remove moisture and to keep them from getting soggy.

10 Serve warm, spread with butter and rolled up like logs.

Æblekage Apple Trifle (Denmark)   SERVES 4

AMOUNT	MEASURE	INGREDIENT
3 cups	18 ounces, 500 g	All-purpose cooking apple (such as Golden Delicious), $\frac{3}{4}$ inch (1.87 cm) dice
$\frac{1}{2}$ cup	$3\frac{1}{2}$ ounces, 98 g	Granulated sugar
$\frac{1}{2}$ teaspoon		Vanilla extract
3 tablespoons	$1\frac{1}{2}$ ounces, 45 ml	Water
$\frac{3}{4}$ cup	3 ounces, 98 g	Fresh bread crumbs
$\frac{1}{4}$ cup	$1\frac{3}{4}$ ounces, 50 g	Granulated sugar
5 tablespoons	$2\frac{1}{2}$ ounces, 70 g	Butter
I cup	8 ounces, 240 ml	Whipping cream
$\frac{1}{4}$ cup	2 ounces, 60 ml	Red currant jelly

PROCEDURE

1   Combine apples, first quantity of sugar, vanilla, and water; simmer, covered, over medium heat until apples are soft but not mushy; check after 10 minutes. Let cool.

2   In a sauté pan over medium heat, toast bread crumbs until golden. Add second quantity of sugar and cook 1 to 2 minutes until nicely browned.

3   Off the heat, add butter and stir until combined with bread crumbs; remove from pan and cool.

4   Layer apples and bread crumb mixture in serving bowl, starting with apples and finishing with bread crumbs.

5   Decorate trifle with whipped cream and jelly.

Borshch Moskovsky
Moscow-Style Beet Soup SERVES 4

AMOUNT	MEASURE	INGREDIENT
1 tablespoon	$\frac{1}{2}$ ounce, 15 ml	Butter
2 tablespoons	1 ounce, 28 g	Bacon, $\frac{1}{4}$ inch (.6 cm) dice
1 cup	4 ounces, 112 g	Onions, $\frac{1}{4}$ inch (.6 cm) dice
1		Garlic clove, minced
$\frac{1}{2}$ cup	2 ounces, 56 g	Celery, $\frac{1}{4}$ inch (.6 cm) dice
$\frac{1}{2}$ cup	2 ounces, 56 g	Carrots, $\frac{1}{4}$ inch (.6 cm) dice
2 cups	10 ounces, 280 g	Beets, peeled, $\frac{1}{4}$ inch (.6 cm) dice
2 tablespoons	1 ounce, 30 ml	Red wine vinegar
$\frac{1}{2}$ teaspoon		Granulated sugar
1 cup	6 ounces, 180 ml	Tomatoes, peeled, seeded, $\frac{1}{4}$ inch (.6 cm) dice
To taste		Salt and white pepper
4 cups	32 ounces, 960 ml	Chicken, beef, or vegetable stock
1 cup	4 ounces, 112 g	Green cabbage, cored and finely shredded
$\frac{1}{2}$ cup	2 ounces, 56 g	Potatoes, peeled, $\frac{1}{4}$ inch (.6 cm) dice
2		Parsley sprigs, tied together with 1 bay leaf
2 tablespoons		Fresh dill or flat-leaf parsley, finely diced
$\frac{1}{4}$ cup	2 ounces, 60 ml	Sour cream

PROCEDURE

1 Heat butter over medium heat and render bacon; do not brown.

2 Add onions and cook, 3 minutes; add garlic and cook 2 minutes until both are translucent.

3 Add celery and carrots; cook 3 minutes.

4 Add beets, stir in red wine vinegar, sugar, tomatoes, 1 teaspoon salt, and white pepper to taste.

5 Add 1 cup stock and simmer, covered, 15 to 20 minutes.

6 Add remaining stock, the cabbage, and potatoes; bring to a boil. Reduce heat, submerge parsley and bay leaf, and simmer, partially covered, until potatoes and cabbage are soft but still hold shape.

7 Stir in dill and serve with sour cream as accompaniment.

Blini Buckwheat Pancakes   SERVES 4

Serve with sour cream or melted butter, topped with thin-sliced smoked salmon, red salmon roe, thin-sliced smoked sturgeon, black caviar, or pickled herring.

AMOUNT	MEASURE	INGREDIENT
1½ teaspoons	3 g	Active dry yeast
¼ cup	2 ounces, 60 ml	Luke warm water, 110–115°F (43.3–46.1°C)
¼ cup	1 ounce, 30 g	Buckwheat flour
1 cup	4 ounces, 112 g	All-purpose flour
1 cup	8 ounces, 240 ml	Lukewarm milk, 110–115°F (43.3–46.1°C)
2		Egg yolks, slightly beaten
Pinch		Salt
½ teaspoon		Granulated sugar
¼ cup	4 ounces, 120 ml	Butter, melted and cooled
1 cup, plus more for serving	8 ounces, 240 ml	Sour cream
2		Egg whites
Garnish		Caviar, smoked salmon, sturgeon, or herring fillets

PROCEDURE

1   Sprinkle yeast over lukewarm water, let stand 3 minutes, make sure it is active, and stir to dissolve. Let stand 3 minutes in a warm, draft-free area.

2   Combine half the buckwheat flour and half the all-purpose flour. Make a well in the center and add half the warm milk and the yeast mixture. Slowly work the flour into the liquid. Cover the bowl and set aside in a warm, draft-free area until the mixture has nearly doubled in size, 2 hours.

3   Beat in remaining flours; let rest 1 hour.

4   Gradually add remaining warm milk, egg yolks, salt, sugar, 1 tablespoon (½ ounces, 15 ml) melted butter, and 1½ tablespoons (¾ ounce, 20 ml) sour cream.

5   Beat egg whites to stiff peaks, fold into batter, and let rest 15 minutes.

6   Preheat oven to 200°F (93°C).

7   Heat a heavy frying pan or flat griddle. Cooking surface is hot enough when a little water sprinkled on bounces off the surface.

8   Grease the cooking surface and pour 3 tablespoons ($1\frac{1}{2}$ ounce, 45 ml) of batter for each pancake; cook 2 to 3 minutes, brushing the top lightly with butter. Turn pancake over and cook 2 minutes, or until golden brown. Keep warm in oven until remaining pancakes are cooked.

9   Serve hot, accompanied with remaining melted butter and sour cream. Garnish with caviar.

Grechnevaya Kasha
Buckwheat Groats   YIELD: 4

AMOUNT	MEASURE	INGREDIENT
1 cup	6 ounces, 168 g	Buckwheat groats
1		Egg, beaten
1 teaspoon		Salt
3 tablespoons	$1\frac{1}{2}$ ounces, 45 ml	Butter
$2\frac{1}{2}$ cups	20 ounces, 600 ml	Boiling water

PROCEDURE

1   Toss together buckwheat groats and egg until the grains are thoroughly coated.

2   Over medium heat in an ungreased pan, cook uncovered, stirring constantly, until groats are lightly toasted and dry.

3   Add salt, butter, and 2 cups (16 ounces, 480 ml) boiling water. Stir, cover tightly, reduce heat to low, and simmer, stirring occasionally, about 20 minutes. After 20 minutes check for tenderness; if necessary, add the additional water and continue cooking until tender and water is absorbed, and the grains are separated and fluffy.

4   Correct seasoning and serve.

Kulebiaka Salmon in Pastry   SERVES 4

AMOUNT	MEASURE	INGREDIENT
Brioche Dough		
3 tablespoons	$1\frac{1}{2}$ ounces, 45 ml	Milk
1 tablespoon	$\frac{1}{4}$ ounce, 7 g	Granulated sugar
1 tablespoon	$\frac{1}{4}$ ounce, 7 g	Active dry yeast
2 cups	14 ounces	Bread flour
3		Eggs
1 teaspoon	2 g	Salt
6 tablespoons	3 ounces, 90 ml	Butter, melted
Rice Filling		
Step 1		
2 tablespoons	1 ounce, 30 ml	Butter
$\frac{1}{4}$ cup	1 ounce, 28 g	Onion, $\frac{1}{4}$ inch (.6 cm) dice
1 cup	7 ounces, 196 g	Rice
$1\frac{1}{2}$ cups	12 ounces, 360 ml	Chicken stock
Step 2		
2 tablespoons	1 ounce, 30 ml	Butter
3 cups	8 ounces, 224 g	Mushrooms, diced
2 tablespoons	1 ounce, 30 ml	Fresh lemon juice
Step 3		
$\frac{1}{4}$ cup	2 ounces, 60 ml	Butter
$\frac{3}{4}$ cup	3 ounces, 84 g	Onion, $\frac{1}{4}$ inch (.6 cm) dice
1		Egg, hard-boiled, finely chopped
1		Egg yolk
1 tablespoon		Fresh dill, chopped
To taste		Salt and pepper
Assembly		
$\frac{3}{4}$ pound	12 ounces, 336 g	Boneless, skinless salmon fillet
As needed		Egg wash

BRIOCH DOUGH

1 Over medium heat bring milk and sugar to 110–115°F (43.3–46.1°C).

2 Sprinkle yeast over warm milk and rehydrate 10 minutes.

3 Combine $\frac{3}{4}$ cup (3 ounces, 84 g) flour, 1 egg, and 1 teaspoon salt. Add yeast mixture, blend until a smooth soft dough, and cut a deep X across top. Cover with plastic wrap and let starter rise at room temperature, 1 hour.

4 Beat remaining eggs with butter.

5 Slowly work remaining flour and egg mixture into starter dough; knead the mixture by hand until the dough is smooth and shiny, 6 to 8 minutes.

6 Lightly butter a large bowl and scrape dough into bowl. Lightly dust dough with flour to prevent a crust from forming.

7 Cover bowl with plastic wrap and let dough rise at room temperature until more than doubled in bulk, 1 hour. Punch down dough and lightly dust with flour.

FILLING

1 **Step 1.** Heat butter and sauté onions until translucent. Add rice and cook 1 minute.

2 Add stock and season. Bring to simmer, cover, reduce heat to low, and cook about 15 minutes. Remove cover and cook 5 minutes longer. Fluff rice.

3 **Step 2.** Heat butter over medium high heat, add mushrooms, and cook until moisture has evaporated. Add lemon juice and cook 30 seconds.

4 **Step 3.** Heat butter over medium high heat, add onions, and cook until translucent.

5 Combine cooked rice, cooked onion and mushroom mixture, hard-boiled egg, egg yolk, and dill. Correct seasoning and cool to room temperature before assembling.

ASSEMBLY

1 Roll out dough to $\frac{1}{8}$ inch (.3 cm) thick and spread $\frac{1}{2}$ inch (1.2 cm) layer of rice mixture in the center of the dough, the size of the salmon fillet.

2 Place salmon fillet on top of rice; add another $\frac{1}{2}$ inch (1.2 cm) layer of rice mixture on top.

3 Brush egg wash over edges of pastry and fold dough over to completely cover the rice and salmon. Trim excess dough. Place seam side down on a parchment lined baking pan. Rest 30 minutes in refrigerator.

4 Brush with egg wash, poke vent holes, and bake at 375°F (190°C) until golden brown and salmon fillet is cooked, around 145°F (63°C). Let set 10 to 15 minutes before cutting.

Chahohbili Georgian-Style Chicken   SERVES 4

AMOUNT	MEASURE	INGREDIENT
5 tablespoons	$2\frac{1}{2}$ ounces, 75 ml	Butter
3 cups	18 ounces, 504 g	Onions, $\frac{1}{2}$ inch (1.2 cm) dice
3 pounds	48 ounces, 1.3 kg	Chicken, cut into 12 pieces
3 tablespoons	$1\frac{1}{2}$ ounces, 45 ml	Tomato paste
1 cup	6 ounces, 180 ml	Tomato, grated
$\frac{3}{4}$ cup	3 ounces, 84 g	Sweet red pepper, minced
1 teaspoon		Hot pepper flakes
To taste		Salt and pepper
2 cups		Italian parsley, rough chopped, packed
1 cup		Coriander greens, rough chopped, packed
2		Garlic cloves, chopped
To taste		Hot pepper flakes

PROCEDURE

1   Heat butter over medium-low heat; add onions and cook until translucent and soft, 20 minutes.

2   Pat chicken dry, turn heat to medium, and add chicken to onions. Cook 2 to 3 minutes, turning often.

3   Add tomato paste, cook 1 minute, then add tomato, sweet pepper, and hot pepper flakes. Cover and simmer until chicken is cooked, 30 minutes.

4   In a mortar, add a pinch of salt to parsley, coriander, and garlic; crush to a coarse paste (this is essential).

5   Add herb mixture, and hot pepper to taste, to saucepan, mix well, and bring to a boil; remove from heat immediately.

6   Serve hot.

Loby String Beans in Sour Cream Sauce SERVES 4

AMOUNT	MEASURE	INGREDIENT
3 cups	12 ounces, 336 g	Fresh string beans
3 tablespoons	$1\frac{1}{2}$ ounces, 45 ml	Butter
1 cup	4 ounces, 112 g	Onions, thinly sliced
$\frac{1}{2}$ cup	2 ounces, 56 g	Green bell pepper, $\frac{1}{4}$ inch (.6 cm) dice
1 cup	6 ounces, 168 g	Tomato, peeled, seeded, $\frac{1}{4}$ inch (.6 cm) dice
2 teaspoons		Fresh basil, chopped
$\frac{1}{2}$ cup	4 ounces, 120 ml	Sour cream
To taste		Salt and pepper

PROCEDURE

1 Cook beans in boiling salted water just until done. Drain, shock in cold water, drain again, and set aside.

2 Heat butter over medium high heat and sauté onions until translucent, 3 minutes. Add green pepper and cook 3 minutes.

3 Add tomato and basil, raise heat to high, and cook 1 minute to remove excess moisture from tomato; cook longer if necessary.

4 Add green beans and sauté until heated completely.

5 Stir in sour cream, correct seasoning, and serve hot.

Syrniki Sweet Cheese Fritter with Berry Kissel

SERVES 4

AMOUNT	MEASURE	INGREDIENT
2 cups	16 ounces, 448 g	Cottage cheese or large-curd pot cheese
4		Egg yolks
$1\frac{1}{3}$ cups	5 ounces, 140 g	All-purpose flour
$\frac{1}{4}$ teaspoon		Salt
2 tablespoons		Granulated sugar
$\frac{1}{2}$ cup	4 ounces, 120 ml	Butter
Berry Kissel		
$\frac{1}{4}$ cup	2 ounces, 56 g	Granulated sugar
2 tablespoons		Cornstarch
Pinch		Salt
1 cup	8 ounces, 240 ml	Water
2 cups	8 ounces, 224 g	Blackberries
2 cups	8 ounces, 224 g	Raspberries
$\frac{1}{2}$ teaspoon, or to taste		Fresh lemon juice

PROCEDURE FOR FRITTER

1   Set cheese in colander, cover with towel, and weigh it down. Let drain 2 to 3 hours.

2   With the back of a spoon, rub cheese through a fine sieve set over a bowl.

3   Beat egg yolks into cheese, one at a time, then gradually beat in the flour, salt, and sugar.

4   Shape into 4 equal portions. On a floured surface, form into 3- to 4-inch (7.2 to 9.6 cm) cylindrical links. Wrap and chill 30 to 45 minutes.

5   Cut into 1-inch (2.4 cm) pieces and fry in butter over medium-high heat 3 to 5 minutes on each side, or until golden brown. Serve hot fritters with berry kissel or sour cream.

PROCEDURE FOR BERRY KISSEL

1   Combine sugar, cornstarch, and salt.

2   Over medium heat combine water and $\frac{1}{4}$ of the berries, simmer 2 minutes. Drain mixture, reserving both liquid and berries.

3   Gradually whisk in reserved hot liquid to the sugar mixture and bring to a boil; stir and cook 3 minutes. Remove from heat and strain.

4   Add all berries and lemon juice to liquid. Chill.

Shchi Cabbage Soup   SERVES 4 TO 6

AMOUNT	MEASURE	INGREDIENT
Beef Stock		
	8 ounces	Lean brisket of beef
$2\frac{1}{2}$ pounds		Beef marrow bones, cracked
2 quarts	1.9 l	Water
I cup	4 ounces, 112 g	Onion, peeled and quartered
I cup	4 ounces, 112 g	Carrot, peeled, large rough chop
		2 celery tops, 6 sprigs parsley, 2 bay leaves tied with string
I tablespoon		Salt

PROCEDURE FOR STOCK

1 In a heavy to 6- to 8-quart pot, bring the beef, beef bones, and water to a boil over high heat, skimming off any foam and scum as they rise to the surface.

2 Add the onion, carrot, tied greens, and salt; partially cover, and reduce the heat to low. Simmer 1 to $1\frac{1}{2}$ hours, or until the meat is tender but not falling apart.

3 Remove meat, cut into small dice, and set aside. Continue to simmer the stock partially covered, 2 to 4 hours longer. Strain the stock through a fine sieve, discarding the bones and greens. Skim off and discard as much of the surface fat as possible.

Soup		
2 tablespoons	I ounces, 30 ml	Butter
I cup	4 ounces, 112 g	Onions, thinly sliced
	12 ounces	White cabbage, quartered, cored, coarsely shredded
I cup	4 ounces, 112 g	Celery root, peeled, julienned
I cup	4 ounces, 112 g	Parsnip, peeled, julienned
$1\frac{1}{4}$ cups	8 ounces, 224 g	Boiling potatoes, peeled, $\frac{1}{4}$-inch (.6 cm) dice
I cup	6 ounces, 168 g	Tomatoes, peeled, seeded, and chopped
I teaspoon		Salt
To taste		Freshly ground black pepper

PROCEDURE FOR SOUP

1 Heat butter over medium heat, add onions, and sauté 7 to 8 minutes, or until soft.

2 Add cabbage, celery root, and parsnips; cover and simmer 15 minutes.

3 Add stock and reserved diced beef. Simmer, partially covered, 15 minutes. Add potatoes and cook until potatoes are tender, 10 minutes.

4 Add tomatoes, simmer 5 minutes, and correct seasoning.

5 Serve hot with vatrushki.

Vatrushki Pot Cheese Tartlets SERVES 4

AMOUNT	MEASURE	INGREDIENT
Dough		
1¾ cups	7 ounces, 196 g	All-purpose flour
½ teaspoon		Baking powder
½ teaspoon		Salt
1		Egg
½ cup	4 ounces, 120 ml	Sour cream
4 tablespoons	2 ounces, 60 ml	Butter

PROCEDURE

Sift together the flour, baking powder, and salt. Make a deep well in the center of the flour and drop in the egg, sour cream, and butter. With your fingers, slowly mix the flour into the liquid ingredients, then beat vigorously with a wooden spoon until it forms smooth, moderately firm dough. Chill 30 minutes.

Filling		
1 cup	8 ounces, 224 g	Large-curd pot cheese (cottage cheese)
2 teaspoons	20 ml	Sour cream
1		Egg
¼ teaspoon		Granulated sugar
¼ teaspoon		Salt
1		Egg yolk, mixed with 1 tablespoon (½ ounce, 15 ml) water

PROCEDURE

Drain the cheese by placing it in a colander, covering it with a double thickness of cheesecloth or a kitchen towel, and weighting it with a heavy dish on top. Let it drain undisturbed 2 or 3 hours, then with the back of a large spoon, rub the cheese through a fine sieve. Beat into it the sour cream, egg, sugar, and salt. Chill at least 30 minutes.

PREPARATION

1   On a lightly floured surface, roll dough into a circle of about $\frac{1}{8}$ inch (.3 cm) thick. With a 4-inch (10 cm) cookie cutter, cut out 8 circles; there will be excess dough. Dough can be reworked and rerolled.

2   Make a border around each circle by turning over about $\frac{1}{4}$ inch (.6 cm) of the dough all around its circumference and pinch in decorative scalloped pleats.

3   Place $1\frac{1}{2}$ tablespoons of the filling into the center and flatten it slightly, leaving a border.

4   Using a pastry brush, coat the filling and borders with the egg yolk and water mixture, then prick the dough lightly with a fork.

5   Bake in the center of a 400°F (204°C) oven, 15 minutes or until pale golden in color.

6   Serve *vatrushki* as an accompaniment to a soup or alone as a first course.

Pelmeni Siberian Meat Dumplings   YIELD: 3 DOZEN

AMOUNT	MEASURE	INGREDIENT
Dough		
2 cups	8 ounces, 224 g	All-purpose flour
$\frac{1}{2}$ teaspoon		Salt
2		Eggs
$\frac{1}{2}$ cup	4 ounces, 120 ml	Water

PROCEDURE

1 Sift together flour and salt and make a deep well in the center. Beat eggs and water together and pour into well. With your hands or a large spoon, slowly mix the flour into the liquid ingredients until the mixture can be gathered into a compact ball.

2 Transfer the dough to a lightly floured surface and knead it by folding it end to end, then pressing it down and pushing it forward several times with the heel of your hand. Sprinkle the dough with extra flour when necessary to prevent it from sticking to the board. Knead about 10 minutes, or until the dough is smooth and elastic. Shape into a ball, cover, and rest 1 hour at room temperature.

AMOUNT	MEASURE	INGREDIENT
Filling		
2 tablespoons	1 ounce, 30 ml	Butter
1 tablespoon	$\frac{1}{2}$ ounce, 15 ml	Vegetable oil
$\frac{1}{2}$ cup	2 ounces, 56 g	Onions, minced
1 cup	8 ounces, 224g	Lean top round or beef chuck, ground twice
1 cup	8 ounces, 224 g	Fresh pork fat, ground twice
1 teaspoon		Salt
$\frac{1}{2}$ teaspoon		Black pepper, fresh ground
$\frac{1}{2}$ cup	4 ounces, 120 ml	Melted butter (optional)

PROCEDURE

1 Melt the butter in the oil over high heat. When the foam has almost subsided, add the onions; cook over moderate heat, stirring frequently, 3 to 4 minutes, or until they are soft and lightly colored. Remove onions from pan, and cool.

2   To the cooled onions, add the meat, pork fat, salt, pepper, and $\frac{1}{2}$ cup (4 ounces, 120 ml) cold water and mix well until the ingredients are well combined and the mixture is smooth.

3   On a lightly floured surface, roll the reserved dough into a rough rectangle about $\frac{1}{8}$ inch (.3 cm) thick. Slide hands under the dough, stretch dough with backs of clenched fists, working from center in all directions until dough is paper thin. Cut out rounds of the dough with a $2\frac{1}{2}$- to 3-inch cookie cutter.

4   Place ground meat mixture in the lower half of each round. Make the dumplings as large as you can, but leave room to seal up the dough; run a finger lightly dipped in water around the edges and fold the exposed dough over the filling. Seal the edges by pressing firmly with the prongs of a fork. Dip your fingers in water again and lift up the two corners, pinching them together to form a round or triangular pouch.

5   Over high heat bring salted water to a vigorous boil, cook dumplings, uncovered, 5 to 7 minutes, or until they rise to the surface of the water. With a slotted spoon, transfer them to a double thickness of paper towels and let them drain while you cook and drain the remaining dumplings.

6   Serve hot with melted butter, if desired.

Frikadellen Meat Patties YIELD: 8

AMOUNT	MEASURE	INGREDIENT
2 tablespoons	1 ounce, 30 ml	Butter
$\frac{2}{3}$ cup	3 ounces, 84 g	Onions, minced
1		Bay leaf
1		Fresh thyme sprig
1		Garlic clove, minced
2 teaspoons		Caraway seeds, ground
1		Egg
$\frac{1}{2}$ cup	2 ounce, 28 g	Bread crumbs, fresh
$\frac{1}{4}$ cup	2 ounces, 60 ml	Milk
6 tablespoons	3 ounces, 90 ml	Heavy cream
$1\frac{1}{2}$ cups	12 ounces, 336 g	Veal, ground
$1\frac{1}{2}$ cups	12 ounces, 336 g	Pork, ground
2 tablespoons	$\frac{1}{4}$ ounce, 7 g	Parsley, chopped
1 tablespoon		Fresh dill, chopped
2 teaspoon		Lemon zest
To taste		Salt and pepper
2 tablespoons	1 ounce, 30 ml	Vegetable oil
2 tablespoons	1 ounce, 30 ml	Butter

PROCEDURE

1 Melt first quantity of butter over medium-high heat, add onions, bay leaf, and thyme, sauté 3 minutes or until onions are soft and translucent.

2 Add garlic, cook 1 minute; add caraway, cook 30 seconds, remove from heat, and cool.

3 Mix together bread crumbs, milk, and heavy cream, let sit 2 minutes.

4 Combine egg, bread crumb mixture, veal, pork, parsley, dill, lemon zest, and onion mixture (remove bay leaf and thyme sprig) until completely incorporated. Test a small portion for seasoning: sauté until done, taste, and adjust seasoning with salt and pepper. Form into oval patties and refrigerate at least 1 hour.

5 Heat pan over medium high heat, add the oil and remaining butter. When butter is melted, add patties. Sauté 3 to 5 minutes on one side, depending on size and thickness of

patties. Turn over and continue to cook an additional 3 to 5 minutes or until juices run clear. Patties can be finished in a hot oven.

6   Serve hot or cold, garnished with pickled beets and marinated cucumbers.

Syltede Rodbeder Pickled Beets
YIELD: 2 CUPS

AMOUNT	MEASURE	INGREDIENT
2 cups	12 ounces, 336 g	Beets, roasted, peeled, cooled, $\frac{1}{4}$ inch (.6 cm) half moon slices or any preferred cut
$\frac{1}{2}$ teaspoon		Caraway, ground
2 tablespoons	1 ounce, 30 ml	Orange juice
2 teaspoons	20 ml	Red wine vinegar
$\frac{1}{4}$ teaspoon		Coarse salt
To taste		Black pepper, freshly ground
$\frac{1}{2}$ teaspoon		Orange zest

PROCEDURE

1   Combine all ingredients and marinate at least 1 hour.

Agurkesalat Marinated Cucumbers
YIELD: 1 $\frac{1}{2}$ CUPS

AMOUNT	MEASURE	INGREDIENT
1 cup	6 ounces, 168 g	Seedless cucumber, julienned
$\frac{1}{2}$ cup	1 ounce, 28 g	Green onion, white and green parts, thinly sliced
To taste		Salt and pepper
1 teaspoon		Sugar
4 teaspoons	$1\frac{1}{3}$ ounces, 40 ml	Cider vinegar
2 tablespoons		Fresh dill, chopped

PROCEDURE

1   Combine all ingredients and marinate 30 minutes before serving.

Beef Stroganov
Sautéed Beef in Sour Cream Sauce   SERVES 4

AMOUNT	MEASURE	INGREDIENT
$\frac{2}{3}$ tablespoon	4 g	Dry mustard powder
$\frac{2}{3}$ tablespoon	8 g	Granulated sugar
1 teaspoon	4 g	Salt
1 tablespoon	10 ml	Hot water
4 tablespoons	2 ounces, 60 ml	Butter
1 cup	4 ounces, 112 g	Onions, julienned
3 cups	9 ounces, 252 g	Mushrooms, thinly sliced lengthwise
$\frac{1}{4}$ cup	2 ounces, 60 ml	Dry white wine
	1 pound, 448 g	Beef, sirloin or filet, trimmed of all fat, cut across the grain into $\frac{1}{4}$ inch (.6 cm) slices, then sliced into $\frac{1}{4}$ inch (.6 cm) strips
To taste		Salt and pepper
$\frac{1}{2}$ cup	4 ounces, 120 ml	Sour cream, warm

PROCEDURE

1   Combine mustard powder, sugar, salt, and hot water to form a paste.

2   Heat 2 tablespoons (1 ounce, 30 ml) butter over medium high heat, sauté onions until soft and translucent, 3 minutes. Add mushrooms and white wine; cook, stirring, until mushrooms are cooked and almost dry. Remove from heat and set aside.

3   Heat remaining 2 tablespoons (1 ounce, 30 ml) butter over medium-high heat and sauté beef until lightly browned. Meat may be cooked a half at a time to ensure sautéing and not stewing.

4   Add mustard mixture to meat and toss to combine.

5   Add mushroom onion mixture to beef; correct seasoning.

6   Add sour cream slowly, working to combine; heat to a simmer, do not boil.

7   Serve hot, with wide noodles, kasha, rice, or straw potatoes.

References

BOOKS

Alford, Jeffrey, and Naomi Duguid. 2000. *Hot, Sour, Salty, Sweet*. Workman Publishing, Inc. New York, New York.

Andres, Jose. 2005. *Tapas A Taste of Spain in America*. Random House, Inc. New York, New York.

Blajekar, Mridula. 2000. *Secrets from an Indian Kitchen*. Pavilion Books, Ltd. London, England.

Burum, Linda. 1985. *Asian Pasta*. Harris Publishing Co. Berkeley, California

Hae-Jin Lee, Cecilia. 2005. *Eating Korean*. John Wiley and Sons, Inc. Hoboken, New Jersey.

Harris, Jessica B. 2003. *Beyond Gumbo*. Simon & Schuster. New York, New York.

Hazan, Marcella. 1986. *Marcella's Italian Kitchen*. Alfred A. Knopf. New York, New York.

Hiremath, Laxmi. 2005. *The Dance of Spices*. John Wiley and Sons, Inc. Hoboken, New Jersey.

Hom, Ken. 1996. *Asian Ingredients*. Ten Speed Press, Berkely, California.

———. 1994. *Chinese Kitchens*. Hyperion. New York, New York.

Ingram, Christine. 2002. *The World Encyclopedia of Cooking Ingredients*. Anness Publishing, Ltd. London, England.

Jaffrey, Madhur. 1999. *World Vegetarian Cuisine*. Random House, Inc. New York, New York.

Johnson, Margaret, M. 2003. *The New Irish Table*. Chronicle Books LLC. San Fransisco, California.

Kamman, Madeleine. 1989. *Savoie: The Land, People, and Food of the French Alps*. Macmillan Publishing Company. New York, New York.

Kennedy, Diana. 2000. *The Essential Cuisines of Mexico*. Clarkson Potter Publishing. New York, New York.

———. 2003. *From My Mexican Kitchen*. Clarkson Potter Publishing. New York, New York.

Lambert-Ortiz, Elisabeth. 1979. *The Book of Latin American Cooking*. Random House. New York, New York.

Law, Ruth. 1990. *Southeast Asia Cookbook*. Donald I. Fine, Inc. New York, New York.

Luard, Elisabeth. 2006. *Classic Spanish Cooking*. MQ Publishers, Inc. New York, New York

Read, Mark. 2001. *Lemongrass and Lime*. Ten Speed Press, Berkeley, California.

Shimbo, Hiroka. 2000. *The Japanese Kitchen*. The Harvard Common Press. Boston, Mass.

Sonnenfeld, Albert. 1999. *A Culinary History of Food*. Penguin Books. New York, New York.

Stow, Josie and Han Baldwin. 2005. *The African Kitchen*. Interlink Books. Northampton, MA.

Tropp, Barbara, 2001. *The Modern Art of Chinese Cooking*. HarperCollins Publishing, New York, New York.

VanAken, Norman. 2003. *New World Kitchen*. HarperCollins Publishers. New York, New York.

Von Bremzen, Anya. 2005. *The New Spanish Table*. Workman Publishing. New York, New York.

Wright, Clifford A. 2003. *Little Foods of the Mediterranean*. Harvard Common Press. Boston, Mass.

Zia Chu, Madame Grace. 1980. *The Encyclopedia of Asian Cooking*. Mandarin Publishers Limited. Quarry Bay, Hong Kong.

WEBSITES

www.HistoryCentral.com
www.NationbyNation.com
www.geographia.com

www.britannica.com
www.AsiaRecipe.com
www.foodbycountry.com